A
HISTORY
IN
FRAGMENTS

A
HISTORY
IN
FRAGMENTS

Europe in the
Twentieth Century

RICHARD VINEN

DA CAPO PRESS

In memory of Matthew Buncombe

Maps by Neil Hyslop

Typeset in Adobe Garamond

First Da Capo Press edition 2001
Reprinted by arrangement with Little, Brown and Company.
ISBN: 0 306 81063 8

Published by Da Capo Press
A Member of the Perseus Books Group
http://www.dacapopress.com

Da Capo Press books are available at special discounts for bulk purchases
in the U.S. by corporations, institutions, and other organizations.
For more information, please contact the Special Markets Department
at the Perseus Books Group, 11 Cambridge Center, Cambridge, MA 02142,
or call (617) 252-5298.

1   2   3   4   5   6   7   8   9   10—05   04   03   02   01

Contents

PREFACE TO THE DA CAPO EDITION   *vii*

ACKNOWLEDGMENTS   *ix*

LIST OF TABLES   *xi*

LIST OF MAPS   *xii*

INTRODUCTION   *1*

PART I
The Belle Époque and the Catastrophe

1. Huddled Masses   *15*
2. Socialism and the Working Class   *32*
3. The Great War   *43*

PART II
From One War to Another

1. The Legacy of the Great War   *69*
2. Youth   *78*
3. Men, Women and the Family   *89*
4. Civil Wars   *128*
5. Modern Times   *151*
6. The Phoney Peace   *172*
7. The Second World War in Europe   *184*
8. Genocide   *199*

CLICHÉS: A PHOTOGRAPHIC ESSAY   *213*

PART III
Postwar Europe
1. Taking Sides 247
2. The Miracle 271
3. Consensus Politics 299
4. The Other Europe 338
5. Rebuilding the Family 368

PART IV
Who Won the Cold War?
1. How Communism Lost 397
2. Did Capitalism Win? 433

PART V
Europe in the New World Order
1. New Frontiers 465
2. Sexual Revolutions 487
3. New Politics? 501

A SORT OF CONCLUSION 521

SOME THOUGHTS ON FURTHER READING 532
NOTES 549
INDEX 595

Preface to the
Da Capo Edition

This book was completed on New Year's Day 2000—though discerning readers will notice that certain parts of later chapters and especially the conclusion were rewritten in the light of events after this date. I have taken advantage of the U.S. edition to correct some errors, but I have not rewritten any part of the book. Some British reviewers commented on the "optimistic" tone of the book. I am not sure that I agree with them. Optimists look to the future; historians think about the past, and no one could deny that the European past contains some grotesque horrors. I do argue that most Europeans had reason to feel pleased with the last decade of the twentieth century, but even this modest assertion must be hedged with reservations, which I hope to have expressed in the conclusion. My own life has certainly given me cause for optimism of a personal kind during the past year, and nothing has contributed more to this than the birth of my son Alexander on the day that I finished correcting the proofs of the first edition, May 23, 2000.

LONDON
June 2001

ACKNOWLEDGMENTS

ANDREW GORDON HAS been a wonderful editor who has stuck by this project through some difficult times. I am also very grateful to Andrew Wille, the copy-editor, and to Fiona Greenway, the picture researcher. Andrew Lownie launched the whole project.

David Stevenson read the first draft of this book and took great pains to help me to express my arguments more clearly even when, as was often the case, he disagreed with them. David Baker commented on the last draft with a characteristic mixture of rigor and tact. Anne Le More's relentless scepticism forced me to rethink many of my ideas; her inexhaustible enthusiasm persuaded me that it was worth doing so. Susan Michell devoted enormous amounts of her time, intelligence and erudition to this book. Her influence on it, and my historical outlook generally, could not be overstated.

Lawrence Block, Robert Frost, Daniel Greenstein, Philip Hanson, Patrick Higgins, Julian Jackson, Jonathan Morris, Kevin Passmore, Joe Vinen and Jim Wolfreys all provided useful advice on all or parts of the text. Katrin Hett's work on the Magnum photography agency made me see the twentieth century through new eyes. Michel Lefebvre and his colleagues at *Le Monde* went to great lengths to help me locate an obscure photograph. Michaela Puchalková's heroic efforts to teach me Czech were not very successful but I did, I hope, learn something about central Europe and life under communism from my conversations with her.

I have also learned a great deal from my students in history and European studies at King's College. The optimistic tone of the closing pages of this book comes partly from my belief that my students and their contemporaries will make a better job of running Europe than their elders have done.

My daughter, Emma, was born in August 1998 as I finished the first draft of *A History in Fragments*. I cannot claim that she has shown much interest in the progress of my work, but I am grateful to her and to her mother, Alison Henwood, for all the benign changes they have brought to my life. For me at least, the twentieth century had a happy ending.

LONDON
New Year's Day, 2000

List of Tables

1   Emigration to the United States by Decade   *17*
2   Military Deaths in the First World War   *59*
3   Ages of European Political Leaders in 1933   *85*
4   War Damage and Reconstruction After 1945   *274*
5   Immigrants in Three Western European Countries,
    1973–74   *286*
6   Estimated Hard Currency Debt of the Soviet Union
    and Eastern European States   *415*
7   Percentage of Economically Active Population in
    Manufacturing   *435*
8   Unemployment Rates   *437*
9   Long-term Unemployment   *439*

10   Days Occupied in Strikes per 100 Workers in Industry
     and Transport   *441*

11   Opinions on Economic Changes in Russia   *470*

List of Maps

1   Europe in 1900   *10*
2   Europe in 1925   *62*
3   Europe in 1949   *238*
4   Infant Mortality in Europe in 1985   *384*
5   Europe in 1994   *462*

INTRODUCTION

WITH CHARACTERISTICALLY POOR timing, I began my career as an academic historian in the year that history ended. As I stumbled through lectures on the origins of the First World War and the Russian Revolution, the political structures brought about by such events collapsed. Of course, 1989 did not really see the "end of history." In some respects, history had come alive like a fossil in a museum smashing out of its display case, but the transformation of Europe by dramatic and unpredictable events did mark the end of history in a limited sense – it made it more difficult to sustain a certain way of writing and teaching Europe's history. It might help to explain what I mean by a "history in fragments" if I outline the assumptions that once governed my approach and show how they have been challenged in the last decade.

The first assumption that governed the writing of history was that there was a clear frontier between the past and the present. Like many traditionalist or conservative assumptions, it is really quite new. Macaulay and Marc Bloch mixed the study of the distant past with that of contemporary events. Only in recent times has the study of recent times been seen to lack intellectual respectability. In part, the separation of history and the present comes from the professionalization of both history and those disciplines – political science and sociology – that are concerned with the present.

The separation of "history" from the present also owes something to the particular nature of the twentieth century. For historians of the period, "history" tends to mean a particular part of the century, from the beginning or end of the First World War until the end of the Second World War. The years 1914 to 1945 were exceptionally violent and dramatic ones; historians were caught up in the very events that they later described. Consider, for example, the career of Moshe Lewin, born in Wilno in Poland (nominally in central Lithuania) in 1921. In 1939 his town was occupied by Soviet forces and annexed to Lithuania; two years later it was invaded by Germany. Lewin, a Jew, ran for his life. He was saved by a group of retreating Soviet soldiers who, defying the orders of their officers, hauled him aboard their truck. Subsequently Lewin worked in a Soviet factory and served in the Red Army, and at the end of the war went to Israel, where he became a farmer and soldier. Eventually he moved to Paris, where he began his historical research on Stalinism. He had been a citizen of four countries and a soldier in two armies. He was thirty-five.[1]

The generation of historians who grew up after 1945 lacked the direct personal experiences of people such as Lewin, but they continued to concentrate their research on the two world wars and the period between them. There was a practical explanation: the defeat of Nazi Germany opened up new sources as the highly bureaucratic regime's archives were captured. The defeat of Germany sometimes facilitated the study of other countries too. Robert Paxton's book on Vichy France was based on German archives that detailed dealings with Pétain's government.[2] An important group of scholars worked on the archives of the Smolensk district of the Soviet Communist Party, which were seized by the Germans when they invaded Russia and later taken by Allied forces.[3] The rapid expansion of western European universities during the 1960s and the subsequent interruption of academic appointments from the mid-1970s froze the view of history that developed in the immediately postwar years. A large group of historians who had been born during or immediately after the Second World War took it for granted that history stopped when their own lives began.

The drama of events between 1914 and 1945 lends a particular tone to much of the writing about them. The innovation and intellectual audacity deployed by those studying earlier periods appear unnecessary when the questions to be asked appear so obvious. Every intelligent historian knows that understanding the world-view of a sixteenth-century miller, for example, requires a use of unusual sources and an imaginative leap into an alien mentality but, curiously, many intelligent historians still assume that the actions of, say, a Polish Stalinist in 1946 can be explained with exclusive reference to explicitly political statements. The playfulness that characterizes some approaches to early periods seems inappropriate when the subject matter is so somber. Simon Schama explains his distaste for twentieth-century history by saying: "After Bismarck the weather turns cold."

The clash of great ideologies and great powers dominates the writing of twentieth-century history, or, at least, the writing of broad pan-European narratives. This is illustrated by the career of the Romanian-born historian Lilly Marcou. Her approach, with its emphasis on relations between powers and international organizations and its attention to very precise questions of chronology, might seem rather old-fashioned to students raised on methods fashionable among early modernists. Her autobiography illustrates the reasons for her interests. Marcou came from a family of Bucharest Jews and was six years old at the time of the Battle of Stalingrad. She understood its consequences very well: if Stalin won she might live; if Hitler won she would certainly die.[4] For her, the idea that relations between the great powers could be considered irrelevant to the lives of ordinary people would be incomprehensible.

The focus on the period 1914 to 1945 sheds a particular light on the history that surrounds the two dates. Most histories of twentieth-century Europe start in 1914, 1917 or 1918. Certain scholars have recently started to talk of the "short twentieth century," as if a secret protocol of the Versailles Treaty had handed almost two decades to the Victorian age. In political terms, the "short twentieth century" hinges around the assumption that the entire history of the century can be seen as a battle between communism and its enemies, which looks more questionable after 1989, and even more so after 1991. In terms of national boundaries, changes have been equally dramatic. Three states created in the aftermath of the Great War – Czechoslovakia, Yugoslavia and the Soviet Union – ceased to exist in the early 1990s.

Most importantly, histories that begin in 1914 are often founded on certain views of European society before that date. The first decade of the century is presented as a bourgeois arcadia of free trade, cheap servants and sound money that was destroyed by the upheaval of wartime inflation and the loss of Russian investments. When the pre-1914 period is examined in detail – rather than seen as just the backdrop to the "short twentieth century" – many of these assumptions dissolve. The bourgeois arcadia was inhabited only by a tiny minority of people.

The attention devoted to the years 1914 to 1945 contributes to a particular interpretation of the years that follow 1945. Historians tend to regard the postwar period with a mixture of optimism and boredom, seeing themselves as pilots who steered between the rocks of war, revolution and repression. Now political scientists can be trusted to sail across the calm open sea of consensus and prosperity. Many narratives simply stop at the end of the Second World War. Others refer to a "golden age" from 1945 to 1975, though any historian who studies the period after 1945 with as much attention as the one before it will have grave doubts about such a concept. The Germans who huddled in the ruins of their houses or in refugee camps in 1945 would certainly have been surprised to be told that they lived at the dawn of a golden age. Even when economies grew, many groups, such as migrant workers, experienced upheaval as much as opportunity. Indeed, some British academic historians look back on the 1950s and 1960s with fond nostalgia because they belonged to one of the few groups that benefited from economic change without having to make any sacrifices in return. Unlike most Europeans, they did not have to up-root themselves or adapt to new types of work, yet they drew great bene-fits from prosperity: British academic salaries increased by 28 percent between 1958 and 1968.

If naïve optimism marks attitudes towards the thirty years after 1945, apocalyptic gloom – or at least a kind of resentful incomprehension – of-ten clouds any examination of the period after the oil crisis of 1973. His-torians formed by study of the interwar period regarded inflation, reces-sion and the revival of the political right with alarm. Such reactions reached a tragi-comic level in the person of Tim Mason. Mason, an emi-nent historian of Nazi Germany, believed that Margaret Thatcher was the British equivalent of von Papen, the conservative politician who brought Adolf Hitler to power. In the last years of his life, Mason advised be-mused leaders of the working class that they should "go underground" before the arrests started.[5] His analysis, and that of many of his contem-poraries who reacted in less extreme ways, ignored the realities of the 1970s and 1980s. During this period, growth never stopped and economies did not contract as they had done in the early 1930s. Far from becoming more polarized, the political system in most of Europe moved to the center and Spain, Portugal and Greece embraced democracy.

The fall of communist regimes in Europe between 1989 and 1991 has provided historians with a new chronological landmark to establish the boundary between history and the present. The end of communist rule, however, was less clear-cut than the end of Nazism: it is a jagged edge, not a clean break. Nazism fell at the apogee of its radicalism and the single project with which it is most associated – the extermination of the Euro-pean Jews – accelerated in the last years of Nazi rule. One moment the Third Reich existed; the next it was gone. Clerks deducted pension con-tributions from the salaries of SS men in April 1945; a month later, their papers had fallen into the hands of the Americans and were soon available to historians.

Communist rule, by contrast, fell as the result of a long process of decline and reform that can be traced back to the 1950s. Hungary and Poland had in effect ceased to be communist by the late 1980s, whereas in Romania, Serbia and Bulgaria party apparatchiks held on to power even after the nominal end of communist rule. Those who criticized commu-nism most eloquently or who tried to reform it in its final years were often the very people who had previously participated in its worst excesses. Historians ought to be acutely conscious of the ways in which the communist past spills over into the post-communist present, because so many distinguished members of our profession – Edward Thompson, Maurice Agulhon, François Furet – were members of the party, often at the height of Stalinist repression. The former communist historian Annie Kriegel summed up the flight from clear-cut judgment that followed the collapse of her communist faith when she entitled her memoirs *Ce Que J'ai Cru Comprendre* ("What I Thought I Understood").

The breakdown of communist rule has provided new perspectives on eastern Europe. Indeed, in some ways it has opened the very idea of "eastern Europe" to question. The existence of the Warsaw Pact imposed unity on the communist states of Europe, even those that were not members. The end of communism suddenly made it clear that the states that were bundled together had little in common. Some inhabitants of what had been labeled "eastern" or "central" Europe indignantly rejected the term.

Information on the former communist countries emerged unevenly. Only in East Germany was there complete transparency. Some governments contrived to make large numbers of documents disappear, and elsewhere there were more pressing concerns than the cataloguing or publishing of historical sources. Academic life in much of the former communist bloc fell apart as impoverished professors and archivists struggled to make ends meet. Some of the most interesting revelations were produced by journalists and sociologists or by the autobiographical writings of anticommunist dissidents rather than by academic historians. Furthermore, the study of the end of communism involves a move away from purely political history. Historians studying the previous upheavals of the century – the two world wars and Nazism – started with a coherent set of documents relating to high policy and used them to try to explain political decisions; only years later did scholars turn their attention to the social histories of those events. Post-communist states were not keen to open their archives, but researchers often made contact with private individuals. One symptom of reform in the Soviet Union was the growth of academic sociology and a rising interest in society rather than the state. As a result, our knowledge is vast, but fragmentary. It is possible to know a good deal about, say, family histories of the Moscow nomenklatura or housing patterns in Brno while much of the political history of the communist bloc remains obscure.

The collapse of communism did not, in any case, lend itself to a purely political history. No individual ever decided to bring the regime down; all powerful individuals thought that they were acting to defend it. Reformers and dissidents throughout the communist world talked of "civil society" and even "anti-politics." It was in the Eastern Bloc after the death of Stalin that public emphasis on the role of the state and ideological mobilization accompanied private emphasis on personal relations, families and children. Many inhabitants of communist countries turned away from public life and entered what Günter Grass called the "niche society." Of course, private lives and the state had never been wholly separable. Intimate matters such as the high incidence of abortion or the violence of parents against children must, at least in part, be explained with reference to government policy, but the state was never a complete explanation, and historians of eastern Europe, even more than their western counterparts, will explain matters in terms of "private spheres."[6]

This book attempts to provide an account of the whole century that gives as much weight to the events of the 1990s as to those of the 1930s. Pulling away from the concentration on the violent conflicts of the period 1914 to 1945 also means pulling away from a history that concentrates on the explicitly political sphere, so a great deal of attention is devoted to social and cultural change. I do not seek to downplay politics or argue that history can be written "with the politics left out." All history is political in that all history is about power, all history is social because it is all about people living in groups, and all history is cultural because all human experience is mediated through various representations.

A focus on the whole century and on experience outside politics does not mean that a "total" history of twentieth-century Europe is being offered. On the contrary, twenty years ago it might have been possible to structure an account of the history of the twentieth century around a single narrative that emphasized, say, the defense of democracy or responses to the Russian Revolution. Now everything is more complicated. There is no single European history but multiple histories that overlap and intertwine with each other. A general account can make sense only by building on a number of arbitrary decisions about what is to be examined. Indeed, the reader should be aware of the artificial architecture of this book: considering and disputing its construction may be the most useful way of engaging with its arguments.

The most artificial and arbitrary choice relates to periodization. The book has five parts, which are divided by the two world wars, the economic slowdown of the mid-1970s and the collapse of communist rule in Europe of 1989–91. It is not suggested that any of those moments were clear "turning points" in European history. Russians might well be bemused by the importance that the British and French attach to November 11, 1918. Similarly, May 8, 1945, did not divide war and repression from "postwar reconstruction"; for many Europeans, the years that followed the end of the Second World War were the worst of the twentieth century. The divisions proposed for the second half of the book are even more arbitrary and in practice much of the analysis, particularly that of the triumph of capitalism and shifting sexual values, transcends chronological divisions. Within each chronological section, a thematic approach has been adopted, and it is hoped that this method will permit a recognition of the speed of change in the twentieth century while avoiding a purely narrative *événementiel* account. It might be objected that the neglect of narrative fails to fulfill what A. J. P. Taylor described as the first duty of the historian: "To answer the child's question. What happened next?" I hope that my approach will go some way towards answering another child's question, more common in my experience: "What does it matter and why should I care?"

Another arbitrary choice involves the balance of coverage given to different countries. I have defined Europe in simple geographical terms as the area bounded by the Atlantic, the Bosphorus, the Urals and the Mediterranean (indeed, the location of such physical landmarks may be the only aspect of Europe that has not changed between 1900 and 2000). Clearly, however, no history of Europe makes sense if it refers only to Europe. Leaders of Britain, France and, for that matter, Portugal regarded themselves as world, rather than purely European, powers for at least the first half of the century. The Soviet Union was both a European state and an Asian one. The Polish peasantry at the start of the century cannot be understood without reference to Ellis Island, and the European bourgeoisie at its end cannot be understood without reference to Wall Street. Within Europe, I have tried to give some attention to all countries and, in particular, to avoid writing a history of the great powers. However, my knowledge of Europe is uneven and my generalizations draw most heavily on the countries that I know best. No doubt the result will amuse or annoy specialists on the history of many countries, but if only those with an equally detailed knowledge of all parts of Europe could attempt a general history of the continent, no such book would ever be written. Besides, this book is not intended to displace earlier works, and one justification for the balance of coverage is that other authors have devoted much attention to areas (such as Germany, Poland and the Balkans) of which I know comparatively little.

The country that certainly receives an attention disproportionate to its population is Britain. This does not necessarily make the book "anglocentric"; there is nothing more anglocentric than works that assume that the history of Britain is so special that it should not be included in histories of Europe. Since the author of this book is British, it seems sensible to describe at some length the ways in which British history fits in with and diverges from that of the continent. Putting Britain at the center of the narrative sometimes reveals how assumptions about Europe that now permeate historical discussion – even on the continent – are really rooted in British experience. The phrase "interwar Europe" (applied to the years 1919 to 1939) would sound odd to Spaniards (Spain was neutral in both world wars but the site of a civil war from 1936 to 1939). Similarly, interest in the experience of the "front generation" makes sense in Britain (where civilian life expectancy increased between 1914 and 1918) but makes less sense in Serbia (where the number of deaths brought about by the First World War exceeded the total number of soldiers mobilized).

A final peculiarity of this book is the lack of reference to historical theory. I am tempted to justify this absence by suggesting that a knowledge of historical theory bears the same relation to writing a history book that a knowledge of the Queensberry Rules bears to being able to box. Clearly my work is based on unspoken assumptions and on the products of theoretical debate that I have absorbed, perhaps unconsciously, from reading the work of other historians. However, I suspect that readers who are interested in such matters would find it more rewarding to unpick the theory for themselves rather than endure my attempts to explain it.

A general introduction to a general book necessarily involves sweeping statements. Some of the remarks above may sound dismissive of other people's work or founded on the assumption that my approach is inherently superior to those of my colleagues. Perhaps I should finish by saying that I doubt whether there is a single subject covered by this book on which I have said the first or the last word. I recognize that this book will one day be read, if it is read at all, as a historical artifact that illustrates the assumptions of a particular kind of European at a particular time. I hope that, before then, it will contribute to debate and help other people formulate their own interpretations – if only by providing them with something to disagree with.

PART I

The Belle Époque
and the Catastrophe

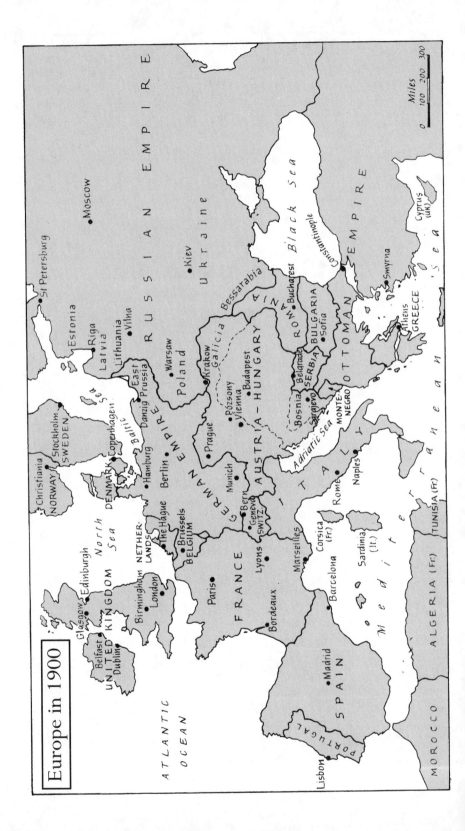

Europe in 1900

MUCH WRITING ON twentieth-century Europe is marked by an aching nostalgia for the period before 1914. Consider, for example, E. M. Forster's novel *Howards End* (published in 1910). The story revolves around the leisured, cultured and wealthy Schlegel sisters, characters based on Virginia Woolf (née Stephen) and her sister Vanessa. We also know of the Schlegel/Stephen sisters through the writings of Virginia herself, as well as the monumental autobiography of her husband Leonard (he devotes an entire volume to the years 1911 to 1918 alone), and the writings by and about the other members of their social circle, which included the painter Duncan Grant, the biographer Lytton Strachey, the philosopher Bertrand Russell and the economist John Maynard Keynes. Most educated Europeans or North Americans probably know more about the couple of dozen people who lived around Gordon Square in Bloomsbury in the first decade of the twentieth century than they do about the whole population of, say, Serbia during the same period.

Forster's vision is, as he knew, restricted. It encompassed a world of economic privilege. The Schlegel sisters have a comfortable private income at a time of low inflation and are not obliged to work or to take risks in order to secure a return on their investments. Virginia Woolf's husband talked of "economic paradise for the bourgeoisie," and recalled that his wife belonged to the "Victorian professional upper middle class which was as impregnably secure as (almost) the Bank of England."[1] Among Forster's acquaintances, even those who worked had jobs – in university teaching or the upper ranks of the civil service – that allowed them a high degree of security and plenty of free time. Such tranquil lives were not typical even of the English bourgeoisie. The other central family of *Howards End*, the Wilcoxes, are rich, but, unlike the Schlegels, they have to work for their money, and consequently lack the time to write books about their lives and opinions. Beneath the Schlegels and the Wilcoxes is Leonard Bast, a clerk, who has neither money nor leisure, and beneath Bast is the great majority of the British population, which, as Forster remarks, is beneath the interest of a novelist and can be dealt with only "by the statistician." The stability and culture that we associate with Europe before 1914 was founded on the labor of those consigned to the statistics. Bourgeois life depended on servants. Consider Keynes's famous passage: "The inhabitant of London could order by telephone, sipping his morning tea in bed, the various products of the whole earth."[2] The telephone was an impossibly exotic object for most Europeans until after the Second World War, so one assumes that those who made telephone calls remembered this life with more regret than those who made the tea.

Turning away from Britain towards continental Europe shows even more clearly how unrepresentative were the rentier bourgeoisie. France contained a substantial rentier population, as did some other European cities (Vienna, Milan, Prague), but few people in other countries had the luxury of living off fortunes accumulated in the nineteenth century.

The lives of the great mass of Europeans before 1914 were utterly removed from those of the British bourgeoisie. For the inhabitants of eastern and Mediterranean Europe, life was hard and insecure, dominated by cholera, malaria and starvation, rather than books and music. It is easy to forget that the mass of Europe's population spent the summer of 1914 in back-breaking labor, preparing to get the harvest in. Those who imagine that the pre-1914 world is to be regretted should ask themselves the question that is posed in Chapter 1: why did so many Europeans want to leave?

Nostalgia for pre-1914 Europe is closely associated with horror of the consequences of the First World War. Members of the Bloomsbury group were, almost to a man and woman, opponents of the war. Leonard Woolf believed that the outbreak of war stopped progress towards civilization and opened the era of "Verdun and Auschwitz." More prosaically, the war brought inflation, and hence the end of the rentiers, and it reduced the availability of servants.

There is one final sense in which our view of pre-1914 Europe is slanted by an emphasis on stability and progress. The writers on whose testimony we depend often present the destruction of their world as though it were the product of purely external forces, as if the violence and upheaval of twentieth-century Europe were entirely separate from themselves. In truth, the very forces that shook Europe came, in part, from within the liberal intelligentsia. Keynes regretted certain forms of pre-1914 stability but his own economic principles implied the "euthanasia of the rentier." Leonard Woolf denounced Nazism and fascism, but defended the Russian Revolution. Virginia Woolf, whose own half-sister had been confined to an asylum, wrote the following entry in her diary in 1915: "On the tow path we met and had to pass a long line of imbeciles . . . everyone in that long line was a miserable shuffling idiotic creature, with no forehead, or no chin, and an imbecile grin, or a wild suspicious stare. It was perfectly horrible. They should certainly be killed."[3]

1

HUDDLED MASSES

Give me your tired, your poor,
Your huddled masses yearning to breathe free,
The wretched refuse of your teeming shore,
Send these, the homeless, tempest-tost to me.
Verse written by Emma Lazarus
for the Statue of Liberty

THE MOST STRIKING feature of Europe in 1900 was that so many of its inhabitants wished to leave; in the twenty-five years leading up to 1900, the United States alone took in 25 million Europeans. Emigrants have not attracted much attention from historians of Europe. They do not fit into narratives that emphasize progress or power and often belonged to groups – such as the Poles, Irish or southern Italians – that regarded themselves as subject races. Furthermore, they tended to come from the parts of Europe that had been least obviously affected by industrialization. Until about 1885, emigration was most common from northern and western Europe; after this, the underdeveloped areas of the south and east (especially southern Italy and Poland) lost the greatest numbers. In the two decades before 1914, 3.5 million Poles left for the United States, while the number of Italians who emigrated between 1898 and 1914 varied from 150,000 to 750,000 per year, most of them coming from the south.

Why did emigrants leave? In part the reasons were political. Countries that received immigrants often regarded themselves as havens of liberty and wished to present the arrivals as motivated by the "yearning to breathe free." This was true of Great Britain, France and, especially, America (though not of Germany, which treated migrants simply as "imported labor"). Correspondingly, some countries were keen to deny that departures were the result of persecution: Romanian authorities obliged departing Jews to sign a declaration that they were leaving for purely economic reasons. Migrants themselves sometimes had an interest in presenting their departures as political. The Aliens Act, passed by the British government in 1905, sought to discourage economic migrants as opposed to political refugees.

European Jews were probably the group most likely to leave for political reasons. Romanian Jews were badly persecuted and 30 percent of them emigrated to the United States between 1871 and 1914, while a large proportion of those who left the Tsarist empire were also Jewish. Tsarism confined most Jews to a strip of land in Lithuania and Poland (the "Pale") and local authorities often connived in the organization of pogroms. Golda Meir, who was born in Russia and raised in Milwaukee before becoming Prime Minister of Israel, recalled her father boarding up the windows of his workshop in preparation for a pogrom in Kiev. Even Jews from central Europe did not always have purely political motives, though. Many came from Austria-Hungary, which was not known for anti-Semitism, and those from the Tsarist empire were driven by desperate poverty as well as persecution (in 1900 there was not a single province of the Pale in which less than one in eight of the population received poor relief).[1] Furthermore, life in the Pale could be claustrophobic; it was not always clear whether the young secularized men who left in greatest numbers wished to escape from the Cossacks or the rabbis.

Other migrants may also have had political reasons for seeking to leave Europe – many came from groups that felt excluded from power in their own lands – but the link between politics and departure is far from clear. In Italy, migration increased at the same time that universal male suffrage was introduced. Migrants often intended to return to their country of origin, and their treatment by officials and employers would have given them little reason to regard the United States as the "land of the free." Simple material advantage encouraged many to leave. The regions from which immigrants came were usually poor, and were afflicted by natural hazards that an inhabitant of northwestern Europe would have regarded as characteristic of Africa or Asia; an earthquake in Messina in 1908 killed 10,000 people, while malaria was common in the swamps of Poland and in southern Italy – a million Italians were estimated to suffer from attacks of malaria in 1898.[2] Growing prosperity, improved technology and modern medicine were making it easier to master these hazards, but such benefits spread relatively slowly to the underdeveloped periphery of Europe. Greater prosperity often led to an increasing population and declining

Table 1: Emigration to the United States by Decade

	1880–89	1890–99	1900–09	1910–19
United Kingdom	810,900	328,759	469,578	371,878
Ireland	674,061	405,710	344,940	166,445
Scandinavia	671,783	390,729	488,208	238,275
France	48,193	35,616	67,735	60,335
German empire	1,445,181	579,072	328,722	174,227
Poland	42,910	107,793	not returned separately	
Austria-Hungary	314,787	534,059	2,001,376	1,154,727
Russia	182,698	450,101	1,501,301	1,106,998
Romania	5,842	6,808	57,322	13,566
Greece	1,807	12,732	145,402	198,108
Italy	267,660	603,761	1,930,475	1,229,916

Source: Alan Kraut, *The Huddled Masses: The Immigrant in American Society, 1880–1921*, (1982), p. 20.

food prices, as it became easier to import food from outside Europe – mixed blessings for those trying to extract a living from the land.[3]

Emigrants were pulled by new opportunities as well as pushed by pressures in their native lands. Railways and steamships made travel easier, and competition between the shipping lines based in Hamburg, Bremen and Liverpool brought the price of tickets to America down sharply in the early twentieth century. Trans-Atlantic migration was big business. By 1914, almost 6 million eastern Europeans had passed through the Baltic ports on their way to America. Albert Ballin, who ran the Hapag line from Hamburg, had built a fleet of 175 ships by 1913; the Hamburg–Amerika line even built its own village, complete with church and synagogue, to accommodate migrants in transit.[4] Shipping lines employed 560 agents to drum up business in southern Italy alone.[5] The governments of Argentina, Brazil and Canada actively sought immigrant labor and cooperated with private business to obtain it – between 1899 and 1906, the North Atlantic Trading Company was paid $367,245 in return for directing 70,000 immigrants to Canada.[6] European governments made some effort to discourage emigration, especially of young men who might be eligible for military service, but, in an age before passports, there was little that governments could do to prevent their citizens from departing. Personal and family contacts also facilitated migration. An individual might send back accounts of his new life, and perhaps even funds for tickets, to encourage his relatives and friends to join him, while supportive family networks and systems of mutual obligation often made it possible to raise the money needed for the journey, as in Consentino in southern Italy.[7] International Jewish organizations also helped Jews move from eastern Europe to the United States, an action motivated partly by charity and partly by the fear among assimilated, prosperous Jews in England, France and Germany that their own position might be undermined if poor, Yiddish-speaking immigrants congregated in western European cities.[8]

Emigrants did not always go far. Some simply headed for the nearest city or crossed a national frontier to find work. France, whose birth rate was barely enough to sustain her population, was particularly dependent on immigrant labor. Some migrants from Russia went to Siberia: indeed, between 1901 and 1910, more Russians headed east than went to America. However, the most dramatic form of emigration, and the one that aroused the greatest interest, took people across the ocean and particularly to America. Around 85 percent of Polish emigrants went to the United States, and in 1910 about four in ten residents of New York had been born abroad.[9]

Migrants were rarely welcomed with open arms. Their reception was influenced by fashionable ideas of degeneracy, and some Americans worried that immigrants would bring poverty, disease and low intelligence. The Ford Committee reported in 1889 that the city of New York was spending $20 million a year on supporting immigrants who were paupers or insane. In 1892, controls were established at Ellis Island, near Manhattan, where new arrivals were tested for disease, "idiocy" and (from 1917) illiteracy. Inspectors watched immigrants climb a steep staircase to gauge whether they were lame, devised puzzles to measure the intelligence of people who spoke no English, and pulled back eyelids to check for trachoma. Of the 12 million people who arrived at Ellis Island, a quarter of a million were turned back. Repatriation often meant family separation and a return to poverty and persecution as well as the prospect of having to endure another period in the appalling conditions of steerage class. Around 3,000 people committed suicide on Ellis Island. The threat of being required to repatriate some immigrants forced shipping companies to institute their own checks on the other side of the Atlantic and, in 1907, 40,000 migrants were turned back at European docks after examination by doctors.[10]

Which immigrants were regarded as desirable varied. French employers were sufficiently close to the countries of origin to make precise distinctions and to seek employees from regions known for political quiescence. The governments of the United States and Canada made a more sweeping distinction between the "desirable" peoples of northern and western Europe, who had provided the first citizens of their country, and the "undesirable" immigrants from southern and eastern Europe, though employers did not always share their governments' preference in such matters. Some recognized that men from relatively underdeveloped countries had the advantage of low expectations and limited traditions of labor organization. Clifford Sifton, head of the Canadian immigration board, wrote, "I think a stalwart peasant in a sheep-skin coat, born on the soil, whose forebears have been farmers for ten generations, with a stout wife and half-a-dozen children is good quality."[11]

Immigrants could be treated harshly. In 1913, Canadian railways transported Russian workers in closed carriages accompanied by armed guards.[12] Immigrants who did not know the language or the customs of their new country were vulnerable and often their hiring was organized by agents such as Antonio Cordasco of Montreal, who claimed the right to provision, and thus exploit, the workers that he provided. In 1900, half the Italian workers in New York were said to be under the control of *padroni*.[13] Sometimes, priests organized immigrant workers: in Johnstown, Pennsylvania, the Polish priest acted as a labor agent and deducted a dollar a fortnight from the wages of every worker hired through his offices.[14] Even secularized immigrants might find themselves thrust into the arms of the Church by the need to find an agency that would provide links to authority.

Migration could change the lives of those involved spectacularly. Bernard Berenson, born in the Lithuanian Pale, grew up speaking Yiddish. His family's move to America allowed him to be educated at the universities of Boston and Harvard, and he died in Florence a world-renowned expert on the Italian art of the Renaissance. Most migrants had more lowly ambitions. They had usually been agricultural laborers in their native lands, and many of them hoped that emigration would enable them to acquire land of their own. As the American frontier closed, such settlement became increasingly unlikely, and immigrants were often forced to take industrial work and to live in cities.[15]

Catholicism – and peasant origins – united Poles, Italians and the Irish, though the latter had the advantage of linguistic integration and, usually, longer residence. The Irish looked down on "lesser" Catholics at least as much as Protestant Americans looked down on the Irish. The hegemony of the Irish over American Catholicism was epitomized by St. Patrick's Cathedral on Fifth Avenue in Manhattan, built in 1878. Every Archbishop of New York since John Hughes, enthroned in 1850, has been of Irish descent.[16]

Irish priests were one link between Catholic immigrants and authority; Irish policemen provided another. Many of the inspectors on Ellis Island were Irish, which accounts for the frequency with which they garbled central European names. In cities such as New York and Chicago, a whole

political system was built on the mobilization of Irish voters, who provided the basis of Democratic Party power.

Emigration to the New World sometimes had a dramatic effect on
Europe itself and bizarre political hopes were fostered by the links that
grew out of it. During the 1930s officials in the Polish foreign ministry
fantasized about the prospect that emigrants from their country might
found a colony in Latin America,[17] while in 1945 some Sicilians proposed that their island might become a part of the United States. More
seriously, central European nationalism was cultivated. During the First
World War a legion of Polish volunteers was raised among emigrants in
the United States, and the influence of emigrants on eastern European
politics was to persist for the whole of the twentieth century. In 1990,
Franjo Tudjman's campaign to become president of Croatia was said to
have raised around $5 million from émigré supporters.[18] In the same
year, Stanisław Tymiński, who had made his fortune in Canada, returned
to Poland to run for president.

Emigration had less obvious effects on parts of Europe. It increased literacy, because families needed to keep in contact by letter. It also created
imbalances of gender and age as young men left: between 1906 and
1915, 4.86 million Italian men emigrated, but only 1.14 million women
accompanied them; in early twentieth-century Calabria, there were three
young women for every two young men.[19] Sexual imbalance may have
produced a self-perpetuating cycle. Carlo Levi suggested that extra-mari-
tal sexual relations in parts of the Italian south were common because
there were not enough men to provide all women with husbands.[20] Illegitimate children in turn were particularly prone to emigrate – in one
village, three-quarters of them did so.[21]

Migration increased prosperity in home countries as money was sent
back or as emigrants returned to buy cherished plots of land. The economic impact of emigration was particularly great in Italy, where links
between emigrants and their places of origin remained close – it was said
that Italy gained $100 million from emigrants who returned between
1897 and 1902.[22] An enquiry of 1931 showed that 2 million hectares of
land were bought by Italians returning from America (though the fact
that they had held industrial employment in America often meant that
they were not very efficient farmers).[23]

Emigration was often linked to political conservatism. Generally, the
areas that sent emigrants abroad during the early twentieth century remained on the political right for the rest of the century. The Finnish
province of Ostrobothnia, which had lost 120,000 people through emigration, fought for the Whites in the civil war of 1918, while the Italian
south was to provide the backbone of Christian democrat support after

1945. Conservatism may have been a cause rather than an effect of emigration; the very social structures that led to emigration also encouraged conservatism. Emigrants generally left rural areas in which there was little industry and were often encouraged by cultures that placed hope in individual initiative – funds for emigration were provided by tight family systems and the incentive for emigration often came from the desire to buy land. Areas of great estates and landless laborers, by contrast, were too poor to support much emigration and tended to place hope in collective action to improve wages rather than in the purchase of land.

However, if emigration often originated in areas that were already prone to conservatism, it increased those tendencies for three reasons. First, the departure of young men removed the group that was most associated with revolutionary politics. Second, remittance money alleviated social discontent and encouraged property-owning. Third, as America became the heart of anticommunist feeling, emigrant communities in the United States were deliberately mobilized to encourage relatives in the old country to support the political right.

Peasants into citizens?

The changes experienced by those who migrated to the cities or to other countries were so spectacular that it is sometimes tempting to assume that those who remained on the land – still the majority of Europe's inhabitants – were an undifferentiated and unchanging mass. In reality, they were neither, and there were huge variations in the lives of the rural population of Europe. The relatively prosperous areas – England, France, western Germany and Scandinavia – were very different from Spain, southern Italy and eastern Europe, where hunger remained the dominant experience of most who relied on agriculture for a living. Europe was also divided up on the basis of land ownership. Areas of great estates were different from areas of sharecropping, tenant farming, or ownership by small farmers. In general, the great estates were in southern Italy, southern Spain, eastern Germany and Hungary, while tenant farming was most heavily developed in England, which was also the only country in Europe with virtually no small peasant farmers.

For all its impact, migration did not directly affect the majority of inhabitants of Europe. What happened to the European peasants who remained behind? Part of the answer to this question is provided in an influential book by Eugen Weber, *Peasants into Frenchmen*, where he argues that between 1870 and 1914 a change occurred in the French peasantry.[24] Before this, he suggests, most peasants were isolated from the culture of the cities. They were poor, their houses were primitive, they spoke local dialects or patois, and they did not interest themselves in politics. Weights, measures and even currencies still varied at the local level one hundred years after they had been standardized in Paris. Weber suggests that peasant isolation was ended by four forces: communications (roads, railways and telegrams), education, military service, and politics.

How far did these forces act across the rest of Europe? The most significant was military service. Armies were national institutions that had means of coercion at their disposal that no civilian agency could match. They took groups of young men out of the village, subjected them to a common discipline, and forced them to make some effort to learn the national language. During the late nineteenth century, military service became increasingly common throughout Europe, every country except Britain had conscription, and mechanisms by which the wealthy could buy their way out of service were increasingly rare. In practice, the direct influence of military service was limited. It was simply not worthwhile recruiting men who were unhealthy, physically small or lacking in basic education, so the most isolated and backward groups were the least likely to undergo military service. Furthermore, not all countries could afford to equip and train whole cohorts of young men. In France, the famously frail Marcel Proust performed military service;[25] in Spain, the famously robust Pablo Picasso bought himself out of his obligation with 1,200 pesetas provided by his uncle Salvador.[26] In 1914, a Frenchman was three times more likely to be conscripted than a man of the same age in Austria-Hungary.

Even peasants who did undergo military service were not necessarily integrated into the national culture by the experience. Many of them regarded the army as a brief and unpleasant encounter with an alien world. Linguistic diversity in the Austro-Hungarian army was so great that during the First World War one regiment was commanded in English.[27]

Hostility to the army was particularly strong in Russia, where conscripts were sometimes mourned as though dead before being bound or rendered paralytic with vodka and taken to the barracks by their village elders, who were responsible for delivering young men. The Russian army did not have the money to train or equip its men properly, and attempts to teach soldiers how to read and write were abandoned after 1881. Much energy was devoted to simple survival, with regiments forced to produce or earn much of what they needed: in 1907, it was estimated that one conscript in eight spent most of his time making or repairing uniforms. Soldiers were often hired out as laborers. Relations between officers and men were bad and discipline was harsh. For those Russian peasants who were unfortunate enough to be conscripted, the army was not so much an introduction to a wider world as a regression to the beatings, humiliations and *corvées* of feudalism.[28] The Russian army mutinied in 1905 and again in 1917. Elsewhere in Europe, former soldiers could usually be relied on to maintain order, but in Russia they were likely to be at the head of peasant disturbances.

Schools were the other great force of national integration. In theory, every country in Europe had some system of universal education by 1914 and, in a very few cases, this system could provide a means of spectacular social mobility. A clever boy with a supportive parent (usually a mother), a good teacher and an enormous amount of luck might escape his social class altogether. The Italian communist leader Antonio Gramsci, born in 1891, grew up in poverty as the son of a disgraced former clerk in Sardinia before winning a scholarship to the University of Turin. Such cases were rare, though, and often inflicted terrible costs on those involved (Gramsci was later to speak of a "Taylorism of the mind"). More common was a social mobility that was spread over more than one generation so that the son of a peasant might become a primary schoolteacher and the son of a teacher might acquire a university education.

Social mobility spread across three generations was particularly common in France. Born in 1896, Marcel Pagnol was the grandson of a stonemason and the son of a primary schoolteacher *(instituteur)*. Pagnol himself won the second highest scholarship to a *lycée* in Marseilles, which provided him with books, food and a daily glass of red wine, before he took a degree in Montpellier and became a *lycée professeur*. The French historian Maurice Agulhon was born in 1926, the grandson of peasants and the son of *instituteurs* (his parents were born in 1899 and 1901). His skill in passing examinations took him to the Lycée du Parc in Lyons, the École Normale Supérieure in Paris and finally to the French academic elite via the *agrégation* examination and the preparation of a *doctorat d'état*. Agulhon wrote: "Nothing could be more classic than such an outcome, which proceeds from plebeian grandparents to parents who are primary schoolteachers to a career as a higher civil servant or academic."[29] The *normalien* with parents who had been primary schoolteachers and grandparents who had been peasants was a common figure in twentieth-century France, with Georges Pompidou, born in 1911 and President of the Republic from 1969 until his death in 1974, the most famous representative of this group. Jean-François Sirinelli's thesis on the educational elites of inter-war France reveals that between 1927 and 1933 over a quarter of all *normaliens* were the sons of teachers and just under half of these were the sons of primary schoolteachers. Less than one in forty were the sons of workers. Sirinelli himself is a *normalien*, and the son of a *normalien;* his book is dedicated to "*mes quatre grands-parents, instituteurs.*"[30]

Hugh Seton-Watson suggested that a similar pattern of three generational social mobility existed in eastern Europe:

Sons of rich peasants obtained higher education in the small towns, and came back to the village as teachers or priests. The children of schoolmasters, Orthodox priests, Calvinist and Lutheran pastors could begin with an advantage over the other peasants' children. If they showed ability, they reached the university, the most important step towards social advancement. The main goal of Eastern European university students of humble origin was the Public Administration.[31]

Most primary schools had a more limited impact on the lives of their pupils – France and Germany had the most extensive school systems and the most literate populations in continental Europe, while Russia, Spain and many parts of the Habsburg Empire trailed behind. The French governments of the Third Republic consciously used schools to propagate national culture and the national language. Their task was made easier by the fact that France already had a relatively homogeneous national culture (even peasants who did not speak French could see the point in doing so) and by the fact that the education system was highly centralized. Elsewhere, matters were different. The Spanish government issued a decree against teaching in the Catalan language in 1902, but the school system was not sufficiently extensive or well funded to stamp out local languages.[32] In eastern Europe, language was a matter of such contention that schools often became centers of dispute. At the Georgian seminary where Joseph Stalin was educated, a nationalist student had assassinated the principal in 1886. The issues raised by the links between schooling, education and language meant that central European men often entered politics young. Stefan Radić, the Croatian peasant leader, made his political debut publicly burning the Hungarian flag at the age of fifteen. Gavrilo Princip was nineteen when he fired the shot at Sarajevo.

There were other limits on the efficacy of schools. Literacy might be drummed into the heads of pupils, but the connection between marks on the page and spoken words was often a mechanical skill that had no wider impact on the minds of those who acquired it.[33] Some peasants recognized the usefulness of reading and arithmetic primarily as a means of protecting themselves against swindling by traders or landlords, but they did not associate such skills with an acceptance of the values of the urban world. Many schoolteachers were underpaid and poorly educated, commanding little prestige in the communities to which they were sent.

Schooling often generated dissatisfactions that could not be appeased. The children who passed through Russian primary schools, which increased in number rapidly during the early twentieth century, were keen to escape from the harsh world of the countryside – one survey showed that only one in fifty peasant children at school wished to inherit their parents' occupation.[34] The nature of Russian society meant that few children stood much chance of escape into anything more desirable than the equally unappealing world of the factory. A little learning proved a dangerous thing for Tsarist Russia; the half-educated sons of peasants were to provide Bolshevism with its mass support after 1917. In France, by contrast, schooling probably eased social tensions more than it exacerbated them. Many peasant children could hope to escape into some form of clerical employment, and even those who stayed on the land might hope to profit from their literacy, if only to read the newspaper.

Transport and communications also began to connect the European peasant to a wider world. Railways and telegraph systems expanded in the late nineteenth and early twentieth centuries, with a dramatic impact. Politicians could visit their constituents regularly, and national newspapers were distributed across a country on the day of publication. Even perceptions of time were changed: for much of the nineteenth century, European countries had contained different time zones; the advent of the railway timetable was probably the most important force in their synchronization. Such developments might have had more impact on small towns, where railway stations and telegraph offices were located, than in the countryside itself, but the improvement of roads created better links for the countryside too, and their use was made easier as the bicycle became more popular. It is not surprising that the Tour de France became a symbol of national unification.

Transport networks created large numbers of secure jobs: by 1914, the Prussian railway system, with 560,000 people on the payroll, was the largest employer in Europe.[35] Such jobs were attractive to the sons of peasants, who realized that a few years in primary school might earn a lifetime of relief from dirt and hard labor. State jobs were particularly appealing to those who had already acquired some experience of obeying – and giving – orders during military service. Former soldiers were also attractive to state agencies that wished to ensure that they had a politically reliable staff: the Prussian police force was reserved for those who had spent between six and nine years in the army. Pagnol regretted the way in which military service and state jobs were combining to empty the Provençal countryside: "Since the sad invention of compulsory military service, their [the peasants'] sons, liberated from the barracks, had remained prisoners of the towns, where they had founded dynasties of crossing keepers, road menders, and postmen."[36] Nevertheless, his own description of the labor of his peasant friend Lili makes it clear why a bright boy would wish to escape such a life.

Roads and railways also helped to bring the market economy to the countryside. Food could be transported, and the industrial economy of the distant city could provide peasants with necessary implements or, increasingly, luxuries that they could be persuaded to want. The results did not always fit expectations about "modernization." Parts of the countryside became more exclusively agricultural as rural industries collapsed in the face of large-scale industrial competition. Peasants sometimes endured considerable hardship, not because they could not produce enough food but because they wished to sell as much of their produce as possible in order to acquire money and land. Milk consumption in the German countryside dropped as its production rose; one family produced 190 liters in two months but drank only 3.5 liters.[37] In France, the capacity of peasants for self-exploitation could be even more dramatic. Inhabitants of Breton villages were said never to taste the oysters that they sent to the city. During the Second World War, mortality rates in many rural areas dropped as the breakdown of legitimate markets encouraged peasants to eat more of their own produce.

Some peasants survived, and even benefited from, the market economy. In Germany and Austria, credit unions made possible the purchase of new equipment and fertilizers, while marketing associations made it easier for peasants to sell their produce. In lower Austria, the first credit cooperative was founded in 1887, and by 1910, 300 such bodies existed. Sometimes the very leaders who denounced the evils of capitalism proved most adept at meeting its challenges. Indeed, the "traditional" ways of life could themselves be the product of market economics: in some parts of Austria, only rich farmers could afford to wear "peasant" clothes.

Politics in the countryside

Two things brought politics to the countryside. First, by 1914, most European countries had introduced something close to universal adult male suffrage, so suddenly the vote of every laborer counted for as much as that of his landlord. Second, industrialization, urbanization and the rise of organized labor meant that the propertied classes needed allies against the left, and they often thought they could be found among the peasantry. Peasants were now presented as the antithesis of the urban working classes, sturdy and healthy when compared with "degenerate" and stunted proletarians; peasants were deferential and conservative while their counterparts in the city were criminal or revolutionary.

Assumptions about the city and countryside were to overshadow the political history of twentieth-century Europe. Bodies such as the French senate were designed to provide a rural brake on dangerous ideas that might come from the cities. Conservatives sought to organize the peasantry into associations such as the German Farmers' League, which was founded in 1893 and attracted the support of 142 Reichstag deputies.

In reality, the distinction between countryside and city was never as clear-cut as either side imagined. In areas of rapid industrialization, many workers had been born peasants and sometimes maintained close contact with the farms from which they came. Workers returned to the land after years in the city, or even commuted to work from small farms on the outskirts of towns, and entire communities from particular rural areas of Ireland or Poland might exist within the urban working class of Britain and Germany. Parts of the countryside were affected by their relationship to industrial work: for example, the Côtes du Nord in Brittany voted for the left because of its links with industrial St-Denis. The pattern of industrial protest in the twentieth century sometimes bore more relation to the *jacqueries* of the countryside than to the disciplined mobilization of socialist imagination.

Nor had rebellion ceased in the countryside itself. Violent conflict was most obvious in Russia, where troops were called out to restore order 1,500 times between 1883 and 1903;[38] in 1908, a quiet year, 1,800 officials were killed.[39] In 1907, French wine growers revolted in protest at declining prices.[40] In the same year, Romanian peasants were behind disturbances that caused thousands of deaths.

Far from being ordained by nature, peasant politics were determined by social position. Peasants' relationships to other groups varied widely. Land-owning peasants – such as those in western Germany or in large parts of France – were reluctant to embrace politics that involved the abolition of private property. In the German political system, economic issues made the peasantry align themselves with the right. In lower Austria, peasants were hostile to both the cities and the large landowners because the weight of feudal obligations had been particularly harsh, so politics were not marked by the aristocratic patronage that characterized their German equivalent: thirty-two out of fifty-nine Christian Social Party candidates in the lower Austrian countryside were drawn from the peasantry itself or from rural businessmen.[41] In France, politics were still largely dominated by the legacy of the Revolution. Many peasants believed that it was the Revolution that had allowed them to acquire land and consequently associated support for the left with the defense of property. Peasant politics were also influenced by the pattern of land settlement. Isolated farms – such as those that prevailed in Brittany – made the organization of collective action difficult and made individual peasants vulnerable to pressure from conservative notables, whereas *vignerons* from southern France lived in small towns rather than in the countryside itself and depended on collective action to maintain cooperative cellars and equipment. In such communities, sociability blended easily into socialism. In parts of southern France in the early twentieth century, almost half the members of the Marxist Parti Ouvrier Français were peasants.[42]

In places where land was worked by sharecroppers, tenants or propertyless laborers, those who lived in the countryside had far less reason to support the established order. Indeed, the landless laborers of Hungary, Prussia, Spain and parts of southern Italy, whose life was divided between bouts of exhausting toil and protracted periods of unemployment, had less to lose than a factory worker with a secure job, social insurance and membership of a friendly society.

Relations between land, peasants and politics in Russia had a particular significance. The emancipation of the serfs in 1861 had freed the peasantry from feudal obligations to their lords and given them ownership of their land, but peasants were still obliged to pay "redemption dues" in return for property. The payment of dues was administered by a village commune, or *mir*, which thus exercised considerable powers, including the right to prevent peasants from leaving the village as well as the allocation of land. No peasant could be sure that he would retain a particular plot for his lifetime, let alone pass it to his children; consequently there was little reason to improve it. The differences between the Russian peasantry and their western European counterparts were reflected in demography and credit. Because land was often distributed according to the number of hands available to work it, Russian peasants had an incentive to have numerous children, which accounts for the high Russian birth rate. In France, by contrast, the division of land among heirs provided an incentive to limit the number of children. Similarly, the expectation that land would be kept and passed down through the generations gave peasants in Germany and Austria an inducement to invest in machinery, fertilizers and the improvement of land. The Russian peasant had no incentive to invest in his property. Surplus money was either spent on drink or lent out. Far from being debtors, many Russian peasants were lenders (kulaks).

Petr Stolypin, Prime Minister of Russia from 1906 to 1911, wished to create a peasantry along western European lines, or at least one similar to the peasantry that he had seen in Poland, where he had been a provincial governor. He encouraged peasants to separate from the commune and to establish efficient private farms that could be passed down from father to son. To this end, he introduced a law in 1906 that gave peasants the right to enclose and consolidate their land, explaining this measure by saying that "the government has placed its wager not on the poor and the drunk but on the strong."

Stolypin's plans failed. Peasants who left the commune threatened the interests of their neighbors and especially those of village elders, whose power was founded on the existing order. This was not a society in which such threats were likely to be met with recourse to law. Surveyors sent to oversee land consolidation traveled with armed guards, and peasants who wished to take advantage of new arrangements had to brave vandalism, beatings and even the threat of murder. Out of 6 million applications for land consolidation made by 1915, more than a third were subsequently withdrawn, and two-thirds of the million consolidations that were completed had to be supported by the authorities against the opposition of the commune.[43] Land consolidation was also opposed by much of the gentry, who resented the prospect of their own land being taken. Most of all, Stolypin's reforms failed because they were founded on the assumption that a strong peasantry could be created from above by government fiat without changing other aspects of the social order. Peasant prosperity in France had been based on dispossession of the Church and the nobility, which was out of the question in Russia. In Germany participation in a market economy meant peasants could enjoy the fruits of industrialization in the form of tools and artificial fertilizer; furthermore, a democratic political system allowed German peasants to benefit from universal suffrage and the need of the propertied classes to find allies against the urban working class. Stolypin had assumed that economic reform was a substitute for, rather than an accompaniment to, political reform.

Peasant politics were also determined by the attitude of the parties that solicited support. French socialists often placed themselves at the head of peasant rebellions; the socialist mayor of Narbonne supported the *vigneron* revolt of 1907.[44] But elsewhere the Marxist left neglected rural areas. This was particularly true of the most powerful European socialist party, the German Social Democratic Party (SPD), whose culture was designed to appeal to urban workers, for whom support for the party fitted in with membership of a union, neighborhood social life and factory work. Furthermore, the SPD rejected attempts, made at the Breslau conference of 1895, to change its policy towards small property in order to appeal to peasants – though party leaders in rural Bavaria seemed to have made more discreet moves in this direction.[45]

Indifference on the part of the European left tied in with pressure from the right to mold peasant politics. Conservatives presented themselves as the natural defenders of the countryside, and often had means to exert influence over rural inhabitants. Tenants, sharecroppers and laborers were all vulnerable to intimidation by landlords, which often counteracted any interest that the lack of property might have given them in voting for the left. In its simplest form, "notable" influence over peasants rested on the control of private resources, such as the power to evict recalcitrant tenants or provide gifts for those who did as they were told. The growth of the state that occurred in the early twentieth century might have threatened this private power, but in practice it often supplemented it. Notables became influential in local government and thus extended their own largesse with the distribution of public goods. In southern Italy, civil service jobs were offered in exchange for votes; in Spain the capacity to secure exemption from military service provided the rural *caciques* with much of their power.

The association of conservatism with the peasantry became so close that sometimes "peasant" simply became a synonym for the political right and lost all relation to those who lived in the countryside. In 1945, the Smallholders' Party won the Budapest municipal election. In 1951, Jacques Isorni, a lawyer, sat in the French parliament as a Peasant Party deputy representing the *beaux quartiers* of western Paris.

Conclusion

The European countryside changed even more rapidly in the three decades before 1914 than ever before – railways, mass migration, schools, the extension of suffrage, and military service all had dramatic effects. But rural society was not just transformed from outside. The forces for change had such an impact because peasants chose to use them, which raises interesting questions about the meaning of progress in the early twentieth century. The word "progress" was most often used by educated bourgeois liberal men who were, if they had any religion, Protestant, yet the illiterate Polish peasant who packed all his possessions in a handkerchief and left his home with a one-way ticket and the name of a distant relative who might get him a job in the Chicago stockyards was, in some ways, more representative of the new industrial world than the liberal who enthused about "progress" in the pages of the *Manchester Guardian* or the *Dépêche de Toulouse*.

Urbanization and migration could in fact strengthen tendencies that were seen as archaic among the European bourgeoisie. Religious practice in New York was higher than in most European cities, often taking forms, such as the Italian propensity for cults of saints, that would have been regarded as the worst kind of superstition by stern Protestant liberals in, say, Berlin. The contrast between the "modernity" of the urban intellectual and that of the migrating peasant can be seen in the book *Christ Stopped at Eboli* by Carlo Levi, a doctor, artist and writer from Milan, who in the 1920s was exiled to a small village in the Italian south (Gagliano) by the Fascist government. He was shocked by his new environment, which he regarded as deeply "primitive," but he also recognized that the most important social influence on his neighbors came from the contact that many of them had had with America through emigration. When the villagers paraded a statue of their patron saint through the streets, Levi noticed that they pinned dollar bills to this totem of "backwardness."

New forms of contact between city and countryside created a fresh awareness of the peasant "problem" on the part of the educated as city dwellers became increasingly likely to come into contact with the peasantry. Immigration in America produced a swathe of studies such as *The Polish Peasant in Europe and America*.[46]

Just as the interaction of city and countryside sometimes changed the city, it sometimes froze the countryside or, at least, froze the city dweller's perception of it. There was a new self-consciousness in folk songs, dances or traditional costume, and, in the process of being recorded and discussed, peasant practices became formalized. America was much associated with such formalization: communities in Chicago or Detroit no longer learned how to be Donegal peasants from their parents but found out how to be Irishmen by attending meetings of cultural associations in church halls, while the culture of the Polish Pale was evoked in the stories that Isaac Bashevis Singer wrote for the Yiddish language newspapers of New York long after the Polish Jews had been wiped out. Literacy and the interest of urban observers meant that folklore was increasingly likely to be written down, and the spread of the gramophone and the photograph meant that music and clothing could be recorded and, eventually, classified in ethnographic studies. Perhaps what was really new about the early years of the twentieth century was not so much that peasant communities changed as that anyone expected them not to do so.

2
SOCIALISM AND THE
WORKING CLASS

"ON AND ON, up and up," wrote Ramsay MacDonald, the future leader of the British Labour Party. It was a phrase that said much about the attitude of European socialists in the first decade of the twentieth century. The size of the industrial working class, the membership of trade unions and the socialist vote were all increasing, and the socialist movement was more unified than ever before. Anarchism still had some influence on the labor movements of France, Spain and Italy, and many British Labour leaders remained resolutely pragmatic, but in general Marxism provided European socialism with a unified and coherent ideology. The Second International, formed in 1889, grouped the various European parties together, while within individual countries socialists were increasingly likely to combine in a single party. The Parti Ouvrier Belge was founded in 1885; Austrian and Swiss socialist parties were founded in 1888; an Italian Socialist Party was founded in 1892; and the French socialist parties united in the Section Française de l'Internationale Ouvrière (SFIO) in 1905. In Germany, the Social Democratic Party (SPD) eventually had 1 million members and attracted the votes of 4 million, and with 110 deputies was the largest group in the Reichstag. Yet the failure of international socialism was exposed in 1914, when it did not prevent the majority of workers in most European countries from uniting with their oppressors to pursue a war against the workers of other countries.

The first problem for European socialists was that the economic analysis on which their political analysis was founded did not match the realities of Europe in the early twentieth century. Many Marxists expected rates of profit to decline as opportunities for investment were used up, encouraging capitalists to seek prosperity by exploiting their workers with ever greater ruthlessness. Capital would become more concentrated until a tiny group of plutocrats confronted a proletariat with nothing to lose but its chains. This did not happen. Working-class living standards in most countries had increased since the mid-nineteenth century, though the scale of such increases varied from country to country. Working-class living standards were highest in Britain, where the fruits of nineteenth-century prosperity meant that increased wages could be spent on cheap cocoa, tea, and food (such as corned beef) imported from outside Europe. Working hours were reduced, and free time was consolidated into the weekend, rather than being taken in the form of long breaks in the working day. Workers' lives increasingly revolved around the home, the family and the neighborhood, especially the local pub, rather than the workplace. George Orwell wrote that revolution in England had been averted by "fish and chips and strong tea."

On the continent, workers were less likely to be absorbed in a depoliticized consumer culture. Cramped housing, in part a product of rapid industrialization, was not conducive to family life; almost one in eight Berlin families took in lodgers in 1905.[1] Working-class culture in areas of heavy industry was rough, hard-drinking and largely masculine: in the Ruhr town of Bochum there were three times as many men aged between eighteen and twenty as women the same age. Far from being tranquil neighborhood pubs, bars on the continent were often located near the workplace and were often centers of left-wing organization – in Hamburg, four undercover policemen devoted all their time to reporting on socialist agitation in working-class bars.[2] This very fact, however, suggests that working-class dispossession had limits. Workers could afford to indulge in at least some nonessential consumption, and contact with bar owners meant that their leadership was often drawn from a group outside the working class itself: of thirty-six socialist councillors in Roubaix, twenty-two managed bistros.[3] Furthermore, certain institutions discouraged labor militancy by making the lives of workers more bearable, with companies such as Schneider in France providing their employees with houses, medical care and schools. In Germany, the SPD and the labor unions themselves created a working-class culture that alleviated working-class discontent, and socialist institutions organized choral societies, football teams and youth clubs – by 1910, socialist sports organizations had 300,000 members.[4] By 1914, the party controlled ninety newspapers with a circulation of almost 1.5 million. Often, the culture that emerged out of such institutions bore curious resemblances to the bourgeois order that the party ostensibly wished to overthrow, and there was a heavy emphasis on educa-

tion and improvement. By 1911 the SPD had established 244 local education boards, and in the same year the Leipzig workers' library had almost
17,000 members.[5]

The conflict between large-scale property owners and the working
class was blunted by intermediate groups, the most important of which
was the lower middle class. Many assumed that the lower middle class
was a historical anomaly that would disappear as production and distribution were concentrated into large units. In reality, however, at the beginning of the twentieth century the size of the lower middle class was increasing. Growing prosperity often meant increased demand for retail
services: the number of cafés in Paris quadrupled during the last years of
the nineteenth century. The arrival of mass politics also gave the lower
middle class a new importance as governments became interested in using the middle class as allies against the parties of the working class. The
multiparty systems of most continental countries granted particular advantages, according great influence to "hinge" parties – such as the
French Radical Party or the German Centre Party – which acquired leverage from their capacity to ally with either right or left and often appealed
to a largely lower-middle-class constituency. The result of such political
influence was that special concessions were made to preserve and appease
the lower middle class. Taxes on shopkeepers were lowered in France,
and, in Belgium, a "*Bureau des Classes Moyennes*" was created in 1899.[6]

Two other things swelled the size of the lower middle class. The first
was the separation of production and distribution, which divided shopkeepers from artisans; the second was the expansion of clerical work in
large companies and public organizations, which produced a change in
the nature of clerical work as well as its scale. For much of the nineteenth
century, clerking had been a means of social mobility that served as an
apprenticeship for higher management. In Lloyds Bank in Britain, for example, all staff, including the chief general manager, were recruited as
clerks after leaving school at the age of sixteen,[7] but as the base of low-
level clerical work expanded and as higher posts became closed to those
without advanced educational qualifications, clerking became a lifetime's
occupation. In 1914, an English bank clerk wrote: "I am the son of a professional man and have a public school education, but no private means. I
cannot possibly expect to get married and I am faced with a solitary life
in lodgings to the end of my days with the continual strains of financial
worries."[8] Such people might respond in two ways. They might accept
their social position and try to improve their financial circumstances by
joining trade unions: the Bank Clerks' Association in England was
founded in 1906 and had 30,000 members by 1922. Alternatively, they
might try to compensate for their diminished chances of material

prosperity by emphasizing the cultural distinctions that separated them from the working class below and united them with the *haute bourgeoisie* above. Many lower-middle-class men who were torn between their romantic aspirations and the drab reality of their daily lives seem to have welcomed the escape to war in 1914.

The lower middle class was to become one of the great villains of twentieth-century history. Contemporaries mocked it as a repository of philistinism and absurd pretensions. Pooter, the clerk portrayed in George and Weedon Grossmith's *Diary of a Nobody*, is a ridiculous figure, while Leonard Bast, the clerk in E. M. Forster's *Howards End*, is out of place in the cultivated circles in which he aspires to move. Later historians would blame the lower middle class for reactionary politics and particularly for the rise of fascism, but such analysis ignores the enormous variation in values and prosperity that existed among this group. Bast lives in a damp basement with a woman who is not his wife; Pooter lives in married respectability in a house in Holloway and employs a servant. Shopkeepers had a natural community of interest with their clients, and often shared the political views of the neighborhood in which they lived, so providers of luxury services in the first *arrondissement* of Paris tended to be right-wing, while their counterparts in working-class Belleville were on the left. Around Milan, those who lived in the working-class suburbs were on the left, while those who lived in the city itself were on the right.[9] Left-wing shopkeepers might provide credit to workers during strikes or join working-class demonstrations.

There was a division between the new lower middle class of clerical workers and the old lower middle class of shopkeepers and artisans. The former were associated with the large enterprises that the latter saw as a threat to their position; the former were often state employees, while the latter often felt overburdened by taxes; the former often had secure employment and pensions, while the latter might be struck by bankruptcy at any moment. The interests of clerical workers and small shopkeepers might even come into direct conflict: in Milan, railway clerks organized their own buyers' cooperatives, cutting out the local retailers.[10] Sometimes socialists succeeded in organizing the new clerical workers, but often, like the peasantry, this potentially powerful group was left to the attentions of the right.

Even the working class itself encompassed many variations. Socialists often ignored the fact that large-scale industry was concentrated in particular areas, such as the Milan–Genoa–Turin triangle, where more than half of all Italian enterprises employing more than ten people were located. They also ignored the fact that particular kinds of industry gave rise to particular kinds of militancy. Often, the most apparently coherent analyses of capitalism were, in fact, based on a single, unrepresentative area. In Britain, the Marxist Social Democrat Federation had its stronghold among the small-scale textile industries of Burnley in Lancashire;[11] the Marxist Parti Ouvrier Français drew a large part of its support from those who worked in the textile industry in the northern city of Roubaix. The effects of industrial growth on working-class political organization were complex. Company towns gave much power to the employer, while highly diversified areas of small factories, such as Birmingham, created interclass relations that undermined socialist organization. Modern large-scale plants – such as those of the chemical and metallurgy industries – required new tactics from labor. Sometimes, industrialists who had indebted themselves to buy expensive equipment could not afford to countenance strikes and consequently proved willing to come to terms with trade unions. Sometimes new industries gave rise to a less skilled working class – often made up of arrivals from the countryside or foreign countries – which broke with the union traditions that had been founded on craftsmen. A single factory might be home to several different working-class cultures – unskilled workers performed repetitive tasks on the production line under the eyes of foremen, themselves a caste apart in the working class, while older traditions of resistance and autonomy survived among the craftsmen in repair shops.

Other divisions impeded labor organization. Race, nationality and religion cut across the working class. Some socialists, such as Rosa Luxemburg, who had been born in the Prussian-ruled part of Poland, regarded nationalism as an irrelevance and hoped that identities other than those of class would fade as the workers became more conscious of their position. This did not happen. Nationality issues caused particular problems in the Habsburg Empire, where the Austrian Socialist Party drew its members almost exclusively from among German-speaking workers.[12] The Austrian Emperor, who felt that his empire was more threatened by national divisions than by social ones, introduced universal male suffrage in the hope that "imperial socialism" might prove a force for unity. Many German-speaking socialists supported the empire, and one, Karl Renner, devised an ingenious scheme whereby people might be allowed their own language and schools regardless of where they lived in the empire. Such unifying initiatives failed, though, and Czech socialists split from their German comrades. In other countries, immigration posed particular problems for the leaders of the working class. There were more than a quarter of a million Polish speakers in the Rhineland and Westphalia in 1910. Trade unions and socialist parties were often suspicious of foreign workers.

Religious divisions overlapped with racial ones. In continental Europe, socialism and Christianity were usually seen as inimical: in 1874, the German socialist Bebel said that they mixed "like fire and water." In Germany, no Catholic priest supported the social democrats, and three Protestant pastors who did so were dismissed.[13] Like middle-class progressives, socialists assumed that religion would decline with economic progress, but they were wrong. Underdeveloped areas such as southern Spain or parts of southwestern France were often de-Christianized, while Belgium was one of the most industrialized countries in Europe and also one of the most devout. Catholicism, which rejected free-market liberalism and proved adept at collective action, often adjusted well to industrial society. In Germany, the Christian Union had 343,000 members by 1914.[14] Sometimes the Catholic Church provided an alternative focus of loyalty for Italian, Polish or Irish workers who were not welcomed by secular workers' organizations.

Socialism faced other problems. Many of its leaders were bourgeois. Emile Vandervelde in Belgium was the son of a lawyer, and Jean Jaurès in France was the highly educated son of a businessman. Trotsky (not exactly a proletarian himself) jibed that one needed a doctorate to become a leader of the Austrian Socialist Party. Such men often had tense relations with their working-class constituents: when Léon Blum, a disciple of Jaurès, became leader of the SFIO, his propensity for writing articles about his friend Marcel Proust in socialist newspapers caused much irritation.

The conditions of the working class in the different countries of Europe produced a variety of political mobilizations. Socialist parties might be reformist (that is, committed to working within the existing system), like the British Labour Party. German social democrats rejected such a stance. At the Erfurt Congress of 1891, the SPD accepted Karl Kautsky's view that revolution should be the party's aim. Eduard Bernstein's "revisionist" advocacy of more limited goals was rejected, though SPD practice, as opposed to its theory, was often reformist. French socialists were divided: the "possibilist" Alexandre Millerand accepted ministerial office in 1899, while hardline Marxists (such as those in Jules Guesde's Parti Ouvrier Français) opposed collaboration with bourgeois parties. In France, a substantial syndicalist current in the trade unions rejected party politics altogether, advocating the destruction of the capitalist order through a general strike.

Debate about reformism was linked to debate about the role of the state. Marxist theory suggested that the bourgeois state was a force for bad. Some labor movements, particularly those with strong traditions of self-help, mistrusted state intervention – workers should protect themselves against employers through strikes and against misfortunes such as illness through insurance funds. State support should be encouraged only for groups – such as women, children or the old – who were excluded, or

ought to be excluded, from work. Other socialists believed that state action might be useful as a means to rally and encourage the working class
(the position of the Parti Ouvrier Français) or was a good thing in itself
(the position of Jaurès). Increasingly, socialist parties showed themselves
willing to accept state interference in certain aspects of the lives of the
working class. In 1894, Bavarian socialists voted in favor of the state
budget; in Hesse, socialists supported the activities of factory inspectors.

Not all labor movements confronted the same kind of state. All governments resorted to some degree of repression, and troops were frequently
called out to face workers (such fighting killed 200 people in Milan in
1898), but the propensity for repression varied from one country to another. Britain had a small standing army, and blatant intervention by the
judiciary on the side of employers in labor disputes was comparatively
rare. Many labor leaders appreciated that legal mechanisms could be a useful weapon: at one London meeting of the Socialist International, the
British organizers threatened to call the police to eject anarchists. In Germany, and especially in Prussia, matters were different. A tough police
force, composed largely of former army sergeants, enforced a ferocious pe-
nal code; in Berlin, even the length of hatpins was regulated by law. In
Russia, where trade unions were illegal and every strike was a potentially
revolutionary act, workers had nothing to gain from legality and union organization often brought them into contact with underground socialist organizers. Skilled workers, the group most likely to be satisfied with their
lot in much of western Europe, were the most radical in Russia.

Reformism was underwritten by the condition of the labor movement
in each country as well as that of its working-class constituency. Organizations with money, buildings and large membership rolls had much to
lose if the system that had allowed them to build up such advantages were
to collapse. German socialist bureaucrats enjoyed bourgeois lifestyles as a
result of their employment by a workers' party. Fifty-five SPD candidates
in the 1912 legislative elections were journalists on party newspapers,[15]
and the income of the average party functionary was 3,000 marks, twice
that of the average worker.[16]

Curious relations between socialist theory and practice sometimes developed. Although all socialists wished to destroy capitalism, they disagreed
over how to do so. Advocates of armed revolution were found alongside
those who favored a more peaceful and gradual process, and it was often
unclear whether a strike or participation in electoral politics was a means to
destroy capitalism or simply a means to alleviate the lot of the workers
while capitalism lasted. Matters were complicated by the fact that many socialists were indifferent to doctrinal debates and by the cohabitation of

revolutionary theory with reformist activity. The very confidence of Marxist predictions encouraged ambiguity, and belief in the inevitability of revolution often made socialists into functional conservatives. Safe in the knowledge that capitalism was doomed, they ignored the mechanisms of revolution and concentrated on day-to-day organization, which actually made revolution less likely.

Conclusion

The contradictions between revolutionary philosophy and reformist practice were exposed most awkwardly by attitudes towards war. According to Marxist theory, workers of all nations had common interests, and the establishment of a bureau of the Socialist International in 1900 seemed to show that European socialists took these shared concerns seriously. However, it was not clear what individual socialists or socialist parties ought to do in the event of war. Some argued for a general strike to paralyze mobilization. Such proposals were easiest to put forward in countries where socialism was weak and the working class was small, so that resistance to mobilization would have little impact and the inevitable state repression would make little difference to socialist leaders, who were often already in exile or prison. A strike in Germany, by contrast, would have had a dramatic effect on mobilization, because such a high proportion of the workforce was unionized, as well as on socialist leaders, because the positions that they stood to lose were relatively comfortable. French socialists were keener on strike action than their German counterparts, but even they would not commit themselves to it.

Even socialists who opposed war faced practical problems if they wished to prevent it. A general strike was hard to organize and in time of war would have brought severe penalties on labor organizers. Socialists lacked contact with two important groups. The first was the peasantry, the largest single element in most European armies. There is evidence that many peasants were hostile to war in August 1914, but collective action or even the diffusion of pacifist propaganda would have been difficult in the countryside, and the socialist movement had paid little attention to peasants in the decades preceding 1914. The second key group was composed of government employees. A strike by railwaymen, government clerks and telegraph operators would have been the one sure way to stop mobilization, but socialist organization was usually weakest among this group. In Prussia, public-sector workers, who made up 5.2 percent of the workforce in 1907, were better paid than their private-sector counterparts[17] and were forbidden to join the SPD, while many key posts were occupied by former professional soldiers whose loyalty could be relied on. The drafting of workers further disrupted established organizations – men who were now in the army lacked contact with the labor movement, and workers who remained in the factory lacked guns. As the war continued, the gulf widened.

Only in Russia and Serbia did the majority of socialist leaders oppose war in 1914. Other parties were divided, though most socialist parliamentarians at first supported the war. The Belgian socialist Camille Huysmans moved the headquarters of the Second International from German-occupied Brussels to neutral Holland, and convened a variety of conferences of socialist leaders from belligerent countries (notably at Zimmerwald in Switzerland in 1915). Huysmans himself was attacked by many members of the Belgian Socialist Party, which became fiercely nationalist as a result of the invasion of Belgium. In Germany the "Independent Socialists" left the SPD in December 1915, while Marcel Sembat and Jules Guesde, who had been a hard-line opponent of all collaboration with the bourgeoisie, joined the French government in August 1914, remaining there until December 1916, by which time almost half of French socialists opposed the war. In Britain, some Labour politicians joined the government in 1915 and 1916, while others opposed the war. Labour leaders could obtain benefits from participation in the war – trade unions secured new degrees of recognition from employers and governments that were desperate to ensure the smooth running of the economy.

War increased divisions among the working classes. Skilled men, especially those involved in arms production, did well. They were, however, joined in the factories by large numbers of women, foreigners (especially in France and Germany), prisoners of war, and youths. Established skilled workers tended to remain loyal to existing socialist parties, whereas women and foreigners were likely to remain "apolitical" (that is, to indulge in forms of protest that were not recognized by any party). Young men who had recently entered factory employment were most receptive to revolutionary socialism.

It was in the most industrialized countries in Europe – Britain, Germany and Belgium – that reformist socialism was strongest. The German case was particularly important, because the German party was the largest in Europe and had vigorously denounced reformist theory before 1914. German labor leaders were influenced by the recognition and influence that they secured in the war economy, and the results of the alliance between the SPD and the German state could be seen after November 1918, when the SPD formed a government. Its formal abandonment of revolutionary principles did not come until 1927, but in practice abandonment was already incarnated in the Groener–Ebert pact, by which a Prussian general agreed to help a socialist Prime Minister repress insurrection by the extreme left.

German labor leaders present a sharp contrast with the leaders of Russian socialism. In Tsarist Russia, levels of industrialization were low, the working class was small, and labor organization was illegal. In such circumstances, no one could imagine that the revolution would come naturally, and socialist leaders were not distracted by the everyday tasks of administering a large organization. They placed their faith in will and action, rather than in patience, organization and theoretical debates about the manner in which some distant revolution might come about. The Russian Bolshevik Party was formed in exile in 1903, at a time when socialists in western Europe were winning parliamentary seats and beginning to discuss the possibility of obtaining ministerial office. The Bolsheviks came into existence as a result of a split in the Russian Social Democratic Party between those who wanted a party with a wide membership, the Mensheviks, and those who stressed the need for a disciplined revolutionary elite. Lenin, the Bolshevik leader, was a Marxist, but he was also influenced by a Russian tradition that emphasized the will, discipline and courage of a revolutionary.[18]

The First World War increased the size of the Russian working class, but it did so under very different circumstances from those that prevailed in the West. Factories were filled with workers who had recently been drawn from the countryside, with no tradition of organization, negotiation or obedience to a trade union hierarchy. When they were dissatisfied – and the conditions of Moscow and Petrograd generated a great deal of dissatisfaction – they turned to strikes and riots of the kind that toppled Tsarism in February 1917. Furthermore, established skilled workers were not drawn into the war effort in the way that some of their counterparts in western Europe were. Trade unions, the key link between workers, employers and the state in western Europe, were weak in Russia. Even the "workers" group on the War Industry Committee (the section of labor leadership that favored the war effort most) insisted in December 1916: "The proletariat . . . will protest decisively against all military coercion and will strive for a peace acceptable to the workers of all countries."[19]

Bolshevism did not replace Tsarism because it had deep roots among the workers. The Bolshevik Party had a large number of members in the summer of 1917, but those members had joined only recently and had a limited idea of what Bolshevism stood for. The leaders certainly did not see themselves as the democratic representatives of the membership. Bolshevik leaders, unencumbered by organizational traditions or a comprehensive body of theory, were able to adopt the flexible tactics that were crucial to the success of revolution and, more importantly, to the failure of counterrevolution. They allied with the very groups from which western European socialists were alienated (peasants and soldiers) and responded to events and seized power at a time that western European theorists would have said was premature. The determinism of western European socialism meant nothing in Russia. The Bolsheviks knew that they had to create circumstances rather than wait for them to arise.

3

THE GREAT WAR

FOR THE BRITISH and the French, the Great War has a time and a place. It began in August 1914, and it ended with the armistice at 11 A.M. on November 11, 1918. It took place in Flanders and in eastern France (more specifically, British memories are dominated by the Battle of the Somme, while those of the French are dominated by that of Verdun). The war cost millions of pounds and millions of lives, but it did not cause much physical suffering to civilians. Indeed, the novelty of the Great War on the western front was that it was confined to such a small area and that casualties were almost exclusively caused by weapons (mostly artillery) rather than starvation and disease. It could be summed up with Pétain's brutal platitude "*le feu tue.*"

For other European countries, things were less clear. Spain, Sweden, Holland, Norway, Denmark and Switzerland did not participate. Italy, Bulgaria, Portugal and Greece joined the fighting between 1915 and 1917. Romania entered the war in August 1916, accepted an armistice with Germany in December 1917, and declared war again in November 1918. The Bolshevik government of Russia tried what Trotsky called "neither war nor peace" before finally accepting the humiliating terms of the Treaty of Brest-Litovsk in March 1918. For Russia, as for much of central Europe, the formal end of war did not mean the end of fighting. Civil war, rebellion and repression continued into the 1920s.

The nature of the war as well as its chronology were different away from the western front. For one thing, there was no single "eastern front." Austrian troops fought against the Italians in the Alps and the Russians in Galicia. Turks held British and Australian troops on the beach at Gallipoli and fought Russian troops in the east of their country. Russian, Austrian and German armies often fought a war of movement, and large numbers of civilians were obliged to flee invading armies (as in Serbia) or were massacred (as in Turkey). Here, war did not just mean "*le feu tue.*" Disease and starvation ravaged the civilian population. The destruction of the war was not contained on the front line but spilt out until it led to the overthrow of a monarchy (in Germany), an empire (in Austria-Hungary) and an entire social order (in Russia). Examining why the war took such dramatically different forms in east and west helps to explain not only who won the war but also what legacy it left for Europe after 1918.

Origins of war

Ten years after the end of the war, the French historian Elie Halévy told an audience in Oxford that "what decided the German government to prepare for an eventual European War was a crisis that was brewing, not in the highly industrialized and capitalistic West, but among the primitive communities of the south-east of Europe. War came to the West from the East; it was forced upon the West by the East."[1]

This is a beguiling explanation. Britain, France and Germany were all industrialized countries with highly educated populations and more or less universal male suffrage. Why should states that were so well placed to calculate their interests rationally embark on a war that was to bring such destruction? Commercial links between the industrialized countries appeared to make their interests inseparable. In a famous book, published in 1909, Norman Angell had argued that the notion that any industrialized power could benefit from war was a "great illusion."[2] A Lloyd's underwriter told the Committee of Imperial Defence that he would feel obliged to pay compensation if the Royal Navy sank a German ship.[3]

The war began with the assassination of Archduke Franz Ferdinand of Austria by Gavrilo Princip, a Bosnian Serb, and the subsequent Austrian attempt to impose humiliating conditions on Serbia, which was blamed for the assassination. Princip came from one of the most economically backward communities in Europe. Serbia was a country of fanaticism and violence (the previous king had been horribly murdered by nationalist officers in 1903). Austria-Hungary was also, by the standards of western Europe, economically backward, and the Hungarian part of the monarchy was probably the least democratic state on the continent. Austrian officers had become increasingly worried by nationalist discontent in the years preceding 1914, and some had come to feel that war would offer a means to assert control over the Slavs, who seemed to threaten the Empire, and to restore the authority of the army.

It is not, however, fair to say that the "primitive communities of the southeast of Europe" caused European war in 1914. Princip himself told a prison psychiatrist in 1916 that he was horrified by the outcome of his actions. He and his accomplices were motivated by resentment at the status of Bosnia Herzegovina, which had been annexed by the Habsburg monarchy in 1908, as well as by bitterness at the poverty of the countryside that was their home and by the example of certain Russian anarchists. But they had no precise aims in mind. Princip himself resented his rejection for service in the Serbian army in the war of 1913 (he was too small). More than anything else, he seemed to have wished to die a hero's death. As it turned out, he was one of the few European men of his generation not to have a chance to die in combat.

Princip and his associates had been supported by conspirators in the Serbian military, but the Serbian government had no desire for a war that would devastate the country. Far from being a nationalist fanatic, King Peter admired John Stuart Mill and had spent most of his life in Switzerland. Serbia did its best to appease the Austrians and only resisted when they insisted on conducting their own inquiries on Serbian soil.

In truth, the actions of Serbia, Austria-Hungary and Russia cannot be explained without reference to those of the western powers. If war "came . . . from the East," then it was sustained by the West. Austria-Hungary would never have acted as she did if Germany had not agreed (on July 5–6) to give her support. Russia would not have mobilized if she had not been allied with France, which had provided many of the resources for Russian armament in the previous decade. Most important of all, the war started by Serbia, Austria-Hungary and Russia was not "the Great War," the extremely destructive nature of which came from the very fact that it was fought by highly industrialized powers. In 1898, Ivan Bloch, a Russian banker, wrote a book that was published in English under the title *Is War Now Impossible?* in which he argued that modern war was so destructive that no state could sustain it; starvation and economic collapse would bring it to an end. Bloch was, in large measure, right. The states of eastern and central Europe could not survive modern warfare. The only one that kept fighting until the armistice of 1918 was Austria-Hungary, kept in the war by pressure from her German ally. In central and eastern Europe, defeat meant general economic and social collapse, not simply the destruction of armies on the battlefield. Bloch was, however, wrong with regard to the western powers. Britain, France and (until 1918) Germany were able to sustain a war of unprecedented destruction, partly because much of the fighting was confined to a small area, and also because suffering was concentrated on a small group of the population (young men). Furthermore, the western powers benefited from high levels of industrialization, organization and education. They could manufacture huge quantities of munitions and transport them to the front. They could rely on the discipline instilled in their populations by education and compulsory military service. It was the bourgeoisie of western Europe that behaved in the most irrational way during the First World War, continuing to obey orders even when such obedience was certain to bring their death. It was the "primitive" peasant populations of eastern Europe who behaved most rationally – they deserted, allowed themselves to be taken prisoner, or mutinied. The fact that the war proved so long and so destructive was the result of the "sophistication" of western European societies, not the "primitive" nature of east European ones.

The nature of fighting

On the western front, the Great War meant trenches. The Germans began with a rapid advance through Belgium into France, and the war was to finish with another burst of movement in 1918. In the intervening period, the two sides dug in and faced each other across distances that were sometimes so short that it was possible to lob hand grenades from one side to the other. Barbed wire, machine guns and the rapid fire of magazine rifles gave defenders an advantage.

Conditions on the western front could be dangerous and squalid: one psychologist described treating a man who had been blown off his feet by a shell and had fallen on a decomposing corpse, so that his mouth filled with rotting entrails.[4] However, no one endured such horrors all the time. There were long periods of calm between attacks, and conditions in the trenches, which seemed so awful to junior officers, may have seemed less shocking to those who had endured poverty and manual labor.

In some respects, the conditions of the western front might even seem benign. In previous wars, especially those that had involved European troops fighting in unfamiliar climates far from hospitals, soldiers were more likely to die of disease than wounds: during the Italian campaign in Libya in 1911–12, 1,432 soldiers died as a result of enemy action, while 1,948 died of disease.[5] On the western front, well-disciplined troops who were close to reasonably good medical facilities often enjoyed better health than they would have done at home. Less than one-tenth of deaths in the German army were due to disease.[6] Army rations were generous: British recruits increased in height when put on a diet of corned beef, while French peasants, who would rarely have eaten meat before 1914, were now provided with up to half a kilogram per day.[7]

War in the east was different from that in the west. Fighting was more mobile. A war that began with the Russian invasion of Germany finished with Germany holding territory in the Russian Empire that exceeded anything Hitler was to gain in the Second World War. The trench system in the east was never as well developed as that in the west. Lines were longer and more difficult to defend. The Russian army did not adopt effective techniques of trench warfare and its trenches often filled with water or collapsed. Defenders did not have the advantage that they had in the west: the Russians retreated 100 miles in 1915. The role of the cavalry illustrated the differences between the eastern and western fronts. In the west, it turned out to be almost useless, though this did not prevent cavalrymen from predominating among the generals who sent infantrymen to their deaths.[8] On the eastern front, and in the various conflicts that followed in Russia and Poland, mounted soldiers had an important role, which may be why the Poles overestimated the value of such forces in 1939. Equipment for the Russian army was poor (some soldiers were not even provided with rifles and had to wait to pick one up from a dead comrade). Conditions were worse than in France. Food rotted. Disease and hunger as well as bullets claimed the lives of Russian, Austrian and Italian soldiers. During a single night in the Carpathian mountains, a Croat regiment lost 1,800 men to hypothermia.[9]

Armies

Why did soldiers put up with it? On the western front, troops often mocked their superiors and discreetly subverted orders, but they rarely rebelled outright. Part of the French army mutinied after a bloody offensive in 1917, but even this was more of a strike than an attempted revolution. Soldiers did not turn their weapons on senior officers or make contact with civilians; neither did they, on the whole, leave their posts. Many made it clear that they would defend their positions if the Germans attacked. The most important burst of ill discipline in the British army, at Étaples in 1917, was even more limited in its aims, directed against an unpopular training program. Mutinies were more common at the end of the war, when troops were being demobilized, or among sailors who had barely seen combat than among soldiers facing the dangers of trench warfare.

In part, soldiers at the front were controlled by brutal discipline. The British army shot several hundred deserters during the course of the war: families were told that the victims had been "killed in action." The French shot fifty-five men after the mutinies of 1917. In the Italian army, men were executed for offenses as trivial as smoking a pipe while on duty:

Italian courts martial passed a total of 4,000 death sentences between 1915 and 1918 (750 of which were carried out).[10] The nature of trench warfare made the exercise of discipline easier. The very fact that troops were stuck in one place made them relatively easy to control. If they moved in one direction they would be shot by the enemy, and if they attempted to fall back, they could be dealt with by reserve troops. Discipline in all armies deteriorated once troops were demobilized and moved away from the trenches (which had a particularly devastating impact on the countries that demobilized after defeat). However, fear of punishment alone cannot explain everything. The German army remained well disciplined despite the fact that penalties were comparatively light, while savage punishments in the Italian army did not prevent chronic desertion.

The separation of soldiers and civilians was important to the maintenance of discipline in the west. Soldiers did not join workers' strikes and, indeed, could be relied on to put such rebellions down. This willingness was rooted partly in a social separation: soldiers were mainly drawn from the peasantry or the lower middle class, while workers were often kept out of the war in order to maintain munitions production. Not surprisingly, soldiers resented those that they perceived as shirkers. The nature of fighting on the western front reinforced the separation, as soldiers were unlikely to encounter workers unless they had been sent to fight them. Reports from the Isère in France cast an interesting light on relations between civilians and soldiers. Protests against the war came from both groups, but the two never worked in concert. On the contrary, soldiers on leave who complained about the war excited animosity from civilians, while civilians who incited soldiers against the war were likely to be beaten up.[11]

Armies were also held together by less obvious forces. Soldiers at the front had little reason to feel hostile to their immediate commanders, junior officers who probably ran even greater risks than themselves. The generalized hostility to distant staff officers may, by helping to bind men at the front together, have lessened the risk of mutiny. Patriotism played little role in the thinking of men at the front. The intercepted letters of French soldiers were written in terms of resignation rather than enthusiasm, and they looked forward to peace rather than victory. However, soldiers often felt a desire to defend territory, which was particularly strong on the part of those fighting on home ground. Such feelings account for the resonance of the defensive battle at Verdun and of Pétain's phrase "They shall not pass." It is significant that morale among French troops serving in Italy and the east was lower than that among troops in France. German troops were not, except briefly in 1914, fighting on home territory, but they too seem to have felt that defense was more legitimate than attack; German soldiers were more prone to remember the defensive battle that they had fought on the Somme than the offensive that they had waged at Verdun.[12]

Discipline away from the western front was worse. Many soldiers in the Austrian, Italian and Russian armies did not feel that they were fighting a defensive war. Austro-Hungarian soldiers, as opposed to officers, regarded the Empire as an abstract concept that bore little relation to their own lives. Russian peasants were equally indifferent. Slav nationalism was a matter for the urban intelligentsia, and they did not believe that German forces threatened their own villages, hundreds of miles behind the lines.

Noncommissioned officers were the linchpins of army discipline. British soldiers were forbidden to approach an officer without an NCO being present. The extent to which NCOs maintained their authority depended partly on military traditions, but also depended on the society from which such men were drawn. Most western European countries had a large reservoir of artisans, foremen, petty clerks and peasants with farms large enough to require the hiring of outside labor: 40 percent of German NCOs were artisans. As such men had some experience of giving orders and of cooperating with their social superiors, it was relatively easy to turn them into corporals and sergeants. Russia, on the other hand, had few such people. Most of her soldiers were peasants and only 3 percent of them hired labor.[13] The Russian army had only one-third as many NCOs, as a proportion of its total size, as the German army.[14] This lack does much to explain the fact that discipline in the Russian army was to break down so badly in 1917.

The fluidity of war in Russia, central Europe and Italy meant that it was more difficult to contain desertion and disobedience. In the aftermath of defeat at Caporetto, more than 350,000 Italian deserters and refugees wandered around the countryside.[15] In Austria-Hungary, hundreds of thousands of men deserted (44,000 were arrested in the first three months of 1918 alone).[16] Far from being stuck in one place under close supervision, Russian soldiers often moved around the front line, and eventually away from it, as looting and ill discipline turned to desertion or mutiny.[17]

Mobile warfare meant the capture of large numbers of prisoners, which contributed to desertion and low morale. The number of prisoners captured from the Habsburg army (2.2 million) was more than twelve times that of prisoners taken from the British army (170,389) and more than four times the number from the French (500,000).[18] Captured men constituted less than a tenth of total British casualties, but roughly a third of all casualties from the Habsburg army and more than half of all casualties in the Russian army: prisoners taken by Austria-Hungary or Russia endured harsh conditions because their captors were already short of food. Furthermore, commanders of some armies regarded their own soldiers who had been taken prisoner with suspicion (surrendering Russians were sometimes shelled by their own forces).[19] The Italian government refused to provide adequate Red Cross parcels for its prisoners (100,000 out of 600,000 died in Austrian captivity).[20] Returning prisoners were bitter, which caused particular problems in Austria-Hungary, where over half a million prisoners came back from Russia after the Treaty of Brest-Litovsk in March 1918. Former prisoners had often been influenced by Bolshevik propaganda, and Austrian authorities treated them with suspicion. Many deserted.[21]

The anarchy of the eastern front was illustrated by the Czechoslovak corps, which was composed of men who had been in Russia in 1914 and had decided to fight with the Russians in the hope of liberating their homeland from Habsburg rule. Swelled by prisoners of war, their numbers reached 40,000 in March 1918. In May, members of the corps, waiting to be sent home, got into a brawl with Hungarian prisoners of war. The Soviet authorities attempted to disarm the Czechs, who fought back. Consequently Czech soldiers, who had initially wanted nothing other than to escape from Russia, became an important element of the anti-Bolshevik forces in the Russian Civil War.

Politics

The military exercised great power in most European countries before 1914 – ministers of war had often been soldiers – and the extent of this influence reached new heights in the early stages of the war. France was virtually under military rule for several months. Military legislation in France had been drawn up on the assumption that the army would advance into enemy territory, and when the Germans advanced into France large parts of the country were defined as "zones of military occupation" and were ruled in a manner that had been devised for a conquered enemy. Military power was reinforced when the civilian government fled to Bordeaux to escape the invading Germans.[22] In Great Britain, General Kitchener was Minister of War from 1914 to 1916. However, in both Britain and France the battle for control of the war was ultimately won by civilians. In France, Georges Clemenceau, a bitter critic of military tactics during the first three years of the war, became Prime Minister and Minister of War in 1917. A man of enormous energy, he was determined to assert his authority over the generals for whom, as a former Dreyfusard, he had no great respect. In Britain, a similar role was played by David Lloyd George, who became Prime Minister in December 1916. Like Clemenceau, Lloyd George had great self-confidence and the vestiges of a radical past that made him dubious about the generals' capacity to win the war (though not about the desirability of their doing so). In Germany, civilian control was less effective – the military had been sheltered from parliamentary scrutiny by the influence of the Kaiser. When war broke out the Kaiser was elbowed aside and the generals gained control over almost all areas of life, which they did not relinquish until the very end of the war. Whereas Clemenceau and Lloyd George were flamboyant, dynamic men from outside the establishment, Georg Michaelis, who replaced Bethmann Hollweg as Chancellor in July 1917, was a colorless civil servant. Charles de Gaulle, observing affairs from the vantage point of a German prison camp, concluded that the need for civilian politicians to keep control of the military was the most important lesson of German failure in the war.

Struggles over the war spilled out of Cabinet rooms. In Britain and France, popular politics played into the hands of effective democratic politicians such as Lloyd George and Clemenceau. In Germany matters were more complicated. The SPD became increasingly dubious about the war and eventually a group of socialists broke away to call for peace. Meanwhile the military establishment itself dabbled in popular politics. Vast quantities of official propaganda were distributed, and in 1917 Admiral von Tirpitz founded the Fatherland Party, which soon acquired 1.25 million members and overtook the SPD as the largest party. In Russia and Austria-Hungary popular politics was more threatening because a large part of the population was unsympathetic to the war.

Popular politics raised the specter of nationalism. Britain and France were little troubled by this. Bretons fought loyally for a state with which they did not even share a language – one was shot by his own comrades because of his inability to explain his presence behind the lines. Welsh speakers flooded into the British army after Lloyd George became Minister of Munitions and persuaded the chapels to abandon their opposition to the war. Only the Irish presented problems. Conscription was never introduced in Ireland, nor (for overseas service) in Australia, where much of the population was of Irish origin. At Easter 1916, the Germans gave some help to an unsuccessful uprising in Dublin.

In eastern Europe, things were different. The Austrian decision to enter the war was provoked partly by fear of nationalism. Some leaders of national minorities appreciated that the war gave them a chance to overthrow foreign domination: Tomáš Masaryk sought support in Britain and the United States for a new Czech state, while in Finland Carl Gustav Mannerheim, an officer trained in Russia, fought with the Russians. Poles had an awkward choice, because some of them lived in the Tsarist Empire while others lived in Austria-Hungary. Józef Piłsudski, another former Russian officer, fought with the Austro-Hungarian army for as long as he believed that to do so served Polish interests, but the Polish national democrats supported Russia against the Central Powers. Germany and Austria-Hungary declared themselves in favor of an independent Polish state in November 1916; in the summer of 1918, the Allies called for a broader state that would encompass parts of the Russian, German and Habsburg empires. The defeat of Russia, a multinational empire, and the entry into the war by the United States, a country populated largely by national minorities from the central European empires, meant that Britain and France were increasingly prone to present their war as one of national liberation.[23]

Economic management

Initially it was assumed that the war would be short and that economics would play little part in its outcome. The length of the war and the scale of resources deployed overturned this assumption, and the transformation of economic management was one of the most dramatic ways in which the war affected Europe.

War production meant breaking with the prewar tradition of laissez-faire. The state became the most important customer for many companies, which meant that the state itself underwent dramatic changes. In France, the total number of government servants increased from 800,000 in 1914 to 1.25 million by 1926.[24]

Dealings with the state encouraged businessmen to develop new forms of organization. In France, the Parisian metallurgical and mechanical producers grouped themselves together in 1917, and by the end of the war firms belonging to the association employed almost 200,000 workers. In Germany, 200 war associations, employing a total of 33,000 people, had been formed by 1918.[25] Firms bought shares in the associations, which then distributed scarce resources among their members. In the absence of a strong state, business could acquire great power. In France, during the early part of the war, the ironmasters' association was granted the sole right to distribute iron and steel.[26] In occupied Belgium, the Société Générale bank was so powerful that it effectively issued its own currency.

Business did not always have things its own way. State bureaucracy became more powerful in all countries as the war went on, and trade unions could also limit activities. This was most conspicuous in Britain, where the engineering trade union imposed strict conditions under which new working practices would be permitted for the duration of the war. In France and Germany, union representatives gained ever greater influence in official bodies as the war went on. In Germany, "yellow" unions, sponsored by employers, gained ground between 1915 and 1916, but thereafter independent unions increased their membership at a faster rate. The 1916 Auxiliary Service Law established factory committees to which union representatives were elected by secret ballot.[27]

Particular trade union leaders, state bureaucrats and leaders of industrial syndicates often acquired such similar outlooks that they seemed to have been fused into a new industrial ruling class, espousing policies that did not fit the normal aims of governments, workers or industrialists. Men like the French minister Albert Thomas or the German industrialist–turned–civil servant Walther Rathenau dreamed of a new industrial order based on coordination and cooperation.

Generally the companies that did well in the war were large, partly because the industries needed by a war economy had to operate on a large scale and also because large companies had the contacts, experience and personnel to gain from an organized economy. Some companies that profited from the war expanded dramatically – Renault became the largest company in France – while mergers brought firms together into larger conglomerations, such as the German chemicals combine, formed in 1916, that eventually became IG Farben. French legislation was eased to make the formation of cartels easier.[28] Conversely, small businesses did badly, as they often produced consumer goods that were regarded as dispensable and lacked the means to lobby for protection. Half a million German artisans were drafted into the army, and one in three artisanal enterprises was shut down.[29]

Countries that had neither an extensive industrial base nor traditions of organization often found that economic mobilization brought political instability. Italian industrialists who were unable to adapt to the restoration of liberalism supported Fascism in the early 1920s. In Russia, War Industry Committees sought a political power to match their economic one: Prince Lvov, the first head of the provisional government established after the February Revolution, had been a member of the central War Industry Committee.

Civilians

Civilian living standards varied from one combatant country to another and from one social group to another. Living standards held up best in Britain and France. France was probably the most agriculturally prosperous nation in Europe, though part of its most productive land had been taken over by battlefields, and Britain was able, for most of the time, to import food. British civilians were almost entirely spared the direct impact of enemy action, while for French civilians fighting was static and confined to a limited area: they did not face the marauding armies that had spread disease and requisitioned food in earlier wars. In Great Britain, life expectancy among civilians increased, while in France it remained at about the same level as before the war.[30]

Civilians elsewhere had less happy experiences. Numerous strikes and disturbances throughout Europe in 1917 were provoked by food shortages: hunger was said to lie behind almost three-quarters of strikes in Austria.[31] The diversion of resources away from agriculture, the poor harvests of 1916, and the British blockade of the Central Powers all reduced the amount of food available. Russia suffered because its railway system, overloaded by the demands of the army, failed to transport enough food to the cities, while Belgium faced the consequences of invasion and occupation by a power that was itself short of resources. A German who tried to live off official rations between November 1916 and May 1917 lost one-fifth of his body weight.[32] Few Germans starved to death during this period, but hunger exacerbated other problems. Civilians wasted hours queuing or in complicated black market operations, changed their diet to include unpopular items such as turnips, and were made more vulnerable to infection (over 200,000 Germans died in the influenza epidemic of 1918).[33]

The countries of central and eastern Europe suffered worst. Fighting was not confined to small areas, and the direct impact of the war on the civilian population was considerable. In Serbia, disease, famine and the movement of refugees resulted in terrible suffering throughout the population: one in ten Serbs died during a typhus epidemic. Half a million Serbs fled the Austrian advance in a march to the Adriatic, and almost half of them died on the journey.[34] In Bulgaria, requisition of food by the German and Austrian armies in 1916 caused starvation,[35] while in Poland 40,000 died of typhus.[36]

The worst civilian suffering of all occurred in Turkey. The Armenian population, which the authorities believed to be sympathetic to the Russians, was subjected to ever increasing persecution. Armenians in the east of the country were caught in fighting between Turkish and Russian forces, and around 200,000 were obliged to seek refuge in Russia. Others were massacred or had to undertake forced marches without food or water. By the end of 1916, foreign observers estimated that only about 600,000 Armenians from a population of between 1,800,000 and 2,100,000 had survived.[37]

Early in the war, workers, like other economic resources, were disregarded. Factories throughout Europe were drained of manpower by recruiting sergeants. Gradually, this changed. In France, 500,000 workers had returned from the front by the end of 1915,[38] and in January 1916, the French metallurgy industry employed the same number of people as before the war. Some workers benefited from employers' need to retain and motivate their staff at a time when labor was so scarce. In France, pay for armament workers increased faster than inflation, while that of other workers fell behind.

The experience of peasants, the largest single social group in most European countries, was mixed. Generals in continental countries regarded peasants as the best soldiers, but in spite, or because, of this many peasants were hostile to war. Conservatives saw peasants as patriotic because they were rarely touched by socialist propaganda, but forgot that they were also often untouched by the nationalist propaganda that had been so widespread in cities before 1914. Many peasants regarded the state as an alien body with which they came into contact only when it collected taxes or conscripted their sons. The outbreak of war in 1914 was particularly resented because it came immediately before the harvest.[39]

Most evidence suggests that the countryside was unenthusiastic about, if not hostile to, mobilization. The Belgian historian Pirenne described his country thus: "Almost all [volunteers] belonged to the urban population. The countryside only took a slight part in this movement. The moral commotion provoked by the war could not shake it as much as it did the intellectual and industrial classes, which were more sensitive, more nervous and more vulnerable to patriotic idealism and, furthermore, more directly affected by the brutal interruption of business and more intimately tied up with national life."[40] Reports by French village schoolteachers showed the trepidation with which many peasants went to war. In Bulgaria, opposition to entry into the war was directed by the peasant leader Alexander Stamboliski.[41]

Hostility to the war rarely translated into peasant support for revolution in western and central Europe. There was an economic reason for this. The price of food rose sharply because imports were lost and armies needed to feed large numbers of men. Furthermore, peasants often profited from inflation when paying off debt: in France, a large part of the 10–20 billion francs of agricultural debt owed in 1914 had been cleared by 1918.[42] Peasants in Germany and Austria drew particular benefits from wartime inflation because they had often borrowed money to buy new equipment before the war: about 13 billion marks of agricultural debt was wiped out in the German inflation that began in the First World War and reached a peak in the early 1920s.[43] Sharecroppers and tenants in Italy gained because they usually bought seed and fertilizer in the high season and paid their debts in arrears during the low season;[44] they used wartime prosperity to buy land – the number of proprietors increased from 2.25 million in 1911 to over 4 million in 1921.[45]

The fate of the Russian peasantry was quite different. The breakdown of the railway system for transporting grain to cities and the activities of rapacious middlemen prevented the peasants from benefiting from inflated food prices; indeed, the price for which they sold their food failed to keep up with the price of tools and other commodities. The collapse of rural industries also hurt the peasants. Furthermore, as the Russian peasantry had rarely borrowed money before 1914, because the commune system provided them little incentive to improve their land, peasants who were losing from inflation often retreated from the market economy altogether and resorted to subsistence farming. This exacerbated the food crisis in the cities that helped to spark revolution in 1917. In western and central Europe, peasants, who had derived at least some economic benefit from the war, fought for counterrevolution; in Russia, they remained indifferent or supported the Bolsheviks.

Defeats

In Russia, defeat and revolution went together. Defeat provoked mutiny, which in turn made defeat more likely. Major mutinies began in the autumn of 1916; the following February, soldiers joined riots and strikes that they had been sent to suppress. Generals persuaded the Tsar to abdicate, in the hope that this would make it easier to prosecute the war. Almost all major political leaders agreed that the war must be continued, the policy followed by the provisional government under Prince Lvov.

In practice, the provisional government's control of the army was weak, with many soldiers refusing to recognize the authority of their officers. The Petrograd Soviet, which claimed to represent workers of the capital, provided a rival for the government. Its "order number one" called for the establishment of soldiers' committees, and it declared that government orders were only valid if authorized by the Soviet. The Germans took advantage of the chaos by transporting Lenin, the most radical leader of the most radical party, the Bolsheviks, from Switzerland to Russia. Lenin's arrival did not settle matters. In spite of "order number one," the majority of members of the Petrograd Soviet did not want to displace the provisional government. However, in June and July, Alexander Kerensky, the Minister of War who became Prime Minister on July 25, ordered an offensive in Galicia. The Russian army, which had done little fighting for the past year, was badly defeated, sustaining 200,000 casualties. Mutinous soldiers and sailors flooded into the capital in July, and in August General Kornilov sent troops into the city in an unsuccessful bid to restore order. Military discipline collapsed. General Alekseev admitted that, "practically speaking . . . we have no army."[46] In October 1917, Lenin and the Bolsheviks overthrew the provisional government with a pledge to secure peace. The Russians signed an armistice with Germany in December, and in March 1918 conceded vast tracts of territory under the terms of the Treaty of Brest-Litovsk.

Germany's defeat was less dramatic than that of Russia. It was a product of attrition. Efficient organization could not disguise the fact that Germany had fewer resources than her opponents, especially after the United States joined the Allies. In 1918, it became clear that Germany would not be able to sustain the confrontation. Her response was to try to break out of trench warfare with an offensive in March 1918. Many of the military assumptions that had governed fighting on the western front for the past four years were abandoned. Both sides had been experimenting with new kinds of assault for some time: instead of using vast numbers of ordinary troops who staggered under the weight of their equipment, small numbers of soldiers were trained to move quickly using light weapons such as machine pistols. In 1916, the Germans established battalions of "storm troopers" to implement such techniques, and in 1918 offensive tactics were applied on a wider scale. One hundred divisions were allocated to defensive duties, while around seventy stronger divisions were allocated to an attack that was to be closely coordinated with artillery barrage, poison gas and the use of aircraft.

The new tactics achieved striking results. Allied lines were driven back thirty miles and, for a time, the Germans seemed to threaten Paris, as they had in 1914. But the Germans became victims of their own success. Infantry troops were left exposed as artillery and machine guns were unable to keep up with them: German forces were ninety miles from their railheads. In addition, the Germans suffered from the very problems of shortage that had made them so keen to escape from a long war of attrition. They did not have enough men, a problem exacerbated by the fact that so many soldiers were tied down holding the vast territories in the east that Germany had acquired at Brest-Litovsk. Hunger and exhaustion sapped the energy of German troops, and half a million of them were incapacitated by Spanish influenza. The tight discipline that had marked static warfare on the western front began to break down as soldiers advanced so fast that they often lost contact with their officers.

The Germans also fell victim to the strategic naïvete of their commander. Ludendorff wanted a rapid advance but was not sure what to do with it. He hesitated between driving the British forces back to the Channel or trying to take Paris, eventually opting for the latter. In July, the French commander, Marshal Foch, counterattacked. He too adopted more mobile tactics. Tanks – a weapon that the Germans had never really exploited – and planes were used, and fresh American troops were thrown into the battle. The Germans suffered 340,000 casualties. They retreated in chaos and, significantly, began to suffer from large-scale desertion.[47] By mid-August, German leaders knew that the war was lost; by October, the Habsburg Empire was breaking up as subject peoples declared their independence, and on November 11 the armistice ended fighting in the west.

Conclusion

The United States, Britain, France, Belgium, Italy, Romania, Serbia, Portugal and Greece were recognized as victors in the negotiations that took place after the end of the Great War; Germany, Austria-Hungary, the Ottoman Empire and Bulgaria were the losers. Russia took no part in postwar negotiations, and only part of the vast territories lost at Brest-Litovsk were restored to her. In purely territorial terms, the biggest winner was Romania, and several countries – Poland, Czechoslovakia and Yugoslavia – that had not existed in 1914 were created. In many respects, however, the emphasis on territory that dominated postwar discussions was a red herring. The country that most increased its power, the United States, gained no territory at all, while Britain gained no territory in Europe, and France acquired a comparatively small amount (Alsace and Lorraine).

The real questions concerned the internal orders of European countries, and the answers to such questions transcended national frontiers. Some workers, peasants, and large-scale industrialists drew economic benefits from the war, while artisans and rentiers lost out. In each of these cases, however, economic gains were matched by physical losses caused by the war itself (in the case of the peasantry) or by the political instability that followed the war.

If national interest and internal order are considered together, then the winners and losers of the First World War are redefined. Romania may have been the largest gainer in terms of land, but she can hardly be said to have gained prosperity or political stability following 1919. Italy was also destabilized, not only because the gains that she made from participation in the war were less than her leaders had hoped for, but also because the war had imposed such social and economic strains. Austria-Hungary saw both the breakup of the empire and social turmoil, which led briefly to Bolshevik revolution in Budapest. Germany's experience was more mixed. In some ways, German society held together remarkably well: soldiers did not mutiny before November 1918, and workers did not rebel. German economic organization was good. On the other hand, Germany's inability to support a long war of attrition was reflected in inflation and, eventually, famine. Defeat and demobilization brought a breakdown of the order that had been preserved for the previous four years and was

Table 2: Military Deaths in the First World War

France	1,398,000	Belgium	38,000
Italy	578,000	Portugal	7,000
Britain	723,000	Romania	250,000
Serbia	278,000	Greece	26,000
Russia	1,811,000	Bulgaria	88,000
Germany	2,037,000	Austria-Hungary	1,100,000
Turkey	804,000		

Source: Niall Ferguson, *The Pity of War* (1998), p. 295. This table includes
military deaths from disease as well as action but not civilian deaths.

reflected in the loss of equipment. During 1918 and 1919, 1,895,000
rifles, 8,542 machine guns and 4,000 trench mortars went missing.[48]
However, in Germany the overthrow of the old order was primarily political – the deposition of the Kaiser. It did not involve the destruction of
entire classes, as in Russia. Many of the foundations on which the German war effort was built (such as the compromise between large-scale industry, organized labor and the army) survived until 1933, and perhaps
beyond.

The upheaval of war did not always end with the armistice. In Russia,
1.8 million died fighting the Central Powers compared with around 5
million who died in the famine of 1921–22.[49] The continued Allied
blockade ensured that the suffering of German civilians between November 1918 and the conclusion of the peace treaty in 1919 was probably
greater than it had been during the war itself. The long-term impact of
wartime expenditure was often reflected in postwar inflation, notably that
which racked Germany in 1923.

In terms of the damage they sustained, Britain and France got off comparatively lightly from the Great War. There was no revolution, no hyper-
inflation, no starvation and no plague. In some ways, of course, such a
conclusion merely reveals how badly everyone suffered. Britain and
France may have endured less than other European participants, but they
still lost more men between 1914 and 1918 than in any other war in history (respectively 1.6 percent and 3.4 percent of their populations).[50]
Many French people concluded that the rapid defeat of the Franco-
Prussian War had been less unpleasant than the slow victory of the Great
War, and this does much to explain their behavior in June 1940.

The suggestion that Britain and France lost least from the Great War
seems odd in view of the intense public regret about the war expressed in
both countries during the 1920s and 1930s. In part, such regret springs

from the very sense that the war was divided from "normal life." Soldiers were bitter about suffering that contrasted so sharply with the relative tranquillity of civilian life. For Russians, the war was merely one element in a period of upheaval that lasted from at least 1905 until at least 1953; in Britain, by contrast, it seemed like an avoidable parenthesis.

For the British, the war had been essentially defensive. It had been designed to preserve the status quo. Since they had nothing to gain, even victory was bound in the long run to seem like the beginning of decline. This was particularly true in terms of overseas empire. Britain commanded even larger areas after 1919 than she had before 1914, but the war sapped her economic capacity to maintain such a position.

In social terms, the British and the French bourgeoisie had special reason to regret the war because it destroyed the stable world of secure investments and low inflation that many of them – those most likely to record their experience in writing – had enjoyed before 1914. In eastern and central Europe, by contrast, the drama of the First World War meant that people were less likely to look back on the pre-1914 world with nostalgia. It had brought a new world into being, and the old world was now unimaginable. The end of the war did not bring a return to "normal," because "normality" had been destroyed. A leader of the German SA wrote that his comrades "marched on to the battlefields of the post-war world just as we had gone into battle on the western front."[51] A Hungarian politician, discussing the prospect that his country's anti-Semitism might attract international disapproval, remarked, "If we'll be accused of being inhuman, or reactionary, these slogans will not move us anymore. The best values of the Hungarian nation have been burnt in the fire of world conflagration."[52] Fascists, Bolsheviks, Nazis and nationalists in the newly created states had all suffered in the war, but they knew that the institutions, movements and states that they supported had come out of that war. The British dreamed of a highly mythologized pre-war idyll in which the clock was stopped at ten to three. For most of Europe, the clock could never be stopped, and the only way forward was into new violence that would often dwarf that of 1914–18.

PART II

From One War
to Another

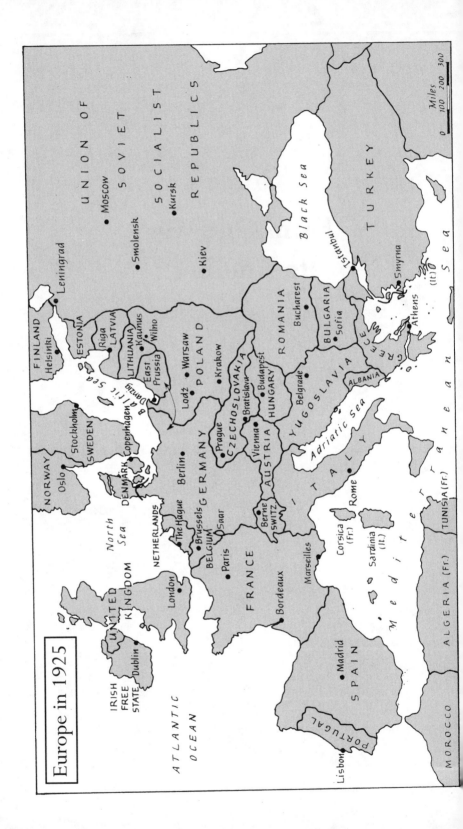

Europe in 1925

IN THE LATE summer of 1940, Europe was at peace. Hitler's victories in Poland, Scandinavia, the Low Countries and France had been decisive. The settlement of the Franco-German dispute, which had overshadowed Europe since 1870, was particularly important, and the armistice that ended French resistance was designed to recall Germany's humiliation twenty-one years earlier. However, the two events were very different. France's new government, headed by its most famous soldier and including the commander-in-chief of the defeated army, accepted the consequences of defeat and genuinely wanted to cooperate with Germany. Only Charles de Gaulle, a junior general of notorious eccentricity, dissented.

German occupation policy in the part of France that she controlled and in the rest of western Europe was sufficiently restrained to avoid provoking resistance. Her occupation policy in Poland was sufficiently ruthless to make it clear that no resistance would be tolerated. The squabbling states of eastern Europe were now overshadowed by a single great power that could arbitrate between them, and the problem of national minorities that had dogged Europe since the Paris peace settlements was to be solved by huge deportations: ethnic Germans were to be brought into the frontiers of an enlarged Reich; Poles were to be pushed east; the Jews were to be sent first into eastern Poland, and later, perhaps, to Madagascar. Hundreds of thousands were bound to die in these operations, but no one had come up with a better solution (and, indeed, mass deportation was to be adopted by the victorious Allies in 1945). It was clear that Germany would have to seal her victory by fighting the Soviet Union but, given the ease of her victories against martial nations such as Poland and

France, defeat of the Bolsheviks did not seem difficult. For the time being, the only conflict in Europe was a small war between Britain and Germany. This merely reflected, as Primo Levi pointed out, the fact that the British ruling class was too stupid to know that it was beaten. In any case, the war was fought almost entirely in the air and caused few casualties.

Of course, for those who know what came after 1941, the lines above seem shocking, but the idea that Europe was at peace in 1940 is no more bizarre than the notion that it had been at peace during what historians call the "interwar" period. There were wars between European states between 1919 and 1939 (Greece fought Turkey and Poland fought Lithuania) as well as occasions when troops from one country entered another without declaration of war (the Franco-Belgian invasion of the Ruhr and the Romanian intervention against the revolutionary government in Hungary), and there were at least three full-scale civil wars (in Russia, Finland and Spain). For the British, war ended in November 1918 and began again in September 1939, but in Russia, Poland, Germany, Hungary, Romania and Spain there was fighting for much of the intervening period. In central Europe, the upheaval of the First World War did not end with the armistice. Equally, 1939 did not necessarily mark the beginning of world war. For Spaniards it was the year in which war ended, and for Czechs it simply marked the last stage in Hitler's bloodless and uncontested takeover of their country. Russians remember the war of 1941 to 1945; French conservatives remember the war of 1939 to 1940.

Our view of interwar Europe is overshadowed by the events that ended the period. Over half of the Europeans who died violent deaths in the twentieth century died between 1941 and 1945. The apocalyptic confrontation between Germany and the Soviet Union and the Nazi attempt to exterminate the European Jews stand out with particular starkness. Not surprisingly, historians have concentrated on the reasons for those two events, which has meant a heavy emphasis on fascism and communism and, more particularly, on the power of Hitler and Stalin. The 1920s and 1930s are often talked about as a "European Civil War," as though a single form of conflict transcended all other divisions.

The striking thing about the interwar period, however, is the number of reasons Europeans found for hating each other. Consider, for example, the career of the Hungarian historian François Fejtö. The mere fact of being Hungarian was enough to earn him the dislike of many from the central European nations that had suffered under the Hungarian yoke before 1914, while the fact that Fejtö worked for reconciliation with the Czechs earned him the dislike of Hungarian nationalists. Fejtö's brief flirtation with communism earned him a year in one of Horthy's prisons; his subsequent departure from the party earned him the hatred of communists throughout Europe that was to blight his life until at least 1956. Fejtö's Jewish origins ensured that he was excluded from the most elite institution of higher education in Budapest, but his formal renunciation of a faith to which he had never subscribed earned him the contempt of the chief rabbi. Fejtö was lucky. His enforced departure from his native country saved him from the fate of most Hungarian Jews, including his father and brothers, who were exterminated by the Nazis. The fact that he never sought refuge in Moscow saved him from the fate of Béla Kun, and many other Hungarian communists, who were killed in Stalin's purges during the late 1930s. The fact that his papers were in order saved him from the fate of his compatriot Arthur Koestler, who was imprisoned by the French.[1]

Even those Europeans who argued that their continent was divided by a single great conflict disagreed about the nature of the conflict. At first, communists played down the importance of national differences and insisted on the importance of a single division between the proletariat and the bourgeoisie, but they later moved away from that position and insisted on the need to unite a broad popular front movement against fascism, a movement often facilitated by an emphasis on specifically national traditions. Conservatives denied the reality of class differences and insisted on national ones. Italian Fascists talked of sexual and generational distinctions that divided "real men" from the old and the female, though in practice the conflicts that they had in mind pitched young men against each other. German Nazis regarded racial divisions as more important than any others.

Why were the various conflicts that divided Europeans during this period so violent? One explanation lies in the upheaval of the First World War. War in itself did not necessarily lead to conflict after the armistice – soldiers from Britain, France and, to a large extent, Germany seem to have returned home to become peaceful citizens after 1918 – but in most countries war had spilled out to affect the civilian population and to generate social and economic disruption that lasted long after demobilization. Often it was not war veterans but their juniors, whose adolescences had been blighted by the war, who proved the most enthusiastic participants in conflict during the 1920s and 1930s.

The Paris peace settlements that brought the war to a formal end often made matters worse. The Versailles Treaty between Germany and the victorious Allies was, as the historian Jacques Bainville put it, too lenient for its harshness. Reparations and the clause on "war guilt" exacerbated the Germans' bitterness without being sufficiently severe to prevent them from contemplating military revenge. The most serious problem, however, was not Germany's relationship with the powers to her west, but that of all powers in central and eastern Europe with each other. Germany never accepted her eastern frontiers, and the treaties that defined the defeat of Hungary, Bulgaria and Austria (Trianon, Neuilly, St-Germain) were bitterly resented from the beginning. Woodrow Wilson's concept of "self-determination" generated new kinds of conflict, and Hungarians and Germans who found themselves outside their state (defined in political and legal terms) were inclined to look to their nation (defined in cultural or linguistic terms) or their race (defined in biological terms). The Jews, the largest ethnic group in Europe to be left without a state of their own, were in an awkward position. The peace settlement did not make their extermination inevitable, but it did make it unlikely that they would have a comfortable time. The Habsburg Empire, which had been relatively tolerant of Jews, was broken up, and Romania, the most anti-Semitic country in Europe, gained the most territory. New states were created in areas that were not famous for tolerance (Keynes jibed that the only viable industry in Poland would be "Jew-baiting"[2]).

The international quarrels created by the Paris peace settlement fed, and fed off, conflicts within countries. When Bulgarian nationalists captured the peasant leader Stamboliski in 1923, the first thing that they did was to cut off the hand that had signed the Treaty of Neuilly.

Economics also made political conflict more severe. Many accounts of the period make much of the Wall Street Crash of November 1929, which is presented as the beginning of an economic depression that divided the playfulness of the 1920s from the somber mood and political extremism of the 1930s. The French writer Robert Brasillach talked of a shift from the "*après guerre*" to the "*avant guerre*" produced by the impact of depression on France. Nightclubs closed; dancing masters stopped teaching the Charleston and started teaching waltzes.[3]

But the division is artificial. Economic depression began not with the Wall Street Crash but with falling agricultural prices in the 1920s. The states of eastern Europe, heavily dependent on agriculture, were already in desperate straits before 1929. Although the British and French middle classes talked a lot about "crisis" after 1929, many of them led rather prosperous lives during this period. Falling prices were good news for those with fixed incomes; Brasillach himself benefited from the fact that rents in the Latin Quarter declined.

More important than the particular problems created by the Wall Street Crash were the general problems caused by the economic legacy of the war itself: chaotic public finances and overproduction of primary goods. In the 1920s and 1930s, more than at any other time in the twentieth century, economics was a "zero sum game"; as resources were limited, one group could increase its prosperity only at the expense of another. Italian peasants, who might once have sought their fortune in

America, occupied land in 1919. Hungarian engineers tried to increase their access to limited professional opportunities by excluding Jews from the education system. British mine-owners cut wages. The Nazi war economy was based on institutionalized plunder.

For all the multiplicity of violent conflicts, it is, in some respects, deceptive to see the interwar period purely in terms of political confrontations. Some of the most important divisions cut across conventional political boundaries. In the 1920s, the fervor of both communism and fascism owed much to youthful rebellion. Similarly in the 1930s, both Stalinism and Nazism displayed similar views about the family and sexual morality, reflected in the repression of abortion and homosexuality.

In some countries, many people seemed indifferent to the sense of political crisis that now haunts history books. For many in Britain, France or Sweden, the late 1930s were a good time, and even the Second World War did not always disrupt "normality." A disconcertingly large number of French autobiographers evoke childhood in Nazi-occupied France with nostalgia.[4] Many intellectuals wanted nothing to do with the great struggle between fascism and its enemies; the philosopher Simone Weil starved herself to death to mark her solidarity with the suffering people of occupied France, but her brother André announced that the study of pure mathematics was more important than the war and deserted from the French army to spend the next five years at the Princeton Institute for Advanced Study.

In Germany, Russia and eastern Europe, most people found it difficult to ignore the great political dramas. Indeed, in many ways the most striking novelty of the times was the fact that "public" life intruded into "private" affairs: Tsar Nicholas II was much more shocked by the prospect that he might not be allowed to bring up his own children than he was by the abolition of the Russian monarchy.[5] But even under the most repressive regimes during the times of most violent upheaval, not everyone believed their lives to be dominated by politics. Anita Grossmann quotes a statement by a Berlin woman who had been raped by a Russian soldier in 1945: "Until that time I had lived so happily with my husband and the children." The surprising – and from Grossmann's point of view deeply shocking – aspect of the testimony is the suggestion that the years before May 1945 – the era of Auschwitz and Stalingrad – could be considered happy and normal.[6]

1

THE LEGACY OF THE
GREAT WAR

"IN ELSIE BENNET'S school, a Thanksgiving service was organized on Armistice Day. When the National Anthem was played, Elsie refused to stand up. The headmaster asked why. 'All the other little boys' and girls' Daddies would be coming home now; but her Daddy would never come home again.' She was caned for disobedience."[1]

Talk of the "legacy of the war" in much of eastern and central Europe meant little, because that legacy was often intertwined with the very existence of the nation (as in Poland, Czechoslovakia or Yugoslavia) or because the postwar period was more violent than the war itself (as in Russia). The war was discussed most in Germany and Italy, and particularly in France and Britain, which had, curiously, suffered least from the direct effects of the war. Even, however, in western Europe the legacy of war varied dramatically from one country to another.

For Britain and France the war itself had been orderly and controlled – fighting had been confined to a small area and suffering confined to a particular part of the population. After 1919, commemoration of the war reinforced the neat distinction between war and peace and between soldier and civilian. Soldiers who had fallen on the western front were gathered together into well-tended cemeteries at a time when unburied bodies were still lying around the battlefields on other fronts. Commemoration was confined to a particular day, November 11, and was marked by smooth ceremonial of which the most striking part was two minutes of silence.

The way in which Britain, France and Germany remembered the Great War contributed to the myth that the war's destructive effects had been exclusively confined to the western front – indeed, the most famous evocation of the First World War was probably Erich Maria Remarque's novel *All Quiet on the Western Front* (published in 1929). British people's interest in the sites of the war was almost entirely limited to Belgium and northern France, not only because so many British soldiers had been killed there but also because such areas were simply more accessible than Gallipoli, Palestine or Italy. French memories concentrated ever more intently on Verdun, where a huge ossuary, inaugurated in 1932, became a repository of national mythology as well as the remains of soldiers. Verdun was even chosen as the site for a highly symbolic meeting between François Mitterrand and Helmut Kohl in 1984.

Neatness and order, of a more macabre kind, also characterized the way in which western European governments dealt with victims of the war, as technocratic expertise was deployed to organize the lives of survivors. Specialists weighed up the virtues of different kinds of false limbs. In Britain, doctors discovered that they could sustain Trooper Samuel Rolfe, who had lost most of his skin after a mustard gas attack, in a warm bath – Rolfe did not die until January 1925.

Vast administrative machines turned widows, orphans and invalids into statistics. The British government paid 3 million war pensions, and William Beveridge complained that "the ministry of pensions is essentially a ministry of war pensions."[2] In Germany, 45,000 people were employed in 1920 simply to process applications for pensions and by May 1928 the German government was making payments to 761,294 invalids, 359,560 widows, 731,781 children without fathers, 56,623 orphans, and 147,230 parents who had lost sons, costs consuming almost a fifth of all central government expenditure.[3] In France, the burden of pensions was particularly heavy because the universal state war pension was introduced just before the effects of the economic depression of the early 1930s were felt, so by the eve of the Second World War pensions and debt repayments from the First World War comprised half of all French government spending. In France, pensions fitted in with a certain social and political structure. They ensured that resources were transferred from the industrial economy, where the majority of taxes were paid, to the agricultural sector, which contained a disproportionate number of veterans. Defense of the war pension became a key political issue. Veterans disliked Pierre Laval, who cut pensions in 1935; conversely François Mitterrand, born during the Battle of Verdun, boasted that, as minister for *anciens combattants*, he had always raised the war pension. Significantly, one of Charles de Gaulle's first moves to modernize France after his return to power in 1958 was the abolition of the universal war pension.

Survivors sometimes had difficulty fitting into postwar society. For some, the war had provided temporary social mobility. Promotion in civilian armies had been slow – officers had spent years in tedious garrison towns waiting for their turn – but this was changed by high casualty rates, the expansion of armies and the need for competent men. Now, however, men who had commanded and been treated with respect had to adjust to life as junior civilian employees or even undergraduates. Promotion had often been granted on an "acting" or temporary basis, and was removed when peace came: Basil Liddell Hart claims that one of his colleagues was demoted from acting brigadier general to lieutenant after the armistice.[4] It was even worse for men who had been promoted from the ranks during the war or who came from classes that would not normally have produced "officer material." Such men were now thrust back into civilian life with stern warnings not to get ideas above their station. About half of British officers commissioned during the First World War came from neither the traditional officer class nor the middle classes; many were clerks. The status of such men had already been uncertain before the war, and there was often a conflict between their pretensions to respectability and their wealth or career prospects. Now the fact that the aspiring clerk might have held an officer's rank made his resentment all the more keen.[5] In Germany, 10,000 men who had been promoted from the ranks to hold temporary commissions formed their own association after the war.[6] The bitterness of those who felt slighted could last a long time. Joseph Darnand, the militia leader who suppressed the French resistance in 1943 and 1944, never forgot that he had not been considered suitable for a permanent commission in 1918.

Political leaders emerged from war, with senior officers often becoming the focus of conservative appeal. Józef Piłsudski, who became dictator of Poland, fell into this category, as did Philippe Pétain in France, Paul von Hindenburg (who became President of Germany) and Erich von Ludendorff (who helped Hitler stage the beer hall putsch in 1923).

Junior or noncommissioned officers – including Hitler, Mussolini, Degrelle, Déat and Mosley – often adopted more radical positions and turned to fascism, but democratic politicians emerged from front-line experience in the First World War too. In Great Britain, Clement Attlee (Prime Minister from 1945 to 1951), Anthony Eden (Prime Minister from 1955 to 1957) and Harold Macmillan (Prime Minister from 1957 to 1963) had all served as junior officers.

All these men sought to justify their subsequent positions by appealing to the war generation and the values that had supposedly emerged from the solidarity of the trenches. Such rhetoric sometimes implied that there was a single experience of combat in the First World War that would unite all ex-servicemen. It was even suggested that the common experience transcended country: attempts were made to establish an international ex-servicemen's association. Such attempts came mainly from the pacifist left, but later the appeasing or defeatist right suggested that French veterans would enjoy a privileged relationship with the veterans who ruled Nazi Germany. In reality, experience of the front did not produce any single form of political thinking, and, in the war's immediate aftermath, veterans' groups were often in conflict with each other. In Italy, Mussolini's Fascists confronted left-wing veterans' groups that had been formed specifically to fight Fascism.

The political impact of the First World War depended partly on the way in which its memory intersected with other circumstances. In Britain, reference to the war remained a patrician affair. This was partly due to conscious control. A report to the War Cabinet in October 1918 warned: "There is a determined attempt among the extremists to capture the Discharged Soldiers' Federation, and the demand for better allowances should be very carefully watched, for if they succeed in getting the soldiers and their wives to back them, they will be a very numerous and dangerous body."[7] The British Legion, created in 1921, became the dominant veterans' organization; its president was Field Marshal Lord Haig and its patron was the Prince of Wales. The Legion was steered away from involvement in controversy.

The political exploitation of war memory in Britain was also affected by the existing culture of military patriotism. This was a country without a tradition of conscription and in which a strong class system operated in the army itself. Public schools, universities and aristocratic families all maintained a cult of the dead. Edward Horner, for example, came from a family of landed gentry, was the brother-in-law of Raymond Asquith (another brilliant member of the "lost generation"), had been educated at Eton and Christ Church, was a barrister, and was killed while serving in a smart cavalry regiment. After the war, all the resources of his class were deployed to perpetuate the name: his mother prepared a memorial volume (for which Lord Birkenhead wrote the introduction),[8] Sir Edwin Lutyens designed a memorial for him in his parish church, and Alfred Munnings sculpted a mounted cavalry officer on top of his plinth.

When the English talked of a "lost generation" of brilliant leaders killed in Flanders, they meant "the sons of the Anglican Tory establishment."[9] Writers – even, and perhaps especially, those who thought of themselves as rebelling against conventional military patriotism – contributed to the image of an officers' war. Rupert Brooke, Siegfried Sassoon, Wilfred Owen, Robert Graves and Guy Chapman were all junior officers.

The careers of individuals show how the English upper classes exploited the First World War. Harold Macmillan, who had been wounded at the Somme, later made much of his wartime experiences, especially during his long retirement. He even reminded Margaret Thatcher's government that striking Yorkshire miners were "the men who beat the Kaiser." However, Macmillan's presentation of the First World War had as much to do with British politics in the 1980s as with the circumstances of the western front in 1916. Recalling the war emphasized Macmillan's difference from the young parvenus who had succeeded him in the leadership of the Conservative Party; it allowed him to contrast himself with such people as a patrician figure imbued with time-honored values, rather than as the middle-class neurotic that he was.

Like Macmillan, Oswald Mosley served as a junior officer. He, too, presented the war as having opened his eyes to the social conditions of the working classes and grew dissatisfied with conventional politics and particularly the failure to tackle unemployment during the 1930s, but his example shows how apparently similar experiences could lead in different directions. While Macmillan became an elder statesman of the Tory party, Mosley founded the British Union of Fascists. He never missed an opportunity to talk about the war or to contrast the heroism of his generation with the cowardice of its successors,[10] all of which fitted in with his image as the dynamic, courageous fascist leader. In fact Mosley had seen little action in the First World War; his only wound was a self-inflicted one that came from crashing his plane while showing off to his mother. He got on badly with his son, a stammering intellectual who won the Military Cross in 1944.

In France, by contrast, memories of the war concentrated on rank-and-file soldiers rather than officers. During the 1930s, veterans' associations, with about 3 million members (a quarter of the electorate),[11] were more fragmented and more explicitly politicized than in England. Some of them became involved in political activity – notably the antiparliamentary riots of 1934 – while one veterans' league, the Croix de Feu, eventually transformed itself into a political party. However, the French veterans' leagues posed only a limited challenge to the established order. Many of them would have preferred a stronger executive, but few of them opposed democracy and none of them opposed the Third Republic. Furthermore, the French war effort fitted into national mythology. It was seen as a defensive war waged by a "people's army" and, as such, was part of a tradition that could be traced back to the revolutionary wars.

The First World War helped to bring two forms of reconciliation to France. First, Catholics were brought back into national life after the separation of Church and state in 1905. Second, some French Jews and a part of the French right were brought together, for a time at least, after the divisions of the Dreyfus case.[12] Alfred Dreyfus himself returned to the army during the war, and a number of his relatives were killed fighting. As the French right became more anti-Semitic during the late 1930s, it often rewrote its histories of the Great War to exclude Jews, but the break was never total: even the Vichy government granted special exemption from its anti-Semitic legislation to Jews who had fought in the Great War.

The manner in which the recollection of war tied in with subsequent political circumstances was also striking in France. Memory of war was cultivated most intensely not in its immediate aftermath but from the early 1930s to the late 1950s. The recollection of victory and unity mattered most at a time of defeat and division. Reference to war was seen in the activities of ex-servicemen's associations during the 1930s, and again under the Vichy government of 1940–44. Pétain, head of state during this period, had an obvious appeal to veterans, and Vichy sought to organize them in a single association – the Légion Française des Combattants.

The political exploitation of the memory of the First World War in Italy was very different from that in France. In Italy, there had been no *union sacrée*. The war had been a divisive experience: many Italians had opposed entry and many conscript soldiers had been prevented from desertion only by brutal discipline. Consequently there was no mythology of the ordinary trench soldier. Rather, the most organized and active veterans were the so-called *arditi*, or shock troops, whose mythology stressed how they differed from the rest of the Italian army.

In Germany, the political memory of the First World War was influenced by the manner in which it ended. Defeat meant that demobilization was more chaotic than in Britain or France, which reduced the chances that the authorities stood of controlling veterans' movements. In addition, the Weimar Republic was widely seen to have emerged out of defeat, so the very recollection of a war that had taken place under the imperial flag challenged Weimar's legitimacy. German veterans were influenced by three other things. First, the severe cut in the size of the army, brought about by the Treaty of Versailles, meant that the number of ex-soldiers was much larger than it would otherwise have been. More particularly, it meant that many former officers who had not felt the need to organize before 1914 now needed to defend their interests. Second, the continuing civil violence and skirmishes with Poles and Bolsheviks meant that ex-servicemen often passed directly into various paramilitary organizations such as the *Freikorps*. Even after the period of open violence had ended, many regular officers still believed that the veterans' movement could be used to circumvent the limitations on the Weimar army imposed at Versailles, and as a result German veterans' associations remained more actively military than their counterparts in other countries. Finally, and paradoxically, German veterans were radicalized by the fact that Weimar was generous in its provision of war pensions and other benefits, thus freeing veterans' organizations from the bread-and-butter lobbying that occupied their counterparts in other countries.

In the long term, German recollection of the First World War was shaped by Hitler's seizure of power in 1933. Hitler made much of his own experience of front-line combat, but, once in power, Nazism looked forward to the victorious wars of the future rather than back to the defeats of the past. The regime's celebration of youth increasingly led to the celebration of a generation that had grown up after the First World War, and most Nazi activists were too young to have served before 1918.[13] Most importantly, Nazism defined the nation in terms of biology rather than military experience: an Aryan Dutchman who had enjoyed tranquil neutrality from 1914 to 1918 was more "German" than a Jew who had fought on the western front for four years. In Minsk during the Second World War, a German policeman beating a German Jew was oblivious to the fact that both men had won the Iron Cross during the First World War.[14] A German family placed an advertisement in a newspaper regretting the "mysterious death" of a relative who had been decorated in the Great War; as the family probably knew, the man in question was a victim of the Nazi euthanasia campaign.[15] In 1941, the Bishop of Münster preached a sermon in which he drew attention to the way in which the Nazi obsession with biological fitness overrode respect for war records: "[It] is only necessary for some secret edict to order that the method developed for the mentally ill should be extended to . . . severely disabled soldiers."[16]

Veterans were not the only ones to suffer as a consequence of war. It created millions of widows and orphans throughout Europe. In Germany alone, the war left almost 2 million orphans and over 500,000 widows, while in France, the "pupils of the nation," who were supported by the state after their fathers were killed in action, became a self-conscious and vociferous group. There were also less obvious victims. Aristocratic mothers sometimes wrote of their grief at the loss of sons, but the distress of illiterate peasants must have been equally intense. The suffering of the western European middle classes was made worse by the fact that before 1914 they had begun to have smaller families in the expectation that all children would survive to adulthood. Loss of sons could have social and economic as well as emotional consequences: aristocratic families lost the prospect that their name would be perpetuated, and peasants lost labor that was vital to the survival of a family farm. Many who had saved to put an only son through school so that he could obtain a safe job in the civil service or railways lost their expectation of support in old age.

The consequences of the First World War reached into the most intimate areas of private life, and views about human nature changed.

Divisions between madness and sanity seemed less clear in 1919 than in 1914. Siegfried Sassoon, known as "Mad Jack" when he displayed the careless heroism that earned him a Military Cross, was sent to a mental hospital when he issued a studiously rational manifesto calling for an end to the war. Study of shell shock prompted an article published in *The Lancet* in 1916 to talk of "a no man's land between sanity and insanity." Shell shock challenged assumptions with particular violence because it questioned conventional ideas about gender and class. Self-control was taken to be an intrinsic part of masculinity, and was associated with the superior characters of men from the upper reaches of society,[17] but shell shock, which exposed the limits of self-control, was an exclusively male affliction that was four times more likely to affect officers than other ranks.[18]

Religious belief was also affected by the war. Conventional religion often seemed inadequate to confront the suffering and loss, and there was a new interest in spiritualism as distraught relatives tried to contact men killed in the war.[19] Curiously, Catholicism survived the war better than Protestantism. At the highest level, this was indicated by a partial reconciliation of Church and state in France, Germany and Italy. On a more individual level, it was reflected in the personal feelings of soldiers. After his wartime encounter with a group of French monks, Robert Graves wrote: "Catholicism ceased to repel me."[20] Anticlerical Frenchmen believed that religious orders exploited their control of medical facilities to gain favor from wounded soldiers,[21] while in Britain Catholic chaplains gained respect because they, unlike their Anglican colleagues, were encouraged to visit the front line.[22]

There may also have been a broader reason for the divergence between the two faiths. Protestantism was often associated with a certain kind of liberal rationality, while in the early twentieth century Catholicism had often been derided as an irrational and archaic superstition appropriate only for women and children – Catholic leaders themselves were worried by the growth of Marian cults in the last years of the nineteenth century. The fact that Catholicism had never succeeded in disassociating itself from such "superstitions" to the same extent as Protestant churches may have made it less vulnerable during and after the war. Some suggested that the Catholic Church's tradition of prayers for the dead meant that its members were less inclined to seek solace in spiritualism, which seems to have been most prevalent in Protestant England.[23] Perhaps soldiers faced with the inexplicable and horrible events of the Somme came to feel that a faith founded on irrationality was more appropriate to the real world. It may be significant that every reported religious vision of the late nineteenth and early twentieth centuries was attributed to women or children except for one – the vision of angels on horseback said to have accompanied soldiers into battle at Mons.

Conclusion

The word "legacy" implies something that is passed from one generation to the next. It is an appropriate word to apply to the Great War because the impact of the war was so often felt even by those born after 1918. However, legacies do not always have a fixed value (a fact particularly evident in the inflation that followed the Great War). The very ubiquity of references to the war can sometimes make us assume that it had a single meaning that transcended all the different European cultures. The truth was that the war had many diverse, sometimes contradictory, meanings. The direct physical impact (reflected in casualty figures), the indirect physical impact (reflected in birth rates) and the economic impact (reflected in national accounts) were all different things, and none of them were easy to measure. The cultural and political meaning ascribed to the war is even more difficult to assess. The new world of the 1920s and 1930s was both a product of the Great War and a prism through which Europeans looked back on it.

2
YOUTH

"The fight that always occurs between the generations was exceptionally bitter at the end of the Great War; this was partly due to the war itself, and partly it was an indirect result of the Russian Revolution, but an intellectual struggle was in any case due about that date."

George Orwell, 1940[1]

"Until ten years ago it was nonsense to talk in any general way about 'The Younger Generation.' Youth and age merged together in a gentle and unbroken gradation . . . But in the social subsidence that resulted from the war a double cleft appeared in the life of Europe dividing it into three perfectly distinct classes between whom none but the most superficial sympathy can ever exist. There is a) the wistful generation who grew up and found their opinions before the war and were too old for military service b) the stunted and mutilated generation who fought c) the younger generation."

Evelyn Waugh, 1929[2]

"Amongst our children it is today fairly easy to distinguish, mainly according to ages, between the war and the post-war generations."

Marc Bloch, 1942[3]

"The rulers of Jugoslavia between 1918 and 1941 consisted partly of the pre-1914 generation, honest and democratic citizens who cared genuinely for the interests of the people, but who were too old to understand the needs of the modern age, and partly of the war generation which had emerged crippled from the catastrophe and was concerned only to compensate itself for its sufferings by riches and power gained at any price. The old generation had lost contact with the people. The middle generation cared nothing for the people. The young generation ignored the first and revolted fiercely against the second."

Hugh Seton-Watson, 1945[4]

THE QUOTATIONS ABOVE show that, throughout Europe, the Great War was seen as inaugurating new divisions between the generations. Waugh was, of course, wrong to say that the conflict of generations was utterly new, and Orwell was right to suggest that such divisions had always existed. In Germany before 1914, there had been 45,000 members of various youth movements. In France in 1913, two authors – Henri Massis and Alfred de Tarde – published a famous enquiry into "*Les jeunes gens d'aujourd'hui*" (young men in elite educational institutions). The British propensity to celebrate youth, especially the "golden youth" of upper-class boys, began before 1914 and explains much of the mythology around the "lost generation" of the First World War. This celebration was epitomized by J. M. Barrie's *Peter Pan*. Barrie himself was fascinated by heroes of the Great War, which gave a few boys the chance to fly and many the chance not to grow up.

Although generational differences had always existed, they were more obvious after the Great War. A new interest in the concept of generation could be found in the writing of Karl Mannheim in Germany, or José Ortega y Gasset in Spain, while in France François Mentré talked about "*générations sociales*" and Jean Luchaire (born in 1901) founded a new journal entitled *Notre Temps: La Revue des Nouvelles Générations*.[5]

Those who talked of a "younger generation" during this period almost always meant young men. Direct involvement in war and political violence was a mainly male experience, and the educational establishments that fostered a self-conscious elite of youth were exclusively male. Often "youth" and masculinity were described as if they were synonymous. Both were presented in terms of action, vigor, and movement. Freud's notion of the "Oedipus complex," which linked youthful rebellion and male sexuality, began to gain wide currency during this period.

A single generation gap did not always operate in the same way throughout Europe, though. Waugh's generation of Oxford undergraduates read Eliot to bemused rowing eights; their contemporaries in Belgrade plotted more serious challenges to the ruling order. Relations between the generations were never fixed. Successive waves of men referred to themselves as "the young generation," but each one was in turn challenged by its juniors. In interwar continental Europe, generational revolt could become a circular process: youthful rebellion contributed to political instability, which in turn produced events that defined a new "younger generation." Thus, for example, Milovan Djilas, born in 1911, attended the University of Belgrade only a decade after the Great War, but for him the defining political event was the institution of royal dictatorship in 1929: "The dictatorship gave rise to a whole new generation, particularly among the intellectuals at Belgrade University, a generation altogether different from the one that preceded it."[6] Even when political drama did not intervene, each younger generation was doomed to be laughed at by its children. Paul Pennyfeather mutated into Gilbert Pinfold in a couple of decades.

The intense preoccupation with generational differences came first from the veterans of the Great War. Those who had fought were hostile to old men, and some presented the war as a kind of child sacrifice: Owen described the old man who "slew his son, and half the seed of Europe, one by one," while Kipling, whose son had been killed in 1915, wrote: "If any question why we died, / Tell them, because our fathers lied." Storm Jameson was the sister of a soldier killed in the war, and the wife and ex-wife of soldiers; one of the characters in her novel *Company Parade* (1934) says, "It is always the young who die of wars, and this creates for the time an elderly experienced world, which smells used."

Returning soldiers did not care for the discipline of educational establishments. At St-Cyr, the French military school, surviving cadets – about half of those who had left in 1914 – were expected to return to their studies as if nothing had happened; three-quarters of them now held the rank of captain.[7] A "one-armed twenty-five-year-old brigadier" led a rebellion against the quality of undergraduate food at St. John's College, Oxford.[8] In Italy, the impact of returning soldiers on universities was more momentous, with special regulations allowing officers to attend lectures while still in uniform and drawing pay. By the summer of 1919, 23,000 officers had taken advantage of this scheme.[9] The rebellious mood of some officer/students found an outlet in Fascism, and such support became so important to the movement that the Fascist Party in Bologna did not begin its activities until after the beginning of the academic year. Youth and the war generation were crucial to the mythology of Fascism, and at first the two were more or less synonymous. In 1924, almost a quarter of Fascist members of parliament were under thirty.

Those who had fought often defined the struggle between the generations as one that pitched young front-line soldiers against old civilians or generals, but those who had been too young to fight soon thought of the generational divide as one that separated themselves from war veterans. Evelyn Waugh's analysis of the generations was rooted in his own experience. The "wistful generation" was that of his father; the war generation was that of his house master at Lancing College, J. F. Roxburgh; and the younger generation was his own. English public schools were tense institutions during the war. Masters – whose age or ill health rendered them unfit to fight and who were often deeply upset by the fate of former pupils – attempted to control boys who knew that they might be dead within months of leaving. Antonia White, whose father was a master at St. Paul's, wrote in her autobiographical novel *The Lost Traveller*: "His [the teacher's] attitude towards the top form became increasingly humble. By 1916 enough of his old pupils had been killed to make him shudder every time a Second Lieutenant came to say goodbye." After the war, matters were made worse by the return of teachers who had been rendered nihilistic by their experiences in France. Waugh argued that his generation of schoolboys "should have been whipped and taught Greek paradigms," but instead "were set arguing about birth control and nationalization."[10]

George Orwell (born, like Waugh, in 1903) wrote of the mood of cynicism that pervaded Eton during the First World War. Orwell also defined youth in terms of rebellion against the war generation: "I have often laughed to think of that recruiting poster, 'What did you do in the Great War, daddy?' (a child is asking this question of its shame-stricken father), and of all the men who must have been lured into the army by just that poster and afterwards despised by their children for not being Conscientious Objectors."[11]

A generation similar to that of Orwell and Waugh in Britain existed in France. Men like André Malraux, born in 1901, or Jean-Paul Sartre, born in 1905, had grown up in the shadow of war. Robert Brasillach epitomized the rebellious youth of the period: he was born in 1909, his father was killed in 1915, and he wrote his first novel at the age of twenty and his memoirs at thirty. He was shot for treason at thirty-five.

This was a restless generation obsessed with travel, especially to dangerous places. Waugh traveled across South America delirious with fever and strapped to a donkey; Orwell had almost died in a Paris paupers' hospital by the time he was twenty-seven; Malraux was arrested for trying to steal ornaments from a temple in Indochina; Graham Greene sought excitement in Russian roulette, spying and opium. But the feelings of such men towards the war generation were more complicated than they first appeared. The fact that they spent such large parts of their lives seeking danger and discomfort suggests that they wished to match the experience of their elders; many were desperate to fight in a war. Orwell, like Malraux, went to Spain and recognized the extent to which he had come to share the values of a generation that he had once despised: "I am convinced that part of the reason for the fascination that the Spanish Civil War had for people of about my age was that it was so like the Great War."[12]

The disruptive effects of the war on youth were not confined to the rich. One French writer remembered that "children were allowed to run wild with only women to teach them and old men to counsel them,"[13] while in Prussia more than half of primary schoolteachers had been called up by 1916.[14] Apprenticeships had often provided discipline for young men, but apprenticeships disappeared as artisanal enterprises closed down,[15] so the young were drawn into work in large factories where they were paid relatively well and were not subjected to the intense surveillance of family enterprises. Male adolescents enjoyed enormous power and freedom. Often they assumed their father's place in the family home and were waited on by their sisters[16] (the employment of women under seventeen in Germany dropped, while that of men under seventeen increased).[17] Georges Simenon had a typical wartime boyhood. He ceased to be an assiduous choirboy and ran wild; his fascination with low life dates from this period. Simenon's own experience of war as a time of rebellion did not prevent him from working for a French veterans' association representing an older generation that talked of the war in terms of order and discipline.[18]

Demographics made the ill-disciplined boys who emerged out of the First World War seem all the more threatening. The generation immediately above them had been depleted by war deaths, while that immediately below them had been depleted by low wartime birth rates. In Leipzig in 1919, there were two and half times as many twelve-year-olds as two-year-olds.[19] The absence of fathers, who were at the front (or dead), and the preoccupation of mothers, who often worked full-time, meant that increasing numbers of young people were left without supervision. In Berlin in 1917, only 8 percent of adolescents working in industry were under the supervision of both parents, and 18 percent had no parents at all.[20]

Adolescents seem to have been particularly hard hit by hunger,[21] and in the absence of the forces that had previously provided discipline, many turned to crime. Juvenile crime in Germany was said to have doubled by the end of the war.[22] Economic crisis further increased the sense that adolescents were escaping from the control of their parents. Unemployed or impoverished men found it hard to command filial respect, and boys were sometimes more able to find work than their fathers.

The problems faced in France, Germany and Belgium were trivial compared to those in the Soviet Union, where the casualties of the civil war had created vast numbers of orphans in a country that was ill equipped to provide for them. By 1921, Russian children's homes contained 540,000 orphans, and still more lived on the streets; throughout the 1920s, hundreds of thousands of adolescents roamed the countryside, living by begging, theft and prostitution. Famine and disease made matters worse.

Furthermore, poor resources forced many children's homes to close. Soviet authorities were buffeted by contradictory impulses: on the one hand, many experts believed in allowing children to enjoy as much liberty as possible; on the other hand, there was increasing fear of adolescent crime and hooliganism. Between 1922 and 1924, 145,052 juvenile crimes were reported in Moscow, most of which were committed by children without a father.[23]

Sometimes relations between the generations that had fought in the war and those who had grown up during it were tense. Precisely because youth was such an important part of the ex-soldiers' self-image, they found it hard to adjust to middle age; there is bitterness in the line, "They shall grow not old, as we that are left grow old." In Italy, there was conflict between the two generations as the young men who had launched Fascism aged. Camillo Pellizzi argued that "youth" could not be defined merely in terms of years lived and that the war generation had "earned" the right to be considered vigorous and healthy in a way that was not true of its successors. By 1931, even the Fascist student movement was composed primarily of men who had joined the party before 1923.[24]

Sometimes the gap between those who had fought the war and those who had grown up during it was bridged. Some veterans' organizations made a conscious effort to reach out to those who were too young to have fought in the war so that the war myth was handed down across the generations. In 1924, the German Stahlhelm, originally restricted to men who had served at least six months at the front, formed its own youth movement for those aged between seventeen and twenty-one,[25] while in Milan, associations originally made up of *arditi* opened their ranks to teenage boys as early as 1920.[26] In the Soviet Union, the military uniform became fashionable among young peasants, including those too young to have fought, because it allowed them to distinguish themselves from their traditionally clad elders.[27] The French Croix de Feu, which had initially limited its membership to men who had been decorated in battle, formed an association of "sons of the Croix de Feu." The extent of the mobilization of the sons of veterans in France was shown in 1954, when Pierre Poujade (a small business leader) attacked the Prime Minister, Pierre Mendès France, with the words: "Our fathers were at Verdun and you M. Mendès were not." Both Poujade (born in 1920) and Mendès France (born in 1907) had served in the Second World War.

Generation gaps in interwar Europe had important political consequences. The most enthusiastic proponents of Bolshevism in the Russian countryside were young men, often radicalized by service in the Red Army, in rebellion against the patriarchs who dominated peasant households. In rural areas, the communist youth organization had three times as many members as the party itself.[28] The split between communists and socialists, which occurred in the early 1920s, was underwritten by a division between young workers, often unskilled and employed in the industries that had grown during the war, and older, more established workers. The division between fascists and conservatives was also partly a matter of generation. The average age of founder members of the Nazi Party (in 1920–21) was thirty-three; by spring 1925 the average age of members had dropped to twenty-nine.[29] Mosley wrote in 1932: "The real division of the past decade has not been a division of parties, but a division of generations."[30]

Generational division was important to the victims of violence as well as to its perpetrators. For example, age made a difference in the way in which Jews reacted to Nazism. Those who had grown up with the comparative tolerance of Third Republic France or Weimar Germany, or even the predictable and limited intolerance of interwar Poland or Romania, were reluctant to accept that things had changed and that the positions that they had established in their native countries were now worthless; Jewish elders sometimes encouraged their communities to stay and to obey the German authorities. It was the younger generation that understood most quickly that the only chance of survival lay in fighting or flight.

An awareness of the importance, and threat, of youth compelled established institutions to take an interest in its affairs. Universities were often at the center of serious political conflict. Salazar, a lecturer in law at Coimbra, became dictator of Portugal, and Louvain was a base for a Catholic radical right that attacked Belgium's established politicians.[31] The assertion of national culture in universities became more important because of the boundary changes of the Paris peace settlement. Marc Bloch returned to Strasbourg, in the region from which his family had fled after the Prussian invasion of 1870, and developed a vision of history that laid particular emphasis on the permanent characteristics of "Frenchness." In eastern Europe, universities were even more strongly linked to the assertion of national identity. Often they had themselves been affected by boundary changes. In Hungary, the proportion of the population who were students doubled between 1913 and 1934,[32] and many of the bitterly nationalistic students who crowded into Budapest came from territories that had been taken away by the Treaty of Trianon. Universities became centers of anti-Semitism as students who were unable to obtain jobs blamed their plight on the comparatively high representation of Jews in higher education and the professions. The combination of elitist disdain, nationalist fervor and intellectual unemployment made eastern European universities dangerous places.

Table 3: Ages of European Political Leaders in 1933			
Socialist and Radical		*Communist*	
Léon Blum (France)	61	Maurice Thorez (France)	33
Edouard Herriot (France)	61	Jacques Doriot (France)	35
Ramsay MacDonald (Britain)	67	Palmiro Togliatti (Italy)	40
Emile Vandervelde (Belgium)	67	Joseph Stalin (USSR)	54
Conservative		*Fascist*	
Stanley Baldwin (Britain)	66	Oswald Mosley (Britain)	37
Paul von Hindenburg (Germany)	86	Adolf Hitler (Germany)	44
Philippe Pétain (France)	77	Léon Degrelle (Belgium)	27
António Salazar (Portugal)	44	José Primo de Rivera (Spain)	30
Neville Chamberlain (Britain)	64	Benito Mussolini (Italy)	50

The Catholic Church took a particular interest in youth. Its priests labored to establish sports teams and scout troops. Jeunesse Ouvrière Chrétienne was established in Belgium in 1924 and had spread to France by 1927; ten years later it had 80,000 members. Its work was matched by that of Jeunesse Agricole Chrétienne and Jeunesse Étudiante Catholique. Significantly, one of the first French Christian democrat parties was called Jeune République. However, Catholic interest in youth was always double-edged. In reality, the Church was a gerontocracy: bishops were old men and youth movements were designed to control, not respond to, the wishes of their members. When Croatian and Polish academic clubs sought too much autonomy, bishops established "seniorites" to keep them in line.[33]

The Church's control over youth movements brought it into conflict with authoritarian regimes; one of the main aims of the concordats that the Church arranged with such governments was the preservation of the autonomy of Catholic youth movements. In France, the struggle pitched the Church against political parties and secular organizations rather than an authoritarian government, and even the French scout movement was divided into Protestant, lay and Catholic associations (the latter being the most important). The struggle to channel youth for political purposes produced strange results. In France, a Trotskyite group split off from the socialist-controlled Red Falcons (and established a Zimmerwald summer camp).[34] Giles and Esmond Romilly, pupils at Wellington, formed an association to incite revolution in English public schools.[35]

Governments, too, tried to organize youth. Nazi Germany established the Hitler Youth and associated bodies and, by the end of 1933, almost half of boys aged ten to fourteen were involved in this organization. Increasingly, the Nazi regime moved away from voluntarism and its commitment to leave the organizations of the Catholic Church alone – by 1939, membership of Nazi youth organizations had become compulsory. The nature of such bodies had also changed. In the early years of Nazism, membership of the Hitler Youth could provide an adolescent with a refreshing chance to rebel against the authority of teachers, parents, employers and pastors, but the passage of time made the Hitler Youth itself seem like an instrument of authority. Its leadership aged, and it became obvious to working-class members that they were likely to be ordered around by middle-class officers from grammar schools and universities. The Nazi youth movement was increasingly concerned to prepare its members for the unpleasant discipline of military service and, eventually, war. Some members of the Hitler Youth accepted such discipline: the unit that fought hardest against the Allied advance in Normandy in 1944 was the 12th SS Panzer Division, named the "Hitler Youth Division" and made up of very young men.[36] But the institution of compulsory membership also brought in reluctant and sullen youngsters.

The outbreak of war widened the gap between the Hitler Youth and those that it sought to control. Discipline was tightened in the movement, and possibilities for excitement out of it often increased. Between the ages of fourteen and eighteen, working-class German boys could escape the constraints of school without having to endure the constraints of the army, and war industries provided the chance to earn good money. Some sought relief in youth gangs such as the Edelweiss Pirates, which mocked Nazi authority and celebrated a world of freedom, parties, sex and popular music (often adapted to fit more subversive ends) and were sometimes associated with opposition to the regime. Much of their activity was simply another form of youthful rebellion, involving, for example, the writing of graffiti on walls, although youth gangs in Düsseldorf did work with the underground Communist Party. The regime took such activity seriously, and in October 1944 Himmler issued a decree on combating youth gangs.[37]

Conservative rulers, unlike those of Nazi Germany, never encouraged youthful rebellion. Salazar's regime established a youth movement in 1936, but its membership was confined to those in full-time education and it was placed under the control of the Ministry of Education, with heavy influence from the Catholic Church.[38] Vichy France inherited a concern with the young from pre-war Catholic organizations, whose power prevented the establishment of a single youth movement. The regime established a "General Secretariat for Youth" and sent men who would normally have been obliged to perform military service to *chantiers de jeunesse*. Here, too, the organization of youth was controlled by the Ministry of Education, although, as in Germany, the young rebelled against movements ostensibly established for their benefit. Juvenile delinquency, or perhaps the state's fear of it, rose, and the number of children under the age of eighteen convicted of criminal offenses doubled between 1938 and 1942.[39]

Conclusion

If the First World War inaugurated a new sense of division between the generations in Europe, what, then, was the effect of the Second World War? In Britain, the armistice was followed by a period of relative political stability. No event ever divided the generations as sharply as the First World War had. The Second World War was less traumatic – the expectations of those who fought were less romantic and casualties were lower. Most importantly, the experience of war was no longer confined to a small group of young men at the front line. Bombing brought the war to civilians, and public understanding of the war effort was as much about industry and administration as fighting. English literature of the Second World War is about garrison duty rather than gas attacks. If the representative Englishman of the First World War had been Sub-Lieutenant Rupert Brooke, who was twenty-eight and acted as though he were eighteen, the representative Englishman of the Second World War was Colonel Kenneth Widmerpool, who was thirty-five and acted as though he were fifty.

In continental Europe, the Second World War created new generational divisions. A Frenchman born in 1917 was old enough to serve in the army that was defeated in 1940, and more than a million such men spent the next five years in captivity. A Frenchman born in 1922 would have been called up for obligatory labor service during the war, and many such men fled to the Maquis. A Frenchman born in 1926 could still be peaceably preparing for school examinations at the time of the Liberation. After this, no dramatic events marked a particular cohort of young people. The young liked to talk about Suez, Algeria or Vietnam, but such events took place a long way from Europe, and even those men who were sent to Suez or Algeria were rarely marked as much as their elders had been marked by the Second World War. The journalist Françoise Giroud, who carried out an enquiry into French youth in 1958, was struck by the fact that no event mobilized the young as much as Spain, Munich and the resistance had mobilized her own generation.[40]

In Germany, divisions between the generations became sharper than ever as a result of the Second World War. In 1945, a man who had grown up before Hitler's seizure of power and been too old to fight in the Second World War had very different experiences from those of someone who had spent five years in the Wehrmacht, and both had a different outlook from that of a member of the Hitler Youth who had grown up knowing nothing but Nazism. Such a divergence in attitudes continued into the postwar period because the recollection of the Nazi past varied so sharply according to age. The generation born after 1945, which learned about the Third Reich from school, was more likely to talk about Nazism than the generation that had lived through it. The postwar generation was highly critical of its parents, which gave the student demonstrations of the late 1960s a particularly sharp edge.[41]

In eastern Europe, 1945 did not mark a break: the Second World War was followed by the communist seizure of power, Stalinism, and a variety of rebellions and "normalizations" rather than by peace and stability. Under these circumstances, generational divides remained important. It made a big difference to a Czech whether he could remember the events of 1948 (the communist coup) or 1968 (the Warsaw Pact invasion). Reactions to Jean-Paul Sartre in the two parts of Europe shed an interesting light on the contrasting perceptions. Part of the rebellious generation that had reached adulthood immediately after the First World War, Sartre was admired by many of his juniors after 1945, but this admiration took different forms in East and West. Young people in the West admired him because the world that he described seemed so different from that in which they had grown up; the students who chanted "CRS/SS" in 1968 were fascinated by the political violence that had been experienced by their elders. In the East, by contrast, Sartre was respected by those who had experienced the very kind of political violence that he described (many of them had experienced it rather more directly than Sartre himself). In 1967, Milan Kundera, born in 1929, described himself as the "contemporary" of Sartre, born in 1905.[42]

3

MEN, WOMEN AND
THE FAMILY

"I DON'T KNOW why people talk about their private parts. Mine aren't private."[1]

The words of Enid Raphael, a 1920s London socialite, seem typical of new thinking about sexual relations after the Great War. Men and, especially, women were seen to behave in ways that previously would have been thought shocking. Barriers between public and private changed. Openness about sexuality went with other developments. The "new woman" is a ubiquitous cliché in writing about the 1920s.[2] Her emancipation was epitomized by short hair, the new fashion for slim, boyish figures, financial independence through paid work and, in many countries, the introduction of female suffrage. The new woman was, of course, a myth. The lives led by a few bourgeois young women in London, Paris or Berlin would have seemed remote to inhabitants of rural Ireland, where priests campaigned to ensure that men and women sat in separate sections of the cinema and where the League of St. Brigid was founded in 1920 to resist "foreign immodest fashions."[3] But that does not mean that changing images of women can be dismissed. Such images were important because they intertwined with thinking about issues of masculinity, war, national strength and the threat of revolutionary politics. Furthermore, because thinking about women was connected to so many other things, it needs to be understood in several dimensions. There was no straight dichotomy between the "emancipated woman" and "traditional values." Defenders of the traditional order might find that their desire to preserve the chastity of single women conflicted with their desire to increase birth rates; similarly, their wish to exclude women from politics conflicted with the need to use women voters as a counterweight to increasingly organized and dangerous male proletarians.

As sex was associated with power, conquest and honor, sexual relations between men and women produced conflicts between men and men. In one area of Calabria, 60 percent of murders in the 1940s were said to have sprung from assaults on female honor – rapes, abductions and broken engagements.[4] Even ostensibly political violence often had roots in sexual relations. One of the most famous assassinations in interwar Europe, that of SA leader Horst Wessel, was in part the product of a conflict among men for the control of women; Wessel lived with a prostitute who had annoyed local pimps by competing with their protégées.[5]

The political dimension of sexual morality was particularly important in Europe after the First World War because sexual relations were no longer seen, if they had ever been, as matters that concerned only two individuals. The fact that sex was associated with so many other things meant that it became the subject of public policy. In 1925, Keynes told a conference of young Liberals that sex, along with peace and government, was one of the great political issues of the day: "Sex questions have not been party questions in the past. But that was because they were never, or seldom, the subject of public discussion. All this is changed now. There are no subjects about which the big general public is more interested; few which are the subject of wider discussion."[6]

The language of interwar politics was shot through with sexual metaphors. Authoritarian politicians were particularly inclined to present the "public" as female, and themselves as the man destined to subdue her. Mussolini had an aggressively sexual style and talked of playing the crowd "like a woman." Hitler adopted a different manner, cultivating a mysterious, solitary air and believing that his appeal depended on public celibacy. Pétain's image stressed paternal authority. One of his admirers wrote: "Public opinion is nervous and feminine; the Marshal is firm and virile."[7]

Sources

Sources for the study of sexual relations pose particular problems. Many apparent changes in sexual behavior came from new ways of collecting information. In Great Britain, for example, the decision to record the parents' marriage date on birth certificates in 1938 revealed that around one-third of women conceived their first child outside marriage.[8] The very quantity of discussion of sex can be confusing and deceptive, not simply because most such works relate to elite opinion and habits – we know more about adultery in Mayfair than about adultery in Bethnal Green – but also because the relationship between the writings of the most celebrated exponents of new ideas and their own lives is sometimes hard to determine. Sigmund Freud said that, personally, he had made little use of the sexual freedoms that he advocated; scholars are divided over whether he had an affair with his sister-in-law.[9] James Joyce, often seen as the most important literary representative of sexual openness, was as obsessed as any Victorian patriarch with establishing whether his wife had been a virgin before meeting him.[10]

Matters are made especially complicated by the fact that many writers deliberately created a mythology around themselves. Furthermore, many influential interpretations of the interwar period come from retrospective accounts written in very different circumstances. Consider, for example, the much publicized relationship between Simone de Beauvoir and Jean-Paul Sartre, which came to be seen as the template of a new kind of sexual freedom in which partners would be free to enjoy "contingent" relations. Yet the two lived a rather conventional life when they were young, describing their relationship, in interestingly bourgeois language, as based on a "leasehold."[11] Furthermore, the fact that the two were not married and had no children was more unusual in the 1950s, by which time they were famous, than it had been in the 1930s.

The complexity of interpreting this relationship also springs from the fact that both sides mined their own lives for literary and political ammunition. Sartre's novel *The Age of Reason*, for example, contains a scene in which a young man seeks to procure an abortion for his mistress.[12] It is tempting to assume that this is an autobiographical account, an impression confirmed by the fact that de Beauvoir signed the petition of 1971, in which 343 women stated that they had had abortions and demanded the legalization of such operations. It would also fit in with her influential claim in *The Second Sex* (1949) that abortions in France were as common as live births. In later life, though, de Beauvoir claimed that she had never had an abortion and merely signed the manifesto out of "solidarity."[13]

The blurring of fact and fiction also creates problems for historians. Novels during the interwar period were often explicit about sexual matters and sometimes seemed very autobiographical. This makes them useful historical sources, but it can also be dangerous. Scholars have devoted much energy to finding the "real experience" behind literary work; Proust's English biographer is keen to prove that his subject was in love with a girl and consequently able to provide an "authentic" account of heterosexuality.[14] The French Sovietologist Alain Besançon was aware that the image of the interwar generation came from the conventions of writing as much as from real behavior: "If one was to believe our French literature, so preoccupied with matters of love, in reading Morand, Pierre Benoit and even Aragon . . . one would say that our parents were concerned only with women, with leading an irreproachable career as a lover. These are literary landscapes that do not have a fixed relation to the state of morals."[15]

Guardians of morality

There was no single kind of sexual morality in interwar Europe, not simply because there were different beliefs about how people should behave but also because there were different conceptions of how behavior should be discussed and regulated. Broadly speaking, morality operated on at least four levels.

The simplest concerned the state, which forbade certain practices, such as homosexuality in Britain, or birth control in France. Such interventions were often more common in the interwar period, and even democratic governments made greater efforts to regulate sex and reproduction. The boundaries of the state sometimes became unclear and in some cases it sought to regulate sex through advice and exhortation rather than compulsion; in 1926, for example, the Prussian Ministry of Social Welfare founded offices to advise couples about their suitability to have children.[16] The state's initiatives often blended into popular morality in a confused way; after the Bolshevik Revolution, enthusiastic officials in one Russian region announced the "nationalization of all women."

Alongside the state stood institutions with explicit moral codes, the most obvious of which was the Church. Church and state sometimes worked in harmony, as the latter sought to impose Christian values. Alternatively, separation of Church and state could create two rival systems of regulation. Before the Lateran Treaty of 1929, the state in Italy refused to recognize Church marriages, while the Church refused to recognize civil ones. Enterprising citizens could exploit this to commit bigamy or evade restrictions on marriage that affected junior army officers or those drawing pensions as widows.[17]

Morality was also expounded in the writings of a wide variety of private individuals. Those who questioned the rules of Church and state were often presented as "immoral" but they rarely saw themselves that way. D. H. Lawrence, for example, wished to redefine morality rather than abolish it. Furthermore, the morality that he propagated does not, in retrospect, seem very radical: he believed in the monogamous heterosexual couple ultimately sanctified by marriage.

Increasingly, discussion of sex was conducted in scientific terms. The works of Sigmund Freud became more widely known, and their dissemination was aided first by the use of psychology in the treatment of shell shock and subsequently by the forced migration of Jewish psychologists from Germany and Austria during the 1930s. In Germany, Magnus Hirschfeld founded an Institute for Sexual Science in 1919.[18] Margaret Mead's anthropological study of growing up in the South Pacific had important implications for what constituted "natural sexual behavior"; she later became an official commentator on the dating patterns of British girls and American troops during the Second World War.[19]

Many who discussed sex in scientific terms would have denied that they were moralists and would have insisted that their work was descriptive, not prescriptive. In practice, however, the distinction was hard to maintain. The study of the subconscious or primitive societies often provided a screen on to which people could project their own values and contrast them with the "artificial" morality of Western society. Although D. H. Lawrence denounced scientific approaches to sex, his emphasis on "naturalness" and on the distortions imposed by civilization often paralleled that of those who rooted their analysis in medicine or anthropology. Words such as "normal," "healthy" and "hygienic" moved out of the medical textbook to acquire a moral connotation. Consider, for example, the statement of a Romanian gynecologist in 1940 that the identity of women "is essentially defined by their procreative function,"[20] or the words of a Soviet doctor in 1937: "Nature has its iron laws and punishes for the slightest failure to observe them. Breast feeding of the baby by the biological mothers is one of these iron laws which cannot be broken without serious consequences."[21] Scientific approaches to sex cut across differences in political regimes to produce strange convergences – Nazi Germany's attitudes towards matters such as homosexuality and the reproduction of "the unfit" look disconcertingly familiar if compared with medically inspired initiatives in the Soviet Union, Sweden and the United States.

An interesting example of ideas on the frontier between science and morality is provided by work on female chastity in France during the 1920s. Some doctors warned of dangerous consequences if women remained virgins as a result of the "deficit of men" produced by the First World War, and some argued that contact with semen was necessary for a woman's healthy development. Such ideas had a moral as well as medical connotation, tying in with a certain kind of socially conservative, though non-Catholic, morality, emphasizing the importance of men and rooted in attempts to deal with the population crisis. Ideas of this kind could have radical consequences even if they had conservative beginnings – they encouraged tolerance of children born outside marriage. Such ideas spread beyond the medical profession, influencing some feminists, such as Josette Cornec, who argued for equal tolerance of male and female sexual activity: "In the opinion of doctors, excessively prolonged virginity can produce a halt in intellectual and physical development."[22]

The Great War and the crisis of masculinity

The most influential commentators on the changing role of women were usually men, and discussion of the changing way in which women were perceived should start by examining the changing way in which men perceived themselves. This perception was much influenced by the Great War. Initially, the war was seen as particularly "masculine," a glorious war of movement, heroism and conquest. Men who went to war often described their action in terms of escaping from close relations with women or a reinforcement of male power over women. Pierre Drieu la Rochelle wrote: "*Les femmes avec leurs bouches rouges dirent: 'Nous sommes vos femmes / O, nos mâles, allez tuer!'*"[23]

Things did not turn out as hoped. Men who had expected to be enjoying a hero's welcome in the arms of their admiring womenfolk within a few months found themselves stuck in trenches on the western front, and such contact as they had with women often took place in the depressing conditions of army brothels. Conditions in the trenches also raised questions about the nature of masculinity. Men avoided the ostentatious heroism that had once been presented as the expression of manhood and learned to crawl, stoop and hide. In the nineteenth century, men had been associated with rationality and robust good health; women had often been associated with illness, especially mental illness. Now, however, large numbers of men were invalided, weak or mentally disturbed: male victims of shell shock in the literature of the 1920s played a similar role to that of women with consumption in the nineteenth century.[24]

War memoirs illustrated a new mood of doubt about male sexual identity. In England, perhaps because of the aftermath of the Wilde case, such doubts often surfaced in references to homosexuality. Robert Graves's *Goodbye to All That* (1929) contains a discussion of homosexuality in an English public school. Guy Chapman's autobiography is even more interesting. His mother avoided sending him to board at his public school because, from what she knew of the Wilde case, she was worried about the influence of exclusively male company on her son. It was, therefore, as a junior officer on the western front that Chapman lived among men for the first time, and he saw war as a peculiarly male experience. A character in a novel about ex-soldiers written by Chapman's second wife remarks, "Perhaps we shall discover why women are so insensitive about war. Is it because they have no imagination? Or only because they lack self-respect?"[25] Chapman quoted Montherlant's remark that war was "the most tender experience that he had lived through." He added: "My love for some of the men I lived with in 1914–1918 is a third sort, sexless in the accepted meaning of the term, completely devoid of the element of fear and strain in sexual love, whether for man or woman, fear of physical failure, of humiliation. Call it, perhaps, essential love, the essence."[26] One of the men for whom Chapman experienced such feelings was Munro Cuthbertson: "That after the war he came to grief when commanding a London territorial battalion and was broken on a homosexual charge is no matter. He remained as much ours as he ever was. And he is dead."[27] Chapman later added, "I have always detested the easy habit of assuming that any man who prefers men and is openly attached to his male friends is a homosexual."[28] Siegfried Sassoon, recovering from shell shock, wrote in his diary about his desire to write a *Madame Bovary* of homosexual life.[29]

Men's doubts about their own sexuality tied in with, and perhaps created, doubts about the women that they had left behind. The war was seen as having produced a burst of sexual expression on the part of women. The excitement of men departing for the front, and the possibility that they would not return, was thought to have encouraged sexual activity on the part of otherwise chaste and demure girls. An article in a Hungarian newspaper read: "At no time have women committed so many mistakes and sins as in the Autumn of this mass fever,"[30] while André Bouton's postwar account of the damage done to the French bourgeoisie by the war included the following passage: "Too many women of austere morality conducted themselves in ways that they would never have considered in the course of a normal existence."[31] Illegitimate births resulting from such liaisons created problems for the guardians of public morality: women who sacrificed their honor in moments of patriotic ardor were not tarred with the same brush as those carried away by mere lust, and the children of war heroes, especially dead war heroes, could not be dismissed as bastards. The German government introduced special legislation allowing women who had borne children by men at the front to be treated as though married. In fact rates of illegitimate births in relation to the total number of unmarried women in Germany do not seem to have risen during the war, but illegitimacy, like venereal disease, became associated with a more general concern about uncontrolled female sexuality.[32]

Sexual activity of women at home was particularly disturbing for soldiers because it reversed pre-war expectations. Men found themselves imprisoned in the passive life of the trenches while women at home seemed to be leading freer and more active lives. If English concerns about the nature of masculinity tended to be expressed in terms of homosexuality, French doubts were expressed in terms of adultery. French war literature was full of accounts of men who went home to find their wives enjoying the company of other men. Alain (Emile Chartier) reports that one of his comrades greeted all new arrivals at the front with the question, "Are you married?" If the answer was yes, he replied, "Then you are a cuckold."[33] Drieu la Rochelle used adultery as a metaphor to express his wider concern about France's inability to win the war without the help of allies: "*Nous n'avons pas couché seuls avec la victoire.*"[34]

The challenge to masculinity presented by the First World War was particularly dramatic in Italy, where entry into the war was less popular than it had been in Britain, France and Germany. In the south, entry into the army was often seen as a sign of effeminacy rather than manhood – it suggested the conscript had been insufficiently resourceful to escape:

> In one quarter of Taurianova [in Calabria], during the war, a peasant woman whose husband was in the army became the love of an *'ndranghetista* [bandit] who had managed – *per diritezza*, he said: because he knew how to stand up for himself – to avoid going to the front. When the husband got back, he realized at once, from the coldness of people's greetings, that something serious had befallen his own and his family's honor. When he had found out from his old father what had happened, he didn't have the courage to kill either his wife or the *'ndranghetista*. A few months later, he had to leave for America. Nobody held him in the slightest regard any longer. Even the children in the street had started to make fun of him.[35]

The war upset relations between men and women. Divorce rates rose as men returned to hastily contracted marriages. The literature of the 1920s reflected the new doubts about sexual relations that had emerged out of the war. Two novels generated particular scandal. Victor Margueritte's *La Garçonne* (1922) concerns a girl who rebels against the bourgeois conformity of her family and her fiancé and resorts to promiscuity and lesbianism before finally finding happiness in the arms of a war veteran. D. H. Lawrence's *Lady Chatterley's Lover* (1928) concerns an aristocratic woman married to a man who has been paralyzed from the hips down by a war wound. The heroine leaves her husband for his gamekeeper – a soldier promoted to officer rank during the war. Lawrence, a pacifist married to a cousin of the German air ace Baron Manfred von Richthofen, had good reason to reflect on the competing visions of masculinity that emerged from the war.

Homosexuality

Much thinking about sex in interwar Europe concerned not relations between men and women but relations among men. Many Europeans had not really thought about homosexuality during the nineteenth century. It was known that men had sexual relations with each other, but the idea of the homosexual as a particular category of person hardly existed. By the beginning of the twentieth century, major trials – of Philipp von Eulenburg in Germany and of Oscar Wilde in Britain – brought homosexuality to wide attention. The Wilde trial was particularly important. It changed people's perceptions of relations between men that had previously been regarded as innocent – in *Lark Rise to Candleford*, Flora Thompson recalls how two old soldiers who lived together were stoned in the street during the trial. It also provided some men with a new sense of their own identity; E. M. Forster's Maurice says: "I am an unspeakable of the Oscar Wilde sort." Doctors and criminologists made increasing efforts to define and explain "the homosexual personality."

Reactions to homosexuality varied between countries and over time. France was more tolerant than Britain. Homosexuality was never illegal in twentieth-century France; even the Vichy government merely passed a law in 1942 forbidding sexual relations between men and boys under the age of twenty-one. French commentators regarded the hysterical British reaction to the Wilde case with amusement. They considered homosexuality to be the product of deficient heterosexual impulses rather than as a specific form of sexuality, and assumed that such practices were more common in England than in France.[36] In Germany, legislation relating to homosexuality became more repressive in 1875 when the Prussian law forbidding sodomy was applied across the Reich.

The interwar period saw two major moves to legalize homosexuality. The first occurred in Russia in December 1917 as a by-product of a more general revocation of the entire *ancien régime* criminal code; the criminal code of 1922 did not reestablish homosexual relations as a crime. But the change did not reflect a new mood of tolerance. The most open attitude towards homosexuals came from anarchists and bourgeois liberals such as Vladimir Nabokov, father of the novelist. Bolshevik leaders disapproved of homosexuality and in many respects Russia in the 1920s was less tolerant than it had been in the aftermath of the February 1917 revolution. The other significant legalization of homosexuality occurred in Germany, where in 1929 an alliance of communist and socialist deputies struck down the Reich laws on sodomy.

In the 1930s both Germany and the Soviet Union reversed the liberalization of homosexuality laws of the previous decade. The Nazi regime stiffened legislation against homosexuality in 1935, and about 50,000 men were prosecuted.[37] In 1936, a Reich Office for the Combating of Homosexuality and Abortion was created, while in the Soviet Union, homosexuality was made illegal in 1934. The Soviet Union and Nazi Germany did not merely restore previous legislation but connected the suppression of homosexuality to wider political projects. In the Soviet Union, homosexuality was now defined as a "crime against the state" and attracted the attention of the political police. In Germany, homosexuality was seen as a crime against the race and convicted men were often sent to concentration camps after completing their official sentences – between 10,000 and 15,000 suffered this fate. Medical science underlay attitudes towards homosexuality in both countries. In 1923, a Soviet authority wrote: "Science has now established, with precision that excludes all doubt, [that homosexuality] is not ill-will or crime, but sickness."[38] Such writers insisted that medicine would soon be able to "cure" homosexuality. In Nazi Germany, links between medicine and repression were even more direct – indeed, the "biological politics" of the Third Reich did not allow for much distinction between diseases and crimes. The SS gave the Danish Dr. Vaernet the chance to try out his cures on the inmates of concentration camps – most of them died.[39]

Many tried to discredit political opponents with accusations of homosexuality. The British government used the private diaries of the Irish nationalist Roger Casement, which detailed his sexual encounters with men, to deter the Americans from protesting about his execution after the uprising of Easter 1916. The German government used accusations of homosexuality to force the resignation of General Fritsch in 1938.

Nazism's enemies used accusations of homosexuality against it as much as it used such accusations against its enemies. In part, such accusations were rooted in what was known of Ernst Röhm, the head of the Nazi SA and an open homosexual. His activities attracted a disproportionate amount of attention, which meant that Nazism was often equated with "sexual abnormality."[40] The Russian writer Maxim Gorky welcomed the outlawing of homosexuality in the Soviet Union in 1934, and explained that the legalization of such activity in Germany had been "the main cause of fascism."[41]

Communist propaganda often referred to homosexuality, associating it with bourgeois decadence and conservative politics. In Yugoslavia, much energy was devoted to publicizing the homosexuality of the Prime Minister, Petar Zivković.[42] At first, communism's attitude towards homosexuality was rendered ambiguous by the Soviet Union's reputation for sexual openness. Communist deputies often voted for the liberalization of legislation on homosexuality – as the German Communist Party did in 1929 – while party propaganda treated individual homosexuals, particularly those from the upper classes, with disdain. Communist attitudes towards homosexuality became less tolerant in the mid-1930s, as Stalin's Russia rediscovered the virtues of sexual conservatism.

Communist writing on Vichy France was full of references to homosexuality, partly because Vichy continued the relative tolerance of the Third Republic, but also as propagandists presented the submission of collaborators to Nazi Germany as a perverted "feminine" act. Sartre argued that collaboration could be explained partly through the homosexual inclinations of its practitioners. Roger Vailland, who had joined the party during the war, wrote a novel – *Un Jeune Homme Seul* (1949) – that linked heterosexuality to proletarian consciousness and homosexuality to bourgeois treason. The hero is a young man from a wealthy background who finds sexual and emotional fullfilment in the working-class movement. Early in his career, he is advised not to attend a communist rally wearing fashionable clothes because he will look like a "*tante.*" The villain of the story is a Vichy policeman, first introduced reading his favorite book, *À la Recherche du Temps Perdu*, and is described as "one of those powerful inverts who reign in secret over prisons and concentration camps."

Rules of the game: male honor and female chastity?

Jean Renoir's film of 1939 (about adultery during a country house shooting party) was entitled *La Règle du Jeu*. Forty years later, Nicholas Mosley used the same title for his account of his father's liaison with Diana Guinness.[43] The use of the word "rules" with reference to adultery is interesting. It reveals that there was no simple dichotomy between "freedom" and "regulation" in interwar Europe. In addition to the varieties of formal and explicit morality described above, there existed an informal morality – or several different kinds of informal morality. Those who broke the explicit rules laid down by public moralists were usually obeying rules that were tacit but widely known. The milieu depicted by Renoir was one in which adultery was tolerated as long as it was conducted discreetly. Sometimes "emancipation" was linked to a lessening of sexual opportunity, because it meant that explicit and tacit rules were brought into harmony. Maurice Agulhon remembered, with some bitterness, that his schoolteacher parents took feminism to mean simply that the puritan code that had previously been applied to girls was now applied to boys too.[44]

The complex interrelationship of formal and informal morality was illustrated in the life of Malcolm Muggeridge. At first glance, Muggeridge's principles were simple: he was an ascetic Christian who believed in chastity. He did not practice what he preached, and had numerous extramarital affairs. This cannot, however, be ascribed simply to hypocrisy; Muggeridge talked about his sexual adventures almost as obsessively as he talked about Gandhi or Mother Teresa of Calcutta. His sexual adventurism and his Christian piety fitted together, both providing a means of rebelling against the worthy Fabianism in which he had been raised. Sex also provided him with material for the confession and repentance that was an essential part of his carefully contrived image as a successor to Aquinas, Rousseau and Tolstoy. In short, Muggeridge's life was governed by two apparently contradictory, but, in reality, complementary, forms of morality – the formal morality of Christianity and the informal morality of the bourgeois womanizer. The latter was not an ethics of complete liberation, but found the idea of sexual freedom for "respectable" women shocking. Muggeridge made much of the saintly qualities of his wife, Kitty, who apparently waited patiently for him to return from his assignations. Only after his death did it emerge that Kitty had made discreet use of the sexual freedom that her husband flaunted and that Malcolm was not the father of one of her children.*

It is sometimes assumed that sexual repression was associated with "backward" societies, while increasing openness was a natural accompaniment of modernization, but this was not always the case. Sexual morals in traditional societies always encompassed a wide range of different standards, and peasant societies were not necessarily less open about such matters than urban ones. In parts of Russia, peasant brides were expected to lose their virginity in front of a crowd of drunken wedding guests (openness about sex in such societies did not, of course, imply respect of female freedom).

Urban observers in the countryside noted a frankness about sexual matters. Gabriel Chevalier's novel *Clochemerle*, published in 1934 and set in the Beaujolais, is regarded as one of the best representations of village life in the Third Republic. Chevalier's world is one in which sex is frankly discussed and widely practiced. Morality in the village does not revolve around chastity – even the priest, who has an "understanding" with his housekeeper, regards the conception of children before marriage as a trivial sin – and adultery is tolerated. The village is contrasted with the city not in terms of chastity versus promiscuity but in terms of healthy sex (with local girls) versus unhealthy sex (with town prostitutes who are likely to carry venereal disease). The outcast woman in *Clochemerle* is not

---

* Richard Ingrams, *Muggeridge* (1996), p. 185. The child in question was Charles, the youngest of Kitty Muggeridge's children and the son of Michal Vyvyan, who was apparently unaware of his paternity. Malcolm Muggeridge seems to have felt little affection for the boy, who died in an accident at the age of twenty.

an adulteress or "*fille mère*" but the spinster Putet, who represents sterility, frustration and the thwarting of natural instinct.

When Carlo Levi was exiled to a village in the south, he had an opportunity to observe peasant attitudes towards sex at close quarters and was surprised by what he found: "All that people say about the people of the south, things I once believed myself: the savage rigidity of their morals, their Oriental jealousy, the fierce sense of honor leading to crimes of passion and revenge, all these are but myths."[45] Illegitimacy in the countryside was common, and children were often born to the mistresses of priests. Sexual imbalance produced by the migration of men to America would in any case have made it impossible for many women to find a legitimate husband. Levi's own housekeeper, Giulia, was the mother of children by several different men, one of them a priest.

In a Spanish village, Gerald Brenan had experiences similar to Levi's. Impressed by the bawdy conversation of his housekeeper, the daughter of a midwife and the publicly acknowledged mistress of his landlord, Brenan later wrote: "Except in chaste, sexless Ireland peasants have coarse minds, and I imagine that, till the folk-lore collector pulls out his notebook and pencil, they nearly always have this character."[46]

If peasant societies could be open about sexual matters, the new society of mass communications was often secretive about them. Indeed, Hollywood films and radio broadcasting created a public sphere from which explicit reference to sex was entirely excluded. Harold Nicolson was forbidden not merely from quoting from James Joyce's *Ulysses* but even from mentioning the title of the book during a radio broadcast of 1935; the British Broadcasting Corporation did not broadcast the word "fuck" until the 1960s. A. J. P. Taylor exposed the prudishness of the BBC, and the ambiguity of relations between modernity and sex: "I was asked, my only invitation, to contribute to a series where the speaker ran into some difficulty, say getting lost on a mountain, and then an expert would be called in to say what he should have done. I offered . . . a very good problem: going to bed with a girl in Berlin . . . and finding that she was a boy with rubber breasts . . . I was not commissioned to give the talk."[47]

Sexual morality was closely connected to language. Most Europeans used two languages: a formal one and an informal one of patois or dialect – sex was usually discussed in the latter. Matters were complicated by the fact that formal language was becoming increasingly important with the spread of education, print and broadcasting. Britain, where prudishness was combined with an obsessive interest in linguistic propriety, saw the most dramatic examples of this phenomenon. Sex was often excluded from the written language, so words spoken daily by vast numbers of people could never be printed; pharmacists could give verbal instructions on the use of contraceptives, but were forbidden from communicating such information in writing.[48] Sexual discussion on an everyday level was conducted in Anglo-Saxon monosyllables; sexual discussion in formal surroundings was conducted, if at all, in the polysyllabic Latinate terms of medical science. Misunderstanding could involve vocabulary as much as morality. A girl who asked a young soldier whether he was a virgin received the reply, "What's a virgin? The only virgin I know of is the blessed Virgin Mary."[49]

Sex and class

Class resentment was entangled with sex in all European societies because rich men often slept with poor women. Prostitution was widespread. Bourgeois men had always exercised economic power over prostitutes (as clients), and increasingly, they also exercised administrative power (as regulators). Many countries in continental Europe had a system of formal registration and control for prostitutes: in 1939, the department of the Seine contained 4,926 registered prostitutes, and officials estimated that another 1,995 were not registered.[50] Men also bought sex in a variety of less formal ways, keeping mistresses or sleeping with household servants, and the economic crisis of the 1930s further increased the sexual availability of poor women. Graham Greene was told that Nottingham girls thrown out of work by the collapse of the lace trade could be had "in return for high tea with muffins."[51] Georges Simenon, a relentless womanizer who conducted a long affair with his wife's maid, was particularly aware of how sexual adventurism by bourgeois men could arouse class resentment – in his novel *Le Chien Jaune* (1931), the male population of Concarneau has been set against a group of notables who have "taken advantage" of the impoverished working-class girls of the town.

The seduction of poor girls by richer men was often perceived as an attack on the honor of the girls' menfolk. At the Magneti Marelli factory near Milan, there was widespread contempt for male workers who had gained advancement by marrying the discarded mistresses of the factory manager. At the liberation, it was said: "In the firm there were numerous men who had got into and kept themselves in good jobs by supplying the two owners with women from amongst the workers and clerks."[52] Such resentment could have political consequences. Sexual relations with female workers was the main accusation leveled against the only Magneti Marelli manager to be executed when Fascism fell.[53]

Just as seduction of working-class women was often perceived as part of bourgeois domination, the seduction of wealthy women by working-class men was sometimes seen as a means of social rebellion or as a sign of the inversion of the social order. Sexual relations between mistresses and servants were a common theme in interwar literature. The stories of W. Somerset Maugham show the connections between sex and class. In "The Colonel's Lady," a landowner's wife – thin, barren and prone to read "advanced" books – publishes a collection of poems that make it clear that she has had an adulterous affair. The landowner expresses his concern about her infidelity thus: "It's rotten not to know what sort of a chap he was. One can't even tell if he was by way of being a gentleman. I mean, for all I know he may have been a farm laborer." *La Règle du Jeu* describes the chaos caused when the sex lives of masters and servants become intertwined (although in this case it is the gamekeeper who is cuckolded by his social betters).

The sexual unavailability of bourgeois women was important to the self-image of the male bourgeoisie, and the prospect that "respectable" women might resort to prostitution was presented as the ultimate symptom of social breakdown. René Benjamin, a conservative Catholic opposed to the education of women, alleged that "three hundred qualified female lawyers were selling themselves on the street in Paris."[54] In Vichy France, "respectability" was defined in terms of the military service of a husband rather than by education or wealth: in 1941 and 1942 various officials claimed that most French prostitutes were married to prisoners of war.[55]

The link between social and sexual challenges explains the shocked reaction of English society to the works of D. H. Lawrence, which often associated the working-class man with "true" masculinity. In response to a poem by Lawrence that questioned the masculinity of middle-class men, George Orwell commented:

> Lawrence tells me that because I have been to a public school I am a eunuch. Well, what about it? I can produce medical evidence to the contrary, but what good will that do? Lawrence's condemnation remains. If you tell me I am a scoundrel I may mend my ways, but if you tell me I am a eunuch you are tempting me to hit back in any way that seems feasible.[56]

More generally, Orwell's writing illustrates the perceived relations between sex and class: "[Unemployment] has not altered the relative status of the sexes. In a working-class home it is the man who is the master and not, as in a middle-class home, the woman or the baby."[57] He also came close to suggesting that patriarchy was a necessary condition of a strong labor movement: "You cannot have an effective trade union of middle-class workers, because in times of strikes almost every middle-class wife would be egging her husband on to blackleg and get the other fellow's job."[58] Orwell was aware that "the strange, obscene burst of popular fury that followed the Wilde trial was essentially social in character."[59] He himself was prone to link homosexuality with a certain kind of bourgeois socialist. He wrote of the "pansy left"[60] and feared that such socialists were often "of the eunuch type with a vegetarian smell who go about spreading sweetness and light and have at the back of their minds a vision of the working class all T.T., well washed behind the ears, readers of Edward Carpenter or some other pious sodomite."[61]

The connections between class and homosexuality in interwar Europe were particularly complicated. Many writers associated heterosexuality with the working classes and homosexuality with the rich, a link probably encouraged by the fact that wealthy people such as Magnus Hirschfeld in Germany or the members of the Bloomsbury group were often the only ones who could afford to face the consequences of leading an openly homosexual life.

Nothing, of course, hid the fact that members of the working classes did commit homosexual acts, often with the wealthy "perverts" who were denounced by the self-appointed exponents of proletarian morality. In some cases, bourgeois men seem to have sought sex with their social inferiors precisely because they shared the view that the workers were "real men." Edward Carpenter wanted "the thick-thighed, hot, coarse-fleshed young bricklayer with the strip around his waist."[62] Sometimes, interest in working-class men interacted with political commitment; the French left-winger Daniel Guerin became involved in politics partly to meet working-class boys but remained convinced that proletarian culture would always be heterosexual.[63]

Homosexual relations across classes could be more equal than heterosexual ones. The clients of a female prostitute had a double privilege, because they were both male and wealthy, while the prostitute herself was usually doubly disadvantaged: she was not only female but also excluded from respectable society. However, a homosexual man who sought company among his social inferiors was already partly excluded from respectable society (or would have been if his activities had been discovered). Male prostitutes, on the other hand, were less likely to be cut off from respectable society than their female counterparts; they were rarely organized or governed by official regulation in the same way that female prostitutes were. Furthermore, young men who took money for sexual favors were not always categorized as either homosexuals or prostitutes.[64]

Sex, race and nation

The linking of male honor to the control of women was even more explicit when sexual relations crossed national frontiers. Such relations seemed particularly threatening in wartime. Many Frenchmen were convinced that large numbers of French women had been raped by German soldiers during the invasion of 1914 and that children had been conceived as a result of such encounters, and attention was devoted to the social and psychological consequences of such attacks for men as much as to their physical effects on women. A newspaper reported that a man threatened to commit suicide when he heard that his wife and daughters were pregnant after being raped by German soldiers. More generally, rape was perceived as an attack on the nation and the race. One doctor wrote that "these children will be the mark of the barbarians' temporary victory." Some argued that women who had conceived babies by German soldiers would be permanently tainted and that subsequent children conceived by Frenchmen would bear the biological imprint of the earlier encounter.[65]

Links between the male defense of national honor and the threat to female chastity reemerged in France between 1940 and 1944. In the early stages of the occupation, some who hoped for Franco-German reconciliation regarded sexual relations between German soldiers and French girls as natural and even desirable; Simone de Beauvoir reported that this was the attitude of a truck driver who gave her a lift back to Paris in 1940.[66] Sometimes the Franco-German relationship was described in sexual terms. A male fascist wrote to Marcel Déat in 1940: "You have said that sometimes rapes finish in marriage. There are also some that leave deliciously troubling memories."[67] Those who opposed collaboration, by contrast, regarded sexual contact between the invader and the conquered as shameful for French men. An early resistance tract (Texcier's "Advice to the Occupied") told men to retaliate against women seen talking to German soldiers, but did not address itself to women at all. One of Vichy France's greatest concerns was to maintain control over the sexual lives of French women. The regulation of prostitution was made more rigorous, and in December 1940 brothel-keepers were given an effective monopoly of the trade in an attempt to drive women off the streets.[68] There was particular concern about women whose husbands were imprisoned in Germany and therefore unable to exercise control of their own. A law of 1942 stated that "living in notorious concubinage" with the wife of a prisoner of war was a criminal offence.[69] At the liberation, women who had "dishonoured" France by sleeping with German soldiers often suffered the most savage

and public forms of humiliation. Several French films about the occupation – *Lacombe Lucien, Une Affaire de Femmes, Une Femme Française* –
portrayed women who were unfaithful to husbands who were prisoners
of war.

The debate on the chastity of French women, with its emphasis on the
wives of prisoners of war and the possibility of sexual relations with the
invader, is put into an interesting light by discussion of French men's relations with German women. Many French prisoners of war were sent to
work on German farms and it was widely alleged that some of these men
had enjoyed sexual relations with German peasant women.[70] Such relations inverted normal power relations between men and women: the
French were inferior in military terms, because they had been defeated,
and socially, because they were farm servants and because only lower
ranks were forced to work – officers and NCOs were condemned to idle-
ness and celibacy. The German authorities considered the French as
racially inferior[71] – though not to the same extent as Russians or Poles,
who would have been executed for having sexual relations with German
women. On the French side, the relations between French prisoners of
war and German women were widely known. Frenchmen seem to have
looked back on such relations with a mixture of amusement, embarrassment and pride.[72] But they never evoked the debate or outrage that was
occasioned by French women's behavior, and no one suggested that a
French man's seduction of a German woman was treasonable.

War and invasion were also associated with a "threat to female honor"
by German commentators, though the Germans were more concerned
about sex and race rather than sex and nationality. The issue first emerged
with reference to children born to black French soldiers posted to the
Rhineland or the Ruhr in the aftermath of the First World War. German
politicians presented the sexual partners of black troops as rape victims,
and a long debate began about what to do with the children born of such
liaisons and how to prevent them from further "corrupting" the race.
Sterilization was suggested as a possible solution by the Bavarian Ministry
of the Interior in 1927 and ten years later this policy was finally put into
effect by the Nazis.[73] One aspect of Nazi anti-Semitic policy was the outlawing of sexual relations between Jews and gentiles under the Law for
Protection of German Blood and Honor (1935), which was primarily directed against Jewish men's sexual relations with "Aryan" women. A
woman who was divorcing her Jewish husband made a special request for
permission to abort the "mixed blood foetus" that she was carrying.[74]

Most dramatically, the threat that the doomed Nazi regime felt from
the invading Soviet forces in 1945 was presented in largely sexual terms
and the risk of rape played a large part in propaganda designed to

strengthen German resistance. Rape was indeed a real experience for many women who found themselves in the path of the Red Army. It was estimated that around one-third of women in Berlin were raped,[75] and figures for Budapest and Vienna were probably similar (all three cities had predominantly female populations in 1945). Such rapes were particularly common in the immediate aftermath of battles, when drunken and angry soldiers roamed freely, but they did not stop with the restoration of discipline. Rape remained common in the Soviet zone of occupation until 1949. Some Soviet soldiers seem to have believed that rape was a continuation of war by other means, and women from nationalities that had been at war with the Soviet Union – Germans, Austrians and Hungarians – were especially prone to be raped. Cultural and linguistic links were important. The strangeness of the Hungarian language made its speakers more vulnerable, but Bulgarian women, by contrast, were often able to establish good relations with Soviet soldiers.[76] The Red Army treated the numerous Russian and Ukrainian women in German factories well, although such women – regarded with suspicion by Soviet authorities – would have had few means to protect themselves. Rape was often linked to a wider sort of revenge that stressed the crimes committed by Germany and her allies as well as German prosperity, which was contrasted with the devastation of the Soviet Union.

Women themselves were reluctant to come forward with accounts of their experiences because they had little faith in the determination of authorities to punish or deter action by the Red Army and were also concerned about the reactions of their own menfolk to their "defilement." Some women may have regarded their relations with Soviet soldiers as springing from forms of constraint that did not involve direct physical violence. The Red Army controlled most resources in a country of desperate penury; in Königsberg, it was said that only women who had been impregnated by Russian soldiers had enough to eat.[77]

The most dramatic accounts of mass rape were written by men, and often reveal as much about their authors as about women's experience. Two authors – the American diplomat Robert Murphy and the Vatican representative Monsignor Montini – were conservative Catholics. The latter's account emphasized the extent to which women had allegedly been infected by venereal disease, which may have reflected fears of women's sexuality as much as concern to defend their safety.[78] Men acted to protect the "honor" of women against Russian assault. One form of such protection was abortion, to prevent "alien children" from being born. Each province in the Soviet zone had its own abortion laws; only in Brandenburg did the law explicitly mention rape,[79] but doctors often acted on their own initiative to end pregnancies believed to be the result of rape.

Some women seem to have been threatened by violence from their German "protectors" as much as from their Soviet attackers. Professor Schüler of Lichterfelde was said to have killed his wife and daughters and then himself as Soviet troops arrived.[80]

Relations between sex, nationality and race intersected in wartime Britain, particularly as about 3 million American soldiers passed through during this time. Young and comparatively wealthy, they often came into conflict with local men over access to British girls, but such disputes did not simply pit British men against Americans. Matters were made more complicated by the presence of black American soldiers (there were about 130,000 by June 1944).[81] The American army was strictly segregated, while Britain had almost no black population and no tradition of racial segregation. White American troops who saw black Americans with English girls might put race above nationality and intervene to protect "their" girls. Eisenhower summarized matters thus: "Our own white soldiers, seeing a girl walk down the street with a negro, frequently see themselves as protectors of the weaker sex and believe it necessary to intervene even to the extent of using force, to let her know what she's doing."[82] In May 1944, an American military court sentenced a black GI to death for the rape of an English woman. The evidence was thin – the woman had accompanied the man into a field, while wearing only her nightdress, in order to "give him directions" – but the GI would have died at the hands of his own countrymen had it not been for an outcry in the British press.[83]

Empire brought the possibility of sexual contact between races. Malcolm Muggeridge, who had a long affair with a Sikh woman during his residence in India, pointed to the fact that English men, who avoided all other forms of intimacy with Indians, slept with Indian women, but the tacit tolerance afforded to sexual contact between English men and Indian women did not extend to English women and Indian men. Novelists such as E. M. Forster and Paul Scott recorded the sense of panic that greeted any report of such sexual contact.

Sexual relations between native male inhabitants of the empire and British women evoked particular outrage when the native men were wealthy and powerful, in other words, when native men enjoyed the kind of relations with British women that British men had always taken for granted with native women. Discussion of such relations often seemed to fit into a broader sense of declining power that accompanied the end of empire. In the 1950s, the British Secretary of State for Colonial Affairs made a statement in Parliament denying that English women in Malaya were sleeping with rich local businessmen.[84] Most famously, the British departure from India was accompanied by rumors about the affair between Edwina Mountbatten, wife of the last Viceroy, and Jawa-harlal Nehru, the first Prime Minister of independent India.

Sexual relations in the French empire were governed by different conventions and were more openly acknowledged. Sometimes, empire brought about an interesting three-cornered confrontation, as different types of European sexual values coexisted with those attributed to native populations. In Orwell's *Burmese Days* (1934), the hero maintains his Burmese mistress, with whom he has a purely commercial relationship, while attempting to seduce an English woman, who is rendered attractive by the sophistication that she has acquired from being "finished" in Paris. In Simenon's *Le Blanc à Lunettes* (1937), the hero is a planter in Africa who keeps an African mistress but reassures his French fiancée that the arrangement has no emotional significance: "I have always had women that I have paid." This happy arrangement is thrown into confusion by the arrival of an aristocratic English woman and her lover. The hero is obliged to hide his African mistress from his English guests ("they never have an open relationship with a native"), but is shocked by the fact that an English woman from a good background should have an open affair (Simenon believed that open sexual relations among social equals was a particularly disgusting English vice).

In 1937, the Italian government passed legislation to regulate sexual relations with the native population of its African empire, and these regulations reflect the complexity of thinking about sex. Sex between African women and Italian men was never forbidden, although "marriage-like relations" between the two were. Italian men prosecuted for enjoying such relations were obliged to prove that they did not regularly share a bed or exchange gifts with their lover. As for Italian women, the authorities took it for granted that such relations were inconceivable. The Minister of Italian Africa said in 1940: "Our laws cannot even allow for such a possibility, which runs counter to all our moral principles."[85] Racial distinctions overrode social ones, and Italian senators took care to ensure that the purity of Italian prostitutes sent to Abyssinia was not compromised by contact with black men.

Women and work

The fact that the changing role of women was seen through a prism of male hysteria does not mean that there were no changes. The aftermath of the Great War saw a change in the number of women working and it was sometimes assumed that this was simply a product of the war itself: women had established themselves in work by replacing men sent to the front. In reality, the number of women working, especially in factories, had increased during the war, but the rise was considered temporary. Women's jobs were often in industries such as munitions, where workers were bound to be laid off after the war. Furthermore, women were regarded as low-quality labor, to be used along with other unsatisfactory expedients – prisoners, children and immigrants. They were categorized as "unskilled" even when doing jobs formerly done by "skilled" men, and less than one in twenty of all British female munitions workers in 1918 were paid skilled men's wages.[86] It was part of the wartime consensus eventually established in most countries between unions, employers and government that the employment of women should not be continued in peacetime,[87] so the very visibility of the wartime positions adopted by women in jobs, such as tram-driving, made them vulnerable after the war. In some countries, notably France, the First World War marked the beginning of a long-term decline of the female proportion of the working population, because it damaged light industries (especially textiles) that had employed large numbers of women. Even in the Soviet Union, where the civil war prevented many men from being demobilized until 1921 and where the government favored women's employment, women made up more than half of the unemployed in the 1920s.[88]

Changes resulting from the Great War were sometimes confused with developments that had begun before it. There had been an increase in office employment for some years as well as an increasing tendency to employ women.[89] Both trends continued after the war: in Germany, the number of female white-collar workers increased from 0.5 million to 1.5 million between 1907 and 1925.[90] However, this increase did not necessarily represent emancipation for women. The expansion of clerical employment was associated with a reduction of pay and status and with diminished expectations of promotion: a survey of girls studying at a secretarial school in Paris concluded that most came from working-class backgrounds and had left school by the age of thirteen.[91] The increased employment of women was in fact both a product and a cause of social decline in the clerical profession. In 1923, an article published by the British Institute of Bankers was explicit about how gender stratified clerical work: "There is . . . no competition in the English Civil Service between the women and male staffs . . . Certain classes of work, mainly of a routine and not very responsible character, are made over to the women staff; and the only result of their employment on that work is that a great mass of clerical labor which would otherwise have to be done by men is done by women."[92]

The fate of female office workers in Fascist Italy casts an interesting light on the feminization of clerical work elsewhere. In Italy, the proportion of office workers who were women increased from 20.3 percent in 1921 to 27.3 percent in 1936,[93] but the process produced a more open contest than in other European countries, partly because comparatively low levels of industrialization meant fewer sources of alternative employment for men, but also as Italians traditionally attached great prestige to nonmanual work, especially state employment, and the Fascist state intervened in the labor market more openly than the democracies. Italian government departments introduced quotas to limit the number of women employed, and significantly the system varied according to rank. Among jobs reserved for university graduates, up to 5 percent of employees could be women; in the middle ranks, up to 15 percent of employees could be women, while up to 20 percent of subordinate posts could be held by women.[94] The largest increase in the employment of female clerical workers in Italy took place outside government departments, in low-status commercial and municipal jobs.

Throughout the interwar period, women were regarded as a reserve army of labor that could be hired and fired more easily than men. In Germany, female wages in 1931 were more than a third lower than those of men. As a result, employers had an incentive to hire women when profits were under pressure and consequently the proportion of women in the workforce increased between 1928 and 1932.[95] Mechanization and rationalization were sometimes associated with the employment of women. Workshops in which skilled male workers had enjoyed a high degree of autonomy and flexibility were replaced by assembly lines in which women performed specific and limited tasks under conditions laid down by time-and-motion experts and controlled by foremen; André Citroën, the French motor manufacturer, redesigned some of his factories on this basis after the First World War.[96] Although employers had an economic interest in hiring women, the state often had a political interest in excluding them from the workforce at a time of high male unemployment. Unemployed male workers were seen as more likely to cause political trouble. In France, where the position of women was particularly weakened by the fact that they did not have the vote, married women were ejected from government service in 1935, and similar measures were taken in Nazi Germany, where marriage loans were granted to couples who agreed that the woman would not work: by the end of 1934, 365,000 such loans had been granted.[97]

Regimes that idealized the nonworking woman for political reasons were often forced to accept female employment for economic reasons as the depression came to an end and, particularly, after the beginning of the Second World War. This was seen most strikingly in Germany, where rates of female employment were high, in spite of the regime's rhetoric.

Hitler's desire to exclude women from the workforce was opposed by fellow Nazis such as Goebbels and Ley,[98] and eventually the Nazis reversed their own policies during the late 1930s as the growth of the war economy generated new needs for labor:[99] in 1937, marriage loans ceased to be conditional on the wife remaining outside employment.[100] By 1939, German women comprised 37.4 percent of the workforce; in Britain, the figure was only 26.4 percent.[101] A similar contradiction existed in Vichy France, where conservative rhetoric about the family coexisted with the absence of over 2 million men in German prison camps or the Maquis.

No regime's attitude towards female employment was entirely straightforward. Each was governed by need, especially in wartime, and also by social and racial assumptions. In Germany, Goering distinguished between "workhorse" women from the lower classes, who were suitable for heavy labor, and "thoroughbred" women from the upper classes, who should be confined to child-rearing.[102] All Nazis distinguished between the "best" Aryan women, who were to be encouraged to breed but not to work, and female laborers imported from Russia, who were to be made to work but forbidden to breed. The British government distinguished between women on a social basis. One of the criteria used to assess whether a woman should be compelled to work in the war economy was whether or not she owned her own home.[103]

The paradoxical relation between female participation in the workforce and other forms of women's emancipation was shown most clearly in the Soviet Union. Soviet policy had been self-consciously feminist in the 1920s: abortion and divorce were made easier, pay and working conditions for the sexes were equalized, and women were encouraged to see themselves as members of the proletariat. However, the most spectacular levels of female participation in work were achieved not as a result of such feminist policies but rather as a result of military and economic necessity during the 1930s and 1940s. Between 1940 and 1945, women came to make up just over half of all workers in large-scale industry.[104] Not only was the increase not the result of feminist policies, but it took place after such policies had been reversed. During the late 1930s, Soviet propaganda placed increasing emphasis on the restoration of women's traditional roles. This shift was illustrated by the abolition, in 1930, of the Special Bureau for Women's Affairs,[105] new legal restrictions on abortion, and a celebration of family life. In 1936, a conference of Soviet wives discussed ways in which the womenfolk of party dignitaries could perform good works and finished with the presentation of a specially embroidered shirt to Stalin.[106] Far from challenging traditional views of women, the encouragement of female work operated through an appeal to such views. Women "Stakhanovites" portrayed in the press were usually young and attractive;[107] they justified their participation in Stakhanovite programs by saying that their bonuses allowed them to buy fashionable clothes.[108] In the Russian countryside, where migration and war had depleted the male population, becoming a successful worker was presented not as a way of doing without men but as a means of attracting the few men who were available.[109]

Changes in the position of women also sprang from the destructive effects of the First World War. The idle wife or daughter was one aspect of the bourgeois rentier society that the First World War destroyed. Simone de Beauvoir might have finished her life as a respectable housewife in Neuilly if wartime inflation had not destroyed the money intended to be her dowry.[110] The war also created an imbalance between the sexes and increased the number of women obliged to support themselves. In some areas, the impact of male war casualties was exacerbated by migration as men moved in search of work. The upheaval of war was so dramatic in European Russia that by 1920 rural areas contained 230 women aged between nineteen and twenty-nine for every 100 men in this age group.[111] This challenge did not always produce the liberated career girls of historical cliché, as the ways in which women could respond to spinsterhood were often defined by conservative expectations. In Italy, religious vocations among women increased: there were 129,000 nuns in 1936 compared with 45,000 in 1911.[112] In England and France, conservative commentators recognized that the war had created a "surplus" of women who were unlikely to get married, and that such women should find appropriate careers. Emphasis was placed on occupations that would give scope to women's maternal instincts.[113] Nursing was one obvious example, and it was suggested that even the judiciary might offer similar opportunities.[114] Teaching in particular appeared to offer the single woman a substitute for motherhood. The influx of women into teaching, especially of girls, had long-term effects as a generation of dedicated and enthusiastic figures, such as Muriel Spark's Miss Jean Brodie, improved women's education. Annie Kriegel, the French historian, attributed the quality of her own schooling partly to the *lycée* teachers whose potential husbands had been killed.[115]

Women in agriculture

"Traditional" views of rural society were often expressed in terms of gender relations. In 1932, a Nazi journalist wrote:

> On one hand we have the strong, robust, virile peasant, moulded by the eternal struggle with nature and the land. A product of the earth, a fighter, a born warrior. At his side is a German woman, a peasant woman, his

faithful companion and proud mother of their children through whom the future and history will be made. On the other hand, the debased city-dweller, weak, effeminate and cowardly. Beside him his wife, masculinized in body and spirit, deliberately childless and therefore self-debased, and instead of healthy descendants he inherits only spiritual conflicts. They are the products of concrete.[116]

In reality, gender divisions in the countryside were not so clearly marked. There had not always been a separation between the woman's world of child-rearing and housekeeping and the man's world of hard agricultural labor. Indeed, such a division was often the product of modernization rather than a feature of tradition.

Women worked in large numbers in agriculture; wives and daughters often provided an alternative to paid labor. In Germany in 1925, there were 4,133,000 female "family assistants," most of whom worked on farms. Their numbers had doubled in the period since 1911, partly because farmers fell back on family labor in hard times.[117]

Martine Segalen suggests that the traditional French peasant family had separate but equal spheres for the two sexes. Men often did heavy work in the fields, while women occupied themselves with milking, poultry, kitchen gardens, baking and cheese making. Men dominated agricultural fairs, where cattle and horses were sold, but women dominated local markets, where eggs, cheese and poultry were traded.[118] Similar arrangements could be found among the Russian peasantry. Indeed, women's power over certain aspects of the household economy was made explicit in Russia. A woman who entered the commune of her husband kept control of her dowry, and the raising of poultry was entrusted to individual women outside the communal farming arrangements.

It is hard to assess the extent to which women's economic usefulness produced a culture of respect and independence for women. Studies based on external signs of power are of limited value. Individual women might assert themselves under a mask of outward conformity: in Marcel Ophuls's film *The Sorrow and the Pity* (1972), two French peasant brothers are interviewed sitting at a table drinking wine. Their sister stands in a stereotypically submissive pose, apparently ready to wait on the men of the household, but this does not prevent her from repeatedly interrupting and correcting them. Furthermore, a woman's power was not dependent simply on her relations with men. Many Russian peasant women seem to have felt that the greatest tyrannies were those exercised by their mothers-in-law.

In the twentieth century, two forces intruded into household economic units. The first was rural "modernization" – the mechanization of

farm work and the organization of farmers. The use of machinery reduced the need for labor, which had the most impact on women, who
were seen as the part of the rural population that was "surplus to requirements." Whereas mechanization in the cities often produced work that
was believed to be appropriate to women, in the countryside it often produced new skills that were seen as the exclusive province of men. Milking
cows, once a quintessentially female activity, was increasingly undertaken
by men with machines.[119]

Agricultural organization further marginalized women. Martine
Segalen writes: "For the women, the family, the intimate, the hidden, the
sexual; for the men, the social, the public, the technical, the economic,
the political."[120] The result of this division was that, as the public, technical, economic and political spheres became more important, women lost
power. This was reflected in the fact that in the first elections to the
French *chambres d'agriculture*, held in 1927, men were assumed to be the
heads of households – women were granted a vote only if they farmed
alone.[121] Women achieved a negligible representation in agricultural organizations during the interwar period, and were increasingly seen as
housewives rather than producers.[122]

Agricultural education reinforced such stereotypes. French peasants
were taught about machinery, veterinary science and accounting, while
their sisters were sent to Catholic *écoles ménagères agricoles* to learn how to
run a home.[123] In Nazi Germany, agricultural organizations also reinforced the housewife/producer distinction: initially the Nazi Agricultural
Association, under Walther Darré, grouped both men and women, but in
1935 it was agreed that women peasants were to be organized in all but
economic terms by the National Socialist Women's Organisation.[124] Not
surprisingly, the proportion of women among the working population in
European agriculture decreased throughout western Europe during the
interwar period.[125]

The Soviet Union provided the one striking counterexample to the
general pattern of women's exclusion from agriculture. The regime made
much of the fact that women had full rights as members of collective
farms, which they had never enjoyed as members of prerevolutionary
communes. Furthermore, women were encouraged to take jobs involving
new machinery such as tractors; indeed, in 1936, tractors in the Soviet
Union were adapted to make them more appropriate to a woman's
physique.[126] The state institutions and organizations that excluded
women from agriculture in other European countries supported them in
the Soviet Union, so by the late 1930s almost one-third of students at Soviet institutes of higher agricultural education were women.[127] However,
barriers to female advancement remained. In part, they were formal. The

regime liked women to occupy prominent positions as workers, but it was less keen to give them managerial positions and in 1936 only 7 percent of those who chaired rural Soviets were women.[128] More importantly, women in the Soviet Union who wished to break out of traditional roles faced great informal resistance. The struggle over women's employment pitted the values of rural communities against those of the state; Pasha Angelica, the Soviet Union's top female tractor driver, was commended by Stalin but divorced by her husband. Women who worked with new machinery faced ostracism and violence, which was most severe in Muslim Russia: nine female Stakhanovites were murdered in Tajikistan in 1937.[129]

The Second World War threw gender relations in the countryside into confusion. The British and German governments drafted urban women on to farms. In France, peasant women were left alone after the departure of large numbers of men. In the Soviet Union by 1945, three-quarters of able-bodied workers on collective farms were women.[130] Many women who entered agriculture during this period did so under unattractive conditions as drafted labor on farms with which they had no connection, but peasant wives who took over family farms may have enjoyed a greater degree of autonomy. In Germany, power was distributed on the basis of race rather than sex, as peasant women gave orders to terrified Polish prisoners of war.

Politics

Only two countries had introduced female suffrage before 1914 – Finland granted women the vote in 1906 and Norway granted it to property-owning women in 1907, extending this to all women over the age of twenty-five in 1913. The end of the First World War saw a burst of female enfranchisement. Women got the vote in England, Germany and the successor states of the Austro-Hungarian Empire (except Yugoslavia). Observers often linked this with the broader changes that seemed to have emerged from the First World War, such as the increased tendency of women to work and the "new woman" of popular imagination. In fact the women who were most readily enfranchised – the relatively old, property owners and war widows – were all welcomed into the political fold precisely because they seemed to offer a counterbalance to the revolutionary male proletariat. The conservative men, who often gave women the vote, were horrified by other signs of women's changing role. Even authoritarian right-wing regimes sometimes gave women new degrees of representation. Vichy France decreed that women should be members of municipal councils, and the first three women to enter the Portuguese parliament did so during the rule of Salazar.[131]

Not only did conservatives look to women for support against the menace of organized labor, but evidence suggests that women did indeed support conservative parties. Such indications are strongest for Weimar Germany, where votes of men and women were counted separately in certain constituencies at certain times. Female support for the Centre Party was so strong in Bavaria that the surplus of women Christian democrat voters over their male counterparts sometimes amounted to one-fifth of all those who voted.[132] By contrast, there is little evidence that women voted for the boisterous and aggressively masculine Nazi Party, though the Nazis did attract increasing numbers of women voters towards the end of the Weimar Republic as they sought to present themselves as more conservative and respectable.

An understanding of relations between political conservatism and women must take account of three forces. The first was nationalism. The granting of female suffrage was often associated with nationalist campaigns in which the whole nation was mobilized against a foreign threat, as in early-twentieth-century Finland. The First World War triggered similar responses. Conservatives were particularly keen to recognize war widows as proxy voters representing their dead husbands – Belgian war widows were enfranchised, and several proposals in the French parliament during the 1920s would have given French war widows the vote too.

The second force was religion. In the nineteenth century, women comprised an increasingly large proportion of those who attended Mass. Furthermore, the political systems of several continental European countries had crystallized at a time when the state was involved in a struggle with the Catholic Church. This was most marked in Italy, where the Pope had banned Catholics from political activity until the early twentieth century, and was also true in France, where, in spite of the Pope's attempts to rally Catholics behind the regime during the late nineteenth century, Church and state had been separated in 1905. All this had an influence on attitudes towards female suffrage. Anticlericals assumed that women would be influenced by the Church and consequently opposed granting them the vote. The sexual/religious divide was most clearly marked in France. Anticlericals in the French senate were the most vociferous opponents of granting women the vote, while parties associated with the Church in France favored it, as did the Vatican in Italy.

The third force was class. Women's experience of work – the dominant influence in the formation of class consciousness – was very different from that of men. Women were less likely than men to work outside the home; if they did work, they were more likely to do so in small enterprises or light industries, and increasingly they were office workers. All this meant that women were less liable to be touched by a labor movement dominated by manual workers in heavy industry. Alienation between women and the labor movement was increased by the fact that male politics often revolved around a social life of drinking, cafés and rough camaraderie from which women were excluded. Some union activists argued that, even if women did not work, they shared the income, and hence the class interests, of men who did. Mary Macarthur of the National Federation of Woman Workers said, "There can be no sex war because the interests of men and women as wage earners are identical."[133] This was questionable. Much labor activity had only a tangential relation to the economic interests of those involved. Strikes by male workers caused economic damage to their families (through loss of wages), and the potential benefits springing from such strikes might not improve the family's standard of living. Strikes might be about hours of work or the struggle for authority inside the factory. Furthermore, labor activity was often concerned with remote and abstract gains – such as revolution or the foreign policy interests of the Soviet Union.

Women were sometimes involved in labor action, though. Indeed, the Russian Revolution was sparked partly by strikes to mark International Women's Day. Spanish tobacco workers were primarily female and struck repeatedly to defend their relatively high wages, job security and artisanal conditions of work (all benefits that were more usually enjoyed by male workers),[134] while Italian women laborers in the rice fields also went on strike on several occasions under Fascism.[135] However, women's protests differed from those of men in several respects. In terms of organization, trade unions were led by men and were designed to mobilize male workers; they laid a heavy emphasis on disciplined and structured action. Women's protests, which tended to occur outside such structures, spread through personal contacts. Further, women's protests tended to concern consumption rather than production.[136] Women were often involved in bread riots and demonstrations about price rises; even women who worked seem to have cared more about matters that had an impact on their life outside the factory – wages – than about conditions in the workplace itself. Perhaps the fact that many women had demanding roles as housekeepers and mothers outside the workplace made them less inclined to see their interests as being centered on the factory.

The gulf between women workers and the male-dominated labor movement was illustrated by the strikes in the Paris munitions industry in 1916 and 1917. At first the strikes were primarily about pay, and female participation was high: sometimes women constituted the majority of strikers. However, in early 1917, strikes became increasingly involved with the issue of peace, and female participation declined. Male pacifists were often bitter about what they saw as women's betrayal, but female attitudes towards pacifist strikes made sense in terms of the material interests of female munitions workers. Unlike their male colleagues, they were not likely to be drafted to the front and most of them knew that the end of the war would mean a drop in their income.[137]

Sometimes political divisions existed within a single family. In France, they were often associated with religion, and, in extreme cases, produced hostility of the kind captured in Mauriac's novel *Le Noeud de Vipères* (1932), whose hero lives in a man's world of business and Dreyfusard politics and is cut off from the world of his wife and children, which is dominated by religion and by the political assumptions of the right. Class divisions might also be felt inside the family: opinion polls in the 1950s showed that French women were indeed more likely than men to define themselves as "middle class."

Divisions between husbands and wives over politics or religion did not necessarily imply animosity. Men accepted that their wives attended church, and women accepted that their husbands were skeptical about religion or even anticlerical: daughters were sent to private religious schools while boys were sent to secular *lycées*. In Hungary, the sexual divide within families was enshrined in law: in mixed marriages, boys were to be brought up in the faith of their fathers while girls were to be raised in accordance with the religion of their mothers.[138] Even in politics, differences between the sexes did not necessarily reflect disagreements. There is evidence that when French women obtained the vote, husbands and wives agreed that it was appropriate for women to vote for the Christian democrat Mouvement Républicain Populaire while their husbands voted for one of the more secular groups.

Many of the women who accounted for the political differences between the sexes were single. Widows – whose numbers had been swelled by the First World War – were particularly important.[139] When French women were finally enfranchised in 1945, it seems to have been largely widows who accounted for the disproportionate number of women's votes gained by the right. In the Soviet Union, widows greeted collectivization with the greatest enthusiasm.[140]

Families

"[The family] will be sent to a museum of antiquities so that it can rest next to the spinning wheel and the bronze axe."[141] These words were written by a Soviet sociologist in 1929. Such people believed that the future lay in communities larger than the household. Housework would be performed efficiently and collectively, meals would be taken in canteens, and sexual relationships would be matters of free choice between individuals. Most of all, the raising of children was to be taken away from jealous, selfish biological parents and entrusted to qualified experts appointed by the state. Another Soviet writer predicted, in 1921, that children would live in special towns, where up to a thousand people between the ages of three and eighteen would be raised under the tutelage of professional educators.[142] Such thinking had a limited impact even in the Soviet Union. The country was too poor to establish the collective child-rearing institutions that some had foreseen, and by 1926 it began to close down state orphanages and offer children out to adoption by peasant families (who often used them as cheap labor).[143] A few years later, some of these children were "orphaned" for a second time as their adoptive families were "de-kulakized."[144]

In the second decade of the interwar period there was a dramatic reaction against attacks on the family. In France, the government enacted a "family code" in 1939, and the Vichy regime, established in 1940, dedicated itself to the defense of "work, family and the fatherland." Even the British royal family was affected by the modishness of family values. After the abdication of Edward VIII, who had contracted a childless marriage with a divorcee, his successor, George VI, was photographed enjoying a life of apparent bourgeois domesticity with his wife and two daughters. Debate on the family reflected wider issues. It was most criticized in the aftermath of the Russian Revolution and the First World War, when it seemed possible and urgent that the whole of society should be remolded, and most defended on the eve of the Second World War, when states and individuals seem to have felt that they needed the security of tested institutions. One 24-year-old woman resigned from her job in a biscuit factory and told her supervisor, "My husband says there's going to be another war, and he'd rather we spent the time together."[145]

Defenders of the family presented it as a traditional institution. It was often associated with rural society and contrasted with the decadence supposedly bred in the cities. In reality, families were complicated, diverse, and subject to constant change. What became seen as the normal family in many countries – that is, one in which a husband supported a non-working mother who raised children – was a relatively recent creation. Before 1914, few children had been raised by their mothers. The children of peasants were often looked after by their grandparents while their parents worked in the fields: Fernand Braudel, raised by his grandmother until the age of seven, attributed the conservatism of peasant society to this habit. The children of the wealthy were brought up by servants, while the children of the urban poor were brought up by old women who earned coppers by child-minding, by their elder siblings, or by no one at all. The "traditional family" was a consequence of urbanization, and especially sub-urbanization, which separated work from home. It was also a consequence of economic change. Many middle-class families could no longer afford servants, and increasing numbers of working-class families were able to afford for wives not to work.

Conservative commentators sometimes presented the family as a "natural institution," to be opposed to the artificial creations of the state. However, different forms of family life were often the creation of state action, and policymakers often weighed up the virtues of various forms of family. Authorities who wished to support the family debated whether child allowances should be channeled directly to women or paid through men's wages, a debate that was connected to a broader discussion about whether families should center on mothers or fathers. At one extreme, this produced a vision in which state-subsidized maternity would be entirely independent of fathers, a vision propounded by the Norwegian Katti Anker Moller.[146] At the other extreme, it produced a vision, propounded by many French conservatives, in which men were rewarded for the numerous children borne by their wives.

Official measures designed to strengthen the family often coincided with other circumstances that weakened it. In the Soviet Union during the 1930s, rapid industrialization uprooted people, drained the countryside of adult men, and ensured that workers were lodged in barracks or overcrowded shared flats that allowed little domestic intimacy. Similar developments could be seen in Nazi Germany. Political mobilization created institutions, such as the Hitler Youth, that operated outside, or even against, families. More importantly, economic mobilization meant that lives increasingly revolved around the workplace rather than the home. Hours of work lengthened, and employers provided food at work as a means of maintaining and motivating their labor force.[147]

The outbreak of war disrupted family life across Europe. Men were sent away to fight; labor was drafted to areas away from the threat of enemy action, and bomb damage forced strangers to share accommodations. Women and children were evacuated from cities and imposed on the – often unwelcoming – population of the countryside. The effects of evacuation in Germany were so great that the population of some villages had doubled by 1945. Sometimes sheer confusion broke up families: it was estimated that 90,000 children became separated from their parents during the French flight from the invading Germans in 1940. The ending of family life that some Utopians had dreamed of in the 1920s was achieved not in municipal crèches but in refugee camps and bomb shelters.

Servant problems

Bourgeois life before 1914 was built on servants. English social commentators drew the line between the middle and the working classes according to whether or not servants were employed. In Hamburg in 1907, over one-tenth of the entire workforce was composed of domestic servants.[148] Many bourgeois children felt more at home with the servants in the kitchen than in the drawing room with their parents. Bourgeois men often depended on their servants for information; Balfour's much quoted remark that he would sooner take the advice of his valet than that of the Conservative Party probably says something about the power of valets as well as the weakness of the Conservative Party.

Servants were important for relations between the sexes for two reasons. First, most servants were women. Second, cheap and plentiful servants liberated bourgeois women from certain kinds of housework and provided them with a sphere in which they exercised authority. Bourgeois feminists of the pre-1914 period had derived freedom from the labors of women from lower social classes, but the First World War and the attractions of industrial work reduced the number of women available for domestic service.[149] The expansion of the middle class also changed relations between employers and servants as ever-larger numbers of people regarded themselves as belonging to the "servant-hiring classes" at a time when smaller numbers of women were willing to endure the conditions of domestic service. Most strikingly, there was a change in the tone of relations between masters and servants. It was harder to take servants for granted in the way that had been possible before 1914. Distinctions of background no longer seemed natural, and employers were forced to recognize that their servants might share their hopes, fears and resentments. Leonard Woolf recalled that a letter written to his wife by an old family servant in 1936 seemed like a relic from a previous age.[150] Woolf's friend Harold Nicolson exemplified the new unease over the servant problem; in spite of precarious financial circumstances, Nicolson's family employed two secretaries, a cook, a lady's maid, a chauffeur, a valet and three gardeners.[151] But Nicolson did not feel at ease with servants. In an autobiographical essay he describes the embarrassment of dealing with the drunken valet who accompanied Lord Curzon to the Locarno Conference. Interestingly, Curzon, a generation older than Nicolson and a good deal higher up the social scale, seems to have regarded the incident with amusement rather than embarrassment.[152]

Relations between servants and employers were a subject of great concern for the interwar middle classes. Some of these anxieties revolved around sexual relations, and sexual rebellion by servants was often associated with violence. In 1933, the French middle classes were shaken by the case of two allegedly lesbian sisters who had murdered their employers.[153] In Britain and France, middle-class housewives often sought to "solve" the servant problem by using new domestic appliances that would allow them to avoid having their incomes and privacy eroded by servants; in England, the very girls who might formerly have entered domestic service now worked for firms that manufactured devices that allowed housewives to manage alone.

The servant problem acquired an explicitly political dimension in Germany. In 1915, the RDH association of housewives was formed to confront the problems raised by the wartime shortage of servants, and in the Weimar Republic it sought to circumvent new rights that servants might acquire under labor laws by defining many servants as "domestic apprentices."[154] In spite of such efforts, some servants were politically mobilized. The Nazi Labour Front sought to enroll servants, much to the annoyance of bourgeois housewives,[155] though the Nazis later reversed their position and distributed subsidies to encourage domestic service as an occupation "fitting for women."[156]

Battles for births

Mussolini believed that Italy needed a "battle for births." The metaphor reflects the extent to which interwar demographic policies were linked to military preoccupations and also how matters that affected women were conceived by men in terms of their own experience: Mussolini also argued that "war is for men what birth is for women." By the late 1930s, the major continental powers – Germany, France and the Soviet Union – were similarly preoccupied with the need to increase the birth rate, and all were eyeing each other's policies nervously as they equated population with military strength. However, not all population policies can be explained by a simple equation between militarism, natalism and an antifeminist defense of the "traditional family"; military needs alone do not explain the obsession with birth rates. Such a preoccupation may have made sense for men in France in the 1920s, who shared Foch's belief that the Versailles peace settlement had been a "twenty-year truce," but it made little sense in any part of Europe by 1939, when natalist campaigns reached their peak. By this stage, it was obvious that war was imminent and that large numbers of children were more likely to be a burden than a benefit. An obsession with demography was as much about images of national rebirth, virility and youth as about the rational calculation of military advantage. Often the denunciation of low birth rates was blended with a general conservative condemnation of modern urban culture or democracy, though neither rural areas nor authoritarian regimes were necessarily associated with fecundity.[157]

Attitudes towards birth rates did not operate across a simple left/right spectrum that pitted "conservative" pro-natalists against "progressive" advocates of birth control. Pro-natalists might be driven to adopt welfare policies that benefited women, or even act to defend women's emancipation. Some regimes sought to push up birth rates by forcing women out of the labor force, but the Swedish government tried to encourage population growth by making it illegal to fire pregnant women.[158] Conversely, the most enthusiastic practitioners of birth control were often concerned not to emancipate women but to improve the "racial stock" by preventing the "least fit" from reproducing. Such attitudes were most obvious among German Nazis, but they could also be discerned in democracies: laws permitting compulsory sterilization were introduced in Denmark in 1929 and in Sweden and Norway in 1934.[159] The British pioneer of birth control, Marie Stopes, advocated the sterilization of up to one-third of the English male population and disinherited her son because he married a woman who wore glasses.[160]

Concern about low population was most acute in France, the one country that had not shared in the general demographic growth of the late nineteenth century. For almost the entire life of the Third Republic (1870–1940), the French population remained virtually unchanged at around 40 million. Before 1914, low population had been primarily seen as a problem by the Catholic right, but the First World War changed matters. The French population had been even more depleted by the loss of large numbers of soldiers and by the fact that birth rates had fallen to half their normal levels during the war, which meant that the number of young men who would be available for military service in the late 1930s was severely reduced, a fact that acquired ever more sinister significance as time went on. France responded to the crisis by introducing a complete ban on all forms of birth control in 1920.

The efforts of French legislators to prevent the practice of birth control failed. Birth rates remained almost unchanged throughout the interwar period. Efforts became ever more intense, culminating in the *Code de la Famille* of 1939 and the natalist policies of the Vichy government. Subsidies were given to women with children and better child-care facilities were provided, while penalties for abortion were tightened. In 1943, a woman was guillotined for having carried out an abortion.

French policy on the birth rate was notably different from that pursued in many European countries. First, eugenics had little influence in France. All births were regarded as good and there was no attempt to improve the racial stock or to prevent those from minority races or the "lower classes" from reproducing. Second, interest in raising the birth rate meant that many commentators, including conservative ones, adopted a relatively tolerant attitude towards sexual morality. Illegitimate children were welcomed, and the sexual expression of women was regarded as good – as long as it produced children. In September 1941, the Vichy government passed a law that allowed children born outside marriage to be retrospectively legitimized.[161] The link between natalism and tolerance of certain kinds of female sexual expression was reflected in the cinema of the 1930s and 1940s. The films of Marcel Pagnol were haunted by the issue of declining birth rates and the need to repopulate the Provençal countryside – in one film, even the pear trees are barren. The possibility of repopulation almost invariably arose from the arrival of a woman with promiscuous sexual habits. In *Regain*, the peasant hero brings life back to his village after setting up house with a former cabaret singer whom he has bought from a traveling knife grinder. In *Angèle*, a farmer's daughter runs away to the city, where she becomes a prostitute and bears a child by an unknown father. Her father imprisons her in a cellar for this deed, but the peasant hero who rescues her treats the child as a blessing and remarks that they will soon give it numerous brothers and sisters. *La Fille du Puisatier* contains a similar sequence of events and finishes with Marshal Pétain's first speech as head of the Vichy state. Another Vichy film, *Le Corbeau*, also revolves around birth. The hero, a doctor unjustly accused of carrying out abortions, would have offended both eugenicists and religious moralists, since he not only conceives a child out of wedlock but does so by a cripple.

Italy did not face the kind of demographic crisis seen in France. Italian birth rates were high, indeed, perhaps too high after the possibilities of emigration to the United States were reduced during the 1920s. In spite of this, Mussolini encouraged Italians to reproduce as fast as possible: taxes were introduced for unmarried people and couples without children, certain jobs in government employment were reserved for parents, and birth control was made illegal. Italian natalist policies were no more successful than those of the French, though. Birth rates declined under Fascism.

In Germany, the Nazis did not encourage the entire population to reproduce but divided the population according to whether they were regarded as biologically desirable. At one extreme, "good Aryans" were

encouraged to produce as many children as possible: births outside marriage were tolerated or even encouraged, and measures that resembled
those taken during the First World War allowed all women with children
to be called "Frau" and ended the dismissal of unmarried mothers from
civil service jobs.[162] At the other extreme, those who were seen as mentally ill, retarded or afflicted with some form of hereditary illness were
prevented from having children – about 0.5 percent of the German population was sterilized during the 1930s.[163]

Soviet policy on birth rates shifted. At first, the government encouraged
the practice of birth control so that by 1934 it was estimated that there
were only 57,000 live births in Moscow in contrast to 154,000 abortions.[164] Subsequently, official attitudes towards birth control changed. In
1936 abortion was outlawed, and the government began to encourage its
citizens to have as many children as possible. This volte-face was imitated
by Western communist leaders, which confused some Western feminists,
who had previously regarded the Soviet Union as the model to which all
nations should aspire. After the outbreak of the Second World War, separation of couples, uncertainty and starvation reduced birth rates. In 1943,
no live births were recorded in the besieged city of Leningrad.[165]

Conclusion

Changing perceptions of women, the family and sexual relations cannot
be separated from thinking about other matters. The two wars and the
advent of states with new ambitions to mold the lives of their citizens
meant that "public" affairs were more likely than ever before to intrude
into private life, but public and private domains did not have fixed frontiers. The bedroom, the inner sanctum of privacy in a bourgeois household, was not at all private in the crowded peasant farmhouses where
much of Europe's population lived. Broadcasting, cinema and publishing
created new sorts of public domains. It should also be remembered that
the private world often showed a remarkable capacity to resist demands
made on it. States that had unprecedented capacities to raise taxes, mobilize soldiers and even exterminate whole sections of their populations often found it impossible to raise the birth rate.

Nuclear families and nonworking wives, often presented as traditional,
were recent innovations. Women's enfranchisement or the toleration of
sexual activity on the part of unmarried women might serve conservative
purposes, and even the most self-consciously "emancipated" women did
not always threaten male authority. The attractiveness of such women
and their sexual availability might be seen as a desirable supplement to
"conventional" femininity rather than its replacement. A number of

interwar feminists became the mistresses of powerful men. The heroine of Rosamond Lehmann's autobiographical novel *The Weather in the Streets* (1936) has an affair with a rich married landowner, while the former Soviet Commissar for Women's Affairs, Alexandra Kollontai, was probably the lover of the King of Sweden during the 1930s.[166]

Most importantly, the simple stereotypical models of family life and sexual behavior passed down to historians through public debate often bore a limited relation to the perception that individual men and women had of their own lives. A striking example is provided by the life of the English woman Kathleen Hale. In her youth, Hale seemed to epitomize the "new woman." She left home to work on a farm during the First World War, and she swore and wore men's clothes. After the war, she lived a life of raffish bohemianism in the city, where she worked as an artist, had a number of affairs (including one with Augustus John) and fell ill as a result of her exhausting and impoverished life. However, eventually she married, moved to the country, gave birth to two sons and devoted herself to the composition of a series of children's books about Orlando the Marmalade Cat (a model of family virtue who lives with his wife Grace and their three kittens). Hale's life might be interpreted as a transition from the questioning of sexual identity in the 1920s to the reassertion of traditional values in the 1930s, but her autobiography suggests that she herself never accepted either set of values; it even raises disturbing doubts about Orlando the Marmalade Cat's own masculinity.[167]

4

CIVIL WARS

THE PERIOD FROM 1917 to 1945 was one of violent internal conflict in most European countries, first seen in the Russian Revolution of 1917 and the Bolsheviks' subsequent efforts to impose their power over the country. Elsewhere, a wave of unrest followed the end of the war. In parts of central Europe, unrest spilled over into revolution, which was bloodily repressed in Hungary, Austria, Finland and Germany. In Ireland, nationalists fought the British and then each other over the form of the new Free State. In Italy, counterrevolution helped the Fascist Party come to power under Benito Mussolini in 1922, and other violent right-wing movements also became known as "fascist" during the interwar period, the most notorious being Hitler's Nazi Party, which came to power in Germany in 1933. In Spain between 1936 and 1939, a coalition of left-wing and democratic forces fought against most of the professional army, the Church, and large parts of the property-owning classes under General Franco. The Soviet Union sent aid to the Republicans; Nazi Germany and Fascist Italy helped Franco. Internal social conflict continued within European countries even after the beginning of international war in 1939. It pitted a largely communist and working-class resistance movement against the conservative Vichy government in France between 1941 and 1944, and Italian partisans against the remnants of their own Fascist government in 1943 and 1944. There were similar conflicts in Greece and in Yugoslavia. Politicians used the language of armed struggle even when the events being described involved no bloodshed, and in spite of, or perhaps because of, the enfranchisement of women in many countries, political styles became more aggressively masculine. Uniforms and clenched fists dominated demonstrations, and speeches were about "struggle," "battle" and "the enemy."[1]

In some countries, rival armies fought pitched battles. This was the case in Russia between 1918 and 1922, when 1.2 million men were killed in fighting; in Finland, where 6,794 men were killed fighting in 1918 (up to 20,000 died as an indirect result of the war);[2] and in Spain from 1936 to 1939 (where 268,500 people were killed as a direct result of the war and another 165,000 died from the effects of disease and hunger).[3] Elsewhere political conflict was expressed in street fighting, which claimed around 50 lives in France from February 1934 until the end of 1938, between 300 and 400 lives in the last years of the Weimar Republic in Germany, and 1,500 lives in Italy between 1919 and October 1921.[4] Levels of violence varied enormously. After the formation of the first Labour government in Britain in 1924, the Conservative politician Duff Cooper joked to his wife that they would have to go into exile "when the massacres begin." Such remarks were being made in deadly earnest in parts of continental Europe. The coup d'état of 1923 in Bulgaria was followed by the slaughter of 20,000 peasants.

In spite of all the differences, it is possible to trace common threads in European political divisions between the Russian Revolution and the end of the Second World War. Many Europeans saw themselves as being part of a wider conflict that transcended national frontiers. When Salazar dissolved the fascist National Syndicalist movement in Portugal, he received a menacing telegram reminding him of the "recent fate of the Austrian Chancellor" (Engelbert Dollfuss, who had been assassinated by Nazis).[5] Defenders of order believed that every disturbance, from the mutinies of French troops on the western front in 1917 to the strikes that accompanied the French Popular Front election victory of 1936, was part of a revolutionary conspiracy. The same individuals were often involved in successive civil wars. Russian advisers applied lessons learned in the Red Army to the Spanish Civil War, while Maxime Weygand began the interwar period fighting against the Red Army in Poland and ended it insisting that the French government sign an armistice with the German invader so that it could keep its army intact to fight the communists. Captain Gyula Gömbös helped Hitler in his beer hall putsch of 1923 before becoming the radical right-wing Prime Minister of Hungary in 1932. International organizations coordinated the various national struggles. The Third International (or Comintern), established in Moscow in March 1919, was the most influential such organization but similar bodies existed on the right: Théodore Aubert in Switzerland produced the *Bulletin de l'Entente Internationale Contre la Troisième Internationale*, which influenced counterrevolutionaries all over Europe, including the young General Franco.[6]

The lefts

The aftermath of the Russian Revolution saw a civil war between different lefts as well as one between left and right as Bolshevism, not the most popular movement in Russia, imposed itself through a mixture of opportunism and ruthlessness. In November 1917, Bolshevik candidates obtained only a quarter of votes cast in elections to the Constituent Assembly. The socialist revolutionaries won the most votes, but their own divisions – over whether to collaborate with the Bolsheviks – made it unclear precisely what the vote meant. The Bolsheviks took no risks and dissolved the Assembly. Some members of the other leftist groups now threw in their lot with Bolshevism; others fought with the Whites.

Conflict on the Russian left continued both during and after the civil war. The Bolsheviks invaded the Menshevik republic of Georgia and crushed a rebellion at the Kronstadt naval base. There was also division among the Bolsheviks. In the summer of 1918, half of the party's 300,000 members were expelled on Lenin's order, and after Lenin's death rival leaders struggled for power. Stalin, the winner of the struggle, imposed his authority with increasing violence, which culminated in the purges of the 1930s.

Explicit opposition was not the only thing that limited the power of Soviet leaders. The party leaders governed a huge country with poor communications and considerable cultural, ethnic and linguistic divisions. An order given in Moscow might have to be transmitted hundreds of miles and be acted on by local officials with interests of their own that might bear only a tangential relation to those of the central party organization, while war and rapid urbanization often created new levels of confusion as people were uprooted and shipped around the country. In Kazan, an intellectual threatened by Stalin's purges could contemplate joining the gypsy bands that still roamed the country.[7] Far from being subject to "totalitarian" control, the Soviet Union was a country in which brigandage and crime intersected with armed resistance to the state, such as that seen during the collectivization program, and with explicit political opposition, such as that seen during the Kronstadt uprising. Until 1935, party members had the right to carry firearms and they used them against all sorts of "enemies of communism." In 1920, Bim the Clown was shot by the Cheka (political police), in the middle of a performance, for making anti-Bolshevik jokes.

Bolshevik leaders assumed that their revolution would be part of a wider movement. Conservatives, too, made much of "international communism" and saw Comintern puppet-masters behind every left-wing movement in Europe. In reality, the relationship between communism in Russia and the

International was complicated. The early leaders of Bolshevism had been cosmopolitan: Trotsky was in New York when the Russian Revolution began. Stalin, by contrast, had spent all his life in Russia. His years of exile had been spent in Siberia rather than Zurich or Paris. Stalin's purges were partly directed against the more internationally minded communists, and Stalin himself, though born in Georgia, was prone to adopt a Russian nationalist outlook. From 1926 onwards, the Comintern was more an instrument of Soviet foreign policy than a center of revolutionary agitation.

Communists loyal to Moscow split away from socialists who remained loyal to the Second International after the Russian Revolution, but the division was not always absolute or clear-cut. Many French socialists who had voted to join the Third International drifted back to the socialist SFIO within a few years, while in Germany the left-wing parties collaborated with each other for several years at the local level and trade unionists from the various factions of the left often cooperated in the factories. In Great Britain and Spain, the communist parties were small. The British left was dominated by the Labour Party, and the Spanish left – until 1936 – was split between anarchism and socialism.

As time went by, the division between communist parties and the rest of the political spectrum became sharper. The communists had a clear center in Moscow, an existing regime to which they were loyal, an international organization and a firm set of rules. Dissidents were purged from the European parties and, in 1927, communists implemented "class against class" tactics, renouncing alliances and condemning every other party, including the socialists. The separation was underwritten by economic conditions: factory rationalization and unemployment broke down working arrangements between socialist and communist trade unions on the shop floor. In 1932, 80 percent of German Communist Party members were unemployed, while around 70 percent of social democrats remained in work.[8] Unemployment widened the gap between relatively old, skilled workers, who tended to support the socialists, and younger workers, who supported the communists.

Even then, though, there were national variations in the relationship of communist parties to other groups. Moscow's discipline was easier to enforce in countries, such as France and Czechoslovakia, where communists operated in the open, but the party's influence shrank dramatically after the implementation of "class against class" tactics, which made communists seem like mere instruments of the Soviet Union. In France, only ten communist deputies were elected to parliament in 1932; in Czechoslovakia party membership dropped from 150,000 to 25,000 in two years.[9] Stalin could call communist leaders from democratic countries to Moscow for instructions or to discipline them. By contrast, a clandestine organization, such as the Italian one, operated with a degree of freedom. Antonio Gramsci, writing in one of Mussolini's prisons, was freer than communists who took refuge in Moscow.

The Nazi seizure of power in Germany in 1933 changed Comintern policy. Communist parties now allied with democratic forces in order to form "popular fronts" to defend democracies against fascism. The success of this policy varied. The British Labour Party rebuffed all attempts at alliance, though a number of dissident socialists worked with the communists. In France, conditions for the Popular Front were propitious. There had been little violence between socialists and communists, and the two movements were able to fuse their antifascism into an older tradition of republican defense dating back to the Dreyfus affair. It was this tradition that facilitated the entry of the centrist Radical Party into the alliance. In 1936, Popular Front governments came to power in France and Spain.

In both countries, the Popular Front failed. The failure was most dramatic in Spain, where the Popular Front provoked a nationalist uprising that eventually brought General Franco to power. In France, large sections of bourgeois opinion remained hostile to the Front. The failure of the Popular Fronts sprang partly from the gulf between workers and those who ostensibly spoke in their name. Workers who flooded into trade unions during this period often had no previous experience of organization, and were not well disciplined. The strikes that accompanied Popular Front election victories had an atmosphere of festival about them, which in Spain was exacerbated by the tradition of anarchism. Workers who had been mobilized by anarchism proved difficult to bring to heel, even when their leaders had decided that they wished to impose order. Strikes and working-class agitation alienated the bourgeoisie, which the Popular Front coalition needed to win over.

Even the communist/anticommunist divide was not clear-cut. The Soviet Union was often defended by those who were not communists or did not accept Moscow's authority. Trotsky became the center of an international movement after leaving Russia in 1929. Stalinists and Trotskyites were divided by vicious mutual antipathy, and Trotsky was assassinated by Stalinist agents in 1940. However, Trotsky continued to express loyalty to the Third International until 1933. He then helped to form a Fourth International, but insisted that the Soviet Union remained a "workers' state" and should be defended. Support for the Soviet Union also came from noncommunist Western intellectuals, some of whom were motivated by admiration for what they took to be a new society of rational organization, technocratic efficiency and sexual freedom. After their return from the Soviet Union in 1932, Sidney and Beatrice Webb summed up their findings with the phrase: "We have seen the future and it works."

The rights

The divisions and complexities of the European right between 1918 and 1945 make those of the left seem straightforward. The right was usually nationalist and often rejected international organization or classification. Many right-wingers argued that their ideas were suited only to the particular circumstances of their own countries: Mussolini said that Fascism was "not for export," and Churchill said that he would have been a Fascist "if he had been Italian." The left stressed the importance of explicit ideological debate and grouped itself around texts such as the works of Stalin, whereas the right defined itself in terms of "tradition," "instinct," the "apolitical" pragmatism of notables or the "apolitical" expertise of technocrats. The French philosopher Alain argued that the identifying characteristic of the French right was its insistence that "right" and "left" had no meaning. The founder of the Romanian Iron Guard brushed aside attempts to define his ideology by saying, "The country is dying for want of men, not of programs."

One way to deal with this confusing situation is to avoid imposing abstract categories on the right and instead to examine particular regimes and movements that provided poles of attraction for right-wingers in Europe. The first such regime was that established by Mussolini in Italy in 1922. Initially, Mussolini did not seem so different from other European rulers – he presided over a parliamentary government with a legal opposition, expressed his admiration for the economic policies of liberalism, and demonstrated his attachment to such orthodoxies by revaluing the lira in 1926 at a level that harmed Italian export industries. Basil Liddell Hart claimed that the Duce subscribed to the *Manchester Guardian*.[10]

The image of the Fascist regime began to change with the murder of Giacomo Matteotti, a socialist deputy, in 1924, for which Mussolini took responsibility, using the subsequent agitation as an excuse to increase repression. Even then, Mussolini's regime did not break with the Western democracies, and communist and socialist newspapers continued to be published until 1926. The Italian senate remained a center of opposition, where men like Benedetto Croce could speak freely until the 1940s. The regime worked through structures – such as prefects, police and the courts – that had existed before 1922.

The fact that Italy had a weak state and a strong civil society limited Mussolini's power. Most Italians felt only loosely bound by the state's desire to collect taxes, conscript soldiers and enforce laws, but felt strongly compelled by the requirements of mutual obligation on which villages and especially families were based. Italian political life had not displaced the network of mutual obligations, but had built on it. Political parties

depended on their capacity to secure jobs and resources for their supporters, and Fascism fitted into the pattern of Italian politics. The movement's initial springboard had been in the north, where communications
were sufficiently good to make Fascism's mass politics possible and technological development made its modernistic rhetoric seem plausible. It
was also in the north that the threat of the left made Fascism seem necessary. However, once Fascism was installed in power, membership of the
party expanded rapidly, especially in the south. It grew from 300,000 in
October 1922, to 783,000 by the end of 1923, to 2,633,000 by 1939.
Far from being a sign that the party was taking over society, this increase
reflected the fact that society was taking over the party. Membership was
distributed indiscriminately: Italian soldiers in Yugoslavia in 1941 found
that partisans, who did not speak a word of Italian and were fighting
against the Italian army, possessed valid Fascist Party cards.[11] Some who
joined the party were notables, who would have exercised power in any
case, or civil servants, dependent on the state. They treated the party as a
means of distributing state resources; Fascism had become the victim of
"*trasformismo*," the process whereby political parties that threatened the
Italian system were absorbed into that system.

Italian Fascism's encounter with German Nazism sheds light on both
movements. They had much in common. Early in his career, Hitler was
influenced by Mussolini and Mussolini ultimately became subordinate
to Hitler. The limits on Hitler's power were less obvious than those on
Mussolini's. German conservatives had helped bring Nazism to power
and they assumed they would be able to control it, and the beginning of
Hitler's rule seemed to suggest that they were right. Like Mussolini,
Hitler came to power as part of a coalition, and his first Cabinet contained only three Nazis, alongside nine members of other parties. Hjalmar Schacht, an orthodox economist, became Economics Minister.
Hitler appeased conservatives by attacking radicals in his own movement – in June 1934, a number of such men, notably the leaders of the
SA, were murdered – but his regime changed during the mid-1930s.
The death of President Hindenburg, in 1934, freed Hitler from one
constraint and allowed him to declare himself head of state and elicit an
oath of loyalty from the army. In 1936, the Nazi four-year plan marked
a shift away from economic orthodoxy towards an autarkic organization
designed to prepare for war. Schacht's dismissal in 1937 illustrated the
regime's radicalization.

The drama of fascism means that it often overshadows the other authoritarian anti-Marxist regimes in Europe. In intellectual terms, the
inspiration for many such regimes owed much to the French royalist
Charles Maurras, who emphasized the virtues of classicism, church

(especially the Catholic Church), the monarchy, the regions, hierarchy and tradition. His ideas aroused admiration in Belgium and Spain and even among Welsh nationalists.

One regime in particular drew inspiration from Maurras – the government of António Salazar in Portugal, which was emphatically on the right although very different from those of Hitler and Mussolini. Whereas Hitler marked his break with bourgeois conventions by dismissing his conservative Economics Minister, Salazar became dictator in 1932 after having been a conservative Finance Minister since 1928. He did not indulge in the theatrical displays beloved of fascist leaders; an Italian envoy described Salazar's politics as "personal rule without a personality." Portugal was home to a National Syndicalist movement that aped certain aspects of fascism in other European countries, but it was only allowed limited power and was dissolved in 1934.

Much attention has been devoted to the distinction between fascism (epitomized by the regimes of Hitler and Mussolini) and conservatism (epitomized by the regime of Salazar). Fascism was a relatively new doctrine, and did not simply defend the established order. Fascists believed in movement rather than order, the "charismatic" leadership of a single individual and the concentration of power in a single party. Such characteristics could be seen in the Spanish Falange, the Portuguese National Syndicalists, the Romanian Iron Guard, the Hungarian Arrow Cross, and the French Parti Populaire Français. Fascists rejected democracy but not mass society. Fascists believed in crowds, and wanted people to think of themselves as part of large entities – the nation, the state, the race. They wished people to be mobilized politically, although they did not intend them to have much say in the direction that mobilization might take. Conservatives, by contrast, rejected mass society and feared crowds. Salazar told the French royalist Henri Massis that his aim was to "make the Portuguese live by habit."

Fascists were active enthusiasts for modernity. Their leaders liked aeroplanes and fast cars, and needed the technology of the radio, the cinema and the loudspeaker. This celebration was particularly visible in Italian Fascism, perhaps because Italy was not a nation of particular technological sophistication. The distinction between the styles of fascism and conservatism could be seen even in their attitudes towards cooking. The conservative Charles Maurras was fascinated by traditional Provençal recipes;[12] by contrast, Marinetti, a friend of Mussolini, denounced the Italian love of pasta, which he associated with sloth, impotence and cowardice: his *Futurist Cooking* (1932) proposed dishes such as pineapples with sardines.[13]

Fascism and conservatism also differed in their ideas about how much power governments should exercise. Conservatives were authoritarian pluralists. They did not believe in freedom or equality, but neither did they believe that power should be invested in any single body. Rather, they wanted to see a variety of agencies – churches, regions, corporations, aristocracies, monarchies – exercise power in appropriate spheres. Fascists, on the other hand, wanted authority to be vested in a single party, fused with a strong state, under a single leader. In the 1920s, Mussolini advocated "totalitarianism."

Finally, conservatives and fascists differed in their attitude towards violence. Conservatives were willing to use violence when it suited them, but they regarded it as a necessary evil and knew that international conflict was likely to bring inflation, revolution and all the forms of instability that they feared. Many of them might have echoed Bismarck's remark: "I do not want war; I want victory." Franco yielded to his generals' desire to keep Spain out of the Second World War, and Marshal Pétain withdrew France from it. The conservative dictators of eastern Europe entered the Second World War only under pressure, and many of them abandoned the conflict as soon as possible. Conservatives applied similar logic to internal politics. For them, the most effective forms of power were those that were least visible, and they valued societies in which men instinctively deferred to their superiors or in which the capacity of authority to inflict punishment was so well known that it need never be used. Pétain had quelled mutinies in 1917 by having dozens of men shot, and accepted even greater degrees of repression as head of the French state from 1940 to 1944, but he preferred to omit the more bloodthirsty part of the "Marseillaise."

Fascists, by contrast, believed that violence was a good thing in itself as well as being a means to their ends: the Romanian Iron Guard shouted, "Long live death." Some fascists were fascinated by bloodshed even when they themselves were likely to be its victims – the French writer Drieu la Rochelle fantasized about death at the hands of a communist before killing himself in 1945. The archetypal conservative died in bed after receiving extreme unction and was then buried in a family vault at a service attended by his faithful retainers. The archetypal fascist lay in an unmarked grave on the battlefield.

In practice, distinctions between fascism and other political movements were rarely clear-cut. The genocidal Nazism of 1943 was different from the Italian regime of 1923, and the shift from one paradigm of fascism to another changed the alignment of European right-wingers. Some moved slowly towards fascism. Jacques Doriot, leader of the Parti Populaire Français, did not describe himself as a fascist until after France's defeat by Germany in 1940, although some of his admirers did. Oswald Mosley's New Party contained some who would follow its leader into the British Union of Fascists, but it also contained others – such as John Strachey or Harold Nicolson – who would return to more conventional political parties. The French peasant leader Henry Dorgères accepted the label of fascist in 1933 but rejected it the following year.[14]

A simple contrast between fascism and conservatism is also made difficult by the ambiguities and contradictions of conservatism. Conservatives implied that they were protecting an order that was hallowed by time, but in practice they were usually trying to re-create certain aspects of social arrangements that were themselves creations of the relatively recent past. Many of the traditions that they defended were the "invented traditions" of the late nineteenth and early twentieth century. They did not reject industrial growth and often used new techniques to defend "old" ways.

Some of conservatism's ambiguities can be seen in views on monarchy. Conservatives often paid lip service to their kings, but in practice many found monarchy an irksome institution. During the Russian civil war, White forces did not campaign for a restoration of the Tsar (Alekseev, commander of the White volunteer army, had helped to persuade Nicholas II to abdicate). Jacques Bainville, the French royalist historian, recognized that the Russian Revolution had displaced the French Revolution in the nightmares of conservatives, and that republican France's aid to the Poles in their fight against the Red Army had made it seem "*le pays de l'ordre par excellence.*"[15] In Portugal, the monarchist associations abandoned restoration in 1923, and one issued a statement saying, "If we shall have no King, let there be a dictator."[16] One of the most characteristic forms of conservative rule in the interwar period was regency. Admiral Horthy, who was regent of Hungary from 1920 to 1944, professed to be an ardent monarchist, but in practice he rejected a Habsburg restoration. Among the Magyar aristocracy, attachment to the dynasty had become so loose that some toyed with the idea of making Lord Rothermere, proprietor of the London *Daily Mail*, King of Hungary.[17] Regencies also existed in Romania and Greece during the interwar period. General Franco anticipated a restoration of the Spanish monarchy after his death, but took care that it did not interfere with his own forty-year rule. French monarchists in Action Française combined enthusiasm for the idea of monarchy with a cool attitude towards the pretender to the French throne. Many were happy to treat Marshal Pétain's regime as a *de facto* regency.

Town versus country

For conservatives, the cities were centers of revolutionary upheaval, while the countryside was the home of deference and tradition, but peasants were as likely to be manipulated as represented by conservatives. The town/country division was the product not of natural differences between peasants and city-dwellers, but of particular circumstances. The European left was structured to appeal to the urban working classes and had paid little attention to the countryside, particularly the property-owning peasantry. The division between the urban working classes and the countryside was exacerbated by the First World War, which strengthened the economic position of the property-owning peasants in most of Europe – and hence their interest in maintaining the established order – while creating hostility between a largely peasant army and an urban working class that seemed to have been spared the worst effects of the war.

The consequences of town/country conflict were most dramatic in Russia. The Bolshevik Party wished to build its power on an urban working class but faced an overwhelmingly peasant population. In addition, the aftermath of the Revolution saw two forms of regression to an earlier pattern of Russian society. First, the Russian population became more rural as people fled from famine-stricken cities, and second, most peasants who had left their communes returned to them.

In the short term, the Bolsheviks responded with a tactical withdrawal. They accepted the peasant desire for property and, although all land was nationalized in 1918, peasants were allowed to control the farms on which they lived. In 1921, the Bolsheviks also introduced the New Economic Policy (NEP): grain requisitions were replaced by taxes and peasants were encouraged to sell their produce for cash. Bolshevik overtures to the peasantry were helped by the fact that Russian peasants, unlike their Western counterparts, had not drawn much profit from wartime inflation and food shortages, so the Russian counterrevolution, unlike that in central Europe, could not depend on peasant support. Some peasants joined the Bolsheviks, others formed "Green" armies to protect territory from the incursions of either side, and some simply retreated into self-sufficient isolation. For the White armies, which had to supply themselves as they fought across the thousands of miles that separated their bases on the periphery of the Russian empire to the Bolshevik heartland, peasant hostility was fatal.[18]

Bolshevik success hinged on the absence of peasant opposition, but this did not mean that the two had good relations. Grain requisition during the civil war and the subsequent imposition of central authority brought violent conflict between the Bolsheviks and the peasants: by 1920, over 8,000 members of requisitioning brigades had been murdered.[19] In addition, Russia's new rulers knew that a society of peasants cultivating small plots of land could never provide a long-term basis of support. To solve this problem Stalin abandoned the NEP in 1928–29 and launched a program of rapid industrial expansion combined with a collectivization of agriculture. By 1937, 93 percent of households that remained on the land lived in collective farms.[20] Peasants did not accept their fate quietly. Many who were ordered to go into collective farms killed livestock and sometimes killed the men sent to enforce the government's decrees. The communists executed or deported rich peasants, whom they blamed for such resistance, while armed bands seized grain with such brutality that large areas of the countryside were afflicted by famine.

Even Stalin's collectivization cannot be interpreted simply as the victory of town over country. The speed of urbanization meant that many of the new "proletarians" were yesterday's peasants, and often the very behavior that the communists derided among the peasantry – drunkenness and violence – was imported into the towns. Many communists were peasants whose horizons had been opened by the expansion of primary education in the decade before 1914 and then by the upheaval of war. Far from being remote urban intellectuals enforcing abstract Marxist theory, some of those who enforced collectivization were peasant sons taking revenge for the humiliations of their youth.

The divorce between rural areas and the European left was not inevitable, and some parts of the European left did succeed in the countryside. Stefan Radić (the Croatian peasant leader) briefly affiliated his party to the Third International.[21] In France, the Radical Party, which had an ideology that was "left-wing" in terms of the republican tradition but was favorable to small property, appealed to the peasantry. Henri Queuille, the Radical Minister of Agriculture in several governments, successfully saw off right-wing challengers in the Corrèze. Even the Marxist parties in France often gained electoral support from the peasantry. Indeed, at the Congress of Tours in 1920, it seems to have been mainly peasant delegates who voted in favor of affiliation to the Third International.[22]

Relations between rural and urban politics were complex. In Poland, Józef Piłsudski's 1926 coup saw the deposition of a peasant government by a military leader with socialist support, though Piłsudski was also supported by some peasants and his links with socialism became weaker as time went on. In Bulgaria, the coup of 1923 was mounted by nationalist officers against the Peasant Party. Most complicated of all was the case of Hungary, where land ownership had traditionally been concentrated in the hands of a few large magnates. After the First World War, Michael Károlyi, himself a magnate, tried to dismember the great estates but was deposed and replaced by the Bolsheviks under Béla Kun, who refused to break up estates for fear of creating a class of conservative smallholders. The Bolsheviks' subsequent defeat at the hands of the conservative Admiral Horthy did not mean a return to land reform; on the contrary, Horthy represented a Magyar aristocracy determined to maintain its privileges.

Defense of the social order in the countryside did not preclude a working arrangement with socialism in the towns; in effect this was a political system based on a town/country division rather than town/country conflict. In 1922, open voting was restored in the countryside, thus securing the power of the aristocracy, but towns retained the secret ballot, while the Socialist Party was legalized on the condition that it confine itself to urban workers and did not attempt to spread propaganda among the peasants. Calls for land reform came not from the left but from the radical right under Gömbös, who in 1932 formed the first government in Hungarian history to contain no aristocrats.

Conflict in the countryside could be as important as that between it and the city. Laborers, sharecroppers and tenants were often hostile to their landlords. In many countries, especially the newly created states of central Europe, redistribution of rural property was the most important political issue after the Great War.[23]

Italy experienced a wave of land seizure as peasants in the south simply occupied the great estates, and sharecroppers demanded full ownership. Elsewhere Italian peasants protested about prices or employment contracts. Italy was unusual in that sympathy was shown to the land occupations of 1919–20 by the government, and particularly by the Christian democrat Minister of Agriculture Luigi Sturzo. The government legislated to provide more secure work for landless laborers. Italian landlords responded to this challenge by turning to agencies that could exert violence against the peasantry – in the south, the Mafia, and in the north and center, the Fascists.

Owners of the great estates in southern Spain faced a variety of threats in the two decades leading up to 1936. Rural agitation spread through the country in 1917, and Miguel Primo de Rivera's dictatorship introduced reforms to benefit landless laborers in the 1920s. The left was divided and hesitant about the problem of the great estates: anarchists wanted to break them up into peasant smallholdings, while socialist trade unions wanted to keep the estates together and collectivize them. In practice, neither solution was applied. The socialist ministers of the Second Republic established an eight-hour day for laborers and legislated to protect them against competition from outside their own locality. Even these limited measures enraged Spanish landowners, encouraging most of them to support Franco's insurrection of July 1936.[24]

One of the novelties of interwar European politics was the advent of peasant parties, which were particularly strong in the successor states of the Habsburg Empire. In Bulgaria, Alexander Stamboliski's Peasant Party saw itself as the representative of a new current in political life and attempted to form a "Green" international that would match the "Red" internationals of communism and socialism. In France, a conservative

Parti Agraire, drawing its support largely from the Massif Central, rivaled Henry Dorgères's Greenshirts, who drew their support largely from the west of the country. Peasant parties campaigned on specifically agricultural issues, pressing for subsidies and protection from foreign competition, and sometimes also allied with the radical right as antiurban rhetoric blended into antimodernism, anti-Semitism and antisocialism. The depression that began in the late 1920s had particularly dramatic effects on agricultural prices and hence on peasant politics. There was a peasant rebellion in Croatia and Dalmatia in September 1932.

During this period, right-wing authoritarian governments often came to power with promises to look after the interests of the peasantry, but those who took such promises seriously were usually disappointed. Italian Fascists talked of the need to establish a strong and independent peasantry, but in fact the regime had come to power partly to protect landowners against just such a peasantry. The Fascist policy of supporting traditional sharecropping arrangements turned out to be a means by which the effects of depression and declining agricultural profits could be imposed on tenants rather than landlords.[25]

The German Nazis also employed ruralist rhetoric and drew much of their electoral support from the Protestant countryside. The party's agricultural expert – Walther Darré – tied the defense of the peasantry to a wider defense of the German race. Peasants were reservoirs of Aryan virtues and their settlement in the east would provide a bastion against the Slav threat, but the Nazis never really resolved their position on the great estates that dominated eastern Prussia. Some talked of breaking these estates up into peasant smallholdings, but aristocratic landlords were a powerful part of the political establishment that had brought Hitler to power. In practice, nothing was done. Furthermore, Darré's policies towards the peasants were based on the assumption that they were simple people who needed protection from the market economy. Such protection took the form of an entail law to prevent peasant property from being mortgaged. In reality, such measures cut off entrepreneurial farmers from funds that they had previously used to invest in new equipment. Similarly, the Nazis' removal of Jewish traders who were seen to have "exploited" the peasantry was sometimes resented by peasants who found themselves deprived of necessary commercial contacts.[26] Finally, the German war economy laid an increasing emphasis on heavy industry; farmers were stripped of resources and were unable to raise prices.

The contrast between proclaimed intention and achievement was most striking in Vichy France, a regime that seemed to hinge on a defense of rural areas at the expense of urban ones. One of Pétain's first speeches as head of state appeared to sum up the attitudes of the regime with the words "the earth that does not lie." In fact, the phrase had been written not by some weather-beaten patriarch from Finistère but by Emmanuel Berl, a half-Jewish Parisian intellectual. Furthermore, Vichy's relations with the peasantry were never as happy as its rhetoric implied. Peasants were oppressed by Vichy's economic regulations and food requisitions and, if they benefited at all during this period, they generally did so by defying Vichy and resorting to the black markets. One French peasant's remark about Pétain says much about the deceptions and self-deceptions that underlay the equation of the peasantry with the political right in Europe: "I like the Marshal because he is like me . . . a good liar."[27]

Churches

Religious differences underlay many of the violent conflicts in Europe between 1918 and 1945. There was still hostility between the various denominations of the Christian faith. Protestants and Catholics sometimes regarded each other with suspicion: on the one occasion when Pope Pius XI met Mussolini, they discussed the problem of Protestant evangelism in Italy. Such disputes rarely caused bloodshed, though, and opposition to the common enemy of socialism often brought Catholics and Protestants together. In France, right-wing Catholics under the influence of Charles Maurras had defined Protestants (along with Freemasons and Jews) as the "*métèques*" from whom they wished to free France, but when the right gained influence at Vichy in 1940 anti-Protestant feeling was almost nonexistent and Protestants such as Pastor Boegner were invited to join the new regime's National Council. There was a similar reconciliation in Germany, where the Protestant Evangelical Group voted with the – mainly Catholic – Centre Party in parliament in the early 1930s, while in Hungary, the Calvinist Magyar aristocracy, exemplified by the Regent Horthy and his Prime Minister, István Bethlen, worked in alliance with a Catholic radical right. In Britain, where conservatism and Anglicanism had once been almost synonymous, many conservatives were attracted by Catholicism, while T. S. Eliot decided that the ideals of his Catholic mentor, Maurras, were best expressed by the Church of England.* Even divisions

---

* Revealingly, George Orwell described the attraction of Catholicism in political terms: "These people went almost invariably to the Roman Church . . . They went, that is, to the Church with a world-wide organization, the one with a rigid discipline, the one with power and prestige behind it . . . Eliot has embraced not Romanism but Anglo-Catholicism, the ecclesiastical equivalent of Trotskyism." "Inside the Whale" in *Inside the Whale and Other Essays* (1962), pp. 9–50, p. 35.

between Christians and Muslims were usually effaced by hostility to common political enemies. Several conservative regimes – such as those in Nationalist Spain, Vichy France and wartime Croatia – maintained good relations with their Muslim subjects.

Struggles between Christian denominations were more likely to spill over into violence when they coincided with national divisions, as happened in Ireland between 1916 and 1922 and, more dramatically, in Yugoslavia, where decades of tension between Serbian Orthodoxy and Croatian Catholicism ended in forced conversion and extermination during the Second World War.

The greatest conflict in which the churches were involved during this period concerned not the struggle of one church against another, but that of Christianity as a whole – and especially the Catholic Church – against its supposed enemies on the political left. The link between religion and the political right was long-established and in many countries the Church and the traditional ruling class were knitted together. In Britain and Hungary, bishops sat with hereditary aristocrats in the upper house of parliament, and in France, religious schools educated many wealthy children. Often the Church itself was a large landowner: in Spain, it owned a total of almost 20,000 properties, reckoned to be worth $13 million.[28]

Church politics were reinforced by the anticlericalism of its opponents. The Russian Revolution and the rise of an international communist movement added a new dimension to the church/anticlerical dispute. Communism was hostile to religion as a whole, not merely to the particular privileges of one church. In Russia, a Union of the Militant Godless was founded in 1921. The Bolshevik Party was itself a kind of secular church, with rituals, gospels and martyrs: Electric Day replaced Elijah Day; the red star replaced the crucifix; "Octobering" (a ceremony in which children were given names such as Paris Commune) replaced baptism; and men who laughed at the veneration of saints queued up to pay homage to Lenin's mummified corpse.

Curiously, the Church/state split that sprang from the Russian Revolution was not always most visible in Russia itself. The Orthodox Church's links with the *ancien régime* were too blatant to make it an effective defender of that regime. Over 100,000 priests had been reliant on the state, and others were dependent on what they could squeeze out of the peasantry in fees for their services. The Church was generally seen as an agent of repression rather than as a representative of the people. Father Gapon, who led demonstrators to the Winter Palace in 1905, was an isolated case – and even he ended up working as a police informer. Peasant religion, with its tendency to blend saints and icons into a pre-Christian pantheistic culture, sometimes had little to do with official dogma.

Unlike Roman Catholicism, Orthodoxy tended to lose touch with peasants who moved to the town: one Moscow industrial suburb had just one
church for a population of 40,000.

In the short term, the Church's links with Tsarism ensured that it was regarded with hostility. Church and state were separated in January 1918 and
in 1921 Lenin used the need to raise money for famine relief as an excuse to
seize Church property and persecute priests who resisted. The regime also
supported the campaign of the "living church" dissidents against the senior
celibate "black" clergy. However, in the long run, the Orthodox Church's
tradition of deference to the state and its lack of interest in popular mobilization were as useful to the Bolsheviks as they had been to their Tsarist predecessors. Furthermore, Russian nationalism sometimes brought Orthodoxy
and Bolshevism together. In 1926, Soviet officials and Red Army generals
joined chanting priests at Marshal Brusilov's funeral in the Novodechie
monastery.[29] The link between communism, nationalism and Orthodoxy
became most pronounced during the Second World War. On September 4,
1943, Stalin, who had been educated in a seminary, received the Patriarch at
the Kremlin and decreed the restoration of the Holy Synod.[30]

Communism's real enemy was not Orthodoxy but Roman Catholicism, and in some ways this enmity sprang from similarity. Catholicism
and communism were both disciplined international movements. Authority in the Catholic Church was more centralized than ever before: in
1931, the papacy even established its own radio station to communicate
instructions directly to the faithful.[31] Mussolini referred to the "rival Vat-
icans of Rome and Moscow." Pius XI, Pope from 1922 to 1939, had
served as Papal Nuncio to Poland during that country's war with Soviet
Russia and had acquired what one Catholic politician described as "an almost physical horror of Bolshevism." The Catholic Church was often the
most prominent member of anticommunist alliances: when people talked
of "clerical" regimes or "Christian democracy" they were always referring
to bodies associated with Catholicism.

Catholicism's success as a counterrevolutionary movement was
founded on the perception that it was not simply the instrument of the
powerful and privileged. Protestants and the various strands of Orthodoxy had strong traditions of respect for the state, which made them reluctant to venture into independent political action, whereas Catholicism
had always emphasized that the commands of the Church took precedence over secular authority. Before 1914, the Catholic Church had been
in conflict with the state in France and Italy. The link between the
Church's perceived history of opposition and its capacity for popular politics was revealed in Germany. In Bavaria, until 1918, the monarch was
Catholic and the Catholic Church was, in effect, the established church.

In the rest of Germany, Catholicism was a minority religion that had been persecuted during Bismarck's *Kulturkampf*, but after the First World War, the Christian democrat Bavarian People's Party obtained the votes of only 56 percent of practicing Catholics while the Christian democrat Centre Party, operating in the rest of Germany, obtained the votes of 70 percent of practicing Catholics. Generally speaking, the Church's influence was inversely proportional to the closeness of its perceived links with secular authority.

After the First World War, the Church usually sought to secure its interests in noncommunist countries through agreement with secular powers, but it maintained the capacity to turn against them. In 1931, the Pope suggested that those required to take an oath of loyalty to the Italian Fascist state should do so "with inner reservations." The independence of the Catholic Church was underwritten by the nature of its representatives. A steady stream of bright peasant boys was recruited to the priesthood, and seminaries gave such recruits a good, if limited, education and a respect for authority. Clerical celibacy ensured that priests were relatively indifferent to their material interests, which meant that Catholic priests could present themselves as leaders of peasant or even workers' movements with a degree of credibility. An Anglican hunting parson with a large rectory and two sons at Marlborough, or a member of the Russian Orthodox noncelibate "white" clergy, squeezing every last ruble out of his sullen parishioners, could not match such behavior.

Even Pius XI did not initially rule out the possibility that the Church might achieve some *modus vivendi* with the Soviet state; indeed, the Church seems to have considered the possibility that the weakening of Orthodoxy during the Russian Revolution might open up chances for missionary work by the Roman Church. Relations between the Church and the left deteriorated as part of the general radicalization of politics that came with economic depression. The papacy marked the abandonment of its missionary efforts in the Soviet Union with an expiatory Mass for Russia in 1930.[32] The following year, the Austrian League of Religious Socialists was dissolved.[33] Also in 1931, the Pope published the encyclical *Quadragesimo Anno*, which was widely interpreted as a model and justification for the corporatist organizations of authoritarian states in Portugal, Austria, Spain and Vichy France. The conflict between political Catholicism and the left first spilt blood in 1934, when forces directed by the Christian Social Party suppressed those of the socialists in Austria. In 1936, the Church and the left came into conflict in Spain. Almost 7,000 members of religious orders were killed by the left during the Civil War. In 1937, the Nationalists defined the state that they wished to create as a Catholic one, and all but three Spanish prelates expressed support for the forces of General Franco, though the Vatican did not recognize Franco as head of government until after the Republican forces had been defeated. Some Catholics in Spain, especially Basques, and a few Christian democrats in western Europe, such as Georges Bidault in France, supported the Republic, but Catholic opinion across Europe was overwhelmingly mobilized in support of the Spanish Nationalists.[34]

Catholic politics in Europe were never entirely uniform. The Vatican's main concern was to ensure that Catholics in various European countries were allowed to practice their religion and to exercise certain rights, especially over education. Good relations with any power willing to guarantee such privileges were not ruled out. In pursuit of such relations, the Vatican signed concordats with a variety of governments during the interwar period, the most important being that with Mussolini's Italy in February 1929, which compensated the Church for land taken by the Italian state, extended religious education, recognized Church marriage and granted the Pope sovereign power in the area around Vatican City. Concordats were also concluded with Bavaria (1924), Poland (1925), Romania and Lithuania (1927), Prussia (1929), Baden (1932), Nazi Germany (1933), Yugoslavia (1937) and Portugal (1940).

Papal diplomacy and Catholic politics were not synonymous. The Catholic Church was disciplined but could not exercise total control over every aspect of the lives of its followers, and the Vatican, unlike the Third International, did not have the power to shoot dissidents. Divisions also existed between national churches and Rome. Bishops, who were linked to the ruling classes of their own country, often regarded previous political orders with nostalgia, while the Pope's diplomatic *Realpolitik* encouraged him to come to terms with whatever regime was in power. Austrian bishops regretted the fall of the Habsburgs, and the Archbishop of Salzburg remained in contact with the exiled pretender to the Austrian throne. More serious divisions were caused when the papacy condemned the royalist Action Française in 1926 – the decision enraged many Catholics and one French cardinal was forced to resign because of his refusal to support Vatican policy. Within national churches, there were further rifts between lower clergy and bishops.

There was also a division between the policies pursued by clergy and the activities of secular Catholics. Catholic Action, founded in the early 1920s, brought together devout laymen and stressed that its activities were independent of both party politics and the direct control of the Church hierarchy. Many Catholic politicians claimed that their activity was religiously inspired: Salazar made much of his Jesuit education, and Franco restored many of the Church's powers in Spain. Pétain was not a man of great personal devotion, but his regime removed some of the anticlerical policies that had been enforced by the Third Republic and was greeted with enthusiasm by many French churchmen.

Not all Catholic politicians opposed democracy. Some parties that worked in the democratic system were explicitly Christian in inspiration – the Belgian Parti Catholique, the German Centre Party, the Italian Popular Party (PPI) and the French Parti Démocrate Populaire. Some parties were led by priests – Jean Desgranges headed the Parti Démocrate Populaire, Luigi Sturzo led the PPI, and Joseph Zender became the first cleric to head the Centre Party in Germany. However, such parties and politicians were not simply the representatives of the Church. It was made clear that secular parties acted independently and had no power to engage the Church. The Vatican signed its concordat with Mussolini even after Sturzo had gone into exile.

Christian parties presented themselves as opponents of class war who denounced both socialism and unrestricted capitalism and, partly as a result, tended to do well in countries that were populated largely by intermediate social groups such as peasants, artisans and small shop keepers. They often occupied a hinge position between right and left and were thus able to extract concessions that were disproportionate to the number of seats that they held in parliament. They also fitted in with Catholic networks of patronage and the need to find jobs in a growing state apparatus for peasant boys from devout families whose education at Catholic schools had made them disinclined to return to the farm. The result was spectacular corruption. Konrad Adenauer, Centre Party mayor of Cologne, became famous for his generosity with public money – he appointed his brother-in-law as city treasurer.[35] Georges Simenon parodied the way in which a Belgian politician was approached with a request for a favor: "He is a good boy, a good Catholic and a good voter."[36]

No single party had a monopoly of Christian support and even in Italy more than one explicitly Christian party competed for the votes of the faithful.[37] In France, Jeune République provided a more socially radical alternative to the Parti Démocrate Populaire, while the Fédération Républicaine attracted more Catholic votes than either, and in Belgium the Parti Catholique lost votes in 1936 to the recently established and more dynamic Rexists.[38]

Relations between the Catholic Church and the politicians who claimed to represent its interests were never simple. Even those regimes that claimed to defend the Church's interests most vigorously, such as those of Pétain and Salazar, did not remove all the anticlerical measures of their predecessors. In Croatia, the Catholic peasant leader Radić welcomed the spread of the Eastern Rite in the hope that it would diminish the influence of the Church hierarchy. For its part, the Church was suspicious of politicians.

Pietro Gasparri, the Vatican secretary, remarked that the PPI was merely the "least bad" of political parties.[39] In some cases, as in the Croatian elections of 1938, priests were forbidden from playing a direct role in politics.

Fascism presented particular problems for the Catholic Church. Mussolini and the German Nazis had records of anticlericalism, and sought to establish control of areas that the Church considered its own domain. Nazism and eventually Italian Fascism distinguished between people on the basis of race rather than religious belief – hence the persecution of baptized Jews. Nazi ideologists explicitly denounced Christianity and proposed an alternative form of religion based on their own rituals and myths, and Nazi leaders, especially Rosenberg, sought to intervene in Church organization and even theology. On the other hand, both Nazism and Italian Fascism were willing to tolerate religion, and both regimes signed concordats with the Vatican. Furthermore, both movements were strong opponents of communism, which seemed to be the greatest threat to Catholicism.

In such circumstances, Catholicism and fascism entered an uneasy cohabitation, which brought considerable benefits to the Church in Italy, where it was unified, intertwined with the institutions of Italian society and untroubled by the presence of rival denominations. Religious practice in Fascist Italy increased – Catholic Action came to have 2 million members, and the number of pupils in Church schools increased from 31,000 in 1927 to 104,000 by 1940.[40] Relations cooled only when the government interfered in Church youth organizations and Catholic Action. In many respects, the Church could limit and control Fascism's attempt to create a totalitarian state. Most significantly, the existence of an independent Vatican City in the heart of Fascism's capital exposed the limits on Mussolini's power and provided a haven for some Christian democrat politicians, such as Alcide de Gasperi.

In Germany, the gulf between the Church and the regime was wider. Possibilities for Christian resistance were limited in a country where the Catholic Church represented only a minority of the population and where its Protestant rivals were influenced by Lutheran ideas about the primacy of secular authority. The churches resisted the Nazi extermination of the handicapped and made less effective protests about Nazi racial policies, but their most pressing concern was the institutional defense of the Church itself. The Centre Party effectively voted itself out of existence soon after the Nazi seizure of power, and senior churchmen were rarely seen as serious opponents by the regime.

Relations between Catholics and fascists outside Germany and Italy were closer. Devout Catholics, such as the Austrian Nazi Artur von Seyss-Inquart, often led violent movements that lent active support to Nazi

Germany, and the Hungarian Arrow Cross, the Romanian Iron Guard and the Belgian Rexists all had strong support among Catholics. In France, Philippe Henriot, who became Vichy's chief of propaganda when the regime moved closer to Nazi Germany, was a Catholic, and the Prime Minister of independent Slovakia (established under Nazi aegis from 1938 to 1945) was a Catholic priest, Josef Tiso. Sometimes the combination of Christian piety and fascist engagement had grotesque results. The rulers of independent Croatia were much influenced by Archbishop Stepinac's campaign against bad language: the new state made swearing a criminal offense and imposed a thirty-day prison sentence for all offenders; at the same time, the Minister of Education was boasting of his intention to exterminate one-third of all his country's Orthodox inhabitants.

Conclusion

Focusing on the violence of interwar politics can be deceptive. Large areas – mainland Britain, Sweden, Denmark – were almost untouched by political violence. Equally, it can be deceptive to assume that the violence of the interwar years was exceptional: politics in parts of eastern and central Europe had been violent before 1914 and in some cases would become even more so between 1945 and 1953. The fate of the Bulgarian peasant leader Petko Petkov, assassinated on June 14, 1924, was anything but unusual – his father, Dimitri, had been assassinated in 1907 and his brother, Nikola, was to be hanged by the communists in 1947.

Generally, however, interwar Europe saw high levels of political violence, which distinguished it from the years before 1914 or after 1945. There are three broad reasons. First, after the Russian Revolution and the establishment of a Bolshevik state, every member of the European bourgeoisie looked anxiously at the left in their own countries as a potential source of revolution. Europe's political frontiers had yet to be frozen by Yalta and the atomic bomb, and communism was seen as something that would arrive as a result of internal subversion rather than foreign conquest. The threat of communism in turn stimulated support for radical right counteroffensives, which further exacerbated conflict. Political language was polarized and pushed to such extremes that Ramsay MacDonald could be denounced as a "social fascist" by the left only shortly after having been described as a Bolshevik by some Conservatives.

The second foundation of internal conflict between 1917 and 1945 was economic. The period before 1914 had been one of rapid economic growth and the period after 1945 would be another one. Interwar economies, by contrast, grew only slowly. Some declined. Crisis was particularly severe in agriculture, which made up a large part of the economy in Spain, Portugal and eastern Europe. Those engaged in violent political conflict rarely expressed their demands in economic terms: the leaders of the radical left would have denied that capitalist systems were capable of producing worthwhile material advances, while the leaders of the radical right would have denied that they were interested in material benefits. However, many of those who supported the two sides clearly had grievances that could have been solved with money. The problem was not simply one of large-scale unemployment in the aftermath of the Wall Street Crash, which Great Britain and the United States both experienced without being afflicted by violent political conflict. Political crises were most severe in countries with long-term economic problems that dated back to before 1929, which was the case in all economies that depended heavily on agriculture and also in those countries, notably Germany, that had never managed to stabilize public finance after the First World War.

The third source of civil war was international war. Civil wars and international wars were very different and sometimes mutually exclusive, but the two forms of conflict were linked. The Russian Revolution led to Russia's withdrawal from the First World War, but was also a product of that war; the Vichy government withdrew France from the Second World War but it and its opponents were products of that war. International conflict repeatedly provoked domestic conflict, exacerbated economic problems and encouraged dissatisfied groups in many countries to look abroad for help.

These pan-European sources of conflict did not, of course, operate in the same way in every country. Levels of violence varied from place to place and at different times. Similarly, the nature of conflict varied. There was not a single struggle of left versus right: indeed, the most violent battles were often those that took place within the right and the left. Political violence sometimes divided families: Franco sentenced his first cousin to death,[41] and Pétain allowed a death sentence to be passed on Charles de Gaulle, his former protégé and the father of his godson. The broad conflicts of the interwar period caused such violence precisely because they overlapped and interacted with a variety of conflicts specific to each country.

5
MODERN TIMES

"He then discourses upon what Bolshevism will mean to central Europe. Work and happiness for all, free education, doctors, Bernard Shaw, garden suburbs, heaps of music, and the triumph of the machine. I ask him what machine? He makes a vague gesture embracing the whole world of mechanics."

Bolshevik commissar, speaking to Harold Nicolson
at Budapest railway station in 1919[1]

THE AFTERMATH OF the First World War saw the birth of a culture that revolved around machines. The importance of motor cars, aeroplanes, radios and telephones had been demonstrated during the war and such technologies were now put to civilian use. Cinema – itself a new technology particularly suited to the representation of rapid movement – captured Europe's obsession with record-breaking flights and fast cars. Machines were built in large, well-equipped factories that lent themselves to new forms of management and the organization of work. Sometimes reorganization on such a scale involved the state and new economic policies as well as new managerial techniques. Often machines were the objects of a new consumer culture or the means by which consumer goods could be produced.

Motor cars illustrated the impact of such changes. Their influence extended beyond ensuring that people could get from one place to another. Car factories had sprung up on a huge scale between 1914 and 1919, and plants such as the Renault works in Boulogne Billancourt or the Fiat works in Turin employed tens of thousands of workers and became centers of industrial conflict. The fact that such plants were built from scratch made them seem particularly propitious for new management techniques. Henry Ford became especially associated with such techniques, and his plants in Highland Park and River Rouge were places of pilgrimage for European industrialists. Ford's book, *My Life and Work*, was published in 1922 and translated into all the major European languages – the German editions had sold 200,000 copies by the end of the 1920s, and Adolf Hitler read it in prison following the failure of the Munich putsch.[2]

Economic variations

It could be objected that the machine age symbolized by the motor car had little impact on the lives of the majority of Europe's inhabitants. In 1925, there were 17 million cars in the United States, about 1 million in Britain, rather more than 500,000 in France and 255,000 in Germany. Further east, mechanization was less advanced. The city of Magnitogorsk was supposed to epitomize industrial modernity in the Soviet Union, but in 1933, when the town's population exceeded 80,000, it contained only 500 motor vehicles.[3]

An emphasis on technological modernization may suggest that there was only one kind of economy in interwar Europe. In reality, there were at least three. The first was agriculture, which dominated most east European nations and played a large role in Spain, Italy and Portugal. Often farms were too small to make the use of tractors, threshing machines or combine harvesters practicable. Peasants would have been too poor to use anything beyond the techniques of their grandfathers, even if they had known about them. Agriculture also occupied an important place in highly developed countries, where its importance was as much political as economic. Inefficient farms might not make money, but they did provide jobs: almost one-third of Germans drew their living from agriculture in the mid-1920s, although it only accounted for around one-sixth of net domestic production.[4] Particular kinds of agriculture had political leverage – in Germany, the large-scale farmers of East Prussia; in France, peasants. The political power of agriculture meant that the suppression of inefficient farming methods was easiest after democracy itself had been suspended, as happened in the Soviet Union and even under regimes, such as Hitler's, that had come to power pledging support for agriculture. Many of the political problems of interwar continental Europe can be traced back to the fact that agriculture was politically powerful and socially important without being economically viable.

The second kind of economy in interwar Europe was based on the heavy industries of the nineteenth century – coal, iron and steel – that dominated northern England, Wales, the Ruhr, Belgium and northern France. Like agriculture, most of these industries were already in difficulty before 1929. Production had increased to unsustainable levels during the First World War. After this, there was a glut, and matters were made worse by growing competition from economies with lower labor costs. Old industries sometimes invested in new equipment – increasing amounts of coal were cut by machine rather than by physical labor – but established industries generally suffered from the problems of old plants and limited funds for new investment. European factories often seemed to owe more to the imagination of Charles Dickens than that of Henry Ford. Heavy industry, like agriculture, was protected from the full impact of economic change by politics. Many governments wanted to ensure that they had an adequate supply of coal and iron because of their value in war, which partly explains why the Soviet Union dedicated so much effort to developing such industries. During the 1930s, military considerations became ever more important and began to overrule conventional business thinking. Hermann Goering's four-year plan of 1936 increased German production even when, as in the case of iron ore, it would have been cheaper to import. War production was rarely associated with modernization. The need for armaments meant that iron and steel manufacturers could sell to the state and not worry about the marketing and design that obsessed newer industries. War, and the preparation for war, also meant that resources for new investment became scarcer and that industrialists were reluctant to spend money to provide for a market that would not last. The French coal industry increased production during the Second World War, but did so by opening poor-quality seams and applying harsh discipline to inexperienced and unskilled workers – techniques that could not be sustained in peacetime.

The third economy comprised the new industries that had emerged after the First World War. These industries took up a small part of the European labor force. Not only were they completely absent from many countries but even in highly developed economies they were confined to certain regions, such as the Midlands and the southeast of England, the industrial suburbs around Paris and northern Italy. Such industries did not form part of the traditional establishment and were often excluded from existing networks of influence, but their newness meant that they often developed close relations with new political movements, notably those of the extreme right. IG Farben, the chemicals combine, was so intimately associated with the Nazi regime that its managers were put on trial along with Nazi leaders at Nuremberg.[5] Louis Renault was the most prominent French industrialist associated with acceptance of the German new order in his country, while in Italy, the managers of Magneti Marelli cultivated close relations with Fascism.[6]

Such economic divisions undermine any attempt to impose a neat chronology on interwar economic history. It is sometimes assumed that the Wall Street Crash of 1929 separated the prosperous roaring twenties from the hungry thirties. In fact, Germany, where there had been heavy investment during the 1920s based on short-term loans from America, was the only part of continental Europe to experience a sharp downturn as an immediate response to the Wall Street Crash, and her economy had already begun to recover by the time Hitler reaped the political harvest of economic discontent in 1933. The primarily agricultural economies of eastern Europe were already in depression before 1929. France, by contrast, and in spite of her largely agricultural economy, survived the beginning of the depression well, and until 1932 some financiers dreamed that Paris might replace London as the financial center of Europe. After this, economic activity declined, but the impact of this crisis was less severe, though longer lasting, than that felt in Germany. France's limited population and the scope for dumping the worst consequences of recession on women and immigrants (neither group possessed the vote) meant that France never faced mass male unemployment.

Some industries, regions and social groups continued to do well throughout the "depression." Magneti Marelli had suffered badly from the loss of export markets after Mussolini's revaluation of the lira in 1926, but thereafter expanded production during the 1930s, as did many consumer industries in Britain. The English middle class benefited from falling prices and new technology. A. J. P. Taylor's investment portfolio, begun with £2,000 at the bottom of the slump, combined with his academic salary to give him a total annual income of £900, and he used the money to buy a record player, an electric cooker and a car.[7] The reconstitution of English bourgeois fortunes during this period could be even more spectacular. Maynard Keynes lost most of his money in 1929, but by 1936 had accumulated half a million pounds.

Machine culture

The fact that modern production did not account for a very large proportion of European production or employment does not mean that the idea of a machine age should be dismissed. Technology may not have had much direct impact on the material circumstances of most Europeans, but it had a vast influence on the culture of Europe's educated classes and on the ambitions of her rulers. Machines provided new metaphors in which economic life was discussed; Keynes wrote: "We have magneto trouble. How, then, can we start up again?"[8] New technology influenced artistic life. Le Corbusier based his architecture on ocean liners and the need to create "machines for living," while Aldous Huxley's novel *Brave New World* (1932) described a society that worshipped "Our Ford," in which everything, including babies, was manufactured on a production line, and in which eugenic science underwrote managerial hierarchies, dividing unskilled "Epsilon Minus" workers from "Alpha Plus" technocrats. The machine age produced new words to describe factory management and economic policy: rationalization, modernization, planning and corporatism. Such words were vague and could mean very different things; even the more precise terms derived from the work of particular men – "Stakhanovism," "Fordism," "Taylorism" and the "Bedaux system" – were often misused. Indeed, the very vagueness of such language accounts for its ubiquity: it could be adjusted to fit different contexts.

Technology sometimes had the greatest influence on culture and language in countries where it had a comparatively small influence on industry, and vice versa. The two most dramatic political movements to emerge out of the First World War – Soviet communism and Italian Fascism – were fascinated by technological modernity. Fascists celebrated fast cars and trans-Atlantic flights; communists looked to the economic possibilities of tractors, hydroelectric projects and shining model factories. In some ways, the cultural and political importance that technology assumed in both countries was due to the fact that Italy and Russia were so technologically backward. By contrast, in Great Britain, the most technologically advanced country in Europe, "ruralism," simplicity and "old world charm" were more likely to be celebrated than modernity. This produced a curious situation in which English writers looked to more backward countries as representatives of the machine age. Wyndham Lewis remarked, of Italian futurism: "You wops insist too much on the machine."[9]

Taylorization, Fordism and the rationalization of production

The impact of machines was first felt in the organization of production. Mechanization and rationalization of production had been discussed in the United States before the First World War. In 1903, Frederick Winslow Taylor had written an article on "shop management" in which he called for factories to be organized by experts working from carefully thought-out principles rather than by tradition, instinct, and the arbitrary decisions of foremen or proprietors. Such ideas had their most dramatic impact in American motor factories, particularly at Ford's plant in Detroit, but they also attracted attention in Europe, especially after the First World War.

In Taylorite projects, the rationalization of work effected other changes. In terms of technology, it brought modernity: rational factories used the most up-to-date machinery – such as the turret lathe and the conveyor belt – and often produced new machines. In terms of corporate structure, it brought larger economic units, because only large companies could afford to invest in new equipment and hire experts. In terms of the workforce, it brought a shift from blue-collar to white-collar employment, as large clerical workforces were needed to process the written rules and complicated reward structures that replaced informal decisions. In terms of power, it brought a reduction in working-class autonomy: craftsmen who had been free to carry out a wide variety of tasks on their own initiative were replaced by workers who were trained to do only a few simple tasks, and foremen who had been responsible for many decisions about hiring, firing and discipline were constrained by formal procedures. The reduction of worker autonomy was most graphically illustrated in the use of assembly lines, whereby the job of each worker was reduced to the repeated performance of a single task and the speed of production was determined entirely by the management.

The rationalization of work was discussed not only by managers and industrial experts but by left-wingers such as Gramsci and Lenin. Even housework was to be rationalized. The Italian National Agency for the Scientific Organization of Work (founded in 1926) produced a journal entitled *Home and Work*.[10] The French engineer Jean Coutrot claimed that France's energy shortage could be solved by persuading housewives to place their saucepans at the center of gas rings.

Rationalized production restructured management hierarchies, factory layout and even the hairstyles of employees. The results could be beyond satire. Charlie Chaplin could never have dreamed up the German office that tried to pay typists by the syllable or the use of light music to set the pace on assembly lines;[11] one English biscuit manufacturer found that foxtrots produced the best results.[12] Orwell chose the Swiss roll as a characteristically graphic image to epitomize the horrors of the machine age,[13] but not even he could have imagined the Lyons factory where twenty-six miles of it slid off the production line every day.[14] The impact of rationalization on the economic, as opposed to the cultural, history of interwar Europe was limited, though. Furthermore, far from being a set of universal scientific principles, rationalization techniques were often refracted through the particular circumstances of individual European countries and applied in ways that bore little relation to the original intentions of the movement's American founders. Taylorization had been devised in an expanding economy with a great reserve of natural resources. Many

American factories were built from scratch in the early twentieth century and therefore designed according to the requirements of new techniques. American business culture was also built from scratch during the early twentieth century, as graduates from new business schools such as Wharton (founded in 1881) and Harvard (founded in 1908) began their careers.[15] Finally, America did not possess strong working-class traditions; there were few craftsmen to guard their skills, and the trade unions that might have protected such privileges were relatively weak.

The interwar European economy fitted none of these conditions. Most production took place in buildings, and often with machinery that had been designed decades before the work of F. W. Taylor. Unions were strong, and even in countries where unions were repressed, such as Fascist Italy, production was often constrained by tacit agreements between workers and managers. Furthermore, the European economy was not growing quickly. In such circumstances, European "Taylorism" often became a means to squeeze more labor out of workers rather than to reorganize production for the benefit of all. For many European industrialists, ideas of scientific management came not directly from Taylor but were mediated by the theories of Charles Bedaux, who produced a scheme that placed a heavier emphasis on the simple speeding-up of work. In 1918, Bedaux established a consultancy in Britain and, by 1937, had 1,100 clients, of whom 200 were British and 150 were French.[16] The crude manner in which most European companies applied such ideas was highlighted by the activities of "revisionist" Taylorites in the United States.[17] While Bedaux and his associates produced a simpler and more disciplinarian version of Taylorism for European consumption, the American revisionist Taylorites were trying to produce a more humane version of rationalization to take more account of workers' needs.

Local cultures influenced the extent and manner of rationalization. Germany had a strong tradition of technical training, the products of which were keen to promote ideas that would increase their status, but the German emphasis on technological rationality did not always produce economic rationality. Novelty and size were often pursued for the sake of prestige rather than profits. Some believed that Germany was particularly vulnerable to depression after the Wall Street Crash of 1929 because such large amounts of money had been tied up in highly expensive projects of dubious value.

Britain presented a sharp contrast to Germany: in 1910, there were only 3,000 British students of science and technology, compared with 25,000 such students in Germany.[18] In Britain, financial rather than technical considerations remained paramount, and "rationalization," which was associated with the professionalization of engineering in America and Germany, was associated with the professionalization of accountancy in Britain.[19]

France lay between the British and German models. She had good engineering schools, but the most prestigious of these, the École Polytechnique, was designed to train sappers and artillery officers. Even though more than half of *polytechniciens* worked in private industry by 1939, the institution never accepted commercial values and its graduates placed technical expertise and loyalty to each other above normal business considerations. Furthermore, they often found their niche in large companies that depended on state contracts, so political contacts were as important as technical ability or commercial acumen. This was illustrated between 1940 and 1944 under the Vichy government, which, more than any other regime in Europe, represented the political triumph of engineers. Jean Bichelonne, Minister of Industrial Production, had graduated with the highest ever marks from the École Polytechnique. The economic bodies established by the new government used the language of efficiency and planning, but in reality, as one industrialist pointed out, such agencies were as much designed to create employment for men like himself as to achieve any useful economic progress.[20] In 1943, in conjunction with his fellow *polytechnicien* and head of the coal industry Aimé Lepercq, Bichelonne arranged to establish a special mine near St.-Étienne to which Polytechnique students could be sent to prevent them from being deported to Germany.

Workers often managed to circumvent the new techniques that were designed to leave them powerless. Even in factories that conducted "scientific" recruitment tests, candidates were presented to foremen by relatives.[21] Workers deliberately slowed down when watched by time-and-motion experts so that work rates would be set at a tolerable pace, hid finished components that could be used to cover up slower work later, and sabotaged conveyor belts to get themselves a break.

Workers also went on strike to defend their position. Sometimes strikes, such as those at Magneti Marelli in the 1920s, were designed to work within the limits of scientific management – that is, to raise the rates paid for a particular kind of work[22] – but other strikes, such as those in the French coal fields in 1941, were directed against the principle of scientific management. Strikes were also organized across many industries, the most famous example being the British General Strike of 1926, although they also occurred after the First World War (particularly in France and Italy) and after Popular Front election victories in 1936 (in France and Spain). These strike waves were facilitated by legal trade unions and in some cases by left-wing governments that were sympathetic to the strikers and unwilling to use force against them. Some industrialists supported authoritarian regimes in the hope that they would make strikes more difficult. However, labor power was not linked only to formal regulations. An authoritarian government might dissolve trade unions and imprison their leaders, but such action did not prevent slow work, absenteeism, job-changing and unofficial strikes, all of which might force employers to make concessions to their workers. Labor power often depended on economic circumstances or the organization of the workplace rather than on the formal role of trade unions. In the 1920s, British coal miners were weakened by the fact that there was overproduction in their industry throughout Europe, and French workers went on strike less during the economic decline of the 1930s, though it is not clear whether that was because of the fear of unemployment or simply because those in work saw their living standards rise as a result of falling prices. By contrast, coal miners in Nazi-occupied Europe benefited from general economic circumstances – the war economy needed coal – and the fact that even the Gestapo found it difficult to exercise control in narrow seams several hundred feet below the ground.

New ways of organizing work did not always produce powerless "deskilled" workers. Sometimes they simply reconfigured skills. Thus the total number of skilled workers in the British food industry remained the same even when established skills – such as baking – had been displaced by new technology.[23] Production lines created new needs for expert, autonomous workers to provide repair and maintenance services. At Magneti Marelli, repair workers wore special badges to allow them to move from one workshop to another, and thus escape the tight control imposed on other workers.[24] Production lines could become blocked if one worker fell behind, which created a need for fast operatives to sort out a backlog of work or fill in while their colleagues were unavailable. At the EMI factory in Middlesex, some women – given the undignified title of "piddle breakers" – were employed to stand in while others went to the toilet.[25]

Concepts of skill were ambiguous. Sometimes, such definitions owed more to cultural or social circumstances than to the specific tasks performed – jobs done by women were often downgraded. New industries also required new skills. On the one hand, they were less likely to require apprentice-trained craftsmen; on the other, the formal rules of a modern factory demanded literacy. Magneti Marelli workers were more literate than most inhabitants of the Milan region, and literacy rates were particularly high among women (who were almost all "unskilled" workers).[26] Workers often possessed "tacit" skills passed on by workmates or picked up on the job.

If "rationalized" production was designed to remove power from workers, who was expected to inherit it? "Capitalists" might be one answer to this question, but it was not the answer that many contemporaries gave.

Frederick Winslow Taylor himself stressed that his techniques were not designed simply to increase return on capital: "Personally my experience has been so unsatisfactory with financiers that I never want to work for any of them . . . As a rule, financiers are looking merely for a turnover. They want to get in and out of their business quickly, and they have absolutely *no pride of manufacture.*"[27] Engineers throughout Europe shared his distaste for "finance" and in some countries, such as Hungary, this took an anti-Semitic form.[28] Taylor saw his world as one in which decisions would pass from capitalists, who owed their position to wealth, to experts, who owed their position to training and qualifications. In 1926 Keynes noted that "the owners of the capital, i.e., the shareholders, are almost entirely dissociated from the management, with the result that the direct personal interest of the latter in the making of great profit becomes quite secondary."[29] The spread of Taylorist ideas was associated with the growing power of the engineering profession and the rise of formal management education. Managers were seen as detached and rational, capable of making decisions that advanced the long-term interests of the firm, and perhaps even of society, rather than the short-term interests of a particular industrialist.

The impact of managerialism was not always as clear as some hoped. Although large firms were increasingly likely to be run by men with a high degree of technical training rather than by those who owned the company, there was no necessary correlation between technological "modernity" and managerial "modernity." French coal mines were modern in terms of managerial culture – they were run by an elite corps of engineers with an almost total separation between management and ownership – but they were backward in terms of equipment and working practices. By contrast, the French car industry was modern in terms of technology, but operated by "old-fashioned" authoritarian owner-bosses such as Louis Renault.

Modern training and traditional recruitment sometimes fused as owners' sons were sent to acquire technical training. The most highly trained manager was often obliged to advance his career in the most traditional manner – by marrying the boss's daughter. Bruno Antonio Quintavalle looked like the epitome of modern managerial expertise – he had studied commerce in Milan and worked in London – but he was a mere clerk until he married the daughter of the proprietor of the firm for which he worked, at which point he was promoted and granted a dowry of 40,000,000 lire. Three years later, he was managing director of Magneti Marelli.[30] The novelist Italo Svevo also began his career with a long period of formal business training, partly undertaken in Germany, but he gained a partnership in a Trieste company because his father-in-law owned the firm. In France, almost two-thirds of a sample of managers between 1912 and 1973 admitted that they had benefited from "useful family contacts."[31]

Managerialism contained a number of contradictions. Its apostles saw the professional manager as a detached, open-minded person who reflected widely on a range of issues. In reality, those who rose up through managerial hierarchies as a result of their own efforts could rarely afford such virtues. They were too absorbed by the specialized decisions of everyday business life and by the need to confront immediate problems. By the time they reached the top they were old men, and the sacrifices that they had made did not incline them to countenance ideas that might challenge their authority. The people with the leisure to spend time in discussion groups or reading reviews on scientific management were the sons, or sons-in-law, of businessmen, who did not have to strive for their position. Men such as Jean Coutrot in France or Walther Rathenau in Germany were more interested in talking about new ideas than in the humdrum business of running a company.

Rationalization in the Soviet Union

The rationalization of work in western Europe was paralleled and thrown into relief by developments in the Soviet Union. Some Soviet leaders had always regarded Western productivity with admiration. Lenin said in 1920: "The Russian is a bad worker compared with the advanced peoples."[32] The very fact that most Russian production took place in conditions far removed from the factories of Chicago gave rationalization a special romance. The leading evangelist of Taylorization in the Soviet Union, Alexei Gastev, was a poet as well as an engineer.

Rationalization in the Soviet Union ran into several problems. The formally trained technicians on which Taylorism depended were conspicuously absent: at the height of Soviet industrialization, only 38 percent of engineers had undergone higher education, while 41 percent were *praktiki* who had picked up their skills on the job.[33] Most technicians and foremen were also *praktiki*. Soviet rationalization was influenced by three considerations. The first was the need to break up the old peasant-based *artel* working group, and in order to achieve this, Soviet managers often carried the Taylorite idea of specialization to much greater lengths than had been attempted in the West. The 12 crafts of metalwork in 1930 had been broken down into 176 by 1939.[34] Subdivision was sometimes counterproductive, and refusal to accept responsibility outside precise limits was one of the ways in which Soviet workers resisted their managers.

The second constraint on Soviet rationalization was political. In the West, rationalization was associated with the "apolitical" expertise of "technocrats," but the Soviet Union, where industrial mobilization was explicitly tied to a political purpose, could not tolerate "apoliticism." The fact that many engineers were not party members caused persistent problems, and policy swung between toleration of "bourgeois specialists" and fierce persecution. Engineers were accused of sabotage when progress seemed slow. Some Soviet companies were run by two-man teams in which a committed and authoritarian but poorly educated "red director" worked in tandem with an engineer.

The third peculiarity of rationalization in the Soviet Union was the role of workers. Soviet workers were presented as active and enthusiastic participants in increasing productivity, rather than as mere subjects of time-and-motion studies. During the 1920s, "shock brigades" volunteered to carry out extra tasks and pushed to raise productivity. In 1932, a miner, Iztov, greatly exceeded his quota of coal cut; he was subsequently treated as a hero and schools were founded to propagate his ideas. In 1937, Stakhanov, another miner, extracted over 100 tonnes of coal – fourteen times his normal quota – during a single shift. Stakhanov inspired a wider movement. "Stakhanovite" workers were used to raise production in plants and to set targets for their colleagues. They were given extra pay, special privileges and much publicity. In many respects, Stakhanovism contrasted with Taylorism, emerging after a period of rapid economic expansion and the state-planning experiments of the early 1930s, whereas Taylorism had been devised for an economy in the process of expansion and preceded experiments in state planning. Stakhanovism presented the worker as a heroic individual, while Taylorism sought to turn him into an anonymous cog in a machine, and whereas Taylorism enhanced the authority of managers, engineers and "experts," Stakhanovism seems to have been devised partly to curb such people's power, which had grown during the early period of Stalinist industrialization.

The differences between Stakhanovism and Taylorism were sometimes more apparent than real. Once the rhetoric of "science" had been stripped away from the latter and the rhetoric of "proletarian dedication" had been stripped away from the former, both provided a means to squeeze more labor out of workers. Both depended on rewards to encourage productivity. Far from marking a break with either the Russian past or the capitalist present, Stakhanovism was often a continuation of techniques that could be traced back to the earliest period of Bolshevik rule and were associated with the early Soviet leaders' admiration for the industrial achievements of the West. Finally, "Stakhanovism," like Taylorism, was rarely applied. Workers in the Soviet Union resisted labor rationalization even more vigorously than their counterparts in the West. An American who worked in a Russian factory dismissed shock workers as the "smoothest boot lickers,"[35] and many of his colleagues had similar feelings. One of the first measures that the local party committee took following Stakhanov's record-breaking shift was to pass a resolution stating that all those who slandered Stakhanov would be considered "vile enemies of the people."[36] Stakhanovites were sometimes murdered.

The Soviet state

Rationalization of work in individual plants was linked to a broader rationalization of the economy, which, at its simplest level, meant increased state intervention. This was most dramatic in the Soviet Union, whose leaders turned away from the relatively free markets of the New Economic Policy. Emphasis was placed on rapid growth to be achieved through ambitious state plans, the first of which was initiated in 1929. Moshe Lewin writes: "This was a unique process of state-guided social transformation, for the state did much more than just guiding: it substituted itself for society, to become the sole initiator and controller of important spheres of life."[37]

New cities were built from nothing. The urban workforce increased from just over 11 million in 1927 to 39 million by 1939. Around 770,000 party members moved from the working class into administrative jobs. However, the new policy was not everything that its defenders claimed, and beneath the apparent clarity of planning was the utter chaos of a system that placed will and fear above rational calculation. The very process by which the five-year plans were arrived at had as much to do with political division as economic needs. Stalin had initially opposed the desire of Trotsky, Zinoviev and Kamenev for rapid industrialization, and only when these potential rivals had been deposed did he adopt their policies and use them against his former allies (Bukharin and Rykov). During the second five-year plan, Stalin seemed to favor a slower pace of growth, but this time his initial intentions were upset by pressure from below (partly produced by the cult of Stakhanov). Debate about the plan's highly unrealistic targets was so intense that, at one point, publication of the planning agency's journal was suspended.[38] Pressure to meet targets meant poor-quality work and inefficient use of resources. Often, an apparently centralized economy saw degrees of destructive competition greater than that of capitalism. At Magnitogorsk, American consulting engineers were horrified when rival teams of workers building a dam from either side of a river competed to see who could reach the center first; the Americans feared that the two halves of the dam would not meet up.[39] Not only was failure common in this system, but its consequences were serious: directors of Soviet planning frequently ended their lives in front of a firing squad.

Soviet industrialization produced odd results because it occurred in such a backward country. Recent migrants from the countryside were often illiterate and unused to the disciplines of factory life. Inexperienced workers operating under great pressure damaged machines or themselves and machinery was scarce. For all the Soviet Union's rhetoric about technology, managers often found it cheaper to use pickaxes and handcarts.

Stalinist economics were also dependent on outright coercion. Western workers might label factories as prisons but a significant part of Russian production took place under the scrutiny of NKVD guards. Plans for 1941 anticipated that over a million forced laborers would account for around 17 percent of the Soviet construction industry's output.[40] The state's odd relations with technical experts meant that some highly advanced research took place in prisons; Tupolev, the aircraft engineer, had an entire workshop in confinement. The difference from Western views of efficiency was marked. Modernizers in the West aimed for predictability: planners predicted economic trends, engineers predicted the output of a particular factory, industrialists predicted their profit levels, and workers predicted the rewards and penalties that would flow from a particular rate of work. In Russia, everything was uncertain. No one knew for sure what demands were about to be made; no one knew whether a machine would work or break down and be left to rust because there were no spare parts, whether a manager would be promoted or disappear, or whether a worker recently arrived from the countryside would settle into the routine of industrial labor with sullen passivity or smash his tools in drunken rage.

Corporatism

Stalinist economic experiments attracted admiration from some non-communists in the West – such as the Webbs and André Gide – but more common was the reaction of John Maynard Keynes: "On the economic side I cannot perceive that Russian communism has made any contribution to our economic problems of intellectual interest or scientific value."[41] Most economic reformers in the West looked not to an all-powerful state but rather to a convergence of the state and private enterprise. Keynes suggested that the future of the economy lay with "semi-autonomous bodies" modeled on the universities, the Bank of England and the Port of London Authority.[42] In continental Europe, many commentators began to talk about "corporatism."

Corporatism meant a wide variety of different things. Its proponents blended references to medieval guilds with more modern thinking on the need for an organized economy. Some saw it as a feature of a just society that would eliminate class conflict and overcome workers' alienation from their work; others saw it as a means to economic efficiency. Some saw corporatism as something to be imposed by government; others saw it as something that would emerge in the natural course of economic development. Some saw it as a means to combat the evils of large-scale capitalism; others saw it as a feature of large-scale capitalism.

Those who argued that corporatism was a natural product of economic progress pointed to an expansion in the number of very large firms. In the 1920s, mergers produced new industrial giants such as IG Farben (founded in 1925) and Imperial Chemical Industries (founded in 1926). In some countries, cartels reduced competition between firms. Such arrangements were often encouraged by government initiatives. State agencies such as the Reich Coal Council (in Germany) meshed with and encouraged the growth of large private-sector interlocutors.[43] Some governments encouraged restructuring to eliminate surplus production – the British government forced closures and mergers in the coal and steel industries during the 1920s. Depression also made governments increasingly prone to coordinate private-sector efforts.

Corporatism was advanced by the changing role of the state. After 1919, most states disposed of a larger proportion of national resources than they had done before 1914, but they did not exercise, or even seek to exercise, the kind of absolute power that the Soviet state aimed at during the 1930s. Most European governments depended on private bodies for much of their information and sometimes for the implementation of their policy. Boundaries between the state and private interest groups became permeable as ministries blended in with the very interests that they were supposed to control.[44]

The "spontaneous" corporatism brought about by the growth of interest groups, companies and the state was paralleled by political corporatism. Political corporatists might talk of the need to restore "natural communities," but in practice they looked to government policy to impose their wishes. Corporatism was formally supported by the papacy in 1931 and became the official basis for economic organization in Fascist Italy and Nazi Germany. Sometimes more than one kind of corporatism existed in the same country – in Vichy France, a formal, and not very successful, corporatism established by the Labor Charter of 1941 sat alongside an informal, though successful, form of corporatism established by large-scale employers under the organization committee system that was set up by the law of August 16, 1940.

Planning

In 1931, a group of British civil servants and businessmen founded a study group that published a journal called *Planning*;[45] Hendrik de Man launched an economic plan at the Belgian Socialist Congress in 1933; in

1936 the Nazis instituted a four-year plan to prepare the German economy for war; and, in 1941 and 1944, the Vichy government of France published industrial plans. All such plans differed sharply from those implemented in the Soviet Union, involving the encouragement and coordination of economic effort rather than the direct control of industry. The extent to which they were implemented varied. The Nazis were probably the most effective because, although they did not exercise detailed control of the means by which industry delivered its goals, they did apply severe penalties if the ends were not achieved. The Vichy government, lacking resources, credibility and even sovereignty in its own country, had less success. Elsewhere, plans remained on the drawing board.

The political climate of the 1930s made the implementation of reformist plans difficult in democratic countries. Many countries were divided between those on the right, who believed that any form of interference with the free operations of capitalism was wrong, and those on the left, who wished to destroy capitalism. The dilemma was summed up by Keynes: "The Capitalist leaders in the City and in Parliament are incapable of distinguishing novel measures for safeguarding Capitalism [i.e., the measures that Keynes himself proposed] from what they call Bolshevism . . . the Labour Party will always be flanked by the Party of Catastrophe . . . This is the party which hates or despises existing institutions and believes that great good will result merely from overthrowing them."[46]

In France, the division between "catastrophists" and economic conservatives was even more extreme. Socialists were still nominally committed to revolution while capitalist thinking was dominated by the liberalism of men such as Charles Rist: Keynes's work was not even translated into French until 1941. This produced an absurd situation in 1936. Léon Blum, who came to power as socialist leader of the Popular Front coalition, argued that left-wingers were as yet unable to destroy capitalism and therefore had no choice but to accept capitalism's rules and govern in the framework of the capitalist system.

New economic thinking during this period was often confined to small parties in big countries or to big parties in small countries. Belgium and Sweden were both good places for economic experiment because they had small communist parties (Keynes's "parties of catastrophe") and strong right-wing socialist parties, willing to countenance "reformism"; they were also countries where socialism was associated with nationalism, a tradition that was reinforced by Sweden's relatively recent secession from Norway and by Belgium's traumatic experience in the First World War. This made them enthusiastic about economic solutions enacted inside their own frontiers. Belgium's Socialist Party adopted the plan proposed by de Man at its 1933 congress, while in Britain the Liberal Party – once the most ardent defender of free-market economics – provided Keynes with his political home and Lloyd George's 1929 electoral campaign was based on a program of public spending to pull Britain out of depression. Dissatisfaction with the blinkered thinking of the major parties encouraged some to admire fascist regimes that seemed to reject conventional economics. Oswald Mosley founded the British Union of Fascists after having left first the Conservative and then the Labour Party, and after having founded his own New Party. In France, Marcel Déat's departure from the socialist SFIO and Jacques Doriot's departure from the Communist Party were largely motivated by frustration at their parties' unimaginative responses to the economic crisis: both men finished up working under the aegis of Nazi Germany during the Second World War, as did de Man in Belgium.

It is tempting to present the various attempts to reform capitalism in the interwar period as though they formed part of a single current. Reformers, keen to enlist allies, often presented themselves as part of a wider movement, but in reality each variety of planning or reformism was designed for a specific purpose. In 1918, Keynes had defended fiscal orthodoxy against Lloyd George's desire to fund the war effort; in 1929, he defended Lloyd George's desire to fund job creation against the guardians of fiscal orthodoxy among his former colleagues at the Treasury. Many in Britain and Germany assumed that economic planning was synonymous with support for large-scale efficient companies, although de Man's plan, devised in a country where the lower middle class exercised great power, was designed to protect small property-owners. Similar thinking informed many in France, and economic modernizers in the Vichy government tried to combine support for efficiency with protection for France's small businessmen and peasants. New thinking about how to manage the economy was inseparable from thinking about how best to use the fruits of prosperity. Keynes's economics went with the hedonistic and cultured life of Bloomsbury, and were designed to support a world in which Victor Rothschild could buy his friend Anthony Blunt a Poussin painting; Hitler's economics were designed to pay for the invasion of the Soviet Union.

State intervention was not always designed to promote a modern industrial society. In many countries, agriculture remained politically powerful and thus obtained state support. In France, spending on supporting the price of wheat in 1935 exceeded spending on national defense.[47] When André Tardieu, France's leading advocate of state-sponsored modernization, entered government in 1931, he took the Ministry of Agriculture. His plan of public works involved spending on rural modernization, and large industrial firms – such as Pont-à-Mousson, which made water pipes – often recognized that such programs offered their best chance to secure state contracts.

Free time

New ideas about consumption and the organization of leisure went with new thinking about production and the organization of work. Rationalization was often perceived as something that would produce more free time for workers and was associated with a clear separation between work and leisure as work became confined to eight-hour days and forty-hour weeks. "Rational" work required "rational" recreation: the relentless pace of the assembly line made no allowance for morning hangovers or the observance of "Saint Monday." The Soviet Union even experimented with an entirely "rational" week in which workers would be allowed leave every fifth day. In such circumstances, mixing work and leisure could seem positively threatening to the neat distinctions on which the modern factory depended: during the factory occupations of 1936, many French workers were said to behave as though they were at a "village festival," and the suppression of playful behavior on the shop floor formed a major part of the employers' subsequent restoration of discipline.

Work and leisure were also linked by the fact that the modern industries that introduced techniques such as Taylorization often produced consumer goods – radios, motor cars, phonograms – associated with new forms of leisure. Orwell pointed out how parts of Britain were transformed by forces that simultaneously produced new forms of industrial production, new social classes and new ways of passing time:

> The place to look for the germs of the future England is in the light-industry areas and along the arterial roads. In Slough, Dagenham, Barnet, Letchworth, Hayes – everywhere, indeed, on the outskirts of great towns – the old pattern is gradually changing into something new. In those vast new wildernesses of glass and brick the sharp distinctions of the older kind of town, with its slums and mansions, or of the country, with its manor houses and squalid cottages, no longer exist. There are wide gradations of income but it is the same kind of life that is being lived at different levels, in labor-saving flats or council houses, along the concrete roads and in the naked democracy of the swimming pools. It is a rather restless, cultureless life, centring round tinned food, *Picture Post*, the radio and the internal combustion engine. It is a civilization in which children grow up with an intimate knowledge of magnetoes and in complete ignorance of the Bible. To that civilization belong the people who are most at home in and most definitely *of* the modern world, the technicians and the higher-paid skilled

workers, the airmen and their mechanics, the radio experts, film producers, popular journalists and industrial chemists. They are the indeterminate stratum at which the older class distinctions are beginning to break down.[48]

However, the lives of the majority of Europeans were not changed by the kind of economic progress that Orwell described, partly because the consumer culture was available only to the rich. The only area of Europe where ordinary people experienced such prosperity was Britain – or rather certain parts of southern England. Modern consumer industries in England could rely on selling most of their goods to the home market, but the Italian car industry often had to sell more than half of its output abroad.[49] In France and Germany, cars were hand-finished for rich men rather than mass-produced for a popular market.

The impact of radio also varied between countries. There were twice as many radios in Britain as in the Soviet Union at the end of the 1930s. The ways in which radios were used varied from country to country. The medium was not the message. At first glance, it seemed that new technology was used most effectively by new political movements. Hitler and Mussolini used the radio to project their speeches to their people and to create an integrated national culture, and Nazi Germany subsidized radio purchase. On closer examination, it might be argued that such obvious and dramatic gestures missed the real possibilities of the medium, whose novelty lay in its ability to create "intimacy" and bring political leaders into the family. Because of this, radio was often used most effectively by those who sought to present themselves as "traditionalists." The British Broadcasting Corporation propagated a cosy conservatism, epitomized by the King's annual broadcast, instituted in 1932.

When commercial consumer cultures were impossible, or regarded as undesirable, working-class leisure was organized. Sometimes, initiatives – such as the Italian Dopolavoro (created in 1925) and the Nazi Strength Through Joy program – came from the state. Democracies – notably Popular Front France – also began to organize leisure in order to match the appeal of the fascist regimes.

Governments were not the only force to organize leisure. In France, the Church took a keen interest in sport and youth organizations, and in many countries political parties organized social activities, outings and sporting clubs. Companies also organized their workers' leisure. Religious paternalism might be one motive for such interventions – the Quaker Cadburys surrounded their factory in Birmingham with cricket pitches and bowling greens. The desire to secure a healthy and loyal workforce might be another. Company paternalism was easiest in capital-intensive modern factories; as labor itself was such a small part of total costs, an increase in the amount spent on each worker would not have a disastrous impact on the balance sheet.[50]

The organization of leisure operated from the top down. "Popular culture" meant the popularization of elite culture rather than the creation of a new culture. In the Soviet Union, attendance at the opera was held up as an appropriate form of recreation for the weary proletarian who had spent a hard day setting new records at the tractor factory.

Leisure in each country was organized to fit the constraints of an existing national culture. In Britain, sabbatarianism was important, and Alderman Roberts campaigned against Sunday bowls matches in Grantham with the humorless determination characteristic of his family.[51] In Italy, Dopolavoro activities were governed by perceptions of what was truly Italian. This produced an absurd situation: Italy won the 1934 World Cup but official agencies sought to suppress football as "un-Italian."

French attitudes towards sport were governed by religious and political assumptions. Catholic priests, who did much to organize sporting activity in Brittany, disapproved of games that were likely to produce excessive physical contact and encouraged basketball as an alternative to football or rugby. Rugby, by contrast, had its stronghold in the anticlerical southwest. There was also a distinction between rugby league (professional and proletarian) and rugby union (amateur and respectable). When the Vichy government came to power, the rugby league association was disbanded and its assets confiscated.

Regulation of leisure was never complete, and institutions were appropriated by those that they were meant to control. Italian Dopolavoro agencies were often subordinated to masonic traditions that predated Fascism, or even to the influence of the clandestine Communist Party, which turned picnics into opportunities for political debate. Sometimes the popular culture of tin pan alley provided symbols of rebellion. The most popular song of the Popular Front era in France was by the commercial artist Tino Rossi, the star attraction at the socialist fête of 1937, although many socialists were disturbed that workers seemed to be playing a purely passive role and absorbing a "debased" commercial culture. But the precise meaning of a hit song could depend on the circumstances in which it was sung. Such songs might provide an expression of defiance and sometimes they were popular precisely because they offered a means of rebelling against the stifling worthiness of the left as well as the explicit authoritarianism of the right. The use of commercial culture as a form of rebellion reached its most extreme form in wartime Germany, where an interest in jazz and Anglo-Saxon fashion, far from reflecting passivity, could mean the risk of execution.

Conclusion

Anyone whose views were based on political speeches, novels or poems would assume that the years 1919 to 1939 were ones of unprecedented technological change. In no other period of the twentieth century did educated Europeans talk so much about the impact of science on their lives. Attitudes towards such matters were central to the two new political doctrines of the age – fascism and communism. Anyone who looked at statistics would take a different view. Economic growth, which had been rapid in the years before 1914 and would be rapid again after 1945, was slow between the wars. The number of Europeans whose lives were directly affected by the machinery that leaders and intellectuals wrote about was quite small. Almost every European must have known the name of Charles Lindbergh, but even the wealthy had rarely set foot in an aeroplane – Neville Chamberlain flew for the first time when he went to Munich in 1938.

The outbreak of war in 1939 reversed the relation between the culture of technology and its physical impact. The pace of technological change increased: the three technologies that were to overshadow the second half of the twentieth century – the jet engine, the atom bomb and the computer – were all developed during the Second World War. The impact of technology on people's lives was also greater than ever before – few urban inhabitants of combatant countries were not directly affected by the aeroplane. Yet, in some respects, the increase in the direct impact of technology went alongside a diminution of its cultural importance. Only in Vichy France, which was not directly involved in the war, did men still discuss the technocratic projects that had absorbed such energy before 1939. The emphasis on precision, novelty and shininess that had marked the 1920s was gone. The "organization of leisure" was now likely to mean the provision of cabbage patches, rather than municipal swimming pools. "Metal" meant melted-down saucepans, rather than gleaming chrome. During the war, and perhaps for a long time after it, surviving the present was more important than fantasizing about the future.

6

THE PHONEY PEACE

ADOLF HITLER CAME to power in 1933 with the stated intention of overthrowing the Treaty of Versailles. In 1936, he sent troops to the Rhineland. In 1938, he integrated Germany and Austria. Later in the same year, at the Munich Conference, Britain and France agreed to his seizure of part of Czechoslovakia (he took more in March 1939). In September 1939, he attacked Poland and divided up the country with the Soviet Union. There then followed a period of military inactivity produced, so it was believed, by the impenetrability of French fortifications along the "Maginot line." This period, which was described as the "phoney war," came to an end in May and June 1940, when German troops swept across the Low Countries, thus circumventing the Maginot line, and invaded France, which they defeated in six weeks.

In some ways, "phoney war" is a good term for the whole period from Hitler's invasion of Poland until his invasion of the Soviet Union. The Poles suffered horribly during this period but they failed to mount effective resistance to German forces. A number of Hitler's other conquests were small, sometimes neutral countries that had no means to defend themselves. Even the French, surprised by the speed and provenance of the German attack, did not put up much of a fight: the French army lost fewer men defending France in 1940 than it had lost defending a few square miles of mud at Verdun in 1916. The most serious fighting in Europe in 1940 took place between the Russians and the Finns.

But if the year or so after September 1939 was a phoney war, then the twenty years that preceded it was a phoney peace. The Paris peace settlements were contested from the very beginning and were often left undefended even by powers, such as Poland, that had been created by them.

Armies that acted without regard to international opinion, or even that of their own governments, settled border disputes by force while the experts at Paris were scrutinizing their maps. The Italian poet Gabriele d'Annunzio led a group of Italian volunteers who occupied Fiume, a city disputed between Italy and Yugoslavia. The city of Wilno/Vilnius was occupied by a Polish general in 1920 as sovereignty over the city was disputed between Poland and Lithuania. Teschen was the scene of fighting between Czechs and Poles, German "free corps" fought Polish troops in East Prussia, the French General Mangin encouraged separatist movements in the Rhineland, and the Turks repulsed Greek efforts to take Smyrna in 1922. Even the Franco-German rapprochement that took place under the aegis of Aristide Briand and Gustav Stresemann during the 1920s did not reflect acceptance of the peace settlement – Stresemann accepted Germany's losses in the west precisely because he hoped to regain some of her lost territory in the east.

It would also be wrong to describe the history of international relations in interwar Europe as if it was simply a matter of treaties and conferences or even wars and battles. Many Europeans, especially those from the new states and new movements that were created after the Great War, believed that conventional diplomacy was finished. On being appointed Soviet Commissar for Foreign Affairs, Trotsky famously declared, "I shall issue a few proclamations and then shut up shop." Trotsky was wrong, in the sense that Soviet diplomats continued to carry out negotiations and even to observe the formalities of their calling (they turned up at conferences wearing frock coats). There were moments when even the most radical regimes found it expedient to behave as if they recognized diplomatic conventions, but relations between states had been transformed by the fact that states themselves were no longer the focus of diplomacy. The Soviet Union claimed to represent the international working class, Nazi Germany claimed to represent "the Aryan race," and the victorious powers of the Great War claimed to represent the "international community." International relations no longer meant a few aristocratic men talking French over the conference table; they could now involve millions of people being displaced from their homes. Everything was done with a new violence and ambition: the German Foreign Office played a large part in plans first to deport and then exterminate Europe's Jews.

The climate of international relations in interwar Europe was illustrated by the marginalization of the very group that might have been expected to defend the status quo – the professional diplomats of Britain and France. Diplomats were drawn from a narrow group. It was united by education[1] (Harold Nicolson was delighted to discover that one of

Mussolini's aides at Locarno was an old Harrovian) and family ties.[2] It contained almost no women (Suzanne Borel was the first woman to pass the French foreign service exams in 1937) and very few Jews. Roger Peyrefitte records that the French Foreign Ministry established a Department of Artistic Works to accommodate three people who could not be posted abroad – Borel (a woman), Jean Marx (a Jew) and Peyrefitte himself (an indiscreet homosexual). Diplomats fussed about protocol, medals and uniforms – Ivone Kirkpatrick felt that Count Galeazzo Ciano's attempts to take precedence over the Duke of Norfolk at the coronation of Pope Pius XII ranked among the major atrocities of Italian Fascism[3] – but they had less and less influence over the course of events. Politicians often took over the running of foreign affairs from professionals. The displacement of foreign offices by new bodies such as the Comintern in the Soviet Union or the Büro Ribbentrop in Germany meant that British and French diplomats could no longer rely on finding interlocutors who shared their own assumptions.

International relations had dramatic effects on people lower down the social scale too. If the period before 1914 had been the age of the migrant, that following 1919 was the age of the refugee: there were 9.5 million refugees in Europe in 1926. One and a half million people were forcibly exchanged between Greece and Turkey; 280,000 were exchanged between Greece and Bulgaria; 2 million Poles were uprooted from their homes, as were 2 million Russians and Ukrainians, 250,000 Hungarians, and 1 million Germans.[4] The flow of refugees eased in the mid-1920s but began again after the Nuremberg laws of 1935 imposed intolerable pressures on German Jews and as defeated Republicans fled Spain in 1939. Germany's victories in 1939 created another great movement of population, as she tried to push Jews and some Poles to the periphery of her new empire. Simultaneously, she agreed with the Soviet Union and Italy to "repatriate" ethnic Germans who lived in areas such as the Baltic and the South Tyrol. About 500,000 people came to the Reich under the terms of these agreements.[5]

The new insistence on passports was in large measure a product of the refugee crisis and population movement during the First World War. By the 1920s, even Lord Curzon, the British Foreign Secretary, was obliged to carry a passport – signed by himself. For less privileged individuals, the correct papers could mean the difference between life and death. Increasingly, the desire to leave a country was seen as a matter of political rather than economic choice, and many governments placed obstacles in the way of such departures. In 1926 Italy outlawed "abusive emigration,"[6] and in 1935 the Soviet Union instituted the death penalty for unauthorized attempts to leave the country.[7] In 1931 the German government introduced special taxes for would-be emigrants, which the Nazis subsequently used to impoverish Jewish refugees.

The reception of refugees in the countries to which they fled became increasingly difficult, especially as their arrival often coincided with economic crisis and political tension. The Swiss authorities asked the Germans to put a special stamp in Jewish passports so that their holders could be turned back at the frontier. By 1939, even France, traditionally the country most sympathetic to refugees, had built camps to confine Spanish Republicans and German Jews.[8]

Refugees were often the cause as well as the consequence of instability in interwar Europe. In November 1938, the assassination of a German diplomat in Paris by a seventeen-year-old Jewish refugee, overcome with despair after his family had been pushed out of Germany and refused entry to Poland, provided the Nazis with an excuse for attacks on Jews, which in turn provoked a further wave of fleeing refugees. In Hungary, refugees were the most bitter opponents of the frontiers established at Trianon and the most enthusiastic supporters of the radical right.

Economics further exacerbated European division after the First World War. In 1914 there had been fourteen currencies in Europe, all of which were tied to gold; after 1919 there were twenty-seven, some of which fluctuated wildly in value. In Germany, the reparations imposed by Versailles aroused great resentment, and German failure to pay provoked the Franco-Belgian occupation of the Ruhr in 1923. Reparations also divided Britain and France, because some British people believed that the French were making impossible demands – Graham Greene volunteered to spy for the Germans during the Ruhr crisis. In reality, reparations sprang not from the personal spite of Georges Clemenceau but from the effects of the Great War. France had inflated her currency and borrowed money; to accept that the losses would never be recouped would have been to accept the death of a whole bourgeois order based on rentiers and stable money. Furthermore, Germany's problems sprang mainly not from reparations, which rarely amounted to more than 3 percent of her gross national product,[9] but from a tradition of high state spending, compounded by the welfare commitments of the Weimar government and the financial legacy of the Great War. To an even greater extent than France, Germany had funded the war by borrowing and printing money, partly on the assumption that she would be able to repay loans and restore her currency with resources extracted from defeated enemies. In short, Germany's problems sprang as much from her inability to impose reparations on others as from the reparations imposed on her.

The relative prosperity of the mid-1920s underwrote Franco-German reconciliation; during this period, foreign – mostly American – investments in Germany exceeded the reparations that Germany paid. In 1924, the American financier Charles Dawes brokered a new arrangement of reparations, allowing Germany to pay relatively low reparations that would increase to their full level by 1928–29. The new mood was reflected in the Locarno Agreement of 1925, by which Germany renounced her claim to Alsace-Lorraine and accepted that the Rhineland should remain free of German troops, and in Germany's entry into the League of Nations.

In 1929, the Young Plan reminded Germany of her long-term obligations to pay reparations. Soon after, economic depression hit Germany, exacerbated by the withdrawal of American loans following the Wall Street Crash.

Depression had wider consequences, too, splitting the international economy into several rival blocs. Britain abandoned the gold standard and introduced "imperial preference" (economic protectionism) at the 1932 Ottawa Conference. During the early 1930s, France also introduced new tariffs, mainly to protect agriculture. Most isolated of all were the economies of the Soviet Union and Nazi Germany, where exchange regulations ensured that trade with foreign countries could be carried out only under strict control. By 1936, the Germans were beginning to plan for an autarkic economy to be as self-sufficient as possible in preparation for war.

International tension was exacerbated by instability in eastern Europe. The Tsarist and Habsburg empires had been broken up, a source of much resentment to diplomats who missed the court life of Vienna and St. Petersburg, and new states – Czechoslovakia, Yugoslavia, Lithuania, Estonia, Latvia, Poland – were created. The peace settlement made Europe more ethnically homogeneous but it did not ensure that every European lived in a country governed by men who shared his or her language and ethnic origin. Talk of "self-determination" in the peace settlement created an expectation, which had never existed before in much of Europe, that the nation-state was the natural form of government.

The fragmentation of eastern Europe was important because containment of Germany depended on an alliance of eastern European states with each other and France (the "Little Entente"): France signed treaties with Poland in 1921, Czechoslovakia in 1924, Romania in 1926 and Yugoslavia in 1927. However, the foundations of this alliance system were frail. France could help its eastern allies only if she was willing to wage offensive warfare, but, after the construction of the Maginot line began in 1929, France's military policy was almost entirely defensive, and during the 1930s French economic power, which had underwritten the alliances, declined. In 1931, Paris had been able to apply financial pressure in order to prevent a proposed customs union of Austria and Germany, but soon afterwards the depression sapped France's financial strength. Increasingly, the eastern European states were obliged to enter Germany's economic orbit as they signed bilateral agreements to provide agricultural products in exchange for industrial imports.

As French influence in eastern Europe declined, Poland tried to assume the leadership of an eastern European bloc, but this bloc was united by little except fear of Nazi Germany and Soviet Russia. Furthermore, the eastern European states had disputes with each other. Poland and Lithuania remained formally at war until 1928 and resumed diplomatic relations only in 1938. After the Munich settlement of 1938, Poland, a supposed ally of the West and soon to fall victim to Hitler's aggression, participated in the German carve-up of Czechoslovakia. When Poland itself was invaded, it could hope for nothing more than neutrality from neighboring countries, and the Romanians refused even to grant the fleeing Polish government a right of passage.

Further problems in international relations were created by the Soviet Union. The Paris peace conference took place against the backdrop of Bolshevik revolution in Russia and parts of central Europe. Russia was not represented at the conference and many were uncomfortably aware that this would cause problems in the long term. The peacemakers left the Germans with an army in order to keep down Bolshevik agitation inside Germany. In practice, both Germany and the Soviet Union felt themselves to be excluded from the Versailles system and gravitated together. This was seen in 1922 when the two countries signed a treaty at Rapallo that restored diplomatic relations and guaranteed that neither country would make economic demands on the other. More importantly, military cooperation began to develop between Germany and the Soviet Union. German soldiers were trained in the Soviet Union in techniques that were forbidden under the Treaty of Versailles.

After the rise of Nazism, as Germany itself came to threaten European peace again, some in the West thought that alliance with the Soviet Union would provide a means to contain Germany. The French and the Czechs concluded such agreements, but enthusiasm was muted. The representatives that the British and French sent to negotiate with Soviet leaders in August 1939 were comparatively junior men who did not have the power to commit their governments, and ultimately it was with Hitler that Stalin concluded a nonaggression pact in August 1939. Indeed, early in the European war of 1939–40, Hitler and Stalin were effectively fighting together. Stalin invaded Poland from the east, while Hitler invaded it from the west. Stalin also attacked Finland and annexed the Baltic states and part of Romania.

Historians who know about the Red Army's role in defeating Hitler often criticize the failure of the Western Allies to bring the Soviet Union

into an anti-Nazi alliance, but hesitation about cooperation with the Soviet Union was not simply the product of anticommunism. There were
good reasons to doubt Stalin's value as an ally. To be of use in 1939, the
Red Army would have had to be capable of an offensive war, and there
was no reason to suppose that it was. The performance of Soviet troops
had not been good: the Red Army had been defeated in Poland in 1920,
and Soviet military advisers had failed to prevent the Spanish Republicans from being defeated in 1939. The ineffectiveness of the Soviet forces
was most dramatically illustrated in the winter of 1939–40, when 1 million Soviet troops had great difficulty in defeating a Finnish force of fewer
than 200,000 men.[10]

Most importantly, it seemed obvious that Stalin's purges of the late
1930s had crippled the Red Army. The purges had eliminated three out
of five Soviet marshals, seventy-five out of eighty members of the
Supreme Military Council[11] and about 7.7 percent of the total officer
corps.[12] The purges fell particularly hard on the Red Army's most original
military thinkers, including Mikhail Tukhachevskii, who had pioneered
new doctrines on the use of armored warfare. Many accused of espionage
had worked closely with the Germans during the period of military cooperation between the two countries and knew about the enemy that
they were likely to confront. The impact of purges on this scale on morale
and organization in the army can barely be imagined. Public denunciations weakened soldiers' respect for their superiors, while fear of political
consequences made military planners reluctant to state their views
frankly. Many officers took to drink, and some killed themselves. Attempts to restore military efficiency in 1940 involved the restitution of
4,000 officers, some of whom had spent the intervening period in labor
camps and torture chambers.[13] Those aware of this black comedy could
only conclude either that the Red Army was genuinely ridden with spies
or that it was a demoralized and disorganized force with yes-men for generals and a psychopath as commander-in-chief. In either case, the Soviet
Union did not seem an attractive ally.

Such developments were especially dangerous because they were accompanied by a shift in the military balance of power that made it possible for
Germany to contemplate war again. The German economy was hit hard by
world depression in the early 1930s, but it recovered fast and gained an advantage over the French economy, which entered the depression relatively
late but did not begin to emerge from it until the late 1930s. France's weakness was compounded by the demographic legacy of the First World War,
which halved the number of conscripts at her disposal in 1939.

Nazi leaders rejected the economic orthodoxy that often restrained
their enemies. The British and French governments were obsessed by the

need to restrain public spending, but Goering simply declared: "We do not recognize the sanctity of some of these so-called economic laws."[14] From 1934 onwards, the German army was excused from the obligation to submit detailed accounts to the Ministry of Finances.

The German economy was no model of efficiency. Disregard of "economic rules" went with a chaotic system in which different agencies competed to manage the economy. Sometimes Hitler's personal arbitration was required to settle such struggles. Furthermore, however ruthlessly Germany mobilized her resources, the fact remained that those resources were smaller than those of her potential adversaries.

Some historians have suggested that the Nazi leaders recognized their economic weakness and that their strategy was devised to circumvent it. According to this interpretation, Germany aimed not to achieve total economic mobilization but rather to direct efforts into concentrated, but short, bursts of war that would be over before Germany's limited resources were strained. Quick and comparatively cheap victories might bring economic benefits. The absorption of Austria had already brought the Germans an extra $200 million worth of gold reserves,[15] and during the invasion of Poland German forces were discouraged from destroying economic targets.[16]

Others have argued that Nazi leaders were seeking total mobilization of the economy, but did not expect to achieve it before 1942 and were therefore surprised by the outbreak of war in 1939. In fact, the chaotic nature of Nazi rule probably meant that both aims were pursued simultaneously. On the one hand, a shrewd strategy recognized that Germany's economic weakness required short victorious wars; on the other, a megalomaniac ambition conceived ever more absurd aims.

Germany gained from the exploitation of new forms of warfare. Military technologies developed during the First World War – tanks and planes – had suggested that highly mobile warfare was possible. The implications were discussed by Basil Liddell Hart in England, by Mikhail Tukhachevskii in Russia, by Charles de Gaulle in France and by Heinz Guderian in Germany. Military debate during the 1930s did not pit modernizers against blind conservatives. By the end of the decade, many of those who had first shown interest in mobile warfare were beginning to express doubts. Tukhachevskii argued that tanks should not be used in isolation from infantry formations, and Liddell Hart had all but abandoned his belief in tank warfare by 1939.

The sheer scale of change in the 1930s made it difficult to calculate the effects of new technology. Tanks became heavier and better armed. Fighter aircraft moved from being biplanes with maximum speeds of around 200 miles per hour to being single-engined monoplanes with maximum speeds of up to 400 miles per hour. Countries that had modernized their armed forces too early were often overtaken by new developments. Italy had the most modern air force in Europe in 1934, but its planes were out of date by 1940. It was hard to assess an air force's strength by simply counting wings: the Luftwaffe reduced its numbers in 1938 while it modernized its machines. Training men to use new equipment could pose problems. By the time of the German invasion in May 1940, French pilots still had not mastered the Dewoitine fighters that had been introduced five months previously.[17]

It was hard to predict how new machines would perform on the battlefield. The performance of tanks in the Spanish Civil War, especially at the Battle of Guadalajara, was not promising,[18] and experienced soldiers knew that machines worked better on the drawing board than in a muddy forest fifty miles from the nearest mechanic. French experts reckoned that tanks would require up to six hours of maintenance a day. Commanders worried about the extent to which new developments in antitank weapons would cancel out new developments in tanks. The French, who calculated that antitank guns were effective at a range of up to 1,000 meters while the guns on tanks could work only at ranges of less than 300 meters, believed that nineteen out of thirty tanks would be destroyed in an assault on antitank weapons. The Germans, who assumed that antitank guns would be effective only up to a range of 800 meters, calculated that only six out of thirty tanks would be destroyed in such an attack.[19] Both the French and the Germans made optimistic assumptions about the training and character of their troops if they believed that tank crews would remain calm and disciplined when faced with such a high chance of an unpleasant death.

The term *Blitzkrieg* or "lightning war," sometimes used to evoke the rapid assault that characterized the German attacks on Poland, France and the Low Countries, was coined by an American journalist, not a German general. The Germans did not plan the war that they fought in 1939–40, and were often as surprised as their opponents by the rapid progress that they made. Only retrospectively, when watching newsreels of their advance – cinema was well suited to the celebration of mobile war – did they realize that they had hit on a new strategy. They did not consciously fight such a war until the invasion of Russia in June 1941.

Military modernization was a matter of culture as well as money and machines. In France, defensive warfare was part of the republican tradition stretching back to the revolutionary wars, as was the mass conscript army that went with such warfare. Many Frenchmen believed that an enlisted army protected democracy against military dictatorship, but it became increasingly doubtful whether such an army protected French democracy against foreign armies. Between 1928 and 1935, French conscripts served for only one year and thereafter were kept as reserve troops called up for short training periods that did not allow enough time to master complicated techniques. Reserve units with which men trained did not always correspond to those with which they would serve in time of war, and this made specialization difficult; the army had to be based on a set of simple interchangeable tasks. Charles de Gaulle's ideas on mechanized warfare became linked to a bitter debate about the professionalization of the army.

In many ways, Germany's exploitation of new techniques of warfare was the product of weakness rather than strength. As a result of the Versailles Treaty, Germany had a small professional army until 1934. German officers were required to serve for twenty-five years, while ordinary soldiers served for twelve. Long service and professionalism allowed plenty of time for reflection on the future of warfare. In 1919 and 1920, 400 officers were members of committees dedicated to learning the lessons of the war that had just ended.[20] When the Germans began to build a large army, they did so from scratch, using the latest techniques. The Luftwaffe enjoyed a privileged position because, having been founded in 1935 (after Hitler's accession to power), it was seen as a particularly National Socialist branch of the armed services.

Most importantly, the reception of military innovation was conditioned by relations between civil and military powers. Generals were conservative. Charles de Gaulle depended on his ability to mobilize politicians, notably Paul Reynaud, against his immediate military superiors. In Germany, Hitler was able to impose risks to which the generals would never have freely consented.

Conclusion

Looking at interwar Europe from a purely European perspective can be deceptive. Most of the major European powers were still very concerned about events outside the continent. The empires of France and Great Britain were effectively enlarged by the peace settlements of 1919 because both powers gained League of Nations mandates. France administered Syria and the Lebanon, while Britain administered Palestine and Iraq. Both powers also had older empires: the French had colonies in sub-Saharan Africa, the Maghreb and Indochina, and the British in Africa, India and the Far East. India was particularly important to the British because it was large and wealthy, while Algeria was important to the French because it had a European population – about 1 million people – who voted in elections to the French parliament. The economic depression encouraged both countries to seek protected economic outlets in their empires.

Empire became inextricably interwoven with British and French military thinking. The French occupied the German Rhineland and Ruhr with African troops, exacerbating the ferocious racism of many Germans, while occupying parts of Africa with German soldiers who had joined the Foreign Legion. Marshal Mangin speculated about the possibility of using the huge "*force noire*" that France might draw from her colonies to compensate for her dwindling population. The British relied on a large navy because it could protect the empire as well as the metropole. Some saw the Anglo-German naval agreement of 1935, by which Germany agreed to limit her navy to a little more than a third of the strength of the British, as a tacit deal whereby Britain preserved her world role while giving Germany a freer hand in Europe. Expansion of the British army during the late 1930s was hampered by the fact that recruits resented service in India.[21]

Imperial considerations were a particular brake on the application of new technology during the late 1930s. Colonial armies were intended to fight low-technology warfare against ill-equipped opponents on terrain that was very different from that of Europe. British discussion of tanks concentrated largely on their usefulness in the North-West Frontier province.[22] The British were preoccupied by the use of aircraft as a cheap means of exercising power over rebels in Iraq and northern India; one-third of the British training manual on air power concerned "control of semi-civilized tribes within our own jurisdiction."[23] In the summer of 1940, the French had twice as many fighter planes in North Africa as in northeastern France.[24]

All the major conflicts that affected Europe in the 1930s were partly colonial affairs. This was true of the Italian war in Abyssinia, and it was even true of the Spanish Civil War, which began in North Africa and was fought largely by Moroccan troops under the leadership of the *africanista* General Franco, who had made his career commanding the Spanish Foreign Legion. The Soviet Union's extra-European commitments were most important of all: its land frontiers in Europe extended for 2,400 kilometers while those in Asia extended for more than 8,000 kilometers. In the late 1930s, its troops fought frontier skirmishes with the Japanese, and in July and August 1938 Soviet forces fought the Japanese around Lake Khasan in a battle that killed 236 Russians and 600 Japanese. Between May and September 1939, a second battle was fought at Khalkin-Gol, involving 35 Soviet infantry battalions, 500 tanks and 500 aircraft; 10,000 Russian and Mongol troops were killed, as well as between 25,000 and 55,000 Japanese.

Only Germany, having lost her colonies at Versailles, was undistracted by extra-European commitments. During the 1920s, German leaders, including Stresemann, recalled Germany's former empire with regret. Lord d'Abernon shrewdly suggested that colonies might prove a restraint on future German policy: "It is clear that any German overseas possessions would largely be under the control of England's sea power, and would increase the desire of Germany to remain on good terms with us."[25] Such suggestions were disregarded by British leaders during the 1920s. After Hitler's accession to power, British policy changed; attempts were made to buy peace in Europe with colonial possessions, but it was too late: the world policy that had dominated German thinking between 1890 and 1912 was now abandoned. Hitler recalled Bismarck's skeptical attitude towards overseas colonies, and his ambitions were focused on the creation of an empire in central Europe. German techniques of warfare were designed for fighting European armies. Germany won the European war of 1939–41 because she was the only purely European power. She lost the world war of 1941–45 for the same reason.

7

THE SECOND WORLD WAR
IN EUROPE

ON THE NIGHT of June 21, 1941, a German soldier, presumably a communist, deserted and, at enormous risk to his own life, made his way across Soviet lines to warn of an imminent attack. The deserter's interrogators telegraphed Moscow to ask for instructions. They received a reply giving Stalin's personal orders that the deserter was an *agent provocateur* who should be shot. Hours later, the Germans attacked.[1] The Second World War had begun.

The invasion of the Soviet Union marked a break with the European war that had been fought over the previous two years. The forces of Germany and the Soviet Union dwarfed anything that had been put into action before, and for the next three years the eastern front was the scene of almost all the serious fighting. In 1942, Hitler had 178 divisions in the east; Rommel's confrontation with British forces in northern Africa, which came to feature so much in British mythology, involved only 4 German divisions. Between the evacuation of Crete in 1941 and the Allied invasion of Italy in 1943, Russian troops were the only ones to fight German forces on European soil. Of the 13.6 million German soldiers who were killed, wounded or captured during the Second World War, 10 million ended their military careers on the eastern front.[2]

At first, the German–Soviet war was a very unequal contest. In the first week of the war, nine-tenths of Soviet tanks[3] and one-seventh of all Soviet front-line warplanes were lost (by midday on June 22, 900 of the latter had been destroyed on the ground).[4] By the end of the first month of fighting, 200 out of 340 military supply dumps had been taken.[5] In October 1941, a Mongolian cavalry division lost 2,000 men attacking

German forces without inflicting a single casualty on their opponents.[6] Such spectacular inequality did not last. The speed of the German advance stretched supply lines, and snow (which began falling unusually early in October) created problems for equipment designed for warmer climates. Most importantly, Soviet forces fought back: by the end of 1941, they had inflicted 750,000 casualties on the German army. They still suffered crushing defeats in 1942, and German forces continued to kill eight Soviet soldiers for every man they lost, but the Red Army had a lot of soldiers, and its leaders were prepared to see a large proportion of them die.

Fighting on the eastern front was more intense than anything seen in the west. Certain groups among the British forces – commandos, airmen, tank crews – ran great risks but British military deaths amounted to only 264,000. Civilians, too, had enjoyed a certain respite between the end of the Battle of Britain and the arrival of the first flying bombs in 1944: only 62,000 British civilians died in the war. Most American troops mobilized never left American soil, and there were no civilian casualties in the United States. For many soldiers in the forces of the Western Allies, "active service" meant short periods of fear combined with long periods of boredom. By contrast, many Soviet soldiers fought almost continuously for the four years that followed June 1941, and were sometimes close enough to the enemy to exchange small-arms fire. Much fighting took place on Soviet soil. Around 9 million Soviet soldiers and 19 million Soviet citizens died in the war.[7]

For Germany, the war in the east was an ideological one (against communism) and a racial one (against Slavs and Jews) as well as a war between nations. This was not just a concern for Nazi theoreticians. The attack on the Soviet Union was desperately important to the aristocrats who composed a large part of the upper reaches of the German officer corps, because their own estates lay in the east. At the beginning of the century, Theobald von Bethmann Hollweg had told his son not to plant oak trees on the family's Prussian estate because "the Russians will be there before they mature." Now Germany was fighting to remove the Russian threat from her border forever; defeat would ensure that Bethmann Hollweg's prophecy came true. Soviet victory meant extinction for the Junkers. Of 8,827 German nobles studied by Norman Naimark, 6,448 were killed in the Second World War. After the war, several hundred were killed by captive foreigners who had been working on their estates, around 500 died in detention and another 500 or so killed themselves.[8]

The war in the east was brutal. Both Soviet and German forces had killed many civilians and prisoners of war during their invasions of Poland in 1939, but brutality was now deployed on an even larger scale and the harshness of the two sides created a spiral of violence. German troops were accompanied by *Einsatzgruppen*, special squads who killed 62,805 civilians in the first five weeks that followed the German invasion.[9] Brutality was rooted in racial contempt for the enemy and in the nature of the war itself. Russian soldiers were fighting on their native soil for several years, often alongside civilians whose casualties in sieges such as Stalingrad and Leningrad were horrible. Both sides knew that they were fighting a war for survival that would end with the crushing and bloody defeat of one side, rather than with negotiation and treaty. In such circumstances any attempt to distinguish between combatants and noncombatants broke down. Germans regarded all Soviet citizens as potential enemies, and the Soviet authorities regarded willingness to deal with the invader as treason.

The extent to which fighting on the eastern front differed from that in other theaters of war was illustrated by the treatment of prisoners of war. In the west, treatment of such men was regulated by the Geneva Convention and supervised by the Red Cross. Over a million Frenchmen spent five years in German captivity, and their welfare became one of the central concerns of the Vichy government. Nineteen out of twenty French prisoners returned home alive. Western prisoners of war did not have a comfortable life, but on the whole their captors respected the rules that governed their treatment: prisoners were fed properly and given medical care, and even those who persistently escaped or broke German laws were rarely executed. Some prisoners of war were better off than their civilian compatriots – French Jewish soldiers in German captivity were usually given the same treatment as their gentile comrades. Officers were not obliged to work, and some British officers seem to have found the atmosphere of their camps reminiscent of their public schools.

In Russia, it was different. Soldiers were ordered not to surrender. Neither side regarded men who disobeyed this order with sympathy – the Russians sent some returning prisoners of war to labor camps in 1945 – so there was no incentive to extend good treatment in the hope that it would be reciprocated. Conditions of prisoners were regulated by nothing other than the desire to exploit their labor. The Germans killed Jews and communist officials among their captives.[10] The gas chambers at Auschwitz were tested on 600 Russian prisoners of war.[11] Of 3.5 million Russians captured by the end of 1941, 2 million were dead by February 1942.[12] Of 5.7 million Red Army soldiers captured by Axis forces, only 930,000 were found alive in 1945. Some had escaped or volunteered to serve in the German army, but more than half the remainder were dead. Just over a third of the 3,155,000 German soldiers that the Soviet Union captured died before their release.[13]

The brutality of war in the east influenced how combatants treated their own soldiers as well as how they treated their enemies. Discipline was harsh. During the entire war the Americans shot only one man – Private Eddie Slovic – for desertion,[14] and only forty British soldiers were executed.[15] The Germans, by contrast, shot around 15,000 of their own men, mostly on the eastern front.[16] German soldiers who managed to stagger back from hellish battles were disciplined for offenses such as "losing a pair of field glasses" or asked to explain why they had retreated when they still had a few rounds of ammunition.

Globalization of war

War was no longer confined to Europe. Russia had a great Asian hinterland into which she moved much of her industrial production, and Hitler's declaration of war on the United States in December 1941 did even more to ensure that the conflict was a global one. War was no longer a matter of short conflicts deploying limited resources (retrospectively labeled *Blitzkrieg*), but now involved huge numbers of men fighting in vast areas, and this changed the nature of the war in ways that eventually determined its outcome. From 1939 until 1941, the scale of the war had diminished. Nations defeated by Germany dropped out until the autumn of 1940, when the European conflict had become a war that pitted Germany and Italy against Britain. The only new operations – in Greece and northern Africa – had been comparatively minor. From June 1941, the number of countries at war increased.

Globalization damaged Germany. The Third Reich was a European power, with almost no surface navy – its resources were based on land and in the air. Britain, by contrast, had always been a naval and imperial power. As the war widened, her capacity to cross oceans mattered more: American equipment and men were shipped to Liverpool; tanks and trucks were shipped to Murmansk. Many German soldiers died at Stalingrad or Kursk without ever having seen the sea. Many British soldiers, by contrast, endured the discomforts of long sea voyages. Evelyn Waugh passed the time on the voyage from Liverpool to Dakar in 1940 by acting as defense counsel for soldiers who had passed the time with buggery.* Later the sea-borne escape from Crete provided him with graphic material for *Officers and Gentlemen*.

---

* *The Diaries of Evelyn Waugh* (ed. Michael Davies, 1979), p. 483. A Marine named Florence, defended by Waugh, got eight months.

The fact that the British and their allies continued to control the seas was crucial to their ultimate success. The sinking of a few big German battleships counted for little, because the German surface fleet was so small; what mattered was the slow war of attrition between the German submarines (or U-boats) and British convoys crossing the Atlantic, a conflict that epitomized many of the differences between the Allies and their enemies. The Germans invested in specialized submarine warfare as a response to their weakness in surface ships. Their U-boats were technically good and their crews brave (28,000 out of 39,000 German submariners lost their lives during the war).

At first, German submarines in the Atlantic claimed great successes: a quarter of all British tonnage was sunk in 1940 alone, and in 1941 the Allies could not build ships as fast as the Germans sank them. Losses of ships taking supplies to the Soviet Union could be even more serious. Of the 36 ships that set sail from Iceland on June 27, 1942, only 11 arrived at Murmansk, and equipment lost on board included 400 tanks, 200 planes and 4,000 trucks.[17] The U-boats were beaten not by a well-equipped elite force, but by a disparate collection of civilian ships, Royal Navy vessels and aircraft. Most of those aboard the convoys were civilian merchant seamen, and their weapons were not sophisticated. Merchant ships were adapted to carry guns and to fire depth charges. Some of the most successful innovations were improvised by individuals (sometimes acting in defiance of higher authority) rather than produced in a sophisticated laboratory. The problem of antisubmarine aircraft's inability to find targets at night was solved by the provision of a very powerful searchlight, and the need to provide air cover in the middle of the Atlantic was partially met by converting oil tankers into makeshift aircraft carriers.

There was no instant victory. The German submarine fleet was not completely destroyed and convoys were never entirely safe, but losses declined sufficiently to make it possible for the Americans and British to replace ships faster than they were sunk. Churchill wrote that the sea war was characterized not by "flaming battles and glittering achievements" but by "statistics, diagrams and curves unknown to the nation, incomprehensible to the public,"[18] a judgment that might have been applied to other aspects of the Allied war effort.

United nations

The globalization of the war placed a premium on the capacity of different and distant powers to work together. Britain and America were strikingly successful at this. The two countries were linked by language, culture and political values, and their ruling classes had been brought together by the Rhodes scholarship program and the need of impecunious British aristocrats to find wealthy brides (Churchill's mother was American). Churchill and Roosevelt liked each other and had been in regular contact before America's entry into the war. Relations with Stalin were less good, but both Western leaders made efforts to get on with him. Churchill claimed that he would have made complimentary remarks about the devil if Hitler had invaded hell.

Germany's capacity for global war was more limited. Her most powerful ally was Japan but the two powers did little to coordinate their actions. Hitler never met senior Japanese leaders, and the key actions that globalized the war – the invasion of the Soviet Union and the attack on Pearl Harbor – were initiated by the Germans and the Japanese respectively without consulting their allies. The invasion of the Soviet Union cut Germany's land links with Japan. Coordination with Germany's allies in Europe was also poor. All of these allies were weak compared to Germany, and many of them were unenthusiastic partners in the new order. Mannerheim's Finland was forced into a German alliance by Soviet aggression, while Hungary and Romania entered the war late and reluctantly – both later came to separate agreements with the Allies. Mussolini was the only foreign leader, perhaps the only human being, for whom Hitler seems to have felt much respect, but Mussolini's control over his country was uncertain. Italy entered the war only when it seemed certain that Germany had won. The King and ruling class withdrew as soon as it was clear that Germany had lost.

War economies

It was widely recognized – although not always by the German leaders themselves – that the short campaigns of 1939 to 1941 had allowed Germany to avoid straining her relatively limited industrial resources. The outcome of a long war fought in numerous theaters depended on economics, which was what Britain and France had always hoped for. Before 1939, they had assumed that a coalition of strong economies would grind down an isolated German economy. In the short term this calculation had proved wrong: military strength overwhelmed economic strength. The invasion of Russia changed matters. Much of Russian production was concentrated in the lands that Germany occupied: by November 1941, most of Russian coal, steel and aluminium production fell into this category.[19] However, the Germans gained little from their advances, because Soviet forces destroyed equipment and even crops in the fields as they retreated. The Russians were also able to transfer large amounts of plant away from the invader. Factories were dismantled, placed on trains and reassembled in Siberia, and between July and November 1941, 1,523 large Russian factories, accompanied by 25–30 million workers, moved east.[20] Most importantly, the fact that Soviet forces continued to fight meant that for the first time the Germans had to replace equipment over the course of a long campaign, rather than recuperate from one short campaign and stockpile for the next. This came as a particular shock because the attack on the Soviet Union had been the first campaign that the Germans had deliberately planned as a *Blitzkrieg*. German industry had already been switched to preparing the next stage of the war before the Russian campaign was completed: when the Red Army counterattacked at Stalingrad, the Wehrmacht was receiving a smaller proportion of total ammunition production than at any previous stage of the war.[21]

The German economy faced several problems in sustaining such a war – it was smaller than that of her opponents and lacked vital commodities (such as rubber). By the end of 1944, total Allied output of munitions was valued at $180,000 million, while total Axis production was valued at $100,000 million.[22] Furthermore, Germany did not always exploit her resources effectively. Much of the area that she controlled had come into her possession as a result of conquest. At first, it was easy to seize gold supplies or a stockpile of finished goods from a factory yard, but such exploitation over the longer term proved more difficult. The most spectacular attempts involved the use of foreign labor to make up the deficit caused by the drafting of German men into the army. Such efforts began with Poles brought to Germany in 1939 and 1940, and continued with prisoners of war (of all nationalities), Soviet labor, and an increasing number of workers drafted from countries such as France. By August 1944, there were 7,615,970 foreign workers in Germany (of whom 2,800,000 were Soviet citizens, 250,000 were Belgian, 1,300,000 were French, 590,000 Italian and 1,700,000 Poles).[23]

The productivity of foreign workers was reduced by poor rations (especially for those from the East), political hostility (especially on the part of those from the West) and the general difficulty of integrating people who often had no industrial experience. In one factory in Essen, the productivity of all foreign workers was lower than that of their German colleagues by 15–43 percent.[24] Furthermore, although foreign workers' wages were lower, the total cost of employing them was higher because of the need to provide transport, special living quarters and extra forms of security and coercion. The most efficient workers from an employer's point of view were young Russian women, not because they were physically strong or skilled, but simply because they were easy to control. The costs of employing foreign labor were cumulative. A skilled worker in an armaments factory might be drafted into the army, and his place would be taken by a farm worker, whose place in turn would be taken by a worker from Poland or the Soviet Union (such people came to make up more than half the German agricultural labor force). At each stage, work was done less efficiently than it would have been done before.

Germany tried to exploit foreign labor by allowing industries to continue to run in defeated countries on condition that they contribute to the German war effort, a policy adopted with some success in France. But exploiting the industries in foreign countries was made difficult by the hostility of both management and workers and the sheer logistical problems of a military administration trying to exercise control over civilian institutions in an unfamiliar setting.

The German war economy was further undermined by conflict between the various agencies that claimed authority over it. Hitler himself took little interest in industrial issues, while Goering (head of the four-year plan and Minister of Economics) clashed with Todt (Minister of Munitions) and Thomas (head of the army's economic agency). After Todt's death in 1942, Albert Speer became Minister of Munitions. As Goering's failings became increasingly evident, Speer was able to impose a degree of control and eventually, in September 1943, to transform the Ministry of Munitions into a Ministry of War Production, though there were still conflicts with army chiefs and with Saukel, responsible for labor.

Matters were made worse by soldiers' power and insistence on putting purely military concerns above economic ones. German troops were better trained and more disciplined than their opponents, and their weapons were usually better, but there were never enough troops or weapons. In France in 1944, the British and Americans had "an effective superiority of twenty to one in tanks and twenty-five to one in aircraft."[25] Such inferiority cannot be blamed solely on perverse military decisions – Germany had fewer resources than its opponents – but the domination of soldiers over economic planning made matters worse, with generals insisting that weapons be manufactured to demanding specifications, but resisting the standardization that helped the Americans produce such large quantities. German thinking, excessively focused on battlefield performance, neglected the question of how appropriate quantities could be delivered to the battlefield. Transport was always a weakness. The German army's much vaunted mobility was based on tanks, but it lacked the trucks needed to carry munitions and food in the wake of a rapid advance, which became a particular problem during the attempt to conquer the yawning spaces of the Soviet Union. German forces took 650,000 horses with them into Russia. The siege of Stalingrad revealed the weaknesses of German supply lines.[26] Goering's assumption that food and ammunition could be conveyed by air turned out to be hopelessly optimistic, while the besieged forces came to appreciate the advantages of primitive forms of transport – they ate 40,000 horses.[27]

German attitudes towards aerial warfare also revealed much about how battlefield priorities prevailed. The Allies used aircraft in a wide variety of different ways. Heavy bombers pounded industrial cities while long-range Liberators were used to help close the "Atlantic gap" (the point at which German submarines had previously been able to operate without fear of attack from the air). The Germans, by contrast, assumed that aircraft should be used mainly to support troops on the ground. Dive-bombing was particularly important in this respect, and the Luftwaffe were forbidden from manufacturing bombers that did not have the capacity to perform such operations. The bombing supremo who took this decision was a former stunt pilot, Ernst Udet, who exemplified the German tendency to put spectacular performance above overall effect.[28]

German economic efficiency was also impaired by enemy action. War on land did not have much of an impact on German industry, and it was not until the Allies penetrated Germany's pre-1938 frontiers that her capacity to continue producing weapons was threatened by loss of territory, a fact that casts an interesting light on Germany's failure to exploit her occupied territories effectively. The air war, by contrast, had a big impact on German production. British and American air force chiefs made optimistic estimates of their capacity to inflict damage. After 1945, economists swung to an opposite extreme, and argued that the German economy had never been exploited to its full potential and that an increase in efficiency had compensated for losses caused by bombs. Neither of these extreme views was true. No amount of bombs could have brought about the collapse of Nazi Germany without war on the land. Equally, it is absurd to imagine that the German economy was not affected by bombing. Effects were cumulative. The well-aimed bomb that blew an entire munitions factory off the face of the earth existed only in the minds of propagandists for Bomber Command, and even the most spectacular British raid of the war – when a squadron of Lancaster bombers tried to flood the Ruhr by destroying dams with bouncing bombs – produced disappointing results. What counted was the frequency with which German industrialists had to slow down production to repair damage or await spare parts (delayed by the bombing of railways), while their exhausted and demoralized workforces took to the shelters yet again (in Mainz in 1944 alarms sounded for 540 hours). Resources were diverted to reconstruction, air defense and moving of production to less vulnerable locations so that in 1944 such activities employed 2 million Germans.[29] Eventually, one-third of German artillery production was devoted to antiaircraft guns.[30] The impact of raids on morale was reflected in a postwar survey of hardships; more than nine out of ten respondents mentioned bombing. The next most commonly cited hardship, food shortage, was mentioned by only one in ten respondents, while Nazi injustices were evoked by one in fifty.[31] Bombing forced the Luftwaffe on to the defensive as it struggled to maintain enough fighter planes to intercept the Lancasters and Flying Fortresses, and this relieved the Red Army from the threat of air attack.

The economies of Germany's enemies benefited from some degree of overall control by civilians who saw the full picture and emphasized the quantity rather than the quality of production. The British aircraft industry concentrated on repair work to ensure that limited resources were stretched as far as possible. In February 1944, 18 percent of all manpower in the aircraft industry was devoted to the production of spare parts.[32]

The United States could devote all of its efforts to improving production unimpeded by direct threat of enemy action. The American economy was not traditionally a war economy. In the period from 1933 to 1938 total military expenditure amounted to £1,175 million – less than half that of Germany (£2,868 million) and Russia (£2,808 million) and little more than that of Italy (£930 million)[33] – but the broad economic base on which the United States built was vastly superior to that of any other nation. She had large natural reserves of almost every raw material required for war, and her coal output was twice that of Germany.[34] Furthermore, America was a dynamic society where capitalists of titanic ambition were used to solving problems as long as they stood to make a profit.

In mobilizing business, America had advantages that were conspicuously absent in the economies under German aegis. By the early 1940s, industrialists in continental Europe knew that large resources had already been devoted to war. Peace – even peace brought by victory – was bound to mean a drop in such production that would prove costly for those who had invested too heavily in it. Furthermore, the increasing likelihood of German defeat meant that many distanced themselves from the Nazi regime – a particularly important consideration for industrialists in occupied countries. For American industrialists, by contrast, their country's victory seemed increasingly likely, and they also had less cause than their European counterparts to regard the postwar economy with apprehension, partly because much American industry was devoted to the production of items, such as jeeps and trucks, that could be used in peacetime, and partly because the American economy was moving from the very low military spending of the 1930s to the comparatively high spending that would characterize the post-1945 period. American industrialists did not necessarily regard government armaments spending as a temporary phenomenon, and many knew that investment in such production made long-term economic sense as well as short-term military sense. Total American production increased during the war (from $88,600 million in 1939 to $135,000 million in 1944).[35] The vast production lines of Chicago and California were the most important source of Allied strength: 40 percent of all weapons used in the European war were manufactured in the United States.[36]

War economies were not designed to produce just military equipment – combatant countries had to maintain food production to feed their soldiers and workers. The Soviet Union – where agricultural production dropped by around one-third between 1940 and 1943 – was the least successful in this. Most Soviet citizens survived on a drab diet of bread and potatoes. In the United States, by contrast, living standards rose. European children associated American soldiers with ice cream, chewing gum and Coca-Cola. Even those countries whose food production fell generally managed to ensure that this did not directly affect their most valuable soldiers and workers. Plenty of people died of starvation in towns that had been isolated by enemy action (such as Leningrad) or by a deliberate decision (such as the Warsaw ghetto). There were also famines – such as those in Greece or Bengal – that were less direct results of the war, but in general no fighting power in Europe was at risk of being starved out. However, living standards were not measured only in terms of calories consumed. In all countries, morale was dramatically affected by the capacity to obtain the small luxuries that made life bearable – nicotine and caffeine were particularly important. The Germans saved their last supplies of real coffee for soldiers about to go into battle; in Haute Savoie, the single most common category of target for Maquis attacks were tobacconists. The British war effort floated on floods of strong, sweet tea.

Leadership

The German military was authoritarian. It depended on orders being passed down from above and obeyed without question. Far from challenging this culture, Nazism exacerbated it, partly because the consequences of disobedience or questioning were now much worse. Senior commanders who disagreed with Hitler's policy (Blomberg, Fritsch) had been disgraced. It is easy to see why Paulus, the German commander who disobeyed Hitler's personal order not to surrender at Stalingrad, threw in his lot with his Russian captors: he knew that nothing but the firing squad would be waiting for him in Germany. A general staff for the German armed forces had been established in February 1938, but Hitler never allowed it to exercise much power, partly for fear that it would become an alternative center of power. In October 1943, two different general staffs were given responsibility for fighting on the eastern front and elsewhere.[37] In the early years of the war, Hitler's personal authority had often proved an advantage, but his interest was erratic and fitful; furthermore, his early successes had given him an excessive confidence in his own judgment and in the capacity of German forces to overcome apparently insuperable obstacles.

Patterns of authority among the Allies varied from one country to another. Roosevelt was a courteous and considerate man and, in any case, his constitutional position forced him to work through consent rather than through issuing of orders. Churchill was less tolerant, but he too could govern only with the consent of Parliament and the Cabinet. His faith in his own judgment may also have been slightly tempered by his responsibility for an early disaster in the war – the Norwegian expedition. Stalin's position was quite different. Soviet generals who said the wrong thing could find themselves, as Marshal Zhukov put it, "invited to coffee with Beria" (the head of the secret police),[38] and those such as Pavlov, held responsible for early defeats, were shot. However, like Churchill and unlike Hitler, Stalin's military career began with catastrophe rather than victory, which may account for the fact that he was more willing to discuss matters with colleagues between 1941 and 1945 than at any point in the previous decade. Zhukov's position was greatly strengthened by the victory at Stalingrad, after which he became the most impressive example of someone who regularly argued with Stalin and survived.

The willingness of Churchill and Roosevelt to discuss their decisions and expose themselves to criticism was illustrated by their relations with Charles de Gaulle. De Gaulle was not the leader of a recognized government, and his official military rank was lower than that held by hundreds of Allied officers. The forces at his disposal were trivial until the end of 1942 and were limited even after this date. De Gaulle was also a difficult character. His violent disagreements with Churchill became famous, and when he met Roosevelt at Casablanca, secret servicemen with machine guns were placed behind a curtain in case he should physically attack the President of the United States. In spite of all this, Allied leaders did receive de Gaulle, take some heed of his advice, and eventually recognize him as the head of government.

The benefits of permitting open discussion can be illustrated by comparing the initiative in favor of a negotiated peace that came from part of the British ruling class in 1940 and a similar one originating with part of the German ruling class in 1944. The most important consequence of the discussion in Britain was that Halifax, leader of the peace faction, ceased to be Foreign Secretary and was appointed ambassador to Washington, where his talents did the British cause much good. By contrast, when a group of German aristocrats and soldiers wanted to discuss peace in 1944, they opened debate by arranging for Colonel Claus von Stauffenberg to place a bomb under Hitler's conference table. The affair finished with Hitler injured, and one of Germany's leading generals, Rommel, was forced to commit suicide. Many of the plotters were executed.

Conclusion

Who won the Second World War? The answer is less obvious than it seems. From 1942 onwards, the forces fighting Nazi Germany described themselves as the "United Nations," but in reality their contribution to the war effort and the rewards that they reaped from them varied hugely. Most Europeans probably did not realize that Argentina, for example, had been a member of the coalition that defeated Hitler. The four key powers that divided the spoils in Europe in 1945 were Britain, France, the United States and the Soviet Union, and it was these four countries that occupied Germany and earned permanent seats on the Security Council of the United Nations, along with China.[39]

France's military contribution to the defeat of Germany was small, and de Gaulle insisted on sending troops to fight largely to earn a place at the victors' negotiating table rather than because he thought that they would be effective against the Germans. Britain's contribution was greater, but still much smaller than that of the Soviet Union and of the United States, the two powers that turned European war into world war. Weighing up the relative contributions of the Soviet Union and the United States is difficult because they were so different. The United States was a great industrial power with a small land army; the Soviet Union was an economically primitive country with a vast number of troops. For every American citizen killed in the Second World War, eighty-five Soviet citizens died.[40]

It is not, however, true to say, as Western admirers sometimes did, that the Soviet Union won the Second World War. Without her allies, the Soviet Union would have faced the full force of German airpower and would have been short of munitions and weapons – in 1943 Lend-Lease provision to the Soviet Union was equivalent to one-fifth of total Soviet production.[41] The Soviet Union could not have held out without Western help. The Western Allies, by contrast, could have won the war without the Soviet Union. The cost of doing so would have been terribly high, but sooner or later bombing would have ground Germany down and America would eventually have mobilized the vast army that could have been drawn from a healthy population of 150 million. If all else had failed, America would, presumably, have settled matters by dropping an atom bomb on Berlin.

The benefits that the Allied powers drew from their victories also varied. In terms of land and military advantage, the Soviet Union was the biggest winner. All the states that had fought the Soviet Union or Russia during the twentieth century – Germany, Japan, Poland, Finland – were devastated in 1945, while the Soviet Union extended its frontiers and increased its influence in eastern and central Europe. The other country to draw obvious gains from the defeat of Germany was France. Some French nationalists had always argued that French security could be guaranteed only by Germany's dismemberment, which the division of Germany into the zones occupied by the Allies effectively brought about. France regained the frontiers drawn at Versailles. Charles de Gaulle and François Mitterrand, both of whom had been brought up in the shadow of the "German problem," built a new relationship with West Germany, based on cooperation from a position of strength.

The gains and losses of Britain and America are harder to measure. In retrospect, it seems obvious that the Second World War marked Britain's decline from, and America's accession to, world power. In 1945, matters were not so clear. America had not gained a square inch of territory in Europe from her victory and was not paid a penny in reparations (she was soon to grant large subsidies to the countries that she had defeated). American hegemony resulted from the technological and economic power that had helped her win the war, rather than from the outcome of the war itself. The British still felt confident, seeing themselves as one of the "big three" powers and regarding the countries of continental Europe with condescension. Many believed that the empire would become more important over the coming years. Only after twenty or thirty years of relative economic decline was it evident that Britain's "world role" was a liability rather than an advantage.

In the euphoria of victory, much was made of the war's moral aspects. Nazi leaders were put on trial for crimes against humanity. The fact that Stalin's prosecutor, Andrei Vyshinsky, turned up at the trial shows that Allied policy and morality never had much to do with each other. States had gone to war with Germany because she threatened their national interest, not because they disapproved of Nazi persecution.

Many ordinary people on the Allied side did, of course, see the war in moral terms, though the impact of Allied propaganda probably makes us overestimate their number and forget that most Allied soldiers had no choice about whether they fought. Some of those who fought on the Allied side had good reason to feel bitter about the way in which their contribution was rewarded. Black American GIs could hardly fail to notice how much better they were treated by the populations of Britain and especially France than by their own segregated army. One black GI recalled seeing German prisoners of war sitting with white civilians in the station restaurant of El Paso: "If I had tried to enter that dining room the ever-present MPs [military policemen] would have busted my skull."[42] In December 1944, Greek communist partisans were suppressed by British forces.[43] Bitterest of all were the Poles, who had fought in the British and Soviet armies and behind the lines in their own country. They had watched Stalin help Hitler dismember Poland in 1939, massacre Polish officers and deliberately allow the Wehrmacht to suppress the Warsaw uprising of 1944 (partly because it suited him to have noncommunist leaders killed). They now learned that Stalin had been offered the predominant influence in postwar Poland.

If any ideology was gained from the Second World War, it was not belief in democracy and freedom, which was preached by the Western Allies, but communism. The Communist Party had new supporters all over Europe in 1945, though never as many as rigged elections in eastern Europe suggested, and the Soviet Union enjoyed the apogee of its prestige. Curiously, the only area where communism's prestige had declined was the Soviet Union, where the war had been fought under the banner of traditional nationalism and many veterans regarded all ideologies with weary cynicism.

The consequences of communist enthusiasm were not, however, apparent in 1945. It was not obvious that eastern and central Europe would become Soviet satellites or that the communist parties of France and Italy would be excluded from government. This illustrates a wider point. What came to be regarded as the "postwar" world was not, in fact, born in 1945. Immediately after the German surrender, many Europeans believed that Britain was a great power that would use victory to make her empire still more secure, and that France was in the grip of irreversible decline. The fate of Poland, where the European war had started, illustrates how interpretations of the war's outcome could change over a few years: in 1945 Poland seemed to have gained from the war, because she had, after appalling losses, been liberated from German occupation. A few years later it seemed possible that the Soviet Union might eliminate the Polish nation altogether. Finally, from 1956, it became clear that the Soviet Union, unlike Nazi Germany, would guarantee Poland some autonomy. The Allies had been united in their desire to destroy Hitler's Europe, but it was only in the years after 1945 that they decided, or had decided for them, what to put in its place.

8

GENOCIDE

THE KILLING OF 6 million European Jews was part of a wider Nazi project. Personnel and techniques from the "euthanasia program" – the killing of the mentally ill – were used against the Jews, and groups who killed Jews in the Soviet Union also killed Soviet commissars. In concentration camps, Jews were confined along with political prisoners, resistance fighters, members of the Polish intelligentsia, gypsies, homosexuals, Jehova's Witnesses and Russian prisoners of war. Elimination of the Jews was accompanied by other efforts to reinforce the "Aryan" race: welfare provision was designed to make the Germans healthier and more fertile, and ethnic Germans from the Baltic Soviet Union or the Italian Tyrol were "repatriated."

However, not all Nazism's projects were pursued with equal intensity. From 1942 onwards, the killing of the Jews was much more systematic than the killing of any other group, except perhaps the gypsies. Every other racial scheme was subordinated to the war effort. The Third Reich took in vast numbers of foreign workers: the SS, which had once required recruits to trace their German ancestry back to the eighteenth century, conscripted Bosnian Muslims, and the extermination of Russian prisoners of war was replaced by an attempt to exploit their labor. Killing the Jews was different. It was done even at the cost of military advantage and was implemented with ever more urgency as German defeat approached.

Some historians have suggested that such large-scale slaughter must have originated in a conscious decision taken by the Nazi leaders at an early stage.[1] If so, it was a decision that was kept well hidden for a long time. In the early stages of Nazi rule in Germany, persecution of Jews seemed designed primarily to drive them out of the country rather than to exterminate them. Jews in Germany were subjected to innumerable humiliations and attacks, but before 1939 only a few hundred had been killed. Much of the violence occurred in the early stages of the regime and in remote towns, where the Nazi rank and file were least likely to observe the rule of law. The assertion of legal control meant that the anti-Semitic policy became official, but it seemed reasonable to assume that it would be limited and predictable. The government had many interests other than anti-Semitism, and some of these concerns, particularly the economic ones, conflicted with anti-Semitic policy. The subordination of Jewish policy to the general interest of the state meant that anti-Semitic persecution was not pursued consistently. There were times – notably before foreign visitors converged on Berlin for the Olympic Games of 1936 – when the lives of German Jews seemed to become more tolerable.

Matters began to change with Nazism's military expansion, which brought ever larger numbers of Jews under the regime's control. The invasion of Poland, which contained 3 million Jews, had particularly dramatic consequences. Poland was an enemy country, where the entire population, not merely its Jewish element, was despised. In such circumstances, legal constraints and the risk of offending public opinion counted for little. Of the 16,336 Polish civilians executed in the six weeks that followed the German invasion of Poland, at least 5,000 were Jews.

The increased violence against Jews that followed the invasion of Poland did not reflect a coherent new policy. In fact, the eighteen months or so following Poland's defeat were marked by confusion and contradiction in the Nazi attitude towards the Jews. Pressure to act came from the increased number of Jews who came under Nazi aegis with each military victory, and from the fact that the "Jewish problem" was associated with wider projects to rearrange populations under Nazi rule. The part of Poland conquered by Germany was divided into an area that was eventually annexed to the Reich and a "General Government" ruled by a civilian governor. Jews, gypsies and a substantial proportion of Poles were to be moved out of the old frontiers of the Reich and the new frontiers created by annexation. The complexity of resettlement projects was increased by the "repatriation" of hundreds of thousands of ethnic Germans.

German officials discussed plans to deport the Jews to the French island of Madagascar, but this project could not be implemented until peace was concluded with Britain, which controlled the seas. They also talked of moving Jews to a reservation in the eastern part of the General Government, but this raised objections from generals who did not want such a strategically sensitive area to be cluttered up with hungry and disaffected people.[2]

A German edict that Jews should not live in communities of less than 500 people drove them into the cities, and local administrators responded by establishing ghettos (notably in Łódź and Warsaw). Some German officials appreciated that Jewish labor could be useful to the war economy and sought to ensure that Jews were provided with some food and raw materials. Other officials simply wished to clear the ghettos and deport their occupants elsewhere.[3] Everyone knew that large numbers of Jews moved around in this way would die of starvation, disease or cold, but they still did not contemplate large-scale deliberate killing.

The invasion of the Soviet Union brought further killing. *Einsatzgruppen* eliminated Soviet commissars and all Jews in Communist Party employment, and along with locally recruited helpers they slaughtered hundreds of thousands of people during the summer of 1941. This still did not amount to a policy of systematic and universal extermination, a policy that seems to have been decided upon at some time between the invasion of the Soviet Union and the end of 1941. The new strategy was explained at the Wannsee Conference on Jewish policy, which in January 1942 brought together fifteen officials responsible for Jewish affairs. It was decided that Jewish flight was to be blocked rather than encouraged. Outright extermination was now the aim.

Europe's Jews were now transported to concentration camps. These camps had existed almost as long as the Nazi regime, but at first they had been used mainly to incarcerate political dissidents. Not all concentration camps were designed solely to kill. Some, such as Bergen-Belsen, were labor camps, where people died from overwork, starvation and disease rather than deliberate execution. Auschwitz, where around a million people died, became the largest and most notorious center of extermination.[4]

Who was responsible for the extermination of the Jews? The simplest answer would be Adolf Hitler, whose anti-Semitism set the tone for that of the Nazi Party and whose personal power was enormous. However, there is no written evidence that Hitler gave explicit orders or even had detailed knowledge about the precise means by which his broad wishes were to be carried out. Senior Nazis often discussed the Führer's wishes, but Hitler's interventions in this matter were strangely discreet. A man who fussed about the design of uniforms never seems to have inquired about the huge operation needed to take people from Salonika, Budapest and Nice to gas chambers in Poland. Orders relating to the killing of the Jews were passed down in an indirect and sometimes secretive manner. For example, when Dieter Wisliceny, who was to be responsible for deporting Greek Jews, visited Adolf Eichmann, the SS Jewish expert, in Berlin in June 1942, Eichmann removed a document from his safe that he said was an order from Himmler expressing the Führer's desire for "a final solution" to the Jewish problem.[5]

The implementation of anti-Semitic policy depended on Nazi functionaries vying with each other to fulfill what they took to be the will of those above them. Among the Nazi leadership, there was a constant struggle over how anti-Jewish policy should be implemented. The attacks on German Jews in November 1938 *(Kristallnacht)* were fostered largely by Goebbels, the Propaganda Minister, in a bid to gain some influence over Jewish matters. Goebbels's initiative was resented by his colleagues, who sought to impose their authority during the aftermath of *Kristallnacht;* Goering, in particular, as Minister of Economics, used the events as an excuse to extract money from German Jews. The Wannsee Conference was opened by Reinhard Heydrich with the claim that he was now plenipotentiary for the preparation of the "final solution of the Jewish question." The Ministry of Propaganda was not even represented there, but Goebbels sought to reassert his authority by ensuring that his men attended a follow-up conference on March 6, 1942.[6]

The extermination of the Jews was not carried out by Nazis alone, but depended on the cooperation of agencies that antedated Nazism. The civil service, the judiciary, the medical profession and the army were all involved, and the Ministries of the Interior, Justice and Foreign Affairs were represented at the Wannsee Conference. The army killed large numbers of Jews in Serbia in reprisal for partisan attacks, and in the Soviet Union soldiers cooperated with *Einsatzgruppen,* while in Greece the army and navy helped with the deportation of Jews.[7] Civil servants and senior officers tended to be older than their Nazi colleagues and were more likely to be members of the traditional German ruling class. Involvement in Jewish questions could provide an opening for bureaucratic entrepreneurs: men such as Hans Luther, Under-Secretary of State at the Foreign Office, increased their power at the expense of their nominal superiors by gaining control of this new area.

Did ordinary Germans participate in the extermination of the Jews? In the sense that they helped bring Nazism to power and failed to resist its subsequent policy towards the Jews, the answer is yes. Many Germans hated Jews and welcomed their persecution, but it is hard to demonstrate that Germans were more anti-Semitic than other nationalities or that their anti-Semitism caused the Nazis to act as they did. Violent outbreaks of anti-Semitism such as that seen on *Kristallnacht* in 1938 seem to have aroused unease rather than admiration. The persecution of the Jews became less open as it became more intense. In the early days of the Nazi regime, anti-Semitic vitriol had poured from the official press, while Jews had been publicly humiliated, but as physical extermination began such openness ceased. Jews were not seen as victims of attack because they were no longer seen at all; they had been removed from public life and ceased to have contact with most German people. The final killing was carried out in camps removed from centers of population, often located outside Germany. The language of anti-Semitism changed. At first, the Nazis had talked of killing, blood and revenge, but in the early 1940s, they talked of "items for transportation," "resettlement" and "final solution." Raul Hilberg lists twenty-five different euphemisms for killing Jews.[8]

As Jews disappeared from Germany, rumors of what was happening were relayed by soldiers, concentration camp guards and released inmates, but knowledge was not diffused precisely or clearly. How much people knew depended on their job, although the relationship between status and knowledge was not obvious: a railway clerk might know more than a high official in the Foreign Office. Knowledge also depended on chance. A brief meeting with a soldier back from the eastern front[9] might reveal more than years of reading the official press or listening to the BBC.

Flickers of illumination did not amount to an overall understanding of what was happening. The Nazi regime hung juvenile delinquents and shot thousands of its own soldiers for desertion or cowardice. It was possible to understand that the Nazi regime was an exceptionally brutal one that was particularly harsh towards the Jews without appreciating that this harshness would eventually extend to total extermination.

Even if Germans had been fully aware of what was happening to the Jews, what could they have done? The Third Reich was, in an odd way, sensitive to public opinion, but its sensitivity was greatest in peacetime, when information flowed reasonably freely, when the state worried about international opinion and before protest could be represented as unpatriotic. Germans were subjected to increasingly harsh penalties for helping Jews. A decree of October 24, 1941 imposed a sentence of three months in a concentration camp for anyone who expressed sympathy for the Jews, and a special leaflet detailing such rules was issued to all German families with their ration cards. Even a casual act of courtesy such as giving up a seat to a Jew on a streetcar (in the days when Jews were still allowed to travel on streetcars) could be a criminal offense.[10]

In such circumstances, quite modest acts required great courage. Little is known about such acts. Resistance to Nazi anti-Semitism in some German-occupied countries is well recorded because a number of Jews survived to recount their experiences and because those people who helped Jews usually operated as part of a wider network. Indeed, in Italy a government official took care to conserve documents detailing the measures that civil servants and soldiers had taken.[11] In Germany, by contrast, individuals had to act alone and usually had to be suspicious of their own colleagues and neighbors. What is known about such acts usually comes from the testimony of the very small number of German Jews who survived in Germany beyond 1939. In 1942 a railway porter found a Jewish woman in a station (she was trying to get to Switzerland) and insisted on taking her home and giving her a bed for the night.[12] Victor Klemperer, a German Jew, recalled being approached by a working-class acquaintance who ostentatiously shook his hand and said, "Now professor, don't let it get you down! Before long they'll be finished, the bloody brothers."[13]

These examples raise a host of questions. Was the railway porter's act an isolated one? He might have helped hundreds of people in a similar situation, but as most of those people would eventually have been killed it is unlikely that any other acts would have been recorded. If he made a habit of helping Jews on the run, it is likely that the porter himself did not survive the war.[14] As for the man who shook Klemperer's hand, was he motivated by political opposition to Nazism (he was a communist), common kindness, or the desire to talk to a social superior on terms of equality and intimacy that would probably have been impossible before 1933? He may well have been driven by a mixture of motives. In any case, as Klemperer recorded in his diary, such heroically indiscreet displays of support did not do their recipients any practical good.

Killers

Not all Germans were merely passive bystanders in the extermination of the Jews. Many were active participants. Camp guards and members of killing squads could not have been under any illusion about what was being done, although, once again, they may not have appreciated the extent to which their actions were part of a systematic extermination program. Who were these people and what motivated them? Killing squads were not composed of dedicated Nazis, and contained at least some representatives from most "Aryan" groups in Germany, but killers were not "ordinary" – indeed, it is hard to see what the word "ordinary" might mean when applied to Germans between 1941 and 1945. Germany was a highly segregated society. It had always been divided by class, a division that overlapped with political differences, which had been greatly exacerbated by the rise of communism and Nazism. It was also divided by sex and generation (a division that was increased by the experiences of the two wars and Nazism). Such distinctions were rarely reflected in an outright refusal to kill, but they were reflected in the differing degree of participation. The most dedicated killers, particularly the junior officers who gave orders and spurred their men on, had certain features in common: they were male, relatively young and likely to be involved in Nazi organizations.

In units that exterminated Jews, some groups were particularly reticent about their task, as can be seen among the men of Police Battalion 101, studied in exhaustive detail by Christopher Browning. The old were less enthusiastic than the young. The commander of the battalion, himself fifty-three years old, offered to excuse "older men" from the killing, and several who subsequently refused to continue explained that their reluctance came from the fact that they were fathers.[15] Former members of the communist and socialist parties seem to have been highly represented among those who refused to kill,[16] and Catholics rebelled against their task more often than Protestants.[17]

Not all those who killed Jews had clear-cut motives: a variety of different feelings seem to have underlain their action. Conformism, ambition and reluctance to seem a coward often played a larger role than sadism or anti-Semitism. Fear was an important motive, too. Much has been made of the fact that men were not sentenced to death for refusing to kill,[18] but German forces exercised very brutal discipline over their members, especially in the areas where most Jews were killed, and there were many ways in which men could be punished without formal process. Some were threatened with summary execution if they refused to kill and, given the casualty rates in some units on the eastern front, "punitive transfer" could amount to a death sentence.

Killing was increasingly broken down into component parts – few deaths resulted from a single act by a single person. Killing was also made easier by the ever more degraded state of the victims. A member of the SA who killed a Jew in 1934 was attacking someone whose language and culture he shared, however unwillingly. His victim's accent, manner and clothing would make it possible to identify his class, region of origin, level of education and age, and such facts presented barriers to large-scale slaughter. Even after 1941, killers were often badly shaken when confronted with some recognizable detail that reminded them of their victims' humanity. Members of Police Battalion 101 were shocked to find among their victims a woman who had run a cinema that they had once frequented.[19]

However, the chances of killers recognizing features in common with their victims diminished all the time. An SS man in Auschwitz in 1944 faced creatures whose identity was uncertain. It was unlikely that the victim would speak the same language as his persecutor. Distinctions of class and education had been eroded by camp uniform and shaved heads, and age became increasingly uncertain among people who were weeks rather than years away from death. In short, everything that might have made the Jews seem like the friends, neighbors or family of those who ran the camps disappeared.

Non-German complicity

The Germans were not the only people to kill Jews. As Soviet forces retreated from the Baltic states, pogroms broke out; some were initiated by Germans, but others seem to have begun before German forces arrived. The Romanian army killed almost 60,000 Jews during a massacre at Odessa in October 1941,[20] and Croat and Slovak fascists attacked Jews with great savagery. German forces also recruited auxiliaries known as Hiwis (volunteers) from occupied countries (Lithuania, Latvia, Estonia and the Ukraine). What motivated the non-German participants in extermination? In some cases, the answer is simple – fear. There may be debate about what would have happened to a German who disobeyed orders, but there is no such debate with regard to the Hiwis, many of whom had been extracted from German prisoner-of-war camps. Participation in killing was the only way to escape the two very unpleasant alternatives of active service against the Red Army or continued incarceration in German camps.

There was also a spontaneous element in attacks by some eastern Europeans on Jews. Anti-Semitic feeling among Latvians and Lithuanians may have been higher than among Germans who participated in killings. However, eastern European participation in the extermination of the Jews did not simply run parallel to that of the Germans. German projects were centrally planned and coordinated, and the men who devised the operations wanted their executors to work in a cold, unemotional way towards the ultimate goal of killing all European Jews. Eastern European attacks on the Jews were sudden, violent and often fueled by vodka. Hilberg writes: "Short violence followed by confession and absolution is one thing; organized killing is quite another."[21]

In Poland and the Soviet Union, matters were more complicated as German persecution of the local population was severe and there was little possibility that local collaborators would be recruited to hunt Jews. Both countries also had strong traditions of anti-Semitism, though, and it might be argued that such traditions contributed to the isolation of the Jews that made them vulnerable after the German invasion. Some Poles, even those fighting against the Germans, were reluctant to help Jews, and Polish pogroms continued after the German departure, when Jews returning from concentration camps were killed by their own compatriots. In the Soviet Union, anti-Semitism was exacerbated by communist rule, not only because some Russians associated communism with Jewry but because the regime itself had begun to encourage anti-Semitism (a policy that tied in with Stalin's struggle against Trotsky and the old Bolsheviks). Some Jews lived under several different anti-Semitic regimes in rapid succession. The city of Wilno was moved from Polish rule to that of Lithuania in 1939, neither country being noted for racial toleration, and it was then annexed by the Soviet Union. Soviet authorities drew up lists of largely Jewish notables to be shot. When the Germans occupied the town in 1941, they found the Soviet lists and shot everyone on them.

Non-German resistance

Participation in the extermination of the Jews by Germany's allies or subjects was neither simple nor universal. Many governments in Europe were anti-Semitic, but until the installation of puppet fascist regimes at the end of the war none of them shared the Nazis' desire to exterminate all Jews. The most extreme example of government resistance to such projects was seen in Finland, where Jewish officers were sent to fight alongside the Waffen SS on the eastern front. Other countries distinguished between "native" Jews and recent immigrants or Jews from outlying areas. Vichy France, Hungary and Bulgaria helped the Nazi authorities to deport Jews, but they also sought to protect at least part of their Jewish populations.

Resistance sometimes came from the population rather than, or as well as, the government. In Italy, a large part of the establishment (including senior army officers) sabotaged attempts to exterminate not only Italian Jews but all Jews under Italian protection in areas such as Greece, Yugoslavia and southern France.[22] In Denmark, arrangements were made to spirit a large part of the Jewish population across to Sweden before the Germans could begin deportation in 1942, and in Holland, popular resistance was manifested in a general strike of 1941 to protest against anti-Jewish measures.

Opposition to the Nazi variety of anti-Semitism did not always come from democrats or liberals. Authorities in Fascist Italy, Bulgaria and Franco's Spain all acted on various occasions to protect Jews. Resistance was easiest in countries with sovereign governments, and especially in countries that were regarded as allies by the Third Reich. It was difficult for the Germans to intervene in such countries until events such as the overthrow of Mussolini or the American invasion of French Algeria gave them a particular reason to do so. Only in Hungary does intervention seem to have been motivated mainly by a desire to accelerate the extermination of the Jews.

Resistance was least difficult in the western European countries, where punishments for sheltering Jews were less severe than in Poland or the Soviet Union – Annie Kriegel believed that the key difference between France, where her immediate family survived, and Poland, where the overwhelming majority of Jews died, was that helping Jews was never made a capital offense in France.[23] Rations were more generous, a crucial consideration for anyone sheltering people without papers. The nature and size of the Jewish population was also important. The countries that did most to protect their Jews – Denmark and Finland – had tiny Jewish populations. This made the logistics of protection easier and may have contributed to low levels of native anti-Semitism.

Poland lay at the opposite extreme. The population of the Warsaw ghetto was greater than the entire Jewish population of France – the Poles could never have hidden a group of this size even if they had had the inclination to do so. The degree of assimilation also counted. Countries in which the Jewish community was long established – where Jews spoke the same language and dressed like their neighbors – tended to be the places where both the desire and the capacity to protect Jews was greatest. France had a community of well-established, relatively wealthy, French-speaking Jews, as well as a population of recent immigrants (often those who had recently fled Nazi persecution). The former benefited from the policy of the government and its contacts in the non-Jewish population, its capacity to blend in and, in the last resort, its capacity to buy protection. Finally, geography played a role. Jews fared best in areas where food could be obtained (even if at inflated black market prices) and where frontiers with neutral countries were accessible. Haute Savoie and Denmark were good places to be; Poland was a very bad place to be.

Jewish resistance and compliance

Why did European Jews not resist their destruction more vigorously? Many did not try to escape from the path of invading German armies, or cooperated with deportations from their native areas to concentration camps, and sometimes Jews who had been in hiding turned up voluntarily to collection points. Physical resistance on the part of Jews began only late, with ghetto uprisings at Warsaw and Łódź and rebellions, sabotage and attempted breakouts in some concentration camps.

The "failure" to resist aroused much bitterness. Some Jews blamed the leaders of their communities for having cooperated with the Nazis. Leaders of the Jewish councils established under Nazi aegis had reassured their followers about Nazi intentions and in some cases had chosen Jews to be deported. Sometimes the decisions of the councils were made on the basis of finding Jews who were capable of work that would be useful to the Nazis, but they also reflected other divisions – between French and foreign-born Jews, or between Viennese Jews who served in the First World War and those who had not. Often the councils and their members' families seem to have benefited (for a time) from their contacts with the Germans. Struggles in the Jewish community became violent. The Warsaw ghetto uprising began with the assassination of Jewish policemen and officials. In 1957, Rudolf Kasztner, a Hungarian Jewish official who had subsequently become a member of parliament in Israel, was assassinated by those who wished to revenge themselves for his alleged role in negotiations with Adolf Eichmann.[24]

Denunciation of the "treason" of Jewish leaders needs to be considered in the context of the constraints on Jewish action. The first was ignorance and misunderstanding. The Jews simply did not know what was in store for them. In some respects, this ignorance was worse among Jews than among the rest of the European population. A Jew in the Warsaw ghetto might know more about individual acts of brutality inflicted on his coreligionists but less about overall Nazi policy towards the Jews than someone on the other side of the wall. Jewish knowledge was restricted by lack of access to any form of communication: Jews were forbidden to own radios and telephones, and postal services in the Warsaw ghetto were strictly controlled. The Jews of the Soviet Union faced a particular problem. After the Hitler–Stalin pact, information about Nazi atrocities was suppressed; furthermore, Jews in this region had memories of the comparatively benign German occupation during the First World War. Although 1.5 million Soviet Jews fled from the German armies, 2.5 million remained, and some seem to have greeted the Germans with enthusiasm.

The Jews' understanding of their fate was filtered through previous experience. German Jews were well established. They had sometimes fought for their country in war, they valued its culture and had professional qualifications that would not be recognized abroad. It was hard to believe that the cost of waiting for the storm to pass in Germany would prove higher than that of beginning a new life in London or New York.[25] Consequently Jews were reluctant to leave during the early years of Nazi rule, although they were also sometimes enthusiastic to leave after about 1936. Once German Jews were pushed out of the professions and the education system, many of them recognized that the country offered no future.

Jews in Poland and the Soviet Union had different experiences. They were used to persecution, but this did not mean that they understood the scale of Nazi projects. On the contrary, communities that had lived through earlier pogroms and discrimination were perhaps least equipped to understand Nazism. Such communities assumed that persecution was a natural part of life, but that it could be survived. They overestimated the capacity of individual Germans to mitigate the impact of Jewish policy, and underestimated the extent to which Nazism's ambitions were greater than those of previous anti-Semitic regimes. Most of all, Jews overestimated the extent to which the Nazis would subordinate the destruction of the Jews to the rational exploitation of Jewish labor. Many ghetto leaders assumed that making themselves useful to the German war economy would ensure their survival.

Even if Jews had known every detail of Nazi plans, what could they have done? Most could not base their plans on their own interests and capacities alone – they lived with their families as part of wider communities. Children played a particularly large part in the passivity of Jews, and parents, especially mothers, focused on providing some semblance of a normal life for them. Primo Levi describes how mothers in an Italian transit camp washed their children's clothes and hung them out to dry on the barbed wire the night before deportation to Auschwitz. In June 1944, the "family camp" at Auschwitz was liquidated and mothers were given the chance to present themselves for selection as workers, but only 2 out of 600 took this offer up. The rest were gassed with their children.[26] Historians find it difficult to judge the choices that Jews made in such conditions. One author treats the Czech Jew Freddy Hirsch as a coward because he took poison when asked to organize armed resistance in Auschwitz;[27] another treats him as a hero because he organized games among the children that may have allowed them to forget their surroundings for a while.[28]

Conclusion

The operation required to ship Jews from all over Europe and kill them required the complicity of many people. The operation might have been initiated by a small number of Nazi leaders, but Hitler, Himmler, Heydrich and Eichmann required thousands of assistants to carry out their plans. Many of these assistants were not Nazis or even Germans. The civil servants who drafted regulations, the policemen who loaded trains and the foreign governments that accepted the deportation of Jews from their territory all participated. Circles of complicity can be drawn even wider. Leaders of the Jewish councils cooperated with the Germans and in some cases deceived their own followers about the fate that awaited them. The British government refused to broadcast everything that it knew about the extermination of the Jews or to take action, such as bombing the railway lines leading to Auschwitz, that might have slowed the rate of extermination. Participants had a wide variety of motives.

Very few wanted to exterminate all the European Jews; some would have been horrified by this outcome. Obedience, ambition, conformism and even the desire to save a particular group of Jews all played a role, along-side cruelty and political fanaticism. Many who would have described themselves as Nazis or anti-Semites did not agree about what such ideo-logical affiliation meant.

The number of people involved in the extermination of the Jews and the complexity of their motives makes explanation difficult. The geno-cide cannot be understood without reference to "scientific" racism and institutions such as the Rhineland Provincial Institute for Neuro-Psychological Eugenic Research, where neatly dressed, educated Germans pored over card index files.[29] On the other hand, it cannot be understood without reference to the eastern front hundreds of miles away, where Latvian auxiliaries sweated, swore and retched amidst the blood and brains and mud. The key to the extermination of the Jews was not that it had no cause but that it had so many.

CLICHÉS

A Photographic Essay

"Photographs, of course, are not arguments addressed to the reason; they are simply statements of fact addressed to the eye."

Virginia Woolf, Three Guineas *(1938)*

FOR MOST OF the twentieth century, hand-held cameras have been available to record dramatic events. Indeed, a succession of photographic images – clichés in the literal sense of the word – have molded our perception of the twentieth century. Say "appeasement" and most people see Neville Chamberlain waving a piece of paper; say "holocaust" and most people see striped pyjamas and shaved heads; say "1960s" and they see miniskirts on Carnaby Street. Photography is not, however, an unproblematic representation of "reality." Photographs are subject to all sorts of manipulation – most notoriously in Stalin's Russia, where purge victims were regularly airbrushed out of group photographs of Soviet leaders. The airbrush was also used in more unexpected ways long after Stalin's departure from power: in 1987, a photograph of Mikhail Gorbachev making a speech in one of the Asian republics was doctored to remove the line of KGB bodyguards who stood between him and his audience.

Photography outside the Soviet Union was also subject to a host of constraints. Governments forbade certain kinds of photographs. British soldiers in the First World War were not allowed to carry cameras. The Nazis banned all photographs of massacres of Jews and Russian prisoners of war carried out on the eastern front.

Most of all, photography, and the ways in which photographs were reproduced, were influenced by considerations other than deliberate and

politically motivated control. In the 1920s and 1930s illustrated magazines generated a new market for photographs. The *Berliner Illustrierte
Zeitung*, which sometimes sold 2 million copies, set the pattern for these
new sorts of publication. It was imitated by the American magazine *Life*,
the French *Vu* and the British *Picture Post*. Commercial and political pressures operated side by side. Many photographers were left-wing, but they
were also obliged to earn a living at a time when wealthy advertisers often
offered the most generous budgets for technical experimentation. *Vu* was
a self-consciously left-wing publication that sought to use techniques
(such as photomontage) that had originated in the Soviet Union, but its
founder, Lucien Vogel, had previously worked for an impeccably bourgeois journal, *La Gazette du Bon Ton*. Robert Doisneau was a left-wing
pacifist but he took some of his best pictures while on the payroll of Renault, a notoriously harsh employer that made much money from munitions contracts. Photographers developed a symbiotic relationship with
the makers of films. The Séeberger brothers provided photographs of
characteristically Parisian scenes that were then used as the inspiration for
Hollywood sets. Stills from films were often reproduced as if they were
photographs of real events; the crowd scenes from Eisenstein's *October*,
which were said to have involved more people than the original revolution, were often reproduced in this way. Robert Capa, perhaps the most
famous photographer of all, had an affair with Ingrid Bergman and wrote
a script based on his own life.

A group of highly talented photographers emerged during the 1930s
to take advantage of the new opportunities. Robert Capa (born André
Friedmann), David Seymour (born David Szymin, and known as
"Chim"), Henri Cartier-Bresson, Robert Doisneau and George Rodger
had much in common. They belonged to the same generation – all were
born between 1907 and 1914. None of them originally intended to earn
their living through photography, which was considered a menial profession. Capa started out as a student of political science, Chim wanted to
be a concert pianist and Cartier-Bresson insisted for most of his life that
he was primarily a painter. Many of them were themselves buffeted by the
political history of Europe. Capa and Chim were Jewish refugees from
central Europe (Hungary and Poland respectively); the former traveled on
a Nansen passport until a marriage of convenience earned him American
citizenship in 1940.

In the 1930s, Paris became the center of the photographic world –
partly because it was a gathering place for political refugees. Chim, Capa
and Cartier-Bresson met each other during this period. The first two
were living in cheap hotels (the marginality of their own lives accounts
for the interest that many photographers took in street life). The Alliance

photo agency, founded by the German Jewish refugee Maria Eisner, promoted their work.

The Spanish Civil War of 1936–39 provided photographers with a rare opportunity – a war fought in an accessible, photogenic country that gripped the imagination of editors around the world. In a few years the communist paper *Regards* printed 456 photographs of Spain. *Paris Soir* sent thirty-five correspondents and photographers to cover the war. Virginia Woolf's remarks about photography, quoted at the beginning of this chapter, are ostensibly about photographs of the Spanish Civil War.* Robert Capa in particular made his reputation in Spain, where his lover and fellow photographer Gerda Taro was killed. In 1938 *Picture Post* described the 25-year-old Capa as "the greatest war photographer in the world." The star status of foreign photographers often eclipsed the work of Spanish photographers, such as the Mayo brothers, whose work, distributed by the Republican government, tended to be dismissed as propaganda.

The Second World War provided another wave of opportunity. Capa, Rodger and Chim all worked with Allied armies (Capa even jumped onto a battlefield with American parachutists). Doisneau and Cartier-Bresson were involved in the war as combatants rather than photographers: both joined the French resistance and the former devoted much of his energies to forging identity papers, but both also seized the chance to take some memorable photographs, notably of the liberation of Paris.

In 1947 five photographers – Capa, Chim, Cartier-Bresson, George Rodger and the American Bill Vandivert – formed their own agency, Magnum, to coordinate their efforts and sell their photographs. Magnum became enormously influential, and magazine editors came to depend on it. The agency was run as a cooperative, and for the first time photographers controlled the copyright to their own pictures. Photographers were admitted as associate members after displaying their work and were then finally allowed to accede to full membership – but the annual general meetings of the agency (held in London, Paris and New York) were notoriously acrimonious.

Curiously, however, Magnum's foundation marked an end rather than a beginning. Magnum photographers, especially Capa, were mainly war specialists, and after 1945 they found little to interest them in Europe, where there were few overtly violent conflicts (indeed, Magnum photographs probably contributed to the notion that European history really

---

* The photographs that Virginia Woolf reproduces in her essay (photographs that represent, and mock, various forms of male power) suggest that Woolf's reference to photography as a simple statement of the facts is ironic.

came to an end in 1945). Photographers found their most striking images outside Europe, in Asia (covered by Cartier-Bresson), Africa (covered by Rodger), or the United States itself (covered by Bill Vandivert). Capa stepped on a landmine in Indochina in 1954; Chim died at Suez two years later. Furthermore, television increasingly displaced the illustrated magazines that had provided photographers with their most reliable source of income. American involvement in Vietnam (1966–75) produced some striking photographs but was mainly brought home to American audiences by television. Photography became increasingly self-conscious, elitist and prone to stage contrived portraits rather than capture action. As photography was perceived more and more as an art form, journalists became increasingly dubious about its capacity to present the truth, and in 1975 a British journalist suggested that one of the most famous photographs of the twentieth century (Capa's shot of a dying Spanish loyalist soldier) had been staged.

The changing image of the photographer was reflected in two films. Alfred Hitchcock's *Rear Window* (1954) portrayed a photojournalist in the classic Magnum mold. The hero is a brave magazine photographer specializing in war zones (he is, presumably, based on Capa, who had hung around the set of *Notorious* during his affair with Bergman). While recovering from a leg injury the photographer notices a murder and eventually traps the culprit – it is a film, therefore, about the photographer's ability to capture a real event. Michelangelo Antonioni's *Blow-Up* (1966), meanwhile, presents a very different image of photography. It portrays a narcissistic fashion photographer (based, it is said, on David Bailey) who believes he has caught a murder on film, but then becomes increasingly doubtful about whether his photograph has captured a real event. *Blow-Up* is a film about photography as artifice rather than as a window on reality.

By the end of the twentieth century, photographs were more ubiquitous than ever before. Technology made images easier to reproduce and almost no document, from a company report to a daily newspaper, was complete without color photographs. Yet, in a curious way, this very ubiquity made photographs less valuable. They were less likely to be seen as rare encapsulations of reality and more likely to be used as all-purpose illustrations of very general themes. Magazines became less concerned with news and more concerned with "lifestyle features," which required attractive illustration rather than the reporting of hard fact. "Image banks" provided photographs that could be used to accompany a whole variety of articles. In 1998 Magnum, the agency set up by left-wing adventurers to cover wars and revolutions, was offering a photograph of a sunflower that could, it was suggested, illustrate any article on "happiness."

EVGENI KHALDEI / VOLLER ERNST

Photograph of photographers, including Yevgeni Khaldei (1917–97), sitting in chairs recently vacated by Stalin, Churchill and Truman at the Potsdam conference, 1945. Khaldei is on the left, in Churchill's chair; the other two are Tass employees Samari Gurari (center) and Vladimir Mukosev. The Second World War was the high point of Khaldei's career – soon afterwards he fell out of favor, partly because he was a Jew and partly because he had been noticed enjoying a joke with Tito during a photo session.

ROBERT CAPA / MAGNUM PHOTOS

Robert Capa's first published
photograph, of Leon Trotsky addressing
a meeting in Copenhagen in 1932.
Trotsky's bodyguards were wary of
photographers and Capa later claimed
that he had to smuggle his camera into
this meeting.

While Capa was making his reputation by photographing Trotsky, Soviet technicians were devoting all their skill to removing him from photographs.

DAVID SEYMOUR / MAGNUM PHOTOS

David Seymour's photograph of
Republicans after looting a church in
Barcelona. The Spanish Civil War was
the midwife of photojournalism.

'MMAGINI NEMICHE / EDITRICE COMPOSITORI, BOLOGNA

Soldiers holding severed heads. This photograph appears to have been taken in Morocco in 1923, but was subsequently published by the Italian newspaper *Corriere della Sera* as an example of "Republican atrocities" in the Spanish Civil War. At one point Magnum distributed this photograph as "an example of Nationalist atrocities found by David Seymour."

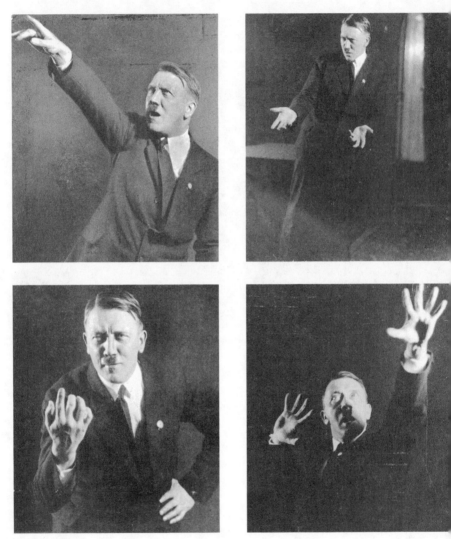

POPPERFOTO

Adolf Hitler practiced for his public speeches by striking poses such as this in front of his personal photographer, Heinrich Hoffmann.

A study of Charles de Gaulle taken by Cecil Beaton. Beaton (1904–80) was a fashion photographer and society portraitist whose skills were turned to the celebration of generals and bomber crews during the war. De Gaulle, an accomplished television performer, photographed badly. In the 1960s, Henri Cartier-Bresson asked to take his photograph but de Gaulle objected, saying, "I am old and wrinkled."

ROBERT CAPA / MAGNUM PHOTOS

Photograph by Robert Capa of a soldier, captioned: "The last man to die: Leipzig, 1945." Of course, people went on dying long after the end of fighting – a fact that was illustrated by George Rodger's photograph of Bergen-Belsen *(opposite)*. It is interesting that Capa, the Jewish Hungarian émigré, should have concentrated so heavily on military action while Rodger, the English public schoolboy, took photographs of concentration camps and refugees.

GEORGE RODGER / LIFE MAGAZINE / TIME INC.

YEVGENI KHALDEI / VOLLER ERNST

Khaldei's famous photograph of Soviet soldiers raising the red flag over the Reichstag in May 1945. Khaldei had used pre-war Baedecker guides to inform himself about landmarks in Berlin. Since no red flags were available at the front, Khaldei got a tailor to sew a hammer and sickle onto three red tablecloths (the other two were flown at Tempelhof and on the Brandenburg Gate). He had to airbrush out a second wristwatch that one soldier was wearing in order to conceal the fact that the soldier had been looting. The airbrushing must have been designed for a Western audience, since most Soviet citizens would have known that any Red Army soldier wearing even one wristwatch had been looting.

YEVGENI KHALDEI / VOLLER ERNST

Khaldei's photograph of a Nazi official in
Vienna who shot his wife and children to
prevent their falling into the hands of
advancing Soviet troops. One of the
daughters, lying on the bench, is said to
have struggled violently before being
shot. In 1945, German, Hungarian and
Austrian women were victims of violence
from both Red Army soldiers and their
own menfolk who wished to "save their
honor."

MGM / REEL POSTER ARCHIVE

"Classlessness." The British poster for
Michelangelo Antonioni's 1966 film
Blow-Up, about a fashionable
photographer. London photographers,
especially David Bailey, born in 1938
and said to be the model for Antonioni's
hero, reflected, or created, the myth of a
classless London in which figures from
the worlds of pop music, film and
gangland mingled on equal terms with
the aristocracy.

ROBERT DOISNEAU / RAPHO / NETWORK

"Class." Robert Doisneau's photomontage of injured and artificial hands against a background of the steelworks at Thionville, Lorraine, in 1973. Doisneau (1912–94) had much in common with Bailey. Both men staged most of their pictures, often in a self-consciously artificial way, rather than attempt to "capture reality." Doisneau was as capable as Bailey of producing a fashion plate for *Vogue* or a portrait of a film star, but he also had strong left-wing commitments. This photograph was taken for *La Vie Ouvrière*, the magazine of the communist-dominated French trade union confederation.

JOSEF KOUDELKA / MAGNUM PHOTOS

Prague, August 1968. The boy's apparent Nazi salute is open to more than one interpretation. Some Warsaw Pact soldiers interpreted gestures such as this to mean that the Czechs were themselves Nazis; in retrospect, the fact that people could indulge in such mockery and not be shot reflects the comparative mildness of the Soviet troops. In 1969 Josef Koudelka (born in 1938) won the Robert Capa Gold Medal, which was awarded anonymously, for his work on the Prague Spring. He left Czechoslovakia in 1970 and joined Magnum the following year. Photographs of Prague in 1968 give the misleading impression that Koudelka is a Capaesque action man; he is in fact a gentle photographer whose first major project concerned Czech gypsies.

CORBIS / BETTMANN

The Albanian communist leader Enver Hoxha. It is interesting to note how
the cliché of the smiling party leader casting his vote was circulated even in
a country where elections meant nothing. Is this the real Hoxha? The dictator
employed a double, a dentist from the north of the country, to fool potential
assassins. The double was made to undergo plastic surgery and fattened up
in order to resemble the leader. After the fall of communism, the double was
attacked by a mob and subsequently put out one of his own eyes while
attempting to mutilate his face with a knife.

JEAN GAUMY / MAGNUM PHOTOS

Polish workers on strike in 1980 by Magnum photographer Jean Gaumy (born 1948). The fact that communist authorities plastered factories with photographs of managers and party leaders made it more difficult for them to evade responsibility for unpopular decisions – at the very time when Western capitalists were becoming increasingly adept at evading such responsibility.

Opposite

A little girl dashes across sniper alley in Grozny to ask for some sweets from a Chechen soldier. This picture was taken by French photographer Éric Bouvet on the last day of the war there in August 1996. Earlier in the morning the Russians were still bombing and dynamiting; by 8 A.M. bodies were being covered up or cleared; by 9 A.M. civilians were out on the streets regarding their devastated homes. The Chechen war seems to have gone some way towards reviving the cliché of the photographer as action man: Bouvet (born 1961) had to disguise himself as a Russian soldier in order to get photographs such as this. He returned to Grozny in 1999, by which time the buildings in the background had all been razed to the ground.

ÉRIC BOUVET

PART III

Postwar Europe

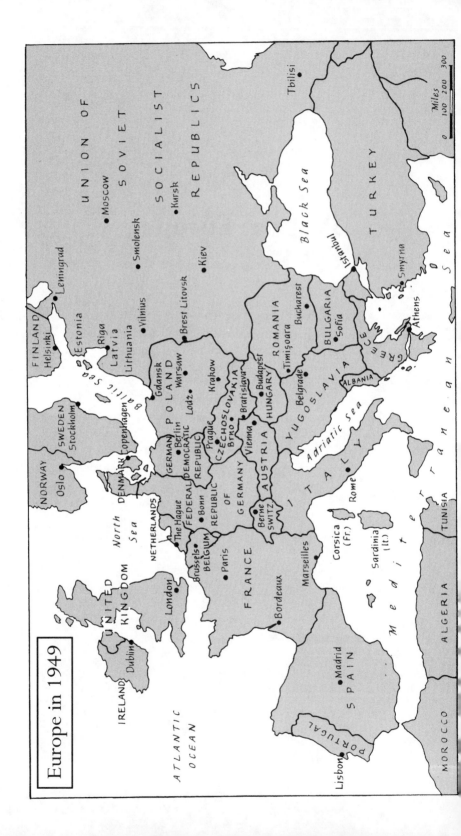

Europe in 1949

"[The] tragedy is vast. It may vary in intensity; the peasantry are reasonably well provided and the rich can use the black market, but the poor urban populations of Europe, perhaps a quarter of its four hundred millions, are all condemned to go hungry this winter. Some of them will starve. The plague spots are Warsaw, where, according to Mr Lehman, Director-General of the UNRRA [United Nations Relief and Rehabilitation Administration], ten thousand people will die of starvation; Hungary, particularly Budapest, where deaths from famine may reach a million; Austria, particularly Vienna and lower Austria, where the rate of calories is below 1,000 a day (the rate needed to maintain reasonable health is well over 2,000), and where in some towns, Wiener-Neustadt for instance, there is already starvation; the Saar, where children are reported to be dying of hunger; Northern Italy, the Ruhr, Berlin and most large towns in Germany, where it is proving difficult to keep the calorie rate up to 1,200. Greece and Western Holland are improving, but are still below full subsistence level. Paris and the larger towns of France face a new food crisis. Nor does this bare recital of calories and diets cover those grisly companions of starvation – tuberculosis, dysentery, typhoid and typhus, rickets – nor the appalling figures for maternal and infant mortality.

"One person in ten in Poland has TB – the figure for Warsaw is one in five – it is rampant in Yugoslavia, and the Czechs say that out of 700,000 needy children 50 per cent have been discovered to be tuberculous. Infant mortality in Berlin has doubled. In Budapest it has risen from 16 to 40 per cent since September. There are no figures for the Ruhr, but English visitors have been told that very few new-born babies are expected to live this winter."

The Economist, *26 January 1946*[1]

For most of Europe, the years immediately after the Second World War were exceptionally grim, sometimes worse than the war itself. Historians tend to write about its last months in terms of "liberation" and "victory," but these were often the months in which fighting caused most suffering. The British army lost more men between the Normandy landings of June 1944 and the defeat of Germany than it had done during the first four years of the war. The battle for Berlin, which took place just before the German surrender, left half a million casualties, and inhabitants of Germany (including the millions of slave laborers who had been deported there) endured bombing by the Western Allies and then random violence, pillage and rape by the Red Army. The Nazi regime had become more radical and barbarous as its end approached, and its full horror dawned on the inhabitants of western Europe only when they saw the first newsreel photographs of concentration camps, where people continued to die of typhus and starvation under the despairing eyes of the troops who had liberated them.

Food and fuel were scarce and the winter of 1946–47 was severe. In Russia, Moldavia and the Ukraine, there was famine. The harvest of 1946 was less than half that of 1940, but the state still stored, and even exported, grain; from 1946 to 1948, about 2 million inhabitants of the Soviet Union starved to death.[2] Many economies collapsed. Inflation in Hungary was the highest ever seen in Europe. Worthless currencies were replaced by bartering in cigarettes, and scrounging from occupying armies was the only way to make a living. In Hamburg two years after the end of the war, 25,000 people made their living from trading on the black market at a time when only 7,000 were employed in the city's shipyards.[3]

The British tend to remember this period with bitter amusement – Elizabeth David first began writing about Mediterranean food to take her mind off the cold and hunger of a weekend in an English provincial town in the winter of 1946. In central and eastern Europe, few found much to laugh about. In Berlin, a man was hanged for having murdered an old woman in order to steal her potatoes;[4] in the Ukraine, a woman driven mad by hunger ate her two children.[5] Matters were particularly bad for the displaced persons in the region, many of whom had been bombed out of their houses or had fled west to avoid the advancing Red Army. Millions of ethnic Germans were expelled from their former homes in Czechoslovakia or Poland, where they were replaced by Czechs and Poles who had themselves been displaced from their homes. Survivors of concentration camps wandered in search of relatives or sat in refugee centers, numbed by the horror of what they had seen.

Many of those who had suffered worst during the previous five years continued to endure misery after the German surrender. Russian prisoners of war were regarded with suspicion by their own compatriots – some went straight from German prison camps to Soviet ones. Not surprisingly, many prisoners tried to avoid falling into the hands of the authorities and turned to crime, which further increased the disorder of eastern Europe. Around 2 million Russian ex-prisoners of war and deserters were at large in Soviet-occupied Europe, and banditry by such men was still being reported in the woods outside Berlin as late as 1948.[6] Former slave laborers in the areas of Germany occupied by the Western powers did not fare much better. Hunger or desire for revenge drove some to attack the German population, and the military authorities suppressed such crimes with a savagery that sometimes recalled Nazi racism. Most of those hanged in the British zone of occupation from July 1945 until December 1946 were Poles. In January 1948 a British judge sentenced a Ukrainian former slave laborer to death with these words: "He is a rather low type of humanity unlikely to be of value to any respectable community at any time."[7]

Stalin's Russia was more powerful in 1945 than ever before. Some Europeans regarded this development with enthusiasm, but they were always a minority: no communist party ever won a fair election. There had been much rhetoric about antifascist unity during the war, but in reality many Europeans had been given the chance to find out that life in the Soviet Union was terrible. Among those who had had the opportunity to inspect the workers' paradise at close quarters were Poles deported in 1939 and Axis soldiers taken prisoner on the eastern front – who often did not get back to their home countries until the 1950s. French resistance leaders had seen communist courage but also learned how ruthless communists could be in pursuit of the party's interests. News of the Katyn massacre, when the NKVD had murdered Polish officers, filtered back to western Europe after German forces discovered mass graves in 1943. British officers charged with deporting Cossacks, who had fought with the Germans, back to the Soviet Union discovered that what awaited these people in their homeland was so terrible that some of them killed their own children.

As Europe became divided between East and West, and as repression in the East became more severe, many Europeans were filled with pessimism. In the West, some feared that another war would sweep across Europe. In the East, many opponents of communism fervently hoped for such a war until American inactivity during the Hungarian uprising of 1956 finally convinced them that the armies of the democracies were never going to liberate them. Western generals believed that Soviet advance was likely to be stopped at the Pyrenees, which was why the integration of Franco's Spain into the Western Alliance became so urgent. Novels written, or set, in the late 1940s reveal much about the atmosphere, and apart from the relentless enthusiasm of Stalinists such as Roger Vailland, the literature of the period was almost universally dark. Graham Greene's *The Third Man* conjured up postwar Vienna as a city of bitter disappointment and ruthless greed. George Orwell's *Nineteen Eighty-Four* anticipated the horrors of a communist future, but the drab, squalid uniformity of a life alleviated only by "Victory Gin" owed something to London in the 1940s as well as to what Orwell knew of the Soviet Union. Two films from opposite ends of Europe capture the atmosphere of the late 1940s: Carol Reed's *Odd Man Out* (made in 1947 and set in Belfast) and Andrzej Wajda's *Ashes and Diamonds* (made in 1958 but set in the Poland of 1945) are both about lone, hunted, dying gunmen.

The bleak pessimism of the late 1940s was dispelled by two changes. The first was the political change in the East. The death of Stalin on March 5, 1953, Khrushchev's subsequent rise to prominence in the Soviet Union and the denunciation of Stalin's crimes reduced communist repression and made the Soviet Union seem less threatening to the West. Curiously, Khrushchev's suppression of the Hungarian rising in 1956 reduced ideological tension in Europe, discrediting communism in the eyes of many western European party members and beginning a long process by which the Soviet Union came to be regarded as simply an imperial power rather than the center of a new religion. The fanaticism and witch-hunting of the Cold War were over.

The second change came from rapid economic growth, which had political consequences. Conflicts that had been intensified in the interwar period by the struggle for scarce resources could now be bought off, which happened on a national level as higher wages sapped working-class militancy, and on an international level as some countries – notably West Germany – used their wealth to secure political concessions from their communist neighbors. Increased prosperity was associated with changes in people's everyday lives, particularly the diffusion of television and cars, which had many social and political consequences.

Some historians describe the thirty years after the Second World War as a "golden age," but for whom was it golden? The answer is: for the very people who comment most on social change. Television producers are an obvious example. Television expanded hugely during the 1950s and 1960s, and broadcasters, especially English broadcasters, were taken more seriously than at any time before or since as catalysts for, and commentators on, social change. Journalists, especially on glossy, style-conscious magazines such as the *Sunday Times Colour Supplement*, also had good memories of the postwar period. Most importantly of all, it was a good time for western European universities. The rapid expansion of higher education offered a route out of the lower middle class for a generation of bright young people. Sociologists, political scientists and, to a much greater extent than they care to admit, historians looked at their own disciplines with enormous confidence. It was the era of ambitious explanatory models, a time when the social sciences seemed to produce answers rather than questions. Malcolm Bradbury's Howard Kirk strutted around the campus of his new university offering to solve any problem with "a little Marx, a little Freud and a little social history."

Many commentators took prosperity for granted, even if they claimed not to believe in the system that had produced it. A. J. P. Taylor casually remarked in a television lecture on the 1930s, "Of course, now we know how to solve unemployment." Eastern Europe did not feature much in such optimistic views. Until 1956, some still believed in the communist experiment, but after the Soviet invasion of Hungary western European intellectuals tore up their party cards. Emmanuel Le Roy Ladurie was so outraged by the news that he cycled to party headquarters in his pyjamas to resign his membership. However, the loss of faith in communism was not accompanied by much interest in the fate of the millions of Europeans who continued to live under communist rule. Many left-wingers in western Europe simply transferred the admiration that they had formerly given to the Soviet Union to "freedom fighters" in Latin America, Algeria or Vietnam. The Prague Spring, the only development in eastern Europe that attracted much interest in the West, was often seen as merely a pale reflection of events in the Boulevard Saint-Michel. A curious dichotomy developed. Scholars who studied communist Europe devoted their attention to "Kremlinology," that is, the high politics of the Soviet leadership, while western Europe was increasingly studied in terms of "society."

Even in western Europe, "society" was defined fairly narrowly, particularly during the 1960s. Indeed, anyone who says "sixties" instantly conjures up an image of young people in one of a few western European cities. It is a view that has become enshrined in historical textbooks – one presents London as "the vanguard of social change" and adds, "'Swinging London' of the 1960s . . . became the European youth nirvana in place of Paris or Munich. The result was a national youth movement which surpassed all class barriers."[8] Michel Winock talks of the 1960s as "*les années anglaises.*"

Almost all the concepts applied to "swinging London" are questionable. "Classlessness" did not mean the abolition of class distinctions but rather the frisson generated by encounters between a small group of young people from patrician backgrounds (such as Kit Lambert, who managed The Who) and an even smaller group of young people who had risen from the working or lower middle class by making money in rock music, film or photography. The English "sexual revolution" did not produce any challenge to established values more radical than those that had been discussed in the 1920s; indeed, it began with the publication of a book – *Lady Chatterley's Lover* – that had been written in the 1920s. In any case, talk of sexual freedom in the 1960s was accompanied by an ever more intense emphasis on the heterosexual couple, marriage and the family. Finally, "youth culture" in the 1960s was a much tamer affair than might be imagined from the portentous declarations of the self-appointed leaders of the "younger generation" or the hysterical reactions of a few middle-aged men (Jeremy Thorpe described the music of Bill Haley as "musical Mau Mau"). During the 1960s the division between young and old in western Europe (especially in England) was much less sharp than it had been after the First World War.

Most importantly, the assumption that London was "in the vanguard of social change" is simply wrong. By any objective measurement, southern England was the most socially static part of Europe: economic growth was slower and started from a much higher base. Cars, consumerism and even television – which transformed postwar continental western Europe – had already been important in London by 1939.

Consider four children born in the last months of the Second World War, one in London, one in the German community in Prague, one in eastern Poland and one in Sicily.* The first child experiences the excitements of "1960s culture": he sees the Rolling Stones perform in Hyde Park, demonstrates against the Vietnam war and gets a job in a boutique selling Mary Quant handbags. However, for all the talk of novelty and youth, the life of such a teenager is hardly incomprehensible to his parents; the very fact that London commentators found so much time to worry about hemlines suggests that they did not have many more dramatic preoccupations. Television producers looking for a teenager to present the program *Ready, Steady, Go* asked candidates, "What is the most important thing for young people today?" Cathy McGowan got the job after saying one word: "Clothes."[9]

It is unlikely that our three other teenagers believed that flared trousers were the most important development of postwar Europe. For at least the first five years of their lives, they would have answered Cathy McGowan's question with the word "food." The German child and the Polish child would have been lucky to reach their first birthday. The experience of all three would probably have involved moving hundreds of miles from their place of birth: the German is ejected from Czechoslovakia; the Pole leaves his birthplace (annexed by the Soviet Union) to settle in an area of Poland

---

* Let us assume that all four children are boys. Their lives would be even more complicated if they were girls.

taken from Germany; and the Sicilian is taken to Belgium where his father seeks work in the coalfields.

Subsequent developments make the lives of our three children even more different from those of their parents. The German's parents are deeply traumatized. His father, assuming that he survived, might be absent for several years and would return to a family that he barely knew after being broken by years in a Soviet prisoner-of-war camp. The child's perception of his parents changes as he grows up. He asks increasingly awkward questions about his parents' relations with the Nazi regime and particularly about his father's behavior as a soldier on the eastern front. An understanding of what his mother endured during the Red Army occupation of Prague might not come until the 1990s (indeed, the mother might talk about such matters with her feminist granddaughter more easily than with her conventionally left-wing, and therefore pro-Soviet, son).

The Sicilian child's alienation from his parents is less extreme. He is grateful for the sacrifices that his father made to secure his education and security, yet this very education creates a gulf. The Sicilian grows up speaking a language (French) that is incomprehensible to his parents (who are really comfortable only with Sicilian dialect) and his world revolves around books that mean nothing to his illiterate mother. Paradoxically, growing up with his parents would make his experiences different from theirs. The Sicilian lives in the "nuclear family," so important to postwar European culture, while his parents never feel happy without an extended family of grandparents, uncles and aunts.

The Polish child's world is changed by industrialization and urbanization. He ends up in a crowded, badly built apartment near the Gdansk shipyards, and his grandmother's stories of peasant life in the 1930s seem to belong to a different world. However, far from rebelling, the Polish child idealizes his family's past. He never misses Mass and he advertises his admiration for an uncle who died fighting with the Polish Home Army. He joins the strikes of 1970 and, in the year that his London contemporary attends the Isle of Wight pop festival, carries a candle in an illegal procession to mourn his fellow strikers who have been shot by the army.

The period described by the following chapters ended in the mid-1970s, which were marked by the slowdown in economic growth that accompanied the rise in oil prices of 1973. Just as our view of the 1950s and 1960s tends to emphasize optimism, rapid change and prosperity, so our view of the mid-1970s emphasizes crisis, decline, loss of confidence and revival of conflict. In Britain, this was the era in which Margaret Thatcher began to challenge the liberal consensus that had been so comfortable for those left-wingers who had pretended not to believe in it, and in which the leaders of the 1960s "youth culture" found themselves spluttering with middle-aged indignation at the irreverence of spotty seventeen-year-olds with safety pins through their noses. Clearly, for western European political leaders and intellectuals, the 1970s were a worrying decade. For the first time since 1956, the intelligentsia began to interest themselves in the affairs of eastern Europe and to look to dissidents living under communist regimes for the certainties that they had lost. However, the great mass of Europe's population did not experience the 1970s as a time of crisis. Economic growth, as measured by statisticians, was slower, but living standards, as experienced by consumers, were higher than ever before, and often continued to rise even as economists insisted that "we are paying ourselves more than we earn." In the 1950s and 1960s many Germans, southern European migrants and, most of all, inhabitants of eastern Europe experienced economic expansion and social change in terms of upheaval and, sometimes, suffering. It was only after growth had slowed that they began to enjoy the fruits of their labor.

1
TAKING SIDES

"I wrote out on a half-sheet of paper:

Romania
Russia 90%
The others. 10%
Greece
Great Britain 90%
(in accord with USA)
Russia 10%
Yugoslavia. 50–50%
Hungary. 50–50%*
Bulgaria
Russia 75%
The others. 25%

---

* In 1957 Árpád Göncz, President of Hungary after the fall of communism, was sent to prison for six years. Like many eastern European intellectuals, he used his time in prison to improve his command of Western languages (Milovan Djilas translated *Paradise Lost* into Serbo-Croat during one of his periods in prison). Eventually the authorities decided to make use of his abilities and asked him to translate Western works for the benefit of party leaders. This produced an absurd situation, very typical of Kádár's Hungary, in which a political prisoner received uncensored copies of the *New York Times*. One of the books that he was asked to translate was Winston Churchill's memoirs. He and his cellmates, all veterans of the Budapest uprising, must have derived some bitter amusement from the reference to the 50 percent Anglo-American influence in Hungary.

I pushed this across to Stalin, who had by then heard the translation. There was a slight pause. Then he took his blue pencil and made a large tick upon it, and passed it back to us. It was all settled in no more time than it takes to set down."[1]

THE DIVISION OF Europe was not settled by this brief exchange between Churchill and Stalin at the Moscow Conference in October 1944. Nothing had been said about most European countries (the absence of Poland was conspicuous). However, the general principle that the Soviet Union and the Western powers would respect each other's sphere of influence was established, and, broadly speaking, the two sides honored the arrangement. There was a decline in the cordiality of relations after 1947, but no attempt to challenge the frontiers that divided a Soviet-dominated East from an American-dominated West. Only once, during the Berlin blockade of 1948–49, did the two camps seriously disagree about who should control a part of Europe. During the late 1940s many Europeans believed that war was imminent, and even the leaders of the two blocs seem to have been frightened that their opposite numbers were planning war. But they were wrong: Soviet and American forces never exchanged a single shot. Soviet military force was not used against Western capitalist countries but against communist states in eastern Europe, Imre Nagy's Hungary in 1956 and Alexander Dubček's Czechoslovakia in 1968. Even between 1948 and 1953, the height of the Cold War, the most savage dispute in Europe was that which divided Tito's communist regime in Yugoslavia from the Soviet Union and its compliant satellites.

American intervention in postwar Europe was less direct and brutal than that of the Soviet Union. American troops never shot European civilians, and American advisers never gave direct orders to western European governments. In part, this was a matter of geography. America was 3,000 miles from Europe and no European army had set foot on American soil for more than a century. It is fairer to compare Soviet intervention in Hungary with American intervention in Nicaragua than with American intervention in Italy. Economics were also important. The Soviet economy was devastated in 1945, and Soviet leaders tried to repair the damage by exploiting their military hegemony. In East Germany, 70,000 Soviet officials pillaged about a third of all productive capacity. America, by contrast, was rich. She could afford to provide generous aid and assumed, rightly, that most Europeans wished to emulate her prosperity.

There was always a division between American and Soviet spheres of influence, but for the first two or three years after the German surrender it did not have much of an influence on the internal politics of the countries involved. In western Europe, there were communist ministers in the governments of France, Italy, Belgium and Finland; in eastern Europe, there were noncommunist ministers in all governments (indeed, at first they comprised a majority in most governments). Coexistence did not last. Gradually, the noncommunist forces in eastern Europe lost power and the most independent-minded ministers were expelled from office, exiled or killed. Noncommunist parties often survived in name, but in practice became appendices to the Communist Party. In western Europe, communist parties continued to exist, often with a large representation in parliament, but their ministers resigned from the governments of France, Italy and Belgium in 1947 and left the government of Finland the following year.

Forms of Soviet influence

There were three ways in which the Soviet Union could exercise influence in its allotted region. First, it could extend its own frontiers. In 1945, the Soviet Union annexed parts of Poland, Germany, Romania, Czechoslovakia and Finland; it had incorporated Estonia, Latvia and Lithuania in 1940.

Second, the Soviet Union could tie states with noncommunist governments into treaties that guaranteed Soviet interests, and at first it seemed possible that this approach would be adopted in most of eastern Europe. Communism was weaker in most eastern European countries than in France or Italy, and in many cases Stalin himself had purged eastern European communist leaders foolish enough to seek refuge in Moscow. After the war, Soviet behavior often seemed designed to exercise hegemony through conventional military and diplomatic means rather than through the establishment of native communist governments. Stalin dealt with representatives of the old regime – including King Michael of Romania, who was decorated by the Soviet Union for his part in the antifascist coup of 1944. Soviet actions seemed likely to weaken support for communism. The harsh terms imposed on defeated Axis powers (Germany, Hungary, Romania, Austria, Bulgaria) were not calculated to evoke waves of pro-Soviet feeling, and the deindustrialization of Germany, which would have resulted from Soviet reparations proposals, did not bode well for the construction of a regime dependent on the German proletariat.

In the end, the only two countries in the Soviet sphere of influence that did not become communist states were Finland and Austria. It is not easy to explain why either attracted the favor of the Soviet Union; both fought against her in the Second World War. Furthermore, both had strong left-wing traditions (the Finnish Communist Party attracted more than 20 percent of the vote) that might have provided a popular basis for communist rule. In spite of this, Austria and Finland were allowed to maintain their internal freedom: Austria was established as a neutral state after the withdrawal of Soviet troops in 1955; Finland was obliged to defer to the Soviet Union in foreign policy matters but was allowed to exclude communist ministers from her government and refuse the offer of Warsaw Pact membership in 1955.

The establishment of communist-dominated governments was the most common method by which the Soviet Union exercised its power – such governments were installed in Poland, Hungary, Czechoslovakia, Romania and Bulgaria (Albania and Yugoslavia, where communists seized power without direct Soviet help, were more complicated cases). Why did Moscow support the establishment of communist governments in eastern Europe? A common response is to blame the Americans. "Revisionist" historians claim that the Soviet Union was forced to indulge in defensive expansionism in order to protect itself from the United States, which pledged to "roll back communism."

It is true that American policy towards communism hardened in 1945 after Truman's accession to the presidency, but the United States never threatened military intervention to save any part of eastern Europe from communism, even though, until 1949, it had a monopoly on the atomic bomb. American passivity was starkly illustrated in Bulgaria, where the United States retained some influence over the communist-dominated government until the peace treaty relating to Bulgaria had been implemented. On June 5, 1947, the day after the U.S. Senate ratified the treaty, Nikola Petkov, the leader of the Agrarian Union, was arrested on the floor of parliament. He was hanged on September 23; the United States recognized Bulgaria on October 1.[2]

The most significant and "provocative" defiance of the Soviet Union came not from America but from communist Yugoslavia. The fact that Marshal Tito's forces had liberated the country with almost no help from the Red Army had given the Yugoslav Communist Party dangerous ideas about its own importance. Exploitative trading arrangements and the brusqueness of Soviet advisers brought a confrontation in 1948, when Stalin incited the Yugoslavs, without success, to overthrow their leader and contemplated military intervention. Purges wiped out communist leaders suspected of "Titoism" (lack of deference to the Soviet Union) in other countries.

The brutality of Soviet intervention in eastern European affairs was not a sign that Soviet leaders enjoyed complete control in the area; events often took a turn that the Soviet Union had not planned or hoped for.[3] It may be wrong to look for too much rationality in Soviet policy during the second half of the 1940s. Stalinism was "rational" in its dealings with external matters – that is, the Soviet Union backed down when confronted by stronger forces – but it was paranoid and irrational when dealing with internal affairs. The problem was that eastern Europe's status was uncertain and changing, which could become a circular process. The closer the countries in the region came to being communist, the more their affairs were seen as "internal matters" and the more opposition was intolerable. Andrei Vyshinsky, who conducted much of Soviet diplomacy from 1945 to 1954, had previously acted as prosecutor in the show trials of the 1930s.

Communists in eastern Europe played on two particular advantages in order to ensure that they eventually dominated the governments of which they were members. The first was control of security. Communists paid great attention to the Ministry of the Interior, the police force and the army, which gave them the power to make life difficult for their opponents. In Czechoslovakia and Poland, the Ministers of Defense were communist sympathizers, and in Czechoslovakia the struggle between communist and noncommunist ministers that led to the coup of 1948 sprang from the use that the communists were making of their control over the police. Communists also benefited from the fact that Ministries of the Interior in eastern Europe were often ministries of electoral management. In January 1947, the Polish Peasant Party's candidates were disqualified in ten electoral districts out of a total of fifty-two.[4]

Control of particular ministries gave communists a chance to exploit the aftermath of war and occupation. Thousands of people had been compromised by their association with Nazism or authoritarian regimes, but communists worked with such people when it suited them. In Hungary, 80 percent of civil servants who had worked under Horthy were still in office in June 1945, and most survived for another two years,[5] while in East Germany 30 of the 312 delegates to a regional meeting of the German Workers' Party in 1954 had been members of the Nazi Party.[6] However, communists also used postwar purges to dispose of their enemies. In Bulgaria, there were said to have been between 20,000 and 100,000 summary executions in the years following the war.[7] Communists also benefited from the distribution of land that had formerly belonged to German inhabitants of Poland and Czechoslovakia. Although the expulsion of Germans was not an exclusively communist policy, communist officials often gained control of redistribution and their powers of patronage were thus expanded.

Eastern European communists also benefited from Soviet support in the former Axis countries under Allied occupation. The Soviet authorities arrested Béla Kovács, secretary of the Hungarian Smallholders' Party, in February 1947. In Bulgaria, General Sergei Biryuzov, the chairman of the

Allied Control Commission, forced the head of the Agrarian Union, who seemed insufficiently malleable, out of office in January 1945.[8]

The communist takeover in eastern Europe was usually portrayed as a Soviet triumph, but in many ways it was a source of vast problems for Soviet leaders. It created a sprawling multinational empire, in which the Soviet Union always exercised ultimate responsibility (because it felt obliged to prevent communist leaders from being thrown out of power) without exercising total power (because local communist leaders had to be allowed at least the semblance of autonomy). The problems that the "people's democracies" presented to Moscow can be illustrated by comparing them with Finland. The people's democracies were expensive; after the early 1950s, all of them stopped paying reparations and the Soviet Union picked up the bill for maintaining troops in its client states. Finland, by contrast, paid reparations to the Soviet Union until the early 1960s. Furthermore, the people's democracies remained a constant source of friction with the West, while Finland provided a bridge between East and West (the accords most associated with "détente" were signed in Helsinki in 1975). On October 29, 1956, the American ambassador to Moscow suggested to Khrushchev that the Soviet Union might be better off if it had relations with eastern European countries of the kind that it had with Finland. Khrushchev, who was on the verge of launching an expensive and risky operation to reinstall Soviet clients in Hungary, agreed.[9]

Western conservatives used the term "Finlandization" to describe the state to which European countries might be reduced if they adopted neutralist policies in the East/West conflict, yet Finland might have provided a good model for many groups. It was not seen as a threat by either side and its people benefited from prosperity and democracy unimaginable in even the most liberal of the communist-ruled states. Indeed, the people really threatened by "Finlandization" were eastern European communist rulers, who feared that the Soviet Union might abandon its eastern European clients, concerns that were particularly acute in East Germany, where it seemed possible that Moscow might accept free elections in return for a united and neutral country. Gorbachev's foreign policy from late 1988 was a belated attempt to "Finlandize" eastern Europe, with the aim of maintaining military alliances with states such as Hungary, Poland and Czechoslovakia even after they had abandoned communist rule.

Once communist regimes had been established in eastern Europe, Soviet military and political intervention could be very direct. The humiliation and threats that Stalin used to cow his foreign allies and Russian subordinates emerges from a description by Jakub Berman (a Pole) of a meeting in Moscow:

BERMAN: "Once, I think it was in 1948, I danced with Molotov."

INTERVIEWER: "You mean with Mrs Molotov?"

BERMAN: "No, she wasn't there; she'd been sent to a labor camp. I danced with Molotov – it must have been a waltz, or at any rate something simple, because I haven't a clue about how to dance – and I just moved my feet to the rhythm."

INTERVIEWER: "As the woman?"

BERMAN: "Molotov led; I wouldn't know how. He wasn't a bad dancer, actually, and I tried to keep in step with him, but for my part it was more like clowning than dancing."

INTERVIEWER: "What about Stalin, whom did he dance with?"

BERMAN: "Oh no, Stalin didn't dance. Stalin turned the gramophone: he treated that as his duty. He never left it. He would put on a record and watch."

INTERVIEWER: "He watched you?"

BERMAN: "He watched us dance."

INTERVIEWER: "So you had a good time?"

BERMAN: "Yes, it was pleasant, but with an inner tension."

INTERVIEWER: "You didn't really have fun?"

BERMAN: "Stalin really had fun."[10]

Eastern European communists were painfully aware of the threat to their security. Often Soviet protégés – those who had spent the war in Moscow – knew most about Stalin's methods. East German communists knew that some of their comrades had been handed over to Hitler in 1939, and the Polish Communist Party had been almost wiped out on Stalin's orders. One Polish communist leader asked Stalin about the fate of his compatriots with tactless insistence until Beria said, "Why do you keep fucking around with Josif Vissarionovich [Stalin]? Why don't you fuck off from him? That's my advice to you. You'll regret it if you don't."[11]

Eastern European communist leaders were not, however, just Moscow's stooges. Many were brave and able people, who had usually joined the party when doing so was highly dangerous. They were often well educated and knew something about countries outside their own (most had been exiled in either Moscow or the West); they resembled the Bolsheviks of 1917 far more than the hack functionaries who dominated the Soviet leadership by the late 1940s. Furthermore, unlike communists in the West, the eastern Europeans did not have many illusions about Soviet behavior. Many knew that participation in government was likely to endanger their lives. They would have defended their actions by arguing that communist rule in their countries was a good thing in the long run, whatever its short-run costs to the country (and themselves). In some ways, they turned out to be right. They succeeded in persuading the Soviet Union that its interests were best maintained by the establishment of communist states in the East, which, for all the postwar seizures of property, remained more prosperous than the military leviathan that ruled over them and (from a communist point of view) protected them from the West. In some respects, the communists who maneuvered Moscow into supporting their vision of communism in Poland and Czechoslovakia resembled Jean Monnet maneuvering Washington into supporting his vision of a modernized France, although being seen to be manipulative carried a far higher price in the East than in the West. Trade ministers who negotiated too hard in their dealings with Moscow were often the first to fall victim to Stalinist purges.

Communist states in eastern Europe were not mere replicas of the Soviet Union. Some – Czechoslovakia and East Germany – were more industrialized than the Soviet Union. Communists such as the German Anton Ackermann had argued that such countries did not need the violent and rapid social transformation deemed necessary in the Soviet Union, and spoke of "national roads to socialism." Communists in eastern Europe did not come to power through revolution and civil war. They governed in coalition with other parties, though such allies were eventually reduced to mere appendices, and had to take the trouble to rig elections, while the Russian Bolsheviks had simply ignored electoral defeat. The specificity of the people's democracies diminished as time went on, and noncommunist parties were maneuvered out of real power or forced to merge with the communists. "National roads to socialism" were abandoned after Tito's defiance of the Soviet Union rendered all displays of independence suspect, but the people's democracies retained some distinctive characteristics, which were to become more important after Stalin's death removed the most severe Soviet constraints.

Moscow always reserved the right to intervene in its clients' affairs. The purges that began in the late 1940s were direct responses to Soviet orders; in some cases, NKVD men attended the interrogation of suspects. Soviet troops were used against Europeans who revolted against the regime imposed on them – in East Germany in 1953, in Hungary in 1956 and in Czechoslovakia in 1968 – but military intervention did not give Moscow unlimited power. The decision to send troops was never taken lightly. At the very least, such action made the Soviet Union unpopular with left-wing intellectuals in the West, damaged the Western communist parties' chances of forming alliances, and jeopardized trade links with Western countries. Intervention was expensive, carrying the risk of Soviet casualties and often obliging the Soviet Union to commit yet more troops to sustain its clients after intervention. There was the risk that Soviet forces might be humiliated if they failed to subdue rebels with sufficient speed, and worst of all there was the terrifying thought that a sufficiently prolonged or bloody conflict might encourage politicians in one of the perplexingly unstable and unpredictable democracies to contemplate giving military aid to the rebels.

Such risks help explain the numerous occasions on which the Soviet Union did not use military force. It refrained in 1948 when Tito broke away from Moscow's leading strings (though a Hungarian general later claimed that a project to invade Yugoslavia in the early 1950s was shelved because of the resolution that the United States showed during the Korean War).[12] It did not invade Poland in 1956 when its government made moves that seemed dangerously similar to those of Hungary. The Soviet navy seems to have had a brief clash with Albanian forces over control of Russian submarines after Albania's break with Moscow, but this conflict was settled by negotiation rather than fighting.[13]

The countries in which the Soviet Union refrained from intervening all presented awkward military problems. Yugoslavia and Albania were mountainous countries where guerrilla forces had operated successfully during the Second World War, and Albania was only accessible via Yugoslavia. Poland presented the most serious problem to Red Army strategists, who knew all too much about the fighting ability of the Poles. The Polish army had defeated Soviet forces in 1920, and the Russian seizure of eastern Poland in 1939 had created strong anti-Russian feeling in the Polish officer corps. Of thirty-one Polish generals who had fallen into Russian hands, only two survived (thirty-five of the fifty-one generals captured by the Germans survived a longer period of captivity).[14] The Polish officer corps had been purged since then and party membership was obligatory for senior officers, but armies have a strong capacity to preserve tradition and remember the dead. Many officers had their own memories of the Soviet Union; one of these was Wojciech Jaruzelski, whose family had been deported to Russia in 1939. The fact that the Soviet Union imposed a Red Army Marshal, Konstantin Rokossovsky, as commander-in-chief of the Polish army reflected their awareness of Polish military resentment and also increased that resentment: the removal of Rokossovsky was one of the concessions that the Poles extracted in 1956. All this made it more likely that the Poles would have fought if Russian troops had entered their country uninvited. Russian generals, who had sat on the banks of the Vistula during the sixty-three days that it took the Waffen SS and the Wehrmacht to crush the Warsaw uprising in 1944, had no desire to send their men into action against Poles. Recent military history also helped determine Soviet relations with Finland. Part of Soviet reluctance to intervene in Finland was the result of the Red Army's memory of two bruising encounters with Finnish forces.

Soviet power in eastern Europe did not mean that states in the region became identical. Huge economic and social variations remained. Highly industrialized countries, such as Czechoslovakia and East Germany, were distinguished from agricultural nations such as Bulgaria and Poland. The cities that had been home to Kafka and Brecht would have seemed strange places to Albanian tribesmen.

Eastern Europe was made up of nations with strong traditions of mutual hostility, which had underlain many conflicts in the interwar period. After 1945, these hostilities continued, and the Soviet Union exploited them. It insisted that Poland's frontiers were moved west, so that part of Polish territory was joined to the Soviet Union while Poland acquired what had been part of Germany, ensuring that Poland felt threatened by the prospect of German *revanchisme* and that the Soviet Union appeared as a potential protector, as well as an oppressor. The extent of division among eastern European states was reflected in the invasion of Czechoslovakia in 1968. The invading armies came not just from the Soviet Union but from several Warsaw Pact states, including Hungary, which only twelve years previously had suffered the same fate.

In spite of such tensions, eastern Europe held together during the period of Soviet hegemony, partly because the rearrangement of frontiers and the movement of peoples – particularly the expulsion of ethnic Germans from many states – ensured that countries were more ethnically and culturally homogeneous than ever before. Eastern Europeans had less in common with each other, but they also had less reason for conflict. States were less likely to present themselves as the defenders of ethnic minorities in neighboring countries. The absence of conflict was also the result of Soviet military power. The interwar settlement in eastern Europe had broken down because the victorious nations of the First World War had refused to intervene, but no one suspected that the Soviet Union would dismiss the states of eastern Europe as "faraway countries of which we know nothing."

The containment of communism in western Europe

If communist rule in eastern Europe was not inevitable, was noncommunist rule in all of western Europe inevitable? If the Soviet leadership's intentions had been all that mattered, the answer would have been yes. Stalin expected Britain and America to honor the bargains that they had struck during the war, but he also expected to honor his pledge to give them a free hand in their sphere of influence. He did not prevent the

British from putting down communist rebels (who had fought the Germans) in Greece. He would probably not have minded very much if the western European communist parties had simply been wiped out – he believed firmly in the sovereign right of governments to murder their own citizens. He is said to have inquired, with mild curiosity, whether de Gaulle planned to have Maurice Thorez, the French Communist Party leader sent back from Moscow at the end of the Second World War, shot. However, Soviet intentions were not all that mattered. The Soviet Union had not planned a takeover in Republican Spain after 1936 any more than it planned a takeover in France or Italy after the Second World War, but events sometimes moved in unanticipated directions. The communist parties of France and Italy seemed to be doing many of the things that their comrades in the East were doing and, if they had made a bid for power, it was not clear that the Soviet Union would have been able to call them to heel. Until their eviction from government in 1947, western European communists used their power ruthlessly, placing their clients in jobs, using the purges of Pétainists and Fascists to dispose of their enemies, and seeking to maintain their own armed formations.

In some respects, the threat of communism in western Europe sprang precisely from the fact that Moscow did not exercise total control. Communists had been active in resistance organizations in France and Italy, and communist parties had taken in many new members who had no experience of party discipline. The Italian party had operated underground, and therefore with some degree of autonomy, for almost twenty years. Some communist resistance leaders had disobeyed the party line in the aftermath of the Hitler–Stalin pact. Not surprisingly, resistance leaders tended to place much faith in guerrilla action: they looked to Yugoslavia, the one European country in which communists had come to power through their own efforts without the aid of the Red Army. Curiously, it was the most "democratic" communists – those who had joined broad, antifascist coalitions – who presented the greatest threat to democracy in the late 1940s, although Moscow's turn against Tito in 1948 and the subsequent Stalinization of communist parties probably decreased this threat. In France, former resistance activists were purged from the leadership at the twelfth congress of the party in 1950, and of the fifty-one members of the party's central committee, fourteen who had been prominent in the resistance lost their positions.[15] The purge coincided with the return of Pétainists to political life on the right of the political spectrum, and marked the end of any chance that an antifascist coalition might provide the communists with a ramp to power.

Communists in western Europe were kept in check. Their opponents were tougher than those who confronted their comrades in the East. This was especially noticeable in France. The centrist politicians of the Fourth Republic were determined and shrewd, and took particular care to ensure that the levers of power did not fall into communist hands. Communists did not control the Ministries of the Interior, Justice or Defense, and were purged from the armed forces and the militarized police force (the CRS). Punishment of former Pétainists was not allowed to turn into a communist-controlled witch-hunt. Numerous small-scale collaborators were punished, but, with a few exceptions, the communists were not allowed to attack members of the ruling class. Furthermore, France's non-communist leaders did not let the communists play them off against the Pétainist right. Even before the liberation, some right-wing resistance leaders decided that a restoration of some Pétainists would be better than allowing the communists into power. De Gaulle's Rassemblement du Peuple Français, founded in 1947, appealed to former Vichy supporters who wished to fight communism; under the skillful direction of Prime Minister Henri Queuille and President Vincent Auriol, the government appealed to Pétainists against both the communists and the Rassemblement du Peuple Français.

American Europe

"I would prefer as the easiest and most sensible [option] . . . to say to the Italians, Now lookahere, we've done more for you than anyone else and will probably continue to do so. It's about time you started behaving like adults if you want us to help you to help yourselves. But remember that it's up to you. The fault with this line, I fear, is that it may be too practical to stand up against the party propaganda being used so adroitly by Togliatti and his friends. Besides, the Italians are still too hungry and too defeated for us to place much reliance on their common sense.

The alternative is a policy so damned pro-Italian that even the dumbest wop would sense the drift, and even the cleverest Italian comrade would have trouble denouncing it. It would be a judicious mixture of flattery, moral encouragement and considerable material aid . . . This policy would of course require a sustained program for a considerable period. It could not be a one-shot cure, but should consist of a kind word, a loaf of bread, a public tribute to Italian civilization, then another kind word, and so on, with an occasional plug from the sponsors advertising the virtues of democracy American style. Naturally, it would not be anti-communist, nor would it need to be, just pro-Italian. Also, it would cost a lot of money and mean a lot of bother, but if I know anything about Italians, it would pay off handsomely."[16]

This document, drafted by a state department official in 1946, says much about the influence that the United States exercised in western Europe. America was richer than its western European clients and had just won a war in which some of them had fought on the other side; these facts underlay the Americans' condescension towards their allies. But America was never able simply to impose its will in western Europe. Local sensitivities made "straight talking" impossible, and the Americans often felt contempt for their local allies and grudging respect for their opponents – "dumb wops" and "clever comrades." The American expenditure of time and money on western Europe did not mold the region in their image. The Communist Party, which was illegal in the United States, remained strong in France and Italy. The Americans were widely blamed for the departure of communist ministers from the French and Italian governments in 1947 – it suited both communists and their domestic opponents that the Americans should be held responsible for this move – but in neither case does American pressure seem to have been applied.[17] Paradoxically, countries with strong communist parties became recipients of especially generous American largesse (designed to assuage social discontent), while Irish politicians' attempts to get their fingers in the honeypot of Marshall aid were undermined by the fact that Ireland was the most right-wing democracy in Europe.[18] Socialism, almost unknown in America, was often the dominant political force in western Europe and the beneficiary of American support. The Americans often found that their most loyal local allies were drawn from groups – such as the French Radical Party or the Italian Christian democrats – that epitomized everything that clean-cut young state department officials most despised about the old continent.

The simplest means by which Americans exercised power in postwar Europe was military. Italy and Germany were both occupied by the American army for a time, and military authorities made important decisions about the reconstruction of both countries. American troops were stationed in many western European countries, and the United States was the leading member of a military alliance that included the most important western European states. But American military influence was limited. Even in Germany in 1945, the American army was subject to the constraint of a civilian government and the rule of law.

The countries in which American troops operated were strange. American generals did not speak the local language or understand local customs, and they were often politically naïve, which made it easy for their local associates to manipulate them. Such manipulation reached its most bizarre form in southern Italy, where the American army faced local notables used to deceiving outside authorities. Some of those notables had links with America – indeed, the American army contained a significant proportion of men from southern Italy. Influenced by such pressures, the military authorities made some peculiar decisions. The inmates of Sicilian jails were released – and sometimes given public office as a reward for their "anti-Fascism." The Americans had soon reversed the consequences of Mussolini's twenty-year campaign against the Mafia.[19]

After the formation of NATO in 1949, American soldiers were even more subject to restraint and manipulation than those who had occupied Europe at the end of the war. They had to cooperate with civilian governments and maintain good relations with civilian populations. Following the establishment of civilian government in West Germany, American troops were never used against western European civilians. European governments had the right to order American troops out of their country – a right that de Gaulle eventually exercised. If most European governments did not do likewise, it was because they feared the reaction of Moscow rather than because they feared the reaction of Washington.

The American army's influence in Europe was not simply a matter of the policy decided by American generals and politicians. Accommodating hundreds of thousands of soldiers had an economic impact on host countries: in 1951 American forces in Germany employed 409,590 German civilians.[20] American soldiers were wealthier than the inhabitants of the countries in which they found themselves, and their clothes, manners and cigarettes diffused an image of the American way of life. Most importantly, American forces' radio stations helped spread early rock-and-roll music. Personal contact between servicemen and civilians remained limited, though. A study of the American air base at Châteauroux found that prostitutes were the only group that had much to do with airmen.[21] Elvis Presley was probably the single American who had the most influence on the lives of young Europeans, but when he was drafted and sent to West Germany he was said never to have eaten a meal off the base.

The second mechanism by which Americans exercised influence was financial. They provided large amounts of money to Europe, most notably the $13 billion given under the Marshall Plan. Such money came with conditions relating to modernization, European cooperation and the defense of capitalism, but all sorts of other American agencies also funded various European institutions. The Central Intelligence Agency (CIA), private companies and American trade unions all supported political groupings in Europe. The aims of these bodies did not always coincide, and there was not always complete congruity of interest between the Americans and the European bourgeoisie, who were seen as the principal beneficiaries of American largesse.

Defending "the interests of capitalism" was a complicated task because it is in the nature of capitalism to have many conflicting interests. Different capitalist countries and different companies competed to benefit from American generosity. Thus the American loan to France in 1946, negotiated between French Prime Minister Léon Blum and American Secretary of State James Byrnes, contained a specific provision to give Hollywood films better access to the French market. Similarly, American officials negotiated with the Italian Air Minister – Mario Cevelotto – to establish an Italian airline in which TWA would have a significant interest, a maneuver that attracted much resentment from the main British airline.[22] Such deals were sometimes connected to the interests of individuals as well as companies. Cevelotto was said to have been offered the presidency of the Italian airline that was to be formed under his aegis.[23]

Sometimes American influence should be understood in terms of individuals rather than groups or institutions. Irving Brown, who toured Europe on behalf of the American Federation of Labour, was not simply an exponent of American or capitalist interests. His activities had much to do with personal conviction and were sometimes subsidized from his own pocket.[24] Support for the right in continental Europe was strong among American diplomats – such as Robert Murphy – who were Catholics. Henry Tasca, at the American embassy in Rome, seems to have been more at home among the Italian bourgeoisie than among his own colleagues, and he eventually married the daughter of an Italian businessman.[25]

The Americans had a different view of the world from that of their European allies, which was reflected in their attitudes towards socialists and trade unionists. The European bourgeoisie had learned to live with the Second International, and conservatives often joined coalitions with socialists, whose strong anticommunism they appreciated. Indeed, it would have been hard to find more effective enemies of communism than Ernest Bevin (the Labour Foreign Secretary who presided over British policy in the Cold War) or Kurt Schumacher (leader of the West German SPD, who presided over his party's break with its East German counterpart). In France, Léon Blum's denunciations of the Communist Party as "a nationalist party with a foreign allegiance" were often cited in the right-wing press, while the socialist Minister of the Interior, Jules Moch, proved so effective in repressing communist agitation that many right-wingers voted for him. The United States, by contrast, had no socialist tradition. Americans often conflated socialists and communists and found it hard to believe that parties that remained, ostensibly, committed to the abolition of capitalism could be their allies. When Blum was sent to negotiate for American loans, the *Wall Street Journal* greeted him with the headline "WHEN KARL MARX CALLS ON SANTA CLAUS."

If the Americans were more hostile than the European bourgeoisie to socialism, they were less hostile to trade unions. America had trade unions, many of which were not seen as enemies of capitalism, and Americans assumed that rapid economic growth would increase working-class living standards without damaging profits. European businessmen, by contrast, were used to economies of low or nonexistent growth, and assumed that wage rises could only damage profits. Furthermore, they were used to facing aggressive and politicized unions. The ones that broke with the communists in the late 1940s were sometimes made all the more radical by the need to outflank communist rivals, so Americans could sometimes be to the left of Europeans with regard to labor relations. When the French government cut its subsidies to the noncommunist Force Ouvrière union in 1949, after it had organized important strikes, the CIA made up the shortfall.[26]

Sometimes American views of their influence on European politics seemed simply naïve. For example, Natalie Zemon Davis, a graduate student in history, had her passport withdrawn, preventing her from visiting the archives in France. The American government took this step because of Davis's left-wing political connections. Judged from a European perspective, it must have seemed unlikely that an earnest young intellectual could have done much to promote communism in a country where a quarter of the adult population already voted for a party that pledged unqualified loyalty to Stalin.

American influence was complicated by the actions of Europeans themselves. The British government, for example, primly insisted that Marshall aid was being used to promote fiscal rectitude (of which the Americans approved) by paying off debt. American officials suspected that the British had deliberately run up such debts by profligate public spending (of which the Americans disapproved).[27] Well-connected and plausible people could present themselves as representatives of America on one side of the Atlantic and of Europe on the other. Jean Monnet, who had spent much of the war in Washington, was a classic example: in Washington he hinted about the threat of communism in France and the dire consequences if American aid was not forthcoming, but in Paris he hinted that American aid might be withdrawn if particular economic policies – those supported by Monnet – were not implemented. A politician who accompanied Monnet on one of his trans-Atlantic trips wearily concluded that it was impossible to tell whether Monnet represented the Americans to the French or vice versa.[28]

Relations between the Americans and their European allies were not governed by deliberate manipulation alone. There was plenty of scope for genuine misunderstanding. The interpretation and reception of American interventions depended on the local context. Matters were simplest in Great Britain: the two countries were united by a common language and wartime alliance – although, even here, attitudes towards socialism and state intervention could seem strange to Americans.

American relations with France were more complex. The Americans had recognized the Vichy government of Marshal Pétain until the end of 1942, while the postwar French authorities penalized supporters of Pétain, so unsurprisingly many French Pétainists assumed that the Americans would be hostile to the new parties established at the liberation. It was also known that the Americans were hostile to General de Gaulle, with whom they had had spectacularly bad relations during the war, and it was assumed, wrongly, that the United States would take steps to exclude de Gaulle from power. Indeed, some believed that de Gaulle's resignation in 1946 was the result of just such an intervention.

Relations between the Italians and the Americans were complicated not so much by mutual ignorance as by the fact that the two sides had too much contradictory information about each other. On the one hand, a section of the northern Italian industrial and intellectual bourgeoisie looked to the Americans to impose free-market economics and break up the interventionist legacy of Fascism. This bourgeoisie was epitomized by Luigi Einaudi – economist, governor of the national bank and eventually President – whose own son was a professor at Cornell University.[29] On the other hand, a large number of poor southern Italian peasants had contacts with America through relatives who had emigrated there. Southern Italians were electorally important in both countries: the Americans were able to incite the relatives of their citizens to vote against the Communist Party, while the Italian electorate in America imposed pressure on the U.S. government to provide aid to Italy. However, the particular form of southern Italian anticommunism – Christian democracy – was characterized by a cavalier attitude towards state resources that horrified stern liberals such as Einaudi and his friends in the Ivy League establishment.

American intervention was resented most in Germany, where the United States was a victor and occupier rather than a collaborator with local politicians. Before the Allied victory, the business elites of Italy and France had detached themselves from the radical strains of authoritarian government (characterized by Marcel Déat in France or the Republic of Salò in Italy) and begun to look to American protection against communism or social reform. The business elites of Germany never had such an option. The Americans made it clear that they regarded German industry as partly responsible for the rise of Nazism, and imposed American antitrust legislation in an explicit bid to break the power of the cartels. Only with the rise of new industries and a new generation of leaders did German business begin to look kindly on the United States.[30]

Finally, it should be emphasized that American influence took many forms other than those directed by official agencies. This was particularly true of American cultural influence. Official policy supported certain aspects of American culture, but the American government could not determine which parts would be adopted with enthusiasm by Europeans or how Europeans would interpret and use them. Sometimes, the European vision of America was quite the reverse of that which American authorities would have liked to project. Official America's vision of its society was white, clean and centered on the family: James Stewart was the archetypal American in this vision. But Europeans were often fascinated by an America of blacks, crime and sexual promiscuity: for many Europeans, Billie Holiday was the archetypal American. Often the Europeans who responded most enthusiastically to a certain vision of America rejected America's political projects most vigorously. Eric Hobsbawm wrote denunciations of American imperialism by day and, by night, under the name of Francis Newton, wrote hymns of praise to American jazz. At the funeral of Georges Marchais, a dour Moscow loyalist who led the French Communist Party from 1972, the music included "In a Silent Way" (Miles Davis) and "Summertime" (Gershwin).[31] The French film director Jean-Luc Godard, fascinated by American cinema but repelled by American political projects, exemplified the misunderstandings generated by trans-Atlantic cultural transmission. His film *Breathless* (1959) is an homage to, and deconstruction of, a Hollywood B-movie, and revolves around Franco-American misunderstanding. In the final scene, the gangster hero, dying in the gutter, says, "It's a bitch." His American girlfriend does not understand and a helpful policeman tells her, "He said, 'You're a bitch.'"

East versus West

The confrontation between the states under the aegis of America and those loyal to Moscow was illustrated and exacerbated by American economic aid. In June 1947, American Secretary of State George Marshall offered help with European economic recovery, an invitation, in theory at least, open to all European countries. The Soviet Union regarded it as an attempt to dominate Europe and ordered its clients – including Czechoslovakia, which still had a noncommunist president and foreign minister – to refuse.

On the western side, the Organization for European Economic Cooperation (OEEC), set up in April 1948 to administer America's Marshall aid, grouped western European countries with the United States and Canada. The economic integration of western Europe was further advanced by the Treaty of Paris (1951), which created the European Coal and Steel Community (ECSC), designed to ensure that France, West Germany, Italy and the Benelux countries had access to raw materials, but also part of a wider project with political as well as economic dimensions. Containing Soviet influence required German participation and this, in turn, created a need to restrain German influence in order to reassure the French. A more explicitly military incarnation of western European integration, the European Defense Community, was defeated in 1954 in the French parliament, but the Common Market, established by the Treaty of Rome in 1957, guaranteed closer economic links between France, Germany, Italy, Belgium, Luxembourg and the Netherlands.

The communist countries set up their own international institutions. The Communist Information Bureau, Cominform, was established in October 1947 to group together the major European communist parties, but the Cominform was never a very substantial body and it was dissolved in 1956, partly because Khrushchev's reconciliation with Tito was facilitated by the dissolution of a body that had been so involved in the denunciation of Yugoslavia. Comecon, set up in 1949 to integrate the eastern European economies, lasted longer than the Cominform and was primarily an instrument of Soviet power.

The relations that the two halves of Europe developed with the rest of the world reflected an interesting shift in their position. Immediately after the war, the two most important states in western Europe thought of themselves in largely non-European terms. Britain and France still had large overseas empires. They believed that these empires would be crucial to their future power and prosperity. Slowly and, especially in the French case, very reluctantly, this conception was abandoned. The British withdrew from their most important colony, India, in 1947; the French abandoned their most important possession, Algeria, in 1962. From this moment on, for all the rhetoric about "world roles," most major western European politicians devised their policy primarily in terms of Europe itself or in terms of relations with America. The communist bloc, by contrast, began with a strong focus on Europe – the Cominform was an exclusively European body. This position soon changed. As revolution in western Europe became less and less likely, opportunities for communist advance presented themselves outside Europe. Communism was grafted onto nationalist movements in Africa, Asia and Cuba, which then became recipients of largesse from the Soviet Union and its European satellites. As the major western European states dismantled their formal empires, the Soviet Union was constructing an informal one.

The division of East and West was also reflected by two military alliances. On April 4, 1949, Belgium, Canada, Denmark, France, Iceland, Italy, Luxembourg, the Netherlands, Norway, Portugal, the United Kingdom and the United States agreed to provide mutual assistance if any one of them was attacked. The North Atlantic Treaty Organization (NATO) was joined by Greece and Turkey in February 1952 and West Germany in May 1955. The Warsaw Pact emerged from a treaty signed on May 14, 1955, between Albania, Bulgaria, Czechoslovakia, East Germany, Hungary, Poland, Romania and the Soviet Union. The Pact provided for mutual assistance in the event of attack and established a unified joint command in Moscow.

Propagandists on both sides presented the opposing alliance as "militaristic." In economic terms, such accusations contained an element of truth: military spending took up a large part of the wealth of Western countries and a disastrously large proportion of the income of the Soviet Union. However, European generals were probably less powerful than at any time in the recent past. Several soldiers had been heads of states in interwar Europe, but the only general to achieve such a position after 1945 was de Gaulle, a comparatively junior general who had always emphasized the need to subordinate military power to civilians. The power of Soviet generals was even more circumscribed than that of their colleagues in the West. Senior officers were party members, but no leader of the Soviet Communist Party was ever drawn from the military. Even the Defense Minister was usually a civilian, and there were long periods during which no general was a member of the Soviet Politburo.

Devised by civilian scientists and deployed on the orders of civilian politicians, nuclear weapons became increasingly important, further reducing the power of armies. Courage, leadership and tactical ability, the values that obsessed traditional soldiers, were useless in what French officers contemptuously labeled the "push-button army," and during the early 1960s both de Gaulle and Khrushchev shifted resources from conventional weapons to nuclear ones. In the French case, this helped provoke the revolt of the army in Algeria in 1961. De Gaulle said much about the new balance of power between civilians and soldiers when he dismissed the officers leading the revolt – all senior to him in military terms – as "a bunch of half-pay generals."

For a time, some Europeans really did expect the two blocs to fight each other. In eastern Europe, some looked to the prospect of war with enthusiasm. The Romanian Lilly Marcou recalled her parents' thinking during the late 1940s and early 1950s thus: "One of the most tenacious legends of my adolescence was that of the imminent arrival of Anglo-American troops."[32] But such expectations did not last: the aftermath of the Hungarian uprising of 1956 shattered illusions about the prospect of NATO intervention. A journalist reporting for a French paper recalled being told by Hungarians that they knew that the Americans would not abandon them;[33] in fact, the American ambassador to Moscow had already told Khrushchev that the United States would not intervene.

The confrontation between NATO and the Warsaw Pact was in some ways more dramatic and extreme than any that had taken place before in Europe. Previous conflicts had involved parties that knew and to some extent understood each other, and previous enmities had involved states that shared many assumptions. The European ruling classes often spoke each other's languages and knew each other's countries intimately. Western leaders may have misjudged Hitler and the Nazis, but they understood the traditional German ruling class, which had retained much influence. The Soviet Union was different. Few Western leaders spoke Russian and, as their behavior in the interwar period had shown, they had little understanding of central and eastern Europe.

Western perceptions of Russia were influenced by a large émigré community. People who had fled from the Soviet Union or its client states provided advice and explanations. Émigrés taught British soldiers Russian and participated in the foundation of Soviet Studies programs at American universities. Another source of information was the group of diplomats that had experience of the Soviet Union, of which George Kennan was the most influential member; such men had often served in Moscow during the terrifying purges of the 1930s. Not surprisingly, both groups regarded the Soviet Union as dangerous. Furthermore, the community of people who studied the Soviet Union had personal as well as ideological reasons for encouraging the United States to take the military threat as seriously as possible: their own livelihoods depended on the perception that the Soviet Union required constant monitoring.

Matters were made more complicated for Western students of Soviet affairs by the inaccessibility of the country that they were studying. Even those who managed to reach the USSR had limited freedom. Only a small number of roads were open to foreign vehicles, and only a small number of towns could be visited (anything connected to the defense industry was off limits); foreigners based in Moscow were not allowed to venture far outside the city. This had a particularly damaging impact on qualitative and social (rather than quantitative and technological) assessments of the Soviet Union. By the 1960s, spy planes and satellites could provide photographs of armaments factories, but only a sociologist conducting interviews on the factory floor could have told American military planners about the drunkenness, poor discipline and chaotic work rhythms that meant that such factories were unlikely to produce at their full potential.

In political as well as military terms, the groups advising the American government tended to adopt a particular line. They emphasized the power exercised by the state over Soviet society and that of its satellites, and played down the possibility of popular support for these regimes. They stressed the role of force in installing and maintaining communist governments, often using the word "totalitarian" and sometimes equating the rule of the Soviet Union with that of Nazi Germany.

Soviet intelligence operatives, unlike their counterparts in the West, were studying an open society. Information that was regarded as a state secret in the USSR, such as the size of the population of the country, could be obtained in any decent library in the West. The Soviet Union could also draw information from the communist parties in a number of western European countries. Curiously, however, the fact that the Soviet Union was a closed society and the West was an open one seems to have meant that the latter was better informed than the former. Western analysts of the Soviet Union were part of a broad debate, and not even the most hawkish Cold War academic could get away with pure prejudice. In the Soviet Union, matters were different. Not only did leaders know little about the West, but they had little inclination to learn. Most had spent their entire careers focused on internal Soviet affairs and the highly absorbing pursuit of surviving Stalinism. Knowledge of the West was not merely redundant, but often dangerous. Those who had lived abroad or had had contact with foreigners were most likely to fall victims of purges. The Institute for World Economics, which had been headed by the Hungarian-born Eugen Varga and had propagated a nuanced view of the West, was dissolved in the late 1940s.[34]

The extent to which the Soviet Union misunderstood its Western rivals was revealed after the fall of communism. One analyst admitted that Soviet economic planners had overestimated the U.S. potential to produce tanks by a factor of almost 120.[35] Another pointed out that the West benefited from the relative independence of research bodies such as the Rand Institution,[36] while the Soviet leadership obtained all its information about U.S. military potential from agencies in the Soviet defense establishment that had interests of their own to advance. The advantages of the West's openness meant that its analysts often knew more about the Soviet Union than Soviet leaders themselves. This was revealed by the career of the Russian economist Gregory Khanin, who began as a student of the West (he wrote a thesis on western European stockmarkets), but quickly understood that such research was unlikely to attract interest in his own country and switched to studying long-term trends in the Soviet economy, coming to the uncomfortable conclusion that Soviet performance was much worse than official statistics suggested. He had great difficulty in publishing his conclusions; his academic colleagues were nervous that such work would attract the attention of the KGB. Finally, he managed to publish some of his findings in 1981 – although he was obliged to couch his theories in such an ambiguous manner that no Soviet analyst seems to have appreciated the importance of his work. The Western scholar Alec Nove, by contrast, read Khanin's article and (in Khanin's own words) "sucked it dry" to provide information for an article that Nove published in 1983.[37]

Soviet–Western understanding was also influenced by the messages that the two sides sent out. If the authoritarianism of the Soviet Union made it difficult to read Western signals, it did at least mean that Moscow could be sure that the signals that it gave were clear. In the 1970s, Jean Kéhayan, a French communist writer, worked for a Soviet propaganda agency in Moscow. Texts were written in Russian by local writers, and then translated by Russians who spoke fluent French (though they would rarely have set foot outside the Soviet Union). French communist writers then reworked the text to ensure that it read smoothly, and finally a Russian read the corrected text to make sure that its original meaning had not been deformed in translation.[38] In such circumstances, the Soviet authorities could be sure that all statements issued on their behalf reflected a consistent line. Matters were much more complicated in the West. The United States was the leading partner in the Western Alliance, but no single agency could hope to impose unity on the opinions and statements of all American government agencies, let alone the statements of private citizens in countries allied with the United States. Failure to control messages could have tragic consequences. In 1956, Radio Free Europe, operating in Austria, told Hungarian listeners to place no faith in the reformist Marxism of Imre Nagy and that Soviet forces could be defeated. Although Radio Free Europe was subsidized by the American government, these provocative remarks, made by right-wing Hungarian émigré broadcasters, did not reflect American policy.

Conclusion

By the mid-1970s, senior officers in both NATO and the Warsaw Pact had spent their entire careers preparing to go to war with each other, but the two sides never fought. The fact that both possessed nuclear weapons from 1949 made them reluctant to risk conflict, at least in an area that mattered to them. The Soviet Union and the United States subsidized and supported rival sides in Cuba, Vietnam and the Middle East, but such conflicts were made safer by their relative indifference to these regions' inhabitants. The Soviet leaders did not care about the humiliation of the Cubans when they agreed to withdraw their missiles from the island in 1962, and the Americans did not care about the fate of their protégés left behind in Saigon.

As time went on, the two sides became increasingly explicit about the mutual tolerance that underlay their cohabitation. John Foster Dulles, Secretary of State from 1953 until 1959, was the last senior American official to talk of "liberating eastern Europe." Khrushchev claimed to want "peaceful competition." In the early 1970s, analysts began to talk of a relaxation, or détente, in relations between the two powers. The new mood was based partly on the removal of ideology from world politics. The rhetoric of diplomacy acquired a reassuringly unconvincing tone – it was hard to believe that Leonid Brezhnev cared about Marxist theory or that Richard Nixon cared about human rights.

The politician most associated with East–West negotiations in this period was Henry Kissinger, U.S. National Security Adviser from 1969 until 1973 and Secretary of State from 1973 to 1977. Kissinger, born in Germany, spoke English with a thick accent, and his view of the world was not based on an evangelical enthusiasm for the American way of life. He admired conservative diplomats of the nineteenth century such as Bismarck, Castlereagh and Metternich (the latter enthusiasm did not make him popular with the Poles).[39] Just as Bismarck had looked back to a world of great-power diplomacy that had been disrupted by the ideological clash of the French Revolution, Kissinger tried to revive a great-power relationship that had been disrupted by the ideological divisions springing from the Russian Revolution. Far from talking of "rolling back communism," he stressed the stability of relations with the Soviet Union: "Today for the first time in our history, we face the stark reality that the [communist] challenge is unending . . . We must learn to conduct foreign policy as other nations have had to conduct it for so many centuries without escape and without respite . . . This condition will not go away."[40]

The supreme moment of American–Soviet cohabitation came in 1975 with the signature of the Helsinki Agreements, whereby the two sides agreed to recognize existing borders in Europe and to limit the number of nuclear weapons deployed (a futile gesture since this number was sufficiently large to destroy the world). The Helsinki Agreements also referred to the defense of human rights – although negotiators on both sides would probably have been very surprised to find how seriously such clauses were taken by some inhabitants of the Soviet Union and its satellite states.

2

THE MIRACLE

THE MEN WHO presided over the western European economies after the Second World War were often devout Catholics, and many of them must have prayed for rapid growth. Few could have expected such a dramatic answer to their prayers. From 1945 until 1975, the European economy grew faster than at any time before or since; average growth during this period was more than twice that of the period before 1939 or after 1973. This expansion laid the foundations for everything else that happened in Europe in the second half of the twentieth century. Indeed, the nature of this period was often much more apparent in retrospect than it had been at the time. Growing prosperity helped alleviate the bitter social struggles that had accompanied economic crisis in the 1930s, stabilizing and legitimizing democracies and underlying the social transformations wrought by migration, urbanization and greater access to education. Even after the oil crisis of the 1970s, the effects of what the French called "*les trente glorieuses*" continued to be felt. No western European economy suffered an absolute decline, and western Europeans continued to get richer, albeit at a less dramatic rate. The prosperity of western Europe at the end of the century and the triumph of western European models over those of the communist-ruled countries owed much to the economic achievements of the decades before 1975.

Statistics, facts, interpretations

The overall statistics of European growth obscure significant variations. Different countries grew at different rates, and those that were already wealthy grew most slowly so that absolute levels of output were inversely proportional to rates of growth in output. There were also variations over time. Generally, growth accelerated in the late 1950s and early 1960s. In some cases chronological distinctions can be made even more precisely: the Italian economic miracle occurred between 1958 and 1963. Timing has important implications for interpretation. If we were to stop the clock in 1949, we would assume that France was one of the least successful postwar economies; twenty years later, it seemed obvious that she was one of the most successful. More generally, historians who stress the role of state intervention in economic growth tend to talk of a postwar period, beginning when the state adopted a more active role in 1945. Recent fashions for economic liberalism have led to a greater emphasis on the late 1950s as a turning point, marked by the liberalization of trade and the creation of the Common Market in 1958.[1] It could also be argued that the focus on a relatively short period is deceptive, and that the rapid growth of 1945–73 should be considered in the context of economic development over a century or so. According to such an interpretation, the postwar boom was not qualitatively different from what went before or came after, but merely a period during which Europe caught up to its "natural" level of development after an abnormal period of depression and war.

Statistics relating to gross national product do not tell us about the goods that made up the statistics. There is a difference between an economy that produces pig iron and one that produces transistor radios or food mixers, which has implications for a wider distinction between the boom in production and the boom in consumption: for many Europeans economic growth was not reflected in the standard of living until comparatively late. In France, relatively slow growth based on capital goods during the 1950s may have been a necessary condition of rapid growth in the production of consumer goods during the 1960s, but sometimes, as in the case of the Belgian coal industry,[2] concentration on heavy industrial production proved a blind alley. Different product mixes also account for the important difference between the economies of capitalist western Europe and those of communist eastern Europe. Rates of growth of GNP, at least as reflected in official statistics, were often higher in the East than in the West, but these rates applied to economies that were starting from low levels and did not produce an abundance of consumer goods.

A history of the postwar European economy must also take into account qualities such as willingness to work, move, and abandon established habits. Sometimes, different qualities were required in different places or at different times. The historian must explain why German workers in the early 1950s were willing to forgo consumption (thus facilitating high investment), as well as how the nation of Goriot and Grandet became a consumer society.

War damage

European economies did not have an equal start in 1945. Some had almost collapsed as a consequence of war and defeat. In Germany, much industry had simply stopped working. Damage was rarely just the direct result of enemy action. War economies had been distorted by diversion of resources to meet short-term priorities, and equipment had suffered from being manhandled by inexperienced workers drafted into factories. Conditions were better in neutral countries or in countries, such as Britain, that had never experienced defeat or invasion. Elsewhere, economic activity had been protected by particular circumstances. In Italy, for example, the economy of the south had been badly damaged by fighting and the need to accommodate large numbers of Allied soldiers. In the north, by contrast, industrialists and workers had sometimes prevented retreating German armies from destroying equipment.[3]

In some ways, the first few years after 1945 were an extension of the war economy, marked by a concern with short-term survival rather than long-term planning or construction. The industries that were central to this concern were often those that had grown during the war. Armament production was run down, but coal and agriculture remained more important than their long-term role in the European economy warranted. The economic techniques used in the immediate postwar period were often very similar to those used during the war. Rationing persisted – indeed, in France bread was rationed for the first time after the war. In Germany, the Allied military government took crucial economic decisions (such as those relating to the stabilization of the currency).[4] Conscripted labor was used after the war. Several countries held on to their prisoners of war for some time and the British continued to send drafted men down coal mines. Even the language of postwar reconstruction resembled that of war, as politicians in Britain and France talked of the "battle for production."

Catching up?

A simple explanation of economic growth in postwar Europe is that such growth merely entailed "catching up": the European economy had been unnaturally constrained by the interwar depression and the war, and after 1945 the European economy simply regained its "natural" level. It might also be argued that the European economies were "catching up" in an international sense. Many of the practices and technologies that contributed to rapid growth in postwar Europe – such as mechanization and production line manufacture – were already well established in the United States:

Table 4: War Damage and Reconstruction After 1945

	Pre-war year in which GDP was equal to that of 1945	*Year in which GDP recovered to its highest pre-war level*
Austria	1886	1951
Belgium	1924	1948
Denmark	1936	1946
Finland	1938	1945
France	1891	1949
Germany	1908	1951
Italy	1909	1950
Netherlands	1912	1947
Norway	1937	1946
Sweden	never	–
Switzerland	never	–
United Kingdom	never	–

Source: Nicholas Crafts and Gianni Toniolo, "postwar growth: an overview" in Crafts and Toniolo (eds.), *Economic Growth in Europe Since 1945* (Cambridge, 1996), pp. 1–37, p. 4.

it was only in the 1960s that the ratio of cars to total population in France and West Germany reached the level achieved in the United States by 1929.[5] Furthermore, European economies converged with each other after 1945 as the fastest growth occurred in the least developed countries – Greece, Spain and Italy – while the most developed ones, particularly Britain, grew more slowly.

There were particular reasons why postwar Europe saw a convergence of underdeveloped and developed economies. War gave all of the European countries a chance to measure comparative economic performance. Defeat, occupation and deportation gave some an intimate knowledge of other economies. While working as prisoners of war on German farms, Breton peasants came to appreciate the benefits of mechanization, and after the war Allied countries sent missions of industrialists to examine German factories.

Most importantly, the war illustrated the superiority of American production methods, a lesson subsequently underlined by deliberate action on the part of governments in both Europe and the United States. "Productivity missions" took workers, industrialists and civil servants to American plants – the British sent around 900 people[6] – and became associated in American eyes with a wider project to diffuse the virtues of the "American way of life." They were to present Europeans with a vision of the mutual benefits of rapidly expanding productivity, rather than conflict over the distribution of resources, and of the links between consumer prosperity and industrial success. Such missions were not entirely successful. The people involved were not representative of their colleagues. Industrialists were often characterized by worthiness rather than by being at the forefront of innovation,[7] while workers were subject to political screening (especially when industrialists were funding the visits). In many cases trade union leaders were excluded in favor of "ordinary workers," and communists, who made up the bulk of trade union leadership in France and Italy, did not go to America. Productivity missions also misunderstood the American economy – or, at least, understood only those parts of it that fitted into their preconceptions.[8]

In spite of such limitations, American propaganda did have an impact in Europe that was reinforced by more general cultural changes. Even if Europeans misunderstood the nature of the American economy, they understood its general principles. Anyone who watched Hollywood films knew that cars and telephones were more common in New York than in Naples. Capital, and particularly the spectacular generosity of the Marshall Plan, would not have been available to Europe if the American economy had not been relatively advanced.

State intervention

After 1945, many European states played a more active role in economic management. Memories of economic depression had rendered the severe economic liberalism of the prewar years unfashionable, and wartime experience had accustomed people to high levels of state intervention. Believers in an economically active state dominated postwar policy-making. In terms of academic economics, John Maynard Keynes, who died in 1946, was the most influential figure, but his prescriptions for government spending to avoid recession did not necessarily imply detailed control of the economy. In any case, Keynes's ideas were interpreted differently in different parts of Europe.

Jean Monnet, founder of France's Commissariat du Plan, was the most notable practitioner of state intervention. His plans were based on the assumption that the state should not merely react to economic crisis but should act to promote modernization, making choices about the economy and deciding which sectors should be supported and which should be allowed to decline. Some forms of state intervention involved no state expenditure. Civil servants and politicians could use planning regulations, rationing of raw materials (a significant power during the postwar penury) or control over access to foreign currency to force industrialists into taking particular decisions. Planning in France was designed to concentrate resources on particular industries and to encourage economic coordination, but it is unwise to place too much emphasis on the *étatisme* of this new institution. Monnet stressed the informal psychological element of his modernization projects. He aimed to create a "mystique of planning," and an American visitor remarked that gatherings of industrialists that took place under the aegis of the Commissariat du Plan often resembled "revivalist prayer meetings."[9]

Elsewhere, state intervention in the economy was even more haphazard. In Britain, intervention did not involve the creation of new institutions. Civil servants worked with existing legislation – such as town planning laws – or regulations left over from the war, but such powers were often used inconsistently. Industrialists in Coventry, a city whose rapid wartime expansion had made it particularly subject to government controls, found that government decisions deprived some factories of workers while others were overburdened with state contracts.[10] The difference between Britain and France lay not so much in the fact that the latter planned while the former did not as in the fact that the latter subjected planning initiatives to centralized control while the former did not.

The most spectacular state intervention took place in Italy, where the Industrial Reconstruction Agency (IRI) controlled shares in large numbers of companies. However, the IRI was not a model of new economic management. It had been founded in 1933 to prevent bankruptcies rather than to promote modernization. It was not run by a tightly knit group of men with a coherent vision, but was a battleground on which Italian industrialists and politicians struggled to increase their power and distribute resources to their clients. The IRI's position in relation to the public and private sectors was ambiguous. It owned shares in companies, but did not always own a controlling interest. Furthermore, the IRI itself was partially controlled by private business, which owned shares in it. One commentator wrote: "One may question whether the Italian state controls it [the IRI] or vice versa."[11]

In some respects, the focus on the state's role in economic management after 1945 is deceptive. There was not always a clear dividing line between state and private business. In much of continental Europe, economic policy did not spring from the imposition of state authority over industry but rather from a convergence of the two. This convergence came partly from changes in the state: new departments were set up to deal with economic matters, and were often staffed by businessmen. The private sector also changed. Small companies run by an owner whose own capital was at risk and who was obliged to spend his own time handling paperwork might feel very alienated from the state. Large companies, however, were run by managers whose own capital was not at risk, and who could afford to take a relatively detached view of many issues. Some companies had departments to negotiate with public authorities or to make long-term plans that ran parallel to those of the state, and many managers had experience of state employment.

Nationalization further complicated matters. Nationalized companies were owned by the state, and their senior managers were sometimes appointed with an eye to political affiliation, but they were usually run in a conservative way that stressed the need to make a profit. The heads of nationalized industries sat alongside their private-sector equivalents in employers' associations; the two had similar problems with labor disputes, the nationalized sector was often a particular target for strikes, and managers migrated between nationalized and private-sector companies. Business associations further helped to bridge the gap between the state and the private sector. Associations tried to take a more comprehensive and long-term view of business interests than that taken by individual industrialists. State powers, such as those relating to the allocation of raw materials, were sometimes delegated to private business associations, and the state often depended on the associations to provide statistics.

In such circumstances, it makes more sense to examine the formation of elites that transcended the state/private-sector division than to examine the expansion of state power. The creation of such an elite was least well developed in Britain, and the British example helps to throw into relief developments on the continent. In Britain the civil service of the post-1945 period had not undergone any major changes since the North-cote–Trevelyan reforms of the mid–nineteenth century. The archetypal civil servant was still a courteous Wykhamist who was good at writing Greek hexameters and solving *The Times* crossword puzzle – the kind of figure who features in the novels of Iris Murdoch (who had herself spent some time at the Treasury before returning to Oxford to teach Greek philosophy). British industrialists, by contrast, often lacked university degrees – as late as 1971, only 40 percent of company managers were graduates.[12] Many had grown up in provincial towns, and in dealings with civil servants seemed inarticulate and ill at ease. If any group in Britain provided an elite that transcended the state/business division, it was to be found among merchant bankers, who shared the background of many civil servants and politicians, possessed social confidence and political contacts, and were accustomed to dealing with state agencies.

By contrast, the formation of an economic elite was most conspicuous in France. Elite institutions of higher education – the *grandes écoles* –

already trained men for both the upper reaches of the civil service and the most senior posts in industrial management. Nationalization and the increased role of business associations in economic life created new opportunities for them after 1945. A new super *grande école* (the École Nationale d'Administration) was created in 1945, and its graduates were just beginning to reach positions of influence in 1958, when the more centralized state of the Fifth Republic was accompanied by a new role for large companies.[13] *Pantouflage*, by which senior civil servants took jobs in the private sector, became increasingly common.

In other countries the economic elite was less explicitly defined. In Italy, as in France, a group of men moved between state service, politics, the nationalized industries and the private sector, although in France the elite was united mainly by education and stressed its "apolitical" nature and the extent to which its judgments were "detached" and "technical," whereas in Italy, political affiliation drew the economic elite together. Its members were united by membership of the Christian Democrat Party (DC), their power sprang from the support of DC politicians, and their economic interventions were often designed to benefit the party's clients. The German state played a less active role in the economy than the French or Italian one, but this did not mean that capitalism operated in an uncoordinated fashion. Business associations planned, encouraged and disciplined their members, and in some cases redistributed resources by collecting levies and subsidizing certain basic industries.[14] It was in these industrial organizations that the economic elite was to be found. The state played a limited role in Germany partly because industrialists had traditions of organization that allowed them to dispense with the discipline imposed by the state elsewhere.

The powers of economic elites everywhere grew because of war and the legacy of authoritarian regimes. Often, economies had been run by institutions that grouped industrialists together under the aegis, but not necessarily the control, of the state. In some cases, such as that of the IRI, these institutions survived into the postwar period, and their legacy often survived even after their formal abolition. In Germany, the Allied occupation authorities aimed to eliminate all economic bodies associated with Nazism, but even after these institutions had been abolished the spirit and the network of contacts that they had encouraged survived.

Sometimes, the political trauma of the 1933 to 1945 period knitted economic elites together (nothing unites men more than shared memories that they do not wish to discuss with outsiders). In Germany, industrialists had often served together in Nazi agencies, and a period of imprisonment provided many such men with a chance to renew their contacts.[15] Economic organizations often provided a discreet base for men whose wartime activities had given them useful political patrons but also precluded an open political career.

The relationship between war experience and authoritarian government and the consolidation of an economic elite was most dramatically illustrated in France. Vichy and the resistance welded the elite more tightly together, rather than dividing it. The lines of communication in the French elite had remained open throughout the war and had crossed the Vichy–resistance divide. After the war, favors were returned and protection was maintained, and sometimes those who had been protected under Vichy were able to return the favor. Georges Villiers had been saved from execution by the prefect of Lyons, André Boutemy. After the war, Villiers became president of the Conseil National du Patronat Français, partly as a reward for his resistance record, and, when Boutemy was sacked as a punishment for Pétainism, Villiers came to the aid of his former protector, arranging for him to be employed as head of the Centre d'Études Économiques, which distributed business funds to politicians.

Armaments and armies

One sector of the economy in which postwar European governments were particularly active was that associated with the military. In the period immediately after 1945, all countries scaled down their military spending, but most of them subsequently increased it, often sustaining it above the levels that had prevailed in previous peaceful eras. Some states, such as the Netherlands, that had been neutral before 1939 now entered the Western Alliance: Dutch military spending rose by 4.9 percent per annum in the period from 1949 to 1968. British, French and Dutch attempts to defend their empires against insurrection all provided reasons – or excuses – for such spending.

Military spending took different forms. In some cases it meant the maintenance of a large conscript army that needed to be fed, clothed and equipped; in all cases it meant the provision of weaponry that increased demand for other industries, such as iron, steel and engineering. Military spending in Britain and France had a special dimension because of the efforts of both countries to develop an independent nuclear bomb. Such efforts account for the relatively high proportion (between 1 and 1.5 percent) of government spending devoted to research and development.[16]

Military spending had a mixed reception. American economic historians have sometimes talked of a "military Keynesianism,"[17] which encouraged American business to tolerate high government spending as long as it was used for military, rather than civilian, purposes. It was acceptable because it provided work for private-sector contractors and did not involve the redistribution of wealth. This view was not shared in Europe, perhaps because business was more willing to accept government spending on purely civilian objectives. Military spending was welcomed by the industries that drew direct benefit from it, but it was not always seen as an inevitable part of capitalist ideology – in Britain it was the Labour government of 1945–51 that took the most momentous decisions in favor of high military spending. Opposition to defense expenditure sometimes came from the right or from interest groups of property-owners. This was particularly notable in France, where representatives of commerce, small business and agriculture resented high taxes and felt that their constituents gained nothing from military contracts. In 1951 the Front Économique tried to rally French voters against increases in government expenditure (including military spending). In 1952, Paul Antier, the leader of the Peasant Party, resigned from the government in protest against increased defense spending.[18]

In France, large-scale business and the military had a tradition of common interest. The École Polytechnique, where a large part of the economic elite were trained, was still nominally a military school, and much defense expenditure benefited the heavy industries that exercised most power in the employers' organizations. However, military salaries declined after the Second World War, and the proportion of *polytechniciens* who took commissions dropped to just 1 percent. Officers felt excluded from postwar prosperity, and many sought refuge in imperial service, where standards of living were propped up by special allowances and cheap servants. France's decision to abandon Algeria in the early 1960s marked both a military and an economic turning point. In military terms, it meant a rejection of conventional infantry warfare in favor of highly technological armed forces, of which the air force would be the most important element and nuclear bombs the most important weapon. In economic terms, it meant turning away from protected colonial markets that had favored industries such as textiles and an integration into more competitive European markets. Opposition to French withdrawal from Algeria became linked to opposition to large-scale capitalism: officers railed against the influence of the CNPF and "*capitalisme apatride*," and some commentators talked of "military Poujadism." The generals' putsch of 1961 was a rebellion against capitalist modernization as well as against decolonization.

Military expenditure illustrates the dangers of a crudely statistical approach to economic history. Such spending increased the figures for gross domestic production, but did not increase the prosperity of Europe's inhabitants very much. Military spending might have increased employment and provided a countercyclical effect in a time of economic downturn, but at a time of rapid growth and tight labor markets it simply diverted resources away from industries that supplied civilian consumers. Some evidence also suggests that the long-term impact of military spending on productivity was bad. The most successful major economy in postwar Europe, that of West Germany, had low military spending; in the least successful, Britain, it was high. The distorting effects were exacerbated by changes in the balance of power. The Western Allies had won the Second World War by subordinating purely military concerns (with high-quality weapons) to business concerns (with cheap and efficient large-scale production), but the West could not hope to use a strategy of mass production during the Cold War. The fact that the Soviet Union was now a potential enemy rather than an ally meant that the West was always likely to have fewer troops in the field than its opponents, and Western powers now shifted to a policy that placed the quality of weaponry above cheapness and efficiency of production.

Three pressures pushed military spending up. First, increasingly sophisticated technology meant that numerous, very expensive, technical upgrades could render previous equipment redundant. Second, the nature of weapons production insulated it from the cost controls imposed in other sectors by ordinary commercial considerations: you cannot buy missiles from China just because they happen to be cheaper, and fighter pilots will not take kindly to being told that their ejector seats have been chosen on the grounds of cost. Third, relations between military industries and governments became so intimate that the latter were unable to exercise control over the former. The small numbers of companies that dominated military production hired retired generals and civil servants to foster their links with government. Eisenhower's warning about the "military/industrial complex" could have been applied to Britain or France as easily as to the United States.

Agriculture

Those who talked most about economic modernization were rarely interested in agriculture: Jean Monnet's first plan contained no provision at all for this sector. Agriculture remained important in most western European countries, though, and the modernization of industry could therefore be accomplished only in parallel with modernization of agriculture. The most important reason for agriculture's continued importance was political. Farmers might contribute a small proportion of the GDP of most European countries, but they made up a relatively large proportion of many countries' electorates. Special circumstances swelled the political influence of agriculture. A large part of the industrial working class in some countries (France, Italy, Finland) voted communist, which made the votes of those outside the working class – that is, those who supported ruling coalitions – all the more important. Farmers were particularly significant because they often voted for "hinge" parties that were at the center of the political spectrum (and therefore overrepresented in coalitions) and also because the peasantry itself (unlike the bourgeoisie) was sometimes volatile in its political affiliations. In countries in which most workers voted consistently communist and most bourgeois voted consistently for conservative parties, farmers provided one of the few groups whose support could be bought with concessions.

Agriculture had two further advantages. The first was cultural. The survival of certain kinds of farms and produce was important to the self-image of many Frenchmen, Germans and Italians. The second lay in the fact that certain groups of farmers had privileged relationships with powerful political parties, which came from their effectiveness at lobbying rather than from the electoral support that they were able to mobilize. The most conspicuous example was provided by the National Farmers' Union in Britain. Although farmers formed a small part of the British electorate and the British two-party system did not give small peasant parties the leverage that they enjoyed in some continental systems, the NFU maintained close contacts with the Conservative Party, which were eventually illustrated by the appointment of the son of the Conservative minister R. A. Butler as leader of the NFU.

What relation did the fate of agriculture bear to that of the rest of the western European economy? On the one hand, protection increased taxes and also ensured that consumers paid higher prices for food (prices that translated into higher wages or reduced demand for other consumer goods). However, agriculture was not static, and the changes that it underwent facilitated industrial modernization. The most important of these changes was mechanization. The demand for tractors, combine harvesters and automatic milking machines increased dramatically and provided orders for industry.

Rural mechanization was related to the large-scale departure of young men from the countryside to seek industrial employment in the cities, but it is hard to determine whether the relation was one of cause or effect. Did farmers mechanize because agricultural labor was becoming scarce and expensive, or did mechanization reduce job opportunities and drive laborers off the land? It seems reasonable to assume that pull was stronger than push in France, where the demand for labor was intense and mechanization was low, and that push was stronger than pull in Germany, a country with a strong tradition of agricultural mechanization, and where labor was relatively abundant. However, relations between mechanization and urbanization cannot be expressed simply in statistical terms. The countryside had also sometimes seemed attractive in the interwar period because it was a refuge from the instability of the city, and because in the last resort it was a place where one could be reasonably sure of finding something to eat. In the 1950s, such considerations counted for less. Most importantly, cities became exciting places in the postwar period. Youth culture in the 1930s had often been rural – it revolved around youth hostels, camping and picnics. Youth culture in the 1950s and '60s was urban – it revolved around dance halls and cinemas.

Young men's migration to the cities was sometimes a response to that of women. Even during the interwar period, when farms had seemed relatively attractive to young men, women had been moving into the cities, and after the war female urbanization became even more dramatic. The mechanization and organization of agriculture marginalized women, and the consumer culture to which women were introduced by magazines and advertising did not imbue Wellington boots and manure heaps with much glamour. Women's departure meant that men who stayed on the farm often knew that their choice meant a celibate life.

If those who left the countryside often did so for nonfinancial reasons, those who stayed on the farm might also be motivated by something other than money. Those who left were likely to be young and to come from groups – such as landless laborers or younger sons – that stood the smallest chance of acquiring land. Those who stayed were older and likely to be proprietors, and their emotional attachment to farming went beyond financial calculation. In some areas, families subsidized the maintenance of farms by commuting to work in nearby factories for some of the time, and some farmers found nonagricultural sources of income, such as running camping sites. Often, farmers survived at a level that would have been regarded as poverty-stricken by inhabitants of the town. However, direct comparison between urban and rural standards of living was difficult. Farmers did not spend their holidays at the Club Med, but they did have large amounts of space, an increasingly expensive commodity in the cities. Farmers sometimes bartered goods and services with each other, which helped preserve an indifference to the money values that dominated city life. As late as 1968, sociologists found that values in a Breton village were often expressed in terms of concrete items, ranging from a liter of wine to a horse, rather than in terms of money.[19]

Energy

The industrial revolution had been powered by coal, access to which defined areas of industrial growth during the nineteenth century. Industry was centerd on the Ruhr, south Yorkshire, the Nord and Pas de Calais, and the Borinage in Belgium. Coal was still important in the immediate postwar period, and governments encouraged production, which peaked in the 1950s.[20] However, other sources of energy were becoming available, and this had a dramatic effect on European industrial geography. In particular, prosperity between 1945 and 1973 was sustained by cheap oil, which underlay some of the spectacular changes in the European economy. Its role in the spread of cars was obvious, but it was also important in the expansion of the shipbuilding, and hence the steel, industries. The most lucrative business for European shipbuilders became the construction of "supertankers." In the early 1970s, a Swedish firm was building a supertanker every forty days.[21]

Energy supply was also changed by the discovery of natural gas in Europe and the growing use of hydroelectric power. Electrification itself was important, as increasing amounts of energy were consumed in this form, and the shift away from the direct use of coal to oil, gas and electricity had important implications, creating forms of energy that were equally useful for industry and domestic consumers. Electrical supplies could be used for aluminium smelting or to turn on a television; petrol could be used in a factory or in a family car, which made the shift from growth centered on capital goods in the 1950s to growth centered on consumer prosperity in the 1960s relatively smooth. Electricity and oil facilitated certain kinds of small-scale production: access to power no longer depended on proximity to a large steam engine. New forms of energy shifted prosperity out of the old centers of heavy industry. They were easier to transport than coal, and in some cases were most easily found where coal was most scarce (as was true for natural gas and hydroelectric power in the southwest of France). Areas without coal reserves (Holland, Greece, Norway) grew fast in the postwar period, while the countries that were most strongly associated with coal mining (Britain and Belgium) had relatively slow growth.

Labor

The interwar economy had proved that abundant labor supplies did not in themselves produce economic growth. Jarrow had not perceived mass unemployment as an opportunity during the 1930s; Hungary and Greece had gained nothing – except high public spending and political instability – from an influx of refugees during the 1920s. Yet similar circumstances often eased economic growth after 1945. This reflects the fact that economic growth after 1945 cannot be explained in terms of any single cause – labor supply was an advantage only when combined with other forces encouraging growth. What mattered was not so much labor supply as potential labor supply. Tight labor markets, notably in France, might have impeded growth, as employers in economies with high levels of employment have very little flexibility to respond to further demands and face the constant risk that workers will exploit their position to obtain wage rises. Keynes, hardly a ruthless proponent of unemployment as an economic weapon, anticipated that a "healthy" economy would have unemployment rates of 3–6 percent – French unemployment in the 1950s rarely exceeded 2 percent. However, European employers had both flexibility and bargaining power because they knew that they would be able to draw on fresh supplies of workers from either the countryside or from abroad. A "reserve army" of peasants and immigrants had the advantage of being disciplined and used to work, unlike those who had endured long-term unemployment, and also had the advantage of not requiring support from the taxpayer while waiting to be used.

Flows of labor often owed something to old colonial relations. Britain took most of the 1,773,000 workers that she imported by 1970 from India, Pakistan and Ireland; France drew about a third of her migrant workers from former colonies in North Africa. Immigration from outside Europe accompanied migration within Europe from comparatively underdeveloped areas (Greece, southern Italy and Portugal) to the industrial cities. Immigrant workers were particularly useful because they had lower expectations than established members of the working class. New arrivals took the most unpleasant jobs, while second-generation workers moved on to more secure and comfortable positions. Migrants and immigrants were often less unionized than their more established colleagues, and less able to resist poor safety standards. In one month alone, July 1961, there were eight fatal accidents on Turin building sites, which were mainly staffed by migrants from the south.[22] In the ten years that followed the war there were 1,000 fatal accidents among Belgian coal miners; three-quarters of those involved were immigrants. On two occasions, the Italian government halted emigration to Belgium in a bid to improve safety – among the 262 miners killed in the Bois du Cazier mining disaster of August 1956, 136 were Italian.[23] Immigrants from abroad were particularly useful to economies in rapid growth, as they were usually young, fit, single men, which meant that they contributed to the economy through production without making the demands on welfare services that came from native workers. This was particularly true of countries that imported labor as "guest workers," who never acquired citizenship or permanent rights of abode. A worker who turned out to be lazy, insubordinate or inconveniently familiar with labor legislation risked losing his work permit as well as his job. In an economic downturn, a

Table 5: Immigrants in Three Western European Countries,
1973–74 ('000s)

From	To	Belgium	W. Germany	France
Algeria		3.0	2.0	450.0
Greece		2.0	268.1	5.0
Italy		86.0	409.7	230.0
Yugoslavia		1.2	466.1	50.0
Morocco		16.5	15.3	120.0
Portugal		3.5	69.1	380.0
Spain		30.0	179.0	270.0
Tunisia		2.1	11.2	60.0
Turkey		12.0	582.2	18.0
Others (EEC)		40.0	156.0	69.0
Others (non-EEC)		93.0	239.5	130.0
Total		*289.3*	*2344.2*	*1782.0*

Source: Lydia Potts, *The World Labour Market: A History of Migration* (1990),
p. 147.

whole section of the workforce could simply be shipped back to Turkey, Portugal or Calabria. Switzerland used guest workers ruthlessly. Here, official unemployment statistics were very low (they averaged 0.1 percent between 1950 and 1969).[24] The Swiss achieved this by having a dual employment market – the native Swiss, who had very secure, highly paid jobs, and foreign workers, who were paid lower wages and could be imported and exported as the need arose.

Political refugees had a particular role in the postwar European economy. In the short term, such people seemed less economically desirable than other migrants. Refugees arrived in unwieldy bulk as a result of political push rather than economic pull, often required a high degree of state support on first arrival, and brought dependants as well as economically active adults. In the long term, however, refugees brought substantial advantages to an expanding economy. They often arrived in a country because they had some cultural affinity with it, which meant that they spoke the language and had often been educated in schools that were compatible with those of their new host country, they identified strongly with their new home, and were forced, by the loss of their possessions and social position, to be dynamic and entrepreneurial.

There are two particularly striking examples of the economic benefits of refugees in postwar Europe. The first was seen in Germany. After German defeat, large numbers of ethnic Germans were expelled from the parts of eastern Europe in which they had formerly lived: by 1960, such people comprised 18.4 percent of the German population. As communist rule was established in the eastern zone, a further wave of refugees fled west, so that about 3 million people had moved from the German Democratic Republic to the Federal Republic by 1960. These refugees caused many problems as they were often dependent on state support, and some extended this dependence by becoming public-sector employees (ultimately a quarter of West German state employees had been expelled from eastern Europe).[25] Some of the refugees brought considerable benefits to the German economy, though. Most had been educated in German-speaking schools, and, because of the social/national stratification of society in Czechoslovakia and Poland, many were well educated or imbued with good business experience. Such advantages became more pronounced as time went on. Those who chose to flee communist rule in the East tended to be those who thought that they would do best in a capitalist system, and the mere willingness to move suggested a certain dynamism. Furthermore, large numbers of refugees were young adults, on the eve of their most productive years. This produced a curious paradox. The East German government invested heavily in education – the number in higher education increased from 28,000 to 57,000 between 1951 and 1954 – yet substantial numbers of those who received this education ended up working in the West. The postwar West German state was able to spend less money on education than had been spent in the Weimar Republic,[26] and one economist calculated that, by 1957, refugees from the German Democratic Republic had brought a total of DM 22,500 million worth of education with them.[27] The construction of the Berlin Wall in 1961 slowed the flow of fresh labor into the West German market, and annual growth of the working population dropped from 1.5 percent to 0.4 percent[28] – though perhaps the need to get past barbed wire and machine guns ensured that those who did get to the West were particularly ingenious, determined or willing to take risks (all useful characteristics in a growing economy).

The French economy also took in an influx of refugees when, in 1962, European residents (the *pieds noirs*) abandoned Algeria, which was about to become independent. A total of 865,000 such people reached French ports between April and September 1962 (about 95,000 had already left Algeria since 1959). This influx was at first seen as a disaster by the authorities: arriving over a short period of time and congregating in a few areas, notably Marseilles, the *pieds noirs* had lost almost all of their possessions (many had just the two suitcases that they were allowed to bring on evacuation boats). The new Algerian government broke its promise to pay compensation for property left behind, and de Gaulle's government refused to make good this shortfall. The *pieds noirs* were often seen as gangsters and terrorists by their compatriots and were not an economic elite. Most had worked in either minor clerical jobs or as shopkeepers in Algeria, and the mainland had few openings in those sectors.

Against all expectations, the *pieds noirs* had a beneficial impact on the French economy. At a time when the French economy needed labor, their desperate circumstances forced them to be flexible and to take whatever jobs were available (often semiskilled factory jobs). Furthermore, having nothing to lose, the *pieds noirs* did not suffer from the caution that characterized so many Frenchmen. They could not hope for the office jobs reserved for those with formal qualifications and the right contacts, so their only chance of prosperity lay in launching their own enterprises. The capacity to succeed in such circumstances depended first on energy and relative youth and second on a reasonable level of cultural assimilation – although the *pieds noirs* did not have the same qualifications as their French-born compatriots, they spoke the language and could eventually escape the damaging constraints of prejudice. They also had two characteristics that are useful for entrepreneurs – strong communal ties and deep distrust of the state. In the Vaucluse in 1963, a third of *pieds noirs* worked in the public sector and less than one in six had their own businesses; ten years later these statistics had been reversed. One *pied noir* summed up the experience: "We were condemned to succeed because we no longer had land and therefore had nothing to lose."[29]

Education also influenced the availability and quality of labor. Almost all countries raised the school leaving age between 1945 and 1975 (in Britain it was raised from fourteen to fifteen and then again to sixteen). In the short term, the measure reduced the size of the workforce, and in the long term, it may have increased productivity. It is difficult to determine the impact of education on postwar economies. The amount spent on education does not tell us much. West Germany, one of the most successful economies, whose workforce was widely seen as well trained, spent less on education than many of its competitors. Average number of years spent at school is also a figure of questionable value. In the highly centralized French education system, it was reasonable to assume that children throughout the country who had spent a certain number of years at school would have acquired the same knowledge. In Italy, by contrast, children moving from the south to the north were often made to drop a class, partly because of the linguistic difficulties of the transition.

The economic value of education was not always as evident as the people whose livelihood depended on it (most of those who studied the subject) claimed. The diffusion of basic literacy probably produced clear

benefits, and most economies probably gained from having large numbers of people with Ph.D.'s in physics. But much education in postwar
Europe provided neither. Universities were often more concerned about
prestige than useful skills and the sociologist Pierre Bourdieu argued that
the function of higher education was to provide the bourgeoisie with a
means of transmitting "cultural capital," which would then give privileged access to certain positions. The great expansion of university education during the 1960s did not improve matters. Much of this boom
was pushed by the social desire of lower-middle-class parents to see their
children achieve status, rather than pulled by an economic need for
more graduates. Overcrowded universities often led to poor education,
and the subjects in which the expansion of student numbers was greatest
(social sciences) were neither obviously useful to employers nor prestigious. Graduates of the new universities were in a difficult position.
They could rarely gain entrance to the traditionally lucrative and powerful professions, but they were not willing to settle for the kind of employment that their parents had taken. The solution was often a spectacular increase in the white-collar public sector: by 1988, only 9 percent of
Danes with a "theoretical" education worked for companies exposed to
competition; 60 percent were employed by the public sector.[30] Even in
the private sector, graduates were often recruited into departments, such
as personnel and marketing, whose habits of work seemed to mirror
those of the civil service. The individuals who made the most obvious
contribution to economic growth – those who started new companies –
were often drawn from among those with least formal education: a survey of small entrepreneurs in Italy during the early 1980s showed that
most had begun life as manual laborers after leaving school at or before
the age of fourteen.[31]

Probably the education that proved most useful for economic growth
was vocational. Germany was widely recognized to have a strong system
of such training, while Britain had a weak one. British government efforts to solve the problem were strikingly unsuccessful. The Butler Education Act of 1944 allowed for three types of school – secondary modern, technical and grammar – but in practice, this tripartite distinction
was ignored. Children were divided: the academically successful went to
grammar schools, which often provided a highly academic education (as
their name suggests, a few of them still regarding the study of classical
languages as the most respectable activity); the unsuccessful went to secondary moderns. In the 1960s, repeated attempts to promote more applied education failed. Polytechnics, designed to provide an applied education, soon concentrated on humanities and social sciences, partly

because teaching such subjects was cheap. Technical colleges established for children who had left other schools at sixteen became known for poorly disciplined, uninterested students, such as those who frequented the "plumbers two" class taught by Tom Sharpe's Wilt.

Elsewhere, technical education was more successful, but in no country did it provide the panacea that some experts had expected. Vocational education sometimes served the same function for the working class that elite higher education served for the upper bourgeoisie: it protected privilege and froze an existing social structure. Vocational schools tended to be monopolized by male, second-generation members of the working class. Women and immigrants were excluded; inhabitants of rural areas were given educations appropriate to farmers, which was not much use to those who were planning to catch the first train to the city. Furthermore, although rapid technological development might make technical skills necessary, it made it difficult to predict which particular ones would be of use in the future. Transistor radios made a generation of radio repairmen redundant; teenagers who learned technical drawing or typing during the 1960s would have been replaced by computers before they reached retirement age.

Industrial concentration

It was often assumed that a modern economy meant a big-business economy, in which large companies would benefit from economies of scale and invest in expensive equipment and research. Large companies would be run by detached, rational managers rather than by ignorant, narrow-minded *petits bourgeois*. European economic growth was accompanied by industrial concentration, but the process was never as complete as some had expected – an important number of small businesses survived, especially in France and Italy. Nor was it clear that small always meant inefficient or backward. In Italy, rapid economic growth was often associated with artisanal workshops and family businesses, whereas large enterprises, especially in the south, were bywords for corruption, paperwork and political backscratching.

The survival or disappearance of small business was partly a political matter. Large-scale enterprises benefited from well-organized and well-funded lobbying and from close links to certain parts of the state's administration, but they suffered from the electoral importance of small producers and the popular hostility to big business that still dominated much political debate in continental Europe, even on the right. Small businessmen and shopkeepers, like farmers, were often "swing" voters or voted for the hinge parties that were crucial to coalition-forming, and they carried an influence that went beyond their mere numbers. Political pressure from this constituency sometimes brought small business tax breaks or exemptions from onerous regulations.

The survival of small business also had an economic dimension. Small enterprises could be more flexible than their large competitors, and family businesses could survive economic downturn by exploiting children and wives, who worked for wages below the market rate. The workforce in a small business was less likely to be unionized, and a small business was less encumbered by regulations governing matters such as safety. Such freedom came partly from the deliberate decision of government to exempt small business – a decision sometimes linked to its associated political leverage – and partly from the fact that inspectors could not hope to enforce rules on every tiny workshop. Some small businesses benefited from the concentration of production elsewhere, as large enterprises subcontracted part of their work to smaller ones that could do jobs cheaper and faster. This was particularly characteristic of the motor industry, and large car factories in Birmingham, Turin and Boulogne-Billancourt were surrounded by companies that manufactured parts.

Productivism

The growth of the European economy was associated with cultural changes. The European economies had always operated with a limited set of resources, and although prosperity had grown quickly during the three decades that preceded the First World War, Europe had never known the sense of infinite possibility imparted to America by an open frontier, an empty land and a nation of immigrants making their fortune from nothing. In the interwar period, Europeans had experienced the constraints of depression. The legacy of the experience varied from country to country. France, which recovered most slowly, was probably most affected by pessimistic assumptions about future economic possibilities, whereas by 1939 parts of the British middle class had already experienced some aspects of the society that would be seen as characteristic of postwar economic growth. Germans remembered not only the severity of economic depression but also the rapid transformation of Hitler's "economic miracle," which, in some respects, anticipated the post-1945 economy.

In general, however, most Europeans shared the assumption that prosperity came from distribution rather than production. The well-being of one group could be achieved only at the expense of others and, if economic growth was possible at all, it could be achieved only by sacrificing present benefits for future ones. This assumption pervaded many statements by European politicians, including those whose names are most associated with modernization. French Prime Minister Pierre Mendès France remarked that "to govern is to choose," and implied that the choices would be unpleasant for some parts of French society. In 1949, an Italian politician called for "more machines and less macaroni," a deceptive phrase, since in Italy, as in other countries in western Europe, wheat production continued to be subsidized, but one that made it clear that present consumption was to be sacrificed to industrial investment. Such statements implied that economics was a "zero sum game," in which winnings in one sphere would mean losses in another. More investment meant less consumption; gains for employers meant losses for workers; expansion of modern industry meant the decline of agriculture and commerce.

After the war, this view of economic life was challenged by the Americans brought to Europe to administer the Marshall Plan, who argued for a vision that focused on production ("productivism") rather than one that focused on distribution and were particularly keen to apply such thinking to the conflict between capital and labor. They tried to persuade European employers and trade unionists that it was possible for wages and living standards to rise at the same time as profits, and that industrial relations could be characterized by cooperation in pursuit of a mutually beneficial goal. American ideas of "productivism" gained little explicit acceptance among workers and employers (it was not clear that they had ever really gained explicit acceptance in American industry, either), but it might be argued that the relatively tranquil industrial relations in most European countries between the late 1940s and the late 1960s marked an acceptance of common interest between workers and employers. The shift away from distributive conflicts could also be seen in many domains other than industrial relations. Growing prosperity meant that the town/country dispute that had bedeviled interwar politics could be assuaged with generous agricultural subsidies. Similarly, inefficient but electorally important small business could be given advantageous treatment at the same time that big business was expanding its profits.

The shift from the old assumptions about limited resources to the new thinking based on expanding opportunities occurred in even the most unexpected corners of the European economy. One was Sicily, where the Mafia dominated much business. Sicily was poor, and Mafia economic thinking centerd on scarcity. The organization's aim was to squeeze the greatest possible benefits out of its victims rather than to increase total wealth, and one mechanism for doing this was water. Control of wells and springs allowed powerful Sicilians to extort money from peasants who needed to irrigate arid land, so the Mafia opposed projects that might have increased the total water supply in any area. After the war, though, a new generation of American mafiosi arrived. These men did not come under the aegis of the European Reconstruction Agency but were sent by the Justice Ministry, which selected particularly dynamic entrepreneurs from Chicago or New York for deportation back to their country of origin. Like the smooth Harvard graduates who gathered in Rome, the American mafiosi tried to explain the virtues of growth to the Italians. They did not oppose irrigation projects. On the contrary, they favored the construction of large dams. In this way everyone could benefit from a new opportunity – though the Mafia, which took big rake-offs from the construction contracts, benefited more than most. Norman Lewis sums up the change thus:

> The mind of the old Mafia had been formed in a feudal past when there was not enough to go round, and it could never free itself from its philosophy of controlled dearth. Now it was opposed by an expansive and capitalistic young Mafia that had no patience with restrictive practices. The old Mafia vetoed dams because a hundred sleepy old villains made a fat living from water pumped up from artesian wells, but the new Mafia wanted them because of the huge profits to be made out of the contracts involved in their construction. For the same reasons they wanted modern roads, bridges and transport systems, urban development and industrial expansion of any kind. Psychologically, Don Calò Vizzini and his followers were still living in the eighteenth century – when not in the Bronze Age itself – whereas the cousins just back from Buffalo, New York or Kansas City were emphatically men of our times.[32]

A second cultural change associated with postwar economic growth came from the increase in "entrepreneurial" activities. Entrepreneurship is an intangible quality, often associated with small business and individuals' willingness to establish new businesses. This was particularly important in Italy, where much growth came from new or expanded family businesses, but was less visible in France, Great Britain and West Germany, whose economies were overshadowed by large enterprises. Big business could take risks, but in practice the gamble taken by a professional manager presenting a project to a board of directors could never be the same as that taken by an individual starting out on his own.

Many of those who set up in business did not do so by choice. Sometimes, as in the case of the *pieds noirs* in France or those whose lack of education excluded them from state employment in Italy, entrepreneurship reflected a lack of more comfortable opportunities, and the willingness to take economic risks often came from precisely the kind of irrational thinking that planners deplored. The desire for independence and obsession with quality that made families set up new enterprises in the "dynamic" northern Italian fashion industry might also encourage a "backward" Breton peasant to stay on his land. The capacity of each economy to produce entrepreneurs was linked to national cultures in curious ways. One Irish historian has suggested that litigation over land rights during the nineteenth century had given the Irish peasantry a tendency to seek prosperity in state handouts rather than through investment; this characteristic meant that the Irish proved less good at economic innovation than the inhabitants of many comparable countries in continental Europe, but it also meant that they were good at exploiting the opportunities presented by the Common Agricultural Policy.[33]

Associated with a new attitude towards production was a new attitude towards consumption. Economic growth was sustained by the Europeans' willingness to buy ever larger quantities of goods and to accept the "need" for commodities that would have seemed luxuries to their grandparents. The result was a huge increase in the sale of certain kinds of consumer goods. The most spectacular growth figures in the postwar period were often achieved by companies such as the French manufacturer of kitchen appliances Moulinex or the Italian firm Candy. In 1947, Candy manufactured one washing machine per day; twenty years later it made one every fifteen seconds.[34] Most of all, consumption was reflected in the spectacular growth of the motor industry: annual sales of cars in Europe increased from 1,595,000 in 1950 to 13,280,000 in 1973.[35] The consumer economy was associated with a shift away from the industries of the nineteenth century, so that by the 1960s increasing amounts of European production revolved around plastic, electronics and light engineering rather than iron and steel.

Europeans' increased willingness to consume was explained partly by imitation of America. Marshall Plan propaganda emphasized the high levels of consumption in the United States. More importantly, individual companies propagated an image of consumption. Hollywood films, Coca-Cola and American advertising agencies presented Europeans with a world of clean white kitchens, big cars on open roads and healthy blonde women. Consumerism was also explained by wider social changes, one of which was the propensity of Europeans to live in nuclear families. The peasant/bourgeois dynasties whose prosperity was based on generations of spectacular meanness were less common. Increasing numbers of Europeans worried more about their children's clothes, toys and holidays than about their dowries and inheritances.

The social mobility promoted by rapid economic growth also contributed to a culture of conspicuous consumption. Many of the people who did well out of such growth were insecure. The aristocracy and the established bourgeoisie had often defined status in terms of things that could not be bought (or at least things that could not be bought in a single generation); country houses, family heirlooms and old school ties defined the social position of such people before they took their first job. The new generation of managers, professionals and entrepreneurs was different. Often its members wished to distance themselves from, rather than display, their family backgrounds. Many such people worked in professions – such as marketing and public relations – in which appearances counted, and defined themselves by what they consumed. Michael Heseltine – who made a fortune in property development and publishing during the 1960s after having been born into a modest, though hardly impoverished, background – typified this generation of parvenu spenders. One Tory grandee was later to remark that Heseltine was "the kind of man who had bought all his own furniture."[36]

New financial arrangements facilitated the acquisition of certain consumer goods. The number of western Europeans with bank accounts greatly increased after the Second World War, and spending money by writing a check was less painful than parting with hard-earned cash. People were often specifically encouraged to buy certain commodities on credit; in Britain, interest repayments on credit could be counted against income tax. Granting credit was made easier by the fact that increasing numbers of people belonged to the salaried middle class and thus had predictable incomes.

The American sociologist Daniel Bell suggested that consumerism was associated with a new kind of capitalism. He argued that the capitalism of the nineteenth century had been based on discipline, restraint and deferred gratification, but eventually it became so successful at mastering the difficulties of production that it had difficulty in selling its goods, at which stage the attention of capitalism shifted from producing goods to producing consumers. This in turn raised particular problems, because the very qualities that capitalism needed to promote in order to sustain consumption – hedonism, exuberance, rebellion – might conflict with the values on which capitalism had been built.[37] The contradiction was summed up by the trite slogan with which Salman Rushdie, then an advertising executive in London, tried to sell cream cakes: "Naughty but nice."

The "cultural contradictions of capitalism" began to appear in Europe, and were seen in the activities of the French holiday company Club Med. Club Med was a highly profitable company that benefited from the rising salaries of the French managerial class, but its appeal lay partly in its capacity to offer clients an apparent break from the pressures of capitalism. In some Club Med colonies, money was replaced by the exchange of beads (which were, of course, purchased at the beginning of the holiday). Club Med's peculiar relation with the rebellious youth culture of the

1960s was exposed when rioting students attacked its headquarters in 1968. The company responded by offering the students free holidays.

Consumer capitalism in Europe never took exactly the same path as in the United States. A culture of consumption did not develop in the same way as in America: in the late 1960s, only about 1 percent of French corporate budgets were spent on advertising. The spread of a consumer culture across Europe was uneven – it was best developed in Great Britain, where the large-scale purchase of cars and electrical equipment had been established during the late 1930s, but large areas of Europe – southern Italy, Spain, Portugal, Greece – remained comparatively untouched. Some features of economic growth insulated parts of the European population from consumerism. Migrant workers who crowded into bedsitters, cooked their meals on primus stoves and sent every penny that they could spare back to Calabria or Galway were not likely to buy fitted kitchens. Increasing numbers of the old in the most developed countries could retire from work, though retirement meant a drop in income and a withdrawal from many forms of consumption. Sometimes the old and the young became part of quite different economies: the old often retired to the countryside and made some effort to recover peasant roots (even if only through the cultivation of an allotment); the young moved to industrial jobs in the cities. The young rushed to buy new possessions, while the old lived with what they already had. Many groups in European society still treated the consumer society with contempt, which could be found in British working men's clubs, among Left Bank intellectuals and throughout the European aristocracy. It did not always preclude a certain participation.

Many different forms of consumption could coexist in a single country. France was a striking example. There was a difference between the spending patterns of a Parisian executive and those of a Breton peasant: the former lived in a post-money economy of credit and banks, while the latter lived in a pre-money economy of exchange and barter; the former celebrated appearance and modernity, while the latter's world revolved around utility and tradition. Sometimes apparently similar objects might have quite different functions for different people. This was conspicuously true of French cars. For some, they were the ultimate consumer status symbol – Roland Barthes evoked the elegance of the Citroën DS in a famous essay – but for small shopkeepers and peasants in isolated parts of rural France, cars were seen as necessities rather than luxuries. Such people were more likely to invest in battered second-hand models than gleaming limousines. In the village of Peyrane, in the Vaucluse, only two cars, belonging to the lawyer and the butcher, were less than five years old; the average age of the remainder was twenty-five years, and one 1923

Renault had been patched together with front wheels from a truck and back wheels from a vine-spraying machine.[38]

Furthermore, the "cultural contradictions of capitalism" made less sense in Europe than in America because parts of Europe had never adopted the Protestant work-and-saving ethic that Bell believed to have characterized an earlier stage of capitalism. The very poor had no culture of saving, because they had so rarely had the opportunity to do so. On the rare occasions that such people did have money, they often preferred to spend it in ostentatious display or spectacular public hospitality, rather than invest it in well-considered saving plans.

Conclusion

Describing European economic growth is not the same as explaining it. It might be argued that many things that are usually described as strengths in the postwar European economy might have been weaknesses in slightly different circumstances. An abundant labor supply was a good thing in Italy in 1958, but it had been a weakness in Britain in the early 1930s and was to be a problem again after 1975. Consumerism, which helped to fuel high growth during the 1960s, helped to fuel high inflation during the late 1970s. Often it is hard to say whether particular developments were causes or effects of growth. Did European agriculture mechanize because rural labor was becoming scarce, or did men leave the land because mechanization threw them out of work? Did European businessmen stimulate growth by becoming more entrepreneurial, or were they willing to launch new initiatives simply because a growing economy gave those initiatives a better chance of paying off?

European growth had no single cause. It was the interconnection of different developments that explained rapid change. Often change snowballed as new habits became both causes and effects of expansion. Growth cannot be separated from its wider context. Events between 1945 and 1975 cannot be discussed without reference to what happened before and after, and the economy was not independent of political and social developments. Many of the economic developments that were regarded as desirable were linked to other changes that were regarded as bad. The groups that succeeded most in economic terms – the *pieds noirs* in France and refugees from the East in Germany – were often those who had the strongest reasons to forget the past. Memories of war, unemployment and displacement underlay much economic transformation.

Of course, memories varied from one place to another and from one generation to another. In Britain, a Welshman born in 1910 would have been formed by the despair and humiliation of mass unemployment, whereas a man born in Coventry a few years later would have left school to enter a relatively buoyant labor market. The Second World War would be remembered as a time of job security, strong unions and generous welfare provision. Consequently, by 1945 much of the British working class had expectations of high living standards. In Germany, by contrast, memories of mass unemployment in the early 1930s were overlain by even more unpleasant recollections of what happened afterwards. Recalcitrant workers who had undergone "reeducation" at the hands of the Gestapo, soldiers who had endured the horrific defeats on the eastern front, and, perhaps especially, the generation of teenagers formed by the Hitler Youth were used to harsh discipline and low expectations. This goes a long way to explaining the work ethic and willingness to forgo consumption that characterized much of the West German population.

West Germany showed that economic success could be based on forgetting, or trying to forget, as well as on remembering. The Bundesbank cultivated the "memory" of the inflation of 1923 but proved much more discreet when it came to the activities of central bankers after 1933 (39 percent of those who sat on the boards of state banks between 1948 and 1980 had been members of the Nazi Party).[39] The Bavarian Christian democrat Franz-Josef Strauss made a revealing remark in 1969: "A people who have achieved such economic performances have the right not to hear any more about Auschwitz."[40]

Finally, it should be remembered that economic growth is always obtained at a price. For many, the 1940s and 1950s were times of hard work and low rewards. Statistics tell us little about the cultural and psychological damage of economic change. It was not only bourgeois sentimentalists who felt that cars and Coca-Cola did not represent a fair exchange for everything that was lost during this period. An Italian laborer explained the qualitative element of economic growth: "The sun, the fresh air, these are beautiful things, my friend, and when I am dead who will give me back the days that have been stolen from me in the factory?"[41]

3
CONSENSUS POLITICS

IN THE LATE 1940s, it seemed possible that western European politics would return to the extreme polarization of the 1930s. Spain and Portugal were right-wing dictatorships. France and Italy had strong communist parties that were countered by aggressive anticommunist movements such as the Gaullist Rassemblement du Peuple Français. In Greece, the right and the communists were fighting a civil war. Against all expectations, however, political violence in western Europe declined from 1948 onwards. Democratic governments succeeded in excluding communists from power without being overthrown or resorting to authoritarianism. The repression that followed the victory of anticommunist forces in the Greek civil war was not, by the standards of 1914 to 1945, severe.[1] In the mid-1970s, even Spain and Portugal acquired elected governments, while the Greek colonels' regime of 1967 to 1974 did not produce the permanent extinction of democracy that many had feared.

Broadly speaking, western Europe united around the values of democracy and capitalism. On an international level, this convergence was a product partly of the Second World War and the reconstruction of West German politics under Allied, especially American, aegis, and partly of the Cold War. The Western democracies now defined themselves against a common enemy and sought unity in bodies such as the North Atlantic Treaty Organization, the Organization for Economic Cooperation and Development and the European Economic Community.

Many political parties began to think of themselves in pan-European, or at least pan-western-European, terms. Before the war, European politics had often pitted "internationalist" communist parties against nationalist parties of the right. After 1945 this changed. Nationalism had been discredited in the eyes of many bourgeois politicians by its association with fascism and Nazism, while the defense of national independence (against American hegemony) was now taken up by communists. Some European communist parties established an international organization – the Cominform – but this was short-lived. In any case, everyone knew that "fraternal solidarity" meant simply obeying Moscow's orders, and, in the late 1960s, some western European communist parties began to make it clear that they found the discipline onerous. International links among the noncommunist parties became stronger. The new Socialist International was founded in 1951, uniting the major socialist parties in every western European country except Italy. Liberal parties had strong international tendencies rooted in free trade and were grouped in a Liberal International. Most striking of all was the internationalism of the Christian democrats, a grouping that had had weak international links in the interwar period; Franco-German disagreements over Versailles had undermined common action. In 1945, Nouvelles Équipes Internationales was formed to bring Christian democrat parties together, and in 1965 a European movement was formed under the aegis of the Italian Christian Democrat Party and the leadership of the Belgian politician Leo Tindemans. European integration brought politicians from different countries together in bodies such as the Council of Europe, the Assembly of the European Coal and Steel Community, and the European Parliament, and in 1976, the European Christian democrats began to prepare for the advent of direct elections to the European Parliament (scheduled for 1979) by launching the European People's Party, which claimed to be the first pan-European party.[2]

Convergence between the political systems of European countries was accompanied by convergence in each individual country. Revolutions and riots were less common than during the 1930s. Some people still advocated the resolution of political conflict through violence, but they were less likely to be leaders of established parties. The dominant political parties agreed about much. In some cases, such agreement had been arrived at before the Second World War. The Swedish consensus about economic management and welfare began as a response to the depression of the 1930s, and was incarnated by the social democrats who governed Sweden from 1936 until 1976. In Britain, the architect of consensus politics was Stanley Baldwin (Conservative Prime Minister 1923, 1924–29 and 1935–37) rather than Clement Attlee (Labour Prime Minister 1945–51); Baldwin persuaded Conservatives to treat Labour leaders as legitimate opponents rather than dangerous revolutionaries. In most of continental Europe, however, the climate of the late 1940s marked a sharp break with the intense political conflict that had begun with the upheavals of the First World War and the economic crisis of the 1930s.

The mechanisms through which agreement was expressed varied from country to country. In some places, two similar political groups competed for power and the same voters; elsewhere, different parties represented different groups but often governed in coalition with each other. Britain was dominated by two parties that competed for power (1945 marked the end of fourteen years of coalition government), but changes of government did not alter the lives of most people. Apart from some nationalizations, neither party tried to reverse measures taken by the other party in government. Labour and Conservative politicians shared views about the preservation of institutions such as the National Health Service and economic management.

The political system in postwar France was more complicated. From 1947 until 1958, it was governed by coalitions that were designed largely to exclude the communists from power. The establishment of the French Fifth Republic in 1958 seemed to end postwar consensus, marginalizing or destroying the groups – socialists, Christian democrats and Radicals – that had dominated Fourth Republic coalitions, and marking a shift away from European patterns. Gaullism was a peculiarly French tradition; the focus of power on a single individual who enjoyed direct relations with the people through television and referenda looked like electronic Bonapartism. De Gaulle was skeptical about international bodies, such as the EEC and NATO, that united western Europe. Most importantly, the early years of the Fifth Republic were accompanied by a revival of political violence. Fighting between Frenchmen over the fate of Algeria spilled over to the mainland. Georges Bidault, a long-serving minister and leader of European Christian democracy before 1958, finished up in political exile because of his links with terrorists. Soldiers plotted coups, and assassination attempts on de Gaulle became so common that he traveled with flasks of his own blood in case he needed a transfusion.

In the long run, however, even Fifth Republic France can be seen in terms of consensus. The political violence of the early 1960s did not last, and in some respects de Gaulle drew the poison of French politics by concentrating on one person all the hatreds that had formerly been directed at entire categories of people. The Fifth Republic was marked by changes at both extremes of French politics. In referenda and presidential elections many French communists supported de Gaulle's policy in Algeria against the extreme right, and the extreme right itself changed. Once France had abandoned Algeria, the last cause that had united right-wingers was gone. Many now looked to a future in European integration and Atlanticism (the politics of the center). Anti-Gaullism kept such people marginalized as long as the general lived, but the way was paved for political reconciliation after his death.

France acquired something like a two-party system in the 1960s, when the moderate right, united under de Gaulle, confronted a left that tried increasingly to unite under a single challenger for the presidency. This role was played in the 1965 election by François Mitterrand, who sought to present himself as leader of the opposition, and even formed a shadow cabinet. The French "two-party system" differed from that of Britain, partly because the "opposition" was composed of two major parties – socialists and communists – that did not always cooperate effectively. More importantly, there was no alternation of right and left in office: right-wing governments held power from 1958 to 1981. Consequently, it was hard to judge how much of the opposition's radical rhetoric should be taken seriously. Mitterrand presented himself as an opponent of the Gaullist system who wished to abolish the Fifth Republic, was willing to flirt with extra-parliamentary agitation and even talked of the need for revolution. Curiously, however, the strikes and riots of 1968 demonstrated the regime's durability. Left-wing politicians did not translate their words into deeds, while the majority of French people showed their attachment to the established order.

The other major European countries were governed by coalitions for much of the postwar period. The supreme example of a stable coalition was Austria, where socialists and Christian democrats, the political descendants of parties that had shed each other's blood in 1934, governed in coalition until 1966. West German social democrats raised the possibility of coalition government in the early 1960s and eventually entered into such a coalition with the Christian democrats in December 1966. In Italy, the Christian Democrat Party, which dominated Italian politics from the late 1940s, was, in some respects, a coalition that brought together the disparate institutions of a socially and regionally fragmented country – institutions such as the clergy, Catholic Action and the Mafia – under weak central leadership. Eventually, the Christian democrats' "opening to the left" created a coalition government (containing Italy's two socialist parties, the Republicans and the Christian democrats) in December 1963.

Whereas two-party politics encouraged both sides to struggle for the center ground, coalition politics encouraged parties to stress their particularity and strengthen their hold on a limited part of the electorate. In many countries, it was impossible for any one party to gain a majority of seats in parliament. In any case, participation in government did not depend on winning a majority of seats.

Coalition government sometimes went with what political scientists labeled "consociational" politics,[3] a term referring to political systems – such as those of Belgium, Holland, Austria or Switzerland – that were divided by language or religion so that different parties emerged to represent different groups. The parties had little hope of attracting each other's electorates and so there was no electoral center ground. However, after 1945, all parties in such countries were united by an acceptance of certain underlying principles. The fact that they did not compete for the same votes often had the curious effect of making electoral rhetoric more fierce but collaboration in government easier. For example, in 1966, the Austrian Christian democrats fought a savage election campaign (presumably as a means of rallying their natural supporters), but they still offered the socialists places in government after the election.[4]

Voters, notables and militants

The phrase "voter-oriented" party was widely used during the 1960s. From an Anglo-Saxon perspective, it sounds strange. European political parties had faced large electorates since the end of the nineteenth century, when universal male suffrage had been instituted in most countries on the continent. Had not all such parties sought to appeal to the largest possible number of voters? In fact, however, at least two other forms of party occupied much of the western European political landscape. The first was the "notable" party, which was concerned with the quality rather than the number of its supporters and valued people who had particular prestige, resources or contacts. Local notables who could deliver the support of a newspaper or of professional associations were particularly important. Sometimes such people were not even party members. Indeed, notables were often keen to stress their "independence": the key notable group in Fourth Republic France was the Centre National des Indépendants, and Felix Kir of Dijon contested the 1951 election as an "independent Independent."

The other sort of party was based on militants, and had a large and committed membership. While the notable stressed his independence of any particular party, the militant derived his influence and even his sense of self from membership. The archetypal militant often had little life outside the party, and was willing to endure hours of excruciating tedium in party meetings. Although the word "militant" was most often used by communists, their parties were not, strictly speaking, militant parties. Communist leaders cared more about Moscow than about the party congress, and were sometimes willing to act in ways – such as supporting the Soviet invasion of Hungary – that alienated a substantial proportion of their militants. Socialist parties were the real centers of militant power, because they offered militants a real chance of controlling party policy. Militants pushed in the opposite direction from notables. While the latter wanted parties with which they were associated to remain in government, so that they could distribute the spoils of office, militants preferred to maintain doctrinal purity even if it meant the party's representatives leaving office. French socialists talked of taking a "*cure d'opposition*" in order to keep their puritan militants happy.

The power of notables and militants, rather than voters, was increased by the fact that the relation between votes cast and governments formed was often unclear. The French *apparentement* law of 1951, designed to limit communist success, gave a disproportionate number of seats to certain parties. The French system gave advantages to parties that were able to form local alliances, which enhanced the influence of the notables who brokered such alliances. Coalition government allowed even a party that had received a small number of votes to exercise influence; if you are one seat away from a majority, then a party with one seat in parliament has as much influence as a party with a hundred. French politics in the Fourth Republic (1945–58) showed that skilful maneuvering could be more important than the ability to attract voters. The Radical Party continually increased its representation in parliament even though its vote fell slightly. The Union Démocratique et Socialiste de la Résistance provided an even more spectacular example of such maneuvers. One of its leaders, René Pleven, became Prime Minister of France at a time when his party attracted so little support that, even with favorable election arrangements, it had only nine seats in parliament.

In the 1950s and 1960s some political systems shifted away from parties that relied on notables and militants to ones that sought direct relations with voters. This shift was based partly on wider social changes. Notable power was more easily exercised in the countryside and small towns, where personal contacts counted for much, than in the anonymity of large cities, and it depended on the wealth of landowners and the discretionary power that individuals could exercise in matters such as the allocation of charity. Urbanization, the decline of the agricultural population, and the provision of state assistance to the poor all undermined such power. Similarly, increasing education and career opportunities meant that a proportion of those whose energies would formerly have found an outlet in political militancy now found jobs that matched their sense of their own abilities. Television and opinion polling created direct links between party leaders and voters, while European integration weakened the power of notables and militants who operated at a local or national level. When party leaders boarded the plane to Brussels or Strasbourg, they could usually forget about the party structures that constrained them in their own countries.

The countries in which "voter-oriented" parties triumphed most clearly were Britain, France and Germany. The British two-party system had always encouraged parties to struggle for the center ground, but voter sovereignty in Britain was never complete. Voters could exercise power only indirectly, by selecting MPs who then selected a Prime Minister (until the early 1960s the Conservative Party continued to insist that prime ministers were chosen by the Queen after party elders had "taken soundings"). On certain issues, such as the abolition of the death penalty, parliament clearly flouted the wishes of the majority of British voters. The British electorate did not exercise direct influence over policy until it confirmed British membership of the Common Market in a referendum in 1975.

Charles de Gaulle's return to power in 1958 transformed French politics. The Gaullist Union pour la Nouvelle République attracted the support of a large proportion of the French electorate. The social basis of its support also resembled the social structure of the French population more closely than had been the case for any previous French party, while the notable-based Radical Party and the militant-based SFIO (socialist party) lost influence. The electoral system changed in a way that clarified relations between votes cast and governments formed. The President was chosen by direct election from 1965 onwards.

In Germany, the triumph of "voter-oriented" politics was associated with that of the Christian Democratic Union (CDU). It looked out to the mobilization required for elections, particularly of Chancellors, rather than in at the congresses and section meetings that preoccupied militant-based parties. Konrad Adenauer had already been elected Chancellor before the party acquired a federal structure (in 1950).[5]

Social change did not always bring the complete triumph of voter-oriented parties. Sometimes the increase in state activity could increase the power of notables by giving them access to new resources with which they could reward their clients. This happened spectacularly in Italy, where the Christian democrats remained a notable-based party. Powerful local barons often exercised more power than the party's ostensible leaders in Rome.

Social change did not necessarily destroy militancy, either. Indeed, in Britain the expansion of local government employment and higher education, as well as the relative generosity of unemployment payments, produced the group of full-time militants that so troubled Labour leaders during the 1980s. Similarly, in Austria, the social democrats remained a militant-based party, with a membership equivalent to one-third of their vote, as late as the 1980s.

The pattern of politics was linked to social change in a wider sense. "Voter-oriented" politics suited homogeneous societies in which politicians could appeal to the entire population with similar policies and rhetoric. Britain was the best example of a society that became more homogeneous after 1945. It was already highly urban and industrial, and after the Second World War income differentials narrowed and employment increased fastest in technical and white-collar occupations that were seen as middle class. British politicians could refer to houses or cars without instantly identifying themselves as representatives of the rich. Elsewhere, matters were more complicated. In France, the middle class expanded and the peasantry diminished in size, but the working class remained a significant group that thought of its interests in different terms from those used by the rest of France: income gaps between bourgeoisie and workers widened during France's postwar economic expansion.

Italy was the most striking example of a society where rapid social change produced fragmentation rather than homogenization. The gap between the prosperous bourgeoisie of the industrial north and the impoverished peasantry of the south widened, and the arrival of southern immigrants in the north created new divisions. The Calabrians who lived six to a room in Turin tenements or built houses out of corrugated iron in the shanty towns around Milan were different from both the agricultural laborers in their native region and the established, unionized, largely communist working class in the cities to which they had moved. Italian Christian democracy's success sprang partly from the fact that its comparatively weak national structure allowed it to adjust its appeal to such a host of local circumstances.

Anticommunism

The first thing about which western European politicians agreed was anticommunism. It was not ubiquitous, and it did not affect politics with equal intensity throughout the entire postwar period. By the 1960s, at the height of consensus politics, many western European governments enjoyed good relations with the Eastern Bloc, and many western European communist parties had accepted significant parts of the political consensus of their countries. Even at the height of the Cold War, communists were not always excluded from contact with other political groups.

Anticommunism did, however, play a role in molding the pattern of western European politics during the late 1940s. The intensity of Cold War divisions eventually subsided, but the institutions it created survived. Indeed, the entry of communist parties into the political mainstream during the 1960s and 1970s often meant their acceptance of bodies, such as NATO, that had been established to fight communism during the 1940s.

Anticommunism produced consensus in several ways. It encouraged the formation of interparty bodies, such as Paix et Liberté in France, that coordinated the actions of different noncommunist parties. The very stability of such coalitions often came from a shared desire to exclude communists from power. Indeed, a perceived decline in the communist threat could undermine the political stability of the system; this was what happened in France between 1951 and 1958. Anticommunism encouraged the nationalist authoritarian right to accept European integration and democracy, encouraged socialist parties to accept American hegemony and encouraged bourgeois parties to accept social reform.

Economic management and welfare

The second foundation of consensus politics was a new approach to economics, based partly on a belief that now seems self-evident – prosperity is a good thing. Before 1945, most governments had wished to increase production of particular goods but were not all persuaded that rising living standards were desirable. Economic liberals feared that too much comfort might blunt people's will to work, fascists feared that it might blunt their will to fight, and some conservatives believed that the simple life of the countryside was superior to the decadent luxury of the city. After the Second World War, this changed. High living standards were welcomed and politicians boasted of their success in this domain. Richard Crossman wrote that the living standard of the English working class was higher than that of any similar group since the time of the Roman emperors.

Politicians tried to increase living standards in two ways. First, they sought to manage the economy to produce growth. Europe was no longer divided, as it had been during the 1930s, between those who refused to reform capitalism because they believed that the free market could not be improved and those who refused to reform capitalism because they wanted to destroy it. It seemed feasible to plan the economy (as was attempted in France) or at least to manage government spending to avoid cyclical crisis (as was attempted in Britain). The extent of state intervention, the mechanisms that directed it and the degree of planning that governed state action varied from country to country: indeed, differences over economic management were usually greater between countries than between opposing parties in each individual country.

Second, politicians embraced welfare states designed to provide benefits to those who needed them (largely groups, such as children, the sick and the old, who were outside the labor market). The creation of a "welfare state" is often linked to William Beveridge's report of 1942, the legislation introduced by the British Labour government of 1945–51, and in particular the creation of the National Health Service. In fact, the 1945–51 government did not mark a sharp break. Universal benefits had been slowly introduced in various European countries ever since the late nineteenth century, and in Britain the sharpest growth in state spending came not under the Labour government of 1945 to 1951, but under the Conservative government of Edward Heath in the early 1970s.

Welfare states did not take a single form. Until the 1960s, most countries in continental Europe lacked the resources to contemplate the comparative generosity of British provision. Furthermore, European welfare states were usually built on preexisting arrangements, which often meant the centralization and streamlining of existing insurance schemes, as in Italy. The Church sometimes continued to play a role in the distribution of welfare, as did political parties, giving rise to opportunities for the exercise of patronage. Many welfare schemes were designed to assist families rather than individuals.

The culture of consensus

Before the Second World War, political divisions had been associated with cultural and social divisions. A party might be linked to a way of life rather than merely with possessing a party card or casting a vote. This was most famously true of the German labor movement, which organized people's leisure as well as their political activity; it was also true of French Radicalism. A Radical was not simply someone who supported a particular set of beliefs or joined a party branch (Radicals were notoriously vague about both doctrine and party membership). Radicalism meant steadfast refusal to attend church and a defense of lay education in state schools, celebration of the rites and anniversaries connected with the French Revolution, and a particular kind of sociability that was centerd on the café and the banquet. It even influenced diet. A true believer ostentatiously ate meat on Fridays and *tête de veau* (to celebrate the beheading of the king) on January 21.

After the Second World War, political cultures became less intensely segregated. Recruitment to the British Conservative Party reflected the way in which party affiliations were becoming less closely tied to other aspects of people's identity. In the 1930s, around two-thirds of Conservatives had been introduced to the party by relatives; by the 1960s, this figure had dropped to less than a third. As Conservatism lost this intimate tie with people's private lives, it gained more general access to society as a whole: by the 1970s a quarter of members had been drawn to the party through canvassing or political broadcasts on television.[6]

The cultural-political ghettos were opened up in several ways after 1945. Economic change was one. The working class was still important – in many continental European countries, it grew after the Second World War – but its experience was less unified and less sharply divided from that of the rest of society. The solidarities of the pithead bath and the workingmen's club mattered less as new industries attracted workers to areas outside traditional industrial heartlands. Prosperity created affluent workers whose life outside work bore some resemblance to that of the middle class, while the entry of non-European immigrants and women into the workforce meant that large numbers were excluded from a working-class culture constructed by and for white men.

The development of consumer capitalism in the more prosperous parts of western Europe during the 1950s and 1960s also changed politics. An American officer in Italy during the mid-1940s wrote:

> The Italians can tell you the names of the ministers in the government but not the names of the favorite products of the celebrities of their country. In addition, the walls of Italian cities are plastered more with political slogans than with commercial ones. According to the opinion of this officer there is little hope that the Italians will achieve a state of prosperity and internal calm until they start to be more interested in the respective merits of different types of cornflakes and cigarettes rather than the relative abilities of their political leaders.[7]

Consumerism directed attention away from the world of production, in which class conflicts had been rooted. Workers spent less of their time at work, and the more prosperous of them thought of their world as revolving around the family, the house and the car rather than around the factory. The new mood was most marked in Great Britain, where sociologists interviewing "affluent workers" in the Luton engineering industry were repeatedly told that "mates" (colleagues) were not the same as "friends";[8] one might add that, *a fortiori*, friends were not comrades.

Consumerism helped create a unified national culture at which politicians could direct appeals. Politics increasingly used the language of consumerism by stressing "living standards." Sometimes it also deployed the methods of consumerism: the British Conservative Party hired an advertising agency for the first time in 1959,[9] and the man behind Giscard d'Estaing's successful presidential campaign of 1974 was Jacques Hintzy, a director of the Havas advertising agency.[10]

Secularization

Before 1945, religious divisions often paralleled social and political ones. After 1945, religion became less important in most European countries. The proportion of the French population regularly attending mass dropped from around one-third in the 1950s to around 15 percent in the 1970s.[11]

Religion did not cease to matter in politics (postwar politics in several countries was dominated by the Christian democrats), but religious conflicts no longer had the same intensity. Churchmen and anticlericals, Protestants and Catholics no longer inhabited different worlds. The sharp divisions of the pre-war period were replaced by what French religious sociologists referred to as "seasonal conformity," meaning that both devotion (characterized by regular attendance at church) and anticlericalism (characterized by complete nonattendance) were less common. Most people attended church at certain times of the year (Christmas and Easter) or at key times in their lives (baptisms, marriages and funerals). The joke about the British national serviceman who tells an army clerk that he has no religion and receives the reply, "We'll put you down as Church of England, then," is revealing. It reflects a society in which church membership had become a matter of outward conformity rather than belief. The days when politicians mobilized in defense of particular religious doctrines, as the British parliamentarians had mobilized against the 1928 prayer book, were over.

Associated with the secularization of society was a new attitude on the part of church leaders. They were less likely to isolate themselves from the rest of society and more willing to work with secular bodies. The change was most dramatic in Catholicism. After the harsh climate of the Cold War, the Vatican II council (1962–65) illustrated a liberalization of the Church. Anti-Semitism, once a cornerstone of most Catholic politics, was denounced, and even systematic anticommunism was abandoned with the 1963 encyclical *Pacem in Terris*. During the 1960s, the Catholic Church and the Italian Communist Party began a curious courtship, and Catholic bodies, which were more responsive to the "post-materialist" politics of the 1960s, sometimes seemed to outflank communists on the left.

Television

Television was central to the culture of consensus. Before the Second World War, much political information was communicated either through local newspapers or through direct contact between politicians and their constituents. Few people on the continent read national papers, and personal contact with politicians was, of necessity, restricted to local rather than national figures. Furthermore, these means of communication were partisan. Meetings brought together individuals of the same party, and discussion among believers was conducted in terms that reinforced their sense of unity and their hostility to their opponents. Newspapers had the same effect. People chose to read a paper partly because they agreed with its politics, and the paper then provided them with information to reinforce their preference.

Even in England, where "papers of record" prided themselves on their detached tone, a reader of the *Manchester Guardian*, which suppressed details of Stalinist atrocities, would have had a different view of the world from that of a reader of the *Morning Post*, which campaigned to raise money for General Dyer after he was disciplined for his role in the 1919 Amritsar massacre. In France, differences could be more severe. *Action Française*, the paper of Charles Maurras's royalist movement, was read by much of the Catholic bourgeoisie, and even those who never shared its royalism can hardly fail to have been influenced by its incessant attacks on Jews, freemasons and parliamentarians. Newspapers – particularly the *Dépêche de Toulouse* – were equally important to the anticlerical and republican Radical Party, so much so that they were represented at the party's annual congress. In Germany, readers of the 200 socialist newspapers in the Weimar Republic read an account of events that would have been unrecognizable to those who subscribed to Nazi papers.

After 1945, many newspapers were banned for political reasons. In some countries, a conscious bid was made to create national papers – such as *Le Monde* in France – that would adopt an "objective" and balanced tone. The decline in the readership of local newspapers was associated with a decline in notable power, and that in the readership of party newspapers was associated with a shift away from militant-based parties. In Lombardy in the mid-1970s, even among relatively active male members of the Christian Democrat Party, less than a fifth read *Il Popolo* (the party paper); by contrast, almost four-fifths of male members of the Communist Party, which preserved a stronger culture of militancy, read *L'Unità*.[12] More importantly, increasing numbers of people began to draw their information and entertainment from the radio and later from television.

The impact of television was particularly dramatic because early broadcasting offered the viewer little choice. Even Britain, the pioneer in this field, had only one television channel until 1955. Consequently, everyone, regardless of political preference, was tuned to the same channels, and broadcasting helped erode politically separate cultures. People of different political persuasions might drink in different bars, sing different songs and send their children to different schools, but they all watched the same television programs and shared a single source of information. Communists or supporters of the extreme right might interpret news broadcasts with more skepticism than their less ideologically committed neighbors, but the conservative historian Philippe Ariès, who stopped listening to the "Gaullist radio" altogether, was a rarity. Significantly, Ariès wrote for the small-circulation right-wing journals that did their best to keep the culture of *Action Française* alive.

Television and radio had an impact on how politicians presented themselves. For the first time, politicians spoke directly to a large section of the population rather than to their own supporters at meetings. "Extreme" political opinions were simply excluded from the options that could be conveyed by television, which was the case of republicanism in England. Although opinion polls showed substantial support for republicanism after the war, the British Broadcasting Corporation decreed that it had a duty to uphold a "national institution." Television broadcasts were used to enhance the royal family's image, and when the broadcaster Malcolm Muggeridge referred to the "royal soap opera" (a revealing image), he was banned from the airwaves. Television focused attention on national party leaders (particularly those in government), and politics increasingly revolved around prominent personalities such as Adenauer, Macmillan, Wilson and de Gaulle.

The impact of broadcasting varied among countries. It was most obvious in France, where de Gaulle's career was intertwined with the new medium. He had first become known to the French people through BBC broadcasts during the Second World War, and while President relied heavily on television and radio. The state broadcasting company – ORTF – was under tight political control, reinforcing the direct relationship with the people that lay at the center of de Gaulle's political thinking. De Gaulle was able to appeal to citizens over the heads of those who might have served as intermediaries, and in 1961 he broadcast directly to French conscript troops, urging them not to follow their rebellious generals. He developed an effective and mannered television style complete with grimaces, dramatic shrugs and striking turns of phrase; Emmanuel Le Roy Ladurie suggested that de Gaulle's use of television to focus attention on the ruler's body recalled the ritual surrounding medieval kings.

British politicians did not enjoy the respect accorded to a head of state, and confronted a less docile broadcasting service. The most effective manipulator of the new medium in Britain was Harold Wilson. While de Gaulle cultivated regal dignity, Wilson used television to project an image of himself as modest and populist; he developed bonds with viewers by emphasising his links with the very individuals whose fame had been spread by television – The Beatles and David Frost.

In Italy, the political use of broadcasting was different. Television spread more slowly than in wealthier parts of Europe: in 1965, less than half of Italian families owned a television set.[13] The state broadcasting service (RAI) was initially influenced by the Christian democrats; Ettore Bernabei, the first director of RAI, had been editor of the Christian democrat *Il Popolo*. In the 1960s, the Christian democrats illustrated the new cordiality of their relations with the socialists, not by making broadcasts on their own channel more balanced, but by creating a second channel to be the fiefdom of the Socialist Party.[14] Television therefore played a smaller role in breaking down separate political cultures than it had done in Britain or France. It is notable that the Christian democrats dominated Italian electoral politics without producing a leader with the national appeal of de Gaulle or Adenauer; indeed, the best-known Italian politicians came from a party that was permanently excluded from power – the Communist Party. Even in Italy, though, television underwrote political consensus. Party-controlled channels could not be as polemical as party newspapers, and the nonpolitical elements of television broadcasting (particularly advertising) helped to create a common culture that transcended parties.

Social science

Social scientists were commentators on and catalysts for a less polarized view of politics. Books such as Daniel Bell's *The End of Ideology*[15] popularized the notion that there were no longer great divisions of general principle in political life, and more generally social science encouraged the idea that many of society's problems were limited, measurable and ultimately soluble. The French Gaullist Roger Frey epitomized the new mood. Quoting the sociologist Raymond Aron, he argued: "In the affluent society towards which western Europe is gradually moving, no political party has a doctrine as such . . . Our society is not without its problems . . . but it does not have one big problem."[16]

The transformation of social sciences had begun in the academic world during the interwar period but began to filter through into practical politics as those educated before the war gained office. Harold Wilson, leader of the British Labour Party from 1963 until 1976, illustrated the new distrust for grand theory. His brilliant career as a student of politics, philosophy and economics at Oxford had, so he claimed, not been damaged by his failure to read a single line of the works of Karl Marx.

Statistics rather than grand theory were now the basis of the social sciences and the inspiration for political action – the French government established a national statistical office in 1946. Precise statistical information reinforced the belief that policies could be agreed to by experts on a basis of mathematical certainty, and should not, therefore, be a subject for political dispute. Statistics also had an important application to the study of public opinion. Opinion polls had begun in Britain and France just before the war, and became common after 1945. The British Labour Party used public opinion polls for the first time during its successful election campaign of 1964.[17] Polls increased politicians' sense of contact with ordinary people – rather than party militants or notables – and encouraged them to focus on reflecting, and molding, the views of "the average person."

Two remarks illustrated the new concern with public opinion. In 1960, Harold Macmillan wrote to a party official: "Who are the middle classes? What do they want? How can we give it to them?"[18] Valéry Giscard d'Estaing is said to have remarked at the beginning of his career: "France wants to be governed by the center-right. I will place myself center-right and one day I will govern France."[19]

Of all the social sciences, economics had the most immediate impact on politics. A training in the subject became a common preparation for public life. This did not mean that the economic policies pursued in every European country were the same. Keynesian principles were more accepted in Britain and France than in West Germany or Italy.[20] Indeed, one of the striking characteristics of postwar economic orthodoxy was its pragmatic adjustment to particular circumstances. Furthermore, the form that economics took in each country depended on the particular institutions in which economists exercised influence. In France, Keynesianism spread not through the universities but through the *grandes écoles*, charged with educating civil servants, particularly the École Nationale d'Administration.[21] In Germany, the Bundesbank, which employed over 1,000 economists at a time when the Finance Ministry employed only 200, was the most important center of economic thinking.[22]

Economists were important not so much because of the particular solutions that they advocated but rather because of the belief that their expertise made the "objective" resolution of problems possible. In 1957, the French established a Centre for the Study of Economic Programmes, and in Germany from 1963, an advisory council of five "wise men" guided government economic policy. In 1930, Keynes had written that economics should be seen as a matter for specialists, like dentistry: "If economists could manage to get themselves thought of as humble, competent people, on a level with dentists, that would be splendid!"[23] After 1945, Keynes's wish came true. It was assumed that experts could create jobs or stimulate investment as easily as they could extract diseased molars. The journalist Alan Watkins recalls an occasion when Hugh Gaitskell, leader of the British Labour Party from 1955 to 1963, was staying with a friend:

[She] arrived at breakfast saying she had had an extraordinary dream about Dick Crossman. Gaitskell expressed polite though perfunctory interest. "Yes," she went on, "he was dressed in a short white coat. I was sitting in a dentist's chair and he was going to take my teeth out or something. 'But Dick,' I said, 'you know perfectly well you're not a dentist.' Dick replied: 'Of course I know I'm not a dentist, you fool, but I can work it all out quite easily from general principles.'" Gaitskell expressed the view that . . . this was a useful and instructive dream which, among other things, illustrated one reason Crossman would not find a place in any future Labour Cabinet presided over by him.[24]

Crossman, who showed such unfashionable enthusiasm for general principles, was a specialist in Greek philosophy; Gaitskell was an economist.

Women voters

Most voters in western Europe were women. In 1945, women voted for the first time in France, Belgium and Italy. How they cast their votes was known with precision, because the advent of female suffrage in some countries coincided with the wide use of opinion polls. Furthermore, in several constituencies in France, men and women voted at different polling stations and their votes were counted separately, and in the British election of 1945 votes of the mainly male overseas forces were counted separately.

All commentators agreed that most women voted for the right. In France, the socialists and communists would have had an absolute majority in parliament in November 1946 if it had not been for women voters.[25]

Some attributed women's electoral behavior to "female nature": Édouard Herriot, Mayor of Lyons, argued that women had "cold political reason" as opposed to the "hot political reason" of men.[26] Others took a more subtle view and argued that the peculiarities of female voting were not linked to sexual differences in themselves but rather reflected more general differences of age, religious practice and work.[27]

The single aspect of women's political character that attracted most attention, at least in continental Europe, was their alleged clericalism. Louise Weiss wrote of French women: "Catholics, born of Catholic mothers, grandmothers and great-grandmothers, they have learned like their ancestors to stammer obedient prayers with their first words."[28] Parties associated with the Catholic Church attracted female votes, which was most obviously true of the Christian democrats. In 1949, 52 percent of West German women voted for the Christian democrats (only 29 percent voted for the SPD); among West German men, only 37 percent voted for the Christian democrats while 38 percent voted for the SPD.[29] In 1951, 61 percent of Christian democrat votes in France came from women (52 percent of voters).[30] The Centre National des Indépendants et Paysans in Fourth Republic France and the various incarnations of Gaullism in the Fourth and Fifth Republics also had predominantly female electorates. Levels of religious practice were higher among women than among men, but clericalism alone does not account for female voting patterns. Women's preference for the Conservative Party in Britain is hard to explain in terms of religion, and impossible to explain in terms of Catholicism. Elsewhere, Church intervention in politics was restrained, and Christian democrat parties were usually keen to present themselves as non-confessional.

The assumption that women were "clerical" was accompanied by the assumption that their behavior was "outdated" and would die out as secularization progressed, but in fact it was anticlerical parties attracting primarily male voters, such as the French Radicals, that suffered most as the Church ceased to be a political issue. In this context it might be better to explain the specificities of women's voting patterns in terms of male anticlericalism rather than female loyalty to the Church.

A second characteristic of women's politics was their apparent distaste for abstract ideology and their loyalty to individual leaders. In France the tendency of women to place personalities above ideology was reflected in the way in which they used the complicated electoral rules of Fourth Republic France, which allowed voters to transfer a portion of their support away from the electoral lists of their preferred party to a particular candidate on another list, and in their support for de Gaulle throughout the period 1945 to 1969.

The differences described above relate mainly to belief or culture, but the material circumstances of men and women also differed. Women lived longer than men. In Britain and France, the preponderance of women among the old had been exacerbated by high male casualties during the First World War (in Germany, which had sustained high male casualties in both wars, matters were not so simple). Since the old tended to vote for the right, women's apparent conservatism was partly a product of age differences. This does not, however, explain everything. In the 1951 French election, for example, the Gaullist electorate was mainly old and female, but the Christian democrat electorate was mainly female and relatively youthful.

Men and women also had different experiences of work. Women were less likely to work than men. Those who did tended to do so in small enterprises rather than large ones and in shops, offices or light industries such as textiles rather than heavy industries such as coal mining or steel production. The kind of work that women did was less unionized than that of men – labor organization was more difficult in small establishments – and women's work was less likely to involve the outward signs of social class. Although they might earn less than male workers, women were less likely to end the working day with dirty clothes or physical injury. Women's jobs often involved dealing with people from a higher social class, and they were therefore encouraged to dress respectably and to speak "correctly."

Public opinion polls showed that women were more likely than men to define themselves as "middle class." Sometimes the division between the classes seemed to run within a family: French workers sometimes referred to their wives as "*ma bourgeoise*." Analysts in the 1950s saw women's failure to define their interests in class terms as a symptom of "false consciousness"; for example, the French political scientists Dogan and Narbonne argued that those whose view of the world was based on reading women's magazines placed their hopes of a better life in individual ascension through marriage rather than collective action: "The heroine of these stories does not work. She waits to meet a young man, the masculine marvel, who she will end up marrying."[31]

Emphasis on false consciousness is deceptive, because it implies that the male working class had a "true consciousness" of its interests. In fact, as it turned out, the vision of the future held out by the "*presse du coeur*" was slightly more realistic than that held out by *Humanité* (some secretaries did marry millionaires, but no western European country experienced proletarian revolution). Furthermore, in some respects women's perception of themselves as belonging to a different class from their menfolk was based on real differences in their economic position. Even women who were dependent on their husbands' pay did not necessarily have an interest in supporting militant trade unions. Many labor disputes concerned dignity or issues of control on the factory floor that had no bearing on the pay of the workers involved. Even when unions did concentrate on pay, the household income might suffer more from loss of earnings during a strike than it stood to gain from increased pay if the strike was successful.

Differences in the interests of men and women were also linked to differences in their attitude towards the state and wealth distribution. Women had no reason to favor nationalization, which mainly affected heavy industries in which few women worked. On the other hand, women had good reason to favor the welfare state, which provided benefits – such as child allowances, maternity care – of direct concern to themselves. The parties that attracted women's votes were all committed to welfare provision of some kind. Christian democrats were often influenced by Catholic assumptions about the desirability of supporting the family and children, and British Conservatives never challenged the main provisions of the welfare state after 1945. Women were generally hostile to parties that advocated economic liberalism: the German Free Democratic Party, for example, attracted 10 percent of the male vote in 1949 but only 8 percent of the female vote.[32]

Male left-wingers sometimes expressed dissatisfaction because the welfare state had failed to redistribute wealth, by which they meant that it had failed to distribute wealth between different social classes, but once again women had different interests. Although welfare states were often bad at redistributing wealth from one class to another, they were good at distributing it from one sex to the other. Money was transferred from single male workers to families, and from husbands to wives.

The gulf between male and female politics looks different when attention is shifted from the "peculiarity" of female behavior to that of men. Such a perspective makes the usefulness of the left/right spectrum itself seem questionable: it never entirely encompassed the experience of any European, and presents particular problems for the description of female experience. The right/left spectrum had been constructed at a time when women had no say at elections, and the politicians who apportioned such labels were still overwhelmingly male (the number of women who held elected office often diminished in the twenty years after 1945). Many male politicians assumed that the political role of women was passive and that they would fit into the categories assigned from above without playing any role in defining those categories. The problems that such thinking could create were illustrated by the Rassemblement des Gauches Républicaines (RGR) in Fourth Republic France. As its name suggests, the RGR defined itself as "left-wing," basing this claim on the anticlericalism of its main component parts (especially the Radical Party) and its celebration of the legacy of the French Revolution. Its support for economic liberalism and the fact that it counted many former Pétainists among its leaders did not prevent male commentators from accepting its claim to be left-wing. The fact that two-thirds of the RGR electorate was male was therefore used to swell statistics suggesting that women voted for the "right."

The truth was not that women preferred the right to the left, but that they preferred a certain type of right to a certain type of left. Women voted for Christian democracy but not for parties associated with extremism, violence or free-market economics. This became even clearer during the 1980s, when new parties emerged on both the right and left. In Austria in 1986, women comprised 56 percent of the Christian democrat vote, but only 39 percent of the vote for the right-wing Freedom Party.[33]

The second common assumption about women voters was that they were less politically "rational" than men. Again, women were judged wanting because of their "failure" to fit into categories that were already established before they had the vote, and commentators assumed that they needed to explain the specificity of female voting rather than that of men. In 1974, two American political scientists wrote: "Rational political

behavior is defined as the male pattern . . . and irrationality is by definition the expression of female roles."[34] Even feminist writers shared the assumption. They often believed that women's behavior could be explained
in terms of the "residue" of past experience, and that women would vote
in the same way as men once they had entered the "modern" world of political involvement, work and secularism. Women's electoral influence
would ensure that they had access to the labor market, while work would
emancipate women by giving them economic independence and an understanding of class structure.

By the end of the 1960s, people began to question the assumption that
explaining the differences between the political behavior of the sexes
meant explaining the peculiarity of women's behavior. The French political scientist Jean Charlot argued that the relatively high proportion of
women among Gaullist voters was "natural" in that it reflected the proportion of women in the electorate as a whole. Charlot shifted attention
from the supposed peculiarities of women's behavior to the peculiarity of
the left's view: "The left's criticism of Gaullism with its electorate comprised mostly of women, old people and a large proportion of the non-
working population, is explicitly or implicitly related to a certain ideal of
society where politics would be essentially the activity of men, young
people and the productive members of the community."[35]

The assumption that women's behavior was "archaic" is also open to
question. Women, whose political behavior was supposedly rooted in the
past, usually voted for parties that had been formed recently (such as the
Christian democrats), and were least attracted to parties that had been established before the Second World War (the socialists, the communists
and the French Radicals). Women's enfranchisement was associated with
the wider shift to "voter-oriented parties," and they were less likely than
men to be party activists. The Italian Christian democrats drew most of
their votes from women, but comparatively few of the party's members
were women, and among those women who did join, more than three-
quarters surveyed in 1977 had not attended a meeting in six months;
among men, the figure was less than half.[36] It should, however, be
pointed out that, while the "old left" of the 1940s and 1950s proved unattractive to women, the various new radicalisms that emerged from the
early 1970s onwards did obtain predominantly female votes. This was
true of the Green Party in Austria – whose electorate was even more predominantly female than that of the Christian democrats[37] – and of the
Parti Socialiste in France.

This raises a wider point. Since writers in the 1940s and 1950s assumed
that women's behavior was "traditional" and that of men was "modern,"
they also assumed that the convergence between the sexes would occur as

women adopted male political behavior. In retrospect, it is clear that the opposite happened. The political behavior of the sexes converged, but around what was seen as the female model. All the features that psepholo-gists in the 1960s identified as characteristic of modern European politics – the shift away from class, the decline of rigid ideological divi-sions, the focus on the personalities of politicians and the arrival of voter-oriented parties – were associated with female political behavior.

Christian democracy

Christian democracy was the most important political movement in post-war western Europe. Christian democrats ruled Germany for most of the period 1949 until 1969, and in Italy they ruled, alone or in coalition, un-til 1994. Austria was ruled by a Socialist–Christian democrat coalition, in which the Christian democrats were the dominant partner, while in France the Christian democrat Mouvement Républicain Populaire (MRP) was the largest party during the first few years of the Fourth Re-public and remained important until 1958. Christian democracy was also crucial to the politics of Belgium and Holland. Even in Franco's Spain, a group of political leaders thought of themselves as "Christian democrats."

The parties that exercised such power were mostly new. There had been important Catholic parties since the late nineteenth century, partic-ularly since the papacy started to encourage Catholics to play a larger role in politics after the First World War, but few had survived the authoritar-ian governments of the 1930s and 1940s. Their successors distanced themselves from purely Catholic politics, and the Church rarely gave ex-plicit instructions about how the faithful should vote. Catholic politi-cians stressed that their parties were not confessional and that they wel-comed support from all quarters.

The precise extent to which Church and party were separated varied from country to country. Divisions were least clear in Italy, where the Vat-ican was able keep a close eye on what was going on in Rome, and where Catholic Action exercised enormous influence, especially in the immediate postwar period. In Germany, Catholics and Protestants formed a single new grouping. The French MRP avoided including the word "Christian" in its name. Christian democrat parties generally became more open as time went on and increasingly prone to present their appeal in terms of opposition to "materialist" politicians rather than as part of a specifically religious project. The Austrian Christian Democrat Party declared in 1972 that it was open to "Christians and all those who from other motives be-lieve in a humanistic view of man."[38] In a survey conducted in 1975, more than three-quarters of Italians said that Christian democrats should follow

"Christian principles of liberty and social justice and economic development independent of religion."[39]

For a time it seemed that Christian democrat parties might be forces of the left. In Germany, for example, the 1947 Ahlen program of the Christian Democratic Union supported public ownership of industry.[40] The German and Italian parties, however, soon turned against public ownership and became the main rallying point for conservative forces. The fate of the French MRP was more complicated. A significant proportion of the party's leaders presented it as a party of the left; it adopted the style of the left, a priggish manner and an attachment to certain general principles, but it never really adopted left-wing policies and opposed nationalization and high public spending. The left-wing pose damaged the party in electoral terms. Conservative voters who had supported the MRP in 1945 and 1946 moved away from it as explicit conservative alternatives emerged in 1951. In spite of, or because of, having been the only MRP leader to have taken a clearly left-wing stand on Vichy and the Spanish Civil War, Georges Bidault argued that the MRP should abandon its left-wing claims and model itself on the Italian or German parties. Bidault eventually broke away to form Démocratie Chrétienne, an initiative that failed partly because his own past alienated voters who might have supported his vision of the future, and partly as his involvement in the Algerian war took him to the violent extreme of French politics.

The left-wing element in Catholic thought never entirely disappeared. It was represented by a variety of experiments outside party politics. The worker-priest movement, which sought to bring Catholicism to the proletariat (and proletarian behavior to the Church), was eventually stopped by the Pope, but Catholic trade unions remained important. During the 1960s, as the Church opened up to new ideas, Catholic-inspired unions sometimes seemed more radical than their communist rivals. In France and Italy, communist unions were associated with the defense of an established, native, skilled, male working class, whereas the Catholic unions were closer to women, immigrants, migrants and the young. This became clear in 1968 and 1969. In Italy, the Catholic unions supported calls, rejected by the communists, for equality of pay, and in France the CFTC, which had emerged from the Catholic unions, was interested in the qualitative "irrational" requests of workers for concessions that could not be expressed in cash.

Some argued that Christian democracy was merely a reincarnation of right-wing authoritarian politics dressed up for democracy, and opponents of the MRP jibed that it was the "*Machine à Ramasser les Pétainistes.*" There is much evidence for such an interpretation. The German CDU contained men such as Kurt Kiesinger, a member of the Nazi Party from

1933 to 1945, while Robert Schuman, a leading member of the MRP, had voted in favor of granting full powers to Pétain in 1940, and Amintore Fanfani, a leader of the Italian Christian Democrat Party (DC), had, as a teacher of law in Milan, supported Fascist legislation in the 1930s.[41] Some of the "resistance records" that members of Christian democrat parties vaunted were hardly heroic. Neither Adenauer nor de Gasperi (who spent the war working in the Vatican library) endured the kind of persecution that many of their countrymen suffered. One MRP deputy stated that her resistance activity was "reading anti-German books."

Such examples help to deflate the smugness of Christian democracy, but do not do much to explain its success. The pre-1945 right had been divided, and had often resorted to violence to achieve its aims. Postwar Christian democracy succeeded in uniting a large part of the electorate and achieved its aims by working through the democratic system. Christian democracy's achievement was not to revive the past, but to embrace certain aspects of the future.

The enfranchisement of women was one aspect of Christian democracy's success; another strength was its distaste for liberalism and its willingness to accept, indeed organize, collectivist institutions, which had always been a feature of Catholic politics. This explains why Catholics had proved better than their liberal rivals at dealing with bodies such as trade unions. Collectivism often blended into corruption as Catholics distributed patronage in return for votes and political favor, and the postwar expansion of state employment and welfare services was perfect terrain for Christian democracy to exercise these talents. The importance of such behavior can be illustrated with a brief comparison. In most of France the Christian democrats refrained from the manipulation of patronage that characterized their counterparts in Belgium, Italy and West Germany. The French party lacked the prewar experience that Italy's Popular Party or Germany's Centre Party had bequeathed to their postwar successors. French Catholicism, perhaps as a result of being a minority bourgeois practice, had a prim air, associated with Boy Scouting, cold showers and healthy team games, and in France it was the anticlerical Radicals rather than the Christian democrats who had learned to buy votes with public money. This goes a long way towards explaining the fact that the MRP failed to live up to its initial success and lost votes after the 1951 election.

Italian Christian democracy presented a spectacular contrast to its French equivalent. Catholicism lay at the center of society rather than at its fringes: the Italian secular state was younger and less powerful than the French Republic. Fascism had strengthened the Church's social position by weakening its rivals, and Italian Christian democracy benefited from this to become the most successful party of its kind in Europe (in fact, probably the most successful election-winning machine in European history). Italian Christian democracy took its appeal to the south, an area that had never been touched by the Popular Party of 1919–26.

Success was often associated with the generosity with which Italian Christian democrat politicians lavished taxpayers' money on their associates and supporters.[42] The differences between the Italian DC and the MRP in France are epitomized by the ministries to which the two parties clung most tenaciously. The MRP always held the Foreign Office, a prestigious ministry that gave great control of policy, but in electoral terms was insignificant; the Quai d'Orsay had a small budget and limited influence inside France's frontiers. The ministries that had the power to reward clients or exercise influence over elections – Public Works, *Anciens Combattants* and, most of all, the Interior – remained in the hands of the Radicals or their allies. By contrast, the ministry on to which the Italian Christian democrats held most tenaciously was that of the Post Office, an unglamorous ministry but one that gave vast powers to hire.[43]

Stories about the corruption of the Italian Christian democrats have reached almost mythical proportions. The Victor Emmanuel hospital in the Sicilian town of Catania is the most notorious example. Not only did the hospital provide jobs for the party's clients, it also provided a convenient residence for voters who needed to be shipped into a key constituency at election time.

It would be wrong to adopt an entirely moralistic or mocking attitude towards such behavior. Italy had a secret ballot, and it is notoriously difficult to obtain votes purely through an appeal to material interests, because any single vote makes such a small difference to the overall result. This suggests that Christian democrat behavior was considered legitimate by many Italians. What a foreign observer might describe as "nepotism" and "political favoritism" would often be regarded as "loyalty to family and friends." Besides, Christian democracy did not "corrupt" Palermo or Naples – it merely succeeded better than its rivals in adjusting to the society that it found there. There is no evidence that other political parties would have behaved differently had they got their hands on the levers of power.

Italian Christian democracy was not simply a friend of the powerful. It offered something to groups that were excluded from other Italian institutions. The DC was particularly valuable for the millions of southern immigrants who poured into cities such as Milan and Turin. Impoverished and disorientated people who spoke southern dialects and did not even have the legal right to live in the cities where they settled could expect nothing from the established bourgeoisie or the established working class, as represented by communist-controlled trade unions. However, migrants

were often looked after by networks linked to the Church or the Christian
Democrat Party. For example, in 1950, Antonio Antonuzzo, born in eastern Sicily in 1938, moved with his family to Massa Marittima in Tuscany,
and they responded to the hostility of the local communist peasants by
joining the Christian democrats. In 1962, Antonio used a letter of recommendation from the Tuscan Christian democrats to get a job in a Coca-
Cola factory in Milan, and later the DC helped him move to a better paid
job at Alfa Romeo.[44] In view of such experiences, it is probably wrong to
draw too sharp a distinction between "principled" left-wing Christian
trade unions and a "corrupt" right-wing Christian Democrat Party. Both
bodies offered something to otherwise underprivileged groups.

Socialism

All the western European democracies had contained socialist parties before
1945, and in some cases, such as that of Weimar Germany, they had dominated politics. However, after 1945, European socialism changed in two
related ways. First, it became more influential. The British Labour Party,
which had held power on its own for a total of less than three years before
the Second World War, governed from 1945 to 1951, from 1964 to 1970
and from 1974 to 1979. In France, the SFIO had participated in governments only briefly in the mid-1920s and the late 1930s, but it was a key element in most coalitions between 1945 and 1958. Second, socialist parties
were more willing to accept the rules of the capitalist system. Sometimes reformist practice ran parallel with doctrinal purity: the SFIO retained Marxist statements of principle at a time when it was pursuing vigorously anticommunist policies and accepting money from big business. In Britain, an
attempt to abolish Clause IV, committing the party to public ownership of
the means of production, was defeated at the party conference of 1959, but
in practice the party carried out only one major nationalization – that of
the steel industry in 1967 – after this date. Elsewhere, changes were more
explicit. In 1957, Austrian socialists recognized that they no longer intended to abolish capitalism, while at the Bad Godesberg conference of
1959, the West German SPD announced that a socialist planned economy
was no longer "a goal in itself."[45] The Dutch Labor Party also moved to reformism in 1959, as did the Swiss socialists, and the Swedish Labor Party
followed in June 1960. Other changes in western European socialism related to foreign policy and interparty alliances rather than capitalism. In
1957, the Norwegian Labor Party expelled a faction opposed to NATO,
while the Italian socialists, who had been loyal allies of the communists,
condemned the Soviet invasion of Hungary in 1956 and thereafter reversed
their opposition to Italy's membership of NATO and prepared to join the
Christian democrats in government.

Why did parties that had resisted reformism in the 1930s succumb in the 1950s? The lessons of experience provide part of the answer. Postwar socialist politicians had been deeply affected by three things: the depression of the 1930s and the mass unemployment that it produced in most of Europe; the rise of fascism; and the behavior of the Soviet Union and its western European clients during and after the Second World War. The memory of unemployment made them determined to manage the economy, and that of fascism made them determined to avoid political polarization. The experience of Stalinism took longest to sink in. Some architects of postwar social democracy, such as Denis Healey in Britain, had themselves been communists. Guy Mollet, who became a savagely anti-communist leader of the SFIO, continued to advocate alliance with the communists even after the Second World War. The Italian Socialist Party actually had such an alliance, and its leader, Pietro Nenni, was awarded a Stalin Prize for such signs of devotion as expelling members of his party who visited Yugoslavia. However, all the mainstream European socialists eventually condemned communism, which greatly facilitated cooperation with center and conservative parties.

Another incentive for European socialists to change came from the changes that they perceived in European capitalism. Socialist parties had been formed at a time when it still seemed possible to argue that the world was becoming divided between a small number of vastly rich capitalists and a large number of utterly impoverished workers, but such arguments were difficult to sustain after the Second World War. Professional and white-collar employment was expanding and absorbing some of the children of the working class. Many socialist leaders had risen from humble origins as a result of academic success, and many were university teachers; they were interested in signs that "new classes" were rising, and perhaps prone to overestimate the impact of such change. Increasingly, socialism directed its appeal at the relatively prosperous. Sometimes it seemed that the political success of socialism was based on the economic success of capitalism. In the prosperous 1960s, the average vote of the western European left increased from 33.4 percent to 39.3 percent.[46]

The increasingly technological nature of society led some socialists to argue that key powers lay not with the owners of capital but with "experts" and "technicians," who were often the supposed beneficiaries of social mobility. Business itself seemed to be changing, operating on a larger scale and planning over a longer term. Certain agencies – such as the French planning commissions – blurred the distinction between the state and the private sector. The merciless competition of prewar capitalism seemed dead, and socialist leaders were increasingly inclined to believe that they could cooperate with capitalism. In 1957, British socialists declared, "The Labour Party recognizes that . . . large firms are as a whole serving the nation well."[47]

Business attitudes towards socialism were sometimes as favorable as socialist attitudes towards business. In the multiparty systems of continental Europe, business often had to operate with several different political parties. Furthermore, anticapitalism had never been confined to the left, so socialist reformers might actually seem more acceptable to business than anticapitalist Catholics or a right opposed to "*finance apatride*." French large-scale business funded all the anticommunist parties, including the socialists, while in Italy the main employers' organization supported the center-left government, which included socialists, from 1965 onwards.[48] Only in Britain did the socialist love for business remain unreciprocated. Harold Wilson regarded parts of British industrial management with the naïve excitement that Ramsay MacDonald had reserved for the aristocracy, but only a few mavericks, such as Robert Maxwell (born in Czechoslovakia), responded to Labour's overtures.

Socialist attitudes towards industrial relations also changed. Before 1945, strikes and socialism had often gone together, and some socialists had seen a general strike as a means to destroy capitalism. After 1945, things changed. In Britain there were no general strikes at all. On the continent, there were strikes affecting several sectors in France and Italy in 1948 and 1968, but such disputes no longer tied in with the strategy of the left. Sometimes, socialists found them embarrassing. Associations between trade unions and socialist parties were weaker than in the past; in France, the socialist SFIO lost its links with the Confédération Générale du Travail, which became dominated by communists, and it never acquired formal ties with the new federation: Force Ouvrière.

Increasingly, the strike was seen as part of capitalism rather than a means to destroy it, and workers bargained with employers just as businessmen bargained with each other. Demands were limited and expressed in quantifiable terms, usually relating to money. The characteristic socialist leader's response to such strikes was that of the arbitrator who convoked both employers and unions to his ministerial office for the proverbial "beer and sandwiches," rather than a partisan who supported workers against employers.

Socialism was changed by the general shift from militant to voter-oriented parties. The reforms of party constitutions in the late 1950s and 1960s, which were supposed to make socialism more attractive to voters, were often resisted by party members, and the increasing frequency with which socialist leaders were in government widened the gulf with party militants. The austere oppositional character of socialism was gone. Party leaders wanted to hold office, and in order to do so they needed either to win votes or, in multiparty systems, form alliances. The more that socialists held power, the more that its elected representatives were aware of the benefits that power could bring. The trappings of office were particularly attractive for those who had not been born into the ruling class. Harold Wilson expressed the feelings of the office-holding strain in socialism when he described the Labour Party as the "natural party of government."

Certain kinds of office could also provide material benefits: Labour local councillors in parts of Britain acquired corrupt links with property developers. The spoils of office had particularly dramatic effects on the Italian socialists; such gains had already been shared by the social democratic group, which split from the main Socialist Party in the 1940s. The DC's "opening to the left" in the early 1960s effectively meant that the PSI was given access to the kind of benefits that the DC had exploited so successfully, and from 1963 until 1972, the Ministry of Public Works – that is, the ministry with greatest powers to award lucrative contracts – was held by socialists for all but thirteen months. In 1971, the socialist Minister of Works, Giacomo Mancini, invoked parliamentary immunity to avoid an investigation into irregularities in the award of contracts.[49] Socialists gained the presidency of two national banks (Christian democrats presided over eleven). *The Times* commented that the socialists had "disappointed their supporters by the eagerness with which they leapt on to the gravy train and the mess which some of their leaders made while spreading it about."[50]

Outside the consensus? Communism

The western European communist parties seem clearly outside the consensus, which in many respects had been constructed precisely to exclude them. Communists ceased to hold ministerial office in most western European countries after 1947 and thereafter were entirely excluded from the coalitions that dominated postwar politics. The Communist Party was one of the largest groups in the French parliament during the 1950s, but it never held a single ministry. Communists opposed everything on which consensus politics was built – NATO, European integration and consumerism – and their leader even ignored the striking evidence of the *trente glorieuses* and insisted that the living standards of French workers were falling in absolute terms.

Communists managed to keep themselves apart from the broad cultural integration that underlay consensus politics. They had their own newspapers and recommended books. Party duties consumed vast amounts of time. Meetings were ritual occasions with a reassuring routine of formulae, and anticommunist propaganda that described the blatant violation of communism's proclaimed principles by communist regimes was a waste of paper. Almost anything that seemed to discredit communism could be dismissed as bourgeois provocation. As observers often pointed out, communism possessed an element of religious fervor, and during the dark days of late Stalinism militants often behaved as if they were believers being tempted by Satan.

At a time when the public world of politics and the private world of family, home and consumption diverged, communists still saw the political and the personal as intertwined. A militant who left the party would lose his friends as well as his faith. The extent to which the personal and the political were connected, and the extent to which western communists were capable of ignoring unwelcome evidence, was shown by the trial of Artur London, a communist minister in the Czech government, who was said to be implicated in the "Slánský plot." The evidence against him and his coconspirators – who were accused by their own comrades of being "Trotskyite, Titoist, Zionist, bourgeois, nationalist traitors" – was ludicrous, as several left-wing noncommunists in the West pointed out. London had spent much of his life in France, was a hero of the French resistance and was married to a French woman. Yet once he had confessed, his French wife accepted his guilt and initiated divorce proceedings. London's brother-in-law, a leading member of the Parti Communiste Français, attended the funeral of Gottwald (the Czech leader who had authorized the persecutions) while London was in prison.

The separation between western European communists and the rest of society can, however, be overestimated. The people who wrote the memoirs, from which the account above is taken, were not necessarily representative. They tended to be the most educated members of the party, and were relatively young at the height of the Cold War. By the time they wrote their memoirs, they had usually left the party, which in itself implies that their commitment was not as total as is sometimes suggested. Members did react to events (such as the invasion of Hungary) in a manner not dictated by the official party line. Perhaps the former communists who stormed out of the party in 1956 or 1968 were really the true believers. Less fanatical members may have had fewer illusions, and thus found events that conflicted with the party's official view less shocking. Working-class communists may have had a different attitude from intellectuals, who valued the party for its ideology, while workers valued the practical impact that trade unions and parliamentary representation might have on their lives. Intellectuals saw the party as setting them apart from bourgeois society. For working-class communists, party membership might be an expression of solidarity with neighbors and colleagues.

The extent to which communism could be integrated into western European society, rather than opposed to it, was most striking in small towns and the countryside. The world described above was an urban world. Party activity was associated with rallies and demonstrations but also, one suspects, with the loneliness of isolated individuals seeking a community. In the villages and small towns of France and Italy, communists were members of a community before they were members of the party. They were linked to their neighbors by bonds of friendship, kinship and shared experiences, such as attendance at the same primary school. The war often increased the fund of such shared experiences. Communist and noncommunist partisans had shivered together in the hills. The solidarity of the resistance – always a myth as far as political leaders were concerned – meant something in Neuvic d'Ussel.

In small towns, communists were not part of an anonymous mass that threatened property holders but were specific, known individuals. Communism was often linked to a tradition of bloody-minded artisans that stretched back to the nineteenth century. Indeed, E. P. Thompson's account of nineteenth-century artisan radicalism in England owed something to his encounter with small-town communism in Italy: "In liberated Italy I would mooch around the town, find the blacksmith's shop – the oxen lifted on a hoist to be shoed – notice the PCI posters, introduce myself as a comrade, and in a trice I would be seated on a bench, incongruous in my British officer's uniform, sampling the blacksmith's wine."[51] The communist described by Thompson could have served as the model for Peppone, the blacksmith hero/villain of the *Don Camillo* novels by Giovanni Guareschi, who describes a village in the Po valley in which the priest Don Camillo confronts the communists, led by Peppone. The two sides denounce each other in violent terms but in reality they remain united by bonds of mutual affection and loyalty. When a communist coup seems imminent, all the prominent communists in the village turn up at Don Camillo's house prepared to hide him "just like in the old days with the partisans."

Guareschi wrote sentimental fiction, but the world that he describes is very close to that which emerges from factual accounts. Peppone had a real-life counterpart in Frégéac, the blacksmith of St-Céré, a small town in southwestern France. Frégéac was a communist, but was integrated into the town of artisans and small shopkeepers, and when his friend Pierre Poujade launched a campaign to prevent tax inspections, Frégéac was one of its most enthusiastic participants. When Poujadism became a national movement, its leader refused to indulge in the kind of general and systematic anticommunism that characterized the main bourgeois parties of France, led by men from Paris. Poujade insisted that the communists he knew were not terrifying revolutionaries or supporters of the Soviet Union, but rough, good-hearted men who, like everyone else, merely wished to defend their interests. Gordon Wright gave a good account of rural communism. He was an American who began his research in 1950, at the height of the Cold War. However, far from treating him as the representative of war-mongering imperialism, his communist interlocutors proved friendly and cooperative. He realized that communism in places such as the village of St-Pierre, in the Lot, or Samazan, in Gascony, was rooted not in class struggle but in the equality of a society in which everyone owned a small amount of property. The communist mayor of Samazan had even, in a gesture that could have come straight out of the Don Camillo novels, campaigned to have a priest restored to the village's empty rectory.[52]

There were other ways in which western European communism fitted into the political consensus better than was apparent at first glance. Indeed, in some respects, the prewar pattern of relations between democracy and communism was reversed. Moscow's most docile supporters in the West came from exiled party members from authoritarian countries, notably Portugal, whereas the parties in France and, especially, Italy became more democratic and more prone to question Moscow as a result of their contact with democracy. The fact that Western communist leaders could see some advantages to living in a democracy was shown by the behavior of the Italian leader Palmiro Togliatti when Stalin offered him the leadership of the Cominform. Stalin took it for granted that an official position in the communist bloc would be preferable to a life of perpetual opposition in the West. Togliatti, on the other hand, took it for granted that leading a large party in a democracy was preferable to being an apparatchik in the Soviet sphere, and turned the offer down.[53]

Western communist parties and the Soviet Union diverged over many issues. The explosion of a Soviet atom bomb in 1949 meant that the USSR no longer needed them as an instrument of its foreign policy (why threaten the West with revolution when it could be threatened with annihilation?). Indeed, Soviet diplomats sometimes made it embarrassingly clear that it suited them to deal with conservative governments. At the same time, Western communists turned away from the prospect of revolution towards the advantages that they could extract from limited participation in the system. Communist deputies benefited from parliamentary immunity and a state salary, which they paid into party funds, and also enjoyed the protection of the law and especially the application of stern Jacobin centralism in France. When the French government tried to exclude communists from the elite École Nationale d'Administration (ENA), the Conseil d'État, which drew its own members from the ENA, ruled that such exclusion would be unconstitutional.

Although communists were excluded from national government, they developed a huge role in local government. By the 1970s, 20,000 municipal councillors in France belonged to the party. Such control provided party leaders with a platform, and the working classes with protection; it even allowed the party to start drawing some of the material benefits of office that went with the award of public works contracts. Some analysts suggested that communist parties in democratic states had ceased to be revolutionary parties seeking to overthrow capitalism and had become "tribune" parties that represented the working classes within the capitalist system, and which in doing so made capitalism more stable.[54]

The practical changes in communism's position in western Europe were accompanied by explicit rethinking of strategy on the part of party leaders, which was most audacious in Italy. Between 1956 and 1964, Togliatti developed the idea of "polycentrism," that is, a refusal to accept that Moscow's line was the only one for communist parties to follow. The Warsaw Pact invasion of Czechoslovakia in 1968 showed that Moscow was not willing to tolerate polycentrism in its own sphere of influence, but it also encouraged Western communist parties to emphasize their independence. The French and Italian leaderships condemned the invasion, and in Italy party leaders began to talk of "Euro-communism," by which they meant a specifically western European model of communism. Their shift was symbolized by their willingness to enter into that supreme symbol of western European consensus: the European Parliament. In electoral terms, the strategy was successful (at least for a time), and the party gained a third of the vote. PCF leaders were less adventurous, but they too began to discuss leaving the ghetto. From 1968 onwards, they contemplated alliances with other left-wing parties, and in 1976, the party congress renounced the idea of "dictatorship of the proletariat" (the political theory that formed the basis of the Soviet state).

Outside the consensus? 1968

In February 1968, François Ceyrac, the leader of the Conseil National du Patronat Français (the French employers' association), met trade union leaders to discuss compensation payments for short-time working. The meeting, which revolved around technical details and small concessions rather than grand principles and confrontation, exemplified the consensus culture of postwar western Europe. At the end of discussions, Ceyrac told his interlocutors that he needed to have a small hernia operation in May, and asked whether that would pose any problems. The union leaders assured him that month would be calm, and the two sides agreed to meet again in September.[55]

In May, Ceyrac lay in his hospital bed while France was gripped by a general strike that involved almost 10 million workers. Factories were occupied, managers were taken hostage, and students and riot police fought in the center of Paris. The head of state fled to West Germany, where he seems to have discussed the possibility of military intervention to restore order. These events were part of wider disturbances that affected much of western Europe. They involved students in France, Belgium, Italy, Spain and West Germany and, in France and Italy, a substantial proportion of the working class.

The protest of the late 1960s seemed to threaten every aspect of political consensus. In Germany and Italy, the demonstrators denounced the compromises that had recently been made between Christian democracy and socialism. They attacked consumerism and the comfortable relations between the leaders of capitalism and the organizations of the working class. They celebrated public, collective life and attacked the private sphere of house, car and family (the most shocking slogan of the Italian students was "I want to be an orphan"). Political violence seemed to return to Europe, with riots and assassination attempts (such as the one that almost claimed the life of the Berlin student leader Rudi Dutschke). Trotskyism and anarchism, ideologies that had barely been considered by most Europeans since the Spanish Civil War, were suddenly the center of attention. The extreme right fought with students in Brussels, Berlin and Rome, though in Paris some of those who had been hurt by the loss of Algérie Française hated de Gaulle even more than they hated the left. Consensus was founded on "maturity" and the assumption that problems could be measured, discussed and ultimately solved. The *soixante-huitards*, by contrast, celebrated irrationality and spontaneity. Posters urged students: "Be realistic – ask for the impossible"; strikers sometimes refused to put forward demands for negotiation. Social science, which had provided a foundation for the consensus society, was an important battleground in 1968. New universities that stressed social science – Nanterre, Trento, the London School of Economics – were all centers of agitation. Students ridiculed quantitative methods and the claims of their discipline to offer "value-free" solutions.

Yet the long-term impact of these dramatic events seemed almost non-existent. Governments did not fall, and violence was contained. Armies were not needed to restore order, and the relative stability of western Europe was highlighted in August 1968, when the rebellious students of Prague were faced with Warsaw Pact tanks. In some countries, the events of 1968 made consensus politics in western Europe stronger. In Spain, protesters were themselves supporters of a certain kind of consensus; many of them wanted the very bourgeois freedoms that their counterparts on the other side of the Pyrenees were denouncing as "repressive toler-ance." Demonstrations against Franco forged an alliance of socialists, com-munists and left-wing Christians, as well as students and professors. A leader of the student underground remarked: "The country continues to live in 1936" (the year of the Popular Front).[56] Far from polarizing Span-ish society, 1968 expedited the transition towards democracy. In France, consensus was strengthened not by the events themselves but by their af-termath. The majority of the population disliked the demonstrations and strikes. Legislative elections in 1969 produced a large majority for the cen-ter right. More importantly, by weakening de Gaulle, who was obliged to resign in 1969, the events strengthened the regime that he had created. It became obvious that the Fifth Republic could function on its own without the intervention of a single man, and de Gaulle's departure made it easier for France to turn its back on the divisions created by Vichy and the Alger-ian war. The new President, Georges Pompidou, had preached reconcilia-tion in the aftermath of both conflicts and helped to prevent bloodshed in Paris in May 1968.

The limited impact of 1968 reflected the complexity of western Euro-pean society. Raymond Aron, who loathed the *soixante-huitards*, had been right to say that society had many problems but no one great problem. The protests of 1968 were not the product of any single discontent, and those involved had different interests. Many students had been motivated by simple material dissatisfaction at the lack of resources in universities, student numbers having expanded hugely during the 1960s, or by the lack of job opportunities, but these discontents were not universal. British students – still a comparatively small group with relatively gener-ous grants – suffered less badly than French or Italian ones. In France, the École Normale Supérieure provided much of the leadership for the revolt, even though its students, a tiny privileged elite, shared none of the material dissatisfactions of the students who were crammed into the new and impoverished campus at Nanterre. Students who subscribed to an ideology did not necessarily agree with each other. Maoism, at least in its 1968 incarnation, did not lend itself to the building of broad fronts, and in any case the simple polarization of left versus right and workers versus exploiters that had motivated earlier political struggles did not seem rele-vant in 1968. Many were looking not to the industrial societies of west-ern Europe but to the peasant wars of the Third World, especially in Viet-nam. Some of the most articulate *soixante-huitards* did not even spend that year in Europe. Luisa Passerini was in Zaire; Régis Debray was in a Bolivian prison. Some students, such as Daniel Cohn-Bendit, were sim-ply not interested in the Marxist theology that obsessed the "old left." The events of 1968 did not so much widen the gap between left and right as complicate it by creating new lefts (revolving around ecology and feminism) and new rights (revolving around race and identity).

Above all, the *soixante-huitards* were divided between workers and students. Students in continental Europe were almost exclusively of bourgeois origin, whereas the workers who were most involved in strikes in 1968 were the most marginal members of their class. Often they were young and/or recent arrivals from the countryside, and were themselves divided from the more established working class and the organizations that claimed to speak in their name (particularly those controlled by the Communist Party). The interests of students and workers were vastly different. The students' demands could, in large measure, be accommodated within the existing social system: greater sexual freedom or more relaxed relations in education would not shake the foundations of capitalism. Indeed, the cultural legacy of 1968 may have contributed to capitalism's success. For all their attacks on consumerism, the hedonism of the students was easily appropriated by advertising, while the assault on rigid hierarchies anticipated the more flexible, fast-moving capitalism of the 1980s. Worker protest, by contrast, posed a real threat. Days lost in strikes increased across Europe, which, along with the pay increases with which employers tried to buy peace, squeezed profits during the 1970s. However, the very fact that workers bargained marked a tacit acceptance of the system. The anarchic rebellion of 1968 was over, with workers back under the control of trade union bureaucracies and strikes focusing on "differentials," percentages and hours of work, rather than on resistance to work itself. This meant that the working class could be contained in the short term, while economic change undermined workers' power in the long term. The triumph of capitalism in the 1980s brought gains for those former students who had entered the bourgeoisie – the great majority – largely at the expense of those former workers with whom the students had been briefly allied in 1968.

Outside the consensus: "terrorism"

As communism was drawn increasingly into the western European consensus, new enemies of the consensus appeared. A spate of bomb attacks and assassinations accompanied French withdrawal from Algeria in the early 1960s, and violence in the Spanish Basque country and in Northern Ireland intensified during the 1970s. The Red Brigades in Italy and the Red Army Faction of Andreas Baader and Ulrike Meinhof in West Germany attracted much attention. The word "terrorism" became an important part of the vocabulary of western European politicians during the 1960s and 1970s.

The various movements described as "terrorist" did not, in fact, have much in common. Groups in Northern Ireland and the Basque country were part of a nationalist tradition that stretched back for at least fifty years. Such movements commanded much support among the communities in which they operated, so that political parties that supported them obtained great electoral success in difficult circumstances. Irish and Basque nationalists came from deeply Catholic areas and espoused rather conservative views on many matters (the Basques opposed immigration into their region until the early 1960s).[57] Eventually this conservatism was challenged by younger members of both groups who justified their violence in terms of "revolutionary" struggle as well as national liberation, and looked to Third World guerrillas for inspiration.

Violence associated with the Algerian war in France was also nationalist in a sense. Frenchmen who aided the Front de Libération Nationale in its struggle to force French withdrawal from Algeria and those who aided the Organisation de l'Armée Secrète to resist French withdrawal were both motivated by a certain idea of Algeria. For a time at least, the OAS's actions commanded support among the European inhabitants of Algeria, and when Tixier-Vignancour, who had made his reputation as a defense lawyer representing OAS leaders, challenged de Gaulle for the presidency in 1965, he obtained 5 percent of the vote, mainly from areas in which the *pieds noirs* (Europeans from Algeria) had settled.

The Red Army Faction and the Red Brigades were different kinds of organization. They saw themselves as international movements, and their origins could be found in the recent past, mainly the student upheavals of 1968. Both aimed primarily for social revolution, whereas ETA and the IRA grafted such aims onto nationalist demands. Neither the Red Army Faction nor the Red Brigades commanded the electoral support of the nationalist movements. The Red Brigades had a small following among the working class, which was expressed in electoral support for the party Lotta Continua; the Red Army Faction was almost entirely isolated from the rest of West German society.

Why did "terrorism" matter so much? The numbers affected by its violence were small. The Red Army Faction were said by the authorities to have killed six people. The annual death toll resulting from terrorist action in Northern Ireland never exceeded that caused by road accidents, and it seems unlikely that the victims of terrorism in western Europe exceeded the number of people killed in an average year by bee stings.

Terrorism was important because it challenged the consensual political system and in doing so revealed interesting things about that system. In part, the mere existence of political violence seemed so unusual and shocking during the 1960s and 1970s: no one would have noticed the Red Army Faction in the last years of the Weimar Republic. Political violence also made an explicit attack on consensus politics. The most prominent victim of terrorist attack, Aldo Moro, who was killed by the Red Brigades in 1978, had been the architect of the alliance between Italian Christian democrats and the socialists during the 1960s. Moro had talked about widening Italian political consensus to include the Communist Party and, significantly, his assassins dumped his body at the exact midpoint between the headquarters of the Christian democrats and that of the Communist Party. Political violence also mattered because it benefited from some of the very things that had helped promote the political system that it attacked, especially television. Attacks provided visually exciting images for news broadcasts, a fact not lost on Andreas Baader, who was a television journalist before he took up arms against the West German state.

Finally, "terrorism" mattered because of the ways in which European states responded to it. Politicians liked to present terrorism as the antithesis of democratic, legitimate politics, but the frontiers between terrorism and the state were not always clearly drawn. In Algeria, the "terrorist" OAS was largely made up of men who had previously been obedient servants of the state using reprisals and torture against the "terrorist" FLN. In Italy, the first bomb attacks to be blamed on "anarchists" were in fact the work of right-wing groups that appear to have been working in cooperation with parts of the secret service.

Government responses to terrorism revealed further similarities between the state and the movements against which they fought. In Italy and West Germany, terrorist suspects developed an alarming propensity to commit suicide in custody – the entire leadership of the Red Army Faction died in this way. Britain and France resorted to torture and internment without trial.[58] The British Parachute Regiment shot dead thirteen unarmed Catholics in Londonderry on "Bloody Sunday" in January 1972, while Paris police killed an undetermined number of Algerians who had defied a curfew on the night of October 17–18, 1961.

Conclusion

It is sometimes suggested that the slowing of economic growth in the mid-1970s was accompanied by the end of consensus politics and the revival of quarrels over the management of the economy and the distribution of wealth. Such suggestions are made with particular frequency in Britain and are associated with the government of Margaret Thatcher (1979–90). As early as 1968, Thatcher said: "There are dangers in consensus; it could be an attempt to satisfy people holding no particular views about anything. It seems more important to have a philosophy and policy which because they are good appeal to a sufficient majority."[59]

Too much importance should not be attributed to such remarks – Britain was an unusual case. The very fact that consensus was so well established meant that challenging it seemed dramatic. The only other country that experienced such an explicit break with the past was Sweden, where the social democrats, who had ruled since the mid-1930s, were defeated in 1976. In most of continental Europe, the political consensus based around social democracy/Christian democracy became more secure from the mid-1970s onwards. The establishment of democracy in Spain and Portugal and *alternance* in France in 1981 all contributed to this security. No German, Italian or Spaniard would have believed that political conflict in the 1980s was more intense than it had been earlier in the century.

4
THE OTHER EUROPE

> "One day, you will be ashamed to have loved a criminal. Remember what I say to you now. One day, you will see that I was right."
>
> *The father of Romanian teenager Lilly Marcou,*
> *on reading a letter that she had written to Stalin*[1]

LOOKING BACK FROM the 1980s, it seemed obvious to many that eastern Europe took a wrong turning between 1945 and 1948. Communist rule brought political oppression and economic failure, even in places, such as Czechoslovakia, that had formerly been democratic and prosperous. Even more strikingly, it seems obvious in retrospect that the early period of communist rule in eastern Europe (that is, the period leading up to Stalin's death in 1953) was one of appalling repression. People confessed to improbable crimes at grotesque show trials, and thousands were executed, imprisoned or driven from their jobs. Yet this was the very period in which enthusiasm for communism was most intense and in which some eastern Europeans, often those who had suffered for their beliefs under earlier regimes, made the deliberate choice to attach the fate of their countries to that of the Soviet Union.

Those who had been most associated with Stalinism, whether as supporters or victims (the two groups overlapped substantially), often had difficulty in explaining what they had lived through. They felt that subsequent generations were simply too removed to understand what had happened. The hero of Milan Kundera's *The Joke* (1967) does not bother to try to explain his expulsion from the party to a 22-year-old woman, the mistress of one of his former persecutors. Lilly Marcou, a Romanian, who, at the age of seventeen, had been devastated by the death of Stalin, wrote in 1982: "The generations that have followed us, those of today . . . have undergone a reversal of values, and they must find it difficult to understand the fever and excitement that seized us in the late 1940s."[2]

The key to the gulf between communists who had reached maturity by the late 1940s and their juniors is simple: some people believed in Stalinism. Astonishing as it seems in retrospect, the period when communist rule in eastern Europe was at its most brutal was also the period during which many intelligent and well-meaning individuals thought that it was a good thing. This partly explains how it was possible to bring about rapid transformations in the societies of eastern Europe, but it also explains much that happened in eastern Europe after 1953. The fact that some people had invested such hopes in something that proved to be so spectacularly bad had an important legacy. For twenty years, debate over that legacy was to be at the center of much eastern European politics, and it accounts for the isolated moments of opposition to communist rule as well as the widespread apathy and cynicism that came to pervade the region.

The purges

The period on which later generations were to look back with such incomprehension began with the break between Tito and Stalin in 1948. Thereafter, Stalin regarded displays of independence by his eastern European clients with suspicion. Attempts to find a road to socialism other than that pursued by the Soviet Union were no longer tolerated. The most spectacular sign of intolerance came in a succession of show trials involving former Communist Party ministers. In Albania, the main victim was Koçi Xoxe, a former Minister of the Interior; in Hungary, it was László Rajk, another former Minister of the Interior. In Czechoslovakia, Rudolf Slánský, a former Minister of Foreign Affairs, was arrested along with thirteen others.

There were patterns to the Stalinist purges. Associates of Tito were obvious targets, as were those who had proved too assiduous in the defense of national economic interests in negotiations with Moscow. As in the Soviet Union during the 1930s, purges in eastern Europe during the 1940s hit those from bourgeois and educated backgrounds. "Cosmopolitanism" was often a target, and there was much anti-Semitism in the communist world at a time when the Soviet Union had just renounced its support for Israel and projects to establish a Jewish-Soviet state in the Crimea had been abandoned. Generally, those who had fought in the internal resistance to Nazism, rather than spending the war in Moscow, were suspect

(Tito's pretensions to independence were based partly on his career as a partisan leader, and an insistence on the primacy of the Red Army in liberating eastern Europe was to become a part of the new orthodoxy). Veterans of the Spanish Civil War often became victims for similar reasons.

But the purges did not operate in a predictable way – indeed, it was their random nature that made them so frightening. Many victims were loyal both to their own party and also to Stalin. Some had proved willing to get their hands dirty in the service of their master, and sometimes people involved in the early stages of the purges later became victims themselves. The head of the Czech security service, Jindrich Vesely, tried to kill himself in 1950 because he knew that "the only way that anyone leaves the service is feet first."[3]

National variations in the intensity and nature of the purges operated in unexpected ways. In Romania, Gheorghiu-Dej directed the purges at Jews, but also at the entourage of the Foreign Minister Ana Pauker, who (unlike Gheorghiu-Dej himself) had spent the war in Moscow. In this sense, the Romanian purges can be seen as a means by which "home communists" asserted their authority when they were being eclipsed elsewhere. Similarly, in Albania, the purges gave the "nationalists" grouped around Enver Hoxha a chance to assert their independence from Yugoslavia, which had sometimes threatened to annex their country, and to take revenge against the most internationally minded members of the Albanian leadership, who had previously been supported by Moscow. The purges were most restrained in East Germany and Poland. Polish party leaders avoided bloodshed and prevented Władysław Gomułka, the most prominent victim, from being formally arrested, though 84,200 Poles were sent to labor camps between 1948 and 1954.[4] Czechoslovakia, on the other hand, which unlike every other eastern European country had a tradition of democracy and the peaceful settlement of dispute, experienced Stalinism in an exceptionally violent form.

Associated with the well-publicized trials and executions of party leaders were sanctions taken against thousands of people lower down the party hierarchy. Eastern European parties had expanded fast after 1945, and now they expelled members: in Bulgaria, 100,000 out of 460,000 members lost their cards.[5] Expulsion was often accompanied by the loss of jobs, houses or university places. People who had lost their jobs were then prosecuted for "parasitism." Students who had been expelled from university lost their exemption from military service, but, not being considered reliable enough to bear arms, would be sent to work in labor brigades.

Stalinism was also associated with a shift in economic policy. Eastern Europe was no longer allowed to proceed gently towards the social transformation that had been carried out in the Soviet Union. Enterprises were to be nationalized and agriculture was to be collectivized, although these operations, particularly the collectivization of agriculture, were never carried out as fully in eastern Europe as they had been in the Soviet Union. This may have been partly a question of time. Soviet leaders were pressing for purges (which had taken place most spectacularly in the USSR during the late 1930s) and collectivization (a policy instituted in the USSR from the late 1920s) to occur simultaneously. The confusion generated by the imprisonment and execution of party leaders did not make large-scale social transformation any easier. Collectivization in the Soviet Union had been made possible by the violence that followed the Revolution, a large army, and the fact that "kulaks" could be deported to the distant and empty spaces of Siberia, but no such conditions were present in Czechoslovakia or Poland.

Administering Stalinism in eastern Europe was a tense business. The widows of ministers such as Hilary Minc in Poland and Rudolf Margolius in Czechoslovakia recalled exhausting hours of work that left their husbands without time to reflect on what they were doing. Party leaders lived in a world of official receptions, chauffeur-driven cars and constant contact with Soviet advisers, often without much sense of what was going on outside this closed circle. Simple fear was important. The Soviet Union began to erect structures of power in eastern Europe that were independent of the local state or party, and the role of Soviet advisers was particularly important in the security services. Just as communists had used their control of the police to evict their noncommunist rivals, now the Soviet Union began to infiltrate police forces.[6] The leaders of eastern European communist states were sometimes terrified and often took to drink. Klement Gottwald staggered around Prague Castle challenging his comrades to drinking contests;[7] Georgi Dimitrov, the leader of the Bulgarian Communist Party, was said to have died of cirrhosis of the liver.

It would be wrong to explain events in eastern Europe purely in terms of orders passed down from the Kremlin. Eastern Europeans possessed some capacity for resistance; furthermore, what was later presented as "Stalinism" suited certain groups in eastern Europe. The establishment of communist states gave rise to all sorts of opportunities, as new jobs were created in an expanded state and party. Men from humble backgrounds suddenly had powers and privileges that they could not previously have dreamed of. The purges provided a means by which the newly privileged could fight each other over their spoils: men of little education could dispose of better qualified rivals on the grounds that they came from bourgeois backgrounds, and men whose membership in the party was recent could outmaneuver veterans of Spain or the anti-Nazi resistance by accusing them of "Titoism." Jobs, cars and apartments – the latter a very precious commodity in most eastern European cities during the late 1940s – suddenly became available.

The role of sometimes quite petty personal interest was repeatedly seen in the operation of eastern European Stalinism. Artur London recalled that the special bonds allowing him to shop in stores that were closed to ordinary Czechs were stolen by his interrogators, while Heda Margolius remembered that the officials who inventoried the property of her husband were keen to see what they could acquire for themselves.[8] Sometimes such operations were grotesque. When the property of the victims of the Slánský trial was sold to senior party leaders, Gottwald's wife bought the bedclothes and porcelain of Vladimir Clementis (whose execution her husband had ordered).[9] The Czech authorities gave a special code name (Plan B) to the project to evict "bourgeois tenants" from desirable houses in first Prague, then Brno and then Pilsen – the order reflected the accommodation needs of party officials – and to send them to frontier regions, which had been cleared by the eviction of Germans.[10]

The purges were ostensibly justified in terms of an international conspiracy, which meant that arrests in one country led to denunciations of "accomplices" elsewhere. Matters were made worse by rivalry among the communist states. No communist leadership wished to be seen as the only national group to have been corrupted. Artur London remembered a conversation with his colleague Siroky, who told him that the Czech party was under pressure from its Hungarian counterpart to initiate purges. Siroky added that this pressure (from a state with which the Czechs had traditionally had bad relations) would be resisted: "Our situation has nothing in common with theirs. We are not emerging from a long period of illegality as they are. Our leadership is united and has worked under the direction of Gottwald since 1929."[11] Siroky's condescension towards the Hungarians was soon swept aside, and Czech purges, which claimed London as one of their victims, began. The Polish party leadership managed to limit the worst effects of the purges in their own borders while encouraging murderous excesses in Czechoslovakia and Hungary.

Stalinism also had an ideological basis. Who believed in Stalinism and why? The first and most obvious answer is those who had been members of the Communist Party before the defeat of Nazi Germany. In some countries the group was very small indeed, though in others, such as Czechoslovakia and East Germany, there had once been relatively large communist parties. Even here communists were never a majority of the politically active population, and their numbers had been depleted by the Second World War, but what they lacked in numbers, they made up for in fervor. They had endured the prisons of interwar dictators, the Nazis and, in some cases, the Soviet Union. Mátyás Rákosi, the Hungarian who was to preside over Stalinist purges in his country, had spent a total of fifteen years in prison; Traïtcho Kostov, the Bulgarian who was to fall victim to purges, was a hunchback as a result of jumping from a prison window.[12] Such men's conception of politics was rooted in the harshness of peasant life, violence and repression. Heroic sacrifices were taken for granted and, for all their talk about party discipline, many communists probably thought about politics in terms that were not very different from those that might have been used by Gavrilo Princip.

Communist leaders who helped establish Stalinism in eastern Europe often became its victims, but this does not mean that their projects failed. In some ways, they were astonishingly successful. They wanted communist rule established in eastern Europe, at a time when it was not clear that Stalin himself did, and communist rule was duly established. Furthermore, it was exercised by native communist parties through nominally independent governments. At first, of course, the independence of those governments was tightly circumscribed by Moscow's orders, but eventually the fact that eastern European nations were not simply federated states of the Soviet Union was to have important implications.

The price to be paid was terribly high, but eastern European Stalinists had never supposed that establishing communism would not involve bloodshed, and may even have been willing to accept the fact that the blood would be their own. Their long-term goals transcended the immediate future and their collective aims transcended the interests of individuals. They remained devoted party men even when they were in secret police torture chambers. In some cases, such loyalty made all the more unbearable the final realization that they were being unjustly accused by their own comrades. Men who had endured the Gestapo sometimes cracked when their own party turned against them. In 1976, the Hungarian communist János Kádár told François Mitterrand: "The worst thing is to doubt one's own people. Horthy took my physical freedom. Rákosi also took my moral freedom."[13] However, Kádár was unusually sentimental for an eastern European communist of his generation, and his experiences at the hands of the secret police do not seem to have shaken his belief that communism must be defended by violence if necessary. A surprising number of purge survivors wanted nothing other than to be reintegrated into the party.

Such behavior did not spring from naïvete about Stalin or about the Soviet Union. Many of those involved in the establishment of communism in eastern Europe knew very well what Stalin was like as an individual, what he had done to their comrades who had been unfortunate enough to fall into his hands in earlier periods, and what he had done in their own countries. Party leaders were loyal to an ideal rather than to an individual.

Although those who lived through the late 1940s often came to define themselves in contrast to the younger generation, Stalinists were composed of at least two generations. The first, described above, comprised those who were old enough to exercise power, but the real enthusiasm for Stalinism came from the people who had been born in the late 1920s or 1930s. They could display an astonishing fanaticism, and teenage Stalinism was, in a strange way, innocent. Zdeněk Mlynář, a Czech born in 1930, wrote: "Our conception of socialism was even more primitive and one-sided than that of older generations of Stalinists."[14] Young Stalinists worshipped Stalin as an individual, and their loyalty was intertwined with the painfully intense emotional experiences of adolescence. Party discussion groups solemnly assessed the political worth of militants' first love affairs, and presentation of the case for the prosecution when a member was threatened with expulsion was often entrusted to the victim's best friend.

Such fanatical enthusiasm does much to explain the foundations on which communism in eastern Europe was built. Teenagers swelled the ranks of the party's youth organizations and provided the most committed elements in armies preparing to ward off the imperialist menace. The Romanian Lilly Marcou recalled the lengths to which she was willing to go in order to serve her faith. Although she had no interest in technical matters (she eventually became a distinguished historian), she was determined to serve communism in a practical way and applied to study chemistry, then to veterinary school, and then to an institution of food science before finally being admitted to a school that specialized in meteorology where, by sheer determination, she made herself into a star pupil.[15]

The fanaticism of the young was sometimes linked to their experiences of the war. For many orphans, the party provided the consolation of a substitute family. Youthful Stalinism was often associated with rebellion against an older generation. The hero of Kundera's *The Joke* becomes a communist partly to spite the self-important bourgeois aunt who brought him up after his father was killed fighting in the anti-Nazi resistance. Curiously, the most violent rebellions often came from the children of communists, who had no contact with a reality outside the party (particularly when both parents were sincere supporters); for them, loyalty to communism could be more important than loyalty to their family. Thomas Frejka, the sixteen-year-old son of one of the accused in the Slánský trial in Czechoslovakia, wrote: "I demand that my father receive the death sentence . . . and it is my wish that this letter be read to him."[16]

The death of Stalin and de-Stalinization

Stalin died of a brain hemorrhage in 1953. The last months of his life and those following his death were ones of chaos and terror as his henchmen jostled for position and strove to avoid annoying an ever more irascible and irrational master. Even when Stalin lay dying, no one wanted to take any decisions that might be held against them (a group of Kremlin doctors had recently been accused of trying to poison Soviet leaders). His funeral was, with grim appropriateness, the occasion for many deaths as vast drunken crowds pressed into the streets of Moscow. Stalin's potential successors now fought it out. It would be wrong to explain the divisions among these men in terms of "de-Stalinization." Khrushchev, the leader who was to become most associated with the destruction of Stalin's legacy, had never shown the slightest sign of disloyalty. At Stalin's seventieth birthday celebrations, he had sat at the old man's left hand (Mao Tse-tung sat on his right). Indeed, if anyone seemed to be a "liberalizer" in the second half of 1953, it was probably Lavrenti Beria, the secret police chief who was later to have much of the blame for Stalinism heaped on his shoulders. Beria favored releases from prison camps and tried to stem Soviet anti-Semitism;[17] Khrushchev was strongly anti-Semitic.

In December 1953, Beria lost his struggle with the faction of the Soviet leadership led by Khrushchev. He was arrested and executed. In retrospect, it is clear that his death was a turning point. Conflict among Soviet leaders was never as violent again; Beria was the last Soviet leader to be shot. When Khrushchev forced Molotov and Malenkov out of their positions in 1957, he sent them to be, respectively, ambassador to Mongolia and manager of an electricity generating station. Khrushchev himself was allowed to enjoy a comfortable, if frustrating, retirement after his own deposition in 1964.

Even as his successors fought each other in Moscow, Stalin's death changed the atmosphere in the communist bloc. There was no public renunciation of the past or attempt to punish Soviet leaders implicated in Stalin's crimes, but the relentless paranoia that had dominated Soviet policy during the previous few years ended: Russian advisers no longer pressed their eastern European colleagues to come up with fresh victims. Some of those who had been arrested, such as Kádár in Hungary, probably owed their survival to Stalin's death, but Soviet attitudes towards real, as opposed to imaginary, opposition had not changed. In 1953, the Red Army suppressed East German workers, who had risen up in protest against changes in regulations that imposed effective wage cuts.

In 1956, Nikita Khrushchev confronted the Stalinist past in his so-called "secret speech" to the Twentieth Congress of the Soviet Communist

Party. The speech was remarkable for what it did not say, concentrating on Stalin's crimes against his own party rather than his crimes against humanity. There was no suggestion that alternative economic policies might have been pursued, or any attempt to rehabilitate those who had advocated such policies. Nevertheless, Khrushchev's speech was important. Along with Khrushchev's more radical denunciations of Stalin during the early 1960s, it raised the possibility that the party had been wrong, inviting a suspicious attitude towards the unquestioning belief that had previously been regarded as the mark of a good communist. It also invited doubt about the cult of personality that had grown up around the "little Stalins" of the "people's democracies."

The impact of Stalinism on many eastern Europeans had been so intense that unraveling its legacy involved a reassessment of many aspects of their lives. Such reassessment could involve the highest people in the land: both Kádár, in Hungary, and Gomułka, in Poland, exercised power while remembering what it was like to be denounced by their own comrades. At the other end of the scale, tens of thousands of small children had to rebuild lives that had been torn apart by forces that they could not have understood. It was only after the beginning of de-Stalinization that the widow of the executed Czech communist Rudolf Margolius dared to tell her son what had happened to his father. The son of László Rajk, the executed Hungarian communist, was put in a children's home after his parents' arrest, and as de-Stalinization began his aunt tried to recover the child. Eventually she was summoned to a Budapest street, where a small boy was deposited from a car; she gathered that the boy was her nephew. Later, the boy's mother was released from prison, although by this time her son was convinced that his aunt was his mother.[18] Zdeněk Mlynář recalled a similar story from his time at Moscow University. One of his contemporaries was a young Russian whose high marks at school had earned him the right to go to university without undergoing military service. Possibly because his experience of life had been confined to the classroom – Moscow University at the time was full of cynical, vodka-swilling war veterans – he was one of the rare Russian students to show a sincere belief in communism. After Khrushchev's "secret speech," he discovered that the couple who had brought him up were merely adoptive parents and that his real family had been killed in the purges of the 1930s. He went mad.

The period after Stalin's death is often described as one of "thaw." This is deceptive. It implies a natural process that happened at an even pace. In reality, the process by which Stalinism was unraveled was anything but natural. Local rulers in communist countries channeled and controlled changes, with regard to their own positions and interests. Moreover, "de-Stalinization" was, in fact, many different processes. First, it involved a challenge by national communist parties to the leading role of the Soviet party. Such challenges were not necessarily associated with internal reform; Albania challenged Soviet authority in 1961, partly because its leaders resented Khrushchev's attempts to dismantle Stalinist politics inside the Soviet Union. On a second level, de-Stalinization affected the inner life of each national Communist Party in two ways. Ending Stalinism could simply mean ending the institutionalized paranoia that had exposed even the most loyal party members to the threat of arrest, torture and execution; liberalization could also mean the toleration of more open discussion in the party and the prospect that it might introduce certain reforms. Third, and most momentously, de-Stalinization could be taken up by those outside the party; it could mean popular revolt against unpopular policies or even against the party's authority. Different kinds of de-Stalinization often conflicted, and every communist reformer from Khrushchev down was dogged by the fear that reform might run out of control.

In the Soviet Union itself, rehabilitation of Stalin's victims came most easily to associates of party leaders, such as Molotov's wife. For less privileged individuals, the past was rarely wiped out. One man had been imprisoned in the 1940s because he had spent the war years abroad (he had, in fact, been a member of the French resistance). He was released in 1955 and granted a pension a year later, but in 1960 his request for a revision of his case was refused. In 1974, he was deprived of his pension again because of his work with a dissident group.[19]

Khrushchev's departure from power in 1964 did not mean the return of Stalinism, but it did mean that the authorities made less effort to atone for what had happened under Stalin. An example of the changed mood is provided by the case of three women who had shared a bunk in a labor camp for seventeen years. They petitioned Khrushchev to be allowed to share a Moscow flat on their release. Their request was granted. Fifteen years later, one of the women died and permission for the remaining two to live together was not renewed.[20] The women were told "the fashion for rehabilitated people is now dead."

There were sharp differences in the way in which de-Stalinization occurred in other communist countries. The Polish party leaders were more successful than their comrades elsewhere at riding the tiger of reform. Polish communists had always been wary of Stalin, and had succeeded in protecting their compatriots from the most severe consequences of Stalinist purges. One of those protected individuals, Władysław Gomułka, could now become Party Secretary without appearing compromised in the eyes of those who had suffered from recent events or threatening in the eyes of those who had previously held power. Poland also benefited from the strength of the Polish army, which discouraged Soviet intervention, and from the ability of the Polish Communist Party to channel and control popular anger. The consequences were, from the point of view of Polish reformers, disappointing. The fact that Gomułka was not a Stalinist did not make him a liberal, and he was to become a focus of workers' discontent during rioting in 1970, at which point he was replaced by Edward Gierek. The fact that the Soviet Union had not intervened in 1956 set a precedent, though. To a greater extent than any other nation in the Warsaw Pact, the Poles would settle their future differences among themselves.

In Hungary, by contrast, part of the communist leadership ended up inside the tiger of reform. Khrushchev's "secret speech" and the increasing explicitness of de-Stalinization in the Soviet Union stimulated desire for reform in Hungary and forced the posthumous rehabilitation of László Rajk in February 1956. In October, students and workers demonstrated in Budapest. Shots were fired and a number of communist militia men were lynched. This had catastrophic consequences. Communists in Hungary and elsewhere were terrified by the prospect of mob violence, and Soviet troops tried briefly to suppress the demonstration, but then the Soviet Union reversed its position and accepted the return of Imre Nagy, a reformer who had served as Prime Minister from July 1953 until April 1955; János Kádár became First Secretary of the party.

Nagy was unable to control the movements that he had partly inspired. He widened his Cabinet to include three noncommunists, and talked of withdrawing from the Warsaw Pact. These changes alarmed the Soviet Union, which reinforced its troops in Hungary. The assault on the Hungarian Communist Party's monopoly of power was brought to an abrupt end by the intervention of the Red Army, when Soviet forces put down the popular uprising, kidnapped Nagy (who was eventually returned to Hungary and executed in 1958) and installed a new government under Kádár. The suppression of the Hungarian uprising had a dramatic impact in the West. The pathetic radio broadcasts from Budapest, the images of teenagers attacking Soviet tanks, and the accounts of the thousands of refugees who fled across Hungary's borders generated the impression of simple conflict between right and wrong, freedom and oppression, the Soviet Union and "the Hungarian people." This impression of simple dichotomies was misleading. The man who took the decision to suppress the rising – Nikita Khrushchev – was also the man who had attacked the Stalinist myth in the Soviet Union, while Nagy had been a protégé of Malenkov, the Soviet leader most linked to Stalin. He had been Minister of the Interior – not a post normally associated with liberal views – during the early period of communist rule in Hungary, and had remained a senior figure in the party throughout the purges of the early 1950s. His

Soviet-installed successor, by contrast, had been imprisoned during the purges.

Nagy did not command the loyalty of all Hungarians. Right-wing Catholics did not forget that he was a communist, and were right not to do so. Nagy remained a convinced supporter of the party, and, when he finally sought refuge in the Yugoslav embassy, he took the communist ministers with him while abandoning the noncommunists to the mercies of the Red Army. The positions of those who evicted Nagy were also complicated. The Yugoslav example had clearly inspired some Hungarian communists, and Tito mediated in the denouement of the crisis – he made ineffectual efforts to protect Nagy – but did not deny the need for military intervention by the Soviet Union. Even Ferenc Münnich, the Hungarian communist most associated with Soviet intervention, cannot simply be dismissed as Moscow's lackey. As a veteran of the Spanish Civil War, he had much in common with the men who had fallen victim to Stalinist purges.

In the long run, Soviet intervention had the curious consequence of making Hungary the most tolerant country in the communist bloc. The basis of the regime was now clear: it rested on force. A government supported by Soviet tanks had no need to ask people to believe in it or even to pretend very hard to believe its own propaganda. In such circumstances, a certain complicity grew up between government and governed. The government could hint that unpopular measures were the product of external constraints, which it was doing its best to loosen.

The post-1956 complicity between the Hungarian government and the people was exemplified by Kádár, who might, at first glance, seem an unlikely recipient of popular approval. He had been a minister in the government that began the purges of the late 1940s, and he had come to power as a Soviet protégé. Before 1956, he had been in favor of reform, but his past made it impossible for him to campaign too hard against the Stalinist old guard: at one point Rákosi, a key figure behind the purges of the early 1950s, humiliated Kádár by playing to the Central Committee of the party a tape recording of Kádár attempting to persuade László Rajk to confess.[21] However, after 1956, Kádár was not identified with outright repression. He was known to have been a victim of the purges, and the Soviet leadership seems to have chosen him as the leader of the Hungarian government, on Tito's advice, precisely because they thought he would command wider support than the more hard-line Münnich.[22] Furthermore, his faults were human ones: he was seen as having betrayed friends and broken promises rather than having gloried in torture and executions. Many Hungarians must have had guilty consciences about similar actions during the late 1940s or the aftermath of 1956, and they may well have felt that Kádár's human vices were better than the inhuman virtues of communist activists (and perhaps also better than the inhuman courage of those who had attacked Soviet tanks with petrol bombs). The popular view of Kádár as a flawed but humane individual who had been forced to commit despicable acts was exemplified by the story, circulated in Budapest during the early 1970s, that he had cried three times in his life: after the execution of Rajk, after the execution of Nagy, and after the participation of Hungarian troops in the suppression of the Prague Spring in 1968.[23]

Kádár's policies were summed up in a phrase that he used in 1961, which he seems to have borrowed from an exiled dissident: "He who is not against us is with us."[24] This meant that the state would protect itself, or ask the Soviet Union to protect it, against open aggression, but that it would not go looking for dissent. The regime did not pretend to be shocked that its inhabitants wanted to listen to Western radio – it stopped jamming broadcasts in 1963[25] – or that they might be tempted to emigrate to the West – a student who overstayed on a study trip abroad would have his passport confiscated for a while but would not be expelled from university.[26] The practical results of such policies were remarkably similar to those produced by the prewar dictatorship of Admiral Horthy. Like Horthy, Kádár was willing but reluctant to use force, and like Horthy, Kádár allowed elections of a limited sort. Voters did not have the option of voting against the ruling coalition, but could vote against particular candidates.[27] Just as Horthy had tolerated socialists in the cities, provided they did not challenge aristocratic power in the countryside, Kádár tolerated discussion among intellectuals, as long as they did not agitate the working classes. Kádár's associate, György Aczél, subsidized a range of journals, publishing houses and film studios that enjoyed a freedom that would have been inconceivable in any other part of the communist bloc.[28] Similarly, entrepreneurship by small businessmen was tolerated as long as they did not challenge the overall control of the economy exercised by the state bodies. All this ensured that Hungary came to be seen as both the freest and the most prosperous of the communist nations in Europe. It also produced a slightly melancholy mood in a country that swapped a faith in sweeping social transformation for the prospect that everyone might be able to afford a Fiat. Between 1955 and 1970 (during the very period in which Kádár's model of socialism had taken shape), the annual suicide rate increased from 20 per 100,000 to 36 per 100,000.[29]

De-Stalinization in Czechoslovakia happened more slowly than in Poland, where Stalinism's roots had been shallow, or Hungary, where the Stalinist period was openly discussed during the uprising. Arrests continued after the death of Stalin and the release of the Moscow doctors; the statue of Stalin that overlooked Prague was constructed after his death (the sculptor eventually committed suicide and the young electrician who had acted as a model took to drink). The last victim of the Czech purges – Osvald Zavodsky – was not executed until March 1954.[30] The Czech Communist Party studiously ignored much of the content of Khrushchev's "secret speech," and references to events in Poland were kept out of the Czech press.[31] The Hungarian uprising dramatically put back the cause of reform in Czechoslovakia – the Czechs had good historical reasons for fearing Hungarian nationalism, which seemed to be part of the Hungarian uprising, and the Czech government even offered to send troops to help restore order in Hungary. Most importantly, the assault on the Communist Party's authority and the lynching of party officials frightened Czech communists who were otherwise sympathetic to liberalization. Zdeněk Mlynář was a Prague lawyer already working to rehabilitate the victims of arbitrary execution and imprisonment during the Stalinist period, but he recognized that there was little point in establishing the freedom of party leaders from arbitrary violence at the hands of the secret police if they were then subject to arbitrary violence at the hands of street mobs. Furthermore, Mlynář knew that his reformist position inside the party would not prevent him from being labeled as a member of the ruling group if antiparty violence should start in Prague. Indeed, knowing something of the injustices perpetrated in his country, he had particular reason to fear the consequences if people started to seek revenge for what had happened. Mlynář's friend Karel Kuehnul had just been expelled for his reformist position, but he too feared the consequences of indiscriminate revenge against the party. He thought it likely that he would end up hanged from the same tree as his neighbor, an unrepentant Stalinist.[32]

The rehabilitation of the victims of Czech Stalinism was slow, discreet and grudging. Between 1955 and 1963, three commissions discussed errors by the party, but they operated in great secrecy – one met in a Barnabite convent – and their conclusions were not widely circulated. Victims were compensated and rehabilitated, but asked not to cause difficulties. Most of those who had been involved in the purges escaped lightly. Karol Bacílek, the most heavily implicated individual after the death of Gottwald, was first sent to preside over the party in Slovakia (not a move that the Slovaks welcomed) and then relieved of his functions "at his own request." The prosecutor in the Slánský trial still held an official post in 1968.[33] The Twelfth Congress of the Czech Communist Party, at which it discussed past errors in the way that its Soviet counterpart had done in 1956, was not held until December 1962.

Czech de-Stalinization, when it did occur, bore some resemblance to what had happened in Hungary after 1956. Both countries were marked by quiet toleration of movements from below rather than explicit reform from above. In Czechoslovakia, such tolerance became particularly marked in the Slovak part of the country, especially after Alexander Dubček became leader of the Slovak party in 1963. There were waves of protest at the writers' conferences in Bratislava in May 1963 and, more dramatically, at the one held in Prague in 1967. Confrontational statements by intellectuals were often regarded as administrative problems to be dealt with by the dismissal of some hapless official in the Ministry of Culture rather than political problems requiring action against the writer concerned.[34]

Czech opposition spilt over in the Prague Spring of 1968, which, like the Hungarian uprising, was partly a product of the Soviet Union's own initiative. Brezhnev effectively withdrew his support for the Czech leader Antonín Novotný, who was replaced as First Secretary in January 1968 by Alexander Dubček. The Czech party, like the Hungarian party in 1956, was divided by debates that cannot be reduced to splits between reformers and conservatives. Dubček was a loyal communist who had spent sixteen of his forty-six years in the Soviet Union. Several men who were normally loyal to Moscow threw in their lot with the cause of reform, perhaps because the Soviet Union wanted to keep change under control. Zdeněk Mlynář, who had worked for reform for many years, tried to prevent moves, such as the abolition of censorship, that he saw as premature and provocative.

As in Hungary, Czech communist leaders failed to control events, but the reasons for their failure were very different. The Hungarian uprising took place after fifteen years of fascism and Stalinism; the Prague Spring came after six years of slow reform in a country that traditionally disliked violence. Religion and nationalism, which had an important influence in Hungary, counted for little in Prague. Czech opinion owed much to reformist Marxism and recollection of the country's democratic past, particularly on the twentieth anniversary of Jan Masaryk's death. Prague crowds in 1968 were much better humored than those in Budapest in 1956. Heda Margolius, whose husband had been hanged in 1952, wrote: "People seemed to understand that violence and revenge, no matter how justifiable, could not be part of the rebirth."[35]

The Soviet Union was uncertain about what to do in such circumstances. Only when talks between the two countries failed to resolve matters did it order military intervention by the Warsaw Pact. At the beginning of August, 250,000 troops from Hungary, Poland, Bulgaria, East Germany and the Soviet Union began to "restore order" in Czechoslovakia, but military intervention was less violent than that which had taken place in Hungary. The Czechs responded not with guns and petrol bombs but with sarcasm, mockery and even attempts to persuade troops to go home. The determined but peaceful protests of August 1968 were in many ways a dress rehearsal for December 1989. Czech leaders were abducted to Moscow but there were no trials or executions; indeed, matters were settled by a kind of compromise between the Czech and Soviet leaders. The Czechs were allowed to return to Prague, and Dubček remained First Secretary until his replacement by Gustáv Husák in 1969. In some respects, Dubček resembled Kádár more than he resembled Nagy. Like Kádár, Dubček was the man chosen by the Soviet Union, in the short term at least, to bring disturbances under control. Like Kádár, Dubček gave the impression that his actions were constrained by the irresistible force of Soviet power. Like Kádár, Dubček seems to have aroused feelings of complicity on the part of a people who believed more in compromise than in pointlessly heroic gestures. A sign in Prague read: "Dubček we understand."[36]

Heda Margolius recalled that the Prague Spring had "all the intensity, anxiety and unreality of a dream come true,"[37] yet in some ways its most important characteristic was realism rather than utopianism. Czech leaders avoided provocative gestures, such as discussion of withdrawal from the Warsaw Pact, and recognized that nothing would be gained from confrontation with an overwhelming military force. Ordinary Czechs understood that debate and persuasion were more important than revenge. Events in Budapest had made Hungary more liberal while setting back the cause of reform in most of communist Europe. Events in Prague made Czechoslovakia less liberal but the example of nonviolent transition provided a lesson that communist reformers were, eventually, to absorb. In 1987, the Soviet Foreign Ministry spokesman Gennady Gerasimov was asked what the difference was between Gorbachev's perestroika and the Prague Spring. "Nineteen years," he replied.[38]

Economics

The end of Stalinism meant a new attitude towards economics in the communist bloc. Previously, the subject had been discussed in dramatic terms. Stalin had emphasized the backwardness of the communist economies and the need for rapid growth that would provide a means to defend and promote socialism and be achieved by heroic acts of will that would provide little comfort for the consumer. After Stalin, policy changed. The economy remained at the center of the communist project, but it was talked about in more complacent terms. Growth was presented as a product of communism rather than as a way of defending it. Where Stalin had talked of the need to catch up with the Western economies if the USSR was not to be crushed, Khrushchev seemed to take it for granted that the USSR would overtake the West and that this process would generate great consumer benefits for the citizens of the communist bloc.

Many in the West found the confidence of communist leaders about their economic prospects convincing. In western Europe, previously underdeveloped economies such as those of Spain and Greece grew rapidly, and it seemed reasonable to assume that parts of Russia and eastern Europe might do likewise. Soviet technological sophistication also seemed impressive. The Soviet Union exploded an atomic bomb in 1949 (only four years after the United States), and put the Sputnik spacecraft into orbit in 1957 (before the Americans). Most importantly, Soviet planning impressed many Westerners. It was widely believed that the anarchic capitalism of the prewar period had produced disaster. The Soviet system of coordinated and well-informed decisions seemed superior, and some believed that it was a model that the West would do well to imitate. The statistics produced by Soviet planning bodies were accepted by some Western economists as proof of Soviet success.

Others in the West argued that the communist economies, and that of the USSR in particular, were in such a bad state that their survival might be endangered. Such interpretations were founded on skepticism about Soviet statistics. It was argued that they were either invented or rendered worthless by neglect of the quality rather than the mere quantity of goods produced. Emmanuel Todd and Alain Besançon suggested that the key to understanding communist economies lay in personal experience of the squalor, deprivation and chaos to be found east of the Iron Curtain. Todd brushed aside details about the number of tonnes of pig iron produced and examined statistics on alcoholism and infant mortality to get a sense of what discipline was like in Soviet factories and what kind of goods reached the Soviet consumer.

The truth was that the communist bloc contained more than one kind of economy. The first distinction to be made was between the economies of the eastern European states and that of the Soviet Union. Several of the people's democracies, notably East Germany and Czechoslovakia, began with levels of industrialization superior to those of the Soviet Union. In the postwar period, this gap widened, and even economies that had been weak grew more quickly than that of the Soviet Union. Eastern European states were more tolerant of private enterprise than the Soviet Union; they had the advantage of capitalist traditions, which gave them a pool of talent that could be used in both small businesses and state companies. They also benefited from their relative smallness: central planning of the economy did less damage in Czechoslovakia, a country with a population of slightly fewer than 15 million in 1975, than in the Soviet Union, which had a population more than ten times greater.

Far from producing an ordered economy, central planning in the Soviet Union exacerbated the chaos that already existed in many factories. In Leningrad, regulations governing the delivery of metals were so onerous that some managers found it easier to send trucks to pick up supplies in Moscow than to handle the red tape required by local authorities. Obtaining spare parts was so difficult that plants often made their own in highly inefficient small-scale workshops. The need to meet planning targets meant that factories worked at an irregular pace. The Azov forge press equipment factory habitually turned out 60–70 percent of production in the last ten days of each month. It did not produce a single machine in the first ten days of May 1958; in the second ten days, it produced three; in the last ten days of the month, it produced thirty-two machines at a frantic rhythm that meant some workers never left their workplace. Such surges were followed by days of absenteeism as workers restored their energies (often with the aid of the vodka that managers had given them in return for their cooperation).[39] Managers hoarded resources in order to be ready for storming sessions when a key component arrived or fulfillment of a planning target was due, and redundant labor was kept on the books. In the factories of one region in 1963, 14,986 pieces of uninstalled equipment were found lying around – many of them irreparably damaged as a result of having been left in the open air.[40]

The second difference was that between agriculture and industry. The pattern of development seen in communist agriculture differed sharply from that of western Europe. In the West, agriculture, especially small-scale agriculture, was protected and subsidized for political reasons, while rapid technological development and the lure of large cities pulled much of the agricultural workforce into industrial employment; in the East, agriculture, especially small-scale agriculture, was disapproved of for political reasons. The state supported the collectivization of agriculture (but with less relentless determination than before the death of Stalin) and sought to divert resources into industrial growth. The policy had disastrous consequences. Collective farms were consistently inefficient. Whereas western Europe could sustain the cost of inefficient small-scale production by obtaining food from highly efficient large-scale farms, eastern European agriculture was propped up by the relatively efficient (by eastern European standards) small-scale farms that had survived in countries such as Poland. The problem was most severe in the Soviet Union, where collectivization had been most extensive and had been undertaken for longest. Soviet backwardness was eventually reflected in the humiliating need to import grain from the United States during the 1970s.

The third division in the eastern European economy was between the military and civilian sectors. Even before the Revolution, the Russian economy had been heavily geared to weapons production, which became all the more important when Soviet governments believed that they needed to protect themselves against aggression from the West (and eventually from China). Some commentators suggested that such pressures had produced a dual economic system in the communist countries, whereby an inefficient civilian sector coexisted with an efficient armaments industry. There are several arguments to support this interpretation. The gulf between Western and communist economies was more marked in the civilian sphere than in armaments manufacture. The Eastern Bloc could isolate itself from competition in civilian goods through import controls, but the military sector was, by definition, exposed to competition with the West. Additionally, some of the weaknesses that a command economy generated in the communist civilian industries were inevitable parts of armaments manufacture in any economy – Western arms manufacture, based on protected monopoly suppliers selling almost exclusively to the state, was less open to competition than, say, the manufacture of transistor radios. Finally, armaments production was the one area in which communist consumers had some power. Indeed, the capacity of a Red Army marshal to make life unpleasant for a company that failed to deliver arms of the required standard was probably greater than that of his NATO counterpart.

Some evidence suggests that the communist war industries were efficient. The Soviet Union matched and exceeded the West in terms of sheer numbers of items it produced. The manufacturers of planes such as the Phantom and the Mirage regarded MiG fighters as providing serious competition in a way that the makers of cars such as BMW or Saab would never have regarded Skodas or Ladas – of course, Western arms manufacturers had a financial interest in persuading their governments that Soviet weaponry posed a threat. Soviet weaponry was characterized by relative simplicity and robustness – the MiG 21 fighter had only one-tenth the number of separate parts used by its NATO equivalent, the F4 Phantom.[41] Soviet military chiefs seem to have been better than their Western counterparts at resisting what defense analysts call "gold plating" (the pressure to produce weapons of greater complexity that were much more expensive but only slightly more effective than their predecessors). The Kalashnikov rifle – which was cheap, easy to produce and difficult to break – epitomized the virtues of Soviet arms manufacture, and was carried by guerrillas and gangsters around the world, including rebels fighting the Red Army in Afghanistan. The Kalashnikov was probably the only Soviet product to achieve international brand recognition.

The Soviet arms industry could not, however, isolate itself entirely from the weaknesses of the Soviet civilian economy, or of Soviet society in general. Weapons manufacturers had to buy raw materials and components from civilian companies noted for poor-quality production or their failure to deliver on time, and to rely on staff who suffered from the same problems of alcoholism, lack of punctuality and indifference to their work found throughout the rest of the economy. The armaments industry could solve this only by investing great resources; armaments consumed a much larger proportion of Soviet investment than was admitted in official figures. For example, the quality necessary in certain processes was sustained by employing almost as many supervisors as workers.[42] This approach may have worked in the short term, but it produced two further difficulties in the long term. First, it created a vicious circle – the backwardness of the Soviet civilian economy was exacerbated by the redirection of resources into military spending, and the backwardness of the civilian economy then forced the military to insist on the diversion of ever larger resources. Second, Soviet techniques worked when production was relatively simple – the Soviet economy was best at producing commodities like iron and steel – but armaments production came increasingly to depend on other industries (especially electronics) that required the sophisticated interplay of different components and a high level of quality control. The Soviet economy lacked the hinterland of high-technology civilian industries that fed, and fed off, armaments industries in the West.

The division between the consumer economy and the capital goods industry was similar to that between the civilian and military sectors. The communist economies, notably that of the Soviet Union, were conspicuously bad at making consumer goods. In the days of Stalinism, this had been the result of an explicit and proclaimed choice, but during the 1960s it came to be seen increasingly as a failure. The most desirable consumer goods were often Western products that could be obtained only on the black market or through special shops reserved for foreigners and members of the nomenklatura. The failings of communist production were often more obvious in consumer goods than in capital goods: it would have taken an expert to distinguish a ton of East German steel from an equivalent amount of West German steel, but a five-year-old could have told a Mercedes from a Trabant.

The failure of communist economies to produce consumer goods was most obvious in the case of motor cars. In the West, cars became the most eloquent symbols of consumerism, associated with comfort, elegance and the imitation of an American way of life. They also became identified with personal autonomy and, in some cases, the maintenance of small enterprises, all features absent from the eastern European economies. Communist economies did not make many cars, and those that they did produce were not very good. The Soviet Union did not even attempt to meet its population's demand – in the 1970s, it produced 4.5 cars a year for every 1,000 inhabitants, while France produced 60 cars a year for every 1,000 inhabitants.[43] When Fiat helped establish a Russian factory, the Soviets exported much of its output, to the horror of the Italians, who had been convinced that sales to the Russian market would prevent cars made there from competing elsewhere with production in Turin.[44] Cars in eastern Europe had more to do with official position than purchasing power, and were allocated by the state; in Czechoslovakia, the right to buy a car was one of the privileges granted to rehabilitated purge victims during the 1960s.[45] This allocation benefited people whose services to the party or state were seen as particularly deserving; in the Soviet Union the perception that only a small section of the population was sufficiently reliable to be trusted with the privilege of uncontrolled travel had much to do with the state's allocation. Possession of cars came to be seen as the distinguishing feature of party apparatchiks. Emmanuel Todd suggested that a car played the same symbolic role for a member of the eastern European nomenklatura that a sword had played for the *ancien régime* aristocracy.[46] East Berliners referred to the suburb inhabited by party functionaries as "Volvograd."[47]

The reasons for the failure of the communist economies to produce consumer goods were linked to the broader nature of their political systems. Western companies were pushed by market competition into recognizing the primacy of the consumer, and Western governments were pushed by voters into trying to raise living standards, which played an increasingly important role in elections. Neither pressure existed in the Soviet Union. Centralized planning made consumer satisfaction hard to obtain; consumer desires were heavily dependent on fashion, whim and the meeting of precise specifications, and men sitting in offices in Moscow found it hard to respond to such a multitude of unpredictable and particular requirements. Consumer goods also depended on quality of production. A transistor radio had numerous components, the failure of any of which might cause the whole device to fail. The result was that a failure rate of just a small percentage in each particular component might produce almost total breakdown among the finished products.

Finally, there was a division in communist Europe between the formal and informal economies. Black markets, moonlighting and the exchange of favors provided many inhabitants of the East with access to much of what they needed. Sometimes, the structure of the "planned" economy made illegality inevitable. For example, the fact that supplies arrived late meant that Soviet factories were often obliged to complete an entire month's production schedule in a week, which obliged them to ask their employees to work an illegally large amount of overtime. To reward workers for such sacrifices, managers might be obliged to provide extra benefits or bonuses that were often obtained by maintaining fictitious workers on the payroll.[48] Entire illegal enterprises grew up: in 1971, there were estimated to be 200 such enterprises in the Odessa region of the USSR.[49]

The impact of the black economy could be beneficial: it could provide services that would not otherwise have been available. Indeed, one of the most successful economies of postwar western Europe, that of Italy, operated extensively outside the law. Illegal activity could, however, damage the economy by diverting resources from other uses. Furthermore, black markets are prone to inefficiency. They operate on the basis of limited information, so "market signals" are not fully relayed, and the need to conceal goods and work through personal contacts limits the extent to which resources can be exploited. Black markets further widened the gap between the people's democracies and the Soviet Union. The former, especially Poland and Hungary, often tolerated a sector of small-scale production, and there was also a high degree of trust among private citizens and a willingness to turn a blind eye to rule-breaking that extended quite far up the official hierarchy. The black economy therefore operated with a reasonable degree of openness, and tended to supplement rather than undermine the official economy. In the Soviet Union since the 1920s, by contrast, little tolerance had been granted to small-scale enterprise; levels of trust among individuals were low and the state sought to repress illegal economic activity with punishments of exemplary savageness. The black economy was driven more deeply underground and became, paradoxically, more damaging. People who had no means of purchasing components simply stole them. Fear of the authorities meant that access to black markets came to depend heavily on personal contacts, and low-level officials added to the confusion and expense of such business by extracting bribes.

Society

The most striking social effect of communist rule was urbanization. In some respects the movement to the cities was part of a wider pattern that could also be discerned in western Europe, but the actual experience of urbanization was felt very differently in West and East (and in different parts of the East). A peasant who moved to Paris or Milan was moving to an established city with schools, cinemas and libraries. Even if he lived in a grim industrial suburb he might draw some benefit from such facilities, and his children would certainly do so. Some towns in the East offered similar advantages – Prague was an ancient city that had escaped wartime damage – but many cities were new creations that offered nothing except the prospect of work, often in a single industry. Furthermore, the fact that cities were created by the fiat of planning committees meant that they often suffered from social as well as economic imbalances.

Such problems were particularly acute in the Soviet Union, where geographical and ethnic privileges reinforced social ones, and the right to live in the major cities, especially Moscow, became a jealously guarded privilege, restricted to those who had been born there or who did certain kinds of work. Muscovites had better access to consumer goods than other Russians, and were able to dump the most menial jobs on temporary migrants. Inhabitants of less well established towns enjoyed no such advantages.[50] The entire town of Rostov-on-Don, with a population of 800,000, was without meat for a period of several months in the early 1970s; meanwhile special herds of cattle were maintained to ensure that the residents of a block of flats for party workers in Moscow could have fillet steak delivered to their door.[51] Worst off were new industrial cities. Bratsk, which was created between 1955 and 1973, had a population of 220,000, but was beset by shortages. There were too few workers to operate the plant there, too few houses for the workers and too few women for the men.[52] "Social and cultural life" in many such places consisted of the vodka bottle.

Mobility was social as well as geographical. The education system expanded in communist states. In 1938, there had been 50,000 students in eastern Europe; by 1966, this figure had increased to 250,000; and, by the mid-1970s, there were almost that number of students in Yugoslavia alone.[53] At first, education was used to promote the children of workers and peasants, and the children of the bourgeoisie were often deliberately excluded from universities. After graduation the newly educated flooded into the white-collar jobs created by the expansion of the state and of the party. In the first seventeen years of communist rule in Hungary, a quarter of workers' and peasants' children who entered the labor market took nonmanual jobs.[54] Some analysts who were interested in the growth of the educated class in eastern Europe discerned the emergence of a class of "specialists" or "technocrats," which would impose rational moderate policies on the communist states. Some believed that there would be a struggle between the specialists, distinguished by qualifications and technical knowledge, and the apparatchiks, distinguished by loyalty to the party.

In fact, the change brought by education and the growth of white-collar employment was less dramatic than it seemed at first glance. The attempt to educate the masses soon ran out of steam, and administrative restrictions reinforced the effects of nepotism in ensuring that children tended to inherit the social position of their parents, particularly in the Soviet Union. Unlike their Western counterparts, ambitious youngsters could not seek their fortunes in the big cities. The right to live in such cities was itself in part hereditary. The children of collective farm workers were forced to stay put because, unlike other Soviet citizens, they were not given passports for internal travel on their fourteenth birthday. Quotas governed the access of certain ethnic groups, notably Jews, to senior positions.[55]

Entry to universities came to depend on connections: Emmanuel Todd argued that Soviet exams had become empty formalities designed simply to grant the children of the nomenklatura access to positions comparable to those their parents enjoyed.[56] The elite Moscow Institute for International Relations did not even advertise its existence in the standard guide to higher education for Soviet school leavers: entry was restricted to candidates who had a personal recommendation from their regional party secretary.[57] Access to university also conferred the considerable advantage of exemption from military service (an advantage enjoyed by less than 14 percent of Soviet men).[58] While the sons of the privileged acquired contacts and prestige at Moscow University, the sons of ordinary Russians endured the bullying and discomfort of the Red Army. Boys from certain ethnic groups and the sons of dissidents had an even harder time because they were relegated to menial labor in noncombat units.

The extent of the change in the Soviet Union was revealed by a French sociologist who, after the fall of communism, embarked on a study of social mobility over several generations. One of the families studied was that of Ivan (1914–88), the son of a wealthy lawyer and bibliophile, who along with his brother Nicholas (1910–45), eventually managed to regain the social status of his father, but only after enormous struggle during the Stalinist period. Nicholas became a sinologist before being killed in a plane crash at the end of the Second World War. Ivan's early life was difficult because it coincided with the upheavals of Stalinism. Being the son of a bourgeois, he stood little chance of being admitted to university, so he took a laboring job building the Moscow underground, which gave him the status of "worker" and thus allowed him to enroll as a student of history at Moscow University in 1937. Almost immediately, disaster struck. Ivan and his entire Komsomol group were arrested and sentenced to ten years in a labor camp for "spreading anti-Soviet jokes." Ivan was released in 1940, after a change of leadership of the NKVD, but a year later war broke out. Ivan volunteered for active service and was severely wounded. In 1945, he resumed his studies at Moscow University, but then in 1948 fled Moscow to teach in a provincial technical school after being warned that he was liable to fall victim to another purge. Finally, in the mid-1950s, Ivan was able to return to Moscow and become editor of a review dedicated to history teaching.

The careers of Ivan's sons (born in 1952 and 1956) and nephew (born in 1941) were easier. Having a successful father was now an advantage rather than a handicap, and both of Ivan's sons became historians. One worked at the review that his father edited and one at the Institute of Oriental Studies that his uncle had founded. Ivan's nephew trained as a chemist, but moved into the history of science, where he presumably benefited from family support. Ivan's great-niece (born 1970) became a chemist, like her father, and his great-nephew (born 1974) became a painter, like his maternal uncle. Patronage and nepotism now underlay almost all success.[59] Even the job of maintaining Lenin's mummified corpse was passed from father to son.[60]

In many eastern European countries, the ranks of the party itself, and particularly its paid officials, became dominated by university graduates so that there was no real conflict between political and technical authority – one Polish authority reckoned that over half of party members were university graduates.[61] The notable exception to the pattern was Czechoslovakia, where the party did not entirely abandon its early egalitarian intentions. Differentials in pay were relatively small and the proportion of leading officials who were university graduates was only 9 percent by the mid-1960s.[62] Perhaps because of this relative lack of privilege, the educated classes played a predominant part in the Czech dissident movement.

The very words "intellectual" and "intelligentsia" were deceptive, often being used in eastern Europe to describe anyone who did not perform manual work. "Technocrat" was also a misleading term. Many in the East graduated with degrees in subjects other than hard science, and there was a slightly surreal quality to such study. What did "law" mean in the country of the Slánský trial? What did "economics" mean in a country where official statistics were works of fiction? Far from subjecting the administration of their countries to rigorous and objective scrutiny, university graduates often spent their days shuffling paper and drafting documents in properly turgid, Marxist style. The emphasis on education and formal qualifications sometimes led to a fierce defense of privilege and to petty demarcation disputes. Two Hungarian sociologists wrote: "An employee with the school leaving certificate will refuse to type a letter on the grounds that typing does not require a school leaving certificate."[63] The emphasis on written skills made eastern Europe even more bureaucratic than it already was. Milovan Djilas, himself the university-educated son of a peasant, argued that in Yugoslavia the "new class" had simply replaced the old Ottoman beys (or landowners). It would be fairer to say that they had replaced the interwar civil service, which itself had absorbed an excess production of graduates. In the 1930s, Hugh Seton-Watson had observed peasants queuing outside a government office while clerks drank coffee and gossiped. The peasants, he wrote, had "waited hundreds of years for justice and they could wait a few more hours." In the early 1970s, many more clerks sat in offices, but they were still drinking coffee and the peasants outside were still waiting for justice (or just for one of the pieces of paper that required an official stamp).

Communism was an international movement, and the communist states of Europe were grouped together in a transnational alliance under the tutelage of the USSR, but complete uniformity was not imposed on communist subjects. The Soviet Union tried to break the consciousness of national groups within its frontiers. Ethnic Germans and Chechens were deported en masse to remote corners of the Union, and the Ukrainians endured continuous efforts to crush their language and religion. Even at the height of Stalinist repression, though, the Soviet Union did not try to extinguish the national culture of communist states outside its frontiers.

Communist governments remained very conscious of being representative of a particular nationality, and the desire for national assertion spilled over into international relations when Yugoslavia, Albania and Romania distanced themselves from the Soviet Union, and when Hungary and Czechoslovakia made less successful attempts to do so. Even in countries that never questioned the authority of the Cominform or the Warsaw Pact, national feeling was not dead. Postwar boundary changes, population movements and the wartime extermination of the Jews had ensured that individual eastern European states were more ethnically homogeneous than ever before. In some ways, communist rule encouraged such feeling, and communism presented itself as the defender of authentic European cultures against the rootless commercial mass culture of the United States: one of Kundera's characters remembers solemn discussions with his friends about the prospect of using Moravian folk music to "redeem" jazz.

National feeling could also be used to divide and rule potential opponents of Moscow or of the various national governments in the Eastern Bloc. Romanian and Polish communists played on anti-Semitic feeling, which was important in the Stalinist show trials of the late 1940s in Czechoslovakia and Hungary. Tito encouraged Croat national feeling in the revival that culminated in the "Croat spring" of 1971, partly so that he could play the Croatians off against other nationalities in the Yugoslav federation. In Czechoslovakia, the Slovaks were seen as more docile than the Czechs – in spite of, or because of, the fact that Bratislava was more liberal than Prague in the 1960s and that Dubček was a Slovak. The Prague Spring of 1968 fatally identified the Czech part of the country with revolt, and thereafter the government deliberately placed Slovaks in positions of responsibility.

Communist rule sometimes unconsciously encouraged the growth of national culture. Eastern European intellectuals had always been fascinated by the West, and many had not even communicated in the language of their native countries. Barbed wire at the frontier now prevented them from following the homing instincts that would have taken them to the Rue Jacob. Foreign languages (other than Russian) were discouraged, so Czech, Polish and Romanian cultures were forced to turn in on themselves. The social changes that accompanied the early years of communist rule reinforced this tendency. Eastern European languages had been regarded as peasant dialects a mere fifty years previously, but now the sons of peasants were likely to be educated and take state jobs. The position of universities as exponents of national culture was reinforced.

One kind of institution occupied a particularly awkward position in national culture – the church. Communist regimes regarded religion with suspicion and tried to purge "traditional" ceremonies such as peasant weddings of their religious dimension and replace baptism with ceremonies of "youth consecration" or "initiation to citizenship." A faculty for the study of atheism was established at the University of Bratislava. Antireligious activity reached its height between 1948 and 1953, when many priests were imprisoned for espionage.

It soon became clear, however, that in religion, as in everything else, the communist regimes could not, and probably did not want to, impose universal measures that took no account of national peculiarities. Attitudes towards churches were heavily determined by the nature of particular churches and the level of religious enthusiasm in each country. Communist rulers confronted several different kinds of religious belief. In terms of religion, postwar Poland was the most homogeneous country in the communist bloc: almost all of its inhabitants had been born into the Catholic Church, and a large proportion were devout Catholics. The East German population was overwhelmingly composed of Lutheran Protestants. Elsewhere, matters were more complicated. In Czechoslovakia, 78 percent of the population was Catholic, though it was already relatively secularized even before the advent of communist rule. In Hungary, 68 percent of the population was Catholic, and most of the remainder was Calvinist, while the Albanian population was 70 percent Muslim, 20 percent Orthodox and 10 percent Catholic. The Bulgarian population contained adherents to the same three religions, though in this case Orthodox Christians formed the majority. In some places, religious divisions overlapped with national ones, as was the case in Yugoslavia, which was divided between Catholic Croats, Orthodox Serbs, and Muslims. In Czechoslovakia, the Slovaks tended to be the most devout element of the population.

The first distinction that communist governments made was between Catholicism on the one hand and Protestantism and Orthodoxy on the other: Islam, seen as a backward religion without allies in the capitalist West, presented much less of a problem to communist governments during this period. Protestantism and Orthodoxy tended to operate within national frontiers and had strong traditions of respect for state authority. Orthodoxy, in so far as it had an international dimension, looked to the patriarch in Moscow, who had more or less arrived at a *modus vivendi* with the Soviet state, and, in Yugoslavia and Bulgaria, Orthodoxy was strongly linked to national identity (though Yugoslav rulers were not entirely enthusiastic about Serbian nationalism or about an institution that might link part of their population to Moscow). In Bulgaria, the special place of the Orthodox Church was officially recognized in 1949, at a time when Catholic churches were closed and three years before a large spy trial involving Catholics.[64] Protestantism could be tolerated as long as it recognized the leading role of the state. In East Germany, an organization of "progressive pastors" was subsidized by the regime.[65] In Hungary, Janós Peter was a pastor who rallied to the regime, served as a diplomat until 1973 and thereafter was a member of the National Assembly (a characteristic example of how Kádár used ostentatious displays of his tolerance to earn international credit).[66] Billy Graham preached near Budapest in the 1970s.[67]

Catholicism presented a different problem. The Catholic Church was a tightly disciplined international organization that demanded that its members disobey secular authorities in certain circumstances. Furthermore, in the late 1940s it was closely associated with the Cold War. Christian democrats in the West were often the leading element in coalitions from which communist parties were excluded, and in July 1949 the Vatican had forbidden Catholics from belonging to the Communist Party. The early period of communist rule in eastern Europe was marked by outright repression and the imprisonment of a number of prominent clerics, notably József Mindszenty in Hungary and Stepan Wyszyński in Poland. In Albania, a "national Catholic Church" that broke links with the Vatican was established in 1951.[68]

The Catholic Church, which had come to terms with regimes as diverse as the French Third Republic and the German Third Reich, eventually sought to establish working relations with the communist states. A new Pope, John XXIII, was invested in 1958 and issued the conciliatory encyclical *Pacem in Terris*. The policy was continued by Paul VI, elected in 1963. A succession of meetings – including one between the Pope and Khrushchev's son-in-law – as well as formal agreements marked the warmer relations between Catholic and communist authorities.

The effects of this new policy were not uniform. In the Church, there were divisions between the national episcopacies, immersed in the political and social struggles of their own countries, and the Vatican, which was conducting a foreign policy designed to protect the interests of the Church. Just as French clergy had often resisted the "*ralliement*" to the Third Republic, Catholics who had spent years in prison were not always pleased to see urbane Papal diplomats such as Cardinal Franz Koenig (the Vatican "secretary for nonbelievers") shaking hands with communist ministers.

There were also divisions in the communist world. Rapprochement with Catholicism worked least well in the USSR, where Catholicism was often associated with national resistance to Russian/Soviet rule. Apart from the release of the primate of the Ukrainian Uniate Catholic Church, there was little sign of increased tolerance on the part of the Soviet authorities. The reconciliation between Church and state was most momentous in Poland, where the Catholic Church was sometimes seen as the true guardian of national legitimacy that the communist state had tried to usurp. The Polish Church laid claim to national legitimacy in its celebrations of the millennium of Polish nationhood in 1966, and even seemed to conduct an independent foreign policy when Polish bishops wrote to their German colleagues in 1965 granting and asking for forgiveness. The Church was also a focus of loyalty for the Polish working class, most of whom were recent migrants from the deeply devout countryside and could hardly look to communist-controlled trade unions to provide protection or support.

Polish communists were not entirely unhappy about the Church's role. The assertion of national culture fitted in with some of the ambitions of the Polish Communist Party itself. Even the conciliatory letter to German Bishops was not wholly inconvenient for the party. It facilitated the *Ostpolitik* (the opening-up to eastern Europe) of the West German leader Willy Brandt, while simultaneously offering Polish communists a rare chance to appear more patriotic than their national Church. Most importantly, the Church's relations with the working class were double-edged. Like the Christian trade unions of early industrialization in Germany, the Polish Catholic Church had the credibility that came from being seen as distanced from the state, but it often used it to prevent violent challenge to the existing social order. The primate of the Polish Catholic Church helped restore peace after the strikes of 1970.[69]

Conclusion

The *modus vivendi* reached by Church and state in many communist countries during the early 1970s was symptomatic of a wider relation between communist governments and those that had formerly been seen as their enemies. On an international level, communism seemed to be reaching an accommodation with the Western powers – an accommodation summed up with the words *Ostpolitik* and détente. Internally, communist governments were less concerned to hunt down enemies. Treatment of dissidents, or people who failed to fit into the system, could still be very harsh (especially in the Soviet Union), but the state's violence was predictable and most people knew how to avoid it. The spirit with which communism was regarded changed. In the late 1940s, at least in eastern Europe, communism had been associated with youth, dramatic change, terrible fear and enormous hope. In the mid-1970s, communist regimes were led by the old or middle-aged. Fewer people regarded them with fear, but almost none regarded them with hope. Stability seemed to be the greatest virtue of the communist world, and even those who wanted communism to reform expected that reform to be a long process.

5

REBUILDING THE FAMILY

AFTER THE SECOND World War, western European discussions of sexual relations placed a heavy emphasis on marriage and the family. In some ways this was simply a continuation of the return to "traditional" values that had begun in the late 1930s. Of course, the experience of Europeans was often very far removed from publicly espoused values. The war had been a time of separation, fleeting liaisons and – for many German, Hungarian and Austrian women – rape. Such experiences may have made western Europeans more enthusiastic to rebuild "normal" family lives. Official policy was heavily influenced by the need to restore "normality" after wartime dislocation – Helmut Schelsky, a member of the committee advising the German government on family affairs, began his career with a study of refugees in the immediate aftermath of the war.[1] A wave of marriage and then an increase in divorce rates followed the Second World War, as it had followed the First, but the aftermath of the Second World War, unlike that of the First, did not create a wider sense of crisis about relations between the sexes. Marriage was held in high esteem, and the names of institutions that interested themselves in sexual matters reflected a concern with families. The British Marriage Guidance Council was founded in 1948.[2] The French talked of "planning familial." No one catered for those who wished to escape marriage or who planned not to have families.

The postwar economy reinforced the "traditional" family. Increasing male pay was often used to support women at home (the proportion of women in the French workforce declined until the early 1960s). Homes became more comfortable and more clearly separated from the public worlds of the workplace and the street. Urbanization meant that the proportion of the western European population who were peasants, for whom the household was an economic unit as well as a center of family life, declined. Advertising bombarded consumers with images of the happy family. Increasingly "instrumental" attitudes towards work in new industries, such as motor manufacturing, meant that the strongest emotional ties of workers tended to be with wives and children. Demography was also important. Except in Germany – where there were 7 million more women than men – the Second World War had not created the imbalance between the sexes that had followed the First World War. The rising birth rate of the postwar years tended to reinforce the "traditional family," now understood to mean the nuclear family.

The postwar emphasis on the family had a political dimension. If the Christian democrat parties, the most important political force in large parts of Europe, stood for anything, it was the family. Their influence, and that of the Church, was particularly strong in Italy and West Germany, where a Ministry for the Family was established in 1953 and a child benefit was paid from 1955. Welfare states were established in much of western Europe to support the family rather than the individual, and many welfare mechanisms regarded the ideal family as one in which a well-paid man supported a housewife and children. The Basic Law, the nearest thing that Germany had to a constitution, was supposed to guarantee sexual equality, although in practice, the civil code was not revised in accordance with the law until 1957, equal pay was not legally guaranteed until 1958, and husbands retained the power to decide on matters related to the upbringing of children until 1959.[3]

European feminism reached its twentieth-century nadir during the 1950s: indeed the word almost ceased to be used in France during this period.[4] The battle for female suffrage had been won in most of western Europe (in 1971 Switzerland was the last European democracy to grant women the vote). Battles over sexual autonomy, and particularly over the right to abortion, did not begin in most countries until the early 1970s.

Permissive society?

Sexual intercourse began
In nineteen sixty-three
(Which was rather late for me)—
Between the end of the *Chatterley* ban
And the Beatles' first LP.

Philip Larkin's lines reflect the widespread belief that a sexual revolution in the 1960s moved from the challenging of taboos and legal restrictions to the association of sexual freedom with a new youth culture. But if there was a revolution, what was the old order that it overthrew? Larkin's own life illustrates some of the complexities. He may have regarded the sexual activity of the younger generation with hostility, but not because he led a chaste life or because he was a defender of traditional morality (he wrote eloquently on the misery of family life). The reference to the *Lady Chatterley's Lover* trial in November 1960 is also interesting, suggesting that the sexual values propagated in the 1960s were not new. In fact, the challenge to existing sexual values in the 1960s was tamer than that of the 1920s. There were none of the radical attacks on the family that had come from people such as Alexandra Kollontai. In many respects, Lawrence's vision of sexual morality – with its emphasis on heterosexual monogamy – was the most conservative on offer in the 1920s.

The second important aspect of the *Lady Chatterley's Lover* trial was its anglocentricity. The English assumed that D. H. Lawrence's novel was a touchstone of obscenity against which other work could be judged: one reviewer wrote that Sartre's *La Nausée* "leaves Lady Chatterley standing at the post." But *Lady Chatterley's Lover* had never been banned in most of Europe, and its discussion of sexual matters was no more explicit than that in works on any educated French person's bookshelf. De Beauvoir was discussing *Lady Chatterley's Lover* as an example of the obstacles to female emancipation ten years before the British legalized it.[5] If England was "in the vanguard of change" during the 1960s,[6] it was changing conventions that had never existed anywhere else in the first place.

Questions about the nature of the "permissive society" become more pressing when we examine marriage statistics. In an age when conventional ways of living were supposedly challenged, young people were more likely than ever to get married. French marriage rates peaked in the mid-1970s. In Britain in the 1960s, four-fifths of women were married; thirty years previously, the proportion had only been three-fifths.[7] In Spain, in 1965, six out of ten of women between the ages of fifteen and forty-nine were married (in 1940 the proportion had been just under half).[8]

Popular culture, which was so often presented as a threat to the "family," actually tended to reinforce it. Rock music, films and fashions all promoted the heterosexual couple, and to a surprisingly large extent popular culture also revolved around marriage and children. Sometimes this produced farcical situations. In a television debate, Mary Whitehouse rebuked Mick Jagger for not marrying his pregnant girlfriend; Jagger could not admit that he had begged her to marry him – and had been turned down.[9] Other rock stars could display their beliefs more openly, and the rock-star wedding became a feature of the social scene in the 1960s and 1970s. Johnny Hallyday's innumerable marriages attracted much attention in France; Jagger himself was finally married in a glare of publicity in St-Tropez in 1971. In Bernardo Bertolucci's 1972 film *Last Tango in Paris*, the heroine is portrayed enjoying anonymous sex with an older man, but her relations with the lover of her own age are tweely conventional and destined to end in what she calls "*le mariage pop*."

Some saw the contraceptive pill, which began to be available during the 1960s, as the basis of a sexual revolution. The pill seemed to offer simple, effective birth control that was under the woman's control. However, its use in the 1960s and early 1970s was restricted. It was taken by a small group of well-educated women in large cities, and in some countries – Italy, Spain and Ireland – it remained illegal. Furthermore, the pill was not as much of a challenge to the family as some believed. It was often used inside marriage, and women who gained autonomy with regard to their husbands were dependent on the largely male doctors who prescribed and controlled its use.

Legislation was also believed to affect sexual relations. In Britain, laws made divorce easier; abortion and homosexual acts between men over twenty-one were legalized. In France, a law of 1967 legalized birth control, and one of 1975 permitted abortion. In West Germany, abortion was legalized in 1976. None of the laws were as revolutionary as they might seem. Abortion, contraception and homosexuality had always existed, whether or not legislators chose to recognize them, and legislative changes were usually brought about not by the campaigns of sexual radicals but by middle-aged male politicians. Sexual reform was presented as a means of preserving the family, much as Keynesianism was a means of preserving capitalism. Undesirable behavior such as homosexuality and abortion was to be brought inside the law, where it could be controlled more easily: the first British law to liberalize regulation of homosexuality was cosponsored by a Conservative MP, and Charles de Gaulle authorized legislation on birth control because he believed that choices about such matters should be "lucid."[10]

In continental western Europe, abortion was the one issue that involved a real challenge to the moral order. Women who had had abortions were increasingly open about their experiences and increasingly prone to talk about them as part of a right to control their own bodies rather than merely a necessity of life. Abortion was often defended by those who wished to avoid having children, rather than simply to "plan" their families, and by those who defended their right to enjoy sex outside marriage. Emma Bonino, the future European commissioner, served a six-month prison sentence in Italy after having publicized her own abortion, and in France a group of women who claimed to have had abortions published their names in the *Le Nouvel Observateur* (a gesture copied by a group of German women in *Stern*). More than any other issue, the campaign in favor of legalized abortion was associated with the rise of radical feminism in the early 1970s.

The focus on the heterosexual couple marginalized two groups that had enjoyed some prominence in certain sections of European society before 1939. The first of these was male homosexuals. France and Germany both retained laws under which homosexuals had been prosecuted by the authoritarian regimes of Vichy and the Third Reich. In Germany, Article 175 of the criminal code, which dealt with male homosexuality, had been revised by the Nazi regime: between 1933 and 1945, 38,000 men were convicted under this law; the number of men convicted under the same law from 1953 to 1965 was 98,700. Homosexual relations between men over the age of twenty-one were legalized only in 1969, and as late as 1979 the German government specifically excluded male homosexuals from compensation paid to victims of Nazi persecution.[11] In France, Vichy legislation on homosexuality was tightened at the beginning of the "permissive" 1960s.[12] In Britain, legislation under which Oscar Wilde had been imprisoned remained in force until 1967, and the way in which it was used became more draconian. The number of prosecutions for homosexuality increased during the 1950s (an era described by Patrick Higgins as "the heterosexual dictatorship").[13]

The authorities that dealt with homosexuality often claimed that their approach was based on medical science rather than morality. A poll in June 1962 showed that most French people regarded homosexuality as a "disease" rather than as a "vice."[14] In practice, however, the distinction between medicine and morality had never been absolute. Doctors wrote in moralistic language: "The clearest normal medical conditions show that most often homosexuality is associated with laziness, social unproductivity and delinquency . . . the inability to be patient, to put up with frustrations, to accept social and family responsibilities, stems in effect from the same infantile persistence which conditions homosexual behavior."[15] The desire of experts to "cure inverts" (often with electric shocks and aversion therapies) could be more unpleasant than the desire of moralists to persecute sodomites.

The process by which male homosexuality was finally legalized in Britain did not reflect an emancipatory desire on the part of legislators or power on the part of those affected by legislation. Debates in Parliament addressed a "problem" to be solved rather than a freedom to be granted. Contributors to the debate were keen to stress their own "normalness." Cartoonist Osbert Lancaster's Maudie Littlehampton remarked: "What I personally admired about the debate was the way in which every speaker managed to give the impression that he personally had never met a homosexual in his life."[16]

Independent women were the other group marginalized by the obsession with the couple. In 1945, European women who believed in the possibility of gaining respect in professions formerly dominated by men and in living outside marriage could look to the future with some confidence. Women had the vote in almost all the European democracies and it was widely believed that suffrage and employment would work together to increase sexual equality. It was true that women still had fewer opportunities at work and generally earned less than men, and that women voted largely for conservative or Christian democrat parties, which were often unsympathetic to women's independence, but over time these short-term problems would resolve themselves. Electoral pressure would force governments to remove obstacles to female employment; women's entry into the workforce would give them the same degree of information and class consciousness as men and thus bring about a political convergence between the sexes.

By the late 1960s, such hopes had been disappointed. Women had entered the labor force in larger numbers but usually did so in comparatively menial and badly paid positions. Cultural and social obstacles to female equality proved more difficult to overcome than legal ones.

Most importantly, the "sexual freedom" of the 1960s tended to exacerbate differences between the sexes rather than diminish them. Sometimes sexual emancipation was linked to a specific rejection of women's right to careers. The theater critic Kenneth Tynan was an evangelist of sexual freedom on stage and in his own life, but he told his wife to give up work because "he did not like girls who got up in the morning."

The children of the revolution?

Postwar western Europe was shaken by a demographic revolution. Birth rates increased after the Second World War so that the children who reached adolescence in the 1960s were far more numerous than their immediate predecessors. In West Germany, the effect was magnified by the very heavy losses of the war years, which affected men born in the 1920s. There was also a social revolution. The young were often the first to benefit from increasing prosperity, education opportunity and social mobility. Most had spent longer in school than their parents, and many had incomes that their parents, growing up in the 1930s, would have regarded as inconceivable.

The newly prosperous youth of the 1950s and 1960s sometimes talked of rebellion against the old. The Who snarled, "Hope I die before I get old" (all but one of them lived long enough to see the line being used in advertisements for pension plans), but in some respects change strengthened the family rather than weakening it. The prosperity that teenagers enjoyed came mainly from their parents', particularly their fathers', income. Increasing educational opportunity (especially the spectacular increase in university education on the continent) meant that young people stayed at home for longer. Even the most rebellious young Europeans often lived with their parents, and such dependence sometimes had tragicomic consequences. In December 1976, Italian police cornered a Walther Alasia, a member of the Red Brigade terrorist organization. Alasia was killed in the subsequent gun battle and became a hero to his organization, but the location in which this confrontation took place was not a revolutionary's garret but his parents' small flat, where he shared a room with his elder brother (a bank clerk).

The generation gap of the 1960s was not evenly spread throughout society. Although those who claimed to speak on youth's behalf often presented themselves as rebelling against "bourgeois values" or as defenders of the proletariat, generational conflict was least intense among the upper ranks of society, who had always enjoyed the wealth and freedom that came to parts of European youth during the 1960s. The upper classes had often tolerated wild behavior or even political radicalism among their young, and many regarded Paris, London or Berlin in the 1960s as tame compared with what they remembered of the same cities in the 1920s. The novels of Anthony Powell evoked youth culture with bored recognition rather than horror.

In France, the student riots of 1968 evoked sympathy from many bourgeois of the older generation. This was rooted partly in the sense that the students had reasonable material demands – relating to job opportunities, the quality of university facilities and so on – but also in class solidarity against the plebeian forces of order: "peasants in plastic clothes," as one student leader described them. The students were, after all, predominantly bourgeois. Raymond Aron bitterly suggested that many parents preferred to see their children throwing stones at the riot police rather than risking their lives in sports cars.

Generational conflict at the top of society was blunted by shared interests as real elites remained small and retained a high capacity to pass on privileges to their children. Underneath the posturing, most Etonians did want to grow up to be their fathers. The same was not true lower down the social scale. Generational splits were most severe among groups that were unable to pass on privileges or whose privileges were not worth having. The French working class fell into the first category. In the immediate postwar period, it had enjoyed a certain degree of security and power, but the changing economic circumstances of the 1960s meant that skilled, safe industrial jobs were no longer available for the sons of what Gérard Noiriel has called "the unique generation."[17] It was the young workers born in the late 1940s who, along with other marginalized groups such as women and immigrants, joined the strikes of 1968, which were in large measure a rebellion against the communist-led Confédération Générale du Travail, the union to which their fathers had been so loyal.

Rifts between generations were caused by social mobility. The widest gulf separated sons who had enjoyed some degree of social or educational success (though often less than they had hoped for) from the parents whose sacrifices subsidized their success. Dennis Potter gave a notorious newspaper interview in the 1950s, in which he spoke of his embarrassment about his working-class parents; Britain's archetypal angry young man, John Osborne, hated his mother even more than he hated everyone else. The hedonism and political radicalism of the 1960s were often a reaction against the deferred gratification and snobbery of lower-middle-class parents who had devoted all their efforts to helping their offspring "get on."

State-sponsored emancipation

Between the end of the Second World War and the death of Stalin, the family in communist Europe was pulled by a particularly complicated set of forces. The first force was official policy. The Soviet Union and the states in eastern Europe that modeled themselves on it proclaimed a commitment to equality of the sexes, but Stalinism had turned away from the radical experimentation of some Soviet thinkers in the 1920s. Abortion and homosexuality were repressed, and divorce was less easy than it had been. Official propaganda presented healthy, smiling babies in the arms of devoted mothers.

There was a less explicit dimension to Stalinism's impact on the family. One aspect of Stalinist paranoia was a denial that any loyalty could supersede that to the party. This attitude affected family relations. Couples sometimes divorced each other so that the arrest of one spouse would not compromise the other. Family and party loyalties cut across each other in painful ways. Thomas Frejka, the Czech sixteen-year-old who demanded the death penalty for his own father, put party above family; Lilly Marcou, who left her beloved party rather than abandon her "Zionist" parents, made the opposite choice. Outside the circle of communist believers, parents were generally able to transmit their private beliefs to their children even when they refrained from making indiscreetly explicit political statements, and this meant that most children passed from one world to another when they left their own home. One Polish girl recalled that she, a young enthusiast, was devastated by the death of Stalin, but at school her classmates seemed happy in spite of the official mourning: "Their parents must have told them that this was good news."[18]

Physical constraints were at least as important as official policy in defining family life in communist Europe. The war left two overwhelming legacies. First, there was a shortage of men, which was most striking in the Soviet Union itself, and which meant that many women had no chance to establish "normal" families. One-third of Soviet women who had reached the age of twenty between 1929 and 1938 remained unmarried in 1959.[19] By 1950, the number of children born outside marriage had increased to almost 1 million per year. Second, there was a terrible shortage of housing, which was, once again, particularly acute in the Soviet Union. Very few families had much private space, and people lived in communal apartments or even barracks. The impact of this lack of privacy was exacerbated by the fact that such a large proportion of the Soviet population was used to living in units other than the family. Soldiers, children brought up in shelters for those whose parents were dead or missing, and workers shipped hundred of miles from home were all used to communal life. Many felt happier in the public spaces established by their peers than in the cramped homes of their relatives.

The death of Stalin in 1953 brought changes in communist attitudes towards the family, but once again they involved multiple and sometimes contradictory forces. The importance given to women's work was perhaps the most striking way in which attitudes towards the family and sexual relations in eastern Europe differed from those in the West. Women made up a large proportion of the workforce in communist countries – in the Soviet Union in 1967, 46 percent of industrial workers were women – and the state celebrated this fact. Although the proportion who worked remained high, and often increased, the nature and effect of women's work changed after Stalin's death. During the 1930s and 1940s, women's entry into the Soviet workforce involved taking jobs that had previously been reserved for men, but during the 1950s, this was no longer the case. The labor shortage – resulting from rapid industrialization, men's absence at the front and high male casualties – became less severe. Women's employment was a matter of convenience rather than pressing need, and communist economies became marked by over-employment. Many people shuffled paper, and managers deliberately kept excessive numbers of employees on their books in order to ensure that they had enough workers for sudden rushes to fulfill plans, so the overall employment rate remained high, even though total production was relatively low. In such circumstances, women were seen as "extra" labor rather than "necessary" workers and were less and less likely to be employed in skilled jobs; for example, the proportion of machine wood-turners who were women fell from 11.7 percent in 1959 to 1.7 percent in 1965.[20] Women were more likely to be employed in services (they comprised three-quarters of such employees in the Soviet Union) than in industry, and those women who did work in industry were increasingly concentrated in unskilled support work in heavy industry and in production-line work in new light industries. Women were less well paid than men, earning less than 70 percent of male wages during the 1960s, and operated under stricter discipline. The relative efficiency of plants in which women acted under tight control may have subsidized the drunkenness, absenteeism and inefficiency of male-dominated industrial plants.[21]

Women's work was not necessarily a liberating experience, and it did not challenge the primacy of the family. As in the West, women rarely acceded to the highest positions and subtle sexual distinctions affected careers. Protective legislation excluded women from some skilled, and highly rewarded, industrial jobs, while they were allowed to do the most dirty and dangerous laboring jobs. Women, especially married women, had less time to study than men and consequently had fewer opportunities for advancement, and their work was seen as an addition, rather than an alternative, to family life. As in the West, working women had to undertake the bulk of domestic chores after they got home. Indeed, the peculiarities of Soviet society meant that they were worse off than their Western counterparts. The inefficiencies of state-owned shops made housekeeping more time-consuming – one study showed that the average Soviet housewife spent an hour a day standing in queues – while the poor performance of Soviet consumer industries meant that there were few labor-saving devices: only one person in ten owned a washing machine, and only one in fifty owned a vacuum cleaner. Soviet women did an average of four hours of housework a day while men did one and one-half hours. The average Soviet woman worker's contribution to housework amounted to 112 working days per year.[22]

After the communist seizure of power in eastern Europe, women entered the workforce in large numbers, but again their labors were a supplement to rather than a substitute for the family. Women rarely had the chance to challenge male authority in the workplace, and men were almost never obliged to take an equal share of responsibility at home.[23] In Poland, women were strongly represented in certain professions, notably medicine, and strongly underrepresented in others, such as engineering; less than one in fifty Polish student mechanics were women, while almost all of those preparing for careers in the textile industry were.[24] In East Germany, too, women were heavily represented in the medical profession, particularly in its least prestigious branch, pharmacy. In Hungary, in 1985, most students of economics, law and administration and almost all of those studying to be kindergarten teachers were women, while more than eight out of ten of those studying engineering were men.[25]

Official communist attitudes towards sexual matters became more liberal after 1953, but there was no return to the radicalism of the 1920s. The Soviet Union legalized abortion (banned in the 1930s), and most communist states enacted similar legislation, but such changes were not motivated by the desire for sexual freedom or increasing female autonomy. They sprang mainly from the desire to control birth rates, and the absence of any other means of birth control. Communist states could still be highly repressive when it suited them. Romania, where the regime wanted to increase birth rates, intruded into the private lives of its citizens to an extent unmatched by any other twentieth century state except Nazi Germany: abortion was made completely illegal in 1966, and couples with fewer than four children were obliged to complete questionnaires about their sexual habits. In any case, abortion was not necessarily a "freedom" for many women in communist countries. Poor medical care meant that legal abortions in the East could be as dangerous and unpleasant as illegal abortions in the West.

Far from marking a new challenge to the family, the post-Stalinist liberalization accompanied a strengthening of family life in communist countries. Stalin's death brought a wave of family reunions. Molotov's wife was one of the first inmates of the Soviet labor camps to be released (she returned to live with her former husband, although the two were never formally married again).

Increasing prosperity made it easier for families to occupy private apartments, although communal living remained an important part of life in the Soviet Union. The relation between family and material circumstances changed. Under Stalin, families had been dangerous – people could lose their liberty or their life for being married to a Trotskyist or the daughter of a kulak. Even Stalin's own relatives derived little physical security from their family. After 1953, the family became a means of access to prosperity rather than a source of danger. Communist societies were no longer shaken by purges, so the powerful stayed in place to guarantee their children's future. Nepotism and contacts became the key to social advancement.

Political disappointment made people ever more inclined to turn to their families. Waves of repression such as that which followed the suppression of the Hungarian uprising in 1956 or the Prague Spring in 1968 drove free discussion out of schools and newspapers, but they were never sufficiently severe to invade kitchens and bedrooms. The family home was often the only place in which people could talk with complete freedom. In the summer of 1968 a journalist interviewed a group of Czech workers about their political beliefs. All had been born after 1945, but they expressed enthusiasm for the political ideas of the first Czech Republic, which had ended in 1939. When the journalist asked them how they knew about a period that had been expunged from official records, they replied simply, "We have parents." When Czech teenagers in the mid-1960s were asked who had the strongest influence on their lives, almost all said their parents. None said the Czechoslovak Youth League.[26] Memories of repression were passed down in families; it is no accident that Mikhail Gorbachev married a woman whose father had been purged in the 1930s.

Families in communist Europe, however, were not always tranquil refuges from repression in the wider world. On the contrary, they could never entirely separate themselves from the wider society in which they lived. Work had an important impact on families, and particularly the role that men played in them. More affluent western Europeans worked relatively short hours at an intense pace, and saw a clear separation between the soulless efficiency of the factory where they worked and the family in which they enjoyed their leisure and for which they reserved most of their emotional energy. Working hours in the communist bloc were longer, and shift work and the lack of adequate childcare meant that couples sometimes barely saw each other. The very inefficiency of communist factories played an important part in the lives of their workers, as "work" involved a vast amount of hanging around. The factory was a place where one smoked, drank, gossiped and made friends, as well as a place where one earned money. The danger and discomfort of life in, say, Magnitogorsk meant that some workers felt a strong emotional attachment to their colleagues.

The violence of the public world often spilled over into the family, and the legacy of suffering from the Second World War and Stalinism could be passed on in families. Purge victims who had been broken in prison were reunited with children who had been toughened in state orphanages. Red Army veterans who had raped in Berlin returned to become fathers in Moscow. The Serbian politician Slobodan Milošević is the son of an Orthodox priest who suffered from psychological problems after the communist takeover; eventually Milošević's father, mother and maternal uncle committed suicide. Milošević's wife is obsessed with the desire to rehabilitate her mother (who was executed by partisans during the war). On a more banal level, millions of men who were confronted with humiliations and petty oppressions every day seem to have vented their frustrations at home. Domestic violence, especially against children, was high in the communist bloc and seems to have been especially common in countries, such as post-1956 Hungary, where the family had a large amount of autonomy – four-fifths of children in a Budapest school in the mid-1960s were beaten at home.[27]

The ubiquity of official "emancipation" in communist Europe concealed a wide range of practices and values in communist societies. Custom and religious practice remained important. In the Soviet Union, for example, family structure varied hugely from Estonia to Uzbekistan. The extent to which pre-communist habits could continue to influence was seen most strikingly in Albania, which was probably the communist regime that liberalized least after Stalin's death, but also a country where ordinary people's behavior and beliefs were heavily influenced by conceptions of honor that predated communism. This survival is illustrated in the novels of Ismail Kadaré; in *The Shadow*, the womanizing hero is disconcerted to find that one of his conquests at Moscow University is a virgin. Virginity, he remarks dryly, is a serious matter in my country. Just how seriously Albanians took female virginity was illustrated by an incident that occurred among the Catholic inhabitants of the northern mountains. In 1949, a member of the Sulejmani family made a girl from the Doda family pregnant. The boy's father began preparations for the appropriate punishment – burning both children alive – but the Doda family refused to hand over their daughter and apparently managed to smooth over the family differences. The peace lasted forty-five years until, in 1994, the Doda family attacked a Sulejmani wedding, killing three guests. In 1997, male members of the Doda family were holed up in their house awaiting a revenge attack. The vendetta had lasted forty-eight years – longer than the entire period of communist rule.[28]

Conclusion

If there was one single thing that united Europe in the early 1970s, it was the family, which was esteemed by the public authorities in both the capitalist West and the communist East. Marriage rates were higher than before the war. Such esteem did not simply mark the survival of "traditional" values. On the contrary, the family, particularly the nuclear family, in which a mother and father lived with their children, dominated European life in an unprecedented way. Before 1945, families had been challenged not only by sexual radicals but by fascists and communists, who believed that loyalty to party, state or race should supersede that to relatives. Even the reassertion of family values in the late 1930s had been driven, on a political level, by the need to increase birth rates and, on an individual level, by the desire to take refuge from a coming war. After 1945, and particularly during the 1960s, the family became valued for itself rather than simply as a means to an end, and, for many Europeans, it was the most important aspect of their lives to be rebuilt after the upheavals of fascism, war and, in the East, Stalinism. However, the discussion of "family values" concealed the range of different kinds of family in which Europeans lived. The family in Sicily was not the same as the family in London, and one in Prague was not the same as one in the Albanian hills. Most importantly, there was a difference between East and West. It was not simply a difference between the "feminism" of communist states and the "traditionalism" of Christian democracy; on the contrary, the hegemony of the family was beginning to be challenged in the West at a time when it was growing stronger in the East. Student radicals in Paris and Turin turned against the family in the demonstrations of 1968, while student radicals in Prague after the Warsaw Pact invasion placed more faith than ever in it. In the East, families were islands of freedom in a repressive society; in the West, families were seen – by some – as centers of repression in a free society.

PART IV

Who Won the Cold War?

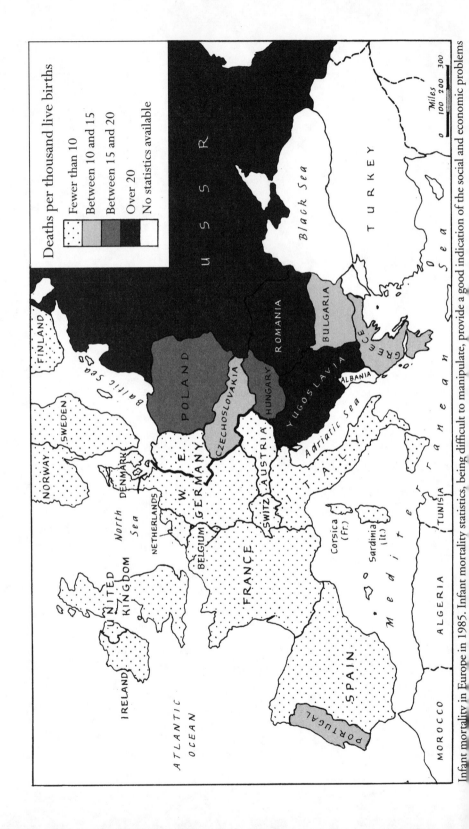

Infant mortality in Europe in 1985. Infant mortality statistics, being difficult to manipulate, provide a good indication of the social and economic problems

"Crisis: A serious rupture in the process of economic growth of capitalism. Crises are inextricably linked to the capitalist economy, and do not appear in any other socio-economic system."

Entry in Polish Universal Encyclopaedia (1965)

"St Paul's Square Clerkenwell. In 1870 the home of Lenin.* Now available to discerning capitalists everywhere. 1, 2, 3 bedroom apartments and duplexes available . . . Call today comrades and you could soon be living in the most sought-after area in London."

Advertisement in Financial Times, 21–22 March 1998

THE MID-1970S were a bad time for the West. The oil price rise of 1973–74 exacerbated long-term problems to bring about a reduction of economic growth, while the Watergate scandal and the resignation of President Nixon in 1974 made the leading power in the Western Alliance seem corrupt and confused. Most importantly, the withdrawal of American advisers in 1975 allowed the installation of a pro-Soviet regime in Saigon. Communist victory in the Vietnam war cheered radicals in the capitalist world, as the Vietcong provided the left with heroes at a time when the gray and aged members of the Soviet Politburo could no longer

---

* Lenin was born in 1870 and did not visit London until he was in his thirties. Presumably they mean Marx.

perform such a role. Vietnam had pitted brave but badly equipped guerrillas against the technology and wealth of the United States, and the atrocities of the Americans had been well publicized. The English journalist Julie Burchill recalls being woken by her father, a communist shop steward in Bristol, after the American departure from Saigon. He said simply, "We won."

Soviet power expanded as that of its enemies contracted. In addition to the new regime in Vietnam, Soviet clients in Angola benefited from Portuguese decolonization. The crisis of capitalist economies seemed not to affect the Soviet world; indeed, the Soviet Union expected to benefit from the rising price of oil, of which it was an exporter. Of course few intelligent people now believed that Soviet rule was benign, but Brezhnev and his associates were less vulnerable to the effects of public disillusionment than were their counterparts in the West. Communist rule was sufficiently authoritarian to secure obedience without being so obsessive as to require its subjects to believe in the regime's propaganda.

Things did not turn out as expected. Communist rule in eastern Europe, and in the Soviet Union itself, collapsed between 1989 and 1991, and the West provided the model that those who overthrew communism wished to imitate. The expansion of communist power, which had seemed a sign of success in the mid-1970s, weakened the Soviet Union. Moscow was now trying to operate a global policy involving far-flung satellite states. It became the epitome of what Paul Kennedy christened "imperial overstretch." Maintaining the empire cost money, but that was not the main problem – the Soviet Union's biased accounting may have caused its leaders to overestimate the scale of the aid and loans that it provided for its clients. The real issue was psychological. Soviet leaders became obsessed with the idea that they confronted an impossibly complicated set of interlocking problems. In 1987 Eduard Shevardnadze burst out in exasperation at a Defense Council meeting: "Is this the basis of our defense strategy? You want to fight practically the whole world."[1]

The Soviet Union's empire was odd. It involved an imperial power that was poorer than many of its colonies. Red Army soldiers stationed in Czechoslovakia or Hungary could hardly fail to notice that life was better in Prague or Budapest than it was in the godforsaken provinces from which many of them were drawn. In the 1980s, many Soviet citizens believed, wrongly, that Soviet food was exported to the eastern European communist states.[2] The acquisition of new spheres of influence during the 1960s and 1970s created a further drain on resources, which squeezed the comparatively wealthy countries of eastern Europe as well as the Soviet Union. Czechoslovakia was in the absurd position of owing Western banks $7.9 billion while having lent almost half this sum to Iraq, Syria,

Libya, Nicaragua and Cuba as part of a design to fit in with a Soviet-sponsored foreign policy. Shortly before the fall of communism, Miloš Jakeš, the Secretary of the Czech Communist Party, toured the Middle East in an unsuccessful attempt to secure the return of these loans.[3]

Loans and aid fed discontent with communism, doing so with particular force because "socialist internationalism" was such an important part of the communist self-image. Communist rulers tactlessly drew the attention of their subjects to the extent of support for extra-European movements, even when the rulers themselves were beginning to have doubts about such support. Questioning such internationalism inevitably led to a questioning of the system itself. When Timothy Garton Ash drank with workers in east Berlin in 1980, he was struck by the frequency with which they complained about the "solidarity" contributions deducted from their pay to subsidize Vietnam and Angola.[4]

Soviet problems of imperial overstretch were exacerbated in December 1979 when Soviet forces intervened to protect communist rulers in Afghanistan, where fighting was made difficult by the terrain and by the naïvete of Western governments, who provided Islamic guerrillas with advanced weapons. This meant a war that was to cost the lives of over 13,000 Red Army soldiers. Afghanistan also highlighted a larger problem for communist rule: Islam. Ever since its break with Israel in the late 1940s, the Soviet Union had allied with Islam and Arab nationalism, but the treatment of the Muslim population of the Soviet Union had not been good. The enormous wealth of Saudi Arabia and the rise of Muslim fundamentalism, particularly when it acquired a center after the Iranian revolution of 1979, provided Islam with new energy and confidence. Soviet planners were concerned by the fact that high birth rates among their Muslim population made the Red Army increasingly dependent on recruits whose loyalty they doubted.

In retrospect, Soviet fears do not appear well founded. Opposition to communist rule was most vigorous in the economically developed and secularized republics of the west, Estonia, Lithuania and the Ukraine. Elites in the Muslim republics adjusted to communist conformism remarkably well in spite of, or because of, the fact that communism seems to have impinged little on their private beliefs.[5] However, perestroika's emphasis on "modernity" made Soviet leaders feel ever more alienated from their Muslim population, and opening up to the West, which was itself gripped by a phobia of Islam in the 1980s, did nothing to allay their fears.[6]

Matters were made worse for the Soviet Union by the fact that its rivals in the West were divesting themselves of world commitments at the very moment that it was acquiring them. After Portuguese decolonization, no western European country had significant overseas possessions. Leninist theory had always assumed that there was a necessary link between capitalism and imperialism and, in view of this, it was disconcerting to see that countries such as France became more prosperous after giving up their empires. The shift also created a problem for communist propaganda: the Western powers had always been denounced as the "imperialists," yet now it was the Soviet Union that seemed, in Ronald Reagan's words, "the Evil Empire."

The Soviet Union's capacity to maintain its empire was undermined by economics, armaments, demography and vodka. The rise in oil prices proved less damaging to capitalism, and less beneficial to the Soviet Union, than had been expected – growth in the West slowed down, but it did not stop. The concentration of Western economies on high technology and consumerism in fact drew attention to the weaknesses of the communist ones. In the 1950s, it had been possible to argue that some Western systems, based on large corporations, heavy industry and state planning, were similar to those of the East. During the 1980s, when economic success in the West depended on speed, flexibility and innovation, this comparison no longer seemed plausible.

Economic decline fed a perception on the part of Soviet leaders that their military power was declining relative to that of the United States. In the 1980s it became increasingly difficult to sustain the separation between a military enclave and the rest of the economy. Strength was seen to depend on battlefield control systems, computers and communications, all of which required sophisticated electronic components, while simplicity, which might once have been considered a Soviet advantage, came to be viewed as a weakness.

The power of Soviet generals and the defense industry, which had once underwritten military strength, became a disadvantage. Western generals were forced, by pressure from civilians, to update their techniques, and defense industries were forced, by free-market competition, to maintain a certain level of efficiency. In the Soviet Union, by contrast, generals who had built reputations as tank commanders opposed change. Even when they advocated new approaches, they often faced resistance from economic planners who feared that a move towards "high-tech" armaments would make labor-intensive armaments industries redundant. Political liberalization in fact weakened Soviet capacity to modernize its armaments, because managers, fearful of public opinion, were reluctant to risk unemployment.[7]

Whether the failure of the Soviet army to embrace certain kinds of modernization had a real impact on the capacity of the Warsaw Pact to fight NATO is impossible to say. NATO's difficulties in Kosovo in 1999 suggested that sophisticated weaponry did not perform as well on the battlefield as on Nevada test sites. Given that both sides possessed nuclear weapons and the means to ensure that at least some of those weapons would reach their target, perhaps the Western emphasis on high-tech weaponry and the Soviet emphasis on tanks were both irrelevant. It might even be argued that the American reliance on high-tech weapons was a sign of weakness. Almost all the most sophisticated technologies were really defensive, being designed to prevent American casualties rather than to inflict casualties on the enemy, and this reflected an unwillingness to accept any losses at all, which did not bode well for American performance in a war against a serious opponent. By contrast, the appalling levels of brutality in the Soviet army might be interpreted as a sign of strength: generals who were indifferent when recruits were beaten to death by their own comrades were not likely to worry too much about the risk of losing men in battle. However, since the two sides never fought except in computer simulations (themselves an example of how technology affected Soviet self-perception), speculation about the real relative strength of the Red Army and its opponents is futile. What mattered was the fact that the Soviet leaders believed that their forces were falling behind in military terms, and this underpinned their general sense of crisis.

Oddly, declining tension between East and West at the end of the 1980s may have increased the sense of inferiority that dogged Soviet commanders. When both sides had believed in the risk of all-out war between them, matching the West was not necessarily important to the Soviet Union. Armies win by exploiting their own strengths, rather than by aping their opponents: technological and economic inferiority had not prevented the Red Army from defeating Nazi Germany. Declining tension brought two important changes. First, Soviet commanders had increasing contact with their counterparts in the West, and were therefore more able to compare the quality of their equipment. Second, "superpower" status was less likely to be measured by a capacity to engage in a hypothetical conflict with another "superpower" and more likely to be measured by an ability to conduct a broader range of conflicts against second-rank powers, which gave the greatest advantage to the sophisticated battlefield control systems of the Americans.

Concern about military decline was associated with concern about falling birth rates. In 1988, the number of young men available for military service was one quarter lower than in 1979.[8] The drop in birth rates was particularly severe among the Slavs, who made up the core of the empire and provided its most trusted troops. By contrast, birth rates remained high among the groups – particularly Muslims – that Soviet leaders trusted least. The non-Slav nationalities in the Soviet Union were not merely more numerous, but were also more assertive. Russians found their position in places that they had formerly regarded as their country to be increasingly uncomfortable. Uzbekistan had taken in 257,000 Slav immigrants between 1961 and 1970; between 1979 and 1989, 507,000 people returned from Uzbekistan to Russia. Even before anyone asked them to leave, the Russians were already going home.[9]

Demographic, economic and military problems were all linked to increasing consumption of alcohol. In the early 1980s it was estimated that more than one in thirty workers was an alcoholic and that almost one-fifth abused alcohol. The medical consequences of drink were particularly severe because Russians, unlike Czechs or Hungarians, derived their alcohol from vodka, rather than beer or wine, and sometimes resorted to even more dangerous substitutes. Liquor increased corruption by providing a hard currency in which bribes were paid. Drink also had humiliating effects on Soviet military power. A tank crew sold their vehicle to a Czech publican for "two crates of vodka and some pickles," while a defecting pilot told his Western interrogators that the MiG 25 fighter/bomber, the braking systems of which contained half a ton of alcohol, was known to ground crews as the "flying bar." The reform programs of Gorbachev and Andropov (who, unlike Brezhnev and Chernenko, were not heavy drinkers) hinged on a drive to cut alcoholism.[10] This caused great resentment, and a drop in state revenue, without having much impact on the livers of Soviet citizens. Sometimes it seemed as though a population that had endured Stalinism would rebel if faced with an interruption of the vodka supply. In December 1988, inmates at a special prison camp for drying out drunks in Magnitogorsk rioted.[11]

The collapse of authoritarian regimes in Spain, Portugal and Greece during the 1970s had looked like an opportunity for communism, which traditionally dominated the opposition in these countries. Portugal seemed briefly to hover on the brink of becoming a communist state, but once democracy was established it was social democracy rather than communism that became the leading force in all three countries. The collapse of authoritarian rule had important implications for the Soviet Union. First, it made western Europe seem a more attractive model for left-wingers – the labels "fascist" and "reactionary" had to be consigned to the dustbin of communist propaganda departments along with "imperialist." Second, it showed that it was possible to manage a peaceful transition from authoritarian to democratic rule. The lesson was not lost on dissidents and communist reformers.

The success of socialism in Spain, Portugal and Greece raises another important question: if communism lost, who won? On the simplest level the answer is clearly capitalism. All the communist states ultimately accepted private property and the market economy. The triumph, however,

should not be overstated. Capitalism was not uncontested or uncon-
strained. One of the most telling arguments of Soviet reformers was precisely that some western European states were more socialist than the Soviet Union.

If capitalism survived better than communism, it was not because it
had managed to avoid challenge but because it had adjusted to new circumstances. Sometimes capitalism thrived from the very changes that
weakened communism. This was true of technology. Capitalist countries
embraced the "total quality management" and "weightless economy"
produced by microchips, while communist attempts to catch up exposed
all the worst failings of centrally planned economies – rigidity and an
emphasis on quantity rather than quality.

Associated with new technologies and a new kind of economy was a
transformation of the elite. This transformation happened in both East
and West, but in the West it took place within the existing system while in
the East it began under communism but only ended after the fall of the
regime. In both parts of Europe, the new elite was better educated than its
predecessors, and was also educated in different ways. Engineering, once
the route to powerful positions in both continental Europe and in the
communist bloc, gave way to economics.[12] The hegemony of economists
was seen in the power that men such as Jeffrey Sachs (of Harvard) or
Gavyn Davies (of Goldman Sachs) wielded in the West and in the role
that figures such as Václav Klaus, Yegor Gaidar and Anatoly Chubais
played in the reform/destruction of communism. The new elite was also
marked by the increasing importance of economic power and the growing
autonomy of business leaders relative to political ones. Political contacts
remained important, especially in eastern Europe, but business leaders
took a more instrumental attitude to such contacts, exploiting political
links but not associating their whole position with a particular political
party. In Britain, the *Financial Times* advised its readers to vote Labour in
1992. In Hungary, four-fifths of economic leaders were members of the
Communist Party in 1987; a few years later less than a fifth of them were
members of any party at all.[13]

The most striking characteristic of the new elite was its relative
youth. The collapse of communism was, in large measure, a generational revolution, as a group that had been excluded from power by a
gerontocratic leadership finally came to the fore. In the West, by contrast, youth exercised greater power inside the existing system. This had
been true for some years. During the 1970s, only in Italy were political
and civil service leaders as old as their Soviet counterparts.[14] During the
1980s and 1990s the gap widened. Established leaders in the communist bloc stayed in post even when they became too decrepit to exercise

their functions, while western European political leaders became younger. Laurent Fabius became Prime Minister of France (and embraced a new degree of economic liberalism) at the age of thirty-seven. When John Major took office in 1990 he was, at forty-seven, the youngest British Prime Minister for over a century. His successor as Prime Minister was younger still, and his successor as leader of the Conservative Party was thirty-six.

Capitalism itself became closely associated with youth in two senses: the leadership of the most dynamic companies, particularly those associated with finance and computers, became younger, and capitalism absorbed the youth culture of rock music and fashion that was seen as such a threat on the other side of the Iron Curtain.

The increasing complexity of capitalist societies made life more difficult for those who opposed capitalism, just as the relative simplicity of the communist system encouraged opposition. Leninism emphasized will and power, so it was hard for communist leaders to evade responsibility when things went wrong. Capitalism emphasized impersonal forces. During the 1980s, Western governments insisted that they were not responsible for every economic development, and a high proportion of their citizens (including those who suffered worst) seem to have accepted those arguments. The contrast between the two systems can be illustrated by comparing the words "internationalism" and "globalization." Internationalism (used in the communist world) implied a conscious decision to intervene in faraway places, and consequently aroused resentment among the inhabitants of communist countries who felt that they suffered from the diversion of resources to prop up remote Third World movements. Globalization implied, by contrast, that developed capitalist countries were themselves unable to resist developments that transcended the control of any government.

The complexity of capitalism versus the relative simplicity of communism had important implications for the working class. Western European labor leaders were ruefully aware in the 1980s that the most successful and militant labor movement was to be found in a communist country (Poland). Industrialization meant that workers comprised an ever larger proportion of the Polish population, who were concentrated in large-scale heavy industries (mining, steel and shipbuilding), and were united by both race (Hitler and Stalin had made Poland ethnically homogeneous) and religion. The working class in the West was different. It was, for one thing, shrinking, as the importance of industry in the economy diminished. Large-scale heavy industry, which had been the center of labor power, was declining particularly fast. Immigration meant that race and religion divided workers. Poles had common grievances because of centrally imposed wages or prices, which united workers with the wider population, while western European workers had a more diverse range of interests, which meant that the grievances of one group rarely coincided with those of another. Public-sector workers were not directly hit by the economic downturns that affected their private-sector counterparts; workers in dynamic fields might be enjoying prosperity at the very moment when the regions of traditional heavy industry were enduring mass unemployment. Most importantly, workers in the West were less likely to translate economic grievances into a broader critique of the whole political system.

The position of dissident intellectuals also reveals much about the difference between opposition to communism and opposition to capitalism. During the 1970s and 1980s, the very term "dissident" came to be used with almost exclusive reference to communist countries, and many Western intellectuals looked admiringly at those who criticized the regime in eastern Europe and the Soviet Union. Of course, dissidents in the West had a much easier time than those in the East. In communist countries, they were usually excluded from higher education, but in the West critics of capitalism dominated some elite institutions of higher education. Education in the Soviet Union itself was a privilege that was reserved exclusively for politically reliable young people from the people's democracies, whereas in the United States it was open to any western European and a large number of European Marxists spent part of their time teaching at American universities. The Soviet Union arranged for its most vociferous critics to be confined in psychiatric hospitals; a western European government (that of France) arranged for a prominent Marxist (Louis Althusser) to be kept out of a psychiatric hospital even after he strangled his wife.

The fact that dissidents in the East had harder lives than those in the West contributed to their influence. Eastern European dissidents had the attention and moral authority that went with persecution, while western European Marxists found themselves in the ludicrous position of being subsidized and protected by the regime that they criticized. Eastern European intellectuals were faced with a simple moral choice: either they supported the regime or they did not, and, if they did not, they united with other anti-regime intellectuals. Western European intellectuals, by contrast, had a confusing range of choices. Some who had once been Marxists, such as Annie Kriegel or François Furet, swung to support liberalism or social conservatism. Others moved on to new forms of radicalism, which stressed gender, race or culture rather than, or as well as, class. Often the fiercest and most incomprehensible debates were those that divided left-wing intellectuals from each other.

Attention to dissidents raises the question of will. Who wanted the changes that came about in both East and West during the 1980s and after? Were those who wanted change the same as those who brought it about, and, if so, did they benefit from it? In parts of eastern Europe, the advocates, agents and beneficiaries of change overlapped substantially. Here, communism fell because a large proportion of the population actively wanted a different kind of society and took steps to bring it about. Most of those who had joined Solidarity or demonstrated in Wenceslas Square believed that their own situation was better after the fall of communism, and probably regarded the even greater benefits drawn by some ex-communist apparatchiks as a small price to pay for the transition. In the Soviet Union itself, communism fell in different circumstances. For communist leaders in Prague, Berlin and, especially, Warsaw, the problem during the 1980s was the active desire of their citizens for change; for Soviet leaders, the problem in the 1980s was apathy rather than activism: they worried about alcoholism and absenteeism rather than unofficial trade unions or human rights' groups. Soviet communism fell not because of revolution from below but rather because a confused and contradictory program of reform from above was followed by a failed counterrevolution. In the USSR only a small group of dissidents wished to end the communist monopoly of power, and, even among dissidents, few dared hope for change as rapid or dramatic as that which occurred in 1991. It was the leadership of the Communist Party itself that brought this end about (although they did so unintentionally) and it was a group of well-connected entrepreneurs who drew the greatest benefits from the change.

Of course, the relation between the advocates, agents and beneficiaries of change was complicated. Communist leaders may not, at first, have been advocates of change, but they (or at least the leaders of the Soviet, Polish and Hungarian parties) all learned something from dialogue with dissidents, who certainly were. Similarly, the relations between the agents and beneficiaries of change were complicated by the fact that some communists did so well in the post-communist regime. Communist regimes were not deliberately brought down by their own leaders, but their downfall was certainly facilitated by the fact that some elements of the communist leadership (particularly its younger and lower-level members) realized that their material position could be protected, and perhaps enhanced, under capitalism.

The distinction between advocates, agents and beneficiaries is also useful for understanding the advance of capitalism. The most enthusiastic advocates of capitalist interests were on the right, which associated free enterprise with a cultural conservatism in matters of race, religion and the family, but the triumph of the free market was accompanied by a continual retreat of the political right. Right-wing authoritarian regimes in Europe collapsed, and socialist parties gained more influence in Europe during the 1980s and were to make even greater gains after the fall of communism. By the 1990s, the major families of the European right – Italian Christian democracy, French Gaullism, British Conservatism – were all in crisis. More generally, capitalist triumph was often accompanied by the kind of cultural change that conservatives deplored.

The relationship between the changing nature of capitalism in the West and the fall of communism in the East can be illuminated through comparison of the most prominent communist reformer, Mikhail Gorbachev, and the most vociferous political advocate of capitalism, Margaret Thatcher. The two leaders faced similar problems when they came to power: both ruled states that had built their identities on imperial power but now found themselves weakened by economic decline (although the decline of Britain was merely relative), and both sought to revive the fortunes of the state with a program of ambitious, wide-ranging and slightly confused reform. For Gorbachev, increased political liberalism was one small part of his program, but it acquired a momentum of its own and ultimately destroyed the very values that he had started out to defend. For Thatcher, economic liberalism was one small part of her program, which also acquired a momentum of its own and ultimately destroyed the very values that she had set out to defend. The history of Europe in the late 1980s and early 1990s needs to be written in terms of the transformation of capitalism as much as in terms of the failure of communism.

1
HOW COMMUNISM LOST

"We have no need to change our policy. It is correct and truly Leninist. We have to pick up speed and move forward [to] . . . our radiant future."
Mikhail Gorbachev to Soviet Politburo, 1985[1]

IN SOME WAYS it is deceptive to talk about the fall of communism. There were many different falls in different parts of Europe. Nine communist regimes came to an end between 1989 and 1991, while the Soviet Union itself fragmented into its constituent republics and in each one of these the endgame of the regime was played out in a different way.

The fall of the regime was most dramatic in Czechoslovakia, Romania and the German Democratic Republic; in these countries, repressive governments were overthrown quickly in late 1989, and in all cases the overthrow seemed to owe something to popular feeling. In Prague, there were demonstrations in Wenceslas Square and similar gatherings occurred in Berlin and Leipzig. The Romanian case was most bizarre of all. A crowd in Bucharest, convoked by the authorities to listen to a speech by Ceauşescu, after demonstrations had been violently suppressed in the town of Timişoara, suddenly began to chant anti-regime slogans. Ceauşescu and his wife attempted to flee, but were captured and then executed on Christmas Day after a summary trial.

Cursory autopsies suggest that these sudden deaths occurred in different ways. Czechoslovakia and East Germany both had influential, if small, dissident movements, which helped to avoid violence. Czechoslovakia had credible leaders, Alexander Dubček and Václav Havel, who assumed power after the old regime fell. East Germany was quickly integrated into West Germany's political structures. Romanian dissent had been ruthlessly crushed, and the men who formed the new government had in fact been prominent members of the Communist Party under Ceaușescu. In Romania, it seems likely that the sudden collapse of the regime was stage-managed from within the elite. The crowd was the hero of the play in Prague and Berlin; in Bucharest, it was an extra with a walk-on part.

Communism in Hungary and Poland died more slowly and with greater dignity. In both cases, the transfer of power had been preceded by a long period of reform, as communist leaders negotiated with their successors in "round tables" before agreeing to give up power. The origins of Hungarian reform could be traced back to the 1960s, and change had been initiated largely from above. Polish reform sprang from pressure applied from below by the Solidarity trade union, founded in September 1980. In Poland, reform was linked to a movement of emotional nationalism; in Hungary, reform was associated with a cool materialism and an insistence on Hungary's weak international position.

Reform in Hungary and Poland accelerated in unexpected directions. Retrospective interpretations of events are very different from those that most people gave at the time. Thus, for example, many saw General Wojciech Jaruzelski's declaration of martial law in 1981 as a rerun of Hungary in 1956, as soldiers were used to suppress a popular movement. By the mid-1980s, the declaration looked more like a rerun of Poland in 1956, when the Polish government had persuaded the Soviet Union that it was capable of dealing with opposition in its own way, without military assistance. In the early 1990s, it was possible to argue that the declaration of martial law was really a rerun of 1926 (Piłsudski's coup d'état), in which an authoritarian, nationalist soldier took over the government.

Communism in Albania, Bulgaria and Yugoslavia was neither overthrown by a sudden burst of popular pressure nor smothered by a slow process of reform. The communist elites themselves managed the transition to democracy (or at least to something that might pass for democracy), but it did not involve any real dialogue with opposition. Communist rulers changed their party labels and embraced demagogic nationalism as a means of remaining in power.

The end of communism in the Soviet Union had elements of all the processes described above. As General Secretary of the Soviet Communist Party from 1985, Mikhail Gorbachev embarked on reforms that resembled those of Hungarian and Polish leaders, but Soviet communism, unlike its Hungarian or Polish equivalent, was not negotiated out of power. Gorbachev himself seems to have turned away from some of the more radical elements of the reform program in the winter of 1990–91, but even this was not enough to appease conservatives in the Soviet leadership.

In August 1991, a group of plotters, mainly in the KGB and the army, staged a coup and Gorbachev was seized at his Crimean villa. From then on events in the Soviet Union resembled those in Czechoslovakia, East Germany and Romania. A repressive communist leadership confronted popular demonstrations and was eventually overthrown by them, mainly, in the Soviet case, because most of the army refused to support the coup. The collapse of communism in the Soviet Union also had a third dimension, which resembled the collapse in the Balkan states: as the Union broke up into its constituent republics, local Communist Party leaders managed and manipulated the shift away from communism with new political etiquettes in order to ensure that they remained in power. The continuity was particularly marked in the Asian republics, and it could also be seen in the Russian Federation, where Boris Yeltsin had been President since May 1990. Yeltsin himself was both a heroic defender of democracy – the man who climbed onto a tank outside the Russian parliament in 1991 to harangue its crew – and a former Communist Party apparatchik who seems to have derived considerable material benefits from the end of communism.

For all the differences and unexpected turns of events, the fall of communism should not be explained simply as a succession of unrelated accidents. Communist leaders and their opponents may have acted in different ways but they were all, to some extent, reacting to the same kind of problems. The first of these, like most problems in communist Europe, came from Moscow.

Perestroika

Mikhail Gorbachev, who became General Secretary of the Soviet Communist Party in March 1985, seemed more pragmatic and liberal than any of his predecessors, but he had spent his whole life serving Soviet communism, his rapid rise suggested that he had never given his superiors cause to doubt his loyalty, and his most important patron had been Yuri Andropov, a former head of the KGB and the Soviet ambassador to Budapest who had coordinated the repression of the Hungarian uprising in 1956. Gorbachev reformed to make the Soviet system stronger rather than to weaken it. Eventually his liberalization began to diminish his own authority and thus, paradoxically, his capacity to promote liberalization, but in the first few years of his leadership his influence increased as he placed his own supporters in important positions, and he also had the enormous power that went with command of the Red Army.

From 1985 to 1991 the policies of the Soviet leadership were described as "perestroika" (restructuring). The word is deceptive, implying that there was one coherent program of reform; the truth is that a variety of different, sometimes mutually counteracting, policies were applied, and the most dramatic changes usually sprang from Moscow's failure rather than its success.

The first problem for Moscow was one of power. Although perestroika was associated with a lessening of East/West tension, Soviet leaders were driven to reform partly by the feeling that they were slipping behind the NATO countries in terms of military power. The Soviet Union could equal its rivals in the production of nuclear bombs and the ballistic missiles that delivered them, but it could not match them in the "smart" technologies based around computers and lasers that increasingly dominated strategic thinking. The Strategic Defense Initiative or "Star Wars" program, announced by the United States in 1983, caused particular alarm among Soviet generals. Curiously, keeping up with the West militarily meant turning away from the purely military sphere. The Soviet Union had to improve its economy in order to be able to support military spending and to improve its high technology industries to match American armaments.

The other element of the economic crisis that confronted the Soviet Union in the mid-1980s affected living standards. In absolute terms, these were higher than ever before, but a slowdown in economic growth meant that expectations of increasingly available consumer goods were not being met. The rural population, still in a majority in some Asian republics, had relatively low expectations,[2] but the population of Russia and the western republics was now mainly urban, relatively well educated and increasingly interested in the kind of comforts that west Europeans took for granted. Under Stalin, this would not have mattered, because simple repression would have prevented discontent from being shown, but the Soviet Union in the 1980s was a more open society. Ordinary people had more chance to compare their living standards with those in the West and to complain about the difference.

Gorbachev's reforms were designed to create an economy that would compete with capitalism without simply imitating it. This was easier said than done. Soviet leaders lurched from one policy to another, and "reform" often exacerbated the problems that it was designed to solve. Increased economic incentives encouraged resentment among the less productive while failing to satisfy the successful, and enterprises were encouraged to take risks without being made fully responsible for the consequences of failure, because they knew that the state would bail them out. The campaign against "corruption," epitomized by the law on "unearned income" of July 1986, meant that one arm of the state often suppressed the very free enterprise that other arms of the state were trying to encourage. Most importantly, increasingly rigorous economic study meant that Soviet leaders themselves were more aware of the scale of the problems that confronted them.

The state itself became more divided and confused. In Moscow, young academic economists drew up ambitious schemes to restructure the economy, while at provincial level power remained in the hands of party bosses who did not countenance any changes that might weaken their own power. Reform often created all the anarchy of capitalism without its corrective mechanisms. Power was taken away from the state without being given to consumers or shareholders, so managers were left answerable to no one. The breakdown of central control meant that companies and local authorities held back ever larger proportions of their production to be used in chaotic barter operations.

Economic restructuring was accompanied by political changes. The Soviet Union never had an uncensored press or free elections and the Communist Party had no intention of surrendering its monopoly of power, but speech did become freer, which meant that discontent was expressed more openly. Contested elections (though not multiparty ones) were held from January 1987. Most importantly, the republics that made up the Soviet Union acquired a new degree of autonomy, exploited first by the Baltic states and then by Boris Yeltsin in Russia itself. All this created further contradictions in perestroika. Power was devolved either to those who did not believe in the reform program envisaged by Moscow at all, or to those who wished to pursue reform to an extent that Moscow had never anticipated.

Soviet reform had implications for other countries. The Brezhnev doctrine of military intervention where necessary had been replaced by what a Foreign Ministry spokesman called "the Sinatra doctrine" of letting satellite countries do it "their way." This was not necessarily good news for those who loved freedom. The Soviet Union respected the autonomy of tyrants such as Ceauşescu as much as that of relatively liberal communist rulers such as Kádár; indeed, those most obviously threatened by Moscow's new line were liberal communists. It was they, in Hungary and Poland, who had tolerated a relatively high degree of debate while hinting to their subjects that exceeding certain limits might trigger Soviet intervention.

It is harder to explain why communism collapsed in the illiberal communist countries (Czechoslovakia, the GDR, Bulgaria and Romania). Some of these regimes looked well equipped to survive. The first two were in better economic shape than the USSR and were unburdened by pretensions to superpower status; the latter two were so repressive that popular discontent seemed to pose no threat to their rulers. Perhaps if such regimes had been left to survive on their own twenty years previously, they would have devised a form of communist autarky, but by the 1980s socialist internationalism had done its work too well to allow the survival of isolated communist regimes. Subjects of the different communist states knew too much about each other.

The leaders of most communist states were old, tired and conventional men, lacking the energy and conviction with which communist states had been built in the 1940s and 1950s. The loss of Soviet support was a crucial blow to their sense of themselves. Significantly, communist rule lasted for longest in Albania, which had broken with the USSR in the 1960s, and in Romania, which had always displayed a certain independence with regard to the Soviet Union. The chances that communist governments would survive were also reduced by the complexity of the administrative machines on which they were based. Communism was no longer controlled by a determined revolutionary vanguard, but was built on a large number of intermediate elites – soldiers, managers and party bureaucrats. This group, more than the upper leadership of the party, decided that communism was no longer worth defending. The fact that it did so can be explained neither simply by pressure from below nor by reform from above. It was the result of interaction between government and people rather than the victory of one over the other.

Dissidents

The period from the mid-1970s until the early 1990s saw the triumph of the "dissidents" – intellectuals who opposed communist rule or some aspects of it. Such people moved from exile or prison to the center of politics. The playwright Václav Havel had written to the Czech President Gustáv Husák in 1975 in an open letter that complained about the lack of freedom in his country. It seemed a brave but futile gesture – as did Havel's subsequent activity in the Charter 77 movement to ensure observance of the Helsinki Final Act that promised respect for human rights – yet in 1990 Havel himself became President of Czechoslovakia. The novelist Alexander Solzhenitsyn, banished from the Soviet Union in 1974, made a triumphal return to Russia in 1994. The physicist Andrei Sakharov, sent into internal exile in Gorky in 1980, was released only in 1986; by the time he died in 1989, he was a member of the Assembly of People's Deputies, and the General Secretary of the Soviet Communist Party came to sign the book of condolences.

Why did dissidents matter so much? The first answer to this question lies west of the Iron Curtain. Communist apologists were right to argue that "dissidents" had been created by the West. Works that were often banned in their authors' own countries became best-sellers in Britain, France, Germany and the United States. Dissidents appealed to the fashion-conscious intellectuals in western European capitals, who were sometimes the very people who had supported communism a couple of decades earlier. The biannual Venice festival of 1977 was dedicated to eastern European culture, and in the same year the General Secretary of the Soviet Communist Party dined in the Elysée Palace while Jean-Paul Sartre and Simone de Beauvoir attended a gala evening in honor of Russian dissidents.[3]

Dissidents exemplified the very qualities that seemed to be missing in the West. Western intellectuals were bombarded with new ideas and opportunities to communicate those ideas. Conservatives talked of the need to reassert a "canon" of great writing and a core of moral belief in an age of relativism. Curiously, the comforting certainties of intellectual life were more secure in the communist world than in the West. Difficult access to books meant that attention in eastern Europe remained focused on a narrow range of "great literature." Philip Roth, returning from a visit to Czechoslovakia in the early 1970s, said: "There nothing goes and everything matters – here [the United States] everything goes and nothing matters."[4]

The difference between the communist and the noncommunist world was illustrated by the fate of the Czech philosopher Julius Tomin. "Flying university" classes on Greek philosophy, conducted in his apartment, were frequented by eminent Western philosophers, and eventually Tomin was exiled. He settled in Oxford, where he claimed that the enforced leisure created by his exclusion from official academic life had given him time to read texts with particular attention and that he had noticed that many Western interpretations of Greek philosophy contained elementary errors. At this point, Tomin's English patrons became less enthusiastic about him, and he finished his career lecturing in a pub. Tomin's son Lukáš, who lived from 1963 to 1995, wrote a novel that captured the sense of dislocation that could afflict a dissident removed from the reassuring routine of a repressive state. The hero of *Kye* lives a life of squalor and drunkenness in north London. All the standard dissident references are in this work. The hero longs for Paris and he lives on the fringes of rock culture with Lou ("who wasn't Reed") and a man who once played with David Byrne. He misses the urgency of life in communist Prague, where "someone was always loved, or arrested or beaten up."[5]

The small size of many eastern European states and the concentration of intellectual life on their capital cities meant that intellectuals in these countries often knew each other personally as well as knowing each other's work. This was particularly true in Prague. The difficulty of publication meant that books that did get into print assumed particular importance. Samizdat texts were devoured by readers who were attentive to every nuance.

The dissidents who attracted such admiration in the West were never a unified group: it would be hard to imagine two individuals with less in common than Alexander Solzhenitsyn and Václav Havel. Many dissidents regarded the label imposed on them by Western journalists with impatience. They felt that an obsession with their political stance distracted attention from their real role as artists or scholars. Havel complained about the propensity of émigrés to "decipher" eastern European writing in an overly political way.[6] Ivan Klíma became positively exasperated when Western journalists asked him about his views on politics,[7] and Milan Kundera talked of his disappointment that "people read me as a political document."[8]

Attention to the writings and ideas of dissidents also risks obscuring the importance of the context in which they operated. It consisted, first of all, in a degree of tolerance on the part of the state, so in this sense dissidence was a response to change in communist rule as much as a means of promoting change. Explicit opposition would have been impossible between 1948 and 1953. Degrees of tolerance varied from one communist country to another. The Soviet Union's abuse of psychiatric hospitals and the exclusion of troublesome people from certain cities made life particularly awkward for independently minded intellectuals. By the mid-1980s, Soviet dissidents seemed to have been removed from the consciousness of their own compatriots. As liberalization began men like Sakharov had an influence on the educated, and notably on Gorbachev himself, but they never attracted the interest of a wide public. As late as March 1991, most Soviet citizens were unable to name a single dissident or even define the word.[9] Hungary and Poland were the most tolerant countries in the Eastern Bloc, and, by the 1980s, it was possible for a Hungarian writer to build an entire career on discreetly tolerated samizdat publications. The possibilities for dissident intellectuals were not defined simply by government attitudes. Geography and economics could be as important as politics. Czechoslovakia was more repressive than Hungary or Poland, but it was also a small, relatively prosperous country in which cultural life was focused on the capital city. Life was much easier for a dissident writer in Prague, even if he had to clean windows for a living, than for his counterpart in the Soviet Union, who was likely to be sent to a closed city hundreds of miles from the nearest library.

Dissident intellectuals counted for nothing on their own. They became important only when they attracted interest from other groups that had more direct means of exercising power. In Poland, support came from the working class, which was mobilized by the Solidarity trade union and the

Church. In Hungary, a kind of backing came from the party itself, which tolerated a degree of debate. Czechoslovak intellectuals lacked help from either quarter, but did benefit from the interest of many in America, France and Britain. Such support came partly from the efforts of Josef Skvorecky in Canada to publish and publicize the writings of his compatriots: he compiled a dictionary of 500 banned writers in Czechoslovakia.[10] It also came partly from the fact that Czech intellectuals were usually multilingual – Havel, whose education had been interrupted by the advent of communism, was the only major figure unable to communicate in English, French or German – and were keen to assert their membership in a western European cultural community. Finally, it came from the fact that Prague was a beautiful city that attracted journalists more easily than, say, Bucharest.

The political attitudes of dissidents varied as much as, and because of, the contexts in which they operated. The Soviet dissident Andrei Amalrik argued that there were three perspectives from which communist regimes could be criticized: reformist Marxism, Christianity and liberal democracy. Reformist Marxism was influential in the early stages of communist liberalization, partly because reformers had access to official means of communication – a point stressed by Leszek Kołakowski, himself a Marxist professor at the University of Warsaw until 1968.[11] Reformist Marxism reached its peak in Czechoslovakia under Dubček in 1968, but it continued to be important in Hungary. Christianity counted for most in Poland and in the Soviet Union itself, though the political meanings of Russian Orthodoxy and Roman Catholicism were very different. Support for liberal democracy was strongest in Czechoslovakia – the only communist country with much experience of such a regime.

Dissent rarely meant outright condemnation of communist rule. In part, this was for reasons of simple prudence; dissidents tried to work within the limits that the regime allowed. Furthermore, few dissidents adopted the stance of unqualified opposition that had characterized attitudes towards earlier tyrannies. Intellectuals in the more tolerant countries of eastern Europe had three particularly strong reasons to regard the communist rule of the 1970s and 1980s as a lesser evil: it was less evil than communist rule in the Soviet Union itself; it was less evil than communist rule in eastern Europe before the death of Stalin; and it was less evil than Nazism. Jews were especially influenced by the memory of Nazism. Ivan Klíma never forgot that the happiest moment of his life was when a Soviet tank crashed through the barbed wire of the Terezín concentration camp where his family was imprisoned.[12]

One result of the perception that communist rule was not as evil as Nazism was that very few intellectuals allowed their lives to be entirely taken over by fighting communism or by any other form of political activity. Many of them were suspicious of all ideologies, and this underlay the reluctance of many anti-regime intellectuals to identify themselves in exclusively political terms. Timothy Garton Ash, citing Thomas Mann's remark that writing about trees was "almost a crime" under Nazism because it implied silence about "so many horrors," wrote: "But are the 'horrors' of the Honecker regime really such as to demand the concentrated artistic attention of the exiled writer? Many of my friends in East Germany would answer no. Indeed, they would rather talk about trees."[13]

Even when dealing with political matters, dissident writers rarely presented matters in a simple light. The West may have seen them as beacons of moral and aesthetic certainty, but they accepted ambiguity and doubt. They were often preoccupied with new issues of ecology or non-European politics, which transcended the communist/noncommunist divide. On one of the many occasions when the Soviet authorities arrested Andrei Amalrik, he was standing outside the British embassy in Moscow protesting about the British delivery of weapons to Biafra.

In one sense, all this limited the effectiveness of dissident intellectuals: they did not present clear rallying cries. In another sense, it was the very emphasis on complexity and ambiguity that made dissidents effective. They did not bring any communist regime down; a determined government with the backing of the army could have had all troublesome intellectuals rounded up and shot in a few days. What dissidents did was influence the way in which regimes fell, which can be seen by comparing the fate of those countries that had important dissident groups – Poland, Hungary, Czechoslovakia and East Germany – with those that did not – Bulgaria, Romania and Albania. The transition in the former countries was smoother and democracy was established more firmly than in those in the latter group. The difference was not exclusively due to intellectual opposition. The countries that fared best were the wealthiest ones, the ones that had had the strongest traditions of democracy in the precommunist period and the ones where communist rule had been most liberal. Yet dissidents were important because they made use of these advantages; it was they who exploited and illustrated liberalization and kept alive the memory of pre-communist traditions.

Dissident intellectuals showed communist rulers that there was a group outside the party with which they could negotiate. In order for communism to fall peacefully, both sides had to show that there would be no repeat of Hungary in 1956, which meant no repression from the regime, but also no lynchings by angry crowds. In Poland and Czechoslovakia, leaders who emerged from the dissident movement were able to ensure that the transition from communism took place without violence.

The overthrow of communism was most violent in Romania, where dissent had been ruthlessly suppressed.

Perhaps the most important effects of dissident activity were felt after communism had fallen. The fact that the foundations of an alternative had been laid meant that it was easier to establish a multiparty system. The states where dissidence had been strong almost all had a period of noncommunist rule immediately after 1989, which, in turn, gave the Communist Party a *cure d'opposition*. It forced communists to rethink their principles and shook out some of the party's most cynical members, who had no interest in an organization that did not have access to the spoils of power. A period of opposition rule also gave the communists a legitimate function as critics of market reform. In countries where there was no alternative leadership – Romania, Albania and Bulgaria – the communist parties remained in power under different names and with slightly different leaderships. In these circumstances, the government often became little more than a cover for the rapacious exploitation of state resources and concealment of past crimes.

The difficulty of dissident life brought a high degree of political maturity. Many knew that democracy would not provide easy answers and that the key to successful politics was that argument should be conducted in a civilized way, rather than that unity should be achieved. Kundera expressed this point of view in 1968, stressing that Czechoslovakia was "going towards new conflicts but conflicts of ideas not conflicts between ideas and their suppression."[14] Even the apoliticism of some dissidents was useful in this respect. The revolutions of 1989 – at least in Hungary, Czechoslovakia, Poland and East Germany – had the advantage of limited expectations. No one talked of "new men" or the Robespierrian incorruptibility of the true revolutionary. It was understood that politics was not an end but simply a means of earning freedom to do something else.

Workers

In much of eastern Europe and the Soviet Union, the working class was a product of communism. The communists built up the working class because they believed that it would provide a natural reservoir of support, and regarded the peasantry, which had previously composed much of the population, as innately reactionary. In retrospect, this looks odd. Peasants were natural conservatives, who generally accepted whatever regime was imposed on them and had little means to protest even if they did not. They might try to swindle the authorities, but they did not organize against the state.

The working class, by contrast, was a source of endless trouble. Timothy Garton Ash pointed out that a working-class quarter of Berlin, which had been a communist stronghold under Weimar, was now marked by the lack of enthusiasm with which its inhabitants participated in elections.[15] Workers joined the Hungarian uprising of 1956 and, to the surprise of its leaders, supported the Prague Spring in 1968. Most importantly, the Polish working class registered its dissatisfaction through strikes and riots in 1956, 1970 and 1976 and in the early 1980s gave enormous support to the independent Solidarity trade union that emerged in the Lenin Shipyards at Gdansk under the leadership of an electrician, Lech Wałesa.

The working-class movement in the East succeeded just when its counterpart in the West faltered. In part, this difference was linked to the more general economic reverses of communism. Communist regimes never delivered the consumer affluence that blunted labor indignation in the West. Class consciousness was easier to maintain in the communist world than in the West. A large part of the communist economy consisted of the large-scale, male-dominated heavy industries that were disappearing in the West. Workers in capitalist countries faced a system of incomprehensible complexity. Those who governed them, those who fixed the prices of the goods they bought, and those who paid their wages were all drawn from different groups. Subcontracting, short-term contracts and convoluted corporate structures meant that many workers had a limited idea of who owned the company for which they worked. Matters were simpler in the East. Labor relations were authoritarian, and the hierarchies of state, party and industrial management ran in parallel. A Polish law of October 1975 specifically authorized employers to deduct up to a quarter of a worker's salary for various offenses.[16] Every worker knew that a decision to raise prices, freeze wages or increase work norms was ultimately authorized by the communist leaders themselves, and, in case he should be in any doubt about who these people were, the regime helpfully plastered factory walls with posters showing their names and photographs.

Workers avoided some of the petty compromises and hypocrisies that overshadowed the lives of white-collar employees. They did not worry about the "political marks" that were necessary to enter university, or about whether party membership would increase their chances of promotion. The nature of manual work spared its practitioners from some of the more onerous attentions of the party: it was hard to argue that a riveter's production would be improved if he had a better understanding of Marxism. Many workers gave up all pretence of believing in the system. In Czechoslovakia, nine out of ten students at academic schools were members of the communist youth organization; among apprentices and young workers, the figures were much lower.[17] In October 1984, one-third of students in Leipzig said that they felt "strongly attached" to the regime; among apprentices, the figure was less than one-fifth.[18]

Such experiences were common to workers everywhere in the Eastern Bloc, but with one important distinction. Workers in most countries showed their feelings about the regime through surliness, withdrawal from party institutions and informal resistance – absenteeism and slow working – but their protest was rarely organized. The culture of apathetic resignation was particularly marked in the two countries that had strong industrial, and hence working-class, traditions stretching back before 1945 – Czechoslovakia and Germany. It may have been precisely because the working class was long established that it was reluctant to confront the regime directly; workers in these countries had the "realism" that came from the collective memory of past defeats. The memory was particularly strong in Germany, where there were still many workers who had been formed by the Hitler Youth.[19]

The great exception to the apathy of the working class under communism was found in Poland. Polish workers benefited from the strength of the Church, which provided a rallying point to unite workers with other groups, and also gained, though this was not always obvious at the time, from the strength of the Polish army, which meant that Polish workers, unlike their German, Hungarian and Czech counterparts, had never faced Soviet tanks. Most of all, Solidarity was built on the relative youth of the Polish working class. The rapid expansion of industry in a formerly peasant nation created a working class that was not yet used to defeat. Solidarity had an optimism and an enthusiasm that could not be found anywhere else in Europe. The rapid expansion of industry cemented links between Church and nation – far from abandoning the Church when they arrived in the city, workers clung to an institution that offered some continuity in a novel and confusing world. The open-air mass in the Gdansk shipyards fitted into this working-class culture as naturally as moaning in the pub fitted into that of Czechoslovakia.

Churches

The *modus vivendi* between communist regimes and Christian churches, which had been established in the 1970s, broke down in the 1980s. It was upset from both above and below. From above, Pope John Paul II, elected in 1978, commanded great respect in parts of eastern Europe, especially in his native Poland, and was less ready than his immediate predecessors to compromise with communism. From below, increasing numbers of ordinary believers began to question the deference that the Church hierarchy in their own countries displayed towards the regime.

People were attracted to the Church precisely because it provided a forum for relatively free discussion, and sometimes the regime itself drove dissident activity into the Church. The East German government's habit of refusing politically suspect students the right to study any subject other than theology produced a cohort of dynamic and independent-minded pastors.[20] In some cases, turbulent priests went well beyond the wishes of their superiors. Gyorgy Bulanyi, a Catholic priest in Hungary who preached against compulsory military service, was denounced by both the Vatican and his own national hierarchy, which eventually requested his transfer to another country.[21]

Religious influence was most obvious in Poland, where the Pope excited wild enthusiasm from a population that was already devout. Polish Catholicism escaped the problems that afflicted religion elsewhere. It held on to the support of men as well as women, the young as well as the old, and workers as well as the peasantry. The capacity to recruit priests, an indicator of the Church's decline almost everywhere else, showed no sign of falling in Poland, and a survey among young people in 1983 showed that the priesthood was regarded as the third most desirable profession (after medicine and law). In the late 1980s, almost a third of all priests ordained in Europe came from Poland.[22] Such signs of devotion did not necessarily mean that Poles obeyed all the Church's teaching. Perhaps because the Church was so associated with Polish national identity, Poles regarded its authority over private morals as less binding than did Western Catholics – the abortion rate was reckoned to amount to almost a million a year during the 1980s.[23]

The influence of religion in secularized countries such as Czechoslovakia and the German Democratic Republic was lower, though the Protestant churches of the GDR benefited from the 2.2 billion marks of subsidy that they obtained from the Federal Republic between 1970 and 1989.[24] There were considerable differences in the kind of influence that churches were able to exercise in the communist bloc. Protestantism had traditionally been least willing to confront the state, but, in the 1980s, Protestant churches in East Germany were often the most important centers of criticism of the regime and in Romania and Hungary evangelical Protestant cults achieved some success. Sometimes, Protestantism's lack of central structure, which had made it reluctant to challenge the regime, made it more liable to engage in confrontation once such a challenge had begun. Catholic priests, by contrast, were always reminded by their own hierarchy that political opposition was not an end in itself and that the interests of the Church were more important than those of any political movement.

Church criticism of communist regimes blended in with that of more secular movements. Some religious leaders had been influenced by the generally left-wing political climate of the 1960s, which was seen most explicitly in the Catholic Church after the Vatican II council. The legacy of this shift to the left made the Church less likely to adopt a position of outright opposition to communist rule, but it could also make it more sympathetic to new left movements, such as ecology, that challenged authority on both sides of the East/West divide.

The Church's involvement with dissent did not mean that the *modus vivendi* established in the early 1970s was wholly broken. Such involvement could be useful, because it allowed the Church to channel and control movements that would otherwise have been more dangerous. Opposition to violence and the desire to defend its own institutional interests made the Church a valuable interlocutor in times of crisis. Catholicism was particularly useful in this context. The Vatican was, after all, an international power with its own diplomatic service, and communist regimes could accept negotiation with such a body more easily than they could with leaders of an internal opposition. Catholicism's discipline was also useful. A comparison illustrates the utility of a powerful and partly independent Church under communism. The Hungarian Church in the early years of communist rule had been led by Cardinal József Mindszenty, a resolute opponent of the regime who was imprisoned by it, which made him all the more dangerous as a focus for radical opposition. Hungarian nationalists broadcasting on Radio Free Europe in 1956 incited the Hungarian people to their suicidal confrontation with the Red Army by insisting that Mindszenty was the "real leader of the country."[25] By contrast, the Polish Church in the 1980s enjoyed many privileges. Polish priests maintained contact with the Solidarity trade union. The primate, Cardinal Glemp, was one of the most powerful people in the country, but he used that power to restrain his followers from aggressive confrontation with the regime. After 1985, he repeatedly refused to meet Wałesa, the leader of Solidarity, while holding frequent meetings with General Jaruzelski, the First Secretary of the Communist Party.

Armies

More than any other body, armies determined whether communist regimes survived. Broadly, the army sponsored the transition from communism to democracy in most eastern European states (a sponsorship that was rendered effective by the fact that most generals were neither communists nor democrats). The precise form of military intervention varied. In Poland, it was long and peaceful; in Romania, it was short and violent. In the Soviet Union, the question to be asked about the army is not so much why it supported reform as why it did not intervene to prevent reform.

The values of officers in communist countries were not, in fact, very different from those of their Western counterparts. Both stressed discipline, tradition, courage and technical proficiency. After the disastrous effect of Stalin's purge of the officer corps in the late 1930s, communist leaders were hesitant about subordinating competence to political loyalty.

If armies subscribed to an ideology, it was nationalism rather than communism, and in most eastern European states nationalism encouraged army officers to view Soviet power, and thus communism, with reservations. The Yugoslav army, which had never been constrained by the military hegemony of the Soviet army in the Warsaw Pact, was the exception to this rule. The primarily Serbian officer corps was worried by the agitation of Muslims and Croats. Nationalism sometimes brought officers together with communists or former communists in defense of the federal state.

The Russian army faced problems that resembled those of the Yugoslav army. The Red Army was dominated by Slavs – Russians, Ukrainians and Belorussians – and eventually there were almost no members of national minorities above the rank of major. In combatant units, eight out of ten soldiers were Slavs; in labor battalions, nine out of ten soldiers were non-Slavs.[26] Nationality divisions presented increasing problems for the Red Army during the 1980s. In part, this was because the non-Slav element of the population was growing faster than the Slav one. In 1977, 18 percent of recruits were Muslims; by the mid-1980s, 24 percent of recruits were Muslims and 15 percent of recruits had a poor command of Russian.[27]

The increasing number of Muslim soldiers was especially awkward because of the Soviet army's role in Afghanistan. More generally, ethnic divisions exacerbated problems of violence, bullying, and separation between officers and other ranks.[28] Men died in brawls between different nationalities in the barracks. Certain groups went to great lengths to avoid military service. In Azerbaijan, some recruits were said to buy exemption in return for 2,000 rubles or a sheep.[29] Recruitment was a chaotic business that seemed to belong to the eighteenth century rather than the twentieth. Regimental "buyers" visited centers in which conscripts were held, and soldiers were shipped across the country – members of national minorities were never posted to their home region – in sealed trains to prevent them from deserting. Some soldiers only found that they had been posted to Afghanistan when they landed at Kabul airport. The French army of the Third Republic had taken Breton peasants and turned them into French citizens; the Soviet army took peasants from Armenia and turned them into Armenian nationalists who knew how to use a gun.

The rising number of non-Russian recruits filled Soviet commanders with alarm, and the prospect of the breakup of the USSR provoked some officers to support the coup of 1991. If most Russian officers had shared such views, they could have blocked reform with force, but a majority shared the low morale of their subordinates. By 1991, many of them seem to have regarded the maintenance of a multinational empire as impossible and perhaps even undesirable. Even senior commanders, such as Alexander Lebed, lost their faith in the Soviet Union as a result of the Afghan war.[30]

In most of eastern Europe, nationalism encouraged officers to support reform rather than oppose it. In many of these countries, Russia was the hereditary enemy. If Polish or Hungarian officers had been in any danger of forgetting this, the patronizing attitude of Red Army marshals towards the "junior partners" of the Warsaw Pact would have reminded them.[31]

The separation between the army and the party sometimes meant that officers toyed with the possibility of presiding over the transition to non-communist rule. In the Soviet Union, a group of colonels discussed what one of their number – Viktor Alksnis – referred to as "the Pinochet model,"[32] meaning market reform under martial law (presumably after having subjected awkward Soviet leaders to the "Allende model").

The army's role in transition was greatest in Poland. Martial law was declared between December 1981 and July 1983, and in his speech announcing its imposition, Jaruzelski did not mention the party once.[33] The Polish army was particularly well equipped to supervise the transition to post-communist rule: it was the strongest army in eastern Europe and had ferociously anti-Russian traditions – Jaruzelski himself had been deported to Siberia in 1939 – and fear of the Polish army had helped prevent the Soviet Union from intervening in Polish affairs in 1956. A survey of 1981 showed that the army was the third most respected institution in Poland (after the Church and Solidarity, but a long way ahead of the party).[34] The army benefited from an unspoken alliance with the Church, which was also powerful, disciplined and conservative. By the late 1980s Poland was effectively a clerical/military state. At a rock concert in 1987, an official censor was sent to suppress lyrics that might be seen as disrespectful of the authorities. However, the authorities referred to were not Marxist ones. The censor explained that his targets were denigrations of military service and words likely to offend Christian morality.[35]

Macroeconomics and microchips

There was nothing new about the economic failure of communism. What changed after 1975 was the widening gap with the West, an increasing awareness of that gap in the communist bloc, and the growing sense that economic failure could be explained only by the inappropriateness of communist economic methods. In part, the problem was that the communist bloc went through a period of relative optimism during the 1970s and early 1980s. High oil prices seemed likely to benefit the Soviet Union, which exported oil. Such optimism sowed the seeds of future problems because it encouraged eastern European states to borrow large amounts of money, a development that was itself encouraged by the increasing size and sophistication of capital markets in the West. By the mid-1980s, many eastern European states were devoting a large part of their income to servicing debt. The indebtedness of communist states depended partly on the degree of repression that they were willing to apply: Romania was able to squeeze living standards until its debt had disappeared, but the Polish and Hungarian regimes, which were trying to buy popularity, had no such option. Debt exacerbated a general crisis of Soviet rule. Western bankers lent heavily to eastern Europe, and the debts of this region were double those of the Soviet Union, which had twice the population. Bankers were willing to make such loans partly for political reasons – the GDR in particular benefited from the largesse of its western neighbors – and partly because they believed that the underlying economic potential of certain eastern European countries was relatively good. Indebtedness forced communist rulers in eastern Europe to look west rather than east, raising questions about the desirability of the Soviet model, as the criteria applied by Standard & Poor's credit rating agency replaced those of *Jane's Infantry Weapons*. A generation of bright young men in eastern Europe began to think in terms of creditworthiness and cost control. Some of them may also have noticed that their interlocutors from Citibank and Goldman Sachs enjoyed higher living standards than the communist nomenklatura.

In an age when the Ruhr and south Wales were deindustrializing, eastern Europe remained dominated by slag heaps and smokestacks. The traditional problems of the Eastern Bloc – lack of flexibility in planning, propensity to waste resources and lack of attention to consumer goods – looked increasingly severe when set against the "customer focus" and "just-in-time management" that were becoming fashionable in the West.

Emphasis on heavy industry created two problems. The first of these was the class consciousness of the workers; the second was pollution,

Table 6: Estimated Hard Currency Debt of the Soviet Union and
Eastern European States (billions of U.S. dollars)

	1975	*1980*	*1985*	*1989*
Bulgaria	2.3	2.7	1.2	8.0
Czechoslovakia	0.8	5.6	3.6	5.7
GDR	3.5	11.8	6.9	11.1
Hungary	2.0	7.7	11.7	19.4
Poland	7.7	23.5	27.7	36.9
Romania	2.4	9.3	6.2	− 1.2
Eastern Europe	18.8	60.5	57.4	79.9
Soviet Union	7.5	14.9	12.1	37.7

Source: Timothy Garton Ash, *In Europe's Name* (1993), p. 654.

which was especially severe in Czechoslovakia. Most of the country's forests had been damaged, almost a third of them irreparably. The life-span of Czech and Slovak men was between three and five years lower than that in neighboring countries, while that in northern Bohemia, the country's most industrialized region, was a further three or four years lower than that in the rest of the country.[36] Political protest in response to such pollution was encouraged by the success of environmentalism in the West, which appealed to young people who were disillusioned with traditional political debates. The fact that environmentalism was a new political issue meant that there was no defined party line on it, and party propagandists could hardly claim that they approved of acid rain or radioactivity. In some cases, communist authorities sought to channel ecological fervor into state-controlled bodies, but this only provided a forum and encouragement for further protest. The issue was brought sharply into focus by the explosion at the Soviet nuclear reactor at Chernobyl in 1986.

Rapid technological advance in the West also highlighted communist failure. Communism had always sought to associate itself with technological modernity, but communist states were not good at translating scientific research into mass-produced goods. This was partly because of the isolation of the scientific community. In the Soviet Union, research was centralized – it sometimes had close links with the military, but rarely with civilian production. Academics would not have felt inclined to have much to do with bureaucratic and hierarchical state enterprises even if those enterprises had shown any inclination to exploit recent scientific research. The problems of Soviet science were vividly exposed after communism fell. In 1997, at a time when some scientists in the West made millions from consultancy work, staff at the Budker Institute for Nuclear Physics near Novosibirsk supplemented their income by growing potatoes.[37]

The political suspicion with which scientists were regarded did not help the economy. The days when 15 percent of all Soviet scientific research had been conducted in prison[38] were over, but many of the country's most eminent dissidents were still men with scientific backgrounds. Indeed, many people seem to have been attracted to the hard sciences by the freedom from ideological conformity that they offered. One incident epitomized both the rift between scientists and the nomenklatura and the separation between advanced research and simple technology. When Mikhail Gorbachev wished to tell Andrei Sakharov of his release from internal exile in 1986, the authorities had to install a telephone in Sakharov's apartment: the Nobel Prize–winning physicist had not previously possessed such a device.[39]

The computer revolution of the 1980s posed particular problems for the communist authorities. At first, it had seemed that computers might fit neatly into the system. They could be used to make central economic planning more efficient, and much computer research was undertaken by the military. The Council of Ministers had talked of the need for more calculating machines as early as April 1948.[40] At the 1971 Party Congress, a grandiose project was presented to build a national computer grid (OGAS) that would link fifteen republican computer systems, 200 regional computer systems and 25,000 "automated management systems." Eventually, all members of Comecon would be plugged into this system.[41]

Soviet efforts to master computers failed. In 1984, experts estimated that they were ten years behind the West in the use of computers and robots;[42] ten years was a long time in computers, and it became longer during the 1980s. Computers became smaller, cheaper and more likely to be used by private individuals than by the state, a change that was marked in the West by the rocky fortunes of IBM and the withdrawal of the French and British governments from attempts to sponsor a national computer industry. No such revolution occurred in the Soviet Union, where the average state enterprise made IBM look like a model of quick-thinking creativity.

The opportunities that computers presented for rapid response were unlikely to be exploited in a system that was built on rigid hierarchies, in which no one would act unless they had written authorization. At a time when Western companies were beginning to talk of the "paperless office," the number of forms used in the Czech mining industry increased from 86 to 265.[43] Communist planning implied a "hardware" economy, and worked best with simple products that could be counted and weighed. A planning official could set targets for the production of pig iron, but no one could assess computer programs except in terms of the willingness of customers to use them. Workmanship and quality control also posed problems. Communist production was dogged by frequent faults, which made it very difficult to produce devices in which every single component had to work. "Total quality management," which came to obsess some Western manufacturers, would have meant nothing to bad-tempered, underpaid workers in a Soviet factory.

The communist failure in computing was sometimes illustrated in farcical terms, especially in East Germany, where the leadership invested much prestige in its ability to master the new technology. When factory managers were given orders to install a certain quota of "robots" in all plants, they responded by redefining existing devices – such as lifts and vacuum cleaners – to fit this new category. At the end of the 1980s, the Stasi still kept its voluminous records on index cards in filing cabinets.[44] The failure in electronics began to have a dramatic effect on living standards. Communist regimes had been relatively successful at simply making sure that their populations had enough to eat, but consumers in the 1980s were increasingly prone to define acceptable living standards in terms of the kind of electronic goods that communist regimes were least good at producing: a Czech had to work 2.5 times as many hours as his West German counterpart in order to buy groceries, but he had to work 65 times as many hours to buy a pocket calculator (assuming, of course, that he acquired it through official channels).[45]

If communism failed to use computers effectively, its critics used them all too well. Cheap Western personal computers flooded into eastern Europe; often they were bought on the black market and used to facilitate black economy enterprise. Poland, where there were said to be half a million private computers, was the most affected by this wave. Computers facilitated the dissemination of information by opposition groups. The days when the state could ensure that it controlled every typewriter in the country[46] were over when any seventeen-year-old with an Amstrad could produce samizdat publications. When the leader of Warsaw Solidarity went underground, he took his Tandy personal computer with him.[47]

Internationalization

In the 1980s, citizens of communist countries became more aware of what was happening elsewhere and more inclined to view their own lives in comparison with such events. Increased travel had an important impact. In 1972, only 11,000 citizens of East Germany had visited West Germany; by 1986, this figure had reached 244,000.[48] Visitors to the

West were particularly struck by differences in living standards, but even travelers in the Eastern Bloc could see how much more liberal and prosperous Hungary was than Czechoslovakia.

Television also had an influence. Communist regimes encouraged television ownership because it provided a means to disseminate propaganda. In practice, it was often Western broadcasts that were most enthusiastically watched, and these provided a glamorized view of capitalism that probably did more to undermine communist regimes than any number of broadcasts on Radio Free Europe. In East Germany, cables were laid to make it easier for inhabitants of Dresden to receive West German broadcasts – it was hoped that this would make them less keen to emigrate. The only inhabitants of East Germany who did not have easy access to Western television were the soldiers in Soviet barracks, where televisions were adjusted to prevent them from receiving Western channels.[49] The aspects of Western culture that often appealed most were precisely those of which high-minded western Europeans – and eastern European dissidents – most disapproved. Ismail Kadaré portrayed Albanians clambering on the rooftops to improvise aerials in the hope of seeing erotic films on Italian television at the very moment when Radio Tirana was beaming out its version of Marxist orthodoxy to an indifferent world. When the first Soviet tanks left Hungary, La Cicciolina, the Hungarian-born porn star and member of the Italian senate, was present at the leaving ceremony.[50]

Reform-minded communist leaders themselves began to learn lessons from abroad. The impact of such lessons was particularly apparent on the entourage of Mikhail Gorbachev. Previous Soviet leaders had been marked by their propensity to look inwards – simply surviving in Stalin's Russia was a full-time occupation, and the study of foreign societies would have been regarded as a suspect activity. Gorbachev was more open. He was a friend of the Czech reformer Mlynář and, though Gorbachev was unwilling to follow Mlynář down the road that led to "socialism with a human face" in 1968, it is clear that Gorbachev learned something from the contemplation of Czech economic experiments.

More importantly, Gorbachev was surrounded by advisers who were well informed about the world beyond the Soviet Union. The international section of the Central Committee Secretariat had already provided Gorbachev's patron Andropov with information and support. Soviet leaders learned by watching what was going on in Hungary and Poland during the 1980s. Oleg Bogomolov, head of the Institute of Economics of the World Socialist System, played an important role in transmitting the results of innovation inside the communist world.[51]

Interest in, and admiration for, other societies did not necessarily encourage Soviet leaders to imitate those societies. Officers of the KGB probably had more access to information about the West than any other group in the Soviet Union, but their desire to copy Western achievement in economics and technology was matched by their desire to avoid copying the West in politics. Gorbachev himself, though, seems to have been increasingly interested in western European political models. He developed close relations with Felipe González, the leader of the Spanish socialists, and with the leaders of the Italian Communist Party.

The shift in perspective implied by such contacts was huge. Traditionally the teacher of its satellite states, the Soviet Union became the student of Hungary and Poland. The Soviet Union had had poor relations with the democratic left, particularly with social democrats and the Italian Communist Party, whose "polycentrism" had challenged the hegemony of the Soviet party. Now those very movements provided a model for the Soviet Union. In the immediate aftermath of the Moscow coup, Yeltsin and Gorbachev both described themselves as "social democrats."[52]

Uncivil societies

One feature of reform in the communist world was the discovery of "society." Academic sociology was marginalized for much of the communist period,[53] but from the 1970s onward the subject began to be taken seriously, first in parts of eastern Europe and then in the Soviet Union itself. Gorbachev's own wife wrote a thesis on the rural sociology of Stavropol. Sociological study often exposed problems that the party claimed to have solved (one of the reasons why it had been discouraged) and also provided reform-minded leaders with information about the people over whom they ruled. An institute for the study of public opinion was established in the mid-1980s,[54] and Soviet newspapers began to publish public opinion polls in the autumn of 1989.[55]

The phrase "civil society" was widely used during this period to mean a network of obligations, customs and rights that was independent of the state. It is misleading for two reasons. First, it implies a clear division between state and society; in fact, the two were closely interwoven, and networks in civil society often existed precisely in order to exploit the resources of the state. Second, it implies a degree of moral approval, yet the ties that bound individuals under communism could be characterized by both heroic altruism and the ruthless pursuit of self-interest. Civil society could mean Charter 77 or the Chechen mafia. For most people, of course, self-interest and altruism were never entirely separate. Their relations with others were marked by a mixture of loyalty, back-scratching and real, if limited, goodwill. Such relations might best be described as those of "uncivil" society.

The strength and nature of bonds between individuals varied from country to country. In Poland by the 1980s, communists were so isolated in a nation of Catholics and Solidarity supporters that they had to make conscious efforts to seek out like-minded people among whom they could relax. Solidarity came close to creating not merely an alternative society, but an alternative state: there were Solidarity publishing houses, Solidarity newspapers and even a Solidarity post office through which people could communicate their thoughts without fear of the censor by using stamps that commemorated events such as the Polish–Soviet war of 1920.[56] In East Germany, by contrast, the Stasi employed a vast network of part-time informers that extended its antennae even into the families of suspected persons.[57]

In economic terms, people needed a range of informal links in order to get by. They might benefit from personal contact with officials or simply organize their own relations with officialdom. In Poland, "queue committees" regulated the lines of people waiting for scarce items and allowed them to reduce the time spent standing on a freezing street. Black and gray economies, which worked on the basis of exchanged favors or private trade, developed in a spectacular fashion (perhaps rather exaggerated by the anecdotal evidence on which students of the phenomena were obliged to rely). In Poland, obtaining quite basic items would have taken an impossibly long time if people had simply saved their official wages: the Fiat cars manufactured under licence in Poland cost 3 million zloty, which was 100 times the average official monthly wage.[58] Yet such items were quite widely possessed. Workers spent large amounts of time, and probably even greater proportions of their energy, moonlighting outside their formal hours of work. It was estimated that 10–13 percent of personal income in Poland came from illegal sources.[59]

The black economy was never entirely separate from the official one, but often depended on access to materials, tools and time that could be obtained only by stealing from the state. Increasing numbers of people were dragged into black economy activity: if the plumber was paid in cash then something had to be done to generate it. Functionaries with nothing to sell other than their ability to generate official papers were bound to become corrupt, and growing black market activity required increasing official complicity to prevent it from being penalized by the authorities. Communist reformers had an ambiguous attitude towards black economies. On the one hand, they saw such activity as a potential basis for more efficient small-scale private-sector enterprise: the Hungarian economy had increasingly hinged on such enterprise since the 1970s, and from 1986, the Soviet Union tried to legalize much "gray economy" activity through recognition of private property. On the other hand, communist reformers were keen to establish a less venal state: perestroika emerged partly from a campaign against corruption.

Most importantly, uncivil society asserted itself in the attitude that people took to the party in their daily lives. Many still joined it in a bid to advance their careers, but increasing numbers regarded it with disdain. Genuine political principle, conformism (with the values of immediate associates rather than the state) and self-interest sometimes mingled. People might refuse to join the party because they disliked the regime, but also because they did not want to be laughed at by their friends or simply because they could not face the boredom of meetings. Authority, power and competence often became entirely separate, as managers, appointed on the strength of their political credentials, were obliged to ask advice of their deputies, appointed on the basis of their ability to do the job.

Youth

Communist rhetoric placed a heavy emphasis on appealing to youth, but communist leaders had grown old: by 1982, the average age of members of the Soviet Politburo was more than seventy.[60] Erich Honecker, who had joined the party's children's organization when he was only eight years old and made his early career as secretary to the communist youth movement in the Saar,[61] seemed by 1989 to incarnate the inflexibility of old age.

Western observers who saw youthful rebellion in the East as a matter of haircuts, clothes and pop music often assumed that youth culture was simply imported from Britain and America. Communist leaders themselves certainly liked to decry Western fashions. In reality, generational rifts in the East were sharper than in the West, because single events such as the Warsaw Pact invasion of Czechoslovakia could make huge differences in how people lived. Eastern Europeans themselves were obsessed by the differences between generations and the way in which an age gap of just a few years could divide the experience of one group from that of another. Zdeněk Mlynář begins his book on the Prague Spring thus: "I joined the Communist Party in the spring of 1946, when I was not quite sixteen. Thus I belong to the generation of Czechoslovak Communists who were around twenty in February 1948 when the Communist totalitarian dictatorship was installing itself, and my political experience is peculiar to that generation."[62] Václav Havel formed a club for those who, like himself, had been born around 1936.

Yet a self-aware "younger generation" did not, in itself, bring down communism. Kundera's hero in *The Joke* was aware of the gap that divided him, born around 1930, from those who were around twenty in the mid-1960s, but this "younger generation" would have been grandparents by the time of the Velvet Revolution. Emmanuel Todd mused at a party in 1974 over whether "dope or the Soviet tanks" would win in the long run, but the students who smoked dope with him in Budapest would have been middle-aged professors – probably writing jargon-ridden papers about the need for a central European derivatives market – by the time of the first multiparty elections in Hungary. It might even be argued that generational differences weakened the opposition to communism by dividing it.

Generations defined by shared experience, political dissent and a commercialized culture of youth imported from the West sometimes blended together. Opponents of communist regimes often turned to jazz and rock music. Václav Havel retained a boyish enthusiasm for such things even after he became head of state. He tried to make Frank Zappa his cultural envoy and once insisted on taking the American Secretary of State to hear the saxophonist John Zorn play at the Knitting Factory nightclub in New York.[63]

Western popular music often changed in meaning as it drifted over the Iron Curtain. Listeners in the East missed the nuances that distinguished one band from another: the gulf between Genesis and The Jam was as incomprehensible to a teenager in the East as that between Stalin and Trotsky was to an average teenager in the West. A concert promoter in Bratislava in 1997 placed the UK Subs (ageing survivors of the 1970s London punk scene) on the same bill as a German techno band. Misunderstanding could impart a significance to Western music that it would never have had in the mind of a Western listener. Thus in 1987, teenagers in east Berlin gathered to listen to the English rock group Pink Floyd, which could be heard playing on the other side of the Berlin Wall. When police tried to disperse them, the teenagers shouted "Gorbachev, Gorbachev."[64] They might have been less enthusiastic about Pink Floyd if they had realized that its members were middle-aged millionaires and that the band's most successful album, *The Wall*, was a self-pitying account of an English childhood during the 1950s, not a reference to the division of Berlin.

Sometimes, rock, folk and jazz music in the Eastern Bloc contained a political message, and the eastern European states saw a few heroic gestures of defiance. The East German singer Wolf Biermann called for a Berlin street to be named after Trotsky,[65] and in Hungary members of Coitus Punk Group were imprisoned for celebrating the death of Brezhnev with the lyric: "The plotter is dead, the animal is dead, now the dictator can become an idol."[66]

Oddly, however, such explicit opposition was becoming less important to youth culture during the years immediately before communism fell. The sharp generational differences of earlier years mattered less. The young eastern Europeans of the late 1980s had rarely experienced dramatic events that divided them from their elders. They became more like their counterparts in the West, defining themselves in conventional opposition to their parents rather than against those a few years older than themselves. Their sense of youth revolved around clothes and music rather than politics. Some eastern European governments sponsored an official rock culture of worthy teenagers willing to sing about oppression in South Africa or the horrors of fascism. Often, the beneficiaries of this tolerance were only too willing to sell out and acquire a party card in return for the right to attend a youth festival in Denmark or obtain a recording contract.

Yet it was this "depoliticized" generation that flooded to the demonstrations that helped to bring down communism. As many communist regimes had encouraged natalism during the 1970s, they faced an exceptionally large cohort of teenagers during the late 1980s, and youth culture in the West had changed in ways that affected the East. The pop music of the 1960s and 1970s had often been associated with protest. Eastern European teenagers who took their ideas from Bob Dylan or The Clash might well have been at odds with their own regime, but they were unlikely to be unqualified admirers of capitalism. However, during the 1980s capitalism infiltrated youth culture, and fashionable bands were associated with consumption and hedonism. Communist authorities found this kind of culture more difficult to control and channel than explicit protest. An East German official was heard talking about the "good old days" of Western protest music.

The nomenklatura

The fall of communism was not the direct result of any of these forces. It was determined not by pressure from below or social and economic problems, but by the way in which the leadership chose to react to those problems. The revolution from above was most clearly visible in the actions of Mikhail Gorbachev in the Soviet Union, but it could also be traced in the hundreds of small-scale decisions made by lesser party functionaries and the leaders of the eastern European states. Few people consciously set out to destroy the regime. Rather, they made negative and limited decisions. Reforms were introduced that had unexpectedly wide consequences and, most importantly, certain leaders ruled out the kind of brutal action that would formerly have been taken to defend the system.

A story told by Zdeněk Mlynář about his time as a student at Moscow University during the early 1950s illustrates the thinking that produced such changes. One day, he was approached by a very drunk Russian who had just voted in favor of excluding a friend from the party for a minor misdemeanor. The Russian was ashamed of himself and he asked Mlynář to "call him a pig." When Mlynář asked the Russian why he wanted to be abused in this way, he received the reply, "Because you are not a pig, you really believe in all this . . . You read Lenin, even when you are all alone. You understand? You have faith in all these ideas."[67] Lack of faith, drunkenness and a propensity to bouts of self-hatred did not turn out to be an impediment to the career of Mlynář's classmate, who went on to be a successful military prosecutor. Writing in the late 1970s, Mlynář added, "No doubt he still gets drunk after a trial and gets someone to call him a pig."

The believers and the pigs both played a role in the undermining of communism. As the regime's failings became undeniable, the nomenklatura was divided into two categories. The first comprised those who still believed that communism was a good idea but recognized that the reality fell disastrously short of the ideal; the second comprised those who were willing to make the most careful display of outward orthodoxy but were really concerned only with the advance of their careers. The two categories were never entirely separate. Mlynář's associate from Moscow clearly felt some respect for "true Marxism" and contempt for himself for falling short of its ideals, even while he was cynically advancing his own career. Mlynář was a believer, although the successful career that he enjoyed in the Czech Communist Party until 1968 suggests that he was not utterly indifferent to worldly success.

Mlynář and his friend at Moscow University, Mikhail Gorbachev, were both examples of Communist Party believers who ended up presiding over dramatic reform. The two men's careers also indicate that the progress of communist reform was not simple and did not take the same form in every country. Gorbachev and Mlynář saw each other for the last time in 1967, when the latter visited the Soviet Union.[68] Gorbachev took a sympathetic interest in the reforms being enacted by the Czech party. Two years later, Gorbachev visited Czechoslovakia as a member of an official Soviet delegation; he did not see his old friend, who had been disgraced and expelled from the party after the Warsaw Pact invasion. By the time Gorbachev joined the Politburo of the Soviet Communist Party, Mlynář was an exiled dissident who supported Charter 77.

Men like Gorbachev and Mlynář were very different from dissident Marxists. Both remained members of the party until they reached the top, and both knew how to keep their heads down when such behavior was useful to their careers. Their transition to support for reform was not the product of a sudden conversion, nor was it the result of a private belief that they had kept hidden throughout their lives – both men seem to have been genuine Stalinists in the early 1950s. Changing beliefs came with experience, and often it was their very success in the party hierarchy that gave them such experience. Mlynář was responsible for unraveling the legal legacy of Czech Stalinism. Gorbachev began to gain access to foreign publications and confidential documents that questioned aspects of the Soviet system. Both men remained discreet about their doubts: Mlynář talked about a generation of functionaries who practiced "self-censorship." Gorbachev made obsequious references to Brezhnev in the early 1980s.

Reformers did not always understand the full consequences of their reforms. In some respects, liberalization acquired a momentum of its own by making it possible for ideas to be discussed more openly and consequently paving the way for yet more radical changes. Dissidents who had been expelled from the party or even imprisoned returned to the political mainstream. Mlynář talked to Eduard Goldstücker, who had been imprisoned during the late 1940s and allowed to return to the party only in 1967. Gorbachev developed some of his ideas through debate with Roy Medvedev and Andrei Sakharov. When reformers did understand the consequences of reform, they did not always like them. Mlynář regarded the decision to allow complete press freedom in Czechoslovakia as a disastrous error, and Gorbachev seems to have had doubts about the reform movement in the Soviet Union during 1990 and 1991.[69]

Moderate reformers' room for maneuver was, however, squeezed by events. The issue ceased to be whether they wanted to go forward; rather, it was whether they preferred going forward to an uncertain, and perhaps unwelcome, future or back into repression. In 1968, Mlynář could either support Soviet intervention or suffer disgrace along with the radicals he had tried to restrain. In 1991, Gorbachev faced a similar choice. The leaders of the Moscow coup seemed to have seriously believed that the Soviet President might side with them. Gorbachev was still General Secretary of the Soviet Communist Party, the role of which was being called into question by radical reform. Siding with the plotters might have given him a chance to destroy dangerous rivals such as Yeltsin, as well as ensure his own physical safety. It was probably not until he stood in the study of his Crimean villa and dismissed the delegation from the coup leaders with a stream of obscenities that Gorbachev himself understood how far he was willing to go.

Alongside the "believers," who tried to reform communism, were the "pigs," who tried to benefit from it. Sometimes the two groups came into conflict with each other. Gorbachev's early reform program was largely a continuation of that begun by Andropov against party corruption, but the cynical self-interest of the nomenklatura did not always lie in the defense of the old regime, and it might be argued that, in the end, self-interest had more to do with the fall of communism than liberalization. This was a point that Mlynář himself appreciated. Writing in the late 1970s, he pointed out that the privileges of party functionaries did not necessarily mean that they would oppose democratization; privileges could exist under democracy, too.

In some ways, capitalism offered greater possibilities for preserving the privileges of the nomenklatura than communism. Private property was easier to protect and transfer down the generations than a party position, which might be vulnerable to a change in policy or a sudden tantrum by a visiting member of the Politburo. Developments in capitalism during the 1980s not only confirmed that capitalism was better than communism at creating wealth, but also suggested that it was pretty good at ensuring that wealth stayed in the hands of a privileged few. The increasing sophistication of capitalism offered subtle varieties of pleasure that could not be obtained by even the most powerful in the communist bloc. Communist regimes had been built in impoverished countries recovering from war, where simply having enough to eat was often the definition of privilege. Early party leaders, men from peasant or working-class backgrounds, had an old-fashioned concept of pleasure and relaxed in ways that would have been more familiar to the nineteenth-century aristocracy than to the late-twentieth-century bourgeoisie. Hunting was a favorite occupation;* visiting spas to work off the effects of a diet of vodka and wild boar was another (Gorbachev's early success came partly from his contacts with party leaders who came to visit spas in Stavropol where he was an official). However, communist leaders began to look wistfully at the trophy wives, designer suits and Porsches of the Western businessmen with whom they came into

---

* The enthusiasm of the nomenklatura for hunting sometimes produced conflicts that seemed reminiscent of the *ancien régime*. One of the few rural areas of Poland where Solidarity succeeded was one in which peasants had been annoyed by the establishment of a government hunting reserve. See C. M. Hann, *A Village Without Solidarity: Polish Peasants in the Years of Crisis* (New Haven, CT, 1985), p. 95.

contact.* Most of all, they were tempted by the open celebration of wealth in the West. Communism hinged on the idea that luxury was wrong. The curtained limousines and discreet hard currency shops hid the privileged from the rest of the population. Capitalists, by contrast, could flaunt their wealth.

The generational revolution and the children of the nomenklatura

Admiration for the capitalist West was particularly strong among the young. A French journalist visiting a management school in Budapest was struck by the fact that those attending it were exactly the kind of people who would formerly have become party apparatchiks.[70] As communism failed or liberalized, a generation of ambitious young men looked over the horizon and began to plan their careers in the successor regime. A prime example was Ivan Pilip, a Czech born in 1963. Clever, ambitious and conformist, he was a central European Valéry Giscard d'Estaing. His family were Catholic property-owners who had suffered under communism, but this did not make him a dissident. He was never imprisoned and did not sign Charter 77. He was getting "A" grades at the Prague School of Economics at an age when Václav Havel had worked in a labor battalion. His views on the regime had as much to do with self-interest as politics: "I counselled my friends not to join the party; not simply because it was immoral, but practically speaking, I saw that the party couldn't survive."[71]

Pilip had backed the winning side. He joined the Christian Democrat Party after the fall of communism, and became Deputy Minister of Education at the age of twenty-nine. Five years later, he was Minister of Finance. There were many like him in eastern Europe. The changes of leadership that accompanied the fall of communism were more dramatic in terms of age than in terms of social background or political principle. The average age of the Soviet/Russian elite dropped by between eight and ten years after 1991.[72] An observer of Bulgarian affairs summed up matters in the mid 1990s: "After 1989 it seems that it was

---

*An early example of the fascination with Western consumer goods on the part of communist leaders came during Brezhnev's visit to West Germany in 1973. He was allowed to test-drive a new Mercedes sports car and became so excited by this rich man's toy that he drove off at high speed (much to the discomfort of his KGB guards). See Timothy Garton Ash, *In Europe's Name*, p. 90.

less a social group than a generation, that of those aged 25–40, whose opportunities for advancement had remained limited under the sclerotic regime of Zhivkov, who benefited from the changes."[73]

One group of young people was particularly important in the generational revolution that accompanied the fall of communism – the children of the nomenklatura. Membership of this category had not always been a privilege. Under Stalin, advantages had been given to the children of workers, and party bosses had been too busy surviving to think about founding a dynasty. Being the child of a party leader in this period had often meant the state orphanage rather than Moscow University. The stabilization of communist rule after 1953 changed all this. Party leaders were able to guarantee their children good educations and secure positions. Except in Romania, which was effectively a dynastic state, the children of the nomenklatura rarely rose to the commanding heights of the party or the state – perhaps to do so would have made nepotism excessively obvious or exposed people who already enjoyed privilege to too many risks. Rather, they fastened on interesting and comfortable positions in journalism, research and management. Because they were seen as politically "reliable," they were often granted an unusual degree of access to the West.[74]

Children born into the nomenklatura after Stalin were very different from their parents. Until the 1980s, most party bosses were characterized by physical courage, cunning and luck. Their children, by contrast, were characterized by high levels of education, smoothness and a knowledge of the West. A classic example of the breed was the son-in-law of Alexei Kosygin, Dzhermen Gvishiani, who was a management specialist who had close contact with Western experts in his role as chairman of the International Institute of Applied Systems Analysis in Vienna. One Western correspondent remarked that he "would make an excellent head of a top management school in the West."[75]

Access to a certain kind of education ensured that the children of communists were more adapted to capitalism than most of their compatriots. In Prague in 1997, a rising star in a Western multinational had a particularly good understanding of Western approaches. He had acquired such skills not in California or London but at the Moscow Institute of International Relations in the late 1980s. An elite institution in perestroika Moscow allowed access to publications that would never have been available to ordinary Czechs – but, of course, no Czech would have been allowed to acquire an education of this kind unless his parents had influence with the communist authorities.

The end of communism as management buyout

The fall of communism offered opportunities to the more quick-witted members of the nomenklatura as well as to the young people who were impatient to replace them, and the people who were already powerful in the system were often the best placed to exploit its demise. The collapse of the regime was accompanied by a period of economic fluidity in which nimble, well-informed and well-connected individuals could exploit lucrative opportunities. The opening-up of foreign trade in the USSR in 1987 created opportunities because private companies were able to hide behind the doubt about who should pay foreign suppliers (a task previously undertaken by the state).[76] Privatization offered opportunities for knowledgeable insiders to acquire assets while granting taxpayers sole ownership of awkward liabilities.

Political transition in eastern Europe often resembled what would be called in corporate finance a "management buyout," which takes place when existing managers borrow money to buy a company from its shareholders. It often offers opportunities for enrichment because managers have inside knowledge denied to ordinary investors. Communist regimes were prime targets for management buyouts – their "investors" (the general public) were naïve about the ways of capitalism, while their "managers" (the communist nomenklatura) benefited from privileged information that came from being the only people who had not been deceived by years of censorship and propaganda.

In Russia, the mechanisms by which political contacts were traded for private wealth were seen from the late 1980s. One prominent Moscow businessman derived his initial investment from a relative who was a general in the KGB, while the Stolitchny Bank, the first private bank to be licensed, was backed by party money. Even the communist youth organization tried to establish private enterprises in the last days of the Soviet Union. Pavel Bunich epitomized the shift from Marxist theory to market practice when he moved from being Professor of Socialism at Moscow University to President of the Association of Entrepreneurs.

Sometimes, the interests of private business and the Communist Party became so closely interwoven that entrepreneurs obtained party cards just as the communist system was collapsing. A. Kadyrov, a doctor and deputy from Bachkirie who created the Vostok Co-operative Bank, which was the seventeenth largest bank in the Soviet Union, joined the party in 1990.[77] The Czech Václav Junek did not join the party's Central Committee until a year after the communist government had fallen. His political contacts remained useful even after the party had lost formal power, and his Chemapol industrial empire soon accounted for 4 percent of the total Czech gross domestic product.[78]

The "management buyout" interpretation of communism's fall does not, of course, mean that there was any conscious conspiracy to engineer the transition to capitalism, or that there was a straight transfer of power from the old elites of the communist regime to the new managers of private firms. The end of communism meant a shift in power within the elite, part of which occurred before the collapse of the regime and part after it. This generally meant that the young replaced the old and that people who exercised economic power benefited at the expense of those who had previously exercised political power. Men who had been slightly removed from the summits of power under the old regime and who might have taken years to reach those summits were able to exploit rapid change. One of Gorbachev's aides talked of a "revolution of the second secretaries."[79] An analyst wrote of Czechoslovakia: "The Velvet Revolution acts as a catalyst for internal elite dynamics accelerating promotion prospects of elites-in-waiting within the enterprises."[80]

No single coherent group of people benefited. The local party boss who grabbed assets in Uzbekistan during the confusion of 1991 was very different from the smooth young economics graduate who ingratiated himself with Western investment banks in Prague. In the Soviet Union, almost all members of the post-communist elite had been members of the Communist Party, and soldiers and KGB officers had particular advantages in circumstances in which physical force was often the only means to assert and maintain ownership. In Poland, by contrast, the Communist Party was by the late 1980s so discredited that membership brought few advantages. The old elite was not entirely replaced, though. Rather, benefits were drawn by those who had been sufficiently low down in the hierarchy to avoid being compromised by martial law. Middle managers were the big winners from the fall of Polish communism.[81]

Curiously, the regime's opponents were more explicit about the possibilities of a "management buyout" than its rulers. In Poland, some dissidents discussed "making owners of the nomenklatura."[82] Members of the elite themselves rarely realized what kind of benefits they would draw until after the event. They groped their way towards capitalism, each joint venture with a Western company or cooperative giving powerful people a glimpse of how capitalism might operate and what their role in it might be. Gradually, parts of the old elite realized that a change in economic system might carry benefits as well as risks, but even at the very last moment they failed to anticipate the drama of the transformation that was to occur, and they certainly did not control every aspect of it. In many ways, the most important impact of contact with capitalism on the elite was a negative one. Such contact did not inspire a coherent program of action, but did rule out certain options that the elite would have pursued in earlier times. When faced with the rapid change of 1988 to 1991, a group of ruthless and quick-witted people devoted their energy to securing their place in the new order rather than defending the old one.

Conclusion

Communist rule in eastern Europe was over by the early 1990s. The recognition of private property and the institution of multiparty elections had brought great changes in the way in which power was exercised, even if not always in the people who exercised it. The new regimes were not always models of democracy or respect for human rights, but it was probably only in Yugoslavia and Russia that a substantial number of people regretted the end of communism.

The fall of communism should be seen not as a single dramatic event, but rather as the culmination of changes that had been going on for years. Particularly important was the widening gap between the economies of the communist bloc and its capitalist rivals, but this did not in itself destroy communism. Some states (such as North Korea) responded to the economic superiority of capitalism with isolation and militarism, some (such as China and Vietnam) with economic but not political reform. What brought communism down in Europe was the way in which communist reformers associated capitalist success with the societies and, increasingly, the political systems of western Europe and the United States.

Communist reform failed. Far from creating communism with a human face, or a Western standard of living, it encouraged dissatisfaction that eventually challenged communist rule itself. This was a predictable pattern – it had been seen in Hungary in 1956 and Czechoslovakia in 1968. The fact that the reforms of the late 1980s were not crushed under the tracks of Soviet tanks was partly because this time the reform movement was sponsored by the leader of the Soviet Union itself. It was also because of a new mood among the critics of communism. The desire to avoid violence was one of the strongest themes in dissident thought during the 1980s. Bodies such as the Polish Church discouraged confrontation with the authorities. A large part of the establishment realized that not only would it be safe after the collapse of communism but that it could do rather well in the new order. The transition from communist rule was therefore generally peaceful.

Some regretted that enlightened self-interest rather than heroic idealism underlay the change. István Csurka of the Hungarian Democratic Forum wrote that his country had been "cheated of its revolution."[83] Those who remembered Stalinism probably thought that there was much to be said for enlightened self-interest.

2

DID CAPITALISM WIN?

ECONOMIC GROWTH THROUGHOUT western Europe slowed down during the mid-1970s. Average annual growth in gross domestic production, which had been 4.6 percent from 1950 to 1973, dropped to 2.6 percent between 1973 and 1979 and then again to 2 percent from 1979 to 1990.[1] Broadly, there were three reasons for slower growth. First, oil prices increased. Western Europe had become very dependent on oil imports during the thirty years of postwar economic growth (at the end of this period, it consumed 749 million tonnes of oil but produced only 15 million). Most of this oil came from Arab countries and in the aftermath of the Yom Kippur war, Arab states tried to boycott certain countries that were seen as supporters of Israel. The boycott failed, but a more general attempt to push up the price of oil succeeded. In the last three months of 1973, the oil price quadrupled, and it rose again in the early 1980s. The oil price rises had severe effects on countries that had few internal sources of energy; they consumed 8 percent of French GDP.[2] Second, monetary instability increased. The convertibility of the dollar had underlain the international monetary system since the Bretton Woods Agreement of 1944. In 1971, the American government suspended the convertibility of the dollar and there followed a wave of competitive devaluations, which contributed to inflation in many European countries. Third, economic growth was constrained by a new worker militancy, and hence increased labor costs, that could be traced back to the strike wave that had begun in 1968.

Economic crisis was most dramatic from the end of 1974 to June 1975, when the economies of some European countries contracted in absolute terms.[3] Previous experience suggested that slower growth meant lower inflation, but now economists began to talk of "stagflation," as rising prices and economic decline coexisted.

The apocalyptic fears (and hopes) that some commentators expressed about the imminent demise of capitalism came to nothing. In many respects, European capitalism was more secure by the late 1980s than it had been fifteen years previously. This security could, in part, be measured in economic statistics. Though growth was slower after 1973, it did not stop, and most western Europeans were richer in 1990 than they had been in 1973.

Capitalism's victory was never as clear-cut as communism's defeat. Some commentators continued to insist that capitalism was on the verge of a terminal crisis throughout the 1990s. Communism was a centralized political and economic system; capitalism's strength lay in the fact that it was a decentralized economic system that could survive under many different political regimes. Its very transformation in the 1980s made its achievements increasingly difficult to measure in statistical terms. Technological advance meant that certain goods (especially electronic ones) became cheaper and required fewer workers to manufacture them; consequently they featured less in statistics designed to measure employment and gross domestic production. Increasingly, western Europeans consumed commodities that were hard to weigh or count. In retrospect, the historian may conclude, with many reservations, that the 1980s saw the triumph of capitalism, but many capitalists experienced the period as one of terrifying uncertainty.

Economic revolution?

Several different, overlapping processes transformed European capitalism in the late twentieth century. First, industry as a whole declined relative to the service sector. As Europeans became more prosperous, their consumption increasingly took the form of services rather than goods. By 1989, the French service sector employed almost two-thirds of workers and accounted for a similar proportion of gross domestic product.[4]

The transition from industry to services did not happen in the same way or at the same time everywhere. Some countries, such as Spain, were becoming industrialized just as other European economies were moving towards services. Indeed, in Greece, the proportion of the population employed in manufacturing peaked in 1990 – at the end of a decade that many saw as characterized by European deindustrialization.[5] Even in the economies that had industrialized early, the shift to services was not uniform. In the late 1980s, around a third of West Germany's gross domestic product still came from industry.[6]

Table 7: Percentage of Economically Active Population
in Manufacturing

	1960–61	*1970–71*	*1980–81*	*1992–93*
Austria	29.8	31.5	30.4	26.6
Belgium	34.6	32.1	21.9	17.7
Denmark	28.5	25.9	17.2	19.9
Finland	21.5	24.7	24.8	18.8
France	27.0	25.8	22.3	18.9
Germany	36.5	37.6	32.7	28.2
Greece	13.4	17.2	18.7	18.8
Holland	29.9	24.0	18.8	16.6
Italy	26.6	31.1	22.3	19.8
Norway	25.5	26.7	20.2	14.3
Portugal	23.3	21.7	24.1	23.7
Spain	17.7	25.4	24.4	19.0
Sweden	34.2	28.3	24.0	16.8
United Kingdom	34.8	32.4	20.6	18.9

Source: Donald Sassoon, *One Hundred Years of Socialism* (1997) p. 169.

Certain industries that had grown up in the nineteenth century declined in absolute terms. Textiles, steel and shipbuilding were hit by competition from non-European producers who could pay lower wages. Coal, steel and shipbuilding had benefited from high levels of government support, first because they were considered "strategically important" and then because of the desire to maintain jobs, but much of this aid was withdrawn in the 1980s. Some politicians, notably Margaret Thatcher in Britain, seem to have regarded large-scale heavy industry with active distaste, in part because they associated it with trade union power.

Economic advance fragmented markets, creating "niches" in which firms with small production runs prospered. The search for mass markets and economies of scale was sometimes replaced by an emphasis on quality and specialization. The wealthy consumers who gained most from the 1980s often valued goods precisely because they seemed archaic, artisanal and remote from the economy that ruled everyone else's life. Paul Smith, the British designer, boasted that he had never carried a Filofax (though he had made a lot of money marketing them) or portable phone and that he did not know how to use a personal computer.[7] Commentators talked of a post-Fordist economy as "flexible specialization" replaced production lines of standard products destined for a mass market.

In these circumstances, macroeconomic theory broke down, because there was no macroeconomy to describe. It became hard to know what was going on in the economy, let alone control it.

Labor relations

In the late 1960s and 1970s, wages increased rapidly. This ate into profits and fed inflation, which reached 7.5 percent per year in western Europe even before the first oil price rise – indeed, in Germany inflation peaked in 1969. In the 1980s, however, wages dropped relative to profits, and inflation slowed down. How was this achieved?

Any account of labor relations in Europe since the 1970s must start with the recognition that many workers did not work. A high proportion of the labor force in most western European countries was unemployed throughout the period. Some assumed that unemployment would play into the hands of capitalism by forcing down wages and breaking union power; others believed that it would destroy capitalism by provoking political upheaval.[8] It did neither. Broadly, the explanation for this lies in the nature rather than the scale of unemployment. A large proportion of western European unemployment was long-term, and concentrated on particular groups. It had remarkably little impact (good or bad) on the majority that remained in work.

In the 1970s, the European economy created jobs more slowly than that of either the United States or Japan, while the total number of people looking for work increased. The proportion of the European population that was of working age rose,[9] and more and more women entered, or tried to enter, the workforce.

Economic theory offered two solutions: governments could expand the money supply, thereby making it easier for firms to take on new workers; or they could control the money supply and, therefore, inflation. In the short term, this might bring bankruptcies and sackings but, in the long run, employers and workers would adjust to the new realities. Wages would fall to realistic levels so that people would be "priced into jobs," and employers would move to areas where they could find supplies of cheap and willing labor.

Neither strategy worked. Reflation did not necessarily create jobs. Employers could use cheaper money to maintain good industrial relations by paying existing workers more, or even to invest in equipment that would allow them to operate with smaller payrolls. Waiting for the market to solve unemployment did not work either. Not only did unemployment grow, but liberal economists were often faced with the puzzling spectacle of incomes for those in work and unemployment rising simultaneously.

Table 8: Unemployment Rates
(as Percentages of Active Population)

	1976	1980	1984	1988	1992
Austria	2.0	1.9	4.5	5.3	5.9
Belgium	6.6	8.9	14.1	11.1	11.2
Denmark	5.3	7.0	10.1	8.7	11.3
France	4.2	6.3	9.7	10.1	10.3
West Germany	4.6	3.8	9.1	8.7	10.5
Italy	6.7	7.6	10.0	12.0	11.5
Netherlands	5.3	5.9	17.2	6.5	5.3
Spain	2.8	9.9	18.4	19.3	14.9
Sweden	1.6	2.0	3.1	1.8	5.3
United Kingdom	5.4	5.0	10.6	7.8	9.9

Source: B. R. Mitchell, *International Historical Statistics: Europe, 1750–1993* (Basingstoke, 1998), p. 169.

Indeed, some countries – such as Spain and Britain – combined high inflation with high unemployment while Germany enjoyed low unemployment and low inflation.

The governments that were most successful in containing unemployment did so through small-scale measures aimed at particular groups of people rather than through macroeconomic strategy. This was the case in West Germany, where a high level of vocational education kept youth unemployment relatively low, and in Denmark, where 5.7 percent of the entire gross domestic product was devoted to measures to integrate the unemployed.[10]

Broad economic solutions to unemployment failed partly because labor markets do not function like stock exchanges. They do not consist of highly informed individuals making rapid choices calculated to maximize economic returns. People's decisions about jobs are influenced by a whole range of constraints. Moving was difficult, especially for those who benefited from subsidized housing, and leaving an industry was difficult for those whose whole identity was built around mining or shipbuilding. Those worst affected by unemployment were usually those least well informed about the overall economy and the possibilities that they might enjoy in it. The relationship between unemployment and "labor flexibility" took a long time to manifest itself. Norman Tebbit famously excited a Tory Party conference with a speech about his father who "got on his bike and looked for work": many were influenced by memories of their own youth or even the experience of their parents rather than by the reality of the labor market that confronted them.

Completely different kinds of labor market often existed within the same country. These markets were partly defined by region (in England in 1985 the male unemployment rate in the north was twice that in the southeast),[11] but also by class, level of education, sex, race and a host of other, less tangible considerations. Thus it was possible for the personnel director of an investment bank in the London docklands to complain that labor shortages were driving up salaries while people queued for dole money a few hundred yards from his office.

At the bottom of the labor market were those who found it almost impossible to adjust once they had lost a job or who never obtained one in the first place. It was this hard core of long-term unemployed that distinguished unemployment in the European Union from that in the United States or Japan.

The long-term unemployed consisted largely of those who lacked simple skills, such as literacy, numeracy or command of the national language: in Belgium, almost half of those without jobs had received no more than a primary education.[12] Employers increasingly required formal qualifications and "transferable skills," and knowledge imparted by apprenticeships or on-the-job training was often useless in rapidly changing economies. The expansion of education accompanied the decline of heavy industry, and the former helped to exclude those laid off in the latter from the labor market. In the mid-1980s in Valenciennes, once the center of the French steel industry, there were more teachers than steelworkers;[13] in 1991 Britain had more university lecturers than coal miners.[14]

Those with criminal records – a large proportion of young men in some countries – found it hard to get work. Youth unemployment also became severe, especially in southern Europe: in Italy in 1986, almost three-quarters of those registered as seeking work were under thirty;[15] in Spain, in the same year, half the unemployed were under twenty-five.[16] Ethnic minorities faced particular problems. Initially, immigrants had been the most flexible element of the labor force – they were drawn by work in the first place and in some countries were simply deported if they became unemployed. As they became established, though, this initial flexibility often disappeared, and immigrants became attached to particular areas and industries. Moving from Bradford to Henley was not easy for someone whose mother spoke no language other than Punjabi. Finding new jobs might also be made difficult by racism from employers or colleagues.[17]

All these problems reinforced each other. Unemployment produced poorly educated, sullen teenagers with criminal records, who consequently

Table 9: Long-term Unemployment (Those Out of Work for Over
Twelve Months as a Percentage of the Total Unemployed)

	1983	*1987*	*1989*	*1990*
United States	13.3	14.0	7.4	5.7
France	42.2	45.5	43.9	38.3
Germany	39.3	48.2	49.0	46.3
Netherlands	50.5	46.2	49.9	48.4
United Kingdom	47.0	45.9	40.8	36.0
Spain	52.4	62.0	61.5	54.0

Source: Valerie Symes, *Unemployment in Europe* (1995), p. 4.

found it hard to find jobs. The stigma of unemployment was reduced on estates where almost no one had a job.

Unemployment often had precisely the opposite effect to that which liberal economists believed it "ought" to have. The unemployed no longer formed a "reserve army of labor," which kept wages among the employed down; rather, they were seen as "unemployables" who were entirely excluded from the labor market – in 1986, a French newspaper suggested that the labor market was "unattainable for those with the lowest skills."[18] Increasing unemployment made "good" workers more scarce and hence more expensive. The sense of division between the prosperous and the unemployable even affected the culture of English football terraces. Fans of London teams taunted Liverpool fans with the refrain: "You'll never get a job."

Why was capitalism able to survive the high rates of unemployment in most European countries with so little political turbulence? In part, the very reasons why certain groups were vulnerable to unemployment also helps explain why unemployment was regarded as tolerable by the majority of the population. Unemployment affected the groups that were often regarded as marginal in politics and labor relations and that had the least power to force themselves on the attention of public opinion: immigrants, women and the young. Thus, in Montpellier in 1990, almost half of immigrant women, but less than one in seven of French-born men, were unemployed.[19] Often long-term unemployment existed in ghettos. Far from being distributed across the population, it was confined to certain areas that had formerly been centers of heavy industry, or to particular minorities, such as young black men.[20] The majority of the population, which did not belong to such minorities or live in such areas, was remarkably unaffected. The fact that the unemployed did not suffer the levels of absolute deprivation that had afflicted their predecessors in the interwar period meant that they were not driven to desperate acts – television and junk food were the most common resorts of the unemployed. They did not do any of the three things that might have forced their plight on the attention of the prosperous – starve, riot or vote. It was also important that unemployment benefit levels were determined nationally, and the kind of direct action to impose pressure on local authorities and welfare offices that had been seen in the 1930s did not make sense in the 1980s.[21] Crime rates increased, but victims were likely to belong to the same underprivileged groups as the unemployed themselves. Most working Europeans were unaffected by the unemployed, except in that they paid slightly higher taxes in order to support increased social security payments. The French conservative Philippe Séguin described this tacit deal among the privileged at the expense of the unemployed as a "social Munich."

The most obvious way in which labor exercised its power was through strikes. The wave between 1968 and 1972 had occurred at a time of rapid growth, but the power of organized labor increased between 1973 and 1979 in many countries even after economic growth slowed. Strikes constrained productivity, and increased wages took money that might otherwise have been used for investment or profits. Mancur Olson developed a theory of "euro-sclerosis," which attributed the poor performance of some European economies to the power of "organized interests" (mainly labor). However, the nature of labor power, and its effects, varied from country to country. While there were many strikes in the United Kingdom in the 1970s, there were few in West Germany, and the Italian economy did well during the 1980s in spite of a large number of strikes. Often, strikes were unofficial and thus outside the control of union leaders, and sometimes workers – as in France and Italy in the late 1960s – were concerned with matters other than pay.

There were defeats for labor in the 1980s. The strike of 1980 at Fiat in Turin and the British miners' strike of 1984–85 failed, as did strikes in the French steel industry during the early 1980s. Gradually, the number of days lost in strikes fell across Europe. This change was rarely a result of government policy. Rather, it was due to general economic changes or the antistrike policies adopted by individual employers. In the most industrialized countries, the number of workers in industry fell – the decline was particularly marked in the heavy industries, in which union power had been greatest. Employers sometimes shifted production away from sites associated with labor militancy, such as the Renault works at Boulogne Billancourt, and more generally production moved away from large plants, where it was relatively easy to organize unions and strikes. In the United Kingdom from 1971 to 1973, plants employing between 11 and 24 workers lost an average of 15 days per year per 1,000 workers

**Table 10: Days Occupied in Strikes per 100 Workers
in Industry and Transport**

	1967–71	*1972–76*	*1977–81*	*1982–87*
France	350	34	23	13
West Germany	8	3	8	9
Italy	161	200	151	93
United Kingdom	60	97	112	88

Source: Philip Armstrong, Andrew Glyn and John Harrison, *Capitalism Since 1945* (1991), p. 263.

through strikes. Plants employing more than 5,000 workers lost an average of 3,708 days per 1,000 workers.[22]

In the past, strike waves had fallen into one of two categories – "opportunistic" strikes, which occurred as workers tried to improve their conditions during a time of economic growth, and "defensive" strikes, which occurred as workers tried to protect themselves during a downturn. The latter kind, which tended to be larger in scale, longer lasting and more bitter than the former, prevailed during the early 1980s. The fact that such strikes usually ended in defeat is not surprising. They were, after all, symptoms of desperation in industries – such as coal and steel – that were already condemned.

On the whole, opportunistic strikes did not return, even when the European economy improved. This did not necessarily reflect the weakness of labor. In some respects, the nature of Europe's most modern enterprises made them more vulnerable to worker unrest, as the fashion for "just in time" management, which assumed that components arrived at exactly the moment they were required, meant that even a short interruption of work could do great damage. In 1984–85, British Coal was able to defeat striking miners partly because it had built up vast stocks of coal (something that only a nationalized industry could afford to do). German car manufacturers, by contrast, were hit hard by a strike of the IG Metall union precisely because, as private-sector companies were obliged to keep prices down, they kept very low stocks. It may be that the decline in strikes reflected a willingness on the part of employers to make preemptive concessions as much as it reflected a weakening of the labor movement. Some companies, notably Japanese ones, were keen to conclude "no strike" deals.

Assessing the shift in the balance of power between employers and workers can be harder than it first appears. Many analysts confuse relations between management and unions with relations between capital and labor, which in turn leads to an emphasis on explicit conflict as the only way in which power was exercised. In reality, unions did not always represent the interests of their members, still less those of the whole working class. Equally, managers did not always represent the interests of shareholders: those who were most keen to tame the unions were often more concerned with their own reputations than with the profits of their companies, and some of the most notorious confrontations between management and unions took place in nationalized industries. Even figures relating to relative levels of wages and profits are not conclusive. Many worker grievances related to matters other than pay such as "dignity," autonomy and tolerable working conditions. The "economism" of trade unions had often caused them to neglect such concerns. The fact that concessions would not cost shareholders anything did not necessarily mean that they were worth nothing to workers.

Sometimes the very changes that produced a decline in union membership or in the number of strikes may have increased other forms of power that workers enjoyed. "Post-Fordist" working practices that replaced the production line were said to grant workers greater autonomy, and more sophisticated technologies required more complex and consequently more independent actions from workers. More demanding markets obliged employers to adopt "total quality management," which in turn meant that they needed to secure commitment rather than mere obedience from their workers.

A good example of the unexpected power of employees is provided by airline cabin crews, a group that epitomized everything that appeared to weaken labor. Cabin crews worked in small groups, in service rather than industry, and were largely female. Levels of unionization were low, and many airlines did not recognize any union. However, given that their main costs were static, all airlines depended heavily on their cabin crews to differentiate themselves from competitors, which gave cabin crews a degree of power. Airlines knew that they could easily defeat an all-out strike, but they also knew that they would lose many of their most lucrative business-class customers as a result of the attitudes of staff during the aftermath of such a confrontation.

The managers of Japanese motor and electronics firms that began to move production into Europe during the 1980s were particularly keen to establish cooperative relations with their workforces. Japanese management techniques – or at least the techniques that the Japanese practiced in their European plants – often inspired emulation. By 1990, 45 of the 100 largest firms in West Germany had established "quality circles," in which workers were encouraged to suggest means of improving production.[23]

One should not, however, overestimate the shifts in labor relations brought by post-Fordism. German workers probably owed the relative autonomy they enjoyed in the workplace to traditions of vocational education as much as to new technology or management techniques. In Italy, a few of the small workshops that aroused such excitement among theorists of post-Fordism built their prosperity on a combination of advanced machinery and craftsmanship, but others exploited underage workers and illegal immigrants, while defying legislation on safety and working hours. Production-line techniques often came into use in one region at the very moment when other regions were moving away from Fordism. Many workers were still subjected to the most onerous forms of discipline – in France, more than a third of manual workers had to ask for permission to stop work for even the shortest period of time, and some were forbidden from talking during working hours.[24]

New technology sometimes produced degrees of discipline that would have exceeded the wildest dreams of Frederick Winslow Taylor. A good example of this is the telephone sales and inquiry services, which eventually employed more British workers than coal mining, steel, and motor manufacturing combined. Telephone services depended on new technologies (particularly the computer consoles from which operatives derived their information), but they granted workers almost no autonomy. Employers knew where each worker was at every moment of the working day, and could log the time taken to handle each call.

Internationalization

All economies were more affected by international considerations after the mid-1970s. Successive rounds of negotiation over the General Agreement on Tariffs and Trade (GATT) made it more difficult to isolate any single economy. The European Economic Community expanded to include Denmark, Britain and Ireland (1973), Greece (1981) and Spain and Portugal (1986), with Austria, Sweden and Finland joining in 1995. Western European states – especially small ones such as Luxembourg and Belgium – were heavily dependent on international trade: by 1992, six out of the ten most important exporters in the world were European, as were six out of the ten most important importers. European integration and the growing prosperity of western Europe meant that this trade was increasingly conducted among European countries themselves.

European monetary integration had a dramatic impact on individual national economies. The European Monetary System (EMS), by which currencies were kept in line with each other, gave great power to the Bundesbank, which controlled the strongest currency. The French franc integrated into the EMS in the 1980s, and the British pound "shadowed the Deutschmark" during the late 1980s. In 1990–92 sterling briefly entered the EMS before withdrawing because the maintenance of parity required excessively high interest rates. Preparation for European Monetary Union (i.e., the creation of a new trans-European currency) was designed, largely by the French, to wrest power away from West Germany and vest it in an independent European bank, and the economic effects of this were even more drastic than those produced by the hegemony of the Bundesbank. The prospect of monetary union forced all western European states who wished to enter to satisfy the "Maastricht criteria" – that is, to cap their public-sector borrowing in accordance with a treaty signed in 1991. This produced sharp cuts in public spending in Italy and deflation in France.

The way in which responses to international circumstances imposed deflationary economics on governments, regardless of political complexion, was reflected in the career of the Dutchman Wim Duisenberg. Duisenberg was Finance Minister in the left-wing government of his country between 1973 and 1977. In spite of his politics and his Keynesian background as a professional economist, he emphasized budgetary stability as the means to confront the aftermath of the oil crisis. In 1982, he was made head of the Dutch National Bank and, from 1997, he headed the European Monetary Institute, which prepared for monetary union. The *Financial Times* wrote approvingly that Duisenberg combined the "grave mien and narrow focus expected of central bankers"[25] with "a reputation for monetary toughness even when judged by the standards of Germany's central bank."[26]

There were other reasons for growing economic interdependence. The shift to luxury consumption, brought by increased prosperity, often meant a shift to imported consumption. Technology also made trade easier. The light electronic goods that dominated the consumer goods market from the 1970s were easy to transport: the cost of shipping transistors from Taiwan to Europe was smaller than the cost of shipping corn or steel over the same distance.

In these circumstances, a government that reflated its own economy ran the risk of passing the benefits on to foreign exporters. This dilemma could be escaped in only two ways. First, an economy could barricade itself behind tariff walls. Some British economists, such as Wynne Godley in Cambridge, advocated this solution but it was rejected by all western European governments. The second solution was to coordinate reflation at an international level. François Mitterrand tried, unsuccessfully, to persuade the seven industrialized countries represented at Versailles in 1982 to mount such an action. Some farsighted individuals, such as Mitterrand and Jacques Delors, suspected that the European Community might one day provide a mechanism to implement a transnational economic policy, but this was not possible in the short term.

Not only did international institutions fail to offer help with reflation, but, in some cases, they were associated with deflation. This was particularly true of the International Monetary Fund. Although the IMF took its money from, and lent to, governments, it behaved like a private banker and pressured the recipients of loans to balance their books. The British adoption of monetary targets and spending cuts in the mid-1970s coincided with the receipt of an IMF loan. In Italy a letter to the IMF of 1977, in which the government agreed to cuts in public spending, was considered so important that an agreement to abide by it was signed by all the major parties – including the communists.[27] Sweden even linked its wage policy to the international economy: an agreement of 1970 tied wage rises throughout the economy to wages in the export sector.[28]

Internationalization of the economy did not affect all European countries in the same way or to an equal extent. West Germany and the United Kingdom both had highly international economies, but the nature of their trade was different. The British economy was still influenced by global links left over from the empire and by the close relations that some companies enjoyed with the United States, and the sector of the British economy that benefited most from this kind of international outlook was that centered around financial services and based in London. By contrast, manufacturing did badly out of its exposure to foreign competition. Japanese investment in the United Kingdom during the 1980s raised interesting questions about the British variety of internationalism – close relations with the Japanese seemed to fit in with the British tradition of global links, but the Japanese came to Britain largely because they wished to use it as an entry point into the protected market of the European Community. Furthermore, Japanese firms in Great Britain invested in expensive plant and emphasized secure, if flexible, employment. Such attitudes seemed to fit continental patterns better than Anglo-Saxon ones.

West Germany was a different kind of economy. Its economic relations with the United States had increased since 1945 and especially since the 1970s, with U.S. investment in Germany increasing from $7,650 billion in 1973 to $16,077 billion in 1981 while German investment in the United States increased from $965 million to $7,067 billion in the same period.[29] Nevertheless, Germany remained a primarily European economy, which had increasingly important relations with the communist-ruled countries of eastern Europe.

Other economies were more capable of isolating themselves from international currents. Austria, for example, preserved a high degree of economic sovereignty because it had few multinationals operating on its soil. Switzerland presented a particularly odd mix of internationalism and particularism. She benefited from high exports, tourism and banking, and provided the headquarters of several multinational companies (such as Nestlé). Yet she repeatedly defied the "international realities" that economists enunciated. She preserved a rigid labor market (at least for Swiss nationals), protected her companies from hostile takeovers with impossibly complicated regulations, and refused to enter the European Community.

Finance and corporate structure

Changes in financial markets and corporate structures meant that all European governments found their economies increasingly difficult to control. The United States ended the convertibility of the dollar to gold in August 1971, and thereafter European governments faced increasingly dramatic fluctuations of their own currencies against the dollar and against each other (sterling lost eight cents against the dollar on a single day in 1976). Exchange controls were abandoned, and governments that wished to support their currencies had to implement policies of which the currency markets approved. Such pressure forced France to abandon reflation in 1983.

The growth of some markets preceded, and perhaps brought about, government liberalization. "Eurocurrency" markets developed during the 1960s as European banks lent to American companies in dollars. Such loans largely escaped the control of either the American or the European authorities, and by 1983 Eurocurrency debt was said to amount to $3,000 billion.

Banks and stock exchanges were subject to progressively less regulation, a process accelerated by the fear that capital would simply move to whichever city offered the most benign climate. The burst of deregulation that affected the City of London in the "big bang" of 1986 was particularly significant.

The scale of international capital markets meant that it was possible for governments to raise vast sums, on condition that they were willing to subject themselves to the kind of discipline that a private debtor would have to accept. It also removed a key justification for *étatisme*, that only the state was capable of providing very large-scale or long-term investment. Indeed, British privatization programs were often justified on the grounds that private companies would be better able to undertake big investment programs, and the most ambitious construction project in European history – of the Channel Tunnel – was handled by a private company.

Financial markets also had an impact on the way in which private-sector companies were run. Changes of this kind were most dramatic in Great Britain. They originated in the activities of certain banks and businessmen during the 1960s. Sigismund Warburg, a refugee from Hamburg who established a merchant bank in London, persuaded some of his clients to launch contested takeover bids for firms quoted in the stock exchange, which meant that any company's management could be evicted by an outsider if that outsider could persuade the shareholders that he could give them a higher return on their investment. Contested takeovers became particularly important in London during the 1980s, and they began to spread to continental Europe. A Frenchman, Bernard Arnault, returned from America during the 1980s to practice contested takeovers with messianic fervor in the European luxury goods industry.

Contested takeovers and, more generally, the emphasis on "shareholder value" stimulated a particular kind of capitalism that concentrated on extracting high returns by ruthlessly "sweating the assets" and was suspicious of large-scale investment. The Anglo-American corporation Hanson Trust was the epitome of this kind of business. Its prosperity was built by acquiring companies through contested takeovers and most of its business involved low-technology enterprises, such as construction firms, in which profits could be pushed up by cutting costs. Hanson Trust's senior managers boasted that they never visited the companies that made up their empire and that any investment over £1,000 required the written authorization of the head office. Companies built on this kind of logic behaved in ways that appeared strange to those who believed that the European economy was dominated by high-technology, post-Fordist enterprises.

Capitalism of this sort marked a sharp break with the pattern that some had believed, or hoped, to be developing during the previous fifty years. Managerialism, which derived its authority from expertise rather than ownership, had been seen as blurring the boundaries between the public and private sectors – Keynes wrote approvingly of the Bank of England (then still a private company): "There is no class of persons in the kingdom of whom the Governor of the Bank of England thinks less when he decides on his policy than of his shareholders."[30] However, the capitalism of the 1980s revolved around the interests of owners (shareholders). The total value of shares quoted on European stock exchanges trebled between 1980 and 1987,[31] and shareholder interests were emphasized against those of managers, who were often presented as idle parasites more worried about their company cars than the efficiency of their businesses.

The capitalism of the 1980s was based on changes in attitude and culture as well as in company structure. In the 1960s, writers such as Andrew Shonfield had argued that capitalism in Europe was marked by the convergence of the private and public sectors. Large companies behaved increasingly like state institutions, and often the same kind of people were at the summits of power in both private companies and the state.

This was most obvious in France, where the "*pantouflage*" of civil servants into business was common, and where graduates of the École Nationale d'Administration, particularly those who had served as *inspecteurs des finances*, exercised enormous power in large companies. During the 1980s, this began to change. Although the same people were in charge, they expressed different attitudes. State institutions remained important, but they increasingly modeled their behavior on private enterprise rather than expecting private companies to model their behavior on the state. A manager from Marks and Spencer was appointed to advise the British civil service. A majority of those entering the École Nationale d'Administration now stated that their long-term aim was to work in the private sector. Just as the state tried to model itself on private enterprise, so large companies sought to model themselves on small companies. Big corporations broke their operations down into autonomous "cost centers."

Changes in European capitalism during the 1980s were linked to the increasing importance of banks, which benefited from booming stock markets. Banks and management consultancies also acquired greater power over industrial companies, which came not from ownership of shares but from their role as advisers and which circumvented normal management structures. Olivier Roux, for example, acted as Finance Director of Guinness plc during its attempt to take over United Distillers, while remaining an employee of the Bain & Co. management consultancy.

Sometimes whole career patterns changed. Bright executives no longer expected to spend years climbing through successive jobs in a single company, but would spend a few years working for a consultancy, which exposed them to a variety of different companies, before finally being hired by one of the consultancy's clients, usually at a high level. Such a firm was McKinsey, which proved particularly successful at placing its protégés in this way. Indeed, in Britain and Italy, McKinsey "graduates" filled the gap that had previously been left by a comparatively underdeveloped management education system.

The management structure of some banks and consultancies differed from that of traditional industrial companies. Divisions between owners and managers were blurred by payment in stock options. Some companies resisted stock market flotation altogether and remained private partnerships – this was true of most management consultancies and of the Goldman Sachs investment bank, which was finally floated in 1999. Managers were subordinated to fee earners: the deal-makers and specialists in investment banks were often more esteemed and highly rewarded than their nominal seniors. Youth was granted great opportunities in an atmosphere of rapid change in which the capacity to deliver results mattered more than number of years served. As Chancellor of the Exchequer, Nigel Lawson complained about the influence of "teenage scribblers" (meaning City economists); in 1995, Rudi Bogni, the Italian head of Swiss Bank Corporation's London dealing operations, who was in his late forties, took a two-year sabbatical to go to Imperial College in the forlorn hope that he might learn to understand the operations being conducted by the young traders who were supposedly subject to his authority.[32]

Technology

The links between new technology and economic success in western Europe were not always direct. The Irish economy grew fast during the 1980s in spite of the fact that Ireland devoted less than 1 percent of its gross domestic product to research and development.[33] Europe's economic base remained in old industries: of the world's five largest companies in chemicals, steel, construction materials and mining, three were European. Only one European electronics company could be considered among the five largest companies in the world in its sector.[34] There was no European equivalent of "Silicon Valley" in California – Europeans with a talent for computers often emigrated to the United States.

It was a commonplace that a capacity for scientific research rarely translated into the capacity to exploit the technology that emerged from it. Britain was the most successful country in terms of research, but her economic performance was poor. West Germany, by contrast, was comparatively weak in terms of abstract scientific research, but was good at making money from the application of new technology.

During the 1980s, the commercial value of technology as well as abstract research began to be questioned, a shift in emphasis that was reflected in the changing status of engineers. For many years, the propensity of British companies to subordinate engineers to accountants had been seen as a weakness; in the 1970s a commission chaired by Sir Monty Finniston, a former chairman of British Steel, suggested that Britain's poor industrial performance could be attributed to the low status of its engineers compared to their counterparts on the continent. Twenty years later, it was clear that attitudes towards engineering in Britain and continental Europe had converged on the British rather than the European pattern. Even in areas where engineering had enjoyed enormous prestige, it was now subordinated to finance. In 1976, the head of the Swedish state telecommunications company was, for the first time, an economist rather than an engineer,[35] and in 1998, the head of the French company Alcatel expressed skepticism about the value of France's elite engineering school: "The motto 'for the country, glory and science' that I was taught at the École Polytechnique is admirable but it is not enough for a modern economy . . . Money is the key to success for all employees."[36]

For all its limitations, technology had an impact on the European economy. In some respects, the important point about technological change in the 1980s and 1990s was that it transcended traditional categories. In the early part of the century, innovation had been expensive and often yielded returns only after many years. Consequently, financiers had often resisted such investments. The information technologies of the late twentieth century, by contrast, were relatively cheap and sometimes yielded spectacular results quickly. Consequently, even the dominance of finance did not preclude investment in new technology; indeed, financiers were sometimes the most enthusiastic supporters of such business.

The growth of technologically advanced industries was often accompanied by a reduction in employment – the number of workers in the European electronics industry fell from 250,000 to 119,000 between 1975 and 1990.[37] Technology shook up labor markets by ensuring that entire professions – such as typists or draftsmen – became redundant. The effect of such change was particularly dramatic in Britain, because trade unions were keen to defend traditional lines of "demarcation" between different jobs. The impact of technology on labor relations was seen most clearly in the printing industry. Printers had been early leaders of organized labor, and print unions such as the Fédération du Livre in France or SOGAT in Britain enjoyed great power. The possibility of setting up newspapers on computers and printing in several different locations (or even in several different countries) changed all that.

Technology also facilitated privatization. State enterprises often controlled industries in which there seemed to be a natural monopoly: it was hard to see how more than one company could control phone lines or how there could be more than a limited number of television stations. Technology promoted competition. The use of fiber-optic cables, mobile telephones, computers and faxes opened up new opportunities for telecommunications companies. British Telecom was widely seen as the most successful of the Thatcherite privatizations because it coincided with a technological revolution that would have exposed it to competition in any case. By 1997, even the French Communist Party accepted the need to privatize France Telecom.

New technology accompanied changes in business culture. Management became younger, as a generation that had been brought up using computers elbowed its elders aside, and business was made more international by the use of faxes and eventually e-mail. Company hierarchies sometimes changed too. The typical large corporation of the twentieth century had come into existence at the same time as the typewriter and the telephone and was built on written procedures and carefully defined structures. Getting something done meant sending an appropriate written request to the appropriate person, who would forward it to the appropriate authority. On an international level, companies sent out young men (they usually were men) to run operations in distant parts of the world, just as district officers had run the British Empire. Someone who had served his time in Brazil or Nigeria might eventually return to work his way up through the grades at the head office. The use of computers challenged this culture. It became less necessary to send people out to run subsidiaries, and it was easier for managers to communicate with each other without dozens of intermediaries. In 1986, it was estimated that more than half of all electronic communication took place *within* companies.[38]

The computer industry itself saw dramatic changes. The first major company in the field, IBM, was the epitome of the 1950s corporation, with a hierarchical and conformist culture. Early computers were large, expensive devices that seemed designed to increase centralization and bureaucracy, and their exploitation was also heavily tied to military purposes. Even when it became apparent that computers would transform civilian business, governments remained convinced that the transformation would take place under the aegis of the state. The conviction was particularly strong in France, where the *plan calcul*, the Bull Computer company and the Minitel (an ancestor of the Internet) were all subsidized by the state. Even in free-market Britain, Kenneth Baker persuaded Margaret Thatcher to appoint him "Minister of Information Technology" with the promise that this sector would create a million jobs.[39]

In the 1980s, computers became smaller, cheaper and simpler to use and it became clear that the companies that would exploit them best would be nimble, flexible ones. European governments gave up trying to direct the industry. The French firm Bull was encouraged to find a private-sector American partner (Honeywell), and the British stopped funding their own Inmos chip manufacturer in 1982.[40] The technological shift also affected the balance of power in the private sector. IBM's hegemony was challenged by smaller, more innovative operations, notably Apple, which makes computers, and Microsoft, which produces software.

Companies associated with high technology operated differently from those in traditional industries. Their key resource was skilled staff and information, and their choice of location was dictated not by proximity to materials or customers but by the desire to attract staff and be close to their competitors/collaborators. Such firms clustered in attractive towns close to good universities (Cambridge, Bologna), and company cultures often owed much to university science departments. In some cases, they were set up by moonlighting academics or by enterprising students. The

Nixdorf computer firm in Germany had been established in 1952 by a
student with a $10,000 loan. Thirty years later, it employed more than
15,000 people.[41] The loyalty of highly skilled and valuable employees was
secured through the issue of stock options, which narrowed the gap between ownership and management that had been seen as a characteristic
of the twentieth-century corporation. Often the traditional division between shareholders, managers and workers broke down entirely. Workers
and shareholders were the same people, while the concept of management often disappeared in "flat hierarchies" where authority sprang from
technical competence on a particular task rather than from formal rank.

It would be wrong to assume that all the different kinds of revolution –
in technology, corporate governance and industrial organization – necessarily worked together or were preordained to produce a particular outcome. Technologies were used in different ways and at different times in
different countries, and companies displaced by one wave of change sometimes regained their position later. This was true of IBM and of the German firm Siemens, which eventually bought the Nixdorf company. In
France, confrontation between management and print unions was headed
off by conciliatory leadership on both sides during the 1980s,[42] but by
1997 *Le Midi Libre*, a French provincial paper, was experiencing the
changes that had racked the Murdoch newspapers fifteen years earlier.[43]

Rolling back the state?

The state became an unfashionable entity in the 1980s. Liberal economists and their political allies believed that welfare states had become excessively expensive, that taxes were too high and that enterprise was being
sapped by state controls on those who wished to succeed or by state support for those who failed. Such talk had little effect. State spending in
western Europe rose. In some countries, the state continued to enjoy high
prestige. This was true in France, where Jacobin centralism continued to
be influential and the *grands corps* of the civil service were highly regarded. In other countries, such as Italy or Austria, the state had little
prestige but was recognized as a useful source of employment for the
clients of the major political parties.

Attempts to cut public spending failed, even when they were not obstructed by institutional or political interests. In Great Britain, the campaign was enthusiastic but almost wholly unsuccessful. Housing was the
only major area in which government spending fell (because the government gave away publicly owned houses at a fraction of their real value).[44]
Welfare payments rose because of high unemployment, and medical costs
increased because science discovered new and ever more expensive ways

to keep an ageing population alive (medical expenditure, which had taken up around 2 percent of western European gross domestic product in 1950, consumed 5 percent of gross domestic product in 1980).[45]

Financial retrenchment and an end to economic planning were not the same thing. It was possible to constrain the decisions of businessmen without spending any money at all, but generally the exercise of such constraints became less common in western Europe in the 1980s. In Britain, the Thatcher government denounced state intervention in the economy with particular fervor. The government wound up consultative bodies that had brought union and business leaders together, and renounced the attempt to "pick winners" in industry. The relationship between rhetoric and reality was not always clear, though. Even in Britain, the government did not cease all attempts to control business, and ministers such as Michael Heseltine and Kenneth Baker continually intervened in the decisions of particular companies, insisted on the need for policies with regard to particular industries, and exhorted businessmen in terms that made it clear that they believed that the government knew what was best for the economy. The British government also tried to exercise one very important form of economic control – it sought to control inflation by reducing the "money supply." This exercise (which was more complicated than it seemed in the textbooks) involved a succession of cumbersome and constantly changing macroeconomic targets.

France presents an interesting contrast with Britain. There was no dramatic ideological "U turn" and in theory the government continued to espouse a planned economy. In practice, however, French planning became more supple, and French governments discreetly abandoned quantitative targets at the very moment when the British government was becoming ever more preoccupied with definitions of the money supply. The government economic plan of April 1979 contained no quantitative targets and justified the omission by saying, "This technique has been rendered obsolete by the fluctuations of a new era and the growing uncertainties that result from them."[46] Perhaps it is indicative of the confusion about how to manage the economy pervading both "*étatiste*" France and "free-market" Britain that both countries saw a very high turnover of industry ministers. The industry ministry in Britain had eight different ministers in ten years and three names in fifteen years; in France in the early 1980s the industry minister changed four times in two years.

The most dramatic way in which the state was curbed was through privatization. This word, supposedly invented by the management guru Peter Drucker, had not appeared in the 1979 manifesto of the British Conservative Party, but by the mid-1980s privatization had become the linchpin of government policy. The policy was based on selling nationalized enterprises. It was the one element of Thatcherite economic policy that seemed an unqualified success. Between 1982 and 1989, the government sold all or part of its interest in oil, telecommunications, gas, airways, airports and motor cars, raising a total of over £23 billion.[47]

The scale of privatizations in continental western Europe was smaller than that in the UK, and they were often used for different purposes. Only Jacques Chirac's government, which came to power in France in 1986, talked in terms similar to those of Thatcher's ministers. French right-wingers planned to privatize 65 companies with 755,000 employees and a total value of 300 billion francs, but they lacked the time in government to implement all their policies, which were in any case often just reversals of nationalizations carried out by their socialist predecessors in the early 1980s. In some countries – notably West Germany – the apparent efficiency of publicly owned companies made privatization seem unnecessary, and elsewhere, privatization was often seen as a means of streamlining rather than reducing the state. IRI, the Italian state holding company, sold off some firms that seemed to have no strategic value, while in France, money earned from privatization was reinvested in improving the productivity of the remaining nationalized industries.[48]

"Us and the Rolling Stones" – capitalism, youth and popular culture

Michael Lewis, who worked as a bond salesman for Salomon Brothers in London and Paris during the mid-1980s, tells a story about an ambitious young man being interviewed by an American investment bank in London. When the candidate mentioned the salary that he hoped to receive, his interviewers laughed and replied, "There's only two groups in town that pay this kind of money. There's us and there's the Rolling Stones."[49] In the 1980s and 1990s, such comparisons were common. The head of Microsoft, twelve years younger than Mick Jagger, was said to have paid £8 million to secure the rights to use a Rolling Stones song – "Start Me Up" – to launch his Windows 95 software.

There are several different ways to interpret capitalism's relationship with rock music. The first would stress its use in marketing. In order to survive, capitalism had to encourage the very behavior that it initially disdained – hedonism, nonconformity and short-term gratification. There was nothing new about all this – rock music had always been exploited by capitalist companies, and the "rebelliousness" of such music had often provided an additional selling point. In the 1960s, Columbia Records produced an advertisement featuring Jim Morrison and Bob Dylan with the line "The revolutionaries are on Columbia," and in the late 1970s

CBS (Columbia's successor) advertised the record "Bank Robber" by The Clash with the slogan "Bank Robber escapes," the implication being that this record – in which the singer celebrates his bank-robber father – was so subversive that the record company had been afraid to release it. The reality was, of course, that the fuss over the record was a marketing device. CBS released "Bank Robber" because they expected it to be a commercial success, as it was. Joe Strummer, who sang the words "Daddy was a bank robber," is, in fact, the son of a senior British diplomat.

The use of rock music as a marketing tool in the 1980s expanded as music was used to promote items other than records. Sometimes this exploitation reached farcical proportions. A teenage band endured the humiliation of having their 1997 tour sponsored by Clearasil spot cream.[50]

It was possible to separate the world of adults and business from the world of teenagers and consumption, but references by 1980s businessmen to rock music hint at a more complicated and intimate relationship. Software houses and corporate finance departments did not, after all, sell their products to teenagers, which suggests that rock music influenced how business saw itself as well as how it saw consumers.

The entry of rock music values into mainstream capitalism was partly just a question of time. Those who had grown up during the 1960s were middle-aged by the 1980s – the would-be investment banker whose experiences were described by Michael Lewis had probably not even been born when the Rolling Stones first stepped onto the stage of the Crawdaddy Club in Dartford. References to the Rolling Stones also pose interesting questions about the meaning of the term "youth." The band's members were older than many of the middle-aged businessmen who admired them. In some respects, youth had become a commercial commodity that could be bought and sold, rather than a phase through which everyone passed; anyone could make themselves young by wearing certain clothes or listening to certain kinds of music. Since youth was commercially available, it was natural that the rich could afford it most easily. Jon Savage, a journalist in his forties, believed that the combination of youth unemployment and middle-aged prosperity under the Thatcher government had broken the link between "youth culture" and youth:

> In the 1960s, youth had been celebrated, not only as a market but also as beatific principle. With its economic *raison d'être* removed, youth became a problem, until it was actively penalized. By the mid-1980s, the late-fifties promise of teenage consumer equality had been reneged upon: it was seen to have referred not to age, but to a style of consumption which was now taken up by an older age group who had been trained to consume teenage products and could still afford to do so.[51]

Capitalism's fascination with rock music also sprang from the fact that music itself had become an ever more lucrative business that increasingly embraced other fields. Bonds were secured against the future royalties produced by performers such as David Bowie. In the late 1980s, executives on the project finance team at Citicorp honed the details of the deal between Virgin Records and Janet Jackson. Virgin itself – founded by Richard Branson, the proprietor of a student magazine – was the supreme example of the infiltration of pop music into mainstream business. Its rejection of conventional English values blended into a proto-Thatcherite attitude towards business and labor relations. A significant, if obscure, industrial conflict of 1977 concerned the record "God Save the Queen" by the Sex Pistols. Enraged workers at the factory pressing the record downed tools in an attempt to prevent the release of a song they regarded as treasonable. Branson won his first confrontation with organized labor and the record was a commercial success.[52]

By the 1990s, Virgin had sold many of its early interests in rock music and moved on to running an airline and selling personal equity plans. Richard Branson was one of the most prominent businessmen in Europe, his image carefully constructed to present him as the antithesis of a geriatric and class-bound establishment. The image bore little relation to reality – Branson was a public schoolboy (he had been to Stowe) and came from a wealthy family – but the fact that a successful businessman should go to such lengths to identify himself with a certain kind of "counterculture" was revealing. The extent of the change that had taken place in business can be illustrated by comparing Branson with a businessman from an older generation: Branson's arch rival, Lord King, chairman of British Airways. Unlike Branson, King was one of the few successful British industrialists to have clawed his way out of the working class, having begun life as a garage mechanic, yet King's image, as contrived as Branson's, stressed his roots in the patrician world of fox-hunting and the upper reaches of the Conservative Party.

The divorce of capitalism and conservatism

The relationship between capitalism and conservatism was always uneasy. In much of continental Europe, the center right of the political spectrum was occupied by groups such as the Christian democrats, who had reservations about the unlimited operation of the free market. Parties that combined free-market economics with conservative stances on matters of culture, morality and race were often on the extreme right. This was true of the Front National in France during the 1980s, and of Austria's Freedom Party (FPO). The FPO distanced itself from the Christian democrats through economic liberalism and stressed its modern, youthful dynamic image, but it also flirted with evocations of a past based on family, hierarchy and the *Volk* – evocations that could seem disturbing in a country that had once given such support to Nazism: the FPO held its last meeting of the election campaign of 1986 in Hitler's birthplace.[53] Liberals elsewhere came to regard the FPO with distaste and, in 1986, the Dutch Liberal Party asked to have it thrown out of the Liberal International.[54] The contradictions between conservatism and capitalism became apparent in the FPO's own rhetoric. One of its candidates fought an election on the slogan "Vienna must not become Chicago."[55] The FPO were using Chicago to evoke the prospect of black ghettos and high crime rates, but forgot that Chicago, the home of Milton Friedman, also incarnated the very capitalism they professed to admire.

Sometimes capitalism explicitly embraced the very values that cultural conservatives abhorred. The student radicalism of the 1960s often blended into the consumer capitalism of the 1980s. The demonstrations of 1968 became a hackneyed motif in advertisements. The French newspaper *Libération*, left-wing in its politics but bourgeois in its tastes, was established by a group of *soixante-huitards*. Henri Weber, who had been a student leader in 1968, went on to write a semiofficial history of the Conseil National du Patronat Français.

The contradiction between conservatism and capitalism was felt most strongly in Britain. The British Conservative Party was more explicitly linked to business than any other party in Europe and it was also more explicitly conservative in terms of values than most parties on the continent: indeed, in theory, the Conservative Party defended institutions – such as the monarchy and the established Church – that would have been regarded as part of the *ancien régime* in much of continental Europe. Thatcherism accentuated both parts of this identity. The Conservative Party praised the virtues of businessmen more than ever before, but Thatcherism was about more than just economics. It asserted the importance of family, patriotism and hard work, which was seen as a good thing in itself as well as being a means to generate wealth.[56]

Thatcherism's attempt to fuse economic liberalism with moral conservatism failed. The capitalists who benefited from its economic aspects did not necessarily feel much sympathy with any other aspect of it, and the Thatcher government presided over the beginning of the breakup of the links between large-scale business and the Conservative Party. This breakup was a slow process, but it is significant that it was often most visible among the very groups that had prospered most under Thatcherism (young people working in finance or high technology). The Pearson Group, which owns the *Financial Times*, illustrated the shift in business culture (it was also the first major British company to appoint a woman as chief executive). It decided to end automatic support for the Conservative Party and instead to distribute equal funds to both of the major political parties.

In economic terms, the Thatcherite revolution benefited the young, the highly educated and the rich. Yet Conservative Party members were old (their average age was sixty-two), poorly educated (over half of them had left school at or before the age of sixteen) and poor (six in ten had an annual income of less than £20,000).[57] In the early 1990s, rank-and-file members of the British Conservative Party – bitter, xenophobic victims of a revolution that their own leaders had started – bore a startling resemblance to members of the Russian Communist Party.

Conclusion: capitalism with a human face?

In one sense, capitalism is a myth. Its opponents grouped themselves into international organizations and defined their struggle in ideologically explicit terms, and to a lesser extent its defenders organized and pontificated in political parties, think tanks and business associations. But the practitioners of capitalism often acted in a quite unselfconscious fashion. Capitalists did not necessarily think of themselves as a united group – ordinary businessmen were as likely to define their interests as being in conflict with those of their competitors as being in conflict with those of their political opponents or their employees. And the kinds of capitalism practiced in western Europe varied hugely. An engineering firm, a supermarket chain and a dress designer had little in common except the fact that they all had balance sheets and tried to make profits. The economic progress of the 1980s and the fragmentation and diversification of national economies increased the gaps between different kinds of companies to even greater levels. All the neat generalizations that economists and sociologists use can conceal enormous differences: "service sector" can mean hamburgers or investment banking; "niche market" can mean running a corporate finance boutique or stitching handbags; "productivity" can mean investment and training or scrapping safety rules. Indeed, to some extent, the success of capitalism came from the very qualities – flexibility and diversity – that make it hard to control or understand.

The victory of capitalism may also have been more apparent to detached – or hostile – observers from the academic world than it was to capitalists themselves. In political terms, several major countries – France, Spain, Sweden – were governed by socialists throughout the 1980s, and by the early 1990s, socialism seemed triumphant – parties affiliated to the Second International governed eleven out of sixteen western European countries. The variety of socialism practiced in the 1980s was, of course, very different from that which some party militants had hoped for. Socialists had stopped talking about revolution, class struggle and the need to abolish capitalism, but such changes were hardly surprising. Socialists in power had always abandoned much of their radical rhetoric.

Nor should it be assumed that socialism was entirely tame or that it was reconciled to administering a system in which its opponents had won. It had retreated from trying to destroy private property and claimed to have accepted that government should not try to run the economy – though in practice, few governments entirely renounced such efforts. It had not, however, renounced its desire to exercise a social and cultural, rather than purely economic, influence. Social spending remained high in most of western Europe (in Thatcher's Britain it consumed a proportion of the gross national product that would have been regarded as impossibly high by the consensus politicians of the 1960s). The left's aims had been achieved in terms of attitudes towards sex, race and family, and even in terms of labor legislation the left had not abandoned efforts to defend job security, safety at work or minimum wages. The European Social Chapter, signed by most members of the European Union in 1991, suggested that such standards might be imposed by governments acting at an international level.

The change in capitalism's attitudes towards certain matters was not simply the result of socialist governments imposing regulations from outside. To some extent, the values that capitalists themselves espoused changed between the mid-1970s and the mid-1990s. Capitalism had often been associated with social and cultural conservatism; it was also associated with sharply differentiated management hierarchies, authoritarian labor relations and the creation of the "company man" who accepted the values of the group that employed him. IBM (the computer company), BATA (the shoe company that was founded in Czechoslovakia and spread through France and Canada across the world) or Royal Dutch Shell (the oil company) had all instilled certain views of the world into their employees. The more flexible, fast-moving capitalism of the 1980s made the transmission of company values much more difficult as rapid labor turnover and the frequency with which corporate restructuring caused entire companies to disappear meant that few people could afford to associate their whole identity with the fate of their employer.

One should not, of course, make too much of all this. The openness and flexibility of capitalism was most visible in a few successful, but not necessarily representative, companies, and its impact was increased by skillful public relations. Furthermore, the changes in western European capitalism came from the interaction of external and internal forces.

Capitalism's own logic of technological progress and competition shook up enterprises, and left-wing governments and social pressures, which interacted with capitalism without being part of it, constrained the freedom of companies to act in particular ways.

Much has been made of the "crisis of the left," when the "multidimensional" politics exemplified by ecology and feminism replaced politics centerd on class and the state. In many ways, such developments complicated the lives of capitalists as much as those of capitalism's traditional opponents. Business faced less of a threat from nationalization or strikes but more of one from consumer boycotts, environmental legislation and shareholder protest. In the sophisticated, property-owning democracies of western Europe, capitalism did not face a simple conflict that pitted it against the "state" or the "workers" or the "left." Rather, it faced a complicated need to negotiate its way around the interests of shareholders, consumers, employees, voters and citizens. Each of these groups overlapped, each of them was, to some extent, part of the capitalist system, and yet each of them also had interests that could not be expressed simply in terms of economic calculation. Capitalism had won, but only at the price of continuous and uneasy cohabitation with those who took a skeptical view of its merits.

PART V

Europe in the New World Order

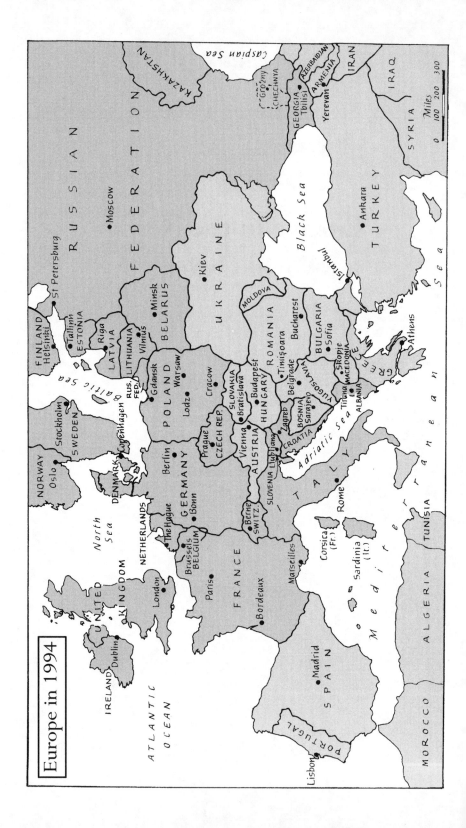

Europe in 1994

"How is it that, in a mere decade, Europe has made the transition from Eurosclerosis to Europhoria? I believe Europe has entered the ascendant phase of a new Kondratiev cycle – the more or less 50-year generational cycle of change in which technological and political innovation overcomes stagnation and generates a new economic boom.

"The new momentum began with a decision by the key European powers to integrate by 1992. In effect, integration was the political response to the necessity of moving from an industrial to a post-industrial society. Already linked by television, fax machines, rapid trains and air travel, Europe's well-educated consumers required more than a vast internal market for merchandising manufactured goods. They required a real, unified economic and cultural space . . .

"East Europeans, especially the young, saw a model of prosperity to which they wanted to belong. This helped trigger the mass migrations and evolutions towards reform in Eastern Europe that (thanks to Mikhail Gorbachev's restraint) produced the revolutions of 1989.

"Today's Europhoria is well founded. Europe will experience in the 1990s the most important economic boom of the century."

Gianni de Michelis, Italian Foreign Minister, 1990[1]

SHORTLY AFTER WRITING the inspiring words cited above, de Michelis was indicted for corruption and chased down a street in his native Venice by an angry crowd accusing him of being a thief. Europe in the 1990s changed dramatically, but not always in the way that had been expected at the beginning of the decade.

The fall of the communist regimes had the most visible effects in the internal affairs of central European countries and in relations between East and West, but its effects could also be discerned in the West. The division of Europe and the struggle between communism and its enemies had underwritten a whole political order, and many aspects of the order were challenged when that basis was removed. Relations of cause and effect were complicated, because it was not always clear which institutions were most dependent on anti-communism: who in 1991 would have predicted that NATO would flourish in a post-communist Europe or that Italian Christian democracy would prove unable to survive? It should also be emphasized that the changes in all parts of Europe during the 1990s cannot be explained solely with reference to events since 1989. The fall of communism was itself part of longer-term social, economic and technological changes that also affected the non-communist and post-communist countries. It is difficult to sum up such changes in a single phrase. Post-Fordism, post-Marxism, post-communism, post-materialism and post-modernism all imply that the 1990s can be defined by contrast with some ostensibly simpler period (though all those terms were in wide use before 1989).

In fact, the fall of communist governments in Europe was neither a beginning nor an end. Rather, the fall of communism was both a product of and a stimulant for other changes. Once the single frontier between East and West had been punctured, other frontiers (especially in eastern and central Europe) that had been frozen since Yalta were called into question. Furthermore, simple cartographic boundaries between states were increasingly replaced by social and cultural ones.

The collapse of communism also raised questions about sexual values and relations between the sexes, because many politicians now encouraged a "return" to "traditional family life" (of a kind that had never existed in most of eastern and central Europe). Even more than any other aspect of European society, sexual values in the 1990s cannot be explained simply with reference to the period after 1989. The notion of a single "sexual revolution" and a dichotomy between "tradition" and "emancipation" that had seemed so clear in western Europe during the 1960s was undermined by developments after 1989.

Finally, there were explicitly political changes associated with the fall of communism. The politics that had revolved around the simple confrontations of the Cold War became more complicated as people in both East and West embraced what dissidents in eastern Europe would once have called "antipolitics."

1
NEW FRONTIERS

THE FALL OF the Berlin Wall did not unite Europe. Rather, it replaced a single, simple division of East and West with several more subtle divisions. The most obvious new frontiers were national, created by the breakup of multinational states, but the end of communist rule also made it clear that each European country was divided by less formal frontiers that separated rich from poor, young from old and country from city. The rise of "nationalism" – which itself had many facets – did not just divide one nation from another; it also divided people who identified themselves in primarily national terms from a transnational elite: internationalization was a complicated process that created new divisions at the same time as it eroded some old ones. After 1989, even history created new divisions in Europe. Recent experience, particularly of communist rule, was remembered in different ways from one country to another, which in turn affected how the slightly more remote experience of the Second World War was recalled. Comforting stories of nations, allies and movements united in an "antifascist" struggle were replaced by more awkward recollections.

Cartographers described the most obvious effects of the fall of communism. Several new nations had come into existence in central and eastern Europe. Czechoslovakia split in two in 1993. Yugoslavia underwent a more complicated and bloody transformation, which began in September 1987, when Slobodan Milošević emerged as leader of the Serbian Communist Party. Milošević played on resentments against Albanians in Kosovo. In March 1989, he abolished the autonomy that Kosovo and Vojvodina had previously enjoyed, and in July 1990, he made the nationalist basis of his politics explicit when he refounded the Communist Party in Serbia as the Socialist Party of Serbia. Slovenia and Croatia responded to Serbian moves. In April 1990, Milan Kučan in Slovenia presided over the creation of multiparty politics and elections, which were won by the nationalist parties of Kučan's DEMOS movement. In Croatia, Franjo Tudjman's HDZ won elections of May 1990. Both countries declared their independence in 1991, followed by Bosnia and, in 1992, Macedonia, while Serbia and Montenegro remained part of the Yugoslav federal state. The newly created states did not, in fact, correspond to ethnic divisions: about a quarter of all Serbs lived outside Serbia. Savage fighting ensued as militias defended the interests of particular ethnic groups, and the Serbs, who inherited many of the arms of the old Yugoslav army, proved particularly ruthless. The Bosnian Muslims suffered most as violence was used to evict them from their homes.

The Soviet Union split into fifteen separate countries as its constituent republics declared their independence, a process that began in Lithuania in February 1991 and ended in Kazakhstan in December 1991.

Alliances

The fate of European military alliances after 1989 was surprising. At first, it seemed likely that the Warsaw Pact would survive. Some eastern Europeans, particularly Poles who were fearful of German attempts at frontier revision, still felt that they had common military interests with the Russians, and several noncommunist governments in eastern Europe were also keen to avoid embarrassing Mikhail Gorbachev. However, Hungary withdrew from the Pact in June 1990, and it was dissolved the following year.

NATO, created to counter a Soviet threat that no longer existed, might have expected to suffer a similar fate. Many eastern European dissidents had claimed that their aim was the disbanding of both alliance systems. Václav Havel told the Council of Europe in 1990: "The present name is so closely linked to the era of the Cold War that it would be a sign of lack of understanding of present day developments if Europe were to unite under the NATO flag."[1] In spite of all this, NATO survived and prospered, and Poland, Hungary and the Czech Republic – where Havel had become an energetic advocate of membership – all joined.

Attitudes towards NATO also changed in the West. France, which had withdrawn from the military structures of the alliance in the 1960s, began to coordinate its actions with NATO more closely. In part, this was because the nature of the alliance changed, its leaders presenting the defense of democracy and human rights as a replacement for anticommunism. NATO generals presided over Western, and even Russian, intervention in the former Yugoslavia, and NATO also benefited from the fact that Germany, which quickly accepted Polish borders, proved less threatening to its eastern neighbors than some had feared, while Russia, riven by political instability, worried its western neighbors.

In some ways, NATO membership became appealing precisely because the conflict for which it was intended was over. States that stayed outside NATO no longer benefited from the prestige of "nonaligned" status. Furthermore, defense could become more difficult for non-NATO European states after the collapse of communism. Before, even non-NATO members knew that they were protected – America and its allies would never have tolerated an assault on any part of western Europe. France's "independent" policy was more or less openly founded on the assumption that America could not disengage herself from the French fate, and French generals admitted that France's nuclear weapons were designed partly as "trip wires": they might not deter aggression on their own, but the threat that they might start a larger conflict would.[2] After the dismantling of the Warsaw Pact, there was less chance that America would come to the aid of European powers that were not members of NATO, and the military challenges that such powers faced were now more complicated. Between 1986 and 1994, France cut defense spending by less than her NATO counterparts, and neutral Sweden increased military expenditure.[3]

NATO adjusted to new circumstances – indeed, the transformation of the alliance illustrated the broader transformation of European politics. This was shown by the war that NATO conducted against Serbia in 1999 in order to protect the Albanian population of Kosovo. The war pitted the Western powers against a former communist state, but it was not simply a rerun of the Cold War. Yugoslavia had never been a member of the Warsaw Pact, and may well have owed her survival during the early 1950s to the Soviet fear of NATO. When communism had been powerful in Europe, the Western Allies had been reluctant to weaken Yugoslavia, while the western European left had often admired Yugoslav models of self-management. Yugoslav writers, including the viciously anti-Muslim Milovan Djilas, were read as critics of Soviet authoritarianism. Support for Kosovan Albanians in the early 1980s had been restrained by the fact that Albania was the last outpost of Stalinism in Europe. By the late 1990s, everything had changed. NATO's action was supported by European left-wingers who would once have been hostile to the organization's very existence, and the Secretary-General of NATO was a Spanish socialist who had been driven into political exile under Franco. The German Foreign Minister who sent his forces into action for the first time since 1945 was a member of the Green Party, whose political outlook had been forged by the anti-American radicalism of the 1960s.

United Europe?

After the destruction of the Berlin Wall, many talked about the "reunifi-cation" of Europe, but it was a deceptive phrase. The fact that divisions were no longer marked by barbed wire did not mean that they had ceased to exist. The countries under communist rule had been socially and eco-nomically diverse, and their differences could now be expressed in politi-cal terms: the end of communism often meant that frontiers were re-drawn. Many eastern or central European intellectuals had been anxious to emphasize their particular country's "Western" credentials rather than to create a united Europe. Kundera described his homeland as "the kid-napped West": the liberation of the kidnap victim implied the increasing isolation of the kidnapper.

The fall of communist rule in eastern Europe coincided with changes in western Europe. A treaty of February 1992, following the Maastricht summit of December 1991, transformed the European Community into a European Union, bringing a freer movement of people and goods within the Union's frontiers and anticipating the monetary union of 1999. The new status of eastern Europe raised further interesting ques-tions for the leaders of the European Union. Their association had always been a purely western European one, designed in its early stages largely to contain communism, and some politicians, especially in Britain, who were skeptical about European integration suggested that Europe now re-quired a wider but looser form of association.

Former communist countries were judged by the extent to which they conformed to a checklist of criteria established by Western governments and bankers, a process that separated Poland, Hungary and the Czech Re-public from their less fortunate neighbors. Slovenia was a candidate for Western recognition in a way that no other part of the former Yugoslav federation could claim to be, while the division between the Czech Re-public and Slovakia, which made little sense to most Czechs and Slovaks, fitted in with the expectations of Western investors, who had concen-trated 92 percent of their investment in the Czech part of the country even before division.[4] Western analysts expressed their judgments in nu-merical terms. A German study rated the republics of the former Soviet Union on the basis of their capacity to integrate into European markets – Ukraine did best with a score of 83 out of 100, Tajikistan did worst with a score of 18.[5]

One of the most important divisions in the former communist states was that between town and country. Prague, Budapest and Warsaw be-came more prosperous as Western companies based their operations in these cities – in 1991, the unemployment rate in Prague was 0.32 percent, when the national rate was 6.61 percent.[6] Divisions between different kinds of towns were reflected in politics. Generally, the parties most associated with economic change performed best in large cities. In Bulgaria, for example, the reforming Union of Democratic Forces drew more than two-thirds of its support from cities with more than 20,000 inhabitants.[7]

Urbanization had been dramatic under communist rule, but the total number of people who earned their living from the land was still greater than in the West. Of 12 million households in post-communist Poland, 2.5 million lived from agriculture.[8] Farming sometimes became more important, and in the poorer countries of the region – Albania, Bulgaria and Romania – the capacity to get the population fed became more significant than any other economic indicator. In Bulgaria, people moved from the city to the countryside, partly in order to replace Turks who had emigrated.

Farmers rarely welcomed free-market economics, and farms in the East were inefficient by Western standards. A survey of 1992 showed that less than a third of Polish peasants had embraced market economics, while more than half had resorted to subsistence farming.[9] In 1989, the average Polish peasant family enjoyed an income above that of the average worker; by 1992 this position had been reversed.[10]

Reformed communist parties sometimes drew votes from the countryside, and peasant parties also reemerged. Such parties had often existed before 1989 as satellites of the Communist Party. In Bulgaria, the Agrarian Party broke away and tried to regain the audience that it had enjoyed in the 1920s under the leadership of Stamboliski, the most important interwar peasant politician. In Poland in 1993, the Peasant Party, trying to distance itself from communism, signed a pact with Solidarnosc 80, which was trying to distance itself from "politicized" Solidarity.[11] The peasant leader Waldemar Pawlak became Prime Minister of Poland in the summer of 1992. Debates on modernization and democratization were often couched in terms of town/country hostility. Sociologists who organized focus-group discussions were disconcerted when one young intellectual suggested that the best thing for his country would be to "shoot the peasants."[12]

The most striking new frontier of the post-communist world was that between generations. The young were generally most favorable to change. It was they who stood the best chance of adapting to new circumstances by learning Western languages or establishing private businesses. Russian opinion of economic reform was determined by age more than by occupation or educational level, and noneconomic opportunities could also be important. The young valued the chance to travel and watch Western films. Those over fifty, by contrast, had learned to live with the certainties

Table 11: Opinions on Economic Changes in Russia
(Percentages in Favor)

	Market economy	*Privatization*
Aged 20–24	74	64
Aged 25–40	54	52
Aged 40+	36	33
Students	81	–
Retired	32	–
Educated to degree level	57	59
Educated to secondary level	52	48
Educated to primary level	40	31
Managers	62	59
Employees	48	45
Skilled workers	54	45
Unskilled workers	33	41

Source: Survey of the Russian Federation Centre for the Study of Public Opinion, cited in Léonid Gordon, "Les particularités du mouvement ouvrier en Russie postsoviétique," *Cahiers Internationaux de Sociologie*, XCV (July–December 1993), p. 266.

of the old regime, and in some cases had made a positive decision to do so – any East German would have found it fairly easy to leave the country until 1961. Many older people felt that the old regimes, for all their faults, were ones that they had built. In the 1990s, all certainties were challenged. Gerontocratic hierarchies that had guaranteed positions were swept aside, and inflation ate into pensions. The separation between those who felt part of a united Europe and those who still felt that they belonged to the East was not simply a matter of geography; it might be found even in a single family.

Private property produced social divisions that were more explicit, though perhaps no wider, than those that had existed under the old regime. Simply deciding who owned what was not easy in former communist countries, and the restitution of property was complicated. Even in east Germany, which had an efficient legal and administrative system, only one in ten requests were satisfied in the first few years after 1989.[13] Political contacts were useful. The old nomenklatura often did well, and the privileges that such people enjoyed were now more explicit and openly flaunted than they had been under communism.

Simply returning the property that people or families had owned before the communist takeover did not work. The collectivizations and nationalizations of communism had been preceded by other transfers of
property. Jews, Germans and aristocrats had been dispossessed, and often
killed or exiled, during the 1940s, and deciding which order was to be restored was difficult. Further problems were created by the transformation
that had been brought about by rapid industrialization and urbanization
under communism. A family that had owned a smallholding near Brno
in 1945 were likely to find that they now had a patch of concrete in the
middle of a housing estate.[14]

The value of assets was unpredictable. Many factories were almost
worthless when forced to face Western competition. An elegant apartment
could be a liability if it had sitting tenants who could not be evicted or
made to pay a market rent, whereas a disused attic in central Prague could –
with imagination, money and some contacts in the town hall – be transformed into a penthouse for which foreign businessmen would pay 2,500
DM per month. Occasionally, restitution could produce unexpected reversals of fortune. One Russian electrician who had grown up in state orphanages after the death of his father in the purges of the 1930s found himself
proprietor of a large estate in Lettonia – though he refused to take possession of his domain because he considered himself a "Soviet patriot."[15]

Governments restored property in various ways. Former proprietors in
the Czech Republic regained their land while those in Hungary were
given bonds. Distinctions were made between land and the machinery
with which it was worked.[16] Factories presented more awkward problems,
because much of their equipment dated from the communist period. The
widow of the former owner of the Taghell lamp factory in east Berlin received only a comparatively small number of shares in the privatized enterprise (which she promptly sold to the former communist manager of
the factory).[17]

Privatization of state assets was no easier than restitution. All governments set themselves ambitious targets that were not fulfilled.[18] Shares
were often given away free to all citizens (a third of Romanian state assets
were supposedly distributed in this way),[19] but the results of such policies
in countries with no recent experience of property, let alone stock markets, were rarely good. Many countries experienced "false privatizations."
In the Czech Republic, state assets that had supposedly been sold to the
public finished up in the hands of the major banks, which were themselves state-owned.

Cash was scarce. Local people either did not have the money to buy state
assets or, more importantly, were unable to invest in the modernization of

businesses. Foreign investment offered one possible solution to the problem, but it was scarce, and Western investors, who had spent the previous twenty years closing their own coal mines and steel plants, were uninterested in much of central European industry.

Lack of clarity about the ownership of property helped produce a particular business culture. Western capitalism depended on explicit rules and financial transparency, but in eastern Europe and the former Soviet Union company law was uncertain. Rapid inflation and the habit, inherited from communist days, of ascribing unrealistic values to assets ensured that company accounts were often fairytales. Sometimes it seemed as though the frontier between capitalism and communism had been replaced by one that divided two sorts of capitalism. George Soros, a leading Western investor, talked of "robber capitalism" in the former Soviet Union.

Political contacts were useful in exploiting the sale of state assets, which were often sold at well below their real value. Contacts were particularly valuable in the Soviet oil and gas industries, where political elites could most easily get their hands on assets with a concrete value. Viktor Chernomyrdin, the former head of the Russian state gas company Gazprom, was said to possess a 5 percent share of a company worth between $250 billion and $1,000 billion, a company that often neglected to pay tax. He moved into politics and became Prime Minister of Russia, at which point he declared a total personal wealth of $47,000 and an annual income of $8,000.[20] Boris Berezovsky owned a car dealership and appeared to have links with Sibneft (an oil company), Aeroflot (an airline), Avtovaz (a car manufacturer), Obedinenny (a bank) and several newspapers and television stations. In 1996, he was made deputy head of the Russian security council under the former communist Ivan Rybkin.[21]

A capitalism based on the exploitation of political contacts produced a particular type of corporate structure. Large holding groups united disparate companies that had nothing in common other than their directors' political influence. In Russia, such enterprises, unimaginatively labeled "Financial Industrial Groups" (FIGs), numbered twenty-eight by 1998. Often the FIGs bought newspapers or television stations to increase their political leverage. Exercising control over FIGs was made difficult by the ambiguity about who owned them. In some cases, shares in nominally privatized companies were bought by state-owned banks, which furthered the interests of those who had good relations with the government. In other cases, "coupon privatization," whereby shares in state companies were given away to the public, created a group of shareholders who had no means of obtaining information about, or influence over, the companies that they were supposed to own.

For a Western company director, the shareholder was king. Shareholder power was asserted every day in the movement of stock market prices, which determined whether a company was likely to become a takeover target and whether its management would survive. In the former communist countries, the shareholder was a remote and abstract figure. Sometimes the nature of privatization meant that shares were distributed among numerous inexperienced holders; sometimes the shareholder was a foreign investor in a distant country; sometimes ownership of companies was obscure. By contrast, the claims of employees, clients and suppliers on the loyalty of an eastern European manager were likely to be strong. Indeed, a manager who had left the employ of a state-owned company to work for a Western multinational might continue to think of those with whom he had worked (who might now be scattered around a number of competitor firms) as "colleagues" while regarding his Western superiors as representatives of foreign interests. Such thinking often produced corruption as managers enriched themselves and their friends, but industrialists also sometimes disadvantaged shareholders by behaving in what they perceived to be a "moral" way. Closing a factory, a regular operation in the West, would have more dramatic consequences if it was the only employer and provider of social services in a desolate Russian provincial town.

Naïvete as much as cynicism underlay eastern European business. Many of the most enthusiastic capitalists in the region were young and had limited experience of free enterprise. Their knowledge of capitalism was acquired from watching *Dallas* and reading the *Harvard Business Review*. They were fascinated by the external trappings of business life – portable phones, smart suits and company cars. Handing over control of a free-market economy to such men (they usually were men) was like handing over the Soviet Union to one of Stalin's innocent Western admirers (say, Sidney Webb). The most spectacular example of the new breed was Kristaq Luniku, head of the Albanian Central Bank between 1994 and 1997, who presided over the financial catastrophe that ruined many of his compatriots. He was not a ruthless former apparatchik with a well-stocked Swiss bank account, but had spent most of his career in a region of Albania where banking was almost nonexistent and salaries were paid in cash. His only serious experience was a brief training period at a provincial branch of the Bundesbank, and he was not quite thirty when he became head of the Central Bank.[22]

Capitalism in eastern Europe was affected by the legacy of communist economic thinking. Planned economies had encouraged managers to take a cavalier attitude towards figures, which had often been fudged in order to "meet targets," and questions of price had meant little when raw materials were bought at way below their market value. The heirs of this system did not pay great attention to balancing books. Whereas their predecessors had been part of a production culture that placed volume above profits, the new capitalists operated in a commercial culture that placed the number of transactions above profits – some salesmen expected to be paid bonuses in return for selling retail goods at below the wholesale price. Rapid inflation did not increase financial clarity or attention to cost control.

In the former Soviet Union, businessmen were obliged to operate outside the limits of what a Western analyst would have considered normal business behavior, just as factory managers had once been obliged to work outside the limits laid down by state plans. Many commodities simply could not be obtained for money, and factories survived by barter, which in turn often depended on a high degree of trust between entrepreneurs, who were willing to deliver goods in the expectation of getting something in return at some point in the future. Jacques Sapir estimated that half of Russian businessmen belonged to a network of confidence in which such arrangements could be made.[23] Deals that looked to an outsider like "crony capitalism" or "clientelism" were often seen by the Russians as honoring tacit contracts without which the economy would have collapsed.

The frontier between "robber capitalism" in the East and "transparent capitalism" in the West was, of course, never entirely clear-cut. Business practice in former communist countries varied enormously. In 1998, a panel of experts rated the level of corruption in central European countries on a scale of 0 to 9: Serbia and Montenegro topped the poll at 7.4, while Slovenia was rated 0.7.[24] Equally, business practice in the West varied among countries and industries. Property developers in the south of France and British arms dealers selling to Saudi Arabia had nothing to learn from the Russians about corruption.

New history

The end of the Cold War brought a rewriting of Europe's history as well as a redrawing of her maps. The process was most dramatic with regard to the history of the communist regimes. The fall of communism was preceded by increasing openness. Events in Hungary in 1956 were now classified as a popular uprising, and the Soviet Union recognized that the Warsaw Pact invasion of Czechoslovakia had been a mistake.

There was a new perspective on, or at least a new frankness about, the communist past. Discussion was most open with reference to the GDR. Parliamentarians who legislated on matters relating to the communist period, being drawn mainly from the western part of the country, could confront the past without fear of embarrassing themselves or their political allies. The East German state had not possessed the national legitimacy claimed by communist Poland and Czechoslovakia – the GDR had always been the denial of a nation rather than its expression, and its leaders, unlike those of Poland and Hungary, could not claim that they had initiated a process of gradual reform before 1989. German attitudes towards the communist past were also influenced by the habits of mind that had developed through confronting the memory of a previous dictatorship. Everyone in the former German Democratic Republic was given the right to consult their secret police files, and a number of officials – particularly those held responsible for the shooting of would-be escapees – were put on trial.

Elsewhere, matters were less clear. Few former communist states could afford to dispense with the expertise of those who had risen to power under the previous regime or the support of those who had believed in that regime. Leaders of anticommunist movements, such as Lech Wałesa and Václav Havel, appealed to their compatriots not to scratch at the scabs of the communist period; Havel refused to examine his own secret police file. Sometimes those in power had an interest in covering up what had happened under communism. In Bulgaria, the "reformed communists" who led the country during the first few years of democracy caused 130,000 out of 280,000 secret police files to disappear.[25]

Romania was particularly reluctant to confront its history. Here, in theory, the break with the past was complete – the Communist Party was made illegal – but in practice, the old communist rulers, with the exception of Ceauşescu himself, remained in power. Not surprisingly, the authorities had little appetite for openness about the past. Constantin Ticu Dumitrescu, a former leader of the National Peasants' Party, became a senator in post-communist Romania. The senate building had formerly housed the Ministry of the Interior, in the cellars of which Dumitrescu had been imprisoned in 1947, but when he applied for permission to visit those cellars, Dumitrescu was told that they were "military property" and therefore out of bounds for parliamentarians.[26] His questions about the past were unwelcome even to the victims of communism. He was expelled from the leadership of the association of former political prisoners, many of whom had been forced to become Securitate informers after their release.[27]

The way in which post-communist countries looked back on their past varied considerably. In Poland, nationalism had always provided common ground between communist leaders and their enemies. In retrospect, General Jaruzelski's rule appeared as a nationalist military regime rather than communist repression, which contributed to the comparative serenity with which Poles recalled their history; in 1997, a round table brought together participants from the Communist Party and Solidarity to discuss the period of martial law. In Hungary, the relative liberalism of communist rule during its final stages meant that some could look back on the period with a mixture of nostalgia and kitsch irony: Budapest had a museum of statues of Stalin and Marxist "theme restaurants," while a "greatest hits of real socialism" album allowed the old to recall the songs that they had sung in the communist youth movement. Such nostalgia would have been inconceivable in Romania or East Germany. In Czechoslovakia, matters were complicated by the fact that different memories existed in Prague and Bratislava: Czechs remembered the "normalization" that followed the repression of the Prague Spring (itself a mainly Czech experience) as a period of extreme intolerance. Slovaks looked back on a time of rising prosperity during which their part of the country was given greater autonomy. Czechs were shocked by the fact that many Slovak dignitaries attended the funeral of Gustáv Husák (the former Communist Party leader) in 1991.[28]

Russians had the strangest attitude of all towards their recent past – a Soviet historian remarked that the opening-up of academic debate made it "more interesting to read than to live."[29] Historical reassessment required a rethinking of almost every family history: citizens of Magnitogorsk, the steel town built from nothing in the 1930s, did not merely have to come to terms with individual stories of purges in their town but also had to recognize that their city had been built not by idealistic young pioneers but by forced labor.[30] However, not all Russians denounced the recent past. The communist period was recalled as one of stability and national pride that sometimes contrasted favorably with the painful confusion that came at its end. One survey in the late 1990s asked under which ruler life was/is good. The results were as follows:*

Leonid Brezhnev	41%
Boris Yeltsin	14%
Yuri Andropov	7%
Tsar Nicholas II	6%
Joseph Stalin	6%
Nikita Khrushchev	4%
Mikhail Gorbachev	3%
Vladimir Lenin	1%
Don't know	17%

---

*Source: VTs/IOM, cited in *The Economist*, February 14–20, 1998.

These statistics reveal disenchantment with official communist historiography, a fact reflected in the low score of Lenin (whose cult had been the basis of Soviet culture for seventy years), the comparatively high score of the last Tsar (who had been killed on Lenin's orders) and the equally high score of Stalin (who had been treated as an embarrassment by official Soviet spokesmen since 1956). They also reveal a disenchantment with post-communist leaders and communist reformers, which distinguished Russia from the West and the former communist states of eastern Europe. Brezhnev's association with the defense of Soviet power, which contributed to his popularity in Russia, made him hated elsewhere: campaigners in favor of Czech membership of NATO distributed posters showing Brezhnev's photograph. By contrast, Gorbachev, still admired elsewhere, was unpopular in Russia.

The reassessment of history extended to the Second World War, which had laid the basis for communist rule, and a certain view of the war continued to provide a justification for that rule. Official accounts in eastern Europe had emphasized the Red Army's role in liberating the region, and the prestige of western European communist parties had rested largely on their supposed role in anti-Nazi resistance.

The challenge to communist rule or Soviet power often went with a challenge to historical orthodoxy. Romanian historians underwrote their country's diplomatic independence by emphasizing the actions of local partisans rather than those of the Red Army, while in Bratislava, historians from the 1960s onwards began to explore the role of the Slovak uprising of 1944 and, implicitly, to question the importance of the Red Army and the Czech resistance. In Belgrade in 1985, Veselin Djuretic published a book that questioned the Titoist monopoly of anti-German resistance.[31]

The fall of communism speeded up such reassessments. In Poland, a country that was mauled at the hands of both Hitler and Stalin during the war, official recognition that the Katyn massacre of Polish officers had been carried out by Soviet, rather than German, forces came in March 1989. Most important was the rehabilitation of the noncommunist resistance in Poland. The Polish leaders who had gone to London in 1939 had spent most of the postwar period eating pork knuckle at the Polish air force club in Kensington while discussing their claims to be the legitimate government of their country in terms that seemed increasingly absurd, yet in December 1990 they secured the recognition of the newly elected President of Poland, Lech Wałesa, who insisted on taking office from them rather than from the outgoing communist leader.[32]

Sometimes the end of communism revived awkward memories of the Second World War. Two states in post-communist Europe – Slovakia and Croatia – had previously existed only under Nazi aegis, and in both countries some nationalists recalled the wartime regime with nostalgia. A plaque to Josef Tiso, the wartime Prime Minister of Slovakia, was unveiled in July 1990.[33] Slovakian school textbooks in the late 1990s stressed the "humane" character of Slovak concentration camps.[34] Memories of the Second World War became associated with the violent disintegration of Yugoslavia: Serbs demanded compensation for Croat wartime atrocities and used the memory of them to justify further racial attacks.[35]

The reassessment of the Second World War was most extreme in Romania, where parallels were often drawn between the crimes of Nazism and those committed during the "red holocaust." Many members of the Romanian political establishment found it more convenient to rehabilitate men who had committed crimes during the Nazi period than to punish those who had committed crimes under communism. In 1991, the Romanian parliament observed a minute's silence in memory of Ion Antonescu, the dictator who had allied with Nazi Germany, and the Romanian chief prosecutor called for the posthumous pardoning of eight of Antonescu's ministers.[36]

The fall of communism sometimes contributed to sympathy for pro-Nazi regimes, as in Slovakia and Romania, or renewed anti-Semitism, which attracted most attention in Poland, where the history of Jewish/gentile relations diverged sharply from that in the West. The Jewish community in Poland, which had been large in 1939, was small by 1945, and was further diminished by departures to Israel in the face of state-sponsored anti-Semitism in the late 1960s. Poland did not participate in the new interest in Jewish suffering that affected western European countries in the early 1970s. The contrast with France, where the Jewish population had increased in the aftermath of the Algerian war, was especially marked.

In other communist states, anti-Semitism was less widespread, and attacks on communism sometimes involved the commemoration of Jews killed under Nazism. Recognition of central Europe's Jewish past was encouraged by Western tourists and Western financial support for surviving Jewish communities. The Czech communist government – not the most liberal in the region – employed Jewish guides to show Western tourists the specifically Jewish sites of Prague during the late 1980s, and the memorial to Jews killed under Nazism became one of the most frequently visited places in the city.

The suffering of Germans expelled from central European countries, particularly Czechoslovakia, after the Second World War was also given new attention. Consideration of the subject had begun in the Prague Spring of 1968, and a collective of historians tackled the matter in an émigré journal in 1981. In 1990, Václav Havel expressed his regret for the expulsions. Such revision obviously involved a criticism of the communist regime, but it went deeper than that: the expulsions had been carried out before communist governments had been established in any central European state, and in Czechoslovakia the policy had been supported by Beneš. Expressions of regret for the expulsions implied a nostalgia for the multicultural Czechoslovakia that had existed before 1938, which raises interesting questions about the innate nationalism of central Europe. Surveys showed that Czechs, especially the young, regretted the brutality with which the Germans had been expelled.[37] This expulsion was sometimes presented as a specifically Czech crime, and was therefore particularly evocative for Slovaks.

The history of the Second World War was revisited in the West, too. Debate about Nazism in Germany was fueled by some historians' desire to rehabilitate German soldiers who had fought against invading Soviet armies in the last days of the war and also by the perception that Nazism had been a reaction to Bolshevism. The history of the French resistance was reappraised. For many years, two political traditions – communism and Gaullism – had claimed the legacy of the resistance, but the presidency of François Mitterrand – a resistance leader who was neither Gaullist nor communist – opened the way for recognition of other *résistants* from outside the two traditions. Dissension over the legacy of the Second World War was also felt in the Parti Communiste Français itself. Its leadership had always emphasized that the resistance was the property of the party as an institution rather than of the particular communists who had risked their lives (indeed, the latter were often suspected of "Titoist" propensities). Matters came to a head in 1991, immediately after the failure of the Moscow coup, when a group of resistance communists from Brittany told Georges Marchais (the communist leader who had spent much of the war working in a German factory) that he would not be welcome at their commemorative ceremonies.

Rethinking the Second World War was not just a by-product of new views of communism. Allegations that Kurt Waldheim, elected as President of Austria in 1986, had been involved in wartime atrocities in the Balkans increased the perception that Austria was a perpetrator rather than victim of Nazi crimes. The passage of time also meant that politicians began to discuss the war in a new way, and this sometimes produced a new willingness to confront the past – Jacques Chirac, born in 1932, discussed the crimes of the Vichy government, including those of the Gaullist former minister Maurice Papon, with an openness that would have been difficult for any previous Gaullist leader. In some respects, the passage of time also encouraged facile assertions that the past was no longer relevant. Helmut Kohl, born in 1930, talked of the "good fortune to have been born late," by which he meant that his contemporaries had been formed by the Hitler Youth rather than the Wehrmacht. In Italy, Gianfranco Fini, the leader of the National Alliance, emphasized that he had been born after 1945, and claimed that his position was "post-fascist."[38]

Nationalism

Some commentators feared that nationalist violence, which had been common in eastern Europe before 1945, would reemerge as soon as communist power ceased to contain it. Nationalism was often seen as a symptom of backwardness, which haunted the impoverished East when the wealthy West was developing international institutions.

The sense that nationalism was the enemy of progress was exacerbated by the career of Mikhail Gorbachev. Gorbachev was seen, in the West at least, as the epitome of reform, but he had no experience of the Soviet nationalities problem and did not seem aware of its potential importance. His reform program was conceived in terms of economics and, later, democracy, but made little allowance for national feeling. He was often tactless in his references to non-Russian parts of the Soviet population. His Western admirers feared that nationalism might "set reform back."

The significance of nationalist violence in eastern Europe can be overstated – many states were utterly unaffected by such currents. One legacy of the Second World War had been the creation of much more ethnically homogeneous states in several eastern European countries as a result of the extermination of the Jews and the postwar expulsion of the Germans. Western visitors used to Brixton or Belleville were struck by the absence of racial minorities in Prague, Warsaw and Budapest. Nationalist agitation still found an outlet against minorities (Hungarians in Romania, Turks in Bulgaria, Gypsies in Slovakia), but few countries experienced the extreme racial tension that had marked the interwar years. Forty years of communist rule had led to an acceptance of existing frontiers in most of eastern Europe. Furthermore, opponents of Soviet rule had sometimes looked to Europe rather than the nation. Poles, Hungarians and especially Czechs associated European unity with culture, liberty and democracy at a time when many western Europeans associated it with committees of middle-aged men in Brussels. The Czech-born Jacques Rupnik wrote: "It is the intellectuals of central Europe, Czesław Miłosz, Milan Kundera or György Konrád . . . who questioned the comfortable, but empty, Europe reduced to the Common Market, to compensatory payments and to agricultural surpluses."[39]

National assertion was not always violent. The separation of Slovakia and the Czech Republic was achieved without apparent ill feeling and most countries in what had been the Soviet Union had tolerable relations with their neighbors. Nationalism did not necessarily mean racism, violence or intolerance – many talked of an "inclusive" or "civic" nationalism that would respect all the nation's inhabitants and allow a variety of cultures to flourish.

Those who feared nationalism sometimes talked in terms of "popular feeling" and implied that international sentiment was felt only by an unrepresentative elite. In reality, referenda and opinion polls often showed that attitudes towards nationality among ordinary Europeans were complicated and nuanced. The Pamyat nationalist grouping in Russia, which attracted much frightened commentary in the West during the last years of the Soviet Union, never gained the support of more than 2 percent of the population.[40] Most of those who lived in Czechoslovakia did not support the division of the state, which was engineered by elites in Prague and Bratislava for reasons of party politics and economic advantage; the breakup of Yugoslavia began with referenda, but the violence that accompanied it was initiated by a small proportion of the population.

Many Europeans thought of themselves as having more than one national identity. Far from being rooted in "age-old conflicts," national feeling, or at least what people said about national feeling when asked by researchers, could change quickly – the number of Northern Irish Protestants describing themselves as "British" increased from 39 percent to 71 percent between 1968 and 1994.[41] Drafting questions about nationhood was difficult. When the Soviet Union organized a poll in the Ukraine about continued membership of a transnational federation, the local authorities simply added another question, implying that continued membership did not exclude the existence of a sovereign Ukrainian government.[42]

Nationalism was not invariably "irrational" or "archaic." Even nationalisms that damaged the national economy as a whole might benefit particular groups – plenty of Slovaks and Serbs grew rich in spite of the relative isolation that nationalist policies imposed on their countries. Some nationalisms were entirely economically rational. The desire of the Baltic states to leave the Soviet Union was increased by the perception that they did badly from the economic arrangements of the state and would benefit from opening up to the West, and the primacy of economic over purely national thinking in the breakup of the Soviet Union was reflected in the support that ethnic Russians in the Ukraine and Lithuania often gave to leaving the Union. Rich nations in transnational states sometimes benefited from breaking with their poorer partners. The Czech Republic gained from divesting itself of responsibility for Slovakia, though, curiously, ordinary Czechs feared the economic consequences of separation more than ordinary Slovaks.[43] Slovenia, which accounted for only 8 percent of the Yugoslav population but 15 percent of gross national product, had an interest in leaving the federation,[44] and by 1997 its annual gross domestic product per head was more than ten times that of Bosnia.[45] The most striking example of economic nationalism was seen in Italy, in Umberto Bossi's Northern League. The state that the League wished to create had no linguistic, cultural or historical roots but was almost entirely based on a desire to see the richest part of the country freed from the need to subsidize the rest.

Internationalization

The growth of nationalism, largely in eastern Europe, was accompanied by the growth of internationalism, mostly in western Europe. Internationalization was often described as though it were eroding all national peculiarities to create a single, homogeneous Europe, but the reality was more involved. A business executive might speak English in the office but still speak Dutch at home. Furthermore, internationalization was not one process but several interrelated ones. First was globalization, a primarily economic process by which flows of trade and communication crossed the world with little interference from government. Second was Americanization, a cultural and economic process that was not new – some Europeans had admired America throughout the twentieth century. In the early 1980s the great success of the American economy in general and certain companies in particular gave America new appeal. Americanization bore a complicated relationship to globalization because increasing numbers of American companies insisted that they were global and multicultural. Third was European integration, a process that owed much to conscious political decision, as governments pooled their sovereignty and constructed pan-European institutions. It was sometimes perceived as a means to resist globalization; European regulations sometimes excluded imports from outside the European Union, and guaranteed certain standards, such as those relating to employment, inside it. A European industrial policy was used, not very successfully, to try to build up European champion companies that would compete with American or Asian rivals.

The impact of Americanization was epitomized by the Disney corporation, which bombarded the world with films and toys and established a theme park near Paris in 1991. McDonald's hamburger restaurants played an even greater role in European demonology, being seen as a symbol of a bland uniformity that had been imposed on Europe. The Prague-born writer Peter Demetz, who had spent most of his career at Yale, pointed out that the Akademická Kavárna on Vodičkova Street, where a generation of Czech writers had gathered, was now a McDonald's.[46] Michael Portillo was said to have lost his seat in the 1997 general election partly because he had not opposed the conversion of the local Conservative Party headquarters into a drive-in McDonald's, while a French peasant leader, José Bové, became a national hero after leading an assault on a McDonald's in the Aveyron.

Such attacks missed the point. American culture had more than one aspect, and Europeans had often mixed these different elements to create their own version of America. Furthermore, America did not simply export its vision of the world without considering the audience at which it was directed. McDonald's restaurants did not, as was so frequently claimed, serve the same food in every country, but made subtle adjustments to suit local tastes, which is why McDonald's survived in the French market while its less flexible rival Burger King was forced to withdraw. Sometimes, aspects of popular culture that seemed peculiarly American to Europeans were designated for export precisely because of limited success in the United States itself. This was true of McDonald's, which chased European markets partly because it had suffered so badly from the competition of (British-owned) Burger King in America.[47]

Sometimes, of course, American efforts to adjust to Europe seemed absurd or offensive to European audiences. Pizza Hut, owned by PepsiCo, produced an advertisement that showed Mikhail Gorbachev in one of their Moscow outlets. Gorbachev was said to hate pizza and the advertisement was not shown in Russia, where most people hated him. The Disney corporation was sued by the descendants of Victor Hugo, who were outraged that the film *The Hunchback of Notre Dame* had been produced without acknowledgment of Hugo's original.[48]

The European elite

As European countries became part of an international economy, a new class of European emerged. The well-dressed young people who flitted through the business-class lounges of international airports brandishing EU passports and corporate American Express cards were probably more international in their culture than any group of Europeans since the aristocratic diplomats of the nineteenth century.

The European elite had a very high – usually postgraduate – level of education. Prestigious universities aimed to recruit and train on an international level. The French École Nationale d'Administration moved some of its operations from Paris to Strasbourg in order to ensure that its candidates were acquainted with the workings of the European Union as

well as those of the French state, and the Institut d'Études Politiques began to conduct part of its teaching in English. INSEAD, the European
business school established at Fontainbleu, threatened to move its operations to Switzerland or Germany when the French state obstructed its expansion. Sometimes European students attended universities in three different countries. When Tristan van der Stegen (Canadian mother,
Walloon father, Flemish name, Parisian upbringing, Anglo-French education) joined the M.Sc. course in Comparative Politics at the London
School of Economics, he found that only two out of forty students in his
class held British passports.

The European elite was also united by a particular kind of relation to
America. Many of them worked, for a time at least, in American companies, particularly investment banks or management consultancies, and an
understanding of American management techniques and of the Anglo-
Saxon world of supposedly ruthless free-market competition was regarded
as a necessary qualification for success. However, members of the European elite did not simply adopt American values. They were contemptu-
ous of many aspects of American popular culture. The impact of Disneyland Paris on the European masses and the elite was quite different. For
the masses it meant Goofy and Mickey Mouse; for the elite it meant the
management philosophy of Philippe Bourguignon, the chairman of the
company until 1997, who believed that his executives should be formed
by the Harvard Business School and McKinsey rather than the French
civil service.

The lingua franca of the elite was English. The hegemony of English
owed much to America's economic power but increasingly it became the
language that continental Europeans spoke to each other. French, the language of diplomacy and the European Economic Community in its early
days, was the main victim of the process. Boutros Boutros-Ghali, *Secrétaire
Général de La Francophonie*, wrote his memoirs in English, and by 1997, 42
percent of European Union documents were first composed in English,
against 40 percent in French.[49] When Jacques Delors chaired a crucial
meeting of central bankers to discuss the prospect of a single currency, he
began speaking in French, but, seeing that his audience was uncomfortable,
switched to English. English became the language of multinational corporations, even when their headquarters were in non-English-speaking countries. The head of ABB, a Swiss–Swedish engineering group, ruefully admitted that his company's language was "bad English." The board of the
Swiss ball-bearings manufacturer SKF contained eleven Swedes, one Swiss,
one German and one Italian; when it met at Gothenburg in 1998, it conducted proceedings in English.[50] The spread of English was encouraged by
the inclusion in the EU of Scandinavian countries, where English was

widely spoken as a second language, and by the fall of communism. Inhabitants of eastern Europe recognized that integration into Europe required them to master a major European language. Once this language might have been French or German, but by the 1990s English was established as the language of capitalism. Curiously, as English was recognized as the lingua franca of eastern European business, French regained its position as the language of eastern European high culture – Ismail Kadaré, the Nobel Prize–winning novelist, moved to Paris from Albania; Milan Kundera's first novel to be written in French, *L'identité*, was published in 1998; and a Russian-born writer, Andrei Makine, won the Prix Goncourt in 1995.

The European elite was not attached to any particular country; indeed, its members were more likely to identify with a city than a country. Particularly important was London. At the end of the century, central London overtook Hamburg to become the richest place in Europe – average incomes were more than twice the European Union average. London provided ambitious young Europeans with a place where they could experience "Anglo-Saxon capitalism" and very high salaries, while remaining three hours away from the Gare du Nord. As a financial center, it dwarfed all other European cities, and in some respects it dwarfed American cities, too: more American banks were represented in London than in New York. The role of London reflected the way in which nation-states were being replaced by units that were both smaller and bigger. Although London was famous for cosmopolitanism and dynamism, it was located in a country famous for insularity and sclerosis. The ambitious young people who thronged into the city were more likely to have visited Kathmandu than Wolverhampton.

Conclusion

The fall of communism created not a united Europe but rather a multiplicity of different Europes superimposed on each other. The gulf between London and Prague narrowed but that between London and Cornwall or Prague and Ostrova widened. Within small areas, different generations, classes and ethnic groups led very different lives. A European banker with a poor sense of direction who caught the Eurostar from Paris to London and lost his bearings in the Gare du Nord might exit at La Chapelle. Instead of being surrounded by sharp-suited business-class travelers, he would be close to the Goutte d'Or, an area celebrated in French working-class mythology but which might now be mistaken for a suburb of Algiers. Similarly, if he were to take the correct exit from Waterloo station, he would cross a bridge with a view of St. Paul's and Big Ben and would arrive in a few minutes for his meeting at Citibank's

London headquarters in the Strand. If he turned in the other direction and walked for a few minutes, he would find himself at the Elephant and Castle – an area of deprivation with architecture reminiscent of east Berlin.

For the most privileged Europeans, the fall of communism created a Europe without frontiers that bore a striking resemblance to the Europe that the privileged had known before 1914. For the least privileged, frontiers were more important than at any time since the 1940s. Gypsies from the former Czechoslovakia were shuttled between two newly created states that refused to recognize their citizenship – the town council of Usti-nad-Labem in the Czech Republic built a wall to enclose its Gypsy population – and Kosovo Albanians saw their identity papers being torn up by Serb policemen before they were pushed across the border. Frontiers of race, age and class divided cities even in the relatively prosperous countries of western Europe. At a time when a rich white European could drive from Paris to Prague with barely any interference from frontier guards, young black men in Sheffield were reluctant to visit the Meadowhall shopping mall because they knew that they would be asked to leave by security guards.[51]

2

SEXUAL REVOLUTIONS

AT THE BEGINNING of the 1980s, it was widely expected that there would be a reassertion of family values after the "permissiveness" that was seen to have characterized the 1960s and early 1970s. This desire to assert traditional morality was made explicit by many conservatives. Some economic projects were specifically tied to the family: the task of social and economic provision for the future was to be shifted from the state to the family. Some assumed that the climate of economic gloom that followed the slowing of growth in the 1970s would automatically result in a return to traditional values, just as the economic crisis of the 1930s seemed to have reversed the sexual innovation of the 1920s.

Against all expectations, the traditional values of conservative morality were challenged in the 1980s. There was irony in the pledges of conservatives to "reverse" the values of the 1960s: in reality marriage, the centerpiece of conservative morality, had become more common and more highly regarded throughout the 1960s. It was in the mid-1970s that marriage rates began to drop. In several countries where the Catholic Church had enjoyed great influence – Ireland, Italy and Spain – the 1980s saw the kind of legislative changes that had occurred in Britain, France and West Germany during the 1960s and early 1970s. Spain, for example, legalized divorce in 1981 and abortion in 1983. Legislative change in the 1980s, perhaps more than in the 1960s, was associated with changes in behavior – birth rates dropped in Spain and Italy, which came to have the lowest birth rates in Europe. Changes in public attitudes were probably most dramatic in Ireland, where legislation on homosexuality and contraception remained unchanged but public opinion, particularly in large cities, became more tolerant of such practices. The Irish Tourist Board even rewrote national history to suit the new mood. A casual visitor might well have assumed that Oscar Wilde and James Joyce – Ireland's best-known sexual dissidents – had spent their lives carousing in Dublin pubs with their broad-minded compatriots.

Women, independence and work

Just as some women had been marginalized in the "permissive" 1960s, so some were allowed a greater public role in the "repressive" 1980s. Their changing status had much to do with economics, as the number of working women increased in every European country. Between 1960 and 1994, the proportion of women in the total workforce increased from slightly more than 20 percent to slightly less than 40 percent in Spain; from just over 30 percent to just under 50 percent in Sweden and France; and from about 20 percent to about 45 percent in the Netherlands.[1] The heavy industries that had traditionally employed only men declined, and light industries such as consumer electronics and service jobs, in which women were numerous, expanded.

It should not be assumed that women always regarded work as emancipatory. The attraction of hiring women for certain employers lay precisely in the fact that they accepted conditions that the unionized male workforce would have resisted. In theory legislation prevented discrimination on grounds of sex in almost every western European country, but in practice laws requiring equal pay for equal work meant little because the kinds of jobs that women did were frequently different from those that men did. Women often worked part-time or on short-term contracts that made it difficult for them to obtain social security benefits or legally enforceable contracts. Much women's work – paid childcare in France, for example – took place in the "black economy." The average woman in Europe seems to have earned about a third less than the average man.[2]

Sometimes women's entry into the workforce simply replicated the separate spheres of home and work in a different context. In Sweden, women took jobs caring for children or the old and were therefore paid for carrying out functions that they might formerly have carried out unpaid at home. In Italy, the fact that children went to school only in the morning meant that a large proportion of women with children sought work in the education system in order to be at home at the same time as their children; in 1981, 91 percent of Italian primary schoolteachers were women.[3]

At the top of society, women's lot seemed better. Having been underrepresented among engineers in most countries, they benefited from the shift of power from industry to finance. In financial institutions, women benefited from expansion. The old-boy networks that had guaranteed male jobs among accepting houses and stockbrokers in the City of London were difficult to sustain in operations with thousands of employees.[4] The market had more to do with women's entry into high-level positions than government policy – the one major financial institution that managed to exclude women almost entirely in the 1980s was publicly owned: the Bundesbank council contained one woman and seventy-five men in 1991.[5]

The professional success of some women was associated with a wider social shift. Increasingly, the most privileged people in society married and/or had children with people who were as professionally and educationally successful as themselves. Ségolène Royal, minister in France since 1997, has four children with François Hollande, Secretary of the French Socialist Party; they met when they were both students at the elite École Nationale d'Administration. Tony Blair met his wife Cherie Booth when they were both pupil barristers.

The diminishing gender gap at the top of society was sometimes accompanied by a widening gap separating the top from the rest of society: a family that contains two partners in Goldman Sachs will be richer than a family that contains one. Indeed, by the 1990s, the most important social gaps separated not families with one adult earning a good income from families with one adult earning a modest income, but families with two adults earning a good income from families with no adults in employment. There were also more complicated social and cultural reasons for the link between certain kinds of sexual equality and economic inequality. A couple of equally successful people were able to provide each other with degrees of support that reinforced both careers, seeking different, but mutually supporting, forms of power. Children who grew up in this new class had the particular advantage of having access to two different sets of role models, contacts and inside information.

Women and politics since the 1980s: the reconciliation with the left

The British Conservative leader Harold Macmillan famously remarked that there were three institutions that a British politician should never annoy – the Catholic Church, the Brigade of Guards and the National Union of Mineworkers. It is revealing that a politician in a country in which more than half of the voters – and considerably more than half the voters who supported the Conservative Party – were women should have been so interested in three institutions that were exclusively male and closely associated with "masculine" virtues – strength, courage, authority. Armies, churches and the industrial working class were key elements of many political cultures, and each was linked to a particular pattern of relations between the sexes. The politics of the industrial working class were usually based on the simple exclusion of women, but the positions of the Church and the army were more complicated. Both institutions had a role for women (albeit a subordinate one). This partly accounts for the fact that conservative parties attracted women's votes more easily than left-wing rivals during the three decades after the Second World War. During the 1980s, though, secularization, the diminishing importance of the military and the decline of heavy industry called into question the primacy of institutions that had been most associated with male power.

In some ways, the Catholic Church was – through the Christian democrat parties – the most important element in the postwar politics of continental Europe. Neither the Church nor its political allies ever excluded women, who composed the majority of those who attended mass as well as the majority of those who voted for Christian democrat parties. However, the role of women was seen as one of passivity and obedience. They were excluded from positions of authority in the Church and were rarely elected as representatives of Christian democrat parties. Catholic agencies were enthusiastic supporters of the "traditional" family in which women devoted themselves to housework and raising children.

Gradually, relations between the Church and women changed. Very few women in western Europe in the 1990s said, as many of their grandmothers would have said, that the Church was the most important thing in their lives. More generally, the radicalization of some parts of the Catholic Church in the 1960s broke the link between the Church and the political right. Christian democrat parties remained powerful, but were less likely to be seen as different from secular conservatives. In spite of the efforts of a very conservative Pope during the 1980s, "traditional" views of the family and sexual matters sometimes seemed to be associated more with the political right than with the Church; in Spain in the early 1990s, only a quarter of practicing Catholics, compared with a third of right-wing voters, opposed birth control.[6] When people talked about specifically Christian, and specifically women's, politics during the 1980s, they were as likely to mean concern with peace, Third World debt or the environment as the defense of the family.

Armies were the second institution that had underwritten a certain vision of relations between the sexes. Although soldiers were predominantly male, the celebration of armies always involved reference to women. Military patriotism was often associated with the defense of a country inhabited by vulnerable women and children, and its political appeal embraced some women. Charles de Gaulle, the postwar politician in western Europe who played most explicitly on his military career, attracted votes from a mainly female electorate. Ultimately, however, placing the army at the center of political life depended on the idea that courage and leadership were particularly male virtues.

During the 1980s, the army's position became less secure in ways associated with changes in the political role of women. Some women rejected their prescribed role as vulnerable beings in need of protection; in Britain and West Germany, women were active in the peace campaigns against nuclear weapons. Perhaps more importantly, the role of armies changed for purely military reasons. After the end of the Cold War large armies, especially conscript armies, were redundant. This marked a crucial change. Citizenship had often been linked to military service; it is no accident that the last country in western Europe to grant women the vote, Switzerland, was also the country with the most universal form of military service. The end of conscript armies broke the citizen–soldier–voter link.

The decline of heavy industry was the most dramatic development to affect the relationship of women and politics. Heavy industries had often excluded women more effectively than the army or the Church. Whereas the political culture of the right granted women a subordinate position, the political culture of the left often denied women any place at all. The segregation of the sexes associated with coal mines and blast furnaces had, of course, already been eroded in the 1950s; the production lines of car factories were still staffed mainly by men, but they did not constitute a world that was unimaginable to women. The physical danger and discomfort that united miners or steelworkers was less common in modern factories.

In the 1980s, heavy industry declined sharply. The British National Union of Mineworkers, which had once represented 600,000 men, came to have less than 30,000 members. The rhetoric of the left changed, and the traditional emphasis on the masculinity of a working class characterized by physical strength became less important. During the British miners' strike of 1984–85, much was made of the defense of "communities" (rather than merely the defense of jobs) and the role that miners' wives played in supporting the strike. The emphasis owed something to the need of left-wing intellectuals to rearticulate their support for the working class in feminist terms.

From the early 1970s onwards, new left-wing parties were formed that sought support among white-collar workers and often aimed to break with the sexism of the old left. In France the Parti Socialiste (PS), formed in 1971, was such a group, and in 1988, a PS candidate (François Mitterrand) became the first left-winger in French history to gain a predominantly female vote in a presidential election. In Spain, the ending of Francoism offered left-wing parties a chance to recast their appeal, and many did so in ways intended to appeal to women. The Spanish Communist Party declared itself the "party of women" in 1975; more significantly, the Spanish Socialist Party (PSOE) acquired a vast number of new supporters and members after its legalization. In 1982, the PSOE broke the center right's hold on the women's vote. It gained a third of all women's votes, while the Union of the Democratic Center, formerly the most successful party among women, gained only 7 percent.[7] Communist parties sometimes saw the incorporation of women as a way of rebuilding their appeal in a world of "postindustrial politics." The Dutch Communist Party embraced feminism in the 1980s, and the British Communist Party appointed a woman leader, Nina Temple, as part of its general "rebranding" in 1990.

The political movements that had the most innovative attitudes towards women were the Green parties that began to have an impact, especially in West Germany, from the early 1980s. The Green parties rejected a key element in right-wing politics – militarism – as well as a key element in left-wing politics, heavy industry. Many of the most prominent Greens – such as Petra Kelly and Dominique Voynet – were women, and Green parties were often the only political parties explicitly committed to equal representation of men and women among their leaders and parliamentary representatives. In Germany, in 1987, 57 percent of Green members of parliament were women; the comparable figures for the social democrats and Christian democrats were 16 percent and 8 percent.[8] Unlike conventional left-wing parties, Green parties secured predominantly female support in elections. Because Green parties had usually been founded at a time when radical feminism was becoming influential on the left, feminism was built into their foundations rather than grafted on as an afterthought. Most strikingly, Greens often used a rhetoric that resembled that of their conservative opponents. They did not argue that differences between the sexes were an irrelevant distraction from differences between classes. Indeed, they often accepted that women had a particular capacity for nurturing and cooperation, but they deployed such qualities in the public sphere rather than at home. The change in women's political behavior in the 1980s was important. For the first time, left-wing parties attracted predominantly female electorates and some political parties were self-consciously feminist. The significance of party politics in terms of the wider distribution of power should not be overestimated, though. In Germany in 1998, one-quarter of members of parliament but less than 3 percent of senior managers in the largest 70,000 companies were women.[9]

Sexuality, politics and economics

Homosexuals were targets of much hostility from the right during the 1970s and early 1980s, and were often used as symbols of the decadence and corruption that could be expected if "family values" were allowed to collapse. Fanfani, a leader of the Italian Christian democrats, warned in 1974: "If divorce is allowed, in Italy it will be possible to have marriages between homosexuals, and perhaps your wife will run off with some pretty young girl."[10] The Tottenham Conservative Association proclaimed that homosexuality was a "bigger threat to family life than even the bombers and the guns of Adolf Hitler,"[11] while the British Conservative government's campaign against the power of local authorities, particularly the Greater London Council, was accompanied by attacks on the alleged promotion of homosexuality by such bodies. Eventually the government introduced a section of a bill on local government designed to prevent the "promotion of homosexuality as a legitimate form of family life."

It is tempting to present the conflict over homosexuality as a simple one, in which the "militant left" was most committed to the emancipation of homosexuals and the "radical right" was most committed to "family values." Things were more complicated. One element of radical right thinking, libertarianism, inclined towards tolerance, and the British Conservative Party's attitude towards sexuality changed dramatically after the departure of Margaret Thatcher in 1990 and again, even more dramatically, after its election defeat of 1997. In 1998 the new leader of the party, William Hague, voted in favor of lowering the age of consent for homosexual men to sixteen. It might be argued that this was not new. Some Conservative MPs had voted in favor of reducing discrimination against male homosexuals in the 1960s, and the mood of the early 1990s might be seen as merely a return to values that had prevailed before the exceptional interlude of early Thatcherism. However, the reforms of the early 1990s, unlike those of the 1960s, were designed to bring homosexuality into mainstream society rather than to control and isolate it. Hague sent a message of goodwill to the 1997 Gay Pride demonstration in London. Continental conservatives, often influenced by Christian democracy, were less tolerant than their British counterparts on matters of sexuality. In 1998 much of the French right mobilized against a plan for a "*union civique*" that included both heterosexual and homosexual households. Just as the right was not always intolerant, so the left was not always tolerant. The most important organization of the British extreme left – Militant – had very conservative views on sexuality.

In the 1980s, the left's view of homosexuality began to change. This was illustrated in French interpretations of the resistance, collaboration and fascism. In the postwar period, many writers had argued that collaboration and fascism went with male effeminacy and homosexuality. Sartre – whose own image was constructed around an aggressive masculinity of boxing, drinking and womanizing – was a prominent exponent of the view, but by the 1980s he gave an interview to *Gai Pied* magazine and expressed admiration for many aspects of homosexual life.

In Britain, homosexuality had rarely been described in the explicitly political terms that continental communists adopted, but in a more general way, middle-class left-wingers had projected onto the working class an image of "authentic" masculinity. In the 1980s, though, the radical left became increasingly interested in gender and sexuality, and this interest sometimes replaced, or intertwined with, its interest in class. The British miners' strike of 1984 illustrated this process; at the 1984 Labour Party conference, the National Union of Mineworkers sponsored a motion in favor of gay rights.[12] The links between struggles over sexuality and those over other matters were reflected by the action of the Union of Democratic Miners. The UDM represented the Nottinghamshire miners, once idealized by D. H. Lawrence, who had continued to work during the 1984 strike – it supported a move by the "Parents' Rights Group" to sue Haringey Council for its support for homosexual causes.[13]

AIDS might well have strengthened a conservative agenda on sexual matters. The British government toyed with the idea of responding to AIDS by discouraging all extramarital sex but such policies were obstructed by the power of civil servants and doctors. AIDS was increasingly seen as a health crisis rather than a moral one, and the experts removed it from the sphere of party political debate. Clause 28 of the Local Government Act of 1987–88, which forbade local authorities from promoting homosexuality, contained a provision that: "Nothing in the subsection (1) above shall be taken to prohibit the doing of anything for the purpose of treating or preventing the spread of disease."

AIDS interacted with medical science in a curious way. During the 1970s and 1980s, historians influenced by Michel Foucault argued that "homosexuality" was an invented category, suggesting that the idea of homosexuals as a group apart had emerged only recently and, in particular, that it had been the product of medical science during the late nineteenth century. In part, of course, such work encouraged a more questioning attitude towards the classification of people on the basis of sexual orientation, but it also interacted with changes in medical science. Scientists had often thought of homosexuality as a disease; British doctors were still offering to "cure" it in the 1960s. In the 1980s, most doctors ceased to regard homosexuality in this way, while much attention was devoted to AIDS as a disease. The treatment of AIDS challenged broad sexual categories by shifting attention to specific sexual acts.

Homosexuality's entry into mainstream culture was facilitated by economics. Adult men were wealthier than the rest of the population and adult men who were unlikely to have dependents from outside this privileged group had particular economic power. More generally, male homosexuals adapted well to the particular consumer culture associated with the capitalism of the 1980s. As "youth" became defined by consumption patterns rather than age, homosexual men came to the fore. Advertising campaigns were structured to appeal to homosexual men; sometimes homosexuals were the leading element in a consumer coalition of the very young and the very wealthy.

The commercialization of homosexuality and its close relations with certain elements of heterosexual society was reflected in urban geography. The gay quarter of Paris moved from the rue Sainte Anne, where discreet nightclubs had operated behind closed doors, to the Marais, where fashionable bars, with a clientele that included both sexes and all sexual orientations, opened directly on to the street,[14] while the London gay scene underwent a similar change when it moved from Earl's Court to Soho. The business interests of the homosexual community in France became so important that in 1990 a Syndicat National des Entreprises Gaies was created. By 1997, the association claimed 900 members in fifteen different sectors with a turnover of a billion francs.[15] David Girard, a successful entrepreneur in the Marais, wrote: "The bar owner who, in the summer, opens a terrace where dozens of guys . . . meet openly, is at least as militant as they [gay rights' activists] are. Even if he earns money from it. By creating two bath-houses, two magazines distributed in every city in France, a much-talked about restaurant and a crowded night-club, I think that I have done more for gays than they ever have."[16]

The changing status of male homosexuals, like that of professionally successful women, was intertwined with social privilege. Homosexual integration was most marked among wealthy young white people in certain cities of northwest Europe – London, Manchester, Edinburgh, Paris, Berlin, Amsterdam.[17] Precisely because it was identified with prominent representatives who had been successful in high-profile professions, male homosexuality came to seem more remote from the life of rural populations or the industrial working class. Reaction to AIDS sometimes marked new divisions between respectability and non-respectability. Homosexuals who practiced safe sex, often represented by articulate middle-class spokesmen, were now part of the respectable, while intravenous drug users and people from parts of east Africa – both groups that were unlikely to be privileged – were increasingly seen as a threat.[18]

Eastern Europe: a sexual counterrevolution?

Changes in the status of women, and of sexual relations, in eastern Europe after the fall of communism presented an interesting contrast to those occurring in the West. Referring to Naomi Wolf's theory of a "genderquake" that had shaken the West, Mary Buckley wrote: "Many women in the post-Soviet states would probably be highly amused by the concept of 'genderquake,' and unlikely to view one as imminent in Russia, Armenia or Uzbekistan."[19]

The assumption that eastern Europe experienced a sexual "counterrevolution" after 1989 is, however, deceptive. The liberation of women in communist countries had always been more apparent than real and the "freedoms" that women lost after 1989 were often obligations imposed on them by the poverty of communist states. These obligations were then covered with a veneer of feminist rhetoric by a state that was controlled almost entirely by men.

Broadly speaking, the position of women after the fall of communism changed in two ways. The first related to employment.[20] In the Czech Republic, unemployment dropped during the 1990s and unemployment rates in Prague were so low that gender differences would have been trivial. In Hungary and perhaps Bulgaria,[21] women seem to have held on to employment better than men.[22] In every other part of formerly communist Europe, unemployment increased as companies that were no longer constrained by social duties or the exigencies of fulfilling government plans tried to increase productivity. Women bore a disproportionate share of that increase; in Poland, in the 1990s, they accounted for more than half the unemployed.[23]

Women who remained in employment tended to lose status. In Russia, men were more likely than women to leave jobs voluntarily, suggesting that men hoped to escape from firms where conditions or pay were declining while women held on for fear of being unable to find alternative employment.[24] Qualified Russian women who lost their jobs were often obliged to accept new posts that did not require qualifications. In Poland, the proportion of senior female managers in the private companies created after communism was even smaller than it had been in the state companies under communism.[25] High levels of education offered women less protection against unemployment than men.[26]

It is not easy to explain this phenomenon in terms of economic theory. Free markets ought to have given employers an interest in hiring the best people, regardless of sex. Besides, the sexual discrimination in terms of training and employment that had operated under communism ought to have made women more employable than men. The sectors in which men were predominant, such as heavy industry and engineering, did worst in the free market, whereas women tended to be trained in foreign languages and commerce, which were highly valued in the new economy. In practice, educational qualifications rarely translated into access to the highest positions. In Hungary, over half of qualified accountants and financial executives but less than a fifth of chief executives were women.[27]

The problem for women was that recruitment and business life depended on networks of informal contacts as much as on formal qualifications or competence. Such networks had existed under communism but their effects had been disguised by government policy and the absence of official unemployment. In the chaotic circumstances of a newly created private sector, contacts became highly important. The impact of contacts was seen in Slovakia, where men who had been members of the Communist Party were half as likely to be unemployed as men who had not been members. For women, by contrast, past membership of the party increased the chances of being unemployed.[28] Hungarian women suffered because the burden of household chores had excluded them from the out-of-hours working in the communist era that had often led to the foundation of private enterprises.

The changing status of women at work was accompanied by changes in the field of birth control. Since the 1950s, most communist states had allowed relatively free access to abortion. In Poland, the number of officially reported abortions was about 120,000 a year, but it was widely believed that the real annual total was much higher.[29] The fall of communism brought this to an end: abortion in Poland was made almost completely illegal, and in east Germany it became more difficult as legislation previously in force only in west Germany was now applied to the entire country.

Western feminists, for whom the right to abortion was a crucial demand, interpreted changes in the East as a sign that women were losing freedom, but such an interpretation is open to question. Access to abortion had always owed more to economics and the state than to women's interests. Communism was rarely associated with a respect for sexual liberty; its values were usually puritan and conservative, and communist states had not hesitated to forbid abortion when it suited them. All communist states had followed the lead of Moscow, which outlawed abortion in 1936, and none had legalized abortion until the Soviet Union did so in the 1950s. Abortion in most communist countries had been performed in primitive conditions, which often threatened women's health, and was common mainly because other forms of birth control were unavailable.[30]

Romania reflected the complexity of attitudes towards abortion and of the reaction that followed the fall of communism. Abortion in Romania had been vigorously repressed since 1966, and illegal operations had been even more dangerous than the legal ones carried out elsewhere in the Eastern Bloc (471 Romanian women died as a result of abortions in 1984). Romanian anticommunists saw the legalization of abortion as an important symbol. When the town of Timişoara declared itself free at the beginning of the Romanian revolution of 1989, abortion was immediately declared free and legal; a week later it was free throughout the country. It was estimated that a million Romanian women had abortions in 1990.[31]

In countries where abortion was restricted after 1989, the impact of such limitations varied according to social position. Even in Poland, wealthy women in large cities may have been better off, because they now had access to Western contraceptives, which was restricted among the poor by money and in rural areas by the pressure that Catholic groups imposed on pharmacists.[32] The least privileged thus lost the freedoms of communism without gaining the freedoms of capitalism.

Changes in access to birth control were accompanied by more general developments in the perception of women. Women's organizations in the West were generally autonomous and became more powerful during the 1990s. By contrast women's movements in the East had been sponsored by the state and had acted as satellites of the Communist Party, lacking credibility in the eyes of the general population, which associated them with the old regime, and in the eyes of women themselves, who knew that such organizations had been of little practical benefit. Many women in the former communist countries were reluctant to use the term "feminist." The end of communism was often accompanied by a reassertion of "traditional" values. In some cases, the process had begun in the 1980s: Soviet educational reform of 1984 emphasized the preparation of women for their family roles,[33] and Gorbachev talked of women "returning" to their "purely womanly mission."[34]

Many politicians in former communist countries talked of women "returning" to the home. Such rhetoric conjured up an image of nuclear families and full-time housewives that resembled American society of the 1950s. The realities of the homes to which women returned varied greatly. Many parts of eastern Europe had moved directly from a peasant society, in which the household was itself an economic unit, to an industrialized communist one, in which women worked outside the home for money, and the "traditional housewife" bore no relation to their traditions. Birthrates in most post-communist countries dropped, so fewer women were occupied as full-time mothers, even as the number who formally declared themselves to be in that category increased. Sometimes the "homes" to which women returned were as much economic units as the peasant farms that their grandmothers had left. Mrs. Kotrba, for example, spent much of her time in the house that had been restored to her family at 17 Kremencova in Prague, but as the building in question contained a dozen apartments, two restaurants, a café and a shop, her chores involved the fax machine more than the vacuum cleaner. Women's feelings about "returning" home were influenced by the prosperity of their societies – in Prague and Budapest, the conservative image of a housewife maintaining the comfortable home that had been bought with her husband's salary was credible, but women in parts of Russia or Romania knew that such a vision was fantasy. Many seem to have preferred even the dangerous and noisy factories in which they worked to the squalid communal apartments in which they lived.

More generally, the images presented to women in former communist countries, particularly the successor states of the Soviet Union, changed sharply with the change of political regime. Raisa Gorbachev, who had a doctorate in sociology, gave way to Boris Yeltsin's ostentatiously deferential wife; a Soviet woman filmmaker commented that the positive view that had formerly been presented of "female shock workers or heroic partisans" had been replaced by the "hard-currency call girl."[35]

The differences between East and West in matters of sex were illustrated in the relationship between sex and power. At a time when relations based on unequal social position, money or force were seen as less acceptable in western Europe,[36] they became more visible in eastern Europe. Prostitutes lined the main roads leading from the German border in the Czech Republic. Sometimes the growth of pornography and prostitution provided ammunition for conservative commentators who insisted on the need for strict sexual morality. Women in eastern Europe often faced a society in which the only publicly discussed models for female behavior seemed to be those of the housewife and the prostitute.

The incidence of the most coercive form of sexual relations – rape – is hard to assess. Societies in which rape is most prevalent are those in which it is least likely to be recorded – the son of a prominent Czech businessman was acquitted of rape on two occasions in the late 1990s. In Russia, 14,400 cases of rape were reported in 1993; some estimated that that was just 10 percent of the real figure.[37] Serbian forces in the Yugoslav civil war of 1991–95 seem to have systematically used rape to advance the "ethnic cleansing" of Bosnian Muslims – the Bosnian Interior Ministry claimed that a total of 50,000 Bosnian women had been raped.[38]

Conclusion

The strongest publicly proclaimed intentions with regard to sexual relations at the beginning of the 1980s were those of the western European right – particularly the Thatcher government in Britain – to restore "family values" and those of the communist regimes in eastern Europe to integrate women fully into national life. By the end of the century, it was in western Europe that traditional values relating to women, sex and the family had been most challenged, and it was in eastern Europe that "traditional" values were most influential. Furthermore, both the "emancipated" West and the "conservative" East contained a wide variety of different attitudes, and the values reflected on television, in advertising and in the statements of publicly prominent people did not always bear much resemblance to the values of the population as a whole. The policies of the state and the proclamations of people who saw themselves as arbiters of morality did, of course, have an effect on the position of women and on sexual morality, but it was not direct or simple. Much more important were the currents of social, economic and cultural change that eddied around divisions of class, race and nation.

3

NEW POLITICS?

THERE IS NOTHING new about "new politics." European politicians have always claimed to be different from their predecessors and called for an end to division, corruption, dogmatism and all the other vices for which politicians are usually blamed. On close examination, some of those who proclaimed the "newness" of their politics most enthusiastically bore an uncanny resemblance to "old" politicians. This was most conspicuously true of the "New Labour Party," which won a spectacular victory in the 1997 British general election. New Labour's leaders presented themselves as having risen above divisions of right and left and politics based on the old industrial working class, yet it operated in the only major European country in which the dominant parties and institutions had existed fifty years previously. The gray eminence of Labour's "rebranding," Peter Mandelson, was the grandson of Herbert Morrison, an archetypal "Old Labour" politician, and Mandelson himself had spent his entire career working as a Labour Party functionary. The three leaders who presided over the birth of "New Labour" – Neil Kinnock, John Smith and Tony Blair – all represented constituencies in established Labour strongholds in, respectively, Wales, Scotland and northern England.

Similar complexities underlay "new" politics in France. The Mouvement des Citoyens, one of the new formations in France, seemed to exemplify "new politics" – "citizen" was a key word in the political lexicon of the late 1990s. However, the Citoyen group was the political vehicle of Jean-Pierre Chevènement. Like a good Jacobin centralist, Chevènement had spent much of the 1980s insisting on the need for a "conquest of the state." In matters of defense, he had been fiercely nationalistic, and in matters of education, he had been elitist. He had derided the lifestyle politics of the "gauche Américaine."[1]

The main political formations of the post-communist period had existed before 1989. Christian democracy collapsed in Italy, but it remained the dominant force in Germany and gained new ground in some eastern European countries. After the elections of 1999, the Christian democrat group was the largest in the European Parliament.

Christian democracy's success after communism resulted from two characteristics that it had displayed throughout the postwar period. First, it benefited from the perception that it had an independent but not entirely hostile attitude towards authority. In Spain, Portugal and Greece, Christian democracy had not been successful after the fall of dictatorships with which the Church had often been closely associated; in parts of communist Europe, by contrast, the Church was widely regarded as a source of opposition to (or at least restraint on) the regime. Christian democrats in eastern Europe retained the credibility with underprivileged groups that they had often lost in the West. In east Germany, a third of members of the CDU were workers; in west Germany, the figure was fewer than one in ten.[2] Second, Christian democracy was not simply a product of religious devotion. The most devout country in the region, Poland, did not have a significant Christian democrat party, and the Polish hierarchy's limited interest in democracy had not been increased by the smooth relations that it had enjoyed with the government during the last years of Jaruzelski's rule. In Poland, the Church preserved its interests through direct negotiations with the state rather than through a parliamentary intermediary: the concordat between Church and state was signed without consulting parliament.

By contrast, a Christian Democratic Party enjoyed great success in the highly secular Czech Republic. Even more strikingly, almost three-quarters of east Germans voted for Chancellor Kohl's CDU, even though less than a third of them described themselves as members of any church.[3] Indeed, the most confessional group in post-communist east Germany was probably the Social Democratic Party, which tried to rebuild its fortunes on the moral authority that some Protestant leaders had acquired under communism.[4]

Social democratic parties did less well in post-communist countries than might have been expected. In some respects, the collapse of communism was a victory of the Second International over the Third. Gorbachev himself had come to talk of his politics as "social democratic," but eastern European social democracy was squeezed by the embrace of Leninism. In the short term, the word "socialism" was indissolubly associated with the old regimes: there was no institutional base on which socialism could be rebuilt because social democrat parties that had existed before the Second World War had been merged with the Communist Party in the late 1940s. In the long term, reconstituted communist parties often took the language, and much of the potential constituency, of social democracy.

In the West, by contrast, social democracy flourished after the fall of communist rule in the East. By 1999, almost every western European country was under the rule of a party affiliated to the Second International. In the 1990s, as in the 1960s, socialism seemed to be the main beneficiary of capitalism's success.

Communist parties sometimes survived after 1989. In some countries, such as Serbia and Romania, where a party led by former communists ruled until November 1996, the survival of communist elites and some communist practices was not linked to any pretence of maintaining communist principles. At least eight presidents of former Soviet republics, including Boris Yeltsin in Russia, had previously been high-ranking members of the Soviet Communist Party, though few of them would have cared to recall the fact.

Elsewhere in eastern Europe, communist parties were refounded under new leaders who promised to embrace democracy. They were launched in Slovakia in December 1989, in Germany, Bulgaria and Poland at the beginning of 1990, and in Albania in June 1991. In Russia, communist parties were re-created after the constitutional court ruled in March 1993 that such groups were legal; almost all these parties changed their names, but the extent of change in ideology varied. The Hungarian and Polish parties virtually abandoned reference to Marxism and embraced economic reform, to the disappointment of many supporters. Most reformed communist parties described themselves as social democratic: those of Hungary, Poland and Slovakia joined the Second International. Former communists sometimes gave different versions of their beliefs to different audiences. The Russian Genadii Ziuganov rubbed shoulders with Western bankers at the Davos economic summit in March 1996 and assured interviewers from France that he supported a "mixed economy like that of Scandinavia." He spoke in different terms to Russian voters.

Reformed communist parties enjoyed an electoral success that would have surprised most observers in 1989 – the German communists obtained up to a fifth of the east German vote in federal elections (but only around 1 percent of the west German vote).[5] In Bulgaria, a refounded communist party won the 1992 elections. In Poland, a communist successor party returned to government days after the last Soviet troops left the country, and a former Communist Party member held the presidency of Lithuania from February 1993 until October 1996. In Russia, the

PCFR, the most important of the reformed communist parties, was the largest party in the Duma for most of the 1990s.

Sometimes more than one party claimed to represent the communist legacy in former communist countries. At least seven such formations existed in Russia. The Polish party divided into two groups, both claiming to be "social democrat," one of which ceased to exist in July 1991. Often groups sprang up to represent "real" communism in opposition to the reformed version – in Hungary, the PSOH under Károly Grósz served such a function. Antireform communist parties existed even in countries where the mainstream communist leadership had hardly been noted for its enthusiastic embrace of reform. The Russian Workers' Communist Party, led by Viktor Anpilov, and the Romanian Socialist Party of Labor, led by Constantin Parvulescu, were such parties.[6]

The only western European communist party to be destroyed by the fall of communist rule in the East was that of Great Britain – its leaders had been too busy exhibiting a sophisticated grasp of Gramsci in the pages of *Marxism Today* to notice that their own organization depended on Soviet subsidy. Elsewhere, western European communist parties flourished. Revelations about the nature of Leninist rule added little to what intelligent people had known since the Budapest uprising and what western European communist leaders had themselves acknowledged since the Prague Spring. In many respects, western European communists, especially in Italy, had anticipated the democratization of communism that occurred in eastern Europe after 1989. By 1997, western European communists held more power in central government than at any stage in the previous fifty years. In France the Parti Communiste Français – the only such party to have retained its original name – was represented in the government of Lionel Jospin, while in Italy, two different refounded communist parties were represented in government. Western communist parties embraced the world of customer-oriented capitalism with a vengeance. Telephonists at the PCF headquarters who had once answered "*Tu veux quoi?*" were taught to say "*Parti Communiste Français, bonjour.*" The Italian party newspaper *Unità* sold three-quarters of its shares to private investors.

In spite of all the continuities, it is possible to argue that European politics escaped from established categories in the 1990s. Previously, rejection of conventional politics had often been a cover for conservatism; technocratic pragmatism, national union or consensus – the forms of "new" politics that had been seen before – were all implicitly conservative in that they all provided means of defending the status quo. During the 1980s and 1990s this changed. People who rejected conventional divisions of left and right often also challenged the status quo.

The most dramatic example of a "new" politician in the late 1990s was Daniel Cohn-Bendit. Born in 1945, Cohn-Bendit became famous as the leader of Paris students during the demonstrations of 1968. His career challenged almost every conventional political category. He was always recognized as a left-winger, even though he had never shown much interest in Marxism, and he eventually became a member of the German Green Party – a personality who did not believe in parties in a party that did not believe in personalities. Of German Jewish parentage, he divided his time between France and Germany, but his politics operated at either the local level, as a municipal politician, or at the transnational level, as a member of the European Parliament. In 1999, he contested elections to the European Parliament on behalf of the French Green Party after having previously represented a German constituency. His support was also transnational – his associates included the Czech President Václav Havel and Tahar Ben Jelloun, a Franco-Moroccan novelist who was himself a candidate for an Italian constituency in the European elections. Cohn-Bendit adopted positions that would have horrified radicals in the previous decade – he was a vigorous supporter of NATO military action in the former Yugoslavia, and he defended the Maastricht treaty (which guaranteed free trade in Europe).

The fall of communism had consequences for political language. The French journalist André Fontaine rejoiced at what he described as the "reunification" of language that accompanied the political reunification of Europe, meaning that the West was no longer obliged to wrestle with the "Newspeak" of communist rulers. The unification of Europe also had more complicated effects on political language – the opponents of communist rule, as well as its defenders, had used language in a particular way, partly because of the need to avoid direct confrontation with the authorities, which might have been produced by excessively explicit attacks, and partly because words acquired meaning from the very contrast that they presented with official language. Thus, for example, Václav Havel's exhortation to his compatriots to "live in truth" made more sense in 1987 than it did ten years later.

The fall of communism challenged the language of left and right. Many writers had pointed out for some time that it was absurd to label communists in power as "left-wing," and the frequency with which former communists took refuge in nationalism, authoritarianism and militarism underlined the point. The Czech-born Jacques Rupnik wrote: "Are Jaruzelski, Ceauşescu and Honecker right or left? For the majority of inhabitants of central Europe the question is quite incongruous. This explains why dissident intellectuals like Adam Michnik, Václav Havel or

György Konrád refuse to use Western political etiquettes to describe the political reality of their country."[7]

The divisions of language that survived the fall of communism were revealed when two Western feminists collaborated with scholars from eastern Europe and the former Soviet Union to edit a work on "gender, politics and post-communism." They discovered that: "The concepts 'left,' 'politics,' 'solidarity,' 'socialism' and even 'women's equality' are not used normatively by post-communist women, but as descriptive terms appropriated by an authoritarian, repressive socialism, referring to disturbing realities imposed by that system."[8]

In this collection a Czech woman commented:

> Thus, similar-sounding political terms and phrases have different meanings and significance for women East and West, rooted in our different historical experiences. This will be a hindrance to our mutual understanding for a long time. In addition, there are ideological currents, philosophical directions and political conceptions in the West with which we are wholly unfamiliar. The isolation of forty years has produced its results: I personally am only just beginning to understand what a difference there is between us! The chasm did not seem as deep while the border was closed and I was unable to travel.[9]

The complexity of political attitudes that developed through opposition to communist rule was shown in an interview given in 1985 by the Polish philosopher Leszek Kołakowski, who had been a communist and was an expert on Marxist thought. He dismissed the socialism of the Eastern Bloc as meaning "nothing but the Soviet Empire." His own views were informed by admiration for certain aspects of Catholicism and for the Solidarity movement, whose novel character he stressed. He approved of the British Social Democratic Party, but not of the social democracy of Kreisky and Palme, which he regarded as excessively pro-Soviet, and he felt some sympathy for the cultural conservatism of the American writer Irving Kristol.[10]

Former dissidents in eastern Europe who entered electoral politics after 1989 had a point of view that the conventional political spectrum could not accommodate. Such people were new to politics in the sense that they did not need to defend a particular party legacy, and under communism many of them had deliberately turned to new political issues in the hope that such concerns might provide them with a space where the state would tolerate independent action. Western politicians were confused about how eastern European post-communist politicians fitted into the political spectrum. The head of the Liberal International admitted: "I have also lost my orientation as to what the word 'liberalism' really means for Polish politicians."[11] The rejection of the left/right spectrum that so confused Western observers sometimes came precisely from the desire of eastern Europeans to integrate into the West. The Pole Władysław Frasyniuk insisted that his Movement for Democratic Action was not left of center but "west of center."[12]

The politics of information

In the 1990s technological change attracted much attention from political commentators. To a large extent, the postwar political order had been based on particular means of communication. Television, in particular, had underwritten a consensus society in which everyone was exposed to the same general culture. Digital, satellite and cable broadcasting meant that more channels became available. Broadcasting became dominated by private entrepreneurs rather than the state. Viewers and listeners had an increasing range of choice, and could use video recorders to watch programs when they wanted to and to escape officially imposed diets of what was "good for them." In 1983, for example, a substantial number of Britons used their video recorders to "screen out" party political broadcasts.[13]

The reception of information became an increasingly individual matter. The number of receivers had increased greatly, with most European households containing more radios than people. Broadcasting was less likely to address itself to an entire family, let alone an entire nation, and radio stations developed to serve highly specialized markets; a resident of Paris could listen to Fréquence Gaie, Beur FM, Radio Shalom, Radio Judaique, Fréquence Protestante, or Féminin Pluriel. Sometimes specializations fitted political categories, and stations advertised explicit political loyalties. In France, Radio Courtoisie advertised itself as "*la radio du pays réel*" (a reference to the royalism of Charles Maurras), and in Poland Radio Maryja was listened to by 2–3 million citizens of what a sociologist described as "a nationalist, integral Catholic, patriotic, anti-Semitic Poland."[14]

Computers offered an even more direct and focused means of communication. Access to the Internet was cheaper and less controlled than access to the airwaves or print, leaving public figures who had previously used the law to prevent information about their private life from being published powerless. When a book about François Mitterrand's fatal illness was banned, an energetic Internet user typed the book's entire contents onto a web site.

The political impact of this revolution should not be exaggerated. New means of communication often had the greatest impact on a relatively privileged and highly educated section of the population, which may be why intellectuals were so excited by its possibilities (Francis Fukuyama thanked "the designers of the Intel 80386 microprocessor" in the acknowledgments for *The End of History*).[15] Well-informed people with access to the right equipment could actively use new communications to widen their choice and to hunt down specific pieces of information. Most people, however, were probably rendered more passive – television channels targeted at specific sections of the population created ghettos of viewers whose access to information was limited to twenty quiz shows. The political uses of broadcasting in the 1990s were crude. The Hungarian military purchased a role in a television soap opera in order to promote membership of NATO. The most important figure to mix television and politics was Silvio Berlusconi, the broadcasting magnate who became Italian Prime Minister, and his channels promoted his platform through simple repetition and the fusion of politics with the enthusiasm generated by football teams.

The state

Political commentators in the 1990s made much of the supposed weakening or marginalization of the state. The shift had several dimensions, the most obvious of which was economic. States decided to withdraw from certain activities, and, in any case, were often unable to control ever increasing and complicated international economic currents, even if they wanted to. Europeans were less willing to accept that state power was an intrinsically good thing, and the very phrase "welfare state," which had formed the basis for much postwar politics, seemed outdated. Western radicals were influenced by critiques, such as those of Michel Foucault, that presented schools, hospitals, and psychiatric institutions as mechanisms for the exercise of power. Former dissidents in eastern Europe were influenced by less abstract perceptions of the damage that could be done by state power in malevolent hands.

States had always justified their existence in terms that went beyond the purely utilitarian. The state was a focus for patriotic loyalty and, in extreme cases, it had the right to ask its citizens to die for it. In the 1990s, its mystique was challenged. Europeans transferred their loyalties to other entities, including nations that did not correspond to the frontiers of any existing state. The key mystical power of the state – its ability to shed the blood of its citizens – seemed irrelevant to most Europeans, or at least to most western Europeans, at a time when a major war seemed unimaginable.

Germany was probably the most important example of a state that lacked mystique. After the Second World War, German leaders had deliberately downplayed the emotional and affective elements of German nationality. In a book published just before the demolition of the Berlin Wall, Harold James worried that Germans had emphasized the purely economic functions of their state to the exclusion of other necessary considerations: "Clio should warn us not to trust Mercury (the economic god) too much. Economies are unlikely to be forever flushed with the rosy bloom of optimism and expansion; when they sicken, it may be helpful to have a dense network of loyalties, traditions, and old institutions which can retain a legitimacy more profound and satisfying."[16]

The reunification of Germany did not create the legitimacy that James advocated. German leaders were reticent about the use of nationalistic language, and the caution of most German citizens was probably increased by the fact that a small number of right-wingers in east Germany adopted nationalist slogans in their attacks on immigrants. East Germans were grateful for the material benefits of unification, but they often felt little sense of belonging to the newly created state. A young economist said: "I have difficulty feeling German. When the question is put, I say that I am a Berliner. The Federal Republic of Germany is not much of a country."[17]

The demystification of the state had important effects in the countries of eastern Europe, which after 1989 often faced a period of economic trouble. This can be illustrated by comparing the fates of Poland and Hungary in the early 1990s. Both countries inherited the debts that communist governments had run up during the 1980s. Western analysts expected Hungary to resolve the problem most easily – in economic terms, she was the most liberal of the eastern European states and the one with most experience of private enterprise – but the very emphasis that Hungary's rulers had placed on economics generated problems. Hungarians had little else in which to believe. In the interwar period, nationalism had focused on opposition to the Treaty of Trianon, but between 1945 and 1989 the Soviet Union had forced Hungarian politicians to abandon such objections. After 1989, the desire to be integrated into a democratic Europe ruled out a challenge to the Trianon frontiers. Even communism in Hungary never claimed much emotional hold on the loyalties of the population after the Soviet invasion of 1956. The Kádár government had built its legitimacy on nothing other than its capacity to improve living standards. Emphasis on living standards and consumerism continued after the fall of communist rule, and the slow compromises that had ended communism did not give rise to a mystique of opposition or democracy. Democratic government was simply judged by the same standards that had been applied to Kádár's communism – that is, in terms of its capacity to improve living standards.

Poland's revolution, by contrast, was political rather than economic. Opposition to communist rule drew on several, not necessarily compatible, traditions – Catholicism, nationalism and support for democracy. The curious result was that the first post-communist Finance Minister, Leszek Balcerowicz, was more able than his Hungarian counterpart to introduce economic policies that resulted in a fall in living standards for many Poles.

State powers were increasingly transferred from long-established nation-states, which had some place in the imaginations and emotions of their inhabitants, to the European Union. The EU had no head of state and no history of military heroism – in short, none of the things that normally moved people who contemplated their state. The absence of mystique struck those from former communist countries for whom Europe had emotional as well as economic significance. Václav Havel remarked that the European Union was "a perfect modern machine but one that lacks something human."[18]

The weakness of the European state in the 1990s should not be exaggerated. States and societies are multifaceted entities that overlap and interact on many levels, and marking the boundaries of the state is difficult. It is easy to confuse an extended or unaccountable state with an effective one. For example, during the 1970s proponents of free-market economics often complained that the state in Italy or in Great Britain was "too large," by which they meant that it spent taxpayers' money on a sprawling empire of public bodies and nationalized industries. Some free-market enthusiasts also recognized that such large states were "weak," in that they had been colonized by private interest groups (particularly trade unions), and were unable to enforce their will (or at least the will of those who nominally commanded the state). In the 1990s, state power was increasingly defined by its capacity to get things done rather than by the number of individuals on its payroll. It may be useful to turn away from analysis that pits the state against the private sector and to examine changes that happened in both the state and the private sector simultaneously. To use the language of corporate reorganization, the state's withdrawal from certain activities was a form of "outsourcing" by which the state focused on its "core competencies."

Sometimes perceptions of the state's weakness did not spring so much from the fact that it had retreated from areas where it had previously exercised power as from the fact that observers were increasingly aware of new domains that had not previously been considered as subjects for state action. Environmental policy illustrated this. Increasing concern with the environment sometimes made the state seem weak – environmentalists often bypassed the state to indulge in direct action, and much damage to the environment occurred at an international level over which individual states had no control. Environmental policy, however, offered the state new areas in which it could exercise power. Environmental regulations presented large companies (supposedly the overlords of a global economy) with problems that they would not have imagined a generation earlier. The very forces that were sometimes presented as limits on state action could become allies of the state. Internationalization was an obvious example. International bodies provided states with the means to coordinate actions and operate on a scale that would not have been possible for any single state.

Corruption, human rights and the rule of law

The redefinition of the state was accompanied by a resurrection of the rule of law at the expense of political parties and private interests. Many political disputes in Europe during the 1990s revolved around allegations of corruption. In Italy in a single year in the late 1980s, £136 million of illegal money was said to have flowed into the coffers of Italian political parties,[19] and by the end of 1992, nearly 100 members of the Italian parliament were under investigation for corruption.[20] In France between 1984 and 1994, the number of condemnations for corruption and peddling influence increased from 44 to 104.[21] In 1999 the entire European Commission resigned after allegations of corruption, and at the beginning of 2000 Helmut Kohl faced awkward questions about donations that he had accepted on behalf of the German Christian Democratic Union. Sometimes politics seemed to be a branch of organized crime. This was most obviously the case in Sicily and in some states of the former Soviet Union, but similar tendencies could be discerned in southern France, where local experts linked violent conflict among gangsters who controlled gaming machines to the fact that the gangsters' former patrons in the UDF had lost power to the Gaullists.[22]

The discovery of corruption was associated with a broader shift of European politics. Turning away from clearly defined ideologies and parties often led to an examination of the personal qualities of prominent individuals. Awareness of corruption was both a cause and an effect of change. Political changes revealed corruption, because the politicians involved no longer had the power to cover up their misdeeds – this was particularly true of groups such as the communists in eastern Europe or Christian democrats in Italy that had been in power for a long time. The discovery of corruption also provoked further scrutiny of the political system, which, in turn, often provoked more political changes.

Changes in capitalism brought increased attention to corruption. Companies that depended on state favor – arms manufacturers or oil companies that needed licences to drill – had been particularly likely to resort to bribery, but such industries became less important in the 1990s. High-technology enterprises, particularly those associated with computers and telecommunications, did not depend on state favor in the same way. Their business depended on direct relations with consumers and on the relatively free flow of information. As capitalism became more widely seen as legitimate, businessmen were more reluctant to pay for treatment that they thought they deserved to receive anyway.

Judges exposed much corruption. In Sicily, Giovanni Falcone and Paolo Borsellino exploited the new independence that Italian judges had been given.[23] Significantly, the judges operated outside traditional categories of right and left. Indeed, the most important figures in the judicial campaign came from opposite ends of the political spectrum (Borsellino had been a member of the neo-fascist MSI and Falcone had flirted with communism) as they united against the practices of the dominant political center.[24] Their action was admired and imitated elsewhere. The 1993 class of the French École de la Magistrature was named after Giovanni Falcone, and French judges began to question politicians such as Roland Dumas, former French Foreign Minister, about their financial dealings.

The new role of the judiciary was associated with a new view of human rights, a fact illustrated in 1999 by the appointment of Carla Del Ponte, the Swiss magistrate who had made a reputation by investigating corruption, as Chief Prosecutor at the International Tribunal of the Hague. The end of the Cold War meant that torturers and murderers were less likely to be protected because they were "on our side." International courts tried those who had committed crimes in Yugoslavia, and a Spanish judge tried to extradite General Augusto Pinochet, former President of Chile. The change in the attitude of the left towards the rule of law was particularly dramatic. Albert Camus and George Orwell had regarded judges as symbols of everything that they despised about power, particularly in the days when European judges passed death sentences. Now they were sometimes seen as the most effective restraint on oppression. When English Law Lords decided to permit the extradition of General Pinochet, Daniel Cohn-Bendit remarked, "Tonight we are all English Lords."

Violence

Europe in the 1990s was a violent place. Racists killed forty immigrants in eastern Germany in the first half of the decade. In Albania, around 1,600 people were killed after the breakdown of government in 1997, and at least 100,000 died in the Yugoslav wars of 1991 to 1995. An as yet un-determined number of people were killed by fighting in Kosovo in 1999 and as a result of the Russian assaults on Chechnya in 1996, 1999 and 2000. The violence of the post-1989 period was thrown into relief by the relative peacefulness of the preceding three decades in Europe. There had been very little fighting among European countries in the forty years after the Second World War, and little support for the kind of internal political violence that had marked the interwar period.

It would, however, be wrong to say that Europeans became more bloodthirsty after the fall of communism. Before 1989, many people had believed that violence was legitimate, a view held by most Europeans in the sense that they believed that the state had the right to use violence against its enemies. The peace between European states was sustained by the colossal latent violence of nuclear weapons. A much smaller propor-tion of the European population believed that it had the right to use vio-lence against the state.

Attitudes changed in the 1990s. Although more Europeans practiced violence, the number who believed that violence was legitimate de-creased. The influence of feminism and an increasingly self-conscious at-titude towards gender on the part of the educated elements of the Euro-pean population was one cause, as the rethinking of masculinity was accompanied by a reassessment of attitudes towards the violence with which it had often been associated. The influence of eastern European dissidents was also important. In the early years of communism, many had believed that it could be overthrown by violence, but they were wrong. Increasingly violence came to be seen as a characteristic of the communist state, and nonviolence was seen by anticommunists as morally right and tactically effective (confrontation with a force that has a monopoly of weapons is pointless). The main Slovak umbrella grouping of democratic forces in 1989 called itself Public Against Violence. The most fervent practitioners of violence in Europe after 1989, in Romania and the former Yugoslavia, were usually former communists who had converted to nationalism.

New views towards violence were accompanied by a decline of revolu-tionary mysticism among the young, and particularly among students. In the 1960s and 1970s, many European students had looked with admiration to Third World guerrillas – in France and Italy, the admiration had sometimes been linked to a cult of the resistance fighters of the Second World War. By the 1990s, admiration for freedom fighters had shifted from Che Guevara to Burmese leader Aung San Suu Kyi. Non-violent protest, patience and negotiation were admired more than guerrilla action. European terrorism persisted among nationalists in Corsica, Ireland and the Basque country, but the activities of the Red Army Faction, Action Directe and the Red Brigades seemed to belong to a different world. Between 1968 and 1978, almost a fifth of students at the University of Konstanz believed that violence was necessary to bring about political change; by 1983, this figure had dropped to fewer than one in ten.[25] Prominent Italian intellectuals argued that it was necessary to draw a line under the "lead years" of terrorism and counterterrorism, and the philosopher Toni Negri, who had been accused of inspiring terrorism, returned from exile to face imprisonment at the end of 1997. The trial of "Carlos the Jackal" in Paris in 1997 evoked an almost forgotten period; Carlos told the judge that the drama of his arrival in court flanked by guards with assault rifles made him feel "nostalgic."

Max Weber had defined the state as a body with a "monopoly of legitimate violence." In the 1990s, many Europeans questioned the meaning of the words "legitimate violence." Attitudes towards two aspects of state violence – capital punishment and military service – evolved in especially significant ways. The last major state of western Europe to abolish capital punishment was France (in 1982) and the Council of Europe required members to renounce the practice from April 1983. States such as Russia and the Ukraine that wished to assert a European identity during the 1990s announced suspensions of the death penalty (though these seem to have been widely disregarded).[26] This was a matter that distinguished Europe from other regions of prosperity, democracy and stability. In February 1998, 3,269 people awaited execution in the United States.

Military service had once been at the center of the European state, which had largely evolved as a mechanism for fighting war. The patriotic culture of European states was intertwined with the official commemoration of wars. After the fall of the Soviet Union, the military threat to most European countries altered. Between 1991 and 1998, the Russian military budget was cut by a factor of fourteen.[27] It was hard for European generals to argue that the survival of their nation depended on the state of its armed forces. The nature of combat changed. Few European powers expected to use their armies in an all-out war against a military equal. Increasingly, soldiers were used as peacekeepers in Yugoslavia, Rwanda and Cyprus.

New forms of warfare encouraged the professionalization of armies as the most important operations required small numbers of highly trained soldiers. Russia announced that it intended to professionalize its army by 2000. Most European countries maintained compulsory military service for men, but it became a less central part of national life. One year of service in the Bundeswehr was a very different matter from three years' service in the army of the German Democratic Republic. The right to conscientious objection, a key demand of dissidents during the last years of communism, was widely accepted.

The most significant move to military professionalization came in 1996, when the French government announced the end of compulsory military service, a momentous declaration because the idea of the "nation in arms" had been such an important part of French national mythology since the Battle of Valmy (1792) and the reality of universal military service had been such an important part of French male experience since 1889. The French army had once been an engine of national integration; by the 1990s, it was an engine of national division. Privileged young men found ways to escape drill and uniforms – one graduate of the Institut d'Études Politiques fulfilled his military obligations by teaching French at the University of the West Indies. The least privileged young men did not acquire even the most simple skills during their military service. A middle-aged Frenchman who lived in rural isolation on social security payments complained that his son had learned how to drive a tank but not a car.[28]

The marginalization of European armies was reflected in the growing gulf between the officer corps and the European economic elite. Armies were national institutions that valued loyalty, tradition and hierarchy; the business elite valued internationalism, rapid change and open discussion in "flat" management structures. Authority in business was increasingly derived from the possession of specialized skills, particularly in finance, rather than from a general ability to exercise "leadership."

Environmentalism

Between 1945 and the mid-1970s, one of the most important assumptions of governments in both eastern and western Europe had been that economic growth in general, and the development of industry in particular, was a good thing. This assumption was questioned most explicitly by environmental groups, which began to attract support in the early 1980s. In March 1983 the West German Green Party won twenty-seven parliamentary seats. By the mid-1990s, the Green share of the vote in continental western Europe ranged from 2.5 percent (Italy) to 8.4 percent (Belgium).

Environmentalism's most obvious origins lay on the *soixante-huitard* left, and, in practice, the major Green parties, in France and Germany, invariably formed alliances with the left. Ecology, however, also had roots on the political right. Charles Maurras had dedicated one of his last essays to an attack on the construction of an oil refinery on the Mediterranean coast. Many conservatives would find the assumptions of environmentalism – for example, that the present generation has obligations to its descendants and ancestors – congenial.

The Greens often rejected conventional political tactics – the German Green Party refused to have permanent leaders – and Greens raised questions about how political influence was exercised. Some of them contested elections and even sought to enter government. The process began in the early 1980s in the German state of Hesse, when the SPD appointed the Green Joschka Fischer as Environment Minister. In France, Greens elected to parliament in 1997 supported the government of the socialist Lionel Jospin; one of their number, Dominique Voynet, became Minister of the Environment. Other Greens rejected participation in government or even in elections (in Germany the division between the two groups was described as that between realists and fundamentalists).

Non-parliamentary environmentalists tried to exercise influence by mobilizing public opinion and through direct action, sometimes outside the law, but the different forms of Green activity did not necessarily represent a split between "realism" and "fundamentalism." Greens operated on several different levels, which were not mutually exclusive, and the distinctive feature of Green politics was its ability to pick its way through a variety of different institutions, adopting whichever strategy was most suited to the occasion. Green success could not, therefore, be measured in the usual ways. The movement had considerable influence even in countries where it attracted little electoral support or held no ministerial office. Greens were particularly adept at manipulating political systems in the 1990s for three reasons. First, they were not locked into the established habits and routines of old parties. Second, the environmental movement had always operated on an international level and therefore grasped the opportunities of internationalization (Green parties did well in elections to the European Parliament). Third, Green politics drew much of its support from the educated middle classes, who understood the mechanisms of the international corporations that they opposed – Nick Mabey, who headed the British office of the World Wide Fund for Nature, was a graduate of the Massachusetts Institute of Technology and had worked at the London Business School. The complexity of the pressure that Green activists could bring to bear was revealed in 1997, when the head of Greenpeace in the United Kingdom, Peter Melchett, sat down to dinner with John Browne, the Chief Executive of British Petroleum, shortly after Greenpeace activists had chained themselves to a BP oil rig.[29]

Sometimes Green activists deliberately used tactics that seemed to belong to their enemies. Market economics was an obvious example. While much of the conventional left regarded the market as their natural enemy, Greens often accepted it as an effective way to allocate scarce resources. When asked for a single measure that would improve the environment, Jonathon Porritt, doyen of British environmentalists, suggested that Sainsbury's should sell the meat of gray squirrels. Greens used boycotts, such as the one deployed by German motorists against Shell in 1996, and the opportunities presented by annual general meetings of shareholders in large companies.

Greens were not simply defenders of the past. Their attitudes towards most matters, such as civil liberties and the family, hardly fitted in with tradition. The Greens of the 1980s and 1990s were usually urban and young, and were not necessarily enemies of economic progress. Advanced industrial processes produced less pollution, and the most advanced economies of all (based on computers and service industries) damaged the environment less than their old-fashioned competitors (based on heavy industry).

Class

The death of class politics – or at least of politics based on support for the industrial working class – was announced frequently in the postwar period. The evidence for such a decline was, however, stronger in the 1990s than at any previous time. For one thing, the proportion of the total population employed in manufacturing was now falling in every western European country, having peaked in some in the previous decade. The various processes by which working-class homogeneity had been undermined in previous generations – the entry of women into the workforce, the increasing wealth of some sections of the working class, the dispersal of production, and the weakening of trade unions – continued.

Politics focused on class were increasingly undermined by new politics of race, gender, sexuality and environmentalism, which displaced class and also made some on the left regard the working class with suspicion. A class based on heavy industry had awkward relations with environmentalists; a class that had been presented in terms of stereotypical masculinity raised problems for feminists; a class that had been defined before large-scale immigration from outside Europe sometimes appeared racist.

The link between progressive middle-class intellectuals and the organized working class that had been epitomized by western European socialists such as Léon Blum seemed fragile. The French and British socialist parties had primarily middle-class memberships. The British "new" Labour Party played down its links with the trade unions, even when the trade unions had supported the reform of the Labour Party. Marxist-influenced analysis had divided society into a "working-class" majority and a capitalist minority (though this analysis had been nuanced to take account of the obvious growth of the middle class), but in the 1990s left-wing politicians were increasingly prone to talk of a division that separated a majority of "citizens" from a minority of "the excluded," who were not defined by income or occupation, but rather in terms of education, family structure, race and propensity to become victims, or perpetrators, of crime. Their sufferings were partly self-inflicted. The underprivileged wreaked damage on each other through violent crime, racism and the neglect of children. Sometimes the "underclass" seemed to be pitted against the very kind of public provision that had originally been intended to improve the condition of the working class. In Manchester, ambulance crews called to certain regions of the city requested police escorts to protect them from stone-throwing crowds, while in France the transport union, a surviving representative of the old working class, was increasingly reluctant for its members to provide services in parts of cities such as Lille because of the frequency with which buses were attacked.

In eastern Europe, the death of the working class was less visible. The communist states had built up industry and, in places like Slovakia, the working class had grown during the 1980s at a time when it shrank in most of western Europe. The fall of communism meant an end to the expansion of large-scale heavy industry, but a substantial working class remained. The former Soviet Union contained 80 million workers, 45 million in Russia alone.[30] Although levels of unionization dropped after the end of communism, they remained higher than in most Western countries. At the end of 1992, most Hungarians, Poles, Czechs and Slovaks were members of trade unions, which also retained a legitimacy in the public mind that they had often lost in the West. In Poland, unions had a special appeal because of their role in the overthrow of communism; in 1992, almost half of Poles said that they believed that trade union influence ought to be greater (less than a fifth said that it should be weaker).[31]

The "underclass," which had replaced the working class in the minds of the western European left, was hard to find in parts of eastern Europe. The stretches of "panel housing" – prefabricated high-rise blocks – that dominated the landscape in areas such as Haje on the outskirts of Prague looked, at a distance, much like the council estates of Chalk Farm or the Paris *banlieue*. Close up, differences were obvious. There was little vandalism in Haje. The system of education (especially primary education) inherited from the communist regime was unimaginative but effective and children were well cared for, partly because the family had been the only private sphere under communism. Rates of crime were low by Western standards, public transport was good, and life in an outlying suburb did not cut people off from entertainment or employment in the city center.

Progressive intellectuals and workers were sharply divided from each other in the political systems of eastern Europe. Educated dissidents often associated the working classes with support for displaced communist regimes, and there was also a gap between an intelligentsia that sometimes traced its origins back to the nobility, as in Poland, or to the prewar bourgeoisie, as in the Czech Republic, and a working class that had been built on a recently urbanized peasantry. Intellectuals who claimed to represent the cosmopolitan, liberal future of their country denounced the "conservatism" and "nationalism" of working-class parties. The division existed even in Poland, the only country where there had been an effective alliance of intellectuals and workers against communism, where intellectuals were disdainful of Lech Wałęsa's candidacy for the presidency, which made much of Catholicism and conservative morality on issues such as abortion.[32] In June 1990, Adam Michnik called his former working-class comrades "pigs," while the rector of Warsaw University said that the intelligentsia was living through its worst period since the end of the Second World War and that the Solidarity government treated it worse than the "old power" had.[33] In Romania, the division was more violent. In June 1990 students protested the policies of President Iliescu's National Salvation Front, a nationalist party built with the personnel of the old Communist Party. The government responded by transporting miners to the capital, where they beat up anyone who looked like an intellectual.

Conclusion

Is it possible to summarize the political developments of the 1990s? It is tempting to suggest that politics in this period was too fragmented and fluid to be encompassed by any single explanation. Before 1989, political divisions operated around right and left, which corresponded to social divisions between rich and poor and international divisions between West and East. After 1989, a multidimensional politics that accommodated issues of gender, race, nationalism and environmentalism created new divisions. The drama of the change can, however, be overstated. Some aspects of the 1990s that evoked excited comment, such as the decline of class as an issue in western European politics, can be traced back to the 1950s, and almost every aspect of "new politics" was visible, to some extent, by the 1970s. The fall of communist regimes in Europe did not mark a complete break with the recent past, but, on the contrary, had been rooted in long-term social, economic and technological changes that were accelerated and made more visible by the end of communist rule.

In the 1990s, people were mobilized around narrow, specific issues that related to their immediate interests. Very few bodies claimed the mystique that once allowed them to appeal to emotional loyalties. The loss of mystique was most dramatic in the case of the state, which was increasingly seen as simply a "large-scale provider of services." Loss of mystique could also be seen in the decline of working-class identity, which had been based on rituals and symbols such as Durham's Miners' Gala and the Red Flag. The arrival of a world without mystique was epitomized by the importance of business and the growing propensity of organizations such as trade unions, political parties and states to conduct themselves as if they were businesses. However, even business itself lost its mystique. In an economy of rapid change, individual companies rarely survived for more than twenty years and the days when company loyalty was regarded as necessary, or even desirable, on the part of employees were gone. Most companies hired on relatively short-term contracts and expected their relationship with their employees to be purely commercial.

Some regretted the quiet, undramatic nature of most European life at the end of the century and felt that Europe had become a colorless place. Francis Fukuyama wrote:

> The end of history will be a very sad time. The struggle for recognition, the willingness to risk one's life for a purely abstract goal, the world-wide, ideological struggle that called forth daring, courage, imagination and idealism, will be replaced by economic calculation, the endless solving of technical problems, environmental concerns and the satisfaction of sophisticated consumer demands.[34]

Those who had once "risked their lives for a purely abstract goal," rather than working for the State Department and the Rand Corporation, often took a different view. Adam Michnik, a leader of Polish Solidarity, came from a country in which dramatic events and mystical idealism had been common for much of the century. In 1997, he was asked whether he regretted the drama of previous times. He replied: "Without the slightest hesitation it is much better to live in a country that is democratic, prosperous and thus boring."[35]

A SORT OF CONCLUSION

THE FIRST OF January 2000 was not a historically significant day for Europe. In the west, the Breton coast was devastated after the wreck of an oil tanker; in the east, Russians were shaken by the unexpected resignation of President Boris Yeltsin. Elsewhere, most Europeans spent the day sleeping off hangovers and cleaning up after the previous night's festivities. Celebration of the millennium itself was remarkably uniform across the continent. Television reflected and defined people's reactions and provided a sense of instant communication with other parts of the world. Attention was focused on a single moment rather than on the preceding century. The uniformity of events marking the millennium is all the more remarkable when compared to the ways in which Europeans experienced the beginning of the twentieth century. In 1900, Europeans did not all use the same calendar, and much of Europe's population would have lacked any accurate means of telling the time, let alone a clear sense of what the rest of the European population was doing at midnight on New Year's Eve.

Few talked of "Europe" during the millennium celebrations. The new frontier for the most ambitious young Europeans seemed not to lie in their own, or any other, continent but in cyberspace. The euphoric predictions about Europe's future that had been made in 1989 and 1990 seemed dated, and the politicians who had been associated with a brave new Europe of post-communist unity had been brought low by the year 2000: Helmut Kohl had been evicted by the electorate and was being pursued by investigators of corruption; Yeltsin also seems to have been forced out of office by a mixture of poor health and allegations of corruption; François Mitterrand was dead, and sometimes was represented at international events by a widow who seemed to regard post-communist

Europe with active distaste; Václav Havel was gravely ill and less popular in his own country than outside it.

The tenth anniversary of the events that brought down communism in most of Europe was often an occasion for gloom rather than celebration. Most accounts emphasized the way in which communist elites had manipulated events rather than the force of public opinion. Images of cheering crowds standing by the Berlin Wall were replaced by descriptions of the turncoat members of the Securitate digging bodies out of a cemetery in Timişoara in order to fake a massacre and discredit Ceauşescu.

Historians reflected the rather melancholy view of Europe at the end of the century. As early as 1993, Eric Hobsbawm suggested that "there is less reason to feel optimistic now than in the mid-1980s." The celebration of "European integration" arouses particular unease among historians. "Europe" did not spring into existence in 1957 with the Treaty of Rome, and it is not made up exclusively of western European states. It is highly questionable whether what are now defined as "European values" have had much influence on most Europeans in the twentieth century, or whether they are incarnated by the political institutions of the European Union. Perhaps in a few years historians will regard all histories of Europe as value-laden and artificial constructions that should be confined to the academic dustbin along with histories of the "Anglo-Saxon race" or "Western civilization."

In the light of these remarks, readers may feel that there is something peculiar about the relatively benign tone of the last few chapters of this book. In some ways, the whole point of this work has been to stress that European experience in the twentieth century, and perhaps especially at its end, has been extraordinarily diverse. An account that stresses the fragmentary nature of European history is ultimately based on arbitrary choices about which particular fragment should be emphasized at which particular time. A Muslim born in Srebrenica – where 6,546 people were reported missing after a Serb attack in 1995 – would produce a very different account of the end of the century. Equally, a Stalinist – and many intelligent Europeans were once Stalinists – would feel extremely pessimistic about Europe in the 1990s; for them, the relative tranquillity of Europe would be the peace of unconditional surrender while the horrors of the 1940s were the birth pangs of a new society.

My view is shaped by those particular fragments of European history that have intersected with my own life. The end of this book reflects the perceptions of a middle-class Englishman born in 1963. The first draft of this book was prepared while I was living in the comfortable apartment of an expatriate executive in Prague. The final chapters would have had a very different tone if the tides of international capitalism had washed me up in Bucharest.

My optimism may come to be seen as naïve. Russia's President, Vladimir Putin, is a former KGB colonel who keeps a portrait of Peter the Great in his office and who has recently extended the circumstances in which Russia might use nuclear weapons. Even if we discount the possibility of general European war, a Russian return to authoritarian government or to the closed frontiers and high arms spending of the Cold War would make life unpleasant for many Europeans. Perhaps more importantly, it may be naïve to write about Europe as if it could be separated from the wider world. There are problems, such as those associated with global warming or the spread of nuclear weapons, that will impinge on Europe's interests but which cannot be solved in a purely European framework.

In moral terms, the wider world also presents Europe with problems. Like the United States, Europe, and especially the European Union, has developed a marked ability to combine universalist rhetoric with insular policy. The contradiction is exposed whenever anyone from outside the privileged circle is foolish enough to take European rhetoric seriously. In July 1999 the bodies of Yaguine Koïta and Fodé Tounkara, respectively fourteen and fifteen years old, were found at the Brussels airport. The children had frozen to death while concealed in the undercarriage of a Sabena jet on which they had hoped to escape from their native Guinea. Discovered with their bodies were letters, addressed to "Excelence Messieurs les membres et responsables d'Europe," in which they begged for help for their country and continent.

For all the qualifications, there are some generalizations that can be made about the state of Europe at the end of the century. First, Europe is more democratic than it has been at any point before in its history. Democracy has, of course, meant lots of different things in the course of the century – right-wing Catholics who described themselves as "Christian democrats" in 1936 did not have much in common with the communists who presided over the "people's democracies" of eastern Europe in the 1960s. Even now, democracy can still have more than one meaning – asked whether Vladimir Putin was a democrat, a Russian commentator replied, "He is a democrat for Russia." In general, however, Europeans have come to agree more about what constitutes democracy – most would assume that it means free speech, pluralism, and defense of certain rights as well as universal suffrage – and also to agree that democracy is a good thing. No European country at the beginning of 2000 does not have at least the formal structure of democracy, which is all the more remarkable in light of the fact that every European country in 1900 excluded at least half of its adult population from suffrage and that democracy in the early 1940s seemed definitively snuffed out in almost every part of the continent. Some have stressed that the fall of communism should be seen as a victory for capitalism rather than for democracy. There is, as any student of Chile in the 1980s will know, no necessary link between capitalism and liberal democracy. However, in the particular circumstances of late-twentieth-century Europe, the spread of democracy and the spread of the free market have usually gone together. Very few countries are perfect democracies, just as very few of them are "perfect" free-market systems, but all central and eastern European countries are now more democratic than they were before 1989. Even the countries that give democrats most cause for concern – Russia, Romania, Serbia – have opposition parties, elections and newspapers in which government ministers are regularly abused. The change since the mid-1980s is so great that we are in danger of forgetting what things were like before. We should listen to Elena Bonner, the widow of Andrei Sakharov, when she denounces Russian aggression in Chechnya as a continuation of Soviet policy, but we should also remember, as she undoubtedly does, what happened to Russians who criticized their government twenty years ago.

Second, Europe is richer than at any previous time in its history. Increased prosperity has been so dramatic that we take it for granted. This is a point that can be reinforced by reading John Maynard Keynes's essay "Economic Possibilities for Our Grandchildren." The tone of this essay was deliberately provocative because it was published in 1930, at a time of economic crisis when most of Keynes's personal fortune had just been wiped out. Some of Keynes's predictions were too optimistic – he based his calculations on the assumption that there would not be another war in Europe – but his general conclusions about economic change have proved remarkably prescient. It does seem quite possible that by the year 2030 "the standard of life in progressive countries will be between four and eight times as high as it is today [i.e., in 1930]." Keynes's prediction that an increase in industrial production would come from the application of American techniques to European industry was correct, as was his prediction that the rapid increase in industrial production would eventually be matched by a similar revolution in agriculture. Measured in purely statistical terms, the great burst of change in the twentieth century came in the thirty years that followed the Second World War. However, events since 1975 have not reversed the economic growth of the immediate postwar years. Growth has continued. It has happened at a slower pace but started from a higher base.

In some respects the last few years recall the period of stability (on which Keynes looked back with a mixture of nostalgia and disdain) before 1914. Once again we have an era of "sound money" in which capitalism functions according to rules that are, more or less, respected by all governments. In 1996, the Russian government even partially reimbursed the holders of pre-1917 "*emprunts russes*" (the worthlessness of which summed up the upheaval of the twentieth century for so many bourgeois Frenchmen). Inflation in eastern Europe after the fall of communism was high, but it never reached the levels experienced by many countries after the two world wars (or the levels experienced in much of Latin America during the 1980s).

Economic success has not been equally distributed across Europe, however. When Keynes talked about the "progressive countries," he meant North America, Britain and, perhaps, a couple of countries in western Europe. Since his time, the circle of economic privilege has widened slightly. The most rapid growth of the postwar period occurred in Spain, Greece and Italy, and some central European countries have become more prosperous since the fall of communism. There are still, however, enormous divisions – gross domestic product per head in Switzerland is about fifty times that in Albania – and within each country the division between rich and poor often overlaps with other divisions between young and old or between city and country. Does this mean that Europe has become more unequal in the last decade of the twentieth century? This is a difficult question to answer. The forms of exclusion and deprivation generated by consumer capitalism are very different from those generated by the authoritarian regimes of the past. Western observers who are horrified by the presence of beggars on the streets of Moscow should remember that the mere right to live in the capital was a carefully guarded privilege as recently as the 1980s.

Determining levels of inequality is even more difficult in the most advanced countries because technology has transformed people's lives in the last few years in ways that are hard to measure statistically. Such changes raise interesting questions for the privileged – how does one compare the benefits of a laptop computer, which most bourgeois Europeans take for granted now, with those of a well-trained parlor maid, which most bourgeois Europeans took for granted in Keynes's day? It may also be that technological change produces new forms of exclusion for the poor. The spread of television may reflect rising levels of prosperity in absolute terms, but it also gives those who have the least access to the consumer society an increasingly strong sense of their relative deprivation – a fact that played an important role in the fall of communism.

What is the effect of prosperity, where it exists, on the lives of Europeans? Keynes anticipated the moment when "the economic problem is not . . . the permanent problem of the human race." At first glance, this looks an odd phrase to apply to contemporary Europe. Economic problems have never occupied a larger share of public debate. Academic economics, which barely existed when Keynes was a student in the early twentieth century, is now a huge discipline.

Yet Keynes's words clearly do apply in one sense to contemporary Europe. For many Europeans at the beginning of the century, economics was a matter of life and death. Their lives were dominated by the struggle to find enough to eat and by the need to perform hard physical labor in order to obtain this goal. Millions of Europeans died of starvation as late as 1946. Simple subsistence has ceased to be a problem for almost all Europeans now. The extent of change can be illustrated by comparing Europe with Africa or much of Asia, where large parts of the population still wake up asking themselves the question, "Will I have enough to eat today?"

The third generalization about Europe at the end of the century relates to the place of violence in public life. There is, of course, still much violence in Europe and 1999 saw two major wars, in Kosovo and Chechnya. This does not, however, mean that Europe is returning to the violence that marked earlier parts of the century or that the postwar order is breaking down. If human suffering can be assessed in purely arithmetical terms, then the violence at the end of the century was on a comparatively small scale compared to that which took place before 1953. The casualties of the Yugoslav civil war of the 1990s are a small proportion of the casualties of the Yugoslav civil war of the 1940s, and the sufferings inflicted on the Chechens during the Russian assault on Grozny are probably less horrible than the sufferings inflicted by the mass deportation of the entire Chechen people in 1944.

Europe since 1989 often seems exceptionally violent because people compare it to the peacefulness that allegedly characterized the years between the end of the Second World War and the fall of communism. This is a deceptive comparison. For one thing, there was substantial violence in Europe, especially in communist countries, during this period. A number of Kosovans – official figures speak of nine; local rumor suggests up to a thousand – were killed during the suppression of riots in 1981. The circumstances of the Cold War did not stop such violence from taking place, they merely ensured that it remained confined to certain areas or that it was not forced on the attention of western Europeans. Furthermore, violence was always latent even when it was not practiced. East–West conflict was held in check by the threat of nuclear weapons;

conflict between the inhabitants of eastern Europe and their political masters was held in check by the threat of the Red Army, and even in the democratic countries of western Europe, the dissatisfaction of marginal groups was held in check by the willingness of democratic states to break their own rules when dealing with the IRA or the Baader–Meinhof group.

There has been a change in the nature of politics which is, in some respects, similar to the change in economics. Both have become less likely to be matters of life and death. Furthermore, just as economics has become as much about consumption as production, so politics has become as much about ends as means. Politics in the middle part of the century emphasized struggle, sacrifice and the necessity of suffering. Political ends were so long-term as to be abstract; political means were violent and immediate. Consider, for example, Auden's lines, written in 1937:

> To-morrow for the young the poets exploding like bombs,
> The walks by the lake, the weeks of perfect communion;
>   To-morrow the bicycle races
> Through the suburbs on summer evenings. But to-day the struggle.
>
> To-day the deliberate increase in the chances of death,
> The conscious acceptance of guilt in the necessary murder;
>   To-day the expending of powers
> On the flat ephemeral pamphlet and the boring meeting.

Auden's words now seem remote. The ends of politics are no longer conceived in such Utopian terms – no one would write about politics in terms of "perfect communion." Equally, few writers would use the phrase "the necessary murder" or celebrate the tedium of political activism. Political ends are more complicated and, in some ways, more limited, but they are also more attainable. Political means are less harsh. The puritanical assumption that suffering produces a better society looks questionable to anyone who compares contemporary Romania with Sweden. Far from emphasizing the need to suffer, political activity at the end of the century sometimes has a self-consciously playful quality. Political demonstrations in the 1930s were modeled on military parades; political demonstrations of the 1990s often seemed to be modeled on the Glastonbury festival.

Some writers seem to regret the passing of the age of heroic sacrifice and believe that Europe at the end of the twentieth century is somehow "mediocre." Such feelings underlie Francis Fukuyama's remark that "the end of history will be a sad time." However, this nostalgia for violent conflict is more pronounced among intellectuals of Britain, France and North America (most of whom escaped comparatively lightly from the great ideological conflicts of the twentieth century) than it is among the inhabitants of eastern and central Europe (who often suffered the effects of such conflicts).

If it is accepted that Europe as a whole is more democratic, peaceful and prosperous at the end of the century, then how does this relate to a more general interpretation of the whole twentieth century? It is often suggested that twentieth-century Europe was a center of unique atrocity. It is hard to know how this suggestion could be assessed or tested. How does a historian decide whether the First World War was "worse" than the Black Death (during which the population of Siena, for example, a rather tranquil place for most of the twentieth century, dropped by two-thirds in the space of six months)? Equally, there is a perverse chauvinism in assuming that Europe must be the center of everything – even suffering. Gabriel García Márquez wrote a story about Colombians, locked in a highly violent civil war, reading newspaper articles about the Franco-British expedition to Suez. Even at the worst moments of its history, the European continent had no monopoly on misery. Europe may have been unique in the scale of *deliberately inflicted* suffering during the Second World War, but it is worth remembering that over 3 million people starved to death in British-ruled Bengal between 1943 and 1946.

Comparison within twentieth-century Europe is more meaningful. There is no doubt that violence in public life increased greatly in the middle part of the twentieth century and that for most Europeans the chances of violent death increased between 1914 and 1953 and, especially, between 1941 and 1945. In some respects, Europe in the last decade of the twentieth century resembled Europe in the first decade. This resemblance is open to different interpretations. On the one hand it may be that western European liberals are living in a fool's paradise that resembles the one inhabited by their great-grandfathers. Accounts, such as mine, that emphasize the peacefulness of contemporary Europe may one day seem as absurd as the entry in the 1911 edition of the *Encyclopaedia Britannica* which said that torture in Europe was a matter of "only historical interest."

An alternative view is to suggest that the whole middle part of the twentieth century was a "parenthesis." Some historians amuse themselves constructing alternative histories in which a slightly different foreign policy on the part of Sir Edward Grey would have averted the First World War, which, in turn, would have averted the Russian Revolution, Stalin, Hitler and Auschwitz. In this Europe-through-the-looking-glass, the Habsburg Emperor, the Kaiser, and perhaps the Tsar of a prosperous and democratic Russia would eventually have signed the Single European Act, which would have marked the culmination of years of peaceful cooperation and economic growth.

A third, and more convincing, interpretation is to suggest that neither present-day prosperity nor the suffering of the middle part of the twentieth century can be dismissed as "parentheses" from the real course of history. The twentieth century is a bloc, and the success of liberalism and democracy at the end of the century cannot be separated from the terror and dictatorship in the middle part of the century. Without the devastation of the Second World War, it is hard to imagine that the West German economy could have enjoyed the spectacular success since 1945 that paved the way for so much else. Without the crushing of the Budapest uprising, it is hard to imagine that Hungary would have undergone the slow liberalization initiated by János Kádár. The uncomfortable truth for liberal Europeans is that the Third Reich and the USSR did much to define the shape of modern Europe. They played a large role in laying down its current frontiers and, especially, its ethnic makeup.

There is another, more subtle and perhaps more important link between the early part of the century and the present shape of Europe. The most influential European values have been formed largely in opposition to the memory of the Third Reich. This was revealed by the horrified reaction of most European leaders when the Austrian Freedom Party, which contains some politicians who seem to admire some aspects of Nazism, was allowed to enter the Austrian government. The whole history of postwar European political thought can be seen as one long meditation on Nazism. This is very obvious in some postwar institutions – Archbishop Temple coined the phrase "welfare state" in explicit opposition to the fascist "warfare state." However, the meaning of an anti-Nazi Europe did not take the shape that it has now straight away in 1945. The victors of 1945 often thought of the conflict as a conventional one between powers or between ideologies. Condemning Nazism did not, therefore, always mean thinking very much about the meaning of repression or violence. The Soviet Union sent Andrei Vyshinsky, prosecutor in the Moscow trials of the 1930s, to the Nuremberg trials of Nazi leaders; the British sent their own hangman to Germany on the mind-boggling grounds that the Germans were insufficiently experienced in this craft. Only as time went on did different groups stress the full extent of Nazism's projects and the ways in which it spilled out into various areas of life, so that eventually Nazism came to be seen not as the antithesis of another ideology but as the antithesis of all human values. Rejection of Nazism in recent years has acquired two, partially contradictory, dimensions. On the one hand, increasing emphasis has been laid on the specificity of Nazism in the sense that it is separated from other repressive and even fascist regimes. On the other hand, increasing emphasis is laid on the way in which some Nazi projects – those connected, for example, to eugenics, sexuality and the "antisocial" – tied in with policies in postwar democracies. Thinking about Nazism has thus become a means by which people reconsider elements of their own society.

The rejection of Stalinism and Soviet communism more generally has also had a considerable influence on postwar politics. The rejection has never been as total as that of Nazism, however: thinking about Stalinism has usually been conditioned by the perception that it was, as Kundera remarked, a distorted form of humanism where Nazism had been the negation of humanism. Likewise, thinking about Soviet rule after 1953 was conditioned by the recognition that it was less repressive than both Nazism and Stalinism. Rejection of Nazism and Soviet communism have rarely, in spite of some well-publicized polemics, been mutually exclusive. Some people in some countries – Romania and Slovakia, for instance – have gone some way to rehabilitating wartime rulers who collaborated with the Nazis, but this has not meant wholesale rehabilitation of the Third Reich. Generally, rejection of Nazism and Soviet communism has blended together to produce a revaluation of certain kinds of human rights. One of the judges who refused to grant Augusto Pinochet immunity from prosecution for crimes against humanity remarked that to do so would be unthinkable because it would imply similar protection for Hitler and Stalin.* In one sense, Hitler and Stalin are the most important political thinkers of late-twentieth-century Europe precisely because so many values come from opposition to them. Without Hitler there would have been no Daniel Cohn-Bendit; without Stalin there would have been no Václav Havel.

Where does all this leave the historian? In many ways the narratives with which we weave together events in the earlier part of the century no longer work. In her memoirs, published in 1998, the novelist Doris Lessing wondered whether she should leave out politics altogether because it might bore her readers. She concluded that she could not do so. For someone like herself, a communist militant in the late 1940s and early 1950s, politics was too intimately tied up with every other aspect of life. Her second husband was unable to see his own son because, as an official in East Germany, he could not risk contact with a foreigner. Her Czech lover was woken by

---

* Pinochet was ultimately returned to Chile on the grounds of ill health – no law court in Europe overturned the view that he was liable to prosecution.

nightmares because his communist faith did not prevent him from knowing that friends executed in the purges were innocent. The implication of Lessing's remark, however, is that politics are not central to most people's lives in the 1990s.

Economic and social history are equally beset with problems. The measurable generalizations on which both are founded are less easy to sustain now. Historians attempting to assess living standards in the early part of the century were able to make relatively simple calculations about average wages and the price of food (which still took up the greater part of most people's spending). Now, everything is more awkward in a world of consumer choice in which the value of objects is determined by culture as much as physical need.

The fact that the historian's task becomes more difficult when writing about the end of the century is linked to the fact that the lives of most Europeans have become easier. In an age of violence and penury, politics and economics are matters of life and death. In an age of peace and prosperity they become less pressing. Recognizing Europe's good fortune does not imply any belief in the innate superiority of European culture or even a naïve faith in the future. We may have done nothing to deserve this, and we may be uncomfortably aware that our privileges have been obtained through the suffering of others, but we should at least have the grace to enjoy it while it lasts.

SOME THOUGHTS ON
FURTHER READING

ANYONE WHO WANTS to understand history should start by trying to understand historians. In France in recent years there has been a fashion for publishing the autobiographies of historians. A number of them are gathered in Pierre Nora (ed.), *Essais d'Ego-Histoire* (1987*). Two particularly revealing and contrasting autobiographies are those of Philippe Ariès and Annie Kriegel. Ariès was a supporter of the monarchist Action Française, who, working outside universities, turned his attention away from political history towards childhood, death and private life. His *Un Historien du Dimanche* (1980) is a wonderful book – although readers who want to find out just how right-wing he was should also read his collected journalism, *Le Présent Quotidien, 1955–1966* (ed. Jeannine Verdès-Leroux, 1997). While Ariès was a former royalist who found himself in sympathy with the *soixante-huitard* left, Kriegel was a former Stalinist who hated 1968; where Ariès turned away from political history, Kriegel was concerned with questions of power, will and party organization. Her memoirs, *Ce Que J'ai Cru Comprendre* (1991), reflect an uncomfortably fierce intelligence. Felix Gilbert, *A European Past, 1905–1945* (1988), tells the story of one of the many Jewish historians forced out of Nazi Germany. It is placed in a wider context by Hartmut Lehmann and James Sheehan (eds.), *An Interrupted Past: German-Speaking Refugee Historians in the United States After 1933* (Cambridge, 1991). Raul Hilberg, *The*

---

* In this chapter, and in the Notes that follow, the place of publication for titles in English is London, and in French, Paris, unless otherwise stated.

Politics of Memory: The Journey of a Holocaust Historian (Chicago, 1996), shows how little attention was paid to the extermination of the Jews in the immediate aftermath of the Second World War. The introduction to Eugen Weber's *My France: Politics, Culture, Myth* (Cambridge, MA, 1991) describes the author's progress from Bucharest to California via Emmanuel College, Cambridge, the Institut d'Études Politiques and the British army. The interview with Moshe Lewin in Henry Abelove, Betsy Blackmar, Peter Dimock and Jonathan Schneer (eds.), *Visions of History* (New York, 1984), describes a progress from Poland to California via Lithuania, Siberia, the Red Army, an Israeli kibbutz and the École Pratique des Hautes Études. Lilly Marcou, *Une Enfance Stalinienne* (1982), tells how the author grew up as a Bucharest Jew in the early 1940s and then cast herself into Stalinist militancy during her teenage years, before finally leaving for the West and becoming a historian of diplomacy and high politics who understood better than most the consequences that political events could have on people's lives. Luisa Passerini, *Autobiography of a Generation: Italy, 1968* (Hanover, NH, 1996), is sad and fascinating. Passerini is an almost exact contemporary of Marcou but their memoirs could not be more different – Marcou's academic view is dominated by conventional diplomatic history while Passerini reflects the intellectual flux of contemporary social history; Passerini experienced the relative material ease, and moral discomfort, of being a "dissident" in the West while Marcou's formative experiences were ones of physical discomfort and moral certainty; Marcou never discusses the impact that her sex might have had on her political or historical outlook; Passerini mentions the subject on almost every page.

British historians have been less frank than their continental counterparts, perhaps because they have so much less to hide. Elizabeth Wiskemann was saved from a career as an academic by the sexism of her Ph.D. examiners. Her subsequent wanderings across central Europe are recounted in *The Europe I Saw* (1968). A. J. P. Taylor, by contrast, enjoyed every privilege of the English establishment (for which he was very ungrateful). His *A Personal History* (1984) is a good read that reflects the contrast between the secure and prosperous lives of most British historians and those of their continental colleagues. Taylor's knowledge of eastern and central Europe was derived from books, from conversations with émigrés and from brief visits, as a privileged tourist, to communist countries. His lifelong defense of Soviet interests came from the mere appearance of Lenin's mummified corpse: "I decided then that Lenin was a good man, an opinion that I have not changed." Taylor's experience should be compared with that of his onetime associate François Fejtö,

who had a rather more intimate knowledge of central Europe and a
more pessimistic view of Leninism. He tells his story in *Mémoires: De
Budapest à Paris* (1986).

Sources

Historians are fond of complimenting each other on their "mastery of the
sources" (as if "the sources" were a rebellious tribe on the North-West
Frontier). Those who work on certain areas of diplomatic or political history may still be able to agree on a limited corpus of documents that specialists need to read (A. J. P. Taylor claimed to have researched two books
in the library of his London club), but generally historians of the twentieth century are faced with too many, rather than too few, sources. Readers should understand that authors make choices about which sources to
use and that the impact of such choices is felt, indirectly, in general books
such as this one. Having said that, the vast capacity of twentieth-century
bureaucracies to produce and record information means that historians
can find out about areas of life that are almost completely closed to their
colleagues researching earlier periods – a single edition of *Social Trends*
(published annually by the British government) contains more information than the Doomsday Book. Ingenious scholars can mine even tedious
works of reference for information. Sheila Fitzpatrick used successive editions of the Moscow telephone directory to investigate Stalin's purges –
only the powerful had phones, and sudden disappearance from the directory was usually a sign that political disaster had befallen the subscriber.

One particular kind of source is available to historians of the twentieth
century and not to their colleagues specializing in earlier periods. Oral
history has been associated with the growing interest in the history of
subordinate and inarticulate groups and, no doubt, with the increasing
availability of small tape recorders. Luisa Passerini, *Fascism in Popular
Memory: The Cultural Experience of the Turin Working Class* (Cambridge,
1987), explores the implications of such research. Oral history in communist states took a very different direction from that in the West. Interviews were often used to uncover episodes that had been deliberately hidden rather than the lives of those whose history had never been written
down. Interviewers were explicit about their political activism and used
their work as an opportunity to confront the powerful rather than to give
voices to the unrepresented. The most influential example of such an approach is the work of the Solidarity activitist Teresa Toranska, *Oni:
Stalin's Polish Puppets* (1987). Karel Bartosek juxtaposes the oral testimony of participants with recently released archival material in *Les Aveux
des Archives: Prague–Paris–Prague, 1948–1968* (1996).

Statistics

The twentieth century is the age of the statistic. The Second World War, with its vast deployment of resources, was a statistician's war – the French statistician Alfred Sauvy said that Allied victory could be predicted with certainty from the moment that the total number of tonnes of shipping produced by the Americans exceeded the tonnes of shipping sunk by German U-boats. Politics in postwar western Europe revolved around statistics, which were believed to provide the material for "objective" solutions to social problems, while the Soviet Union's claims about its economic successes were expressed in statistical form.

Statistics pose their own problems. They hide qualitative distinctions and sometimes numb the mind to human realities (Stalin said that one death is a tragedy and a million deaths is a statistic). The ways in which statistics are compiled and digested can be subject to all sorts of manipulation, which was particularly evident in the communist states. Falsification occurred at every level as managers attempted to give the impression that targets, which extended to matters as diverse as the borrowing of library books in east Berlin, were being met. In any case, statistics were often meaningless because quality of production was disregarded in the search for simple quantity. Under Stalin, certain kinds of statistical study, especially demographics, could become physically dangerous if they revealed unwelcome truths, and even in the 1980s, Soviet statistics were still hampered by the difficulty of persuading officials to put in truthful returns and by the fact that Soviet statisticians were unable to accept that there was a random element in the economy and consequently refused to use sampling techniques.

Statistics in the West should also be treated with caution. In 1987, Italian economists "increased" Italian gross national product by 18 percent through the simple but unprecedented expedient of making allowance for their country's black economy. Between 1979 and 1986, the British government changed the way in which unemployment statistics were calculated twenty-six times (almost all the changes had the effect of making unemployment appear lower).

General accounts

Four general histories are of particular interest. Eric Hobsbawm's *Age of Extremes: The Short Twentieth Century, 1914–1991* (1994) is a history of the whole twentieth-century world rather than just Europe, and has laid down much of the framework (the "short twentieth century," the "golden age") within which subsequent historians have operated. Norman Davies,

Europe: A History (Oxford, 1996), has a wider scope in chronological terms. Since Davies's own area of expertise is Poland, it is not surprising that he has a more hostile view of the Soviet Union than Hobsbawm. Donald Sassoon, *One Hundred Years of Socialism: The West European Left in the Twentieth Century* (1996), contains almost as much for those interested in the history of capitalism as for those interested in socialism. Mark Mazower, *Dark Continent: Europe's Twentieth Century* (1998), is an excellent book, with particularly strong chapters on interwar national/racial tension and constitution-making in the 1920s.

Any British, and especially English, reader ought to remember that their view of Europe is likely to say as much about the nature of their own country as it does about the "peculiarity" of any continental European state. Stimulating surveys of recent British history are provided by Peter Clarke, *Hope and Glory: Britain, 1900–1990* (1997) and Ross McKibbin, *Classes and Cultures: England, 1918–1951* (Oxford, 1998). The most penetrating analysis of Englishness, and of so many other things, is provided by George Orwell. His essay "England Your England," first published in 1941, manages in a very Orwellian, perhaps very English, way to be both sentimental wartime propaganda and a caustic scrutiny of national myth.

Europe before 1914

For the evocation of Europe as a bourgeois idyll before 1914, see André Bouton, *La Fin des Rentiers* (1932). Eugen Weber, *Peasants into Frenchmen: The Modernization of Rural France, 1870–1914* (1977), continues to raise questions even for those who disagree with Weber's answers. See also Ben Eklof and Stephen Frank (eds.), *The World of the Russian Peasant: Post-Emancipation Culture and Society* (1990); Richard Evans and W. Lee (eds.), *The German Peasant: Conflict and Community in Rural Society from the Eighteenth to the Twentieth Centuries* (1980); and Gavin Lewis, "The peasantry, rural change and conservative agrarianism: Lower Austria at the turn of the century" in *Past and Present,* 81 (1978). On workers, see Dick Geary, *European Labour Protest, 1814–1939* (1981); R. J. Evans, *Proletarians and Politics: Socialism, Protest and the Working Class in Germany Before the First World War* (1990); Robert Stuart, *Marxism at Work: Ideology, Class and French Socialism During the Third Republic* (Cambridge, 1992); Ross McKibbin, *The Ideologies of Class: Social Relations in Britain, 1880–1950* (Oxford, 1990); and Stefan Berger, *The British Labour Party and the German Social Democrats, 1900–1931* (Oxford, 1994). On the lower middle class see Geoffrey Crossick and Heinz-Gerhard Haupt (eds.), *Shopkeepers and Master Artisans in Nineteenth-Century Europe* (1984). On the bourgeoisie generally, see Jürgen Kocka and Allan Mitchell (eds.), *Bourgeois Society in Nineteenth-Century Europe* (Oxford, 1993).

The Great War

David Stevenson's history of the First World War (Penguin, forthcoming) will undoubtedly be comprehensive. See also Niall Ferguson, *The Pity of War* (1998), and Holger H. Herwig, *The First World War: Germany and Austria-Hungary, 1914–1918* (1997). Norman Stone's *The Eastern Front, 1914–1917* (1975) should be supplemented by Allan Wildman, *The End of the Russian Imperial Army: The Old Army and the Soldier's Revolt (March–April 1917)* (Princeton, NJ, 1980).

Much research in recent years has focused on the social impact of the war and, in spite of the fact that this impact was greatest in eastern Europe, research has concentrated on western Europe. See Richard Wall and Jay Winter (eds.), *The Upheaval of War: Family, Work and Welfare in Europe, 1914–1918* (Cambridge, 1988); Avner Offner, *The First World War: An Agrarian Interpretation* (Oxford, 1991); Jürgen Kocka (ed.), *Facing Total War: German Society, 1914–1918* (1984); Patrick Fridenson (ed.), *The French Home Front, 1914–1918* (Oxford, 1992); John Horne (ed.) *State, Society and Mobilization in Europe During the First World War* (Cambridge, 1997); Jean-Jacques Becker and Stéphane Audoin Rouzeau (eds.), *Les Sociétés Européennes et la Guerre de 1914–1918* (1990); and Eric J. Leed, *No Man's Land: Combat and Identity in World War One* (Cambridge, 1979).

The legacy of the war is covered implicitly in almost any book on any aspect of post-1918 European history. It is covered explicitly in Stephen Ward (ed.), *The War Generation: Veterans of the First World War* (1975); Robert Weldon Whalen, *Bitter Wounds: Germany's Victims of the Great War, 1914–1939* (Ithaca, NY, 1984); Antoine Prost, *In the Wake of War: Les Anciens Combattants and French Society, 1914–1939* (Oxford, 1992); Adrian Gregory, *The Silence of Memory: Armistice Day, 1919–1946* (Oxford, 1994); Richard Bessel, *Germany After the First World War* (Oxford, 1993); and Martin Petter, "'Temporary gentlemen' in the aftermath of the Great War: rank, status and the ex-officer problem" in *Historical Journal* 37, 1 (1994), pp. 127–52. Jay Winter, *Sites of Memory, Sites of Mourning: The Great War in European Cultural History* (Cambridge, 1995) is good on concrete detail.

From one war to another

E. H. Carr's *The World Crisis, 1919–1939: An Introduction to the Study of International Relations* (1951) had a huge influence. So too did John

Maynard Keynes, *The Economic Consequences of the Peace* (1919), which is an astonishing mixture of wit, insight and offensive prejudice – it should be read alongside Étienne Mantoux, *The Carthaginian Peace, or the Economic Consequences of Mr Keynes* (Oxford, 1946). Orlando Figes' *A People's Tragedy: The Russian Revolution, 1891–1924* (1996) is long and bleak. Sheila Fitzpatrick, *The Russian Revolution* (Oxford, 1994), is short and, relatively, optimistic. For the career of the most important revolutionary see Robert Service, *Lenin* (2000).

Eastern and central Europe were at the heart of European political instability during the 1920s and 1930s. Many of the best accounts of tensions in the region come from personal observation rather than research in archives. Rebecca West's *Black Lamb and Grey Falcon* (two volumes, 1942) describes a journey through Yugoslavia in 1937. Hugh Seton-Watson, *Eastern Europe Between the Wars, 1918–1941* (Cambridge, 1946) is also worth reading. More academic accounts can be found in Antony Polonsky, *The Little Dictators: The History of Eastern Europe Since 1918* (1975), and Joseph Rothschild, *East Central Europe Between the Two World Wars* (Seattle, WA, 1974). Mária Kovács, *Liberal Professions and Illiberal Politics: Hungary from the Habsburgs to the Holocaust* (Oxford, 1994), is an important book. Jacques Rupnik, *Histoire du Parti Communiste Tchécoslovaque: Des Origines à la Prise du Pouvoir* (1981), is excellent.

Diplomacy involving central and eastern Europe was made difficult by the fact that British diplomats knew so little about the region and so often regarded the successor states of their beloved Habsburg Empire with contempt. Readers from continental Europe who believe that the British ruling classes are snobbish, anti-Semitic and antidemocratic will find their prejudices confirmed in the memoirs of eminent British diplomats. See especially Ivone Kirkpatrick, *The Inner Circle* (1959), and David Kelly, *The Ruling Few, or, the Human Background to Diplomacy* (1953). Neville Henderson's *Water Under the Bridges* (1945) reveals the relationship between anti-Czech feeling and British diplomacy. By comparison with such works, Roger Peyrefitte's autobiographical novel about the Quai d'Orsay – *Les Ambassades* (1951) – looks fairly tame.

On Stalinism, J. Arch Getty, *Origins of the Great Purges: The Soviet Communist Party Reconsidered, 1933–1938* (Cambridge, 1985), revises the totalitarian model established by Merle Fainsod in *Smolensk Under Soviet Rule* (Cambridge, MA, 1958), even though the two historians use almost exactly the same sources. J. Arch Getty and Roberta Manning (eds.), *Stalinist Terror: New Perspectives* (Cambridge, 1993), is a curious work that was published just before the avalanche of new work made possible by perestroika. The avalanche is represented by Sarah Davies,

Popular Opinion in Stalin's Russia: Terror, Propaganda and Dissent, 1934–1941 (Cambridge, 1997); Sheila Fitzpatrick, *Stalin's Peasants: Resistance and Survival in the Russian Village After Collectivization* (Oxford, 1994), and *Everyday Stalinism: Ordinary Life in Extraordinary Times – Soviet Russia in the 1930s* (Oxford, 1999); Stephen Kotkin, *Magnetic Mountain: Stalinism as a Civilisation* (Berkeley and Los Angeles, CA, 1995); and Amy Knight, *Beria: Stalin's First Lieutenant* (Princeton, NJ, 1993). See also Lewis Siegelbaum, *Stakhanovism and the Politics of Productivity in the USSR, 1935–1941* (Cambridge, 1988); Moshe Lewin, *The Making of the Soviet System: Essays in the Social History of interwar Russia* (1985); and Nick Lampert and Gábor Rittersporn (eds.), *Stalinism: Its Nature and Aftermath* (1992). Eugenia Ginzburg, *Into the Whirlwind* (1967), is a wonderful account of Stalinism by a woman who was a believer in, and a victim of, Stalinism. On women in the Soviet Union, see Wendy Z. Goldman, *Women, the State and Revolution: Soviet Family Policy and Social Life, 1917–1936* (Cambridge, 1993); Rosalind Marsh (ed.), *Women in Russia and the Ukraine* (Cambridge, 1995); and Beatrice Farnsworth and Lynne Viola (eds.), *Russian Peasant Women* (Oxford, 1992).

On the Church in interwar politics, see Tom Buchanan and Martin Conway (eds.), *Political Catholicism in Europe, 1918–1965* (Oxford, 1996), and R. Wolff and J. Hoensch (eds.), *Catholics, the State and the European Radical Right* (New York, 1987). On the peasantry in politics see George Jackson, *Comintern and Peasant in East Europe, 1918–1939* (New York, 1966), and Robert Paxton, *French Peasant Fascism: Henry Dorgères's Greenshirts and the Crises of French Agriculture, 1929–1939* (Oxford, 1997).

Cyril Connolly's *Enemies of Promise* (first published in 1938) shows how the storms of continental politics rattled the tea cups of English literary life. It is placed in a wider context by Valentine Cunningham, *British Writers of the Thirties* (Oxford, 1988). Robert Brasillach's *Notre Avant-Guerre* (first published in 1941) is, in many ways, a French counterpart to *Enemies of Promise* (both works contain much sentimental reminiscence of the authors' schooldays); it should be read alongside Jean-François Sirinelli, *Une Génération Intellectuelle: Khâgneux et Normaliens dans l'Entre-Deux-Guerres* (1988).

On Vichy France, the publication of Robert Paxton's *Vichy France: Old Guard and New Order, 1940–1944* (New York, 1972) was itself a historical event, the consequences of which are described by Henry Rousso in *The Vichy Syndrome: History and Memory in France Since 1944* (Cambridge, MA, 1991). Those wishing to know about the social impact of the Second World War in France should start with Philippe Burrin, *France Under the Germans: Collaboration and Compromise* (1996). Julian Jackson's *France. The Dark Years, 1940–1944* (Oxford, 2001) summarizes the vast literature published on this subject in the last decade. On Portugal see António Costa Pinto, *Salazar's Dictatorship and European Fascism: Problems of Interpretation* (Boulder, CO, 1995). On the Spanish Civil War see Paul Preston, *A Concise History of the Spanish Civil War* (1996), and a collection of essays edited by the same author, *Revolution and War in Spain, 1931–1939* (1993).

Debate over the nature of fascism and its relations to other political currents has consumed a vast amount of energy. Stuart Woolf (ed.), *The Nature of Fascism* (1968), encapsulated debate at an early stage. Eugen Weber, *Varieties of Fascism* (1964), is short and informative about little-studied movements. Two recent collections are Martin Blinkhorn (ed.), *Fascists and Conservatives: The Radical Right and the Establishment in Twentieth-Century Europe* (1990), and Richard Bessel (ed.), *Fascist Italy and Nazi Germany: Comparisons and Contrasts* (Cambridge, 1996). Kevin Passmore's *From Liberalism to Fascism: The Right in a French Province, 1928–1939* (Cambridge, 1997) is not really about fascism, or liberalism, but it is well worth reading.

Works on Nazi Germany are now very numerous and the debates on this subject sometimes generate more heat than light. Michael Burleigh and Wolfgang Wippermann, *The Racial State: Germany, 1933–1945* (Cambridge, 1991), is refreshingly clear. On society under Nazism see Richard Overy, *War and Economy in the Third Reich* (Oxford, 1994); Tim Mason, *Nazism, Fascism and the Working Class* (Cambridge, 1995), and *Social Policy in the Third Reich: The Working Class and the "National Community"* (Cambridge, 1993). The most recent serious biography of Hitler is Ian Kershaw, *Hitler, 1889–1936: Hubris* (1998) and *Nemesis, 1936–1945*. For Hitler's relations with the German people see the same author's *The "Hitler Myth": Image and Reality in the Third Reich* (Oxford, 1989). Two recent and important books on Nazism are Michael Burleigh, *The Third Reich: A New History* (2000) and Robert Gellately, *Backing Hitler: Consent and Coercion in Nazi Germany* (Oxford, 2001).

In recent years, fascism has become less widely used as a unifying concept. Some historians have emphasized Nazism as a regime of institutionalized mass killing, and in this context the Third Reich can only really be compared to Stalin's Russia. Such a comparison is attempted in Ian Kershaw and Moshe Lewin (eds.), *Stalinism and Nazism: Dictatorships in Comparison* (Cambridge, 1997). In some ways a more interesting, though highly polemical, approach is taken in Stéphane Courtois, Nicolas Werth, Jean-Louis Panné, Andrzej Paczkowski, Karel Bartosek and Jean-Louis Margolin (eds.), *Le Livre Noir du Communisme: Crimes, Terreur, Répression* (1997). The latter book launched a fashion for comparative works in France. Henri Rousso (ed.), *Stalinism et Nazisme: Histoire et*

Mémoire Comparées (1999), and Marc Ferro (ed.), *Nazisme et Communisme: Deux Régimes dans le Siècle* (1999), compare the historiography as well as the history of the two regimes.

Another approach to Nazi Germany emphasizes "biological politics" and race. At the center of such work is the extermination of the European Jews and the less systematic assaults on other groups. Students of this subject should start with Raul Hilberg's *The Destruction of the European Jews* (1973) and move on to Christopher Browning's minutely detailed reconstruction of the motives of a particular group of killers in *Ordinary Men: Reserve Police Battalion 101 and the Final Solution in Poland* (1992). Collections of essays by Browning, *The Path to Genocide: Essays on Launching the Final Solution* (Cambridge, 1992), and Hilberg, *Perpetrators, Victims, Bystanders: The Jewish Catastrophe, 1933–1945* (1993), are also useful. In *"Final Solution": Nazi Population Policy and the Murder of the European Jews* (1999), Götz Aly places the Jewish fate in the wider context of the resettlement of ethnic minorities in the Nazi order. David Bankier, *The Germans and the Final Solution: Public Opinion Under Nazism* (1992), and Robert Gellately, *The Gestapo and German Society: Enforcing Racial Policy, 1933–1945* (Oxford, 1991), show how severe were the measures applied against the small group of Germans who resisted Nazi racial policy.

One aspect of "biological politics" is an emphasis on gender, women and reproduction, which sometimes associates studies of Nazism with wider research on Europe. Specific works on the Third Reich include Claudia Koonz, *Mothers in the Fatherland* (1987); Renate Bridenthal, Anita Grossmann and Marion Kaplan (eds.), *When Biology Became Destiny: Women in Weimar and Nazi Germany* (New York, 1984); and Anita Grossmann, *Reforming Sex: The German Movement for Birth Control and Abortion Reform, 1920–1950* (Oxford, 1995). Women under Italian Fascism are discussed by Victoria de Grazia in *How Fascism Ruled Women: Italy, 1922–1945* (Berkeley, CA, 1993) and by Perry Willson, *The Clockwork Factory: Women and Work in Fascist Italy* (Oxford, 1993); the latter work can usefully be read alongside Miriam Glucksmann, *Women Assemble: Women Workers in the New Industries in interwar Britain* (1996). Sian Reynolds, *France Between the Wars: Gender and Politics* (1996), is explicitly a work of "women's history" rather than gender history; Mary Louise Roberts, *Civilisation Without Sexes: Reconstructing Gender in postwar France, 1917–1927* (Chicago, 1994), is gender history and mainly about men, as is Joanna Bourke, *Dismembering the Male: Men's Bodies, Britain and the Great War* (1996). Women and the welfare state are covered in Susan Pedersen, *Family, Dependence and the Origins of the Welfare State: Britain and France, 1914–1945* (Cambridge, 1993), and Gisela Bock and Pat Thane (eds.), *Maternity and*

Gender Policies: Women and the Rise of the European Welfare States, 1880–1950s (1991).

On the Second World War in Europe, Richard Overy's *Why the Allies Won* (1996) provides an overview. John Erickson's *The Road to Stalingrad* (1975) and *The Road to Berlin* (1983) describe the apocalyptic confrontation in the East. John Barber and Mark Harrison, *The Soviet Home Front, 1941–1945: A Social and Economic History of the USSR in World War II* (1991), is excellent. Alan Milward, *War, Economy and Society* (1987), is informative but dated.

Western European politics and society since 1945

There are many excellent monographs on western Europe since 1945 but few good syntheses. Alan Milward, *The European Rescue of the Nation-State* (1992), has been very influential. Nick Crafts and Gianni Toniolo (eds.), *Economic Growth in Europe Since 1945* (Cambridge, 1996), contains a number of good essays on individual countries. Peter Hall (ed.), *The Political Power of Economic Ideas: Keynesianism Across the Nations* (Princeton, NJ, 1989), shows how economic ideas could have different meanings in different countries. American influence in Europe is described in Antony Carew, *Labour Under the Marshall Plan: The Politics of Productivity and the Marketing of Management Science* (Manchester, 1987); John Lamberton Harper, *American Influence and the Reconstruction of Italy, 1945–1948* (Cambridge, 1986); Volker Berghahn, *The Americanization of West German Industry, 1945–1973* (Leamington Spa, 1986); and Irwin Wall, *The United States and the Making of postwar France, 1945–1954* (Cambridge, 1991). The work of French scholars in the 1950s on female suffrage has not been bettered. See Mattei Dogan and Jacques Narbonne, *Les Françaises Face à la Politique* (1955), and Maurice Duverger, *The Political Role of Women* (Paris, 1955). On individual countries see Paul Ginsborg, *A History of Contemporary Italy: Society and Politics, 1943–1988* (1990), and Melanie Sully, *A Contemporary History of Austria* (1990). Robert Moeller (ed.), *West Germany Under Construction: Politics, Society and Culture in the Adenauer Era* (Ann Arbor, MI, 1997), contains some interesting essays. On Portugal, see the work of Costa Pinto (cited above). On Spain, Paul Preston has written three important books. *Franco: A Biography* (1993) provides a general narrative; *The Triumph of Democracy in Spain* (1990) gives a detailed account of the end of the dictatorship; and *The Politics of Revenge: Franco and the Military* (1990) brings together some wide-ranging general essays. Stanley Payne, *The Franco Regime, 1936–1975* (Madison, WI, 1987), is also good.

On individual political parties see Jean Charlot, *The Gaullist Phenomenon* (1970), which says a great deal about the whole pattern of western European politics in the 1960s. Annie Kriegel, *The French Communists: Profile of a People* (Chicago, 1972), is a brilliant book. On Christian democracy see David Hanley (ed.), *Christian Democracy in Europe: A Comparative Perspective* (1994). The characteristics that made Italian Christian democracy into such a successful political machine are described in Robert Leonardi and Douglas Wertman, *Italian Christian Democracy: The Politics of Dominance* (1989). The roots of the Italian political system are also analyzed in James Walston, *The Mafia and Clientelism: Roads to Rome in postwar Calabria* (1988), and Judith Chubb, *Patronage and Poverty in Southern Italy: A Tale of Two Cities* (Cambridge, 1982).

The student protests of 1968 have probably received more attention than they deserve from academics who were often supporters or victims. David Caute provides a useful summary in *The Year of Barricades: '68* (1988). Henri Weber's *Vingt Ans Après: Que reste-t-il de '68?* (1988) is the best work produced by a participant in the Paris events. Paul Hoch and Vic Schoenbach, *LSE: The Natives are Restless – A Report on Student Power in Action* (1969), captures the absurdity of events in London.

No one should try to understand postwar society without reading two local studies of France – Lawrence Wylie, *Village in the Vaucluse* (Oxford, 1974), and Edgar Morin, *Commune en France: La Métamorphose de Plodémet* (1967). John Goldthorpe, David Lockwood, Frank Bechhofer and Jennifer Platt, *The Affluent Workers: Industrial Attitudes and Behaviour* (Cambridge, 1968), also has implications that extend well beyond the local level on which research was conducted.

Scott Lash and John Urry, *The End of Organized Capitalism* (Cambridge, 1987), is better at describing organized capitalism than explaining its alleged demise. Valerie Symes, *Unemployment in Europe: Problems and Policies* (1995), uses a series of local studies to reach the unsurprising conclusion that living in Barcelona is nicer than living in Manchester. The energy devoted to the study of the largely unsuccessful Thatcherite experiment in Britain has probably distracted attention from the real reasons for capitalism's political victory at the end of the century. Denis Kavanagh, *Thatcherism and British Politics: the End of Consensus* (Oxford, 1990), provides a straightforward account. Paul Whitely, Patrick Seyd and Jeremy Richardson, *True Blues: The Politics of Conservative Party Membership* (Oxford, 1993), raises some interesting questions, as does Andrew Gamble, *The Free Economy and the Strong State: The Politics of Thatcherism* (Basingstoke, 1994). Peter Hall, *Governing the Economy: The Politics of State Intervention in Britain and France* (Cambridge, 1986), puts Thatcherism in an international perspective. Anna Marie Smith, *New Right Discourse on Race and Sexuality* (Cambridge, 1994), says much about the contradictions of political conservatism and economic liberalism, as do some of the essays in David Higgs (ed.), *Queer Sites: Gay Urban Histories Since 1600* (1999).

Communist Europe

Eastern Europe under communism was seen, perhaps wrongly, as a more coherent bloc than western Europe, and this has made it easier for historians to produce general narratives (often dominated by politics and ideology at a time when such concepts were becoming unfashionable in the West). Joseph Rothschild, *Return to Diversity: A Political History of East Central Europe Since World War II* (Oxford, 1993), is good. Richard Staar, *Communist Regimes in Eastern Europe* (Stanford, CA, 1977), is rooted in the Cold War (which does not necessarily mean that it is wrong). Norman Naimark, *The Russians in Germany: A History of the Soviet Zone of Occupation, 1945–1949* (Cambridge, MA, 1995), illustrates the wealth of information that is becoming available since the fall of communist rule. Mary Fulbrook, *Anatomy of a Dictatorship: Inside the GDR, 1949–1989* (Oxford, 1995), takes up the story. The new research being done on the GDR is reflected in unpublished Ph.D. dissertations such as that by C. R. Ross, "Constructing Socialism at the Grass-Roots: The Transformation of East Germany, 1945–1965" (University College, London, 1998). On the purges and Stalinism see two heartbreaking autobiographies, Heda Margolius Kovaly, *Prague Farewell* (1988), and Artur London, *L'Aveu: Dans l'Engrenage du Procès de Prague* (1969). Eugen Steiner, *The Slovak Dilemma* (Cambridge, 1973), reveals much about communism and nationalism. Paul Neuburg, a Hungarian-born journalist, exploited the comparatively liberal climate in many communist countries during the late 1960s to extract the information on which he based *The Hero's Children: The postwar Generation in Eastern Europe* (1972). On Soviet society see Leonard Schapiro and Joseph Godson (eds.), *The Soviet Worker from Lenin to Andropov* (1984); Blair Ruble, *Soviet Trade Unions: Their Development in the 1970s* (Cambridge, 1981); Ellen Jones, *Red Army and Society: A Sociology of the Soviet Military* (1985); Timothy Colton and Thane Gustafson (eds.), *Soldiers and the Soviet State: Civil Military Relations from Brezhnev to Gorbachev* (Princeton, NJ, 1990); Donald Filtzer, *Soviet Workers and De-Stalinization: The Consolidation of the Modern System of Soviet Production Relations, 1953–1964* (Cambridge, 1992); and Mervyn Matthews, *Privilege in the Soviet Union: A Study of Elite Lifestyles Under Communism* (1978).

Three novels have had a vast influence on Western perceptions of communist Europe. Alexander Solzhenitsyn's *One Day in the Life of Ivan Denisovich* did more than any other work to reveal the world of the Soviet labor camps. It was published in 1962 and by 1974, when Solzhenitsyn was expelled from the Soviet Union, it had been translated into seventy-nine languages. The impact of the book is described by Zhores Medvedev in *Ten Years After Ivan Denisovich* (1973). Milan Kundera's account of youthful enthusiasm and disillusionment in *The Joke* (1967) is so convincing that Lilly Marcou says it dispenses her from any need to give an account of her own expulsion from the Romanian Communist Party. Readers should, however, remember that Kundera never thought of himself as a primarily political writer, that much of his work was written for translation, and that the Czechs knew him, if at all, from the film version of his work, which has a very different tone from the novel. For a view of Kundera before "normalization" turned him into a political exile and European literary star, see Antonin Liehm, *Trois Générations: Entretiens sur le Phénomène Culturel Tchécoslovaque* (1970). For a view of Kundera after the fall of communism see Ivan Klíma, *The Spirit of Prague* (1994). For Kundera's translation onto the Czech screen see Josef Skvorecky, *All the Bright Young Men and Women: A Personal History of Czech Cinema* (1971). Ismail Kadaré's novels provided Western intellectuals with pretty much their only window on communist Albania. His *Le Grand Hiver* (1982) mixes an account of Soviet–Albanian diplomacy with the snakes and wolves of the Albanian mountains. It should, however, be remembered that *Le Grand Hiver* was written in strange circumstances. As an eminent novelist, Kadaré was more or less obliged by 1971 to write a novel that featured his country's leader, Enver Hoxha. He later claimed that he had tried, unsuccessfully, to present a model of a romantic hero that would inspire Hoxha himself to change his policy. Kadaré, like Kundera, wrote mainly for the translator, and one of his later novels was smuggled out of Albania wrapped around raki bottles.

The fall of communism

Given that so many intelligent analysts failed to predict the fall of communism, it is only fair to begin any reading on this subject with three people who did predict it. The French demographer Emmanuel Todd based his *La Chute Finale: Essai sur la Décomposition de la Sphère Soviétique* (1976 and 1991) partly on widely available statistics and partly on personal observation. The Soviet dissident Andrei Amalrik based his *Will the Soviet Union Survive Until 1984?* (1980) partly on the information about the Soviet economy that he gleaned while exiled to a remote collective farm. The Czech Stalinist, turned reformer, turned dissident Zdeněk Mlynář was remarkably prescient in *Night Frost in Prague: The End of Humane Socialism* (1980). His views are particularly interesting because he was, until 1967, an associate of Mikhail Gorbachev. His views on Gorbachev are expressed directly in *Can Gorbachev Change the Soviet Union? The International Dimensions of Political Reform* (Boulder, CO, 1990). Gorbachev's own career is described in Archie Brown, *The Gorbachev Factor* (Oxford, 1997). Michael Ellman and Vladimir Kontorovich (eds.), *The Destruction of the Soviet Economic System: An Insiders' History* (New York, 1998), shows that the highly intelligent advisers behind perestroika did not have much idea what was going on. Anyone flicking through the index of recently published books on eastern Europe might well conclude that Timothy Garton Ash's role in the fall of communism was only slightly smaller than that of Mikhail Gorbachev. Garton Ash's engagement does not always produce interesting analysis but his evocation of life in east Berlin in the 1980s – reprinted in *The Uses of Adversity* (1989) – is wonderful. Stephen Kotkin is another historian who seems to have learned as much from talking in bars as he did from reading archives. His *Steeltown USSR: Soviet Society in the Gorbachev Era* (Berkeley, CA, 1991) describes a fascinating encounter between a rich post-Marxist left-winger (one of Kotkin's books is dedicated to Michel Foucault) and the inhabitants of the godforsaken town of Magnitogorsk. Kotkin's book should be read in conjunction with the account of an earlier observer in the same town – Andrew Smith, *I Was a Soviet Worker* (1937). The career of the economist Philip Hanson spanned all the extremes of the Cold War. He was taught Russian while doing national service, was thrown out of the USSR for "spying" in 1972, and returned to Moscow in 1988 as part of the delegation that George Soros took to advise Soviet leaders on economic reform. His insights are brought together in a lucid collection of essays, *From Stagnation to Catastroika: Commentaries on the Soviet Economy, 1983–1991* (New York, 1992). Elizabeth Teague, *Solidarity and the Soviet Workers: The Impact of Polish Events of 1980 on Soviet Internal Politics* (1988), reveals much about the way in which problems in one part of the empire affected another. C. M. Hann, *A Village Without Solidarity: Polish Peasants in the Years of Crisis* (New Haven, CT, 1985), shows how the countryside became the last island of quiescence in some parts of communist Europe. Veronique Soulé, *Avoir Vingt Ans à l'Est* (1989), is a superb book on youth culture under communism. Stanisław Gomułka and Antony Polonsky (eds.), *Polish Paradoxes* (1990), describes the society that resisted communism best. Jacques Rupnik, *L'Autre Europe: Crise et Fin du Communisme* (1993), is good. The morgue is an appropriate place from which to survey Soviet history, and this is the starting point for Ilya Zbarsky and Samuel Hutchinson in *Lenin's Embalmers* (1998).

Europe after the fall of communism

"Post-communist studies" is a rapidly expanding discipline. Misha Glenny, *The Rebirth of History: Eastern Europe in the Age of Democracy* (1993), is wide-ranging and informative. Much interesting empirical work is contained in two special issues of *Cahiers Internationaux de Sociologie*, XCV (1993) and XCVI (1994). The breakup of supranational states is handled in Ian Bremmer and Ray Taras (eds.), *Nations and Politics in the Soviet Successor States* (Cambridge, 1993), and Jiří Musil (ed.), *The End of Czechoslovakia* (Budapest, 1995). The literature on the breakup of the former Yugoslavia is vast. David Dyker and Ivan Vejvoda, *Yugoslavia and After: A Study in Fragmentation, Despair and Rebirth* (1997), is a good place to start. On individual countries see Marcin Frybes and Patrick Michel, *Après le Communisme: Mythes et Légendes de la Pologne Contemporaine* (1996), and Jerzy Szacki, *Liberalism After Communism* (Budapest, 1995). On the prosperity of post-communist elites, which also reveals something about why communism was not defended more vigorously, see John Higley, Jan Pakulski and Włodzimierz Wesołowski (eds.), *Post-Communist Elites and Democracy in Eastern Europe* (1988). Some of the most interesting effects of the fall of communism were seen in the study of women and gender. This subject is treated in Mary Buckley (ed.), *Post-Soviet Women: From the Baltic to Central Asia* (Cambridge, 1997); Nanette Funk and Magda Mueller (eds.) *Gender, Politics and Post-Communism: Reflections from Eastern Europe and the Former Soviet Union* (1997); Barbara Łobodzinska (ed.), *Family, Women and Employment in Central Eastern Europe* (1995); Barbara Einhorn, *Cinderella Goes to Market: Citizenship, Gender and the Women's Movement in East Central Europe* (1993); Sabrina Ramet (ed.), *Gender Politics in the Western Balkans: Women and Society in Yugoslavia and the Yugoslav Successor States* (Pennsylvania, 1999); Jacqueline Heinen, *Chômage et Devenir de la Main d'Oeuvre Féminine en Pologne* (1995); and Jacqueline Heinen and Anna Matuchniak-Krasuska, *L'Avortement en Pologne: La Croix et la Bannière* (1992).

Italy is the only western European country where "post-communism" has been treated as self-consciously as in eastern Europe. The comparison with former communist states is made explicit in Robert Putnam, *Making Democracy Work: Civic Traditions in Modern Italy* (Princeton, NJ,

1993). The breakup of the Italian political system is described in Stephen Gundle and Simon Parker (eds.), *The New Italian Republic: From the Fall of the Berlin Wall to Berlusconi* (1996). Alexander Stille, *Excellent Cadavers: The Mafia and the Death of the First Italian Republic* (1996), says something about the more sinister side of this story. On western Europe generally, see Martin Rhodes, Paul Heywood and Vincent Wright, *Developments in West European Politics* (1997).

NOTES

Introduction

1 "Moshe Lewin" in Henry Abelove, Betsy Blackmar, Peter Dimock and Jonathan Schneer (eds.), *Visions of History* (New York, 1984), pp. 279–308.
2 Robert Paxton, *Vichy France: Old Guard and New Order, 1940–1944* (1972 and 1982).
3 Merle Fainsod, *Smolensk under Soviet rule* (1958 and 1989).
4 Lilly Marcou, *Une Enfance Stalinienne* (1982).
5 Lutz Niethammer, in Patrick Fridenson, Lutz Niethammer and Luisa Passerini, "International reverberations. Remembering Raphael," *History Workshop Journal*, Spring 1998, pp. 250–60.
6 For an exposition and critique of the niche society interpretation see Charles Maier, *Dissolution: The Crisis of Communism and the End of East Germany* (Princeton, 1997), pp. 36 and 43.

PART I

The Belle Époque and the Catastrophe

1 Leonard Woolf, *Beginning Again: An Autobiography of the Years 1911–1918* (1964), pp. 54 and 90.
2 John Maynard Keynes, *The Economic Consequences of the Peace* (New York, 1919), p. 11.
3 Cited in Hermione Lee, *Virginia Woolf* (1997), p. 104.

1. Huddled Masses

1 Michael Marrus, *The Unwanted: European Refugees in the Twentieth Century* (Oxford, 1985), pp. 30–39.

2 Martin Clark, *Modern Italy, 1871–1982* (1984), p. 162.
3 Falling agricultural prices sometimes even drove those who had been born rich to emigration. The only male heir of Count Carlo Brogila di Casalborgone died in 1896 while working as a miner in Brazil. Anthony Cardoza, *Aristocrats in Bourgeois Italy: The Piedmontese Nobility, 1861–1930* (Cambridge, 1997), p. 199.
4 Alan Kraut, *The Huddled Masses: The Immigrant in American Society, 1880–1921* (1982), p. 48.
5 Ibid., p. 16.
6 Donald Avery, *Reluctant Host: Canada's Response to Immigrant Workers, 1896–1994* (Toronto, 1995), p. 25.
7 Pino Arlacchi, *Mafia, Peasants and Great Estates: Society in Traditional Calabria* (Cambridge, 1983), p. 58.
8 Marrus, *The Unwanted*, p. 39.
9 Hugh McLeod, *Piety and Poverty: Working-Class Religion in Berlin, London and New York, 1870–1914* (1996), p. 52.
10 Kraut, *The Huddled Masses*, p. 47.
11 Avery, *Reluctant Host*, p. 24.
12 Ibid., p. 39.
13 Kraut, *The Huddled Masses*, p. 91.
14 Ewa Morawska, "'T'was hope here': the Polish immigrants in Johnstown, Pennsylvania, 1890–1930" in Frank Renkiewicz (ed.), *The Polish Presence in Canada and America* (Ontario, 1982), pp. 29–45.
15 Klaus J. Bade, "German emigration to the United States and continental immigration to Germany in the late nineteenth and twentieth centuries," *Central European History*, 13 (1980), pp. 348–77. By 1900, 51 percent of German Americans lived in cities with more than 25,000 inhabitants while only 35 percent of Germans lived in cities with more than 20,000 inhabitants.
16 McLeod, *Piety and Poverty*, p. 57.
17 Marcin Kula, "Polish emigration to Latin America" in Renkiewicz (ed.), *The Polish Presence in Canada and America*, pp. 63–78.
18 Misha Glenny, *The Rebirth of History: Eastern Europe in the Age of Democracy* (1993), p. 127.
19 Clark, *Modern Italy*, p. 166.
20 Carlo Levi, *Christ Stopped at Eboli* (1982), p. 102.
21 R. Bosworth, *Italy and the Wider World, 1860–1960* (1996), p. 133.
22 Kraut, *The Huddled Masses*, p. 10.
23 Arlacchi, *Mafia, Peasants and Great Estates*, p. 65.
24 Eugen Weber, *Peasants into Frenchmen: The Modernisation of Rural France, 1870–1914* (1977).
25 George Painter, *Marcel Proust: A Biography* (1966), I, p. 72.
26 John Richardson, *A Life of Picasso: Volume 1, 1881–1906* (1992), p. 249.
27 Norman Stone, "Army and society in the Habsburg monarchy, 1900–1914," *Past and Present*, 33 (1966), pp. 95–111.

28 John Bushnell, "Peasants in uniform: the Tsarist army as a peasant society" in Ben Eklof and Stephen Frank, *The World of the Russian Peasant: Post-Emancipation Culture and Society* (1990), pp. 101–14.

29 Maurice Agulhon, "Vu des coulisses" in Pierre Nora (ed.), *Essais d'Ego-Histoire* (1987), pp. 9–59, p. 16.

30 Jean-François Sirinelli, *Génération intellectuelle: Khâgneux et Normaliens dans l'Entre-Deux-Guerres* (1988), p. 169.

31 Hugh Seton-Watson, *Eastern Europe Between the Wars, 1918–1941* (Cambridge, 1946), p. 126.

32 Adrian Shubert, *A Social History of Modern Spain* (1992), p. 183.

33 For a discussion of the possible impacts of literacy see Ben Eklof, *Russian Peasant Schools: Officialdom, Village Culture and Popular Pedagogy, 1861–1914* (Berkeley, CA, 1986), pp. 1–16.

34 Orlando Figes, *A People's Tragedy: The Russian Revolution, 1891–1924* (1996), p. 109.

35 Alastair Thompson, "Honours uneven: decorations, the state and bourgeois society in Imperial Germany," *Past and Present*, 144 (1994), pp. 171–204.

36 Marcel Pagnol, *Le Temps des Secrets* (1960), p. 84.

37 Gisela Griepentrog, "Peasants, poverty and population: economic and political factors in the family structure of the working village people in the Magdeburg region, 1900–39," pp. 205–23 in R. Evans and W. Lee (eds.), *The German Peasant: Conflict and Community in Rural Society from the Eighteenth to the Twentieth Centuries* (1986), p. 212.

38 Figes, *A People's Tragedy*, p. 57.

39 Sheila Fitzpatrick, *The Russian Revolution* (Oxford, 1994), p. 35.

40 J. Harvey Smith, "Agricultural workers and the French wine-growers' revolt of 1907," *Past and Present*, 79 (1978), pp. 101–25.

41 Gavin Lewis, "The peasantry, rural change and conservative agrarianism: Lower Austria at the turn of the century," *Past and Present*, 81 (1978), pp. 119–43.

42 Tony Judt, *Socialism in Provence, 1871–1914: A Study in the Origins of the Modern French Left* (Cambridge, 1979), p. 297.

43 Figes, *A People's Tragedy*, p. 237.

44 J. Harvey Smith, "Agricultural workers and the French wine-growers' revolt of 1907."

45 William Harvey Maehl, "German Social Democratic Agrarian Policy 1890–1895, Reconsidered," *Central European History*, 13 (1980), pp. 121–57.

46 William I. Thomas and Florian Znaniecki, *The Polish Peasant in Europe and America* (New York, 1927, two vols).

2. Socialism and the Working Class

1 V. R. Berghahn, *Modern Germany: Society, Economy and Politics in the Twentieth Century* (Cambridge, 1987), p. 9.

2 Richard Evans, *Proletarians and Politics: Socialism, Protest and the Working Class in Germany Before the First World War* (1990), pp. 124–91.

3 Robert Stuart, *Marxism at Work: Ideology, Class and French Socialism During the Third Republic* (Cambridge, 1992), p. 371.

4 Berghahn, *Modern Germany*, p. 25.

5 Stefan Berger, *The British Labour Party and the German Social Democrats, 1900–1931* (Oxford, 1994), pp. 148–9.

6 Ginette Kurgan-van Hentenryk, "A forgotten class: the petite bourgeoisie in Belgium, 1850–1914" in G. Crossick and H.-G. Haupt (eds.), *Shopkeepers and Master Artisans in Nineteenth-Century Europe* (1984), pp. 120–32.

7 Michael Savage, "Career mobility and class formation: British banking workers and the lower middle class" in Andrew Miles and David Vincent (eds.), *Building European Society: Occupational Change and Social Mobility in Europe, 1840–1940* (Manchester, 1993), pp. 196–216.

8 Ibid.

9 Jonathan Morris, *The Political Economy of Shopkeeping in Milan, 1886–1922* (Cambridge, 1993), p. 88.

10 Ibid., p. 146.

11 Ross McKibbin, *The Ideologies of Class: Social Relations in Britain, 1880–1950* (Oxford, 1990), p. 7.

12 Dick Geary, *European Labour Protest, 1848–1939* (1981), p. 97.

13 Berger, *The British Labour Party and the German Social Democrats*, p. 196.

14 Geary, *European Labour Protest*, p. 101.

15 Alex Hall, "The war of words: anti-socialist offensives and counter-propaganda in Wilhemine Germany, 1890–1914," *Journal of Contemporary History*, 11 (1976), pp. 11–42.

16 Evans, *Proletarians and Politics*, pp. 124–91, p. 139.

17 Alastair Thompson, "Honours uneven: decorations, the state and bourgeois society in Imperial Germany," *Past and Present*, 144 (1994), pp. 171–204.

18 Orlando Figes, *A People's Tragedy: The Russian Revolution, 1891–1924* (1996), pp. 131–3.

19 Cited in David Mandel, *The Petrograd Workers and the Fall of the Old Regime: From the February Revolution to the July Days, 1917* (1983), p. 20.

3. The Great War

1 Elie Halévy, *The World Crisis of 1914–1918: An Interpretation* (Oxford, 1930), p. 28.

2 Norman Angell, *The Great Illusion* (1909).

3 Quoted in Paul Kennedy, *Strategy and Diplomacy* (London, 1984), p. 96.

4 Eric Leed, *No Man's Land: Combat and Identity in World War I* (Cambridge, 1979), p. 19.

5 John Whittam, *The Politics of the Italian Army, 1861–1918* (1977), p. 178.

6 Robert Whalen, *Bitter Wounds: German Victims of the Great War, 1914–1939* (Ithaca, 1984), p. 42.

7   Pierre Barral, "La Paysannerie française à l'arrière" in Jean-Jacques Becker and Stéphane Audoin-Rouzeau (eds.), *Les Sociétés Européennes et la Guerre de 1914–1918* (1990), pp. 237–43.

8   Haig was particularly keen on generals from the cavalry – Allenby, Gough, Kavanagh and Byng all fitted into this category. See Tim Travers, "The hidden army: structural problems in the British officer corps, 1900–1918," *Journal of Contemporary History*, 17, 3 (1982), pp. 523–44.

9   Norman Stone, *The Eastern Front, 1914–1917* (1975), p. 314.

10 Macgregor Knox, "Expansionist zeal, fighting power, and staying power in the Italian and German dictatorships" in Richard Bessel (ed.), *Fascist Italy and Nazi Germany: Comparisons and Contrasts* (Cambridge, 1996), pp. 113–33, p. 128.

11 Cited in P. J. Flood, *France, 1914–1918: Public Opinion and the War Effort* (1990), p. 169.

12 Annick Cochet, "Les soldats français" in Becker and Audoin-Rouzeau (eds.), *Les Sociétés Européennes et la Guerre de 1914–1918*, pp. 357–66. Patrick Facon, "Les Soldats expatriés: orient et italie, 1915–1918" in ibid., pp. 385–92, and Gerd Krumeich, "Le soldat allemand sur la Somme" in ibid., pp. 367–74.

13 Stone, *The Eastern Front*, p. 167.

14 Richard Luckett, *The White Generals* (1971), p. 8.

15 Holger H. Herwig, *The First World War: Germany and Austria-Hungary, 1914–1918* (1997), p. 344.

16 Ibid., p. 363.

17 Allan Wildman, *The End of the Russian Imperial Army: The Old Army and the Soldiers' Revolt (March–April 1917)* (Princeton, 1980), p. 94.

18 Niall Ferguson, *The Pity of War* (1998), p. 369.

19 Stone, *The Eastern Front*, p. 169.

20 Paul Corner and Giovanna Procacci, "The Italian experience of 'total' mobilization, 1915–1920" in John Horne (ed.), *State, Society and Mobilization in Europe During the First World War* (Cambridge, 1997), pp. 223–40, p. 231.

21 Mark Cornwall, "Morale and patriotism in the Austro-Hungarian army, 1914–1918" in ibid., pp. 173–92.

22 J. C. King, *Generals and Politicians: Conflict Between France's High Command, Parliament and Government, 1914–1918* (Westport, CT, 1971), pp. 24–35.

23 Clemenceau wrote: "Our war of national defence was transformed by force of events into a war of national liberation." Cited in Etienne Mantoux, *The Carthaginian Peace or the Economic Consequences of Mr Keynes* (London, 1946), p. 36.

24 John Godfrey, *Capitalism at War: Industrial Policy and Bureaucracy in France, 1914–1918*, (Leamington Spa, 1987), p. 296.

25 Jürgen Kocka, *Facing Total War: German Society, 1914–1918* (1984), p. 29.

26 Gerd Hardach, "Industrial mobilization in 1914–1918: production, planning and ideology" in Patrick Fridenson (ed.), *The French Home Front, 1914–1918* (Oxford, 1992), pp. 57–88, p. 76.

27 Kocka, *Facing Total War*, pp. 71 and 72.

28 Robert Paxton, "The calcium carbide case and the decriminalisation of industrial ententes in France, 1915–1926" in Fridenson (ed.), *The French Home Front*, pp. 153–80.

29 Kocka, *Facing Total War*, p. 102.

30 Jay Winter, "Some paradoxes of the First World War" in Jay Winter and Richard Wall (eds.), *The Upheaval of War: Family, Work and Welfare, 1914–1918* (Cambridge, 1988), pp. 9–42.

31 Reinhard Sieder, "Behind the lines: working-class family life in wartime Vienna" in ibid., pp. 109–38, p. 125.

32 Avner Offer, *The First World War: An Agrarian Interpretation* (Oxford, 1991) p. 33.

33 Ibid., p. 34.

34 Michael Marrus, *The Unwanted: European Refugees in the Twentieth Century* (Oxford, 1985), p. 49.

35 R. J. Crampton, *A Short History of Modern Bulgaria* (Cambridge, 1987), p. 68.

36 Guy Hartcup, *The War of Invention: Scientific Developments, 1914–1918* (1988), p. 173.

37 Gerard Chaliand and Yves Ternon, *1915, La Memoire du siècle: Le Génocide des Arméniens* (1984), p. 12.

38 Hardach, "Industrial mobilization in 1914–1918."

39 Robert Moeller, "Dimensions of social conflict in the Great War: the view from the German countryside," *Central European History*, 2, 14 (1981), pp. 142–68.

40 Cited in Jean Stengers, "La belgique" in Becker and Audoin-Rouzeau (eds.), *Les Sociétés Européennes et la Guerre de 1914–1918*, pp. 75–92, p. 85.

41 Crampton, *A Short History of Modern Bulgaria*, p. 66.

42 Barral, "La Paysannerie française à l'arrière," p. 242.

43 Gustavo Corni, *Hitler and the Peasants: Agrarian Policy of the Third Reich, 1930–1939* (Oxford, 1990), p. 5.

44 Frank Snowden, *The Fascist Revolution in Tuscany, 1919–1922* (Cambridge, 1989), p. 36.

45 Piero Melograni, "Les soldats et la population civile italienne en 1917" in Becker and Audoin-Rouzeau (eds.), *Les Sociétés Européennes et la Guerre de 1914–1918*, pp. 333–9, p. 335.

46 Sheila Fitzpatrick, *The Russian Revolution* (Oxford, 1994), p. 60.

47 Herwig, *The First World War*, pp. 392–428.

48 Leed, *No Man's Land*, p. 198.

49 Evan Mawdsley, *The Russian Civil War* (1987), p. 287.

50 Jean-Jacques Becker, *The Great War and the French People* (Leamington Spa, 1985), p. 6.

51 Cited in Leed, *No Man's Land*, p. 213.

52 Mária M. Kovács, *Liberal Professions and Illiberal Politics: Hungary from the Habsburgs to the Holocaust* (Oxford, 1994), p. 57.

PART II

From One War to Another

1 François Fejtö, *Mémoires: de Budapest à Paris* (1986).
2 John Maynard Keynes, *The Economic Consequences of the Peace* (New York, 1919), p. 291.
3 Robert Brasillach, *Notre Avant-Guerre* (Paris, 1992; first published 1941), p. 136.
4 Jacques-Alain de Sédouy, *Une Enfance Bien-Pensante sous l'Occupation, 1940–1945* (1998).
5 Sheila Fitzpatrick, *The Russian Revolution* (Oxford, 1994), p. 45.
6 Anita Grossmann, "A question of silence: the rape of German women by occupation soldiers" in Robert Moeller (ed.), *West Germany Under Construction: Politics, Society and Culture in the Adenauer Era* (Ann Arbor, MI, 1997), pp. 33–52.

1. The Legacy of the Great War

1 Jay Winter, *Sites of Memory, Sites of Mourning: The Great War in European Cultural History* (Cambridge, 1995), p. 47.
2 David Englander, "Soldiers and social reform in the First and Second World Wars," *Historical Research*, 67 (1994), pp. 318–26.
3 Richard Bessel, *Germany After the First World War* (Oxford, 1993), pp. 275, 276.
4 Basil Liddell Hart, *Memoirs*, Vol. 1 (1965), p. 50.
5 Martin Petter, "'Temporary gentlemen' in the aftermath of the Great War: rank, status and the ex-officer problem," *Historical Journal*, 37, 1 (1994), pp. 127–52.
6 James Diehl, "Germany: veterans' politics under three flags" in Stephen Ward (ed.), *The War Generation: Veterans of the First World War* (1975), pp. 135–86.
7 Quoted in Stephen Ward, "Great Britain: land fit for heroes lost" in ibid., pp. 10–37.
8 Francis Horner, *Time Remembered* (1933).
9 Barry Doyle, "Urban liberalism and the 'lost generation': politics and middle-class culture in Norwich, 1900–1935," *Historical Journal*, 38, 3 (1995), pp. 617–34.
10 Oswald Mosley, *My Life* (1969), p. 49.
11 Antoine Prost, *In the Wake of War: Les Anciens Combattants and French Society, 1914–1939* (Berg and Oxford, 1992), p. 44.
12 David Weinberg, *Les Juifs à Paris de 1933 à 1939* (1974), p. 106.
13 Bessel, *Germany After the First World War*, p. 259.
14 Raul Hilberg, *The Destruction of the European Jews* (1973), p. 278.

15 Michael Burleigh and Wolfgang Wippermann, *The Racial State: Germany, 1933–1945* (Cambridge, 1991), p. 150.

16 Ibid., p. 153.

17 A doctor, addressing a postwar enquiry, expressed the optimistic opinion that "any soldier above the rank of corporal seemed possessed of too much dignity to become hysterical." Cited in Ted Bogacz, "War neurosis and cultural change in England, 1914–1922: the work of the War Office Committee of Enquiry into 'shell shock,'" *Journal of Contemporary History*, 24, 2 (1989) pp. 227–56.

18 Elaine Showalter, "Rivers and Sassoon: the inscription of male gender anxieties" in Margaret Randolph Higgonet, Jane Jenson and Margaret Collins Weitz (eds.), *Behind the Lines: Gender and the Two World Wars* (New Haven, CT, 1987) pp. 61–9.

19 Winter, *Sites of Memory, Sites of Mourning*, pp. 55–77.

20 Robert Graves, *Goodbye to All That* (1957, first published 1929), p. 253.

21 Alain, *Souvenirs de Guerre* (1937), p. 170.

22 Robert Graves, *Goodbye to All That*, p. 189. Guy Chapman, *A Kind of Survivor* (1975), p. 68. Michael Monynihan argues that Graves is unfair and fails to allow for the fact that Anglican chaplains were allowed to visit the front after 1918. Michael Monynihan (ed.), *God on Our Side: The British Padres in World War I* (1983), p. 12. The casualty figures cited by Monynihan himself suggest that Anglican padres stood a better chance of surviving than Catholic ones.

23 Winter, *Sites of Memory, Sites of Mourning*, p. 63.

2. Youth

1 George Orwell, *The Collected Essays, Journalism and Letters, Vol. 1: An Age Like This, 1920–1940* (1970), p. 553.

2 Evelyn Waugh, "The war and the younger generation," *Spectator*, April 29, 1929.

3 Cited in D. Nasaw, "From inquiétude to revolution," *Journal of Contemporary History*, 11, 2 and 3 (1976), pp. 149–72.

4 Hugh Seton-Watson, *Eastern Europe Between the Wars, 1918–1941* (Cambridge, 1946), p. 230.

5 On the obsession with generation in interwar Europe, see Robert Wohl, *The Generation of 1914* (1980).

6 Milovan Djilas, *Memoir of a Revolutionary* (1973), p. 12.

7 Jacques Nobécourt, *Une Histoire Politique de l'Armée: De Pétain à Pétain* (1967), p. 51.

8 Robert Graves, *Goodbye to All That* (1957, first published 1929), p. 292.

9 Michael Ledeen, "Italy: war as a style of life" in Stephen Ward (ed.), *The War Generation: Veterans of the First World War* (Port Washington, NY, and London, 1975), pp. 104–34.

10 *Spectator*, April 13, 1929.

11 George Orwell, *The Collected Essays, Journalism and Letters, Vol. 1: An Age Like This, 1920–1940*, p. 589.

12 Ibid., p. 590.

13 Paul Demasy cited in Nasaw, "From inquiétude to revolution."

14 Richard Bessel, *Germany After the First World War* (Oxford, 1993), p. 24.

15 Ibid., p. 23.

16 Reinhard Sieder, "Behind the lines: working-class family life in wartime Vienna" in Richard Wall and Jay Winter (eds.), *The Upheaval of War: Family, Work and Welfare, 1914–1918* (Cambridge, 1988), pp. 109–39, p. 116.

17 Bessel, *Germany After the First World War*, p. 21.

18 Patrick Marnham, *The Man Who Wasn't Maigret: Portrait of Georges Simenon* (1992), pp. 52–4.

19 Bessel, *Germany After the First World War*, p. 225.

20 Ibid., p. 24.

21 Avner Offer, *The First World War: An Agrarian Interpretation* (Oxford, 1991), p. 59.

22 Bessel, *Germany After the First World War*, p. 241.

23 Wendy Z. Goldman, *Women, the State and Revolution: Soviet Family Policy and Social Life, 1917–1936* (Cambridge, 1993), pp. 60–80.

24 Bruno Wanrooij, "The rise and fall of Italian Fascism as a generational revolt," *Journal of Contemporary History*, 22, 3 (1987), pp. 401–18.

25 James Diehl, "Germany: veterans' politics under three flags" in Stephen Ward (ed.), *The War Generation*, pp. 135–86.

26 Michael Ledeen, "Italy: war as a style of life" in ibid., pp. 104–34.

27 Sheila Fitzpatrick, *Stalin's Peasants: Resistance and Survival in the Russian Village After Collectivisation* (Oxford, 1996), p. 36.

28 Ibid., p. 34.

29 Mark Roseman, "Introduction: generation conflict and German history 1770–1968" in Mark Roseman (ed.), *Generations in Conflict: Youth Revolt and Generation Formation in Germany, 1770–1968* (Cambridge, 1995), pp. 1–46, p. 25.

30 Eugen Weber, *Varieties of Fascism* (1964), p. 172.

31 Martin Conway, "Building the Christian city: Catholics and politics in interwar francophone Belgium," *Past and Present*, 128 (1990), pp. 117–51.

32 Mária M. Kovács, *Liberal Professions and Illiberal Politics: Hungary from the Habsburgs to the Holocaust* (Oxford, 1994), p. 53.

33 Stella Alexander, "Croatia: the Catholic Church and Clergy, 1919–1945" in R. Wolff and J. Hoensch, *Catholics, the State and the European Radical Right, 1919–1945* (1987), pp. 31–66, p. 41. Marcin Przeciszewski, "L'association catholique de la jeunesse académique. 'Odrodzenie' (La Renaissance). Aperçu historique," *Revue du Nord*, LXX, 227 (1988), pp. 333–47.

34 Pascal Ory, *La Belle Illusion: Culture et Politique sous le Signe du Front Populaire, 1935–1938* (1994), p. 766.

35 Jessica Mitford, *Hons and Rebels* (1960), p. 3.

36 Macgregor Knox, "Expansionist zeal, fighting power, and staying power in the Italian and German dictatorships" in Richard Bessel (ed.), *Fascist Italy and Nazi Germany* (1996), pp. 113–33, p. 131.

37 Detlev Peukert, "Youth in the Third Reich" in Richard Bessel (ed.), *Life in the Third Reich* (Oxford, 1987), pp. 25–40.

38 António Costa Pinto, *Salazar's Dictatorship and European Fascism* (1995), p. 187.

39 William Halls, *Politics, Society and Christianity in Vichy France* (Oxford, 1995), p. 276.

40 Françoise Giroud, *La Nouvelle Vague* (1958), p. 328.

41 Joyce Marie Mushaben, *From Post War to Post-Wall Generations: Changing Attitudes Toward the National Question and NATO in the Federal Republic of Germany* (Boulder, CO, 1998).

42 Antonin Liehm, *Trois Générations: Entretiens sur le Phénomène Culturel Tchécoslovaque* (Paris, 1970), p. 106.

3. Men, Women and the Family

1 Enid Raphael, cited in footnote to Michael Davies (ed.), *The Diaries of Evelyn Waugh* (1976), p. 315.

2 For this cliché, and indeed almost every other cliché about twentieth-century history, see Harold Perkin, *The Rise of Professional Society: England Since 1800* (1990), p. 219: "The shortening of women's skirts marked the approach towards greater freedom for women and more equality between the sexes."

3 Dermot Keogh and Finín O'Driscoll, "Ireland" in Tom Buchanan and Martin Conway (eds.), *Political Catholicism in Europe, 1918–1965* (Oxford, 1996), pp. 275–300, p. 279.

4 Pino Arlacchi, *Mafia Business: The Mafia Ethic and the Spirit of Capitalism* (1986), p. 8.

5 Eve Rosenhaft, *Beating the Fascists? The German Communists and Political Violence, 1929–1933* (Cambridge, 1983), pp. 22–3.

6 John Maynard Keynes, "Am I a liberal?" *Essays in Persuasion* (1931, 1952), pp. 323–38, pp. 331–2.

7 René Benjamin, *Le Grand Homme Seul* (1943), p. 10.

8 David Reynolds, *Rich Relations: The American Occupation of Britain, 1942–1945* (1995), p. 273.

9 Peter Gay, "The dog that did not bark in the night" in *Reading Freud: Explorations and Entertainments* (New Haven, CT, 1990), pp. 164–79.

10 Brenda Maddox, *Nora: A Biography of Nora Joyce* (1988), p. 44.

11 Simone de Beauvoir, *La Force de l'Âge* (1960), p. 28.

12 Jean-Paul Sartre, *The Age of Reason* (1947, first published in France in 1945), p. 53.

13 Deirdre Bair, *Simone de Beauvoir: A Biography* (New York, 1990), p. 547.

14 George Painter, *Marcel Proust: A Biography*, 1 (1966), p. xii: "Readers who have felt all along that Proust's picture of heterosexual love is valid and founded on experience will be glad to find their instinct justified."

15 Alain Besançon, *Une Génération* (1987), p. 111.

16 Anita Grossmann, *Reforming Sex: The German Movement for Birth Control and Abortion Reform, 1920–1950* (Oxford, 1995), p. 10.

17 David Kertzer and Denis Hogan, *Family, Political Economy and Demographic Change: The Transformation of Life in Casalecchio, Italy, 1861–1921* (Madison, WI, 1989), pp. 118–24.

18 Michael Burleigh and Wolfgang Wippermann, *The Racial State: Germany, 1933–1945* (Cambridge, 1991), p. 186.

19 Reynolds, *Rich Relations*, p. 265.

20 Maria Bucar, "In praise of wellborn mothers: on the development of eugenicist gender roles in interwar Romania," *East European Politics and Societies*, 9, 1 (1995), pp. 123–42.

21 Elizabeth Waters, "The modernization of Russian motherhood, 1917–1937," *Soviet Studies*, 44, 1 (1992), pp. 123–35.

22 Cited in Christine Bard, *Les Filles de Marianne: Histoire des Féminismes, 1914–1940* (1995), p. 224.

23 Frank Field, *Three French Writers and the Great War* (Cambridge, 1975), p. 86.

24 Ted Bogacz, "War neurosis and cultural change in England, 1914–1922: The work of the War Office Committee of Enquiry into 'shell shock,'" *Journal of Contemporary History*, 24, 2 (1989), pp. 227–56.

25 Storm Jameson, *Company Parade* (1982), p. 99.

26 Guy Chapman, *A Kind of Survivor* (1975), p. 76.

27 Ibid., p. 73.

28 Ibid., p. 122.

29 Elaine Showalter, "Rivers and Sassoon: the inscription of male gender anxieties" in Margaret Randolph Higonnet, Jane Jenson, Sonya Michel and Margaret Collins Weitz (eds.), *Behind the Lines: Gender and the Two World Wars* (New Haven, CT, 1987), pp. 61–9, p. 69.

30 Cited in Eric Leed, *No Man's Land: Combat and Identity in World War I* (Cambridge, 1979), p. 45.

31 André Bouton, *La Fin des Rentiers: Histoire des Fortunes Privées en France depuis 1914* (Paris, 1932), p. 70.

32 Richard Bessel, *Germany After the First World War* (Oxford, 1993), p. 233.

33 Alain, *Souvenirs de Guerre* (1937), p. 20.

34 Cited in Jacques Nobécourt, *Une Histoire Politique de l'Armée: de Pétain à Pétain, 1919–1942* (1967), p. 16.

35 Interview cited by Pino Arlacchi, *Mafia Business: The Mafia Ethic and the Spirit of Capitalism*, p. 8.

36 Nancy Erber, "The French trials of Oscar Wilde," *Journal of the History of Sexuality*, 6, 4 (1996), pp. 549–88.

37 Burleigh and Wippermann, *The Racial State*, pp. 196–7.

38 Simon Karlinsky, "Russia's gay literature and culture: the impact of the October Revolution" in Martin Bauml Duberman, Martha Vicinus and George Chauncey (eds.), *Hidden from History: Reclaiming the Gay and Lesbian Past* (1991), pp. 347–64, p. 358.

39 Burleigh and Wippermann, *The Racial State*, p. 195.

40 Erwin Haeberle, "Swastika, pink triangle and yellow star: the destruction of sexology and the persecution of homosexuals in Nazi Germany" in Duberman, Vicinus and Chauncey (eds.), *Hidden from History*, pp. 365–79, p. 369.

41 Simon Karlinsky, "Russia's gay literature and culture: the impact of the October Revolution," p. 361.

42 Milovan Djilas, *Memoir of a Revolutionary* (New York, 1973), p. 21.

43 Nicholas Mosley, *Rules of the Game: Sir Oswald and Lady Cynthia Mosley, 1896–1933* (1982).

44 Maurice Agulhon, "Vu des coulisses" in Pierre Nora (ed.), *Essais d'Ego-Histoire* (1987), pp. 9–59, p. 12.

45 Carlo Levi, *Christ Stopped at Eboli* (1982), p. 102.

46 Gerald Brenan, *South from Granada* (Cambridge, 1980), p. 19.

47 A. J. P. Taylor, *A Personal History* (1983), p. 167.

48 Ross McKibbin, *Classes and Cultures: England, 1918–1951* (Oxford, 1998), p. 313.

49 Joanna Bourke, *Dismembering the Male: Men's Bodies, Britain and the Great War* (1996), p. 160.

50 Sarah Fishman, *We Will Wait: Wives of French Prisoners of War, 1940–1945* (New Haven, CT, 1991), p. 48.

51 Graham Greene, *A Sort of a Life* (1971), p. 156.

52 Perry Willson, *The Clockwork Factory: Women and Work in Fascist Italy* (Oxford, 1993), p. 154.

53 Ibid., p. 227.

54 Miranda Pollard, *Reign of Virtue: Mobilizing Gender in Vichy France* (Chicago, 1998), p. 78.

55 Fishman, *We Will Wait*, p. 48.

56 George Orwell, *The Road to Wigan Pier* (1962), p. 147.

57 Ibid., pp. 72–3.

58 Ibid., p. 103.

59 Ibid., p. 111.

60 George Orwell, *The Collected Essays, Journalism and Letters, Vol. 1: An Age Like This, 1920–1940* (1970), p. 365.

61 Ibid., p. 245.

62 Cited in Jeffrey Weeks, "Inverts, perverts and Mary-Annes: male prostitution and the regulation of homosexuality in England in the nineteenth and early twentieth centuries" in Duberman, Vicinus and Chauncey (eds.), *Hidden from History*, pp. 195–211, p. 203.

63 Anthony Copley, *Sexual Moralities in France, 1780–1980: New Ideas on Family, Divorce and Homosexuality* (1992), p. 181.

64 Weeks, "Inverts, perverts and Mary-Annes."

65 Ruth Harris, "The child of the barbarian: rape, race and nationalism in France during the First World War," *Past and Present*, 141 (1993), pp. 170–206.

66 Philip Burrin, *La France à l'Heure Allemande, 1940–1944* (1995), p. 29.

67 Roger Chabaud cited in Robert Zaretsky, *Nîmes at War: Religion, Politics and Public Opinion in the Gard, 1938–1944* (Pennsylvania, 1995), p. 75.

68 William Halls, *Politics, Society and Christianity in Vichy France* (Oxford, 1995), p. 262.

69 Fishman, *We Will Wait*, p. 136.

70 Henry Charbonneau, *Les Mémoires de Porthos* (1980), p. 296. The German authorities believed that around 20,000 children had been fathered by various foreign workers or prisoners of war in Germany (mainly French and Italians). See Ulrich Herbert, *Hitler's Foreign Workers: Enforced Foreign Labour in Germany Under the Third Reich* (Cambridge, 1997), p. 269. See also p. 126: "The authorities showed special interest in cases of 'prohibited contact' between German women and French men."

71 Note the reference to a German telephonist seduced by a French prisoner who was a "Latin type" in Burleigh and Wippermann, *The Racial State*, p. 263.

72 Laurence Wylie, *Village in the Vaucluse* (1974), p. 117. A inhabitant of the southern village is quoted as saying: "I can't say I've always been faithful to my wife. During the war when I was in the army and then a prisoner on a farm in Germany . . . well, it was different."

73 Burleigh and Wippermann, *The Racial State*, pp. 128–9.

74 Grossmann, *Reforming Sex*, p. 150.

75 Ibid., p. 193.

76 Norman M. Naimark, *The Russians in Germany: A History of the Soviet Zone of Occupation, 1945–1949* (Cambridge, MA, 1995), p. 70.

77 Ibid., p. 74.

78 Ibid., pp. 80 and 81.

79 Ibid., p. 123.

80 Ibid., p. 81.

81 David Reynolds, *Rich Relations*, p. 303.

82 Ibid., p. 218.

83 Ibid., p. 234. Other black Americans were executed for rape in Britain.

84 Ronald Hyam, *Empire and Sexuality: The British Experience* (Manchester, 1990), p. 109.

85 Carl Ipsen, *Dictating Demography: The Problem of Population in Fascist Italy* (Cambridge, 1996), pp. 188–9.

86 Susan Pedersen, *Family, Dependence and the Origins of the Welfare State: Britain and France, 1914–1945* (Cambridge, 1993), p. 95.

87 The weakness of the unions probably meant that this consensus was less powerful in France than in Britain. Ibid., p. 104.

88 Wendy Goldman, *Women, the State and Revolution: Soviet Family Policy and Social Life, 1917–1936* (Cambridge, 1993), p. 110.

89 Sian Reynolds, *France Between the Wars: Gender and Politics* (1996), p. 93.

90 Tim Mason, *Nazism, Fascism and the Working Class* (Cambridge, 1995), p. 139.

91 Reynolds, *France Between the Wars*, p. 94.

92 Michael Savage, "Career mobility and class formation: British banking workers and the lower middle classes" in Andrew Miles and David Vincent (eds.), *Building European Societies: Occupational Change and Social Mobility in Europe, 1840–1940* (Manchester, 1993), pp. 196–216.

93 Victoria de Grazia, *How Fascism Ruled Women: Italy, 1922–1945* (Berkeley, 1993), p. 193.

94 Ibid.

95 Richard Overy, *War and Economy in the Third Reich* (Oxford, 1994), p. 41.

96 Pedersen, *Family, Dependence and the Origins of the Welfare State*, p. 104.

97 Overy, *War and Economy in the Third Reich*, p. 49.

98 Eleanor Hancock, "Employment in wartime: the employment of German women during the Second World War," *War and Society*, 12, 2 (1994), pp. 43–68.

99 Overy, *War and Economy in the Third Reich*, p. 50.

100 Burleigh and Wipperman, *The Racial State*, p. 250.

101 Overy, *War and Economy in the Third Reich*, p. 304.

102 Hancock, "Employment in wartime."

103 Ibid.

104 Chris Ward, *Stalin's Russia* (1993), p. 178.

105 Barbara Alpern Engel, "Women in Russia and the Soviet Union," *Signs*, 12, 4 (Spring 1992), pp. 781–800.

106 Sheila Fitzpatrick, *The Russian Revolution, 1917–1932* (Oxford, 1994), p. 161.

107 Roberta T. Manning, "Women in the Soviet countryside on the eve of World War II, 1935–1940" in Beatrice Farnsworth and Lynne Viola (eds.), *Russian Peasant Women* (Oxford, 1992), pp. 206–35, p. 216.

108 Mary Buckley, "Why be a shock worker or a Stakhanovite?" in Rosalind Marsh (ed.), *Women in Russia and Ukraine* (Cambridge, 1996), pp. 199–213, p. 206.

109 Sheila Fitzpatrick, *Stalin's Peasants: Resistance and Survival in the Russian Village After Collectivization* (Oxford, 1994), p. 278.

110 Simone de Beauvoir, *Memoirs of a Dutiful Daughter* (1963), p. 104: "My father was no feminist . . . But, after all, necessity knows no law: 'You girls will never marry,' he often declared, 'you have no dowries.'"

111 Fitzpatrick, *Stalin's Peasants*, p. 25.

112 Martin Clark, *Modern Italy, 1871–1982* (1984), p. 256.

113 Certain occupations had been presented as appropriate outlets for the maternal feelings for women who did not experience physical motherhood ever since the late nineteenth century. See Irene Stoehr, "Housework and motherhood: debates and policies in the women's movement in Imperial Germany and the Weimar Republic" in Gisela Bock and Pat Thane (eds.),

Maternity and Gender Policies: Women and the Rise of the European Welfare States, 1880s–1950s (1994), pp. 213–32.

114 Cheryl Koos, "Gender anti-individualism and nationalism: the Alliance Nationale and the pro-natalist backlash," *French Historical Studies*, 19, 3 (1996), pp. 698–724.

115 Annie Kriegel, *Ce que j'ai cru comprendre* (1991), p. 132.

116 Gastavo Corni, *Hitler and the Peasants: Agrarian Policy of the Third Reich, 1930–1939* (Oxford, 1990), p. 28.

117 Renate Bridenthal and Claudia Koonz, "Beyond Kinder, Kuche, Kirche, Weimar Women and politics and work" in Renate Bridenthal, Anita Grossmann and Marion Kaplan (eds.), *When Biology Became Destiny: Women in Weimar and Nazi Germany* (New York, 1984), pp. 33–65.

118 Martine Segalen, *Love and Power in the Peasant Family: Rural France in the Nineteenth Century* (Oxford, 1983).

119 Lena Sommestad, "Gendering work, interpreting gender: the masculinization of dairy work in Sweden, 1850–1950," *History Workshop*, 37 (1994), pp. 57–75.

120 Segalen, *Love and Power in the Peasant Family*, p. 141.

121 M. C. Cleary, *Peasants, Politicians and Producers: The Organisation of Agriculture in France Since 1918* (Cambridge, 1989), p. 52.

122 Ibid., p. 159.

123 Ibid., p. 161.

124 Corni, *Hitler and the Peasants*, p. 81.

125 De Grazia, *How Fascism Ruled Women*, p. 181: in Italy the proportion of women in the working agricultural population fell from 59 percent to 45 percent, in France from 46 percent to 40 percent, and in Germany from 43 percent to 38 percent.

126 Manning, "Women in the Soviet countryside on the eve of World War II, 1935–1940," p. 218.

127 Ibid., p. 224.

128 Fitzpatrick, *Stalin's Peasants*, p. 182.

129 Manning, "Women in the Soviet countryside on the eve of World War II, 1935–1940," p. 224.

130 Fitzpatrick, *Stalin's Peasants*, p. 315.

131 António Costa Pinto, *Salazar's Dictatorship and European Fascism: Problems of Interpretation* (Boulder, CO, 1995), p. 198.

132 Maurice Duverger, *The Political Role of Women* (Paris, 1955), p. 65.

133 Pedersen, *Family, Dependence and the Origins of the Welfare State*, p. 100.

134 Adrian Shubert, *A Social History of Modern Spain* (1990), p. 40.

135 De Grazia, *How Fascism Ruled Women*, p. 199.

136 Temma Kaplan, "Female consciousness and collective action: the case of Barcelona, 1910–1918," *Signs* (Spring 1982), pp. 545–66.

137 Mathilde Dubesset, Françoise Thébaud and Catherine Vincent, "The female munitions workers of the Seine" in Patrick Fridenson (ed.), *The French Home Front, 1914–1918* (Oxford, 1992), pp. 183–218, p. 206 and 207.

138 Jörg K. Hoensch, *A History of Modern Hungary, 1867–1994* (1996), p. 45.
139 Duverger, *The Political Role of Women*, p. 46.
140 Beatrice Farnsworth, "Village women experience the Revolution" in Farnsworth and Viola (eds.), *Russian Peasant Women*, pp. 145–66.
141 Cited in Goldman, *Women, the State and Revolution*, p. 1.
142 Ibid., p. 9.
143 Ibid., p. 100.
144 Fitzpatrick, *Stalin's Peasants*, p. 219.
145 Quoted in Miriam Glucksmann, *Women Assemble: Women Workers in the New Industries in Inter-War Britain* (1996), p. 108.
146 Ida Blom, "Voluntary motherhood, 1900–1930: theories and politics of a Norwegian feminist in an international perspective" in Bock and Thane (eds.), *Maternity and Gender Policies*, pp. 21–39.
147 On the provision of benefits in the workplace see Tim Mason, "Labour in the Third Reich," *Past and Present*, 33 (1966), pp. 112–41.
148 Niall Ferguson, *Paper and Iron: Hamburg Business and German Politics in the Era of Inflation, 1897–1927* (Cambridge, 1995), p. 51.
149 Pedersen, *Family, Dependence and the Origins of the Welfare State*, p. 91.
150 Leonard Woolf, *Beginning Again: An Autobiography of the Years 1911 to 1918* (London, 1964), p. 51.
151 Harold Nicolson, *Diaries and Letters, 1930–1939*, edited by Nigel Nicolson (1966), p. 109.
152 Harold Nicolson, "Arketall," *Some People* (1958), pp. 187–216.
153 Robert Frost, "Machine civilization: home appliances in interwar France," *French Historical Studies*, 18, 1 (1993), pp. 109–33.
154 Renate Bridenthal, "Professional housewives and stepsisters of the women's movement" in Bridenthal, Grossmann and Kaplan (eds.), *When Biology Became Destiny*, pp. 153–73.
155 Claudia Koonz, *Mothers in the Fatherland: Women, the Family and Nazi Politics* (1987), p. 163.
156 Overy, *War and Economy in the Third Reich*, p. 49.
157 Mary Nash, "Pronatalism and motherhood in Franco's Spain" in Bock and Thane (eds.), *Maternity and Gender Policies*, pp. 160–77, p. 164.
158 Ann-Sofie Ohlander, "The invisible child? The struggle for a Social Democratic family policy in Sweden, 1900–1960s" in ibid., pp. 60–72, p. 69.
159 Gisela Bock and Pat Thane, "Introduction" in ibid., pp. 1–20, p. 12.
160 Deborah A. Cohen, "Private lives in public spaces: Marie Stopes, the mothers' clinic and the practice of contraception," *History Workshop*, 35 (1993), pp. 95–116.
161 Pollard, *Reign of Virtue*, pp. 64–6. Pollard would not agree that Vichy's legislation involved any liberalization of attitudes towards female sexuality, but argues that the law merely recognized the apparent irrepressibility of male sexuality.
162 Burleigh and Wippermann, *The Racial State*, p. 252.
163 Ibid., p. 253.

164 Chris Ward, *Stalin's Russia*, p. 198.

165 John Barber and Mark Harrison, *The Soviet Home Front, 1941–1945: A Social and Economic History of the USSR in World War II* (1991), p. 92.

166 Orlando Figes, *A People's Tragedy: The Russian Revolution, 1891–1924* (1996), p. 741.

167 Kathleen Hale, *A Slender Reputation* (1988). The title for this book is taken from the remark of the artist Cedric Morris, "Do you mean to tell me, Kathleen, that you have hung your slender reputation on the broad shoulder of a *eunuch* cat" (my italics).

4. Civil Wars

1 Eric Weitz, "The heroic man, the ever-changing woman: gender and politics in European Communism, 1917–1950" in Laura Frader and Sonya Rose (eds.), *Gender and Class in Modern Europe* (Ithaca and London, 1996), pp. 311–52.

2 On the Finnish civil war see D. G. Kirby, *Finland in the Twentieth Century: A History and Interpretation* (1979), p. 64.

3 Stanley Payne, *The Franco Regime, 1936–1975* (Madison, WI, 1987), p. 219.

4 Kevin Passmore, "Boy scouting for grown ups: paramilitarism in the Croix de Feu and the Parti Social Français," *French Historical Studies*, 19, 2 (1995), pp. 527–57.

5 António Costa Pinto, *Salazar's Dictatorship and European Fascism* (Boulder, CO, 1995), p. 162.

6 Paul Preston, *Franco: A Biography* (1993), p. 61.

7 Eugenia S. Ginzburg, *Into the Whirlwind* (1968), p. 26.

8 Dick Geary, "Employers, workers and the collapse of the Weimar Republic" in Ian Kershaw (ed.), *Weimar: Why Did German Democracy Fail?* (1990), pp. 92–119, p. 115.

9 Jacques Rupnik, "The roots of Czech Stalinism" in Raphael Samuel and Gareth Stedman Jones (eds.), *Culture, Ideology and Politics* (1982), pp. 302–19, p. 309.

10 Basil Liddell Hart, *Memoirs* (1965), Vol. 1, p. 106.

11 Jonathan Steinberg, *All or Nothing: The Axis and the Holocaust, 1941–1945* (1990), p. 25.

12 On the importance of Provençal cooking to Maurrasians, see Raoul Girardet and Pierre Assouline, *Singulièrement Libre* (1990), p. 36.

13 Elizabeth David, *Italian Food* (1987), p. 65.

14 Robert Paxton, *Le Temps des Chemises Vertes: Révoltes Paysannes et Fascisme Rural, 1929–1939* (1996), p. 252.

15 Jacques Bainville, *Les Conséquences Politiques de la Paix* (1920), p. 250.

16 Costa Pinto, *Salazar's Dictatorship*, p. 116.

17 Elizabeth Wiskemann, *The Europe I Saw* (1968), p. 108.

18 Orlando Figes, *Peasant Russia, Civil War* (Oxford, 1990).

19 Orlando Figes, *A People's Tragedy: The Russian Revolution, 1891–1924* (1996), p. 753.

20 Sheila Fitzpatrick, *The Russian Revolution* (Oxford, 1994), p. 138.

21 George Jackson, *Comintern and Peasant in East Europe, 1919–1930* (New York, 1966), p. 106. The relationship seems to have involved considerable reservations on both sides.

22 Dick Geary, *European Labour Protest, 1848–1939* (1981), p. 149.

23 Antony Polonsky, *The Little Dictators: The History of Eastern Europe Since 1918* (1975), p. 81.

24 Paul Preston, "The agrarian war in the South" in Paul Preston (ed.), *Revolution and War in Spain, 1931–1939* (1993), pp. 159–81.

25 Paul Corner, "Fascist agrarian policy and the Italian economy in the interwar years" in John Davis (ed.), *Gramsci and Italy's Passive Revolution* (1979), pp. 239–74.

26 Ian Kershaw, *Popular Opinion and Political Dissent in the Third Reich* (Oxford, 1983), p. 241.

27 Gordon Wright, *Rural Revolution in France: The Peasantry in the Twentieth Century* (Stanford, CA, 1964), p. 224.

28 Stanley Payne, "Spain: the Church, the Second Republic and the Franco Regime" in R. Wolff and J. Hoensch (eds.), *Catholics, the State and the European Radical Right* (1987), pp. 182–98, p. 183.

29 Figes, *A People's Tragedy*, p. 818.

30 Isaac Deutscher, *Stalin: A Political Biography* (1966), p. 478.

31 Martin Conway, "Introduction" in Tom Buchanan and Martin Conway (eds.), *Political Catholicism in Europe, 1918–1965* (Oxford, 1996), pp. 1–33, p. 12.

32 Peter Kent, *The Pope and the Duce: The International Impact of the Lateran Agreements* (New York, 1981), p. 113.

33 Erika Weinzierl, "Austria: state, politics and ideology, 1918–1938" in Wolff and Hoensch (eds.) *Catholics, the State and the European Radical Right*, pp. 5–31, p. 21.

34 Stanley G. Payne, "Spain: the Church, the Second Republic and the Franco regime" in ibid., pp. 182–98.

35 Harold James, *The German Slump: Politics and Economics 1924–1936* (Oxford, 1987), p. 92.

36 Georges Simenon, *Le Bourgmestre de Furnes* (1939), p. 163.

37 John Pollard, "Italy" in Conway and Buchanan (eds.), *Political Catholicism in Europe, 1918–1965*, pp. 69–96, p. 79.

38 Martin Conway, *Collaboration in Belgium: Léon Degrelle and the Rexist Movement* (1993).

39 John Molony, *The Emergence of Political Catholicism in Italy: Partito Popolare, 1919–1926* (1997), p. 124.

40 Martin Clark, *Modern Italy* (1984), p. 256.

41 Payne, *The Franco Regime*, p. 212.

5. Modern Times

1 Harold Nicolson, *Peacemaking, 1919* (1945) p. 244.
2 Mary Nolan, *Visions of Modernity: American Business and the Modernisation of Germany* (Oxford, 1994), pp. 32–4.
3 Stephen Kotkin, *Magnetic Mountain: Stalinism as a Civilization* (Berkeley and Los Angeles, CA, 1995), p. 131.
4 Harold James, *The German Slump: Politics and Economics, 1924–1936* (Oxford, 1987), p. 246.
5 Peter Hayes, *Industry and Ideology: IG Farben in the Nazi Era* (Cambridge, 1987 and 1989).
6 Perry Willson, *The Clockwork Factory: Women and Work in Fascist Italy* (Oxford, 1993), p. 33.
7 A. J. P. Taylor, *A Personal History* (1983), pp. 68, 139, 155.
8 John Maynard Keynes, "The Great Slump of 1930," *Essays in Persuasion* (1951, first published 1931), pp. 135–47, p. 140.
9 Valentine Cunningham, *British Writers of the Thirties* (Oxford, 1988), p. 404.
10 Willson, *The Clockwork Factory*, p. 39.
11 Tim Mason, *Nazism, Fascism and the Working Class* (Cambridge, 1995), p. 89.
12 Miriam Glucksmann, *Women Assemble: Women Workers and the New Industries in Inter-War Britain* (1990), p. 97.
13 "Look at a sixpenny Swiss roll . . . Wherever you look you will see some slick machine-made article triumphing over the old-fashioned article that still tastes of something other than sawdust." Orwell, *The Road to Wigan Pier* (1937 and 1962), p. 179.
14 Glucksmann, *Women Assemble*, p. 127.
15 Scott Lash and John Urry, *The End of Organized Capitalism* (1987), p. 173.
16 Ibid., p. 181.
17 David Noble, *America by Design: Science, Technology and the Rise of Corporate Capitalism* (Oxford, 1977), pp. 264–5. Note that some interest in revisionist Taylorism was displayed by European industrialists; see Willson, *The Clockwork Factory*, p. 65.
18 Lash and Urry, *The End of Organized Capitalism*, p. 188.
19 Glucksmann, *Women Assemble*, p. 76.
20 Roger Martin, *Patron de Droit Divin* (1984).
21 Glucksmann, *Women Assemble*, p. 98; Willson, *The Clockwork Factory*, p. 75.
22 Willson, *The Clockwork Factory*, p. 97.
23 Glucksmann, *Women Assemble*, p. 157.
24 Willson, *The Clockwork Factory*, p. 135.
25 Glucksmann, *Women Assemble*, p. 122.
26 Willson, *The Clockwork Factory*, pp. 106–7. Illiteracy among female workers in the factory was just 0.7 percent, compared with a rate for the population of the region (itself better than that for most of Italy) of 5.6 percent.

27 Cited in Lash and Urry, *The End of Organized Capitalism*, p. 170.

28 Mária Kovács, *Liberal Professions and Illiberal Politics: Hungary from the Habsburgs to the Holocaust* (Oxford and Washington, 1994), p. 75.

29 John Maynard Keynes, "The end of laissez-faire" (1926) in *Essays in Persuasion*, pp. 312–22, p. 314.

30 Willson, *The Clockwork Factory*, p. 29.

31 Maurice Lévy-Léboyer, "Le Patronat Français 1912–1973" in ibid. (ed.), *Le Patronat de la Seconde Industrialisation* (1979), pp. 137–68, p. 144.

32 Lewis Siegelbaum, *Stakhanovism and the Politics of Productivity in the USSR, 1935–1941* (Cambridge, 1988), p. 1.

33 Moshe Lewin, *The Making of the Soviet System: Essays in the Social History of Interwar Russia* (1985), p. 244.

34 Ibid., p. 250.

35 Cited in Siegelbaum, *Stakhanovism and the Politics of Productivity in the USSR*, p. 51.

36 Ibid., p. 72.

37 Lewin, *The Making of the Soviet System*, p. 209.

38 J. Arch Getty, *The Origins of the Great Purges: The Soviet Communist Party Reconsidered* (Cambridge, 1985), p. 15.

39 Kotkin, *Magnetic Mountain*, p. 91.

40 J. P. Depretto, "Construction workers in the 1930s" in Nick Lampert and Gábor Rittersporn (eds.), *Stalinism: Its Nature and Aftermath* (1992), pp. 184–210, p. 200.

41 John Maynard Keynes, "A Short View of Russia" (1925) in *Essays in Persuasion*, pp. 297–322, p. 306.

42 Keynes, "The end of laissez-faire," p. 314.

43 James, *The German Slump*, pp. 154 and 155.

44 C. S. Maier, *Recasting Bourgeois Europe: Stabilization in France, Germany and Italy in the Decade after World War I* (Princeton, 1975), p. 9.

45 Glucksmann, *Women Assemble*, p. 78.

46 Keynes, "Am I a liberal?" (1925) in *Essays in Persuasion*, pp. 323–38, pp. 327–8.

47 Robert Paxton, *Le Temps des Chemises Vertes: Révoltes Paysannes et Fascisme Rural, 1929–1939* (1996), p. 33.

48 George Orwell, "England Your England" in *England Your England and Other Essays* (1953), pp. 192–224, p. 223.

49 Willson, *The Clockwork Factory*, p. 24.

50 Mason, *Nazism, Fascism and the Working Classes*, p. 91.

51 Hugo Young, *One of Us* (1990), p. 9.

6. The Phoney Peace

1 Three-quarters of French diplomats were educated at the École Libre des Sciences Politiques. Richard Challener, "The French Foreign Office: the era of Philippe Berthelot" in Gordon Craig and Felix Gilbert (eds.), *The Diplomats, 1919–1939* (Princeton, 1994), pp. 49–85, p. 63.

2 In 1935, more than a tenth of the entire French diplomatic corps came from just twelve families. Jean-Baptiste Duroselle, *La Décadence, 1932–1939* (1979), pp. 269 and 518.

3 Ivone Kirkpatrick, *The Inner Circle* (1959), p. 141.

4 Michael Marrus, *The Unwanted: European Refugees in the Twentieth Century* (Oxford, 1985), p. 51.

5 Götz Aly, *Final Solution: Nazi Population Policies and the Murder of the European Jews* (1999).

6 Marrus, *The Unwanted*, p. 126.

7 Ibid., pp. 126 and 139.

8 Anne Grynberg, *Les Camps de la Honte: Les Internés Juifs des Camps Français, 1939–1944* (1991).

9 Harold James, *The German Slump: Politics and Economics, 1924–1936* (Oxford, 1987), p. 21.

10 John Erickson, *The Road to Stalingrad* (1975), p. 28.

11 Donald Cameron Watt, *How War Came* (1990), pp. 109–10.

12 Roger Reese, "The Red Army and the great purges" in J. Arch Getty and Roberta Manning (eds.), *Stalinist Terror: New Perspectives* (1993), pp. 198–214, p. 199. Reese argues that Erickson's estimate that 30,000 to 40,000 officers – or half the total officer corps – were purged is excessively large.

13 Erickson, *The Road to Stalingrad*, p. 34.

14 Quoted in P. M. H. Bell, *The Origins of the Second World War in Europe* (1986), p. 142.

15 Paul Kennedy, *The Rise and Fall of the Great Powers: Economic Change and Military Conflict from 1500 to 2000* (1988), p. 398.

16 D. C. Watt, *Too Serious a Business: European Armed Forces and the Approach to the Second World War* (1975), p. 68.

17 Kennedy, *The Rise and Fall of the Great Powers*, p. 403.

18 Watt, *Too Serious a Business*, p. 66.

19 Eugenia C. Kiesling, "'If it ain't broke don't fix it': French military doctrine between the World Wars," *War in History*, 3, 2 (1996), pp. 208–23.

20 James S. Corum, "From biplanes to Blitzkrieg: the development of German air doctrine between the wars," *War in History*, 3, 1 (1996), pp. 85–103, p. 87.

21 Harold Nicolson, *Diaries and Letters, 1930–1939* (1966), p. 303. Thomas Inskip, Minister of the Coordination of Defense, told Nicolson in July 1937 that "people absolutely refuse to volunteer owing to the necessity of service in India."

22 Basil Liddell Hart, *Memoirs* (1965), pp. 111, 244, 246.

23 Richard Overy, "Air power, armies, and the war in the west," *The Harmon Memorial Lectures in Military History*, No. 32 (United States Air Force Academy, Colorado, 1989), p. 9.

24 Ibid.

25 Cited in Andrew Crozier, "The colonial question in Stresemann's Locarno policy," *The International History Review*, IV (1982), pp. 37–54.

7. The Second World War in Europe

1 John Erickson, *The Road to Stalingrad* (1975), pp. 150, 151.
2 John Erickson, *The Road to Berlin* (1983), p. xi.
3 Richard Overy, *Russia's War* (1997), p. 112.
4 John Barber and Mark Harrison, *The Soviet Home Front, 1941–1945: A Social and Economic History of the USSR in World War II* (1991), p. 27.
5 Overy, *Russia's War*, p. 102.
6 Ibid., p. 147.
7 Barber and Harrison, *The Soviet Home Front*, p. 42.
8 Norman M. Naimark, *The Russians in Germany: A History of the Soviet Zone of Occupation, 1945–1949* (Cambridge, MA, 1995), pp. 142–3. Of those killed in the war, 4,948 were killed fighting, mainly on the eastern front. I assume that this study refers only to adult men.
9 Christopher Browning, *The Path to Genocide: Essays on Launching the Final Solution* (Cambridge, 1995), p. 100.
10 Ibid., p. 101.
11 Martin Gilbert, *The Holocaust: The Jewish Tragedy* (1987), p. 239.
12 Barber and Harrison, *The Soviet Home Front*, p. 41.
13 Michael Burleigh, "'See you again in Siberia': the German–Soviet war and other tragedies" in *Ethics and Extermination: Reflections on Nazi Genocide* (Cambridge, 1997), pp. 36–110, p. 61.
14 David Irving, *The War Between the Generals* (1982), p. 209.
15 Richard Overy, *Why the Allies Won* (1995), p. 293. See also David French, "Discipline and the death penalty in the British Army in the war against Germany during the Second World War," *Journal of Contemporary History*, 33, 4 (1998), pp. 531–46.
16 Macgregor Knox, "Expansionist zeal, fighting power and staying power in the Italian and German dictatorships" in Richard Bessel (ed.), *Fascist Italy and Nazi Germany: Comparisons and Contrasts* (1996), pp. 113–133, p. 128.
17 Erickson, *The Road to Stalingrad*, pp. 544–5.
18 Cited in Overy, *Why the Allies Won*, p. 61.
19 Alan Milward, *War, Economy and Society, 1939–1945* (1987), p. 83.
20 Barber and Harrison, *The Soviet Home Front*, p. 130.
21 Milward, *War, Economy and Society*, p. 80.
22 Ibid., p. 59.
23 Ulbricht Herbert, *Hitler's Foreign Workers: Enforced Labour in Germany Under the Third Reich* (Cambridge, 1997), p. 1.
24 Ibid., p. 300.
25 Liddell Hart cited in Paul Kennedy, *The Rise and Fall of the Great Powers: Economic Change and Military Conflict from 1500 to 2000* (1988), p. 453.
26 Overy, *Why the Allies Won*, p. 5.
27 Erickson, *The Road to Berlin*, p. 48.
28 Overy, *Why the Allies Won*, p. 219.
29 Ibid., p. 131.

30 Ibid.

31 Richard Overy, *The Penguin Historical Atlas of the Third Reich* (1996), p. 103.

32 Sebastian Ritchie, "A new audit of war: the productivity of Britain's wartime aircraft industry reconsidered" in *War and Society*, 12, 1 (1994), pp. 125–47, p. 129.

33 Milward, *War, Economy and Society*, p. 25.

34 Ibid., p. 48.

35 Ibid., p. 63.

36 Ibid., p. 70.

37 Geoffrey P. Megargee, "Triumph of the null: structure and conflict in the command of the German land forces, 1939–1945," *War in History*, 4, 1 (1997), pp. 60–80.

38 Timothy Colton, "Perspectives on civil/military relations in the Soviet era" in Timothy Colton and Thane Gustafson (eds.), *Soldiers and the Soviet State: Civil/Military Relations from Brezhnev to Gorbachev* (Princeton, NJ, 1990), pp. 3–43, p. 19.

39 China was taken to mean nationalist China and this meant that the Chinese government was taken to be based in Taiwan from 1949. Communist China was only recognized in 1971.

40 Barber and Harrison, *The Soviet Home Front*, p. ix.

41 Ibid., p. 192.

42 Staff Sergeant David Cason, cited in David Reynolds, *Rich Relations: The American Occupation of Britain, 1942–1945* (1995), p. 443.

43 Mark Mazower, *Inside Hitler's Greece: The Experience of Occupation, 1941–1944* (1993), pp. 363–8.

8. Genocide

1 Lucy Dawidowicz, *The War Against the Jews, 1933–1945* (1990).

2 Götz Aly, *"Final Solution": Nazi Population Policy and the Murder of the European Jews* (1999), pp. 14–18.

3 Christopher Browning, "Nazi Ghettoization policy in Poland, 1939–1941" in *The Path to Genocide: Essays on Launching the Final Solution* (Cambridge, 1995), pp. 28–56.

4 Raul Hilberg, *The Destruction of the European Jews* (1973), p. 572.

5 Mark Mazower, *Inside Hitler's Greece: The Experience of Occupation, 1941–1944* (1995), p. 240.

6 Hilberg, *The Destruction of the European Jews*, pp. 264 and 276.

7 Mark Mazower, *Inside Hitler's Greece*, p. 253.

8 Hilberg, *The Destruction of the European Jews*, p. 216.

9 In July 1944 a woman was reported to the Gestapo by her own apartment mate when she said that an acquaintance of hers in the SS had recalled being "up to his knees in blood" during the killing of 40,000 Jews. Robert Gellately, *The Gestapo and German Society: Enforcing Racial Policy, 1933–1945* (Oxford, 1991), p. 211.

10 David Bankier, *The Germans and the Final Solution: Public Opinion Under Nazism* (Oxford, 1992), pp. 127–8.

11 Jonathan Steinberg, *All or Nothing: The Axis and the Holocaust* (1990).

12 Bankier, *The Germans and the Final Solution*, p. 125.

13 Cited in Michael Burleigh and Wolfgang Wippermann, *The Racial State: Germany, 1933–1945* (Cambridge, 1993), p. 94.

14 On the difficulty of assessing the extent of German resistance to the persecution of the Jews see Gellately, *The Gestapo and German Society*, p. 180.

15 Browning, *Ordinary Men: Reserve Police Battalion 101 and the Final Solution in Poland* (1992), p. 57.

16 Ibid., p. 75.

17 Ibid., p. 87. Rudolf Höss, commander at Auschwitz, seems to have seen his career partly as a reaction against a strict Catholic upbringing (his father had intended him to become a priest). Hilberg, *The Destruction of the European Jews*, p. 575.

18 Burleigh and Wippermann, *The Racial State*, p. 101.

19 Browning, *Ordinary Men*, p. 153.

20 Hilberg, *The Destruction of the European Jews*, p. 201.

21 Ibid., p. 330.

22 Steinberg, *All or Nothing*.

23 Annie Kriegel, *Ce Que J'ai Cru Comprendre* (1991), p. 146.

24 David Cesarani, "Introduction" in David Cesarani (ed.), *Genocide and Rescue: The Holocaust in Hungary* (Oxford, 1997), pp. 1–28, p. 8.

25 Jews were also faced by the increasing difficulty of selling their property and by the high taxes imposed on those who departed. See Saul Friedlander, *Nazi Germany and the Jews: the Years of Persecution, 1933–39* (1997), p. 62. The number of Jews leaving ran at about 25,000 per year from 1933 to 1937. I assume that it increased from 1937 to 1939.

26 Ruth Bondy, "Women in Theresienstadt and the Family Camp in Birkenau" in Dalia Ofer and Lenore Weitzman (eds.), *Women in the Holocaust* (New Haven, CT, 1998), pp. 310–26.

27 Raul Hilberg, *Perpetrators, Victims and Bystanders: The Jewish Catastrophe, 1933–1945* (1993), p. 177.

28 George Eisen, *Children and Play in the Holocaust: Games Among the Shadows* (Amery, MA, 1988), p. 47.

29 See photograph on p. 51 of Burleigh and Wippermann, *The Racial State*.

PART III

Postwar Europe

1 Cited in Philip Armstrong, Andrew Glyn and John Harrison, *Capitalism Since 1945* (Oxford, 1991), p. 4.
2 Elena Zubkova, *Russia After the War: Hopes, Illusions, and Disappointments, 1945–1957* (New York, 1998), pp. 40–47.
3 Alan Kramer, "Law abiding Germans? The social disintegration, crime and the reimposition of order in postwar western Germany, 1945–1949" in Richard Evans (ed.), *The German Underworld: Deviants and Outcasts in German History* (1988), pp. 238–61, p. 242.
4 Richard Evans, *Rituals of Retribution: Capital Punishment in Germany, 1600–1987* (1996), p. 765.
5 John Keep, *Last of the Empires: A History of the Soviet Union, 1945–1991* (Oxford, 1996), p. 17.
6 Norman Naimark, *The Russians in Germany: A History of the Soviet Zone of Occupation, 1945–1949* (Cambridge, MA, 1995), p. 105.
7 Evans, *Rituals of Retribution*, pp. 752–3.
8 Anthony Sutcliffe, *An Economic and Social History of Western Europe Since 1945* (1996), p. 157.
9 Philip Norman, *The Stones* (1985), p. 107.

1. Taking Sides

1 Winston Churchill, *The Second World War, Vol. VI: Triumph and Tragedy* (1954), p. 198.
2 Joseph Rothschild, *Return to Diversity: A Political History of East Central Europe Since World War II* (Oxford, 1993), p. 118.
3 Alexei Filitov, "The Soviet administrators and their German 'friends'" in Norman Naimark and Leonid Gibianskii (eds.), *The Establishment of Communist Regimes in Eastern Europe, 1944–1949* (Boulder, CO, 1997), pp. 111–22.
4 Rothschild, *Return to Diversity*, p. 83.
5 Ibid., p. 98.
6 Mary Fulbrook, *Anatomy of a Dictatorship: Inside the GDR, 1949–1989* (1995), p. 63.
7 Rothschild, *Return to Diversity*, p. 115.
8 Ibid., p. 116.
9 François Fejtö, *Budapest: L'Insurrection de 1956* (1990), p. 13.
10 Interview between Teresa Toranska and Jakub Berman in *Granta*, 17, (Autumn 1985), pp. 47–65, p. 48.
11 Ibid., interview with Stefan Staszewski, p. 66.
12 *L'Autre Europe*, 1 (1984).
13 Richard Staar, *Communist Regimes in Eastern Europe* (1977), p. 21.

14 M. B. Biskupski, "The military elite of the Polish Second Republic, 1918–1945: a historiographical review," *War and Society*, 14, 2 (1996), pp. 49–86.

15 Roger Faligot and Rémi Kauffer, *Les Résistants: De la Guerre de l'Ombre aux Allées du Pouvoir, 1944–1989* (1989), p. 220.

16 John Lamberton Harper, *American Influence and the Reconstruction of Italy, 1945–1948* (Cambridge, 1986), p. 109.

17 Irwin Wall, *L'Influence Américaine sur la Politique Française, 1945–1954* (1989), p. 9; Harper, *American Influence and the Reconstruction of Italy*, p. 111.

18 J. J. Lee, *Ireland, 1912–1985: Politics and Society* (Cambridge, 1989), p. 304.

19 Norman Lewis, *Naples '44: An Intelligence Officer in the Italian Labyrinth* (1978).

20 Anthony Sutcliffe, *An Economic and Social History of Western Europe Since 1945* (1996), p. 147.

21 F. Jarraud, *Les Américains à Châteauroux (1951–1967)* (1981).

22 Harper, *American Influence and the Reconstruction of Italy*, pp. 83–4.

23 Ibid., p. 185.

24 Anthony Carew, *Labour Under the Marshall Plan: The Politics of Productivity and the Marketing of Management Science* (Manchester, 1987), p. 64. Note that Brown was officially employed by the Free Trade Union Committee until 1950.

25 Harper, *American Influence and the Reconstruction of Italy*, p. 124.

26 Carew, *Labour Under the Marshall Plan*, p. 102.

27 Ibid., p. 14.

28 Michel Debré, *Trois Républiques pour une France: Mémoires, II, 1946–1958* (1988), p. 33.

29 Harper, *America and the Reconstruction of Italy*, p. 83.

30 Volker Berghahn, *The Americanisation of West German Industry, 1945–1973* (Leamington Spa, 1986).

31 *Le Monde*, November 22, 1997.

32 Lilly Marcou, *Une Enfance Stalinienne* (1982), p. 97.

33 Thomas Schreiber, *Hongrie: La Transition Pacifique* (1991), p. 5.

34 Bruce Parrott, *Politics and Technology in the Soviet Union* (Cambridge, MA, 1983), p. 88.

35 V. V. Shlykov interviewed by Sergei Belanovsky, "The arms race and the burden of military expenditures" in Michael Ellman and Vladimir Kontorovich (eds.), *The Destruction of the Soviet Economic System: An Insiders' History* (1998), pp. 40–69, p. 43.

36 M. A. Gareev, interviewed in ibid., p. 48.

37 Gregory Khanin, "An uninvited advisor" in ibid., pp. 76–84.

38 Nina et Jean Kéhayan, *Rue du Prolétaire Rouge* (1978), p. 57.

39 Adam Michnik, "L'éclat de Tocqueville, l'ombre de Metternich" in *L'Autre Europe*, 5 (1985).

40 Cited in Francis Fukuyama, *The End of History and the Last Man* (New York, 1992), p. 8.

2. The Miracle

1 For this perspective see Pierre Sicsic and Charles Wyplosz, "France, 1945–1992" in Nick Crafts and Gianni Toniolo (eds.), *Economic Growth in Europe Since 1945* (Cambridge, 1996), pp. 210–39, p. 211.

2 Alan Milward, *The European Rescue of the Nation-State* (1992), pp. 46–118.

3 John Lamberton Harper, *America and the Reconstruction of Italy, 1945–1948* (Cambridge, 1986), p. 1.

4 Harold James, *A German Identity, 1770–1990* (1989), p. 180.

5 Karl-Heinz Paqué, "Why the 1950s and not the 1920s? Olsonian and non-Olsonian interpretations of two decades of German economic history" in Crafts and Toniolo (eds.), *Economic Growth in Europe Since 1945*, pp. 95–106, p. 102.

6 Anthony Carew, *Labour Under the Marshall Plan: The Politics of Productivity and the Marketing of Management Science* (Manchester, 1987), p. 137.

7 Jacques Warnier from Reims, who went on a French productivity mission in 1951, was an example of this type; see Richard Vinen, *Bourgeois Politics in France* (1995), pp. 64 and 65.

8 Carew, *Labour Under the Marshall Plan*, p. 149.

9 Charles Kindleberger, cited in Maurice Larkin, *France Since the Popular Front: Government and People, 1936–1986* (1988), p. 185.

10 Nick Tiratsoo, *Reconstruction, Affluence and Labour Politics: Coventry, 1945–60* (1990), p. 26.

11 Cited in Allan Williams, *The Western European Economy: A Geography of Post-War Development* (1987), p. 81.

12 Harold Perkin, *The Rise of Professional Society: England Since 1880* (1990), p. 461.

13 Pierre Birnbaum, *Les Sommets de l'État: Essai sur l'Élite du Pouvoir en France* (1977).

14 Wendy Carlin, "West German Growth and Institutions, 1945–1990" in Crafts and Toniolo (eds.), *Economic Growth in Europe Since 1945*, pp. 455–97, p. 466.

15 Volker Berghahn, *The Americanisation of West German Industry, 1945–1973* (Leamington Spa, 1986).

16 Milward, *The European Rescue of the Nation-State*, p. 40.

17 Robert Collins, *The Business Response to Keynes* (New York, 1982).

18 Milward, *The European Rescue of the Nation-State*, p. 247.

19 Edgar Morin, *Commune en France: La Métamorphose de Plodémet* (1967), p. 73.

20 Williams, *The Western European Economy*, p. 99.

21 Ibid., p. 173.

22 Paul Ginsborg, *A History of Contemporary Italy: Society and Politics, 1943–1988* (1990), p. 223.

23 Milward, *The European Rescue of the Nation-State*, p. 51.

24 Ibid., p. 30.

25 James, *A German Identity*, p. 187.

26 Carlin, "West German Growth and Institutions, 1945–1990," p. 467.
27 Volker Berghahn, *Modern Germany: Society, Economy and Politics in the Twentieth Century* (Cambridge, 1987), p. 227.
28 Carlin, "West German Growth and Institutions, 1945–1990," p. 468.
29 Anthony Rowley, "La réinsertion économique des rapatriés" in Jean-Pierre Rioux (ed.) *La Guerre d'Algérie et les Français* (1990), pp. 348–52.
30 Peter Pedersen, "Postwar growth of the Danish economy" in Crafts and Toniolo (eds.), *Economic Growth in Europe Since 1945*, pp. 541–75, p. 557.
31 Ginsborg, *A History of Contemporary Italy*, p. 234.
32 Norman Lewis, *The Honoured Society: The Sicilian Mafia Observed* (1984), pp. 215–16.
33 Cormac O Gráda and Kevin O'Rourke, "Irish economic growth, 1945–1988" in Crafts and Toniolo (eds.), *Economic Growth in Europe Since 1945*, pp. 388–426, p. 413.
34 Ginsborg, *A History of Contemporary Italy*, p. 215.
35 Williams, *The Western European Economy*, p. 186.
36 Michael Jopling cited in Alan Clark, *Diaries* (1993), p. 350.
37 Daniel Bell, *The Cultural Contradictions of Capitalism* (1976).
38 Lawrence Wylie, *Village in the Vaucluse* (Oxford, 1957 and 1974), p. 174.
39 David Marsh, *The Bundesbank: The Bank That Rules Europe* (1992), p. 19.
40 Tony Judt, *A Grand Illusion: An Essay on Europe* (1996), p. 36.
41 Ginsborg, *A History of Contemporary Italy*, p. 225.

3. Consensus Politics

1 David Close, *The Origins of the Greek Civil War* (1995), p. 220. Close estimates that there were only 5,400 political prisoners in Greece by 1955.
2 David Hanley, "The European People's Party: towards a new party form?" in David Hanley (ed.), *Christian Democracy in Europe: A Comparative Perspective* (1994), pp. 185–201.
3 Such democracies are described in a memorable passage in Donald Sassoon, *One Hundred Years of Socialism: The West European Left in the Twentieth Century* (1996), p. 293.
4 Sassoon, *One Hundred Years of Socialism*, p. 291.
5 David Broughton, "The CDU–CSU in Germany: is there any alternative?" in Hanley (ed.), *Christian Democracy in Europe*, pp. 101–18, p. 104.
6 Paul Whitely, Patrick Seyd and Jeremy Richardson, *True Blues: The Politics of Conservative Party Membership* (Oxford, 1994), p. 79.
7 Cited in Paul Ginsborg, *A History of Contemporary Italy: Society and Politics 1943–1988* (1990), p. 248.
8 John Goldthorpe, David Lockwood, Frank Bechhofer and Jennifer Platt, *The Affluent Worker: Industrial Attitudes and Behaviour* (Cambridge, 1968).
9 Denis Kavanagh, *Thatcherism and British Politics: the End of Consensus* (Oxford, 1992), p. 39.

10 J. R. Frears, *France in the Giscard Presidency* (1981), p. 15.

11 Suzanne Berger, "Religious transformation and the future of politics" in Charles Maier (ed.), *Changing Boundaries of the Political: Essays on the Evolving Balance Between the State and Society, Public and Private in Europe* (Cambridge, 1987), pp. 107–50, p. 107.

12 Robert Leonardi and Douglas Wertman, *Italian Christian Democracy: The Politics of Dominance* (1989), p. 154.

13 Ginsborg, *A History of Contemporary Italy*, p. 240.

14 Donald Sassoon, "Political and market forces in Italian broadcasting," *West European Politics*, 2, 8 (April 1985), pp. 67–83.

15 Daniel Bell, *The End of Ideology: On the Exhaustion of Political Ideas in the Fifties* (Chicago, 1960). Bell's book is about America although it clearly had implications for Western countries generally.

16 Cited in Jean Charlot, *The Gaullist Phenomenon* (1970), p. 65.

17 Kavanagh, *Thatcherism and British Politics*, p. 39.

18 Ibid.

19 Frears, *France in the Giscard Presidency*, p. 6.

20 Peter Hall (ed.), *The Political Power of Economic Ideas: Keynesianism Across Nations* (Princeton, NJ, 1989).

21 Pierre Rosanvallon, "The development of Keynesianism in France" in ibid., pp. 171–93.

22 Christopher S. Allen, "The underdevelopment of Keynesianism in the Federal Republic of Germany" in ibid., pp. 263–89, p. 277.

23 Keynes, "Economic possibilities for our grandchildren" (1930) in *Essays in Persuasion* (1951), pp. 358–73, p. 373.

24 *Spectator*, April 7, 1979.

25 Mattei Dogan and Jacques Narbonne, *Les Françaises Face à la Politique: Comportement Politique et Condition Sociale* (1955), p. 181.

26 Francis de Tarr, *The French Radical Party from Herriot to Mendès-France* (Oxford, 1961), p. 5.

27 Dogan and Narbonne, *Les Françaises Face à la Politique*, p. 90. "It would be inexact to believe that the gap between male and female voters for the parties are specifically linked to differences of sex."

28 Cited in Christine Bard, *Les Filles de Marianne: Histoire des Féminismes, 1914–1940* (1995), p. 25.

29 Dogan and Narbonne, *Les Françaises Face à la Politique*, p. 183.

30 Ibid., p. 89.

31 Ibid., p. 69.

32 Ibid., p. 184.

33 Melanie Sully, *A Contemporary History of Austria* (1990), p. 50.

34 S. L. Bourque and J. Grosshultz, "Politics, an unnatural practice: political science looks at female participation," *Politics and Society*, 4, 2 (1974), pp. 225–66.

35 Charlot, *The Gaullist Phenomenon*, p. 67.

36 Leonardi and Wertman, *Italian Christian Democracy*, p. 155.

37 Sully, *A Contemporary History of Austria*, p. 50. Of all Green voters, 60 percent were women.

38 Ibid., p. 51.

39 James Walston, *The Mafia and Clientelism: Roads to Rome in Post-War Calabria* (1988), p. 62.

40 Sassoon, *One Hundred Years of Socialism*, p. 159.

41 Elizabeth Wiskemann, *Italy Since 1945* (1971), p. 21.

42 Judith Chubb, *Patronage, Power and Poverty in Southern Italy: A Tale of Two Cities* (Cambridge, 1982).

43 Walston, *The Mafia and Clientelism*, p. 77.

44 Ginsborg, *A History of Contemporary Italy*, pp. 217, 218.

45 Sassoon, *One Hundred Years of Socialism*, p. 134.

46 Ibid., pp. 282–3.

47 Cited in Kavanagh, *Thatcherism and British Politics*, p. 155.

48 Ian Birchall, *Bailing Out the System: Reformist Socialism in Western Europe, 1944–1985* (1986), p. 105.

49 Ibid., pp. 105–6.

50 Cited in Walston, *The Mafia and Clientelism*, p. 58.

51 Bryan D. Palmer, *E. P. Thompson: Objections and Oppositions* (1994), p. 50.

52 Gordon Wright, *Rural Revolution in France: The Peasantry in the Twentieth Century* (Stanford, CA, 1964), pp. 189–96.

53 Lilly Marcou, *Le Kominform* (1977), p. 228.

54 Georges Lavau, *A Quoi Sert le Parti Communiste Français?* (1981), p. 36.

55 Henri Weber, *Le Parti des Patrons: Le CNPF (1946–1986)* (1986), p. 161.

56 Cited in David Caute, *The Year of Barricades: '68* (1988), p. 64.

57 John Sullivan, *ETA and Basque Nationalism: The Fight for Euskadi, 1890–1986* (1988).

58 On the use of torture against IRA suspects see Tim Pat Coogan, *The IRA* (1993), pp. 697–712.

59 Kavanagh, *Thatcherism and British Politics*, p. 11.

4. The Other Europe

1 Lilly Marcou, *Une Enfance Stalinienne* (1982), p. 139.

2 Ibid., p. 118.

3 Karol Bartosek, "Europe centrale et sud-est" in Stéphane Courtois, Nicolas Werth, Jean-Louis Panné, Andrzej Paczkowski, Karel Bartosek and Jean-Louis Margolin (eds.), *Le Livre Noir du Communisme: Crimes, Terreur, Répression* (1997), pp. 429–96, p. 474.

4 Andrezj Paczkowski, "Pologne, la nation ennemi" in ibid., pp. 397–428, p. 418.

5 Richard Staar, *Communist Regimes in Eastern Europe* (1977), p. 34.

6 Artur London, *L'Aveu: Dans l'Engrenage du Procès de Prague* (1969), p. 32.

7 Heda Margolius Kovaly, *Prague Farewell* (1988), p. 118.

8 Ibid., p. 154.

9 Zdeněk Mlynář, *Night Frost in Prague: The End of Humane Socialism* (1980), p. 66.

10 Ibid., p. 38.

11 London, *L'Aveu*, p. 376.

12 Robin Okey, *Eastern Europe, 1740–1980: Feudalism to Communism* (London, 1982), p. 192.

13 Thomas Schreiber, *Hongrie, la Transition Pacifique* (1991), p. 16.

14 Mlynář, *Night Frost in Prague*, p. 3.

15 Marcou, *Une Enfance Stalinienne*, p. 150.

16 Kovaly, *Prague Farewell*, p. 163.

17 Amy Knight, *Stalin's First Lieutenant* (Princeton, NJ, 1996).

18 Roger Stéphane, *Rue László Rajk: Une Tragédie Hongroise* (1991), p. 114.

19 Albert P. Van Goudoever, *The Limits of Destalinisation in the Soviet Union: Political Rehabilitations in the Soviet Union Since Stalin* (1986), p. 40.

20 Roy Medvedev, *Khrushchev* (Oxford, 1982), p. 98.

21 Stéphane, *Rue László Rajk*, p. 120.

22 Schreiber, *Hongrie, la Transition Pacifique*, p. 17.

23 Olivier Todd, *La Chute Finale: Essai sur la Décomposition de la Sphère Soviétique* (1976 and 1990), p. 84.

24 The phrase was coined by Tibor Méray; see Schreiber, *Hongrie, la Transition Pacifique*, p. 23.

25 Ibid., p. 25.

26 Todd, *La Chute Finale*, p. 80.

27 Schreiber, *Hongrie, la Transition Pacifique*, p. 24.

28 François Fejtö with Ewa Kulesza-Mietkowski, *La Fin des Démocraties Populaires: Les Chemins du Post-Communisme* (1992), p. 178.

29 Todd, *La Chute Finale*, p. 213.

30 London, *L'Aveu*, p. 373.

31 Pavel Tigrid, *Le Printemps de Prague* (1968), p. 59.

32 Mlynář, *Night Frost in Prague*, p. 42.

33 Tigrid, *Le Printemps de Prague*, pp. 92 and 99.

34 Eugen Steiner, *The Slovak Dilemma* (Cambridge, 1973), p. 142.

35 Kovaly, *Prague Farewell*, p. 211.

36 Ibid., p. 223.

37 Ibid., p. 211.

38 Timothy Garton Ash, *In Europe's Name: Germany and the Divided Continent* (1994), p. 124.

39 Donald Filtzer, *Soviet Workers and De-Stalinisation: The Consolidation of the Modern System of Soviet Production Relations, 1953–1964* (Cambridge, 1992), pp. 19 and 20.

40 Ibid., p. 87.

41 Thane Gustafson, "The response to technological challenge" in Timothy Colton and Thane Gustafson (eds.), *Soldiers and the Soviet State: Civil Military Relations from Brezhnev to Gorbachev* (Princeton, NJ, 1990), pp. 192–238, p. 205.

42 Alain Besançon, *Anatomie d'un Spectre* (1981), p. 56.
43 Todd, *La Chute Finale*, 105.
44 Besançon, *Anatomie d'un Spectre*, p. 127.
45 Steiner, *The Slovak Dilemma*, p. 111.
46 Todd, *La Chute Finale*, p. 49.
47 Mary Fulbrook, *Anatomy of a Dictatorship: Inside the GDR, 1949–1989* (Oxford, 1995), p. 39.
48 On the use of illegal overtime see Blair Ruble, *Soviet Trade Unions: Their Development in the 1970s* (Cambridge, 1981), p. 56.
49 David A. Dyker, "Planning and the Workers" in Leonard Schapiro and Joseph Godson (eds.), *The Soviet Worker from Lenin to Andropov* (1984), pp. 39–76, p. 65.
50 Vladimir Andrle, *A Social History of Twentieth-Century Russia* (1994), pp. 256–7.
51 Mervyn Matthews, *Privilege in the Soviet Union: A Study of Elite Lifestyles Under Communism* (1978), pp. 38 and 39.
52 Moshe Lewin, *The Gorbachev Phenomenon* (Berkeley, CA, 1991), p. 106.
53 Okey, *Eastern Europe*, p. 219.
54 Fejtö, *La Fin des Démocraties Populaires*, p. 74.
55 Andrle, *A Social History of Twentieth-Century Russia*, pp. 256–7.
56 Todd, *La Chute Finale*, p. 203.
57 Matthews, *Privilege in the Soviet Union*, p. 48.
58 Ellen Jones, *Red Army and Society: A Sociology of the Soviet Military* (1985), p. 55.
59 Daniel Bertaux, "Révolution et mobilité sociale en Russie soviétique," *Cahiers Internationaux de Sociologie*, XCVI (1994), pp. 77–97, pp. 85–87.
60 Ilya Zbarsky and Samuel Hutchinson, *Lenin's Embalmers* (1998).
61 Fejtö, *La Fin des Démocraties Populaires*, p. 76.
62 Staar, *Communist Regimes*, p. 61.
63 György Konrád and Iván Szelényi, *La Marche au Pouvoir des Intellectuels: Le Cas des Pays de l'Est* (1979), cited in Fejtö, *La Fin des Démocraties Populaires*, p. 75.
64 Starr, *Communist Regimes*, p. 45.
65 Ibid., p. 100.
66 Schreiber, *Hongrie, la Transition Pacifique*, p. 22.
67 Okey, *Eastern Europe*, p. 221.
68 Staar, *Communist Regimes*, p. 12.
69 Dennis Dunn, "The papal-communist détente, 1963–1973: its evolution and causes" in Bernard Eissenstat (ed.), *The Soviet Union: The Seventies and Beyond* (1975), pp. 121–40.

5. Rebuilding the Family

1 Robert Moeller, "The homosexual man is a 'man,' the homosexual woman is a 'woman': sex, society and the law," *Journal of the History of Sexuality*, 4, 3 (1994), pp. 395–429, p. 408.

2   Ross McKibbin, *Classes and Cultures: England, 1918–1951* (Oxford, 1998), pp. 300, 320.

3   Ingrid Sharp and Dagmar Flinspach, "Women in Germany from division to unification" in Derek Lewes and John R. P. McKenzie (eds.), *The New Germany: Social, Political and Cultural Challenges of Unification* (1997), pp. 173–91.

4   Christine Bard, *Les Filles de Marianne* (1995), p. 22.

5   Simone de Beauvoir, *The Second Sex* (1953, first published in French in 1949), pp. 223–33.

6   The view that "London was in the vanguard of social change" is advanced in Anthony Sutcliffe, *An Economic and Social History of Western Europe Since 1945* (1996), p. 157.

7   Harold Perkin, *The Rise of Professional Society: England Since 1880* (1989), p. 430.

8   Adrian Shubert, *A Social History of Modern Spain* (1992), p. 212.

9   Philip Norman, *The Stones* (1985), p. 287.

10   "Exposé de Lucien Newirth" in *De Gaulle en son siècle, 3, Moderniser la France, Actes des Journées Internationales Tenues à l'UNESCO, Paris 19–24 Novembre 1990* (1992), pp. 331–3, p. 333.

11   Robert Moeller, "The homosexual man is a 'man', the homosexual woman is a 'woman': sex, society and the law," p. 427.

12   Antony Copley, *Sexual Moralities in France, 1780–1980: New Ideas on the Family, Divorce and Homosexuality* (1992), p. 216.

13   Patrick Higgins, *Heterosexual Dictatorship* (1996), p. 158. Higgins points out that changes in statistical techniques probably led people to exaggerate the extent of increase in prosecutions for homosexuality.

14   Copley, *Sexual Moralities*, p. 219.

15   André Morali-Daninos, cited in Copley, *Sexual Moralities*, p. 218.

16   Cartoon of July 1, 1960, reprinted in *The Life and Times of Maudie Littlehampton* (1982).

17   G. Noiriel, *Workers in French Society in the 19th and 20th Centuries* (Oxford, 1990).

18   Paul Neuburg, *The Hero's Children: The Post-War Generation in Eastern Europe* (1972), p. 133.

19   John Barber and Mark Harrison, *The Soviet Home Front, 1941–1945: A Social and Economic History of the USSR in World War II* (1991), p. 207.

20   Donald Filtzer, *Soviet Workers and De-Stalinization: The Consolidation of the Modern System of Soviet Production Relations* (1992), p. 185.

21   Ibid., pp. 177–209.

22   Ibid., pp. 198 and 199.

23   Jacqueline Heinen, *Chômage et Devenir de la Main d'Oeuvre Féminine en Pologne* (1995), p. 138. In 1984, Polish women devoted an average of 6 hours and 29 minutes per day to domestic chores; men spent an average of 2 hours and 20 minutes on similar duties.

24   Ibid., pp. 130–1.

25 Marilyn Rueschemeyer and Szonja Szelenyi, "Socialist transformation and gender inequality: women in the GDR and Hungary" in David Childs, Thomas Baylis and Marilyn Rueschemeyer (eds.), *East Germany in Comparative Perspective*, pp. 81–109, p. 92.
26 Neuburg, *The Hero's Children*, p. 100.
27 Ibid., p. 193.
28 *Financial Times*, November 8–9, 1997.

PART IV

Who Won the Cold War?

1 A. A. Danilevich, cited in Sergei Belanovsky, "The arms race and the burden of military expenditures" in Michael Ellman and Vladimir Kontorovich (eds.), *The Destruction of the Soviet Economic System: An Insiders' History* (New York, 1998), pp. 40–69, p. 42.
2 Elizabeth Teague, *Solidarity and the Soviet Worker: The Impact of Polish Events of 1980 on Soviet Internal Politics* (1988), p. 139.
3 Misha Glenny, *The Rebirth of History: Eastern Europe in the Age of Democracy* (1993), p. 34.
4 Timothy Garton Ash, *The Uses of Adversity* (1989), p. 7.
5 Gregory Gleason, "Fealty and loyalty: informal authority structures in Soviet Asia," *Soviet Studies*, 43 (1991), pp. 613–28. See also Yaacov Ro'i (ed.), *Muslim Eurasia: Conflicting Legacies* (1995).
6 Mark Saroyan, "Rethinking Islam in the Soviet Union" in Susan Gross Solomon (ed.), *Beyond Sovietology: Essays in Politics and History* (New York, 1993), pp. 23–52.
7 M. A. Gareev, interviewed by Sergei Belanovksy, "The arms race and the burden of military expenditures" in Ellman and Kontorovich (eds.), *The Destruction of the Soviet Economic System*, pp. 40–69, p. 48.
8 Ellen Jones, *Red Army and Society: A Sociology of the Soviet Military* (1985), p. 58. Jones pointed out that the draft pool would increase again after this date. She could not, of course, know either that Soviet power would have been fatally damaged by the time that it did so or that birth rates would be declining again by the late 1980s.
9 Anatol Lieven, *Chechnya: Tombstone of Russian Power* (1998), p. 187.
10 Stephen White, *Russia Goes Dry* (Cambridge, 1996), pp. 52–4.
11 Stephen Kotkin, *Steeltown USSR: Soviet Society in the Gorbachev Era* (Berkeley, CA, 1991), pp. 39–42.
12 On the shift in the Soviet Union, see David Lane and Cameron Ross, "The Russian political elites, 1991–1995: recruitment and renewal" in John Higley, Jan Pakulski and Włodzimierz Wesołowski (eds.), *Post-Communist Elites and Democracy in Eastern Europe* (1988), pp. 34–66. From a sample of 109 members of the Soviet elite, 42 had graduated in engineering.

13 György Lengyel, "The Hungarian economic elites in the first half of the 1990s" in ibid., pp. 203–12, p. 204.

14 David Lane and Cameron Ross, "The Russian political elites, 1991–1995: recruitment and renewal" in ibid., pp. 34–66.

1. How Communism Lost

1 John Keep, *Last of the Empires: A History of the Soviet Union* (Oxford, 1996), p. 333.

2 Vladimir Shlapentokh, "Standard of living and popular discontent" in Michael Ellman and Vladimir Kontorovich (eds.), *The Destruction of the Soviet Economic System: An Insiders' History* (New York, 1998), pp. 30–39.

3 F. Hourmant, "Autour de la dissidence: intelligentsia française entre célébration et identification ennoblissante," *Revue Historique*, 601 (January–March 1997), pp. 223–50.

4 "Return to Prague: A conversation between Ivan Klíma and Philip Roth" in Ivan Klíma, *The Spirit of Prague* (1994), p. 51.

5 Lukáš Tomin, *Kye* (Prague: Twisted Spoon Press, 1997).

6 Antonin Liehm, *Trois Générations: Entretiens sur le Phénomène Culturel Tchécoslovaque* (1970), p. 305.

7 "On conversations with journalists" in Klíma, *The Spirit of Prague*, pp. 91–4.

8 Interview with Ian McEwan, in *Granta*, 11, 1984.

9 Archie Brown, *The Gorbachev Factor* (Oxford, 1997), p. 10.

10 Jacques Rupnik, *L'Autre Europe: Crise et Fin du Communisme* (1993), p. 289.

11 Leszek Kołakowski, *Main Currents of Marxism, 3: The Breakdown* (Oxford, 1987), p. 457.

12 Klíma, *The Spirit of Prague*, p. 24.

13 Timothy Garton Ash, *The Uses of Adversity: Essays on the Fate of Central Europe* (1989), p. 15.

14 Cited in Pavel Tigrid, *Le Printemps de Prague* (1968), p. 212.

15 Garton Ash, *The Uses of Adversity*, p. 7.

16 Emmanuel Todd, *La Chute Finale: Essai sur la Décomposition de la Sphére Soviétique* (1990), p. 107.

17 Veronique Soulé, *Avoir 20 Ans à l'Est* (1989), p. 65.

18 Timothy Garton Ash, *In Europe's Name: Germany and the Divided Continent* (1994), p. 201.

19 Alexander von Plato, "The Hitler Youth generation and its role in the two postwar German states" in Mark Roseman (ed.), *Generations in Conflict: Youth Revolt and Generation Formation in Germany, 1770–1968* (1995), pp. 210–26.

20 Mary Fulbrook, *Anatomy of a Dictatorship: Inside the GDR, 1949–1989* (Oxford, 1995), p. 89.

21 Soulé, *Avoir 20 Ans à l'Est*, p. 41.

22 Ibid., pp. 34–5.

23 Janine Wedel, "The ties that bind in Polish society" in Stanisłsaw Gomułka and Antony Polonsky (eds.), *Polish Paradoxes* (1991), pp. 237–60, p. 259.

24 Garton Ash, *In Europe's Name*, p. 153.

25 François Fejtö, *Budapest: L'insurrection* (1990), p. 100.

26 M. Julien, "Le problème national dans l'armée soviétique," *L'Autre Europe*, 3 (1984), pp. 48–53.

27 Mikhaïl Tsypkin, "Les conscrits," *L'Autre Europe*, 3 (1984), pp. 35–47.

28 The gulf between officers and other ranks was increased by the weakness of the NCO culture in the Soviet army, a problem inherited from Tsarist days. In 1971 a warrant officer program was introduced but this does not seem to have been very successful. See Ellen Jones, *Red Army and Society: A Sociology of the Soviet Military* (1985), p. 95.

29 Julien, "Le problème national dans l'armée soviétique."

30 Anatol Lieven, *Chechnya, Tombstone of Russian Power* (1998), p. 205.

31 The rudeness of Marshal Koulikov to his colleagues was well known: see François Fejtö with d'Ewa Kulesza-Mietkowski, *La Fin des Démocraties Populaires: Les Chemins du Post-Communisme* (1992), p. 89.

32 Alec Nove, *An Economic History of the USSR, 1917–1991* (1992), p. 412.

33 Rupnik, *L'Autre Europe*, p. 202.

34 Ibid., p. 204.

35 Soulé, *Avoir 20 Ans à l'Est*, p. 125.

36 Misha Glenny, *The Rebirth of History: Eastern Europe in the Age of Democracy* (1993), p. 32.

37 *The Economist*, November 8–14, 1997.

38 Bruce Parrott, *Politics and Technology in the Soviet Union* (Cambridge, MA, 1983), p. 117.

39 Brown, *The Gorbachev Factor*, p. 165.

40 Parrott, *Politics and Technology*, p. 134.

41 John Keep, *Last of Empires*, p. 238.

42 Basile Kerblay, "Coup d'oeil sur la robotique en URSS," *L'Autre Europe*, 1 (1984), pp. 48–50.

43 These figures refer to the years 1975–86. George Shöpflin, *Politics in Eastern Europe, 1945–1992* (Oxford, 1993), p. 199.

44 Fulbrook, *Anatomy of a Dictatorship*, p. 49.

45 Glenny, *The Rebirth of History*, p. 34.

46 Rupnik, *L'Autre Europe*, p. 291. All typewriters in Romania were registered.

47 Soulé, *Avoir 20 Ans à l'Est*, p. 222.

48 Garton Ash, *In Europe's Name*, p. 655.

49 Tsypkin, "Les conscrits."

50 Thomas Schreiber, *Hongrie, la Transition Pacifique* (1991), p. 55.

51 Hanson, *From Stagnation to Catastroika: Commentaries on the Soviet Economy, 1983–1991* (New York, 1992), p. 49.

52 *Le Monde*, August 30, 1997.

53 Moshe Lewin, *The Gorbachev Phenomenon* (Berkeley and Los Angeles, 1991), p. 86.

54 Brown, *The Gorbachev Factor*, p. 8.
55 John Dunlop, "Russia: confronting a loss of empire" in Ian Bremmer and Ray Taras (eds.), *Nations and Politics in the Soviet Successor States* (1993), pp. 43–74, p. 61.
56 P.M. "En Pologne," *L'Autre Europe*, 1 (1984), pp. 22–3.
57 Fulbrook, *Anatomy of a Dictatorship*, pp. 48–50. By 1989 the number of paid Stasi employees was between 85,000 and 105,000, while it was estimated that the number of informers was between 109,000 and 180,000.
58 Janine Wedel, "The ties that bind in Polish society" in Gomułka and Polonsky (eds.), *Polish Paradoxes*, pp. 237–60, p. 239.
59 Ibid., p. 243.
60 Brown, *The Gorbachev Factor*, p. 67.
61 Richard Staar, *Communist Regimes in Eastern Europe* (1977), p. 93.
62 Zdeněk Mlynář, *Night Frost in Prague: The End of Humane Socialism* (1980), p. 1.
63 *Le Monde*, October 28, 1997.
64 Garton Ash, *In Europe's Name*, p. 201.
65 Soulé, *Avoir 20 Ans à l'Est*, p. 133.
66 Ibid., p. 128.
67 Mlynář, *Le Froid Vient de Moscou: Prague 1968* (1978), p. 22. There is a slightly different version of this story on page 13 of the English-language version (cited for note 62).
68 Brown, *The Gorbachev Factor*, p. 41.
69 Ibid., p. 269.
70 Soulé, *Avoir 20 Ans à l'Est*, p. 203.
71 Quoted in profile by Richard Allen Greene, *The Prague Post*, October 29–November 4, 1997.
72 Olga Kryshtanovskaya and Stephen White, "From Soviet nomenklatura to Russian elite," *Europe–Asia Studies*, 48, 5 (1996), pp. 711–733, p. 725.
73 Bernard Lory, "L'histoire Bulgare au fil de ses traumatismes: 1878, 1944, 1989," *Revue d'Europe Centrale*, IV, 1 (1996), pp. 13–22, p. 18.
74 On the children of the nomenklatura, see Mervyn Matthews, *Privilege in the Soviet Union: A Study of Elite Lifestyles Under Communism* (1978), p. 159.
75 Cited in Hanson, *From Stagnation to Catastroika*, p. 79.
76 Nove, *An Economic History of the USSR*, p. 403.
77 Olga Yartseva, "Russie, les entrepreneurs et le marché d'hier et d'aujourd'hui," *L'Autre Europe*, 26 (1993), pp. 107–15.
78 *The Economist*, January 25–30, 1998.
79 Kryshtanovskaya and White, "From Soviet nomenklatura to Russian elite," p. 729.
80 Ed Clark and Anna Soulsby, "The re-formation of the managerial elite in the Czech Republic," *Europe–Asia Studies*, 48, 2 (1996), pp. 285–303.
81 Kazimierz M. Slomczynski and Goldie Shabad, "Systemic transformation and the salience of class structure in East Central Europe," *East European Politics and Society*, 11, 1 (1997), pp. 155–89.

82 Jerzy Szacki, *Liberalism After Communism* (Budapest, 1995), pp. 125 and 136.
83 Schöpflin, *Politics in Eastern Europe*, p. 254.

2. Did Capitalism Win?

 1 Nicholas Crafts and Gianni Toniolo, "Post-war growth: an overview" in Crafts and Toniolo (eds.), *Economic Growth in Europe Since 1945* (Cambridge, 1996), pp. 1–37, p. 25.
 2 Peter Hall, *Governing the Economy: The Politics of State Intervention in Britain and France* (New York and Oxford, 1986), p. 197.
 3 Yves Gauthier, *La Crise Mondiale de 1973 à nos Jours* (1989), p. 81.
 4 Ibid., p. 259.
 5 Donald Sassoon, *One Hundred Years of Socialism: The West European Left in the Twentieth Century* (1997), p. 651.
 6 Gauthier, *La Crise Mondiale*, p. 259.
 7 *Financial Times*, November 1–2, 1997.
 8 On the assumption that full employment was necessary to capitalism's survival, see Bill Warren: "It is precisely because the capitalist state is a class state that it operates a full employment policy," cited in Peter Hall, *Governing the Economy*, p. 7.
 9 Bernadette Galloux-Fournier, *Histoire de l'Europe au XXe siècle: 1974 à nos Jours* (1995), p. 97.
10 Ibid., pp. 97 and 108.
11 Paul Bagguley, *From Protest to Acquiescence: Political Movements of the Unemployed* (1991), p. 7.
12 Armand Spineux, "Trade unionism in Belgium: the difficulties of a major renovation" in Guido Baglioni and Colin Crouch (eds.), *European Industrial Relations: The Challenge of Flexibility* (1990), pp. 42–70, p. 47.
13 Gérard Noiriel, *Workers in French Society in the 19th and 20th Centuries* (Providence, RI, 1990), p. 223.
14 Mike Savage and Andrew Miles, *The Remaking of the British Working Class* (1994), p. 11.
15 Serafino Negrelli and Ettore Santi, "Industrial relations in Italy" in Baglioni and Crouch (eds.), *European Industrial Relations*, pp. 154–98, p. 160.
16 Jordi Estivill and Josep M. de la Hoz, "Transition and crisis: the complexity of Spanish industrial relations" in ibid., pp. 265–99, p. 270.
17 On the severity of unemployment among immigrants in the British Midlands, see Ken Spencer, Andy Taylor, Barbara Smith, John Mawson, Norman Flynn and Richard Batley, *Crisis in the Industrial Heartland: A Study of the West Midlands* (Oxford, 1986), p. 42. For unemployment among French immigrants see Noiriel, *Workers in French Society*, p. 225.
18 Noiriel, *Workers in French Society*, p. 225.
19 Valerie Symes, *Unemployment in Europe: Problems and Policies* (1995), p. 57.

20 In Manchester 59.7 percent of black men of African origin under the age of twenty-five were unemployed. Symes, *Unemployment in Europe*, p. 82.

21 Paul Bagguley, *From Protest to Acquiescence.*

22 Philip Armstrong, Andrew Glyn and John Harrison, *Capitalism Since 1945* (Oxford, 1991), p. 267.

23 Otto Jacobi and Walther Müller-Jentsch, "West Germany: continuity and structural change" in Baglioni and Crouch (eds.), *European Industrial Relations*, pp. 127–153.

24 Noiriel, *Workers in French Society*, p. 231.

25 *Financial Times*, November 6, 1997.

26 *Financial Times*, November 8 and 9, 1997.

27 Sassoon, *One Hundred Years of Socialism*, pp. 588 and 615.

28 Ibid., p. 481.

29 V. R. Berghahn, *Modern Germany: Society, Economy and Politics in the Twentieth Century* (Cambridge, 1987), p. 241.

30 John Maynard Keynes, "The end of laissez-faire" in *Essays in Persuasion* (1952), pp. 312–22, p. 315.

31 Galloux-Fournier, *Histoire de l'Europe*, p. 67.

32 SBC made him head of their private banking section as soon as he returned from his sabbatical.

33 Galloux-Fournier, *Histoire de l'Europe*, p. 84.

34 Ibid., p. 87.

35 Jeremy Richardson, "Policy, politics and the communications revolution in Sweden," *West European Politics*, 9, 4 (October 1986), pp. 80–97.

36 *Le Monde*, February 10, 1998.

37 Galloux-Fournier, *Histoire de l'Europe*, p. 101.

38 Kenneth Dyson, "West European states and the communications revolution," *West European Politics*, 9, 4 (1986), pp. 10–55, p. 13.

39 Keith Middlemas, *Power, Competition and the State, 3: The End of the Post-War Era: Britain Since 1974* (1991), p. 355.

40 Ibid., p. 358.

41 Walter Laqueur, *Germany Today: A Personal Report* (1985), p. 182.

42 Jean-Marie Charon, *La Presse en France de 1945 à nos Jours* (1991), p. 77.

43 *Le Monde*, June 28, 1997.

44 Alan Murie, "Housing and the environment" in Denis Kavanagh and Anthony Seldon (eds.), *The Thatcher Effect: a Decade of Change* (Oxford, 1989), pp. 213–25.

45 Jan Pen, "Expanding budgets in a stagnating economy: the experience of the 1970s" in Charles Maier (ed.), *Changing Boundaries of the Political: Essays on the Evolving Balance between State and Society, Public and Private in Europe* (Cambridge, 1987), pp. 323–62, p. 335.

46 Peter Hall, *Governing the Economy*, p. 186.

47 Alan Murie, "Housing and the Environment" in Kavanagh and Seldon (eds.), *The Thatcher Effect*, pp. 213–25, p. 219.

48 John Vickers and Vincent Wright, "The politics of industrial privatisation in western Europe: an overview," *West European Politics*, 11 (October 1988), No. 4.

49 Michael Lewis, *The Money Culture* (1991), p. 122.

50 *Financial Times*, October 11–12, 1997.

51 Jon Savage, *England's Dreaming: The Sex Pistols and Punk Rock* (1991), p. 356.

52 Ibid., p. 349.

53 Melanie Sully, *A Contemporary History of Austria* (1990), p. 68.

54 Ibid., p. 64.

55 Mark Mazower, *Dark Continent: Europe's Twentieth Century* (1998), p. 354.

56 On the moral basis of Thatcherism's enterprise culture see Paul Morris, "Freeing the spirit of enterprise: The genesis and development of the concept of enterprise culture" in Russel Keat and Nicholas Abercrombie (eds.), *Enterprise Culture* (1991), pp. 21–37.

57 Surveys conducted in 1992 cited in Paul Whitely, Patrick Seyd and Jeremy Richardson, *True Blues: The Politics of Conservative Party Membership* (Oxford, 1994), pp. 43–4.

PART V

Europe in the New World Order

1 "Europe: a golden opportunity not to be missed" originally published in the *Los Angeles Times*, reprinted in Lawrence Freedman (ed.), *Europe Transformed: Documents on the End of the Cold War* (1990), pp. 514–16.

1. New Frontiers

1 Misha Glenny, *The Rebirth of History: Eastern Europe in the Age of Democracy* (1993) p. 223.

2 On the basis of French foreign and defense policy before the fall of communism, see Philip Cerny, *The Politics of Grandeur: Ideological Aspects of de Gaulle's Foreign Policy* (Cambridge, 1980). On the attempts to adapt this policy after the fall of communism, see Philip H. Gordon, *A Certain Idea of France: French Security Policy and the Gaullist Legacy* (Princeton, NJ, 1993).

3 Philip Gummet, "Foreign, defence and security policy" in Martin Rhodes, Paul Heywood and Vincent Wright (eds.), *Developments in West European Politics* (1997), pp. 207–25, p. 217. France's spending dropped from $42,918 million (in 1993 prices) to $42,724 while Britain's spending dropped from $41,891 million to £33,861 million. Swedish spending went from $4,194 million to $4,818 million.

4 Misha Glenny, *The Rebirth of History*, p. 244.

5 Bohdan Krawchenko, "Ukraine: the politics of independence" in Ian Bremmer and Ray Taras, *Nations and Politics in the Soviet Successor States* (Cambridge, 1993), pp. 75–98, p. 88.

6 Jan Keller Sylvaine Trinh, "Marché et société en République Tchèque," *Cahiers Internationaux de Sociologie*, XCVI (1994), pp. 113–63, p. 117.

7 Jacques Capdevielle, Henri Rey and Anthony Todorov, "Bulgarie: la difficile construction d'un système partisan pluraliste," *Cahiers Internationaux de Sociologie*, XCVI (1994), pp. 191–211, p. 201.

8 Marcin Frybes and Patrick Michel, *Après le Communisme: Mythes et Légendes de la Pologne Contemporaine* (1996), p. 162.

9 Marie Halamska, "Les paysans polonais dans le processus de transition," *Cahiers Internationaux de Sociologie*, XCVI (1994), pp. 33–56, pp. 43–5. In the late 1980s most peasants had believed that the state of the country was "satisfactory"; by 1992, 90 percent of peasants, compared to 72 percent of Poles overall, believed that the state of the country was bad.

10 Frybes and Michel, *Après le Communisme*, p. 162.

11 Marcin Frybes, "Le syndicalisme en Europe centrale à la recherche d'une nouvelle légitimité sociale et politique," *Cahiers Internationaux de Sociologie*, XCV (1993), pp. 275–87, p. 286.

12 Frybes and Michel, *Après le Communisme*, p. 133.

13 François Bafoil, "Du plan au marché: le grand bouleversement" in Gilbert Casasus, Sylvie Lemasson and Sophie Lorrain (eds.), *L'Autre Allemagne, 1990–1995: L'Unification au Quotidien* (1995), pp. 179–93, p. 181.

14 Anne Olivier, "Stratégies d'appropriation du logement à Brno: vers une différenciation sociale et spatiale des quartiers" in Centre Français de Recherche en Sciences Sociales, *Cahiers du CEFRES: Anciens et nouveaux propriétaires: stratégies d'appropriation en Europe centrale et orientale*, 11 (March 1997), pp. 95–129.

15 Daniel Bertaux, "Révolution et mobilité sociale en Russie Soviétique," *Cahiers Internationaux de Sociologie*, XCVI (1994), pp. 77–97.

16 Marie-Claude Maurel, "Terre, capital, travail, vers de nouveaux rapports sociaux en Europe centrale," *Cahiers Internationaux de Sociologie*, XCVI (1994), pp. 7–31.

17 Birgit Müller, "Pouvoir et discipline, du monde du plan à celui du Marché," *Cahiers Internationaux de Sociologie*, XCV (1993), pp. 333–53, p. 343.

18 Jacqueline Heinen, *Chômage et Devenir de la Main d'Oeuvre Féminine en Pologne: Le Coût de la Transition* (1995), p. 683. In Poland 2,909 enterprises had begun to be prepared for privatisation by 1996 but only 1,000 had been sold. Among the 683 enterprises employing over 500 people that were considered in a good state, only 124 had been sold by the end of 1994.

19 Pavel Campeanu, "Roumanie: Les méandres de la privatisation," *Cahiers Internationaux de Sociologie*, XCV (1993), pp. 355–68.

20 *Le Monde*, July 30, 1997.

21 *The Economist*, November 8–14, 1997.

22 *Le Monde*, May 7, 1997.

23 Jacques Sapir, *Le Chaos Russe: Désordres Economiques, Conflits Politiques, Décomposition Militaire* (1996), p. 65.

24 *The Economist*, January 24–30, 1998.

25 *Le Monde*, October 27, 1997.

26 *Financial Times*, January 2, 1998.

27 *Le Monde*, October 27, 1997.

28 Petr Příhoda, "Mutual perceptions in Czech–Slovak relationships" in Jiří Musil (ed.), *The End of Czechoslovakia* (Budapest, 1995), pp. 128–38, p. 137.

29 Natan Eidelman, quoted in translator's introduction in Elena Subkova (translated by Hugh Ragsdale), *Russia After the War: Hopes, Illusions and Disappointments, 1945–1957* (New York, 1988), pp. vii–x, p. ix.

30 Stephen Kotkin, *Steeltown, USSR: Soviet Society in the Gorbachev Era* (Berkeley, CA, 1988), pp. 204–42.

31 Jacques Rupnik, *L'Autre Europe: Crise et Fin du Communisme* (1993), p. 114.

32 Joseph Rothschild, *Return to Diversity: A Political History of East Central Europe Since World War II* (Oxford, 1993), p. 234.

33 Glenny, *The Rebirth of History*, p. 43. The chairman of the Slovak parliament, who was against the plaque, attributed admiration for Tiso to ignorance and misunderstanding. Petr Příhoda, "Mutual perceptions in Czech–Slovak relationship," in Musil (ed.), *The End of Czechoslovakia*, p. 137.

34 *Le Monde*, May 10, 1997.

35 Glenny, *The Rebirth of History*, p. 138.

36 *Le Monde*, January 27, 1998. Note the letter of protest about aspects of this article from Ana Blandiana of the Civic Academy foundation of Bucharest in *Le Monde*, February 10, 1998.

37 Milan Hauner, "Tchèques et Allemands: hier et aujourd'hui," *L'Autre Europe*, 26–7 (1993), pp. 29–58; 42 percent of Czechs regretted the brutality of expulsion though only 4 percent supported the restitution of German goods.

38 "Introduction" in Stephen Gundle and Simon Parker (eds.), *The New Italian Republic: From the Fall of the Berlin Wall to Berlusconi* (1996), pp. 1–15, p. 11.

39 Rupnik, *L'Autre Europe*, p. 12.

40 John Dunlop, "Russia: confronting a loss of empire" in Bremmer and Taras, *Nations and Politics in the Soviet Successor States*, pp. 43–74, p. 62.

41 Thomas Hennessy, *A History of Northern Ireland* (1996).

42 Bohdan Krawchenko, "Ukraine: the politics of independence" in Bremmer and Taras (eds.), *Nations and Politics in the Soviet Successor States*, pp. 75–98, p. 82.

43 Sharon L. Wolchik, "The politics of transition and the break-up of Czechoslovakia" in Musil (ed.), *The End of Czechoslovakia*, pp. 225–44, p. 235. In April 1992, 75 percent of Czechs and 61 percent of Slovaks believed that standards of living would not be better if the countries separated.

44 Glenny, *The Rebirth of History*, p. 139.

45 In Slovenia it was $9,279, in Yugoslavia (i.e., Serbia and Montenegro) it was $1,456 and in Bosnia it was $815.

46 Peter Demetz, *Prague in Black and Gold: the History of a City* (1997), p. 355.

47 *Financial Times*, January 5, 1998.
48 *Libération*, March 20, 1997.
49 *Financial Times*, January 3–4, 1998.
50 *Financial Times*, April 4–5, 1998.
51 Ian Taylor, Karen Evans and Penny Fraser, *A Tale of Two Cities: Global Change, Local Feeling and Everyday Life in the North of England* (1996), p. 214.

2. Sexual Revolutions

1 *The Economist*, July 18, 1998.
2 Ingrig Sharp and Dagmar Flinspach, "Women in Germany from division to unification" in Derek Lewis and John Mckenzie (eds.), *The New Germany: Social, Political and Cultural Challenges of Unification* (Exeter, 1995), pp. 173–98, p. 182.
3 Alisa del Re, "Vers l'Europe: politiques sociales, femmes et état en Italie entre production et reproduction" in Annette Gautier and Jacqueline Heinen (eds.), *Le Sexe des Politique Sociales* (1993), pp. 37–57, p. 47.
4 Paul Thompson, "The pyrrhic victory of gentlemanly capitalism: the financial elite of the City of London, 1945–1990," *Journal of Contemporary History*, 32, 3 (1997), pp. 283–304.
5 David Marsh, *The Bundesbank: The Bank that Rules Europe* (1991), p. 67.
6 Anny Brooksbank Jones, *Women in Contemporary Spain* (1997), p. 85.
7 Ibid., p. 15.
8 Sharp and Flinspach, "Women in Germany from division to unification," p. 182.
9 *The Economist*, July 18, 1998.
10 Paul Ginsborg, *A History of Contemporary Italy: Society and Politics, 1943–1988* (1990), p. 350.
11 Anna Marie Smith, *New Right Discourse on Race and Sexuality: Britain, 1968–1990* (Cambridge, 1994), p. 187.
12 Scott Lash and John Urry, *The End of Organized Capitalism* (Cambridge, 1987), p. 279.
13 Smith, *New Right Discourse on Race and Sexuality*, p. 194.
14 Michael Sibalis, "Paris" in David Higgs (ed.), *Queer Sites: Gay Urban Histories Since 1600* (1999), pp. 10–37.
15 *Le Monde*, June 28, 1997.
16 Cited in Sibalis, "Paris," p. 34.
17 On the "gay village" where wealthy homosexual men spent money in one city (Manchester), see Ian Taylor, Karen Evans and Penny Fraser, *A Tale of Two Cities: Global Change, Local Feeling and Everyday Life in the North of England* (1996), pp. 190–97.
18 The importance of the "respectable homosexual" is stressed by Smith, *New Right Discourse on Race and Sexuality*.

19　Mary Buckley, "Victims and agents: gender in post-Soviet states" in Mary Buckley (ed.), *Post-Soviet Women: From the Baltic to Central Asia* (Cambridge, 1997), pp. 3–16, p. 7.

20　Jacqueline Heinen, *Chômage et Devenir de la Main d'Oeuvre Féminine en Pologne: Le Coût de la Transition* (1995).

21　Bistra Anachkova, "Women in Bulgaria" in Barbara Łobodzinska (ed.), *Family, Women and Employment in Central-Eastern Europe* (1995), pp. 55–68, p. 65.

22　Éva Fodor, "Gender in transition: unemployment in Hungary, Poland and Slovakia," *East European Politics and Society*, 11, 3 (1997), pp. 470–500.

23　Heinen, *Chômage et Devenir de la Main d'Oeuvre Féminine en Pologne*, p. 101.

24　Sarah Ashwin and Elaine Bowers, "Do Russian women want to work?" in Mary Buckley (ed.), *Post-Soviet Women from the Baltic to Central Asia*, pp. 21–37, p. 25.

25　Heinen, *Chômage et Devenir de la Main d'Oeuvre Féminine en Pologne*, p. 133. An inquiry of 1993 found that 60 percent of private firms (as compared to 7 percent of public ones) had no women at all among their senior employees.

26　Ibid., p. 103. In Poland a man with a secondary education was four times less likely to be unemployed than a man with a primary education; among women unemployment among the two groups was roughly the same. Only the small minority of women with higher education were less likely than men to be unemployed.

27　Éva Fodor, "Gender in transition: unemployment in Hungary, Poland and Slovakia," *East European Politics and Society*, 11, 3 (1997), pp. 470–500.

28　Ibid.

29　Jacqueline Heinen and Anna Matuchniak-Kraususka, *L'Avortement en Pologne: La Croix et la Bannière* (1991), pp. 73 and 80.

30　Ibid., p. 77.

31　Doina Pasca Harsanyi, "Women in Romania" in Nanette Funk and Magda Mueller (eds.), *Gender Politics and Post-Communism: Reflections from Eastern Europe and the Former Soviet Union* (1993), pp. 39–52, p. 49.

32　Jacqueline Heinen and Anna Matuchniak-Kraususka, *L'Avortement en Pologne*, pp. 185–215.

33　Lynne Attwood, "The post-Soviet woman in the move to the market: a return to domesticity and dependence?" in Rosalind Marsh (ed.), *Women in Russia and Ukraine* (Cambridge, 1996), pp. 255–66.

34　Sarah Ashwin and Elaine Bowers, "Do Russian women want to work?" in Buckley (ed.), *Post-Soviet Women from the Baltic to Central Asia*, pp. 21–37, p. 22.

35　Elena Stishova, "'Full frontal': perestroika and sexual policy" in Marsh (ed.), *Women in Russia and Ukraine*, pp. 188–95.

36　Georges Vigarello, *Histoire du Viol, XVI–XX siècle* (1998).

37　Lynne Attwood, "'She was asking for it': rape and domestic violence against women" in Buckley (ed.), *Post-Soviet Women from the Baltic to Central Asia*, pp. 99–118, p. 99.

38 Barbara Einhorn, *Cinderella Goes to Market: Citizenship, Gender and the Women's Movement in East Central Europe* (1993), p. 106.

3. New Politics?

1 Suzane Berger, "Religious transformation and the future of politics" in Charles Maier (ed.), *The Changing Boundaries of the Political: Essays on the Evolving Balance Between the State and Society, Public and Private in Europe* (Cambridge, 1987), pp. 107–50, p. 120.

2 David Broughton, "The CDU–CSU in Germany. Is there an alternative?" in David Hanley (ed.), *Christian Democracy in Europe: A Comparative Perspective* (1994), pp. 101–118, p. 106.

3 Etienne François, "L'unité dans la diversité" in Gilbert Casasus, Sylvie Lemasson and Sophie Lorrain (eds.), *L'Autre Allemagne, 1990–1995: L'Unification au Quotidien* (1995), pp. 33–40, p. 34.

4 Gilbert Casasus, "Une succession difficile" in ibid., pp. 41–51, p. 46. Manfred Stolpe, who became Socialist Minister-President of Brandenburg, had presided over the evangelical consistory of East Germany until 1989.

5 Etienne François, "L'unité dans la diversité" in ibid., pp. 33–40, p. 35.

6 Information about surviving communist parties has been taken from Lilly Marcou, *Le Crépuscule du Communisme* (1997).

7 Jacques Rupnik, *L'Autre Europe: Crise et Fin du Communisme* (1993), p. 185.

8 Nanette Funk, "Introduction: women and post-communism" in Nanette Funk and Magda Mueller (eds.), *Gender Politics and Post-Communism: Reflections from Eastern Europe and the Former Soviet Union* (1993), pp. 1–14, p. 4.

9 Jiřina Siklová, "Are women in Central and Eastern Europe conservative?" in ibid., pp. 74–83, p. 80.

10 *L'Autre Europe*, 5 (1985), pp. 87–109, interview with Wojciech Karpinski.

11 Jerzy Szacki, *Liberalism After Communism* (Budapest, 1995), p. 8.

12 Misha Glenny, *The Rebirth of History: Eastern Europe in the Age of Democracy* (1993), pp. 64–5.

13 Jean Seaton, "Political parties and the media in Britain," *West European Politics*, 8, 2 (April, 1985), pp. 9–25.

14 *Le Monde*, September 20, 1997.

15 Francis Fukuyama, *The End of History and the Last Man* (New York, 1992), p. ix.

16 Harold James, *A German Identity, 1770–1990* (1989), p. 4.

17 "Je suis Berlinois," interview with "Ralf" by Sophie Lorrain in Casasus, Lemasson and Lorrain (eds.), *L'Autre Allemagne*, pp. 24–9.

18 Françoise de la Serre, Christian Lequesne and Jacques Rupnik, *L'Union Européenne: Ouverture à l'Est?* (1994).

19 Yves Mény and Martin Rhodes, "Illicit governance: corruption, scandal and fraud" in Martin Rhodes, Paul Heywood and Vincent Wright (eds.), *Developments in West European Politics* (1997), pp. 95–113, p. 109.

20 "Introduction" in Stephen Gundle and Simon Parker (eds.), *The New Italian Republic: From the Fall of the Berlin Wall to Berlusconi* (1996), pp. 1–15, p. 5.

21 *Le Monde*, November 15, 1997.

22 *Le Figaro*, July 26 and 27, 1997.

23 David Nelken, "A legal revolution? The judges and *Tangentopoli*" in Gundle and Parker (eds.), *The New Italian Republic*, pp. 195–205.

24 Alexander Stille, *Excellent Cadavers: The Mafia and the Death of the First Italian Republic* (1996), pp. 24–5.

25 Hans Josef Horchem, "The lost revolution of West German terrorists," *Terrorism and Political Violence*, 1, 3 (July 1989), pp. 353–60.

26 *Le Monde*, February 5, 1998.

27 Ibid., January 15, 1998.

28 Ibid., January 10, 1998.

29 *Financial Times*, December 30, 1997.

30 Léonid Gordon, "Les particularités du mouvement ouvrier en Russie post-Soviétique," *Cahiers Internationaux de Sociologie*, XCV (1993), pp. 255–73, p. 256.

31 Marcin Frybes and Patrick Michel, *Après le Communisme: Mythes et Légendes de la Pologne Contemporaine* (1996), p. 96.

32 Joseph Rothschild, *Return to Diversity: A Political History of East Central Europe Since World War II* (Oxford, 1993) p. 232.

33 Fybes and Michel, *Après le Communisme*, pp. 51 and 101.

34 Francis Fukuyama quoted in Ralf Dahrendorf, *Reflections on the Revolution in Europe*, p. 34.

35 Interviewed by Jan Krauze in *Le Monde*, November 11, 1997.

Index

Page numbers in *italics* refer to the photographs.

ABB engineering group, 484
Abortion, 6, 67, 91, 106, 107, 112, 124, 126, 369, 371–372, 375, 378, 410, 487, 497–498, 519
Absenteeism, 394, 409
Abyssinia, 109, 182
Ackermann, Anton, 254
Action Française, 137, 146, 311
Aczél, György, 350
Adenauer, Konrad, 147, 305, 312, 322
Adultery, 90, 95, 99, 100
Advertising, 283, 294, 295, 296, 309, 334, 369, 495, 500
Afghanistan, 357, 387, 412, 413
Africa, 180, 182, 184, 187, 218, 265, 496, 526
Age of Reason, The (Sartre), 91
Agrarian Party (Bulgaria), 469
Agriculture, 19, 21, 26, 54, 55, 70, 149–150, 176, 191, 194, 256, 273, 281–283, 304, 469, 524; crisis in, 149, 154; vs. industry, 292, 355; political power of, 152, 167, 281–282; prices (*see* Food, prices); subsidies for, 292; women in, 113–116. *See also* Collective farms; Food
Agulhon, Maurice, 5, 23, 99
AIDS, 494, 495–496
Aircraft, 57, 151, 155, 171, 179–180, 182; antisubmarine, 188; dive-bombers, 192; F4 Phantoms, 356; MiG fighters, 356, 390; in Second World War, 180, 184, 188, 191, 192, 193, 196
Air forces, 280

Airlines, 261, 442
Alain, 95–96, 133
Alasia, Walther, 374
Albania, *233*, 250, 255, 347, 407, 418, 467, 473, 513, 525, 545; agriculture in, 469; Albanians in Kosovo, 465; communist party refounded in, 503; dissent in, 406; fall of communism in, 398, 402; and female virginity, 380; purges in, 339, 340; religion in, 364, 365; and Soviet Union, 363; vendetta of Sulejmani/Doda families in, 379
Alcatel, 449
Alcoholism/drinking, 341, 346, 354, 355, 357, 360, 394. *See also* Vodka
Alekseev (General), 56, 137
Algeria, 87, 181, 207, 243, 265, 280, 287–288, 301, 321, 332, 333, 334, 335, 336, 478
Alksnis, Viktor, 413
Alliance photo agency, 216–217
All Quiet on the Western Front (Remarque), 70
Alsace and Lorraine, 58, 176
Althusser, Louis, 393
Altruism, 419
Aluminium, 189, 284
Amalrik, Andrei, 405, 406, 545–546
Ambiguity, 406
American Federation of Labor, 261
Americanization, 482–483
Amritsar massacre, 311
Anarchism, 32, 38, 45, 50, 131, 132, 140, 332, 336

Andropov, Yuri, 390, 399, 418, 426; and survey of Soviet rulers, 476
Angelica, Pasha, 116
Angell, Norman, 44
Anglicanism, 142
Anglo-German Naval agreement of 1935, 182
Angola, 386, 387
Anpilov, Viktor, 504
Antiaircraft guns, 192
Antier, Paul, 280
Anti-Semitism, 60, 66, 74, 84, 106, 141, 160, 200, 201, 202, 206, 310, 311, 339, 345, 363, 538; and fall of communism, 478. See also Jews, extermination of
Antonescu, Ion, 478
Antonioni, Michelangelo, 218, *230*
Antonuzzo, Antonio, 324
Apparatchiks, 360, 399, 427
Apple computer company, 451
Apprenticeships, 82, 159, 408–409, 438
Argentina, 17, 196
Ariès, Philippe, 311, 532
Aristocracy, 75, 137, 139, 140, 142, 143, 185, 189, 196, 230(caption), 294, 296, 358, 426, 471
Armaments, 273, 279–281, 356, 400. See also Industry, war industries; Second World War, munitions in
Armenians, 54, 413
Armies, 22–23, 38, 40, 43–44, 47–50, 279–281, 490–491; in Algeria, 266; American, 108, 197–198, 259–260; black American soldiers, 108, 197–198; colonial, 182; demotions/promotions in, 71; desertions, 47, 48, 49, 50, 58, 187, 203, 412; and effeminacy, 96; French, 413, 515; generals, 181, 191, 195, 196, 200, 241, 255, 259, 266, 280, 281, 388, 389, 400, 411; morale in, 48, 49, 178; mutinies in, 47, 56, 266; and nationalism, 412, 413; officers, 49, 71, 72, 73, 74, 76, 80, 92, 106, 139, 178, 185, 186, 207, 241, 255, 280, 412, 413, 477; peasants in, 39, 46, 48, 49, 138, 413; Polish, 178, 255, 348, 409, 413, 477; professionalization of, 514–515; recruitment for, 412; Red Army, 107, 129, 178, 185, 190, 240, 254–255, 256, 340, 345,

348, 356, 361, 379, 386, 387, 389, 399, 412, 413, 477; Russian White army, 137, 138; soldier/civilian relations, 48; and transition to democracy, 411–413; 12th SS Panzer Division, 86; Yugoslav, 412. See also Conscription; Military spending
Arnault, Bernard, 447
Aron, Raymond, 313, 333, 374
Ashes and Diamonds (film), 242
Asquith, Raymond, 72
Assassinations, 24, 44, 90, 132, 133, 134, 149, 175, 209, 301, 332, 334, 336
Assembly lines, 156, 168
Atheism, 364
Atom bomb, 171, 197, 250, 330, 354. See also Nuclear weapons
Attlee, Clement, 71, 300
Aubert, Théodore, 129
Auden, W. H., 527
Aung San Suu Kyi, 514
Auriol, Vincent, 258
Auschwitz, 186, 201, 205, 210
Australia, 51
Austria, 28, 93, 128, 179, 302, 452, 456; Austrian League of Religious Socialists, 145; Christian democrats in, 302, 303, 318, 320; coalitions in, 302; economy, 445; and European Economic Community, 443; female enfranchisement in, 116; and First World War, 44–45, 51, 66; integration with Germany, 172; market economy in, 26; peasants in, 27, 55; after Second World War, 249–250, 479; socialism in, 32, 36, 37, 302, 303, 305, 324
Austria-Hungary, 16, 22, 24, 36; and First World War, 44, 45, 49, 50, 51, 58, 66; starvation in, 239; successor states of, 140
Austrian Socialist Party, 36, 37
Azerbaijan, 412
Azov factory (Soviet Union), 355

Baader, Andreas, 334, 336, 527
Bacílek, Karol, 351
Baden, 146
Bad Godesberg conference of 1959, 324
Bailey, David, 218, 230–231(captions)
Bainville, Jacques, 65, 137
Baker, Kenneth, 451, 453

Balcerowicz, Leszek, 510
Baldwin, Stanley, 300
Ballin, Albert, 17
Baltic states, 206, 481
Bank Clerks' Association (England), 34
Bank of England, 164, 447
"Bank Robber" (record), 455
Banks, 52, 277, 295, 296, 298, 327, 386, 414, 429, 438, 446, 448, 454, 472, 473, 485
Banning of books, 402–403
Barrie, J. M., 79
Bartering, 474
Barthes, Roland, 296
Bartosek, Karel, 534
Basques, 146, 334, 335, 514
BATA shoe company (Czechoslovakia), 459
Bavaria, 29, 38, 106, 117, 298; Catholic Church in, 144–145, 146
BBC. *See* British Broadcasting Corporation
Beatles, The, 312
Beaton, Cecil, *225*
Bedaux system, 155, 157
Belgium, 32, 34, 37, 84, 85, 117, 135, 249, 265, 284, 302, 443, 515; Bois du Cazier mining disaster (1956), 285; Christian democrats in, 320, 322; education in, 438; and First World War, 46, 52, 54, 58, 166; immigrants in, 286(table); industry in, 153, 272; Socialist Congress (1933), 165; Social Party in, 40, 166
Belgrade University, 80
Bell, Daniel, 295, 297, 313
Bengal, 194, 528
Benjamin, René, 103
Berenson, Bernard, 19
Berezovsky, Boris, 472
Bergen-Belsen concentration camp, 201
Bergman, Ingrid, 216
Beria, Lavrenti, 253, 345
Berl, Emmanuel, 142
Berlin, 33, 38, 82, *228*, 241, 374, 394, 397, 398, 408, 422; battle for, 240; Berlin Wall, 287, 465–466, 468; blockade of, 248; East Berlin, 358, 471, 535; infant mortality in, 239; rapes by Red Army in, 107

Berliner Illustrierte Zeitung, 216
Berlusconi, Silvio, 508
Berman, Jakub, 252–253
Bernabei, Ettore, 312
Bernstein, Eduard, 37
Bertolucci, Bernardo, 371
Besançon, Alain, 91–92, 354
Bethlen, István, 142
Bethmann Hollweg, Theobald von, 51, 185
Beveridge, William, 70, 307
Bevin, Ernest, 261
Bichelonne, Jean, 158
Bidault, Georges, 146, 301, 321
Biermann, Wolf, 422
Bim the Clown, 130
Birkenhead (Lord), 72
Birth control, 92, 124, 125, 371, 378, 490, 497, 498. *See also* Abortion; Contraceptives
Birth rates, 18, 28, 77, 82, 89, 123–126, 369, 373, 378, 380, 487, 499; among Muslims, 387, 389
Biryuzov (General), 251–252
Bishops, 146
Black Death, 528
Black markets, 54, 142, 208, 240, 357, 358–359, 417, 420, 535
Blacks, 108, 197–198, 264, 439, 457, 486
Blair, Tony, 489, 501
Blitzkrieg, 180, 187, 190
Bloch, Ivan, 45
Bloch, Marc, 1, 78, 84
Bloody Sunday, 336
Bloomsbury group, 11–12, 104, 167
Blow-Up (film), 218, *230*
Blum, Léon, 37, 166, 261, 517
Boegner (Pastor), 142
Bogni, Rudi, 448
Bogomolov, Oleg, 418
Bohemia, 415
Bois du Cazier mining disaster (1956), 285
Bolshevism, 25, 41–42, 56, 57, 58, 60, 83, 92, 131, 138, 144, 151, 254, 479; divisions in, 130; as secular church, 143
Bonino, Emma, 371
Bonner, Elena, 524
Booth, Cherie, 489

Borel, Suzanne, 174
Borsellino, Paolo, 512
Bosnia, 466, 500
Bosnia Herzegovina, 45
Bossi, Umberto, 482
Bourdieu, Pierre, 289
Bourgeoisie, 3, 7, 11, 12, 30, 33, 34, 37, 38, 40, 46, 60, 65, 89, 95, 113, 120, 122, 126, 132, 162, 260, 261, 263, 282, 294, 306, 328, 334, 339, 341, 342, 374, 426, 525, 536; Catholic, 311; and education, 289, 360, 361; English, 154; and homosexuality, 99, 104; and prostitution, 102, 103. *See also* Middle class
Bourguignon, Philippe, 484
Boutemy, André, 279
Bouton, André, 95
Boutros-Ghali, Boutros, 484
Bouvet, Éric, *235*
Bové, José, 483
Bowie, David, 456
Boycotts, 433, 460, 517
Bradbury, Malcolm, 243
Brandenburg, 107
Brandt, Willy, 366
Branson, Richard, 456
Brasillach, Robert, 66, 81
Bratislava, 352, 363–364, 422, 476, 477; University of Bratislava, 364
Bratsk, 360
Braudel, Fernand, 120
Brave New World (Huxley), 155
Brazil, 17
Breast feeding, 93
Breathless (film), 264
Brenan, Gerald, 101
Breslau conference (1895), 29
Brest-Litovsk, Treaty of, 43, 50, 57, 58
Bretton Woods Agreements, 433
Brezhnev, Leonid, 270, 352, 386, 390, 422, 427(n); Brezhnev doctrine, 401; and survey of Soviet rulers, 476, 477
Briand, Aristide, 173
Bribes, 359, 390, 512
Britain, 7–8, 15, 18, 21, 22, 27, 33, 34, 36, 40, 52, 67, 90, 92, 101, 166–167, 284, 309, 468, 491, 528; abortion in, 371; aircraft industry, 193; Aliens Act in, 16; British Union of Fascists in, 73, 137, 167; Butler Education Act of 1944, 289; cars in, 152; Civil Service

in, 110, 277; Clause IV in, 324; coal industry in, 441; colonies of, 181, 183, 197, 265, 285; Communist Party in, 492, 504; consensus politics in, 300; diplomats in, 173–174; divorce in, 371; economic elite in, 277; economy, 167, 176, 274, 276, 277, 291, 293, 301, 437, 438, 445, 446–447, 449, 453; education in, 81, 85, 288, 289; EMI factory in, 159; and European Economic Community, 443; and extermination of Jews, 210; female employment in, 113; female enfranchisement in, 116; and First World War, 43, 44, 46, 47, 49, 50, 51, 52, 53, 54, 58, 59–60, 69, 72–73, 81; foreign workers in, 285; homosexuality in, 371, 372–373, 494, 495; industry in, 153, 165, 193, 276, 277, 449; and Japan, 445; labor supply in, 297; leisure in, 168–169, 170; life expectancy in, 54; literature of Second World War in, 87; marriage in, 370; middle class in, 66, 154; Militant organization in, 494; military spending in, 279, 281; Minister of Information Technology in, 451; National Health Service, 301, 307; navy of, 182, 183, 187, 188; Nazi Party in, 84; newspapers in, 311; Parliament in, 305, 372; planning initiatives in, 276; political homogeneity in, 305–306; public schools in, 81, 85; public spending in, 452; rationalization of production in, 157–158; religion in, 310; royal family in, 120, 312; and Second World War, 64, 108, 193, 196, 197, 240; SOGAT in, 450; strikes in, 440–441; unemployment in, 438; and United States, 188–189, 263; war pensions in, 70. *See also* Conservative Party; Labour Party; Thatcher, Margaret
British Broadcasting Corporation (BBC), 101, 169, 312
British Coal, 441
British Institute of Bankers, 110
British Legion, 72
British Marriage Guidance Council, 368
British Petroleum, 516
Brittany, 27
Brooke, Rupert, 72, 87
Brown, Irving, 261

Browning, Christopher, 205
Brusilov (Marshal), 144
Bucharest, 397, 398
Buckley, Mary, 496, 547
Budapest, 30, 58, 65, 84, 107, 348, 350, 352, 353, 365, 386, 476, 480, 499, 504, 529; infant mortality in, 239. *See also* Hungary, uprising of 1956
Budker Institute for Nuclear Physics, 416
Bukharin, Nikolai, 163
Bulanyi, Gyorgy, 410
Bulgaria, 4, 43, 66, 107, 139, 149, 174, 207, 249, 250, 251–252, 256, 407, 496; agriculture in, 469; communist party refounded in, 503; coup d'état (1923), 129; dissent in, 406; executions in, 251; fall of communism in, 398, 401–402, 427–428; and First World War, 54, 55, 58, 66; purges in, 340, 341, 343; religion in, 364, 365; secret police files in, 475; Union of Democratic Forces in, 469
Bull Computer company, 451
Bulletin de l'Entente Internationale Contre la Troisième Internationale (Aubert), 129
Bundesbank, 298, 314, 443, 444, 489
Bunich, Pavel, 429
Burchill, Julie, 386
Burger King, 483
Burmese Days (Orwell), 109
Business associations, 277, 278
Butler, R. A., 282
Byrnes, James, 261

Calabria, 20, 90, 96
Camus, Albert, 512
Canada, 17, 18–19, 265, 405
Capa, Robert, 216–217, 218, *220, 226*
Capital goods, 272, 284, 357
Capitalism, 7, 33, 36, 38, 39, 150, 165, 166, 167, 193, 260, 261, 280, 299, 325, 332, 334, 354, 458–460, 543; and communism, 331, 426, 472, 504, 524; complexity of capitalist societies, 392, 408, 458; and conservatism, 456–458, 459; consumer capitalism, 309, 495, 525; and corruption, 512; crises in, 433–434 (*see also* Depression period); cultural contradictions of, 295–296, 297; in Eastern Europe, 473,

474; and fall of communism, 395, 430–431; and imperialism, 388; in 1980s, 447–448, 495; and privileges of nomenklatura, 426; reforming, 307; and rock music, 454–456; and socialism, 503; success of, 390–391, 394–395, 503; transformation of in 1980s, 434; as winner, 433–460; and youth, 392, 423, 427
Carlos the Jackal, 514
Carpenter, Edward, 104
Cars, 151–152, 155, 160, 169, 242, 244, 274, 275, 284, 291, 356, 357–358, 420, 427(n); sales of, 294, 296–297. *See also* Motor industry
Cartels, 165, 264
Cartier-Bresson, Henri, 216–217, 218, 225(caption)
Casement, Roger, 98
Casualties, 182. *See also under* First World War; Second World War
Catholic Action, 146, 148, 302, 320
Catholicism, 19, 37, 73, 84, 85, 86, 92, 103, 117, 124, 142, 142(n), 143, 144, 205, 261, 271, 310, 317, 349, 405, 487, 489–490, 539; Catholic parties, 320; Catholic women in France, 315; concordats of, 146, 147; divisions in, 146; and Fascism, 148, 165; left-wing of, 321; Marian cults, 76; and national cultures, 364, 365–366; and secular authorities, 365–366, 367, 409–410, 411, 502; and trade unions, 321, 322, 324; and women, 315, 490; and working class, 366, 409. *See also* Christian democrats; Religion
Cavalry, 47
CDU. *See* Christian Democratic Union
Ceauçescu, Nicolae, 397, 401, 522
Celibacy, 106, 145, 283
Censorship, 352, 413, 420, 429
Central Intelligence Agency (CIA), 260, 262
Centre Party (German), 117, 142, 145, 147, 148, 322
Cevelotto, Mario, 261
Ceyrac, François, 331–332
Chamberlain, Neville, 171, 215
Change, 291, 394, 430, 448, 464, 515, 519; in politics/economics, 470(table); 514, 520, 524, 527. *See also* Social change

Channel Tunnel, 446
Chaplains, 76
Chaplin, Charlie, 156
Chapman, Guy, 72, 94–95
Charlot, Jean, 319
Chartier, Emile. *See* Alain
Chastity, 89, 93, 99, 100, 105, 106
Chechnya, *235*, 363, 513, 524, 526
Cheka, 130
Chemapol industrial empire, 430
Chernenko, Konstantin, 390
Chernobyl, 415
Chernomyrdin, Viktor, 472
Chevalier, Gabriel, 100
Chevènement, Jean-Pierre, 501
Chicago, 457
Children, 24–25, 28, 70, 75, 76, 82–83,
    92, 96, 106, 112, 121, 122, 124, 168,
    194, 210, 239, 288, 294, 307, 317,
    325, 375–376, 489, 518, 523; born in
    last months of Second World War,
    244–245; of communists, 344, 346,
    428; illegitimate, 90, 93, 95, 101, 125,
    126, 376; killing of, 241; knowledge of
    the West of, 428; of nomenklatura,
    428; of peasants, 360, 364; raising,
    120–121, 369, 490; of rapes, 105, 106;
    violence against, 6, 379–380; of work-
    ers, 360, 428, 488; working, 291. *See
    also* Students; Youth
Chile, 512, 524, 530(n)
China, 431
Chirac, Jacques, 479
Christian Democratic Union (CDU,
    Germany), 305, 315, 321–322, 502,
    511. *See also* Germany, Christian
    democrats in
Christian democrats, 300, 301, 305, 310,
    320–324, 365, 369, 395, 427, 456,
    464, 492, 502, 523, 543; and social
    democracy, 337; and socialists, 324,
    332; success of, 322. *See also under*
    Women; *individual countries*
Christian Social Party (Austria), 27
Christian Union (Germany), 37
Christ Stopped at Eboli (Levi), 30
Chubais, Anatoly, 391
Churchill, Winston, 133, 188, 189, 195,
    248
CIA. *See* Central Intelligence Agency
Cigarettes, 194, 260
Cinema, 180. *See also* Films

Citicorp, 456
Cities, 120, 201, 282, 323, 374, 485, 486,
    487, 495; building new, 163, 360; capi-
    tals, 403, 404; vs. countryside, 26–27,
    31, 137–142, 282, 292, 296, 307, 468
    (*see also* Countryside, migration to
    cities from); right to live in, 360, 361.
    See also Urbanization
Citroën, André, 111
Civil service, 289, 314, 363, 448, 452
Civil society, 133, 419–421
Civil wars, 43, 64, 128–150, 528; sources
    of, 149–150. *See also under* Greece;
    Russia; Spain; Yugoslavia
Clarke, Peter, 536
Clash, The (rock group), 455
Class issues, 65, 72, 76, 102–104, 169,
    204, 205, 230(caption), 316–317, 320,
    393, 486, 500, 517–519; class conflict,
    131, 147, 309; class consciousness, 408,
    414; classlessness, 243; and homosexu-
    ality, 104; new classes, 325, 362, 483,
    489; and working women, 117–118,
    517. *See also* Bourgeoisie; Middle class;
    Underclass; Upper/ruling classes;
    Working class
Clemenceau, Georges, 50
Clementis, Vladimir, 342
Clerical work, 34–35, 71
Clochemerle (Chevalier), 100–101
Clothes/fashions, 244, 260, 294, 317,
    370, 392, 421, 423
Club Med, 295–296
Coal, 152, 153, 158, 159, 160, 162, 165,
    189, 193, 272, 273, 283–284, 316,
    435, 438, 441, 472, 491; Bois du
    Cazier mining disaster (1956), 285
Coalitions, 301, 302, 304, 307, 327
Coffee, 194
Cohn-Bendit, Daniel, 333, 504, 512, 530
Coitus Punk Group, 422
Cold War, 242, 248, 281, 299, 306, 365,
    466, 526
Collective farms, 115, 116, 119, 130,
    138–139, 341, 355, 361
Colonialism, 181–182, 183, 387–388
Columbia Records, 454–455
Comecon, 265, 416
Cominform, 265, 300, 330, 363
Comintern, 129, 130–131, 132, 139, 174
Common Agricultural Policy, 294
Common Market, 265, 272, 305, 480

Communes, 28, 29, 114, 115, 138
Communication(s), 22, 25, 101, 130, 134, 209, 310, 388, 507–508
Communism, 65, 83–84, 98, 99, 132, 171, 198, 205, 299, 300, 325, 327–335; and abortion, 497–498; anti-communism, 306–307, 324, 326, 328, 464, 466, 475, 513; attitudes toward the family, 376; belief in vs. career advancement, 424, 426; and Catholic Church, 144, 148, 365, 365, 411; communist-dominated governments, 250; communist parties, 249, 257, 330, 331, 347, 363, 416, 503–504; communist parties and Soviet Union divergence, 330, 331, 363; communist reformers, 420, 421, 469, 503–504; communist rule remembered, 465; compared with Nazism, 405–406, 540; containment of, 256–258; crisis of, 386; and democracy, 330; de-Stalinization and national Communist Parties, 347; economic failure of, 414; end of, as management buyout, 429–431; Euro-communism, 331; fall of communist rule, 4–6, 268, 386, 391, 394, 397–432, 464, 465, 467, 468, 477, 478, 485, 486, 498, 504, 505, 513, 518, 519–520, 524, 525, 545–548; and generational divisions, 422, 423; and humanism, 530; liberal communists, 401; and nationalist movements, 265; Party Congress of 1971, 416; reformed communist parties, 503–504; rejection of, 243, 530; and religion, 143; simplicity of communist system, 392; social effects of communist rule, 359–366; and technology, 155; Twelfth Congress of Czech Communist Party, 351; writers' conferences, 352; youth organizations, 408, 429. *See also* Bolshevism; Comintern; Eastern Europe; Leadership, communist; Lenin, V. I.; Stalin, Joseph
Company Parade (Jameson), 80
Competition, 165, 356, 358, 388, 483; and technology, 450
Computers, 171, 388, 389, 392, 400, 416–417, 435, 449, 507, 512, 517, 525; and business culture, 451
Concentration camps, 98, 186, 199, 201, 203, 208, 240, 405; camp guards and

killing squads in, 204–206; Slovak, 478
Concordats, 146, 147
Confédération Générale du Travail, 326, 375
Conformism, 421, 451
Congress of Tours (1920), 139
Conscription, 22, 40, 51, 53, 55, 72, 178, 180, 181, 279, 491
Consensus, 336–337. *See also* Cultural issues, culture of consensus; Politics, consensus politics
Conservatism, 20–21, 26–27, 29, 30, 39, 55, 65, 84, 93, 98, 112, 120, 307, 403, 487, 504, 519; ambiguities of, 137; and capitalism, 456–458, 459; and communism, 497–498; vs. fascism, 135–136, 137; and religion, 142, 143; and women, 117–118. *See also* Politics, political right
Conservative Party (Britain), 73, 122, 282, 301, 305, 308, 309, 310, 315, 317, 371, 392, 395, 456, 457–458, 483, 489
Consociational politics, 302–303
Conspicuous consumption, 294–295
Conspiracies, 342
Consumer goods, 272, 281, 282, 294, 295, 354, 356, 357–358, 360, 400, 427(n), 444
Consumerism, 244, 294, 295, 296, 309, 327, 332, 388, 509
Contested takeovers, 447
Contraceptives, 102, 371, 487, 498. *See also* Birth control
Convoys, 188
Cooper, Duff, 129
Cooperatives, 26, 35, 217
Cordasco, Antonio, 19
Cornec, Josette, 93
Corporations, 450, 472; multinationals, 445, 446, 473, 484, 516
Corporatism, 145, 155, 164–165
Corruption, 147, 290, 322, 323, 390, 400, 420, 421, 426, 463, 473, 474, 493, 511–512, 521
Cosmopolitanism, 339
Council of Europe, 300, 514
Countryside, 83–84, 100, 113, 115, 125, 164, 296, 304, 366; communism in, 329–330; evacuations to, 121; and First World War, 55; gender relations in,

114, 116; migration to cities from, 282, 283, 296, 323, 469; politics in, 26–30. *See also under* Cities
Coutrot, Jean, 156, 161
Coventry, 276
Credit, 26, 28, 35, 295, 296
Crete, 184, 187
Crime, 98, 130, 203, 241, 264, 438, 440, 457, 511, 518, 519; juvenile, 82, 87
Crises, 66, 385, 386, 389, 395, 411, 414, 433; of the left, 460
Croatia, 20, 24, 85, 141, 143, 148, 149, 206, 363, 412, 465–466, 477–478
Croce, Benedetto, 133
Croix de Feu, 73, 83
Crossman, Richard, 307, 314–315
Csurka, István, 432
Cuba, 265, 269, 270
Cult of personality, 346
Cult of the dead, 72
Cultural issues, 170, 393; and agriculture, 282; American cultural influence, 264, 482–483; business culture, 450–451; cultural assimilation, 208, 288; cultural capital, 289; cultural change and economic growth, 291; cultural contradictions of capitalism, 295–296, 297; culture of consensus, 308–309, 310; national cultures, 363, 364, 366; popular culture, 370–371. *See also* Youth, youth culture
Currencies, 154, 175, 273, 276, 390, 433, 443–444, 446
Curzon (Lord), 122, 174
Cuthbertson, Munro, 95
Czechoslovakia, 3, 36, 64, 88, 131, 176, 177, 240, 248, 249, 251, 252, 254, 264, 287, 403, 418, 428; Charter 77 movement in, 402, 424; Church in, 364; Communist Party in, 351, 352, 387, 421, 424; communist past in, 476; de-Stalinization in, 350–353, 358; dissent in, 404, 405, 406, 424; economy, 354, 418, 430; educated classes in, 362; expulsions of Germans from, 479; fall of communism in, 397, 401–402, 407, 465; first Czech Republic, 379; and First World War, 50, 51, 58; life expectancy in, 415; loans of, 386–387; mining industry in, 416; and NATO, 466; purges in, 338, 339, 340, 342, 344, 351, 358; reformist Marxism in,

405, 424; Slovaks in, 363–364, 365, 476, 477, 479 (*see also* Slovakia); and Soviet Union, 363; students in, 408; tuberculosis in, 239; workers in, 409. *See also* Czech Republic; Prague
Czech Republic, 466, 471, 481–482, 486, 496, 519; Christian Democratic Party in, 502

d'Abernon (Lord), 183
Dalmatia, 141
d'Annunzio, Gabriele, 173
Darnand, Joseph, 71
Darré, Walther, 115, 141
David, Elizabeth, 240
Davies, Gavyn, 391
Davies, Norman, 535–536
Davis, Natalie Zemon, 262
Dawes, Charles, 176
Déat, Marcel, 105, 167, 263
Death penalty, 174, 305, 344, 375, 512, 514
de Beauvoir, Simone, 91, 105, 113, 370, 403
Debray, Régis, 333
Debt, 414, 446, 490
Defenders of territory, 47, 48–49
Deflation, 445
de Gasperi, Alcide, 148, 322
de Gaulle, Charles, 51, 63, 70, 150, 179, 181, 196, 197, *225*, 257, 258, 260, 263, 266, 302, 316, 332, 333, 395, 479; assassination attempts on, 301; and birth control, 371; and Churchill and Roosevelt, 195; return to power in 1958, 305; and television, 312; and women voters, 319, 491
de Man, Hendrik, 165, 166
Delors, Jacques, 444, 484
Del Ponte, Carla, 512
Demetz, Peter, 482–483
de Michelis, Gianni, 463
Democracy, 4, 29, 73, 135, 147, 152, 180, 257, 259, 299, 307, 322, 333, 405, 426, 466, 509–510, 520, 523–524, 529; and communism, 330; transitions to, 398, 406, 407, 411–413
Démocratie Chrétienne, 321
Democratic Party (U.S.), 20
Denmark, 43, 124, 207, 208, 289, 437; and European Economic Community, 443
Dépêche de Toulouse, 311

Deportations, 63, 139, 363, 413, 526. *See also under* Jews
Depression period, 66, 70, 111, 141, 145, 157, 159, 165, 176, 181, 291, 325, 487
Desgranges, Jean, 147
de Tarde, Alfred, 79
Détente, 252, 270, 367
Diary of a Nobody (Grossmith and Grossmith), 35
Dimitrov, Georgi, 341
Diplomats/diplomacy, 173–174, 175, 251, 267, 270, 538
Discharged Soldiers' Federation (Britain), 72
Disease, 12, 16, 44, 46, 47, 54, 82, 98, 100, 129, 201, 239, 240; venereal, 107. *See also* AIDS
Disney corporation, 482, 483, 484
Dissidents, 5, 146, 201, 246, 361, 362, 367, 390, 410, 416, 418, 422, 425, 466, 508, 513, 51, 533; apoliticism of, 407; and avoiding violence, 431; as created by the West, 402–403; East/West comparison of, 393; and fall of communism, 397–398, 402–407, 430, 464, 505, 506; in Soviet Union, 394; states' tolerance of, 404
Divorce, 96, 112, 368, 371, 375, 487, 493
Djilas, Milovan, 80, 247, 362–363, 467
Djuretic, Veselin, 477
Doisneau, Robert, 216, 217, *231*
Dollars, 433, 446
Dollfuss, Engelbert, 129
Don Camillo novels (Guareschi), 329
Dorgères, Henry, 137, 141
Dorriot, Jacques, 136, 167
Doubles, 233(caption)
Dowries, 114, 160
Dreyfus, Alfred, 73–74
Drieu la Rochelle, Pierre, 94, 96, 136
Drucker, Peter, 453
Drugs, 496
Dubček, Alexander, 248, 352, 353, 364, 397, 405
Duisenberg, Wim, 444
Dulles, John Foster, 270
Dumas, Roland, 512
Dumitrescu, Constantin Ticu, 475
Dutschke, Rudi, 332

Earthquakes, 16
Eastern Europe, 5, 18, 20, 21, 45, 46, 56, 63, 64, 65, 66, 88, 149, 177, 240, 241, 243, 246, 267, 338–367, 413, 463, 472, 473, 480, 528, 538, 544–545; capital cities in, 403; cars in, 358; change in, 394, 464; communist parties refounded in, 503–504; compared with noncommunist world, 403, 417; compared with Soviet Union, 386; computers in, 417; debt in, 414, 415(table); dissidents in, 393, 402–407, 418; economies in, 354–359, 408, 525; education in, 360–361; emancipation in, 375–380, 464; expulsion from political parties in, 340; and extermination of Jews, 206; fall of communism in, 397–432 (*see also* Communism, fall of communist rule); and First World War, 51, 54, 60, 69; fragmentation of, 176; generational rifts in, 421 (*see also* Generational divisions); and Germany's economic orbit, 177; and great literature, 403; languages in, 364; opposition to communist rule in, 387; purges in, 339–345 (*see also* Stalin, Joseph, purges of); and sexual equality, 375; and sexual revolution, 496–500; social democratic parties in, 502–503; social mobility in, 23–24; Soviet influence in, 197, 198, 249–256; universities in, 84; women's work in, 376–378, 496; workers in, 407–409 (*see also* Working class). *See also* Warsaw Pact; *individual countries*
East Germany, 5, 248, 249, 251, 252, 254, 256, 297, 345, 354, 414, 470, 509, 513; abortion in, 497; CDU in, 502; communist party refounded in, 503; communist past in, 474–475; dissent in, 406; education in, 287; fall of communism in, 397, 401–402, 407; religion in, 364, 365, 410; Soviet barracks in, 418; Stasi in, 417, 420; students in, 410; visits to West Germany from, 417; women in, 377–378
Ecology, 334, 406, 411, 415, 459
Economic issues, 20, 32, 65, 82, 102, 271–298, 353–359, 481, 531; and American army in Europe, 260; black and gray economies, 420, 488 (*see also* Black markets); booms, 463; consumer economy vs. capital goods industry, 357; convergence of developed/unde-

veloped economies, 274; cost controls, 281; differences in communist bloc economies, 354–359; economic crisis of 1974–1975, 433–434; economic elite, 277–279, 489, 515; economic failure of communism, 414; economic growth, 149, 162, 163, 171, 242, 244, 245, 246, 262, 271–272, 273, 274, 284–285, 287, 289, 290, 291, 294, 296, 297, 298, 307, 336, 353–354, 385, 400, 433, 434, 515, 524, 525; economic liberalism, 307, 318, 392, 395, 457; economic management, 307–308; economic risks, 293; economics as zero sum game, 292; economic value of education, 288–290; economists, 391, 401, 452, 526; and education, 288–290; and First World War, 52–53, 66, 77, 175; formal vs. informal economies, 358–359 (*see also* Black markets); free markets, 167, 263, 307, 318, 394, 456, 469, 473, 484, 497, 510, 524; gross domestic product (GDP), 430, 433, 434, 437, 453, 482, 525; gross national product (GNP), 272, 459, 482, 535; household economic units, 114–115; and international considerations, 443–446; in interwar Europe, 152–154, 157; macroeconomics, 436, 453; market economies, 25–26, 29, 56, 141, 388, 390, 473, 484, 517, 524; mixed economies, 503; new economy, 497; planning, 155, 162, 163, 164, 165–168, 191, 275–276, 307, 324, 354–355, 358, 360, 391, 416–417, 453, 473; quantity vs. quality, 391, 435; and refugees, 286–288; and Second World War, 189–194; and Stalinism, 340–341; and technology, 449–452; and war, 45, 194. *See also* Inflation; Politics, and economics; Rationalization of production

"Economic Possibilities for Our Grandchildren" (Keynes), 524

Economist, The, 239

ECSC. *See* European Coal and Steel Community

Edelweiss Pirates, 86

Eden, Anthony, 71

Education, 22, 23, 24, 34, 36, 44, 46, 79, 80, 81, 86, 101, 139, 161, 205, 242, 271, 277–278, 286, 287, 293, 304, 305, 308, 360–361, 362, 373, 374, 391, 428, 438, 483, 488, 497, 518; agricultural, 115; Catholic, 143, 145, 146, 148; economic value of, 288–290; exclusion from, 65, 66, 209, 290, 360, 393; in management, 160; and quality of labor, 288; vocational, 289, 290, 437, 443; of women, 103, 498. *See also* Literacy; Universities

Edward VIII, 120

Eichmann, Adolf, 201–202, 209, 210

Einaudi, Luigi, 263

Einsatzgruppen, 186, 201, 202

Eisenhower, Dwight, 108, 281

Eisner, Maria, 217

Elections, 358, 401, 408, 483, 502, 515, 516, 524; and reformed communist parties, 503–504

Electricity, 284, 296

Electronics, 357, 388, 417, 434, 442, 444, 449, 450, 488

Eliot, T. S., 142, 142(n)

Elites, 374, 387, 398, 402, 472, 483–485, 522, 547; age of Soviet/Russian, 427; new elites, 391–392; post-communist, 430–431; transnational, 465. *See also* Economic issues, economic elite; Upper/ruling classes

Ellis Island, 7, 18, 19

Emigration, 15–21, 174–175, 350, 418. *See also* Immigration

Émigrés, 267, 478

Employment, 25, 28, 35, 82, 151, 240, 280, 323, 333, 341, 357, 360, 445, 459, 482; by American army in Europe, 260; clerical, 34–35, 110–111, 156; during First World War, 54–55; and moonlighting, 420, 451; in public sector, 30, 39, 52, 70, 111, 125, 126, 277, 287, 288, 289, 293, 305, 322, 393, 452; quotas concerning, 111; in service sector, 434; and technology, 450; white-collar, 156, 289, 306, 325, 360–361, 408, 491; of women, 109–113, 126, 159 (*see also* Women, and work). *See also* Labor; Working class

EMS. *See* European Monetary System

Encyclopaedia Britannica, 528

End of Ideology, The (Bell), 313

Energy, 283–284

Engineers/engineering, 158, 160, 161, 162, 164, 279, 377, 378, 391, 488, 497; engineering vs. finance, 449
Entrepreneurs, 289, 293–294, 295, 350, 394, 429, 474, 507
Environment, 415, 460, 490, 511, 515–518, 519. *See also* Ecology; Pollution
Espionage, 178, 364
Estonia, 176, 206, 249, 387
ETA, 335
Ethnic cleansing, 500
Eton, 81
Eugenics, 125, 211, 530
Eulenburg, Philipp von, 97
Eurocurrency, 446
Europe; ages of political leaders in 1933, 85(table); alternative history of, 528–529; Central Europe, 472, 474, 479, 480, 528, 538 (*see also* Eastern Europe); empires of, 387–388; first/last decades of, 528; generalizations about, 523–527; integration of, 301, 307, 327, 443, 463, 468, 482, 522; interwar period, 64–67, 79–80, 92, 97, 99, 104, 111, 115, 146, 149, 150, 152–154, 157, 167, 171, 172–183, 242, 256, 283, 291, 439–440, 537–542 (*see also* First World War, postwar period); in 1900, 10(map); 1914–1945 period, 1–3, 6; in 1925, 62(map); in 1949, 238(map); in 1950s/1960s, 245, 283, 304; in 1994(map), 462; at peace in 1940, 63, 64; postwar spheres of influence in, 248, 264–269; pre–1914 period, 12–13, 122, 124, 149, 171, 486, 525, 536; rewriting of history in, 474–480; unification of, 468–474, 505; western Europe, 248–249, 256–258, 390, 391, 468, 486, 500, 504, 542–544. *See also* Eastern Europe
European Coal and Steel Community (ECSC), 265, 300
European Commission, 511
European Community, 444, 445, 446, 468
European Defense Community, 265
European Economic Community, 299, 301, 443, 484
European Monetary System (EMS), 443–444

European Parliament, 300, 331, 502, 505, 516
European People's Party, 300
European Social Chapter, 459
European Union, 438, 459, 468, 482, 483, 484, 485, 510, 522, 523
Euthanasia, 75, 199
Executions, 102, 106, 124, 136, 139, 146, 149, 163, 170, 186, 187, 195, 196, 203, 205, 206, 241, 250, 257, 279, 340, 342, 345, 348, 397, 514
Experts/technicians, 325

Fabius, Laurent, 392
Falcone, Giovanni, 512
False consciousness, 317
Families, 6, 33, 112, 119–122, 126, 127, 264, 309, 317, 332, 368–381, 394, 420, 518; East/West differences concerning, 381; family contacts, 160; and party loyalty, 375, 380; and state-sponsored emancipation, 375–380; traditional/nuclear, 121, 123, 245, 294, 368, 369, 380, 464, 490, 498. *See also* Values, family values
Famine, 54, 58, 59, 82, 138, 139, 144, 194, 240. *See also* Hunger/starvation
Fanfani, 493
Fascism, 35, 60, 64, 65, 67, 71, 73, 84, 171, 307, 325, 540; and Catholic Church, 148; and homosexuality, 98, 494; and modernity, 135; and Nazism, 134; and technology, 155; and youth and war generation, 80. *See also under* Conservatism; Italy
Fatherland Party, 51
Federal Republic of Germany. *See* West Germany
Fédération Républicaine (France), 147
Fejtö, François, 64–65, 533–534
Feminism, 99, 112, 122, 127, 334, 369, 372, 460, 491, 492, 496, 497, 513, 517
FIGs. *See* Russia, Financial Industrial Groups in
Films, 101, 114, 135, 151, 216, 243, 264, 294, 350, 370, 469, 482; about female sexuality, 125; about German occupation of France, 106; about photographers, 218; after Second World War, 242, 275
Finance, 445, 446–449, 457, 488–489, 497

Financial Times, 391, 444, 457

Fini, Gianfranco, 480

Finland, 20, 51, 64, 116, 117, 128, 172, 177, 189, 197, 207, 208; and European Economic Community, 443; after Second World War, 249–250, 252, 255–256

Findlandization, 252

Finniston, Sir Monty, 449

First World War, 3, 20, 22, 43–60, 79, 93, 94–96, 113, 153, 174, 175, 300, 528, 537; armistice of November 11, 58; casualties in, 8, 43, 46, 47, 48, 50, 56, 58, 59(table), 77, 172, 316; and civilians, 43, 44, 53–56, 65, 80; desertions in, 47, 48, 49, 50, 58; discipline in, 47–48, 49, 56, 74; eastern front, 47, 57; equipment loss in, 59; Jews in, 209; legacy of, 66, 69–77, 116, 175, 178, 537; opposition to, 39, 40, 41, 48, 55; origins of, 44–46; and photography, 215; postwar period, 60, 69, 106, 109, 368, 369 (*see also* Europe, interwar period); prisoners captured in, 49–50; Russian-German armistice, 57; survivors of, 70–71; trench warfare in, 46, 47, 48, 57, 71, 94; western front, 43, 46, 47, 48, 57, 69–70; winners/losers, 56–60

Fischer, Joschka, 516

Fitzpatrick, Sheila, 534, 538

Fiume, 173

FLN, 336

Foch (General), 57, 123

Folklore, 31

Fontaine, André, 505

Food, 121, 135, 208, 239, 244, 308, 386, 417, 426; food industry, 159; imports, 53; junk food, 440; prices, 17, 55, 56, 167, 282, 531; rationing, 273; and Second World War, 191, 192, 193, 194; shortages, 54, 193, 356, 360. *See also* Famine; Hunger/starvation

Football, 170, 439, 508

Force Ouvrière, 262, 326

Ford Committee, 18

Ford, Henry, 152; Fordism/post-Fordism, 155, 435, 432, 443, 464

Foreign Legion, 182

Forests, 415

Forster, E. M., 11, 35, 97, 108

Foucault, Michel, 494, 508

FPO. *See* Freedom Party (Austria)

France, 7, 12, 15, 18, 21, 25, 26, 28, 32, 33, 34, 37, 52, 55, 81, 92, 131, 249, 393, 483, 528; abortion in, 371; agriculture in, 115, 154, 280; *alternance* in, 337; apparentement law of 1951, 304; birth control in, 371; birth rates in, 123, 124–125; cars in, 152, 274, 296–297, 358; catastrophists in, 166; Centre d'Études Économiques, 279, 314; Centre National des Indépendants, 303, 315; Conseil National du Patronat Français, 279; *chambres d'agriculture,* 115; Christian democrats in, 315, 316, 320, 321, 322; civil servants in, 278, 452; colonies of, 181, 265, 285, 388; Commissariat du Plan, 275–276; Communist Party in, 257, 259, 261, 299, 302, 306, 327, 329, 330–331, 334, 450; computers in, 451; Conseil d'État, 330; Conseil National du Patronat Français, 279, 331; consumption in, 296; corruption in, 511; defense spending in, 467; defensive warfare in, 180–181; and depression period, 66, 167, 176, 177; diplomats in, 174; École Nationale d'Administration in, 278, 314, 330, 448, 483, 489; École Normale Supérieure, 333; École Polytechnique in, 158, 280; economic elite in, 277–278, 279, 280; economy, 177, 272, 276, 277–278, 285, 287–288, 290, 291, 293, 306, 433, 434, 444, 446, 453; education in, 288, 483–484; factory occupations of 1936, 168; family life in, 120; Fédération du Livre in, 450; female employment in, 113; female enfranchisement in, 117, 119; and First World War, 43, 44, 45, 46, 47, 48, 49, 50, 51, 52, 53, 54–55, 58, 59–60, 69, 73–74, 75, 95–96, 105, 110, 178; Fifth Republic, 301, 302, 315, 333; Fourth Republic, 258, 301, 303, 304, 315, 316, 318; French Revolution, 308, 318; Front de Libération Nationale, 335; Front Économique, 280; Front National in, 456; General Secretariat for Youth, 87; German invasion/occupation of, 63, 67,

105, 121, 172; homosexuality in, 97, 99, 372, 494, 495; immigrants in, 286(table); industry in, 153; Institut d'Études Politiques in, 484; Jews in, 207, 208, 478; Keynesianism in, 314; at the liberation, 105–106, 217, 263; life expectancy in, 54; marriage in, 370; middle class in, 66, 306; military spending in, 279; Mouvement des Citoyens in, 501; and NATO, 466, 467; new politics in, 501; newspapers in, 311; nuclear weapons of, 467; ORTF in, 312; peasants in, 21–22, 26, 27–28, 29, 46, 114, 116, 140–141, 152, 274, 285, 306; and Poland, 137; political system in, 301–302; Popular Front in, 129, 132, 158, 166, 169, 170; protests of 1968 in, 331–334, 374, 375, 543; Radio Courtoisie in, 507; reconciliation of Church and state in, 76; religion in, 309; resistance in, 479, 494, 514; and Second World War, 136, 191, 196, 197, 479, 540; service sector in, 434; sexual relations in French empire, 109; socialism in, 32, 37, 39, 166, 170, 302, 304, 319, 458; social mobility in, 23–24; Third Republic, 84, 99, 100, 124, 147, 365, 413; trade union leaders in, 275; treaties of 1920s, 176; two-party politics in, 302; veterans in, 72, 73–74, 83; Vichy government, 74, 86–87, 97, 99, 103, 105, 112, 116–117, 120, 124, 125, 137, 141—142, 143, 146–147, 158, 165, 166, 171, 207, 279, 333, 372, 479, 539 (see also Pétain, Philippe); voting in, 315; war literature of, 95–96; war pensions in, 70; and West Germany, 197, 444; workers in, 374–375, 443; working women in, 488; youth in, 85. See also Paris; under United States

Franco, Francisco, 128, 129, 132, 136, 137, 140, 146, 150; demonstrations against, 333; and Spanish Foreign Legion, 182. See also Spain, Civil War in

Franco-Prussian War, 59

Franz Ferdinand (Archduke of Austria), 44

Frasyniuk, Władysław, 507

Free Democratic Party (Germany), 317

Freedom fighters, 243

Freedom Party (FPO, Austria), 318, 456–457, 529

Frégéac (blacksmith), 329

Freikorps (Germany), 74

Frejka, Thomas, 344, 375

French Telecom, 450

Freud, Sigmund, 79, 91, 92

Frey, Roger, 313

Friends, 309

Fritsch (General), 98

Frost, David, 312

Fukuyama, Francis, 508, 520, 527

Furet, François, 5, 393

Futurism, 155

Futurist Cooking (Marinetti), 135

Gaidar, Yegor, 391

Gaitskell, Hugh, 314–315

Galeazzo Ciano (Count), 174

Galicia, 56

Gallipoli, 43

Gapon (Father), 143

Garton Ash, Timothy, 387, 406, 408, 546

Gasparri, Pietro, 148

GATT. See General Agreement on Tariffs and Trade

Gaumy, Jean, 234

GDP. See Economic issues, gross domestic product

Gender, 20, 76, 110, 204, 316, 393, 519, 533, 547; divisions in countryside, 114, 116; equality of the sexes, 375, 489; genderquake, 496; imbalance between the sexes, 369, 376; and interests, 317; male power, 490 (see also Masculinity); men/women relations, 90, 122, 368, 373, 464; and voting, 315; and work, 377, 489

General Agreement on Tariffs and Trade (GATT), 443

Generals. See under Armies

Generational divisions, 78, 79, 80, 81, 83, 87, 204, 205, 244, 373–374, 374–375, 391–392, 427–428, 430, 469–470, 486; in East vs. West, 421; and opposition to communism, 422, 423

Geneva Convention, 186

Genocide, 199–211

George VI, 120

Georgia, 24, 130

Gerasimov, Gennady, 353

German Democratic Republic. *See* East Germany
German Farmers' League, 27
Germany, 2, 16, 18, 21, 26, 27, 28, 37, 52, 71, 82, 93, 128, 174–175, 182–183, 256; agriculture in, 114, 152; American army in, 260; birth rates in, 123; cars in, 152; Catholic Church in, 144–145; Christian democrats in, 315, 320, 322, 502 (*see also* Christian Democratic Union); Communist Party in, 86, 98, 131; and depression period, 178; divided into zones, 197; economy, 55, 59, 157, 178, 278, 287, 293; education in, 24, 157, 289; ethnic Germans, 240, 256, 363, 478–479, 480; female enfranchisement in, 116; female wages in, 111; and First World War, 44, 45, 46, 48–49, 50, 51, 57, 58–59, 65–66, 69, 74–75; generational division in, 88; homosexuality in, 97, 372; industry in, 263–264, 278, 409; Law for Protection of German Blood and Honor (1935), 106; market economy in, 26, 29; peasants in, 27, 55, 113–114, 116, 141; reconciliation of Church and state in, 76; reunification of, 509; and Second World War, 63–64, 88; servant problem in, 123; socialism in, 38, 40, 311; trade unions in, 52–53; veterans in, 74–75; war pensions in, 70, 75; Weimar Republic, 74, 75, 84, 117, 123, 129, 175, 287, 311, 324, 336; youth movements in, 79. *See also* East Germany; Nazi Germany; West Germany
Gheorghiu-Dej, 340
Gide, André, 164
Gierek, Edward, 348
Gilbert, Felix, 532
Girard, David, 495
Giroud, Françoise, 87
Giscard d'Estaing, Valéry, 309, 314, 427
Glemp (Cardinal), 411
Globalization, 392, 482, 511
GNP. *See* Economic issues, gross national product
Godard, Jean-Luc, 264
Godley, Wynne, 444
"God Save the Queen," 456
Goebbels, Joseph, 112, 202
Goering, Hermann, 112, 179, 191, 202

Gold, 176, 179, 446
Goldman Sachs investment bank, 448
"Gold plating" weapons, 356
Goldstücker, Eduard, 425
Gömbös, Gyula, 129, 140
Gomułka, Władysław, 340, 346, 347, 348
Göncz, Árpád, 247
González, Felipe, 419
Goodbye to All That (Graves), 94
Gorbachev, Mikhail, 215, 252, 353, 379, 397, 398–399, 404, 416, 419, 424–425, 466, 480, 483, 498, 502, 546; advisers of, 418; early success of, 426; and survey of Soviet rulers, 476, 477. *See also* Reforms, of Gorbachev
Gorbachev, Raisa, 419, 499
Gorky, Maxim, 98
Gottwald, Klement, 341, 342, 351
Government spending, 275, 307, 308, 321, 444, 452, 510
Graham, Billy, 365
Gramsci, Antonio, 23, 132, 156, 504
Grant, Duncan, 11
Graves, Robert, 72, 76, 94
Great War. *See* First World War
Greece, 4, 43, 64, 128, 173, 174, 266, 284; Christian democrats in, 502; civil war in, 299; democracy in, 390; economy, 274, 354, 434, 525; and European Economic Community, 443; and First World War, 58; Jews in, 201, 202, 207; and Second World War, 187, 194, 257
Greene, Graham, 81, 102, 175, 242
Green parties, 492, 505, 515–517; Green Party (Austria), 319; Green Party (West Germany), 467, 492, 505, 515, 516
Grey, Sir Edward, 528
Groener-Ebert pact, 41
Grossmann, Anita, 67
Grossmith, George and Weedon, 35
Grósz, Károly, 504
Grozny, *235*, 526
Guareschi, Giovanni, 329
Guderian, Heinz, 179
Guerin, Daniel, 104
Guesde, Jules, 40
Guinea, 523
Guinness, Diana, 99
Gurari, Samari, *219*

Gvishiani, Dzhermen, 428
Gypsies, 199, 200, 480, 486

Hague, William, 493
Haig (Field Marshal), 72
Hale, Kathleen, 127
Halévy, Elie, 44
Haley, Bill, 244
Halifax (Lord), 195
Hallyday, Johnny, 370
Hamburg, 33, 122, 240
Hamburg-Amerika line, 17
Hanson, Philip, 546
Hanson Trust corporation, 447
Hapsburg Empire. See Austria-Hungary
Hart, Basil Liddell, 71, 133, 179
Harvard, 157
Havel, Václav, 397, 402, 404, 405, 421,
    422, 466, 475, 478–479, 505–506,
    522; and European Union, 510
Healey, Denis, 325
Heath, Edward, 308
Helsinki Agreements (1975), 270, 402
Henriot, Philippe, 149
Herriot, Édouard, 315
Heseltine, Michael, 295, 453
Heydrich, Reinhard, 202, 210
Higgins, Patrick, 372
Hilberg, Raul, 203, 206, 532–533
Himmler, Heinrich, 86, 202, 210
Hindenburg, Paul von, 71, 134
Hintzy, Jacques, 309
Hirsch, Freddy, 210
Hirschfeld, Magnus, 93, 104
Historians, 1–2, 3, 4, 6, 15, 35, 64, 137,
    177, 199, 240, 242, 243, 272, 279,
    294, 311, 344, 476, 477, 478, 494,
    522, 530, 531; alternative histories
    constructed by, 528–529; autobiogra-
    phies of, 532–534; revisionist, 250;
    sources of, 534
Hitler, Adolph, 63, 71, 75, 90, 112, 152,
    154, 179, 181, 183, 189, 191, 224; and
    beer hall putsch of 1923, 129; and
    extermination of Jews, 201–202 (see
    also Jews, extermination of); and
    Mussolini, 134; policies in Second
    World War, 194–195; and radio broad-
    casts, 169; and Stalin, 177, 209. See also
    Nazi Germany
Hitler Youth, 86, 88, 121, 298, 409, 480
Hiwis (volunteers), 206

Hobsbawm, Eric, 264, 522, 535
Hoffmann, Heinrich, 224
Holiday, Billie, 264
Holland. See Netherlands
Hollande, François, 489
Holocaust, 215. See also Jews, extermina-
    tion of
Home and Work (journal), 156
Homosexuality, 67, 92, 93, 94, 95, 96–99,
    104, 174, 199, 372, 375, 493–496;
    commercialization of, 495; legalizing,
    97, 371; lesbians, 123
Honecker, Erich, 421
Horner, Edward, 72
Horthy (Admiral), 137, 139, 142, 251,
    343, 350
Housework, 377, 490, 497
Housing, 33, 341–342, 360, 376, 378,
    437, 452, 471, 499, 518
Howards End (Forster), 11, 12, 35
Hoxha, Enver, 233, 340, 545
Hughes, John, 19
Hugo, Victor, 483
Humanism, 530
Human nature, 75–76
Human rights, 270, 402, 431, 466, 512, 530
Hunchback of Notre Dame (film), 483
Hungary, 4, 21, 28, 50, 60, 64, 65, 66,
    67, 84, 129, 137, 139–140, 142, 160,
    174, 175, 207, 247, 248, 249, 251,
    252, 284, 401, 418, 471; Church in,
    364, 410, 411; communist party
    refounded in, 503; communist past in,
    476; de-Stalinization in, 348–350,
    351–352; dissent in, 404, 405, 406,
    422; economic leaders in, 391; econo-
    my, 350, 359, 414, 420, 509; fall of
    communism in, 398, 407; female
    enfranchisement in, 116; Hungarian
    language, 107; inflation in, 240; Iron
    Cross in, 135, 149; and NATO, 466,
    508; Protestants in, 410; PSOH in,
    504; purges in, 339, 342, 343, 349;
    and Second World War, 189; sexual
    division in, 119; and Soviet Union,
    363, 419; uprising of 1956, 241, 242,
    243, 254, 255, 267, 303, 324, 328,
    348, 351, 352, 378, 399, 406, 408,
    431, 474, 529; and Warsaw Pact, 466;
    women in, 116, 378, 496, 497
Hunger/starvation, 12, 21, 44, 45, 47, 54,
    57, 82, 126, 129, 194, 201, 239, 240,

526, 528. *See also* Famine
Hunting, 426, 426(n)
Husák, Gustáv, 353, 402, 476
Huxley, Aldous, 155
Huysmans, Camille, 40

IBM, 451, 452, 459
Ideology, 320, 328, 332, 342, 406, 416
IG Farben, 53, 153, 165
IG Metall, 441
Il Popolo, 312
IMF. *See* International Monetary Fund
Immigration, 30, 36, 101, 154, 271,
    286(table), 290, 390, 392, 438, 517;
    desirable/undesirable immigrants,
    18–19; repatriation of immigrants, 18;
    treatment of immigrants, 19; women
    immigrants, 20. *See also* Emigration
Imperial Chemical Industries, 165
Incomes, 295, 306, 317, 373, 374, 436,
    485; of Soviet scientists, 416. *See also*
    Wages
Independents, 303
India, 108–109, 181, 182, 265, 285
Indochina, 181
Industry, 25–26, 35, 53, 56, 84, 112, 141,
    152–153, 176, 256, 267, 272, 275,
    280, 283–284, 309, 316, 321, 472,
    482, 515, 524; vs. agriculture, 292,
    355; consumer, 169, 272, 377 (*see also*
    Consumer goods); deindustrialization,
    249, 414, 434; export, 133; after First
    World War, 153; heavy industry, 393,
    408, 414, 435, 438, 439, 440, 488,
    490, 491, 492, 497, 517, 518; indus-
    trial cities, 360; industrial concentra-
    tion, 290–291; industrialization, 15,
    27, 29, 33, 36, 46, 111, 121, 138, 152,
    245, 254, 354, 376, 434, 471; industri-
    al relations, 292, 326, 408 (*see also*
    Strikes); luxury goods industry, 447;
    ministers of, 453; nationalized, 454 (*see
    also* Nationalization); printing industry,
    450, 452; war industries, 86, 110,
    118–119, 122, 153, 280, 356, 400 (*see
    also* Armaments)
Inequality, 525
Infant mortality, 239, 354, 384(map)
Inflation, 3, 4, 12, 55, 56, 58, 59, 60, 77,
    113, 136, 240, 297, 298, 433, 434,
    436, 453, 470, 472, 474, 525
Influenza, 54, 57

Informers, 420, 475
INSEAD business school, 484
Institute for Sexual Science, 93
Institute for World Economics, 268
Institute of Economics of the World
    Socialist System, 418
Intelligentsia, 12–13, 49, 199, 246, 296,
    328, 350, 352, 362, 514, 517;
    Eastern/Central European intellectuals,
    393, 480, 528 (*see also* Dissidents);
    Western intellectuals, 403
International Institute of Applied Systems
    Analysis (Vienna), 428
Internationalism, 392, 402, 417–419,
    443–446, 465, 482–483, 511, 515
International Monetary Fund (IMF), 445
International relations, 173, 174, 177, 363
International Tribunal of the Hague, 512
International Women's Day, 118
Internet, 507. *See also* Computers
Invalids, 70
Investments, 175–176, 193, 272, 314,
    445, 446, 447, 450
Iran, 387
Iraq, 181, 182, 386
Ireland, 27, 51, 89, 128, 143, 259, 285,
    514; contraception in, 371; economy,
    449; and European Economic
    Community, 443; Irish immigrants, 15,
    19–20, 31; Irish Tourist Board,
    487–488; Northern Ireland, 334, 335,
    481, 527
IRI. *See* Italy, Industrial Reconstruction
    Agency
Iron, 52, 152, 153, 279, 354, 357
Irrigation, 292, 293
Islam, 387. *See also* Muslims
Isorni, Jacques, 30
Israel, 339, 433
Is War Now Possible? (I. Bloch), 45
Italian Popular Party (PPI), 147, 148
Italy, 21, 28, 30, 32, 35, 55, 80, 92, 129,
    174, 249, 258, 285, 309, 332, 358,
    438, 443, 480, 504, 515, 547–548;
    agriculture in, 152; airforce of, 180;
    American army in, 259–260; birth
    rates in, 125, 487; challenge to mas-
    culinity in, 96; Christian democrats in,
    259, 263, 278, 300, 302, 305, 306,
    311, 312–313, 319, 320, 322–324,
    327, 336, 395, 464, 493, 502, 512,
    543; Church/state relations in, 76, 117,

146, 147; Communist Party in, 170,
257, 259, 263, 299, 310, 311, 313, 329,
330, 331, 336, 419; contraception in,
371; corruption in, 511; Dopolavoro
in, 169, 170; economic elite in, 278;
economy, 272, 273, 274, 276, 278,
290, 293, 359, 440, 444, 445, 525,
535; education in, 288; Fascism in 53,
65, 72, 80, 83, 102, 110–111, 118,
125, 128, 133–134, 135, 140, 141,
145, 148, 153, 155, 157, 322, 391,
541; female office workers in,
110–111; and First World War, 43,
47–48, 49, 50, 58, 69, 74; generational
divisions in, 83; gross national product
of, 535; Industrial Reconstruction
Agency (IRI), 276, 278, 454; Italian
immigrants, 15, 17, 18, 19, 20, 125;
Jews in, 203, 207; labor supply in, 297;
and Libya, 46; malaria in, 16; military
spending in, 193; Ministry for the
Family in, 369; Ministry of Public
Works, 327; National Agency for the
Scientific Organization of work, 156;
Northern League in, 482; nuns in, 113;
peasants in, 66–67, 140; RAI in, 312;
Red Brigade in, 334, 335, 336, 374,
514; and Second World War, 189, 273;
sexual relations in African empire, 109;
socialism in, 32, 312–313, 324, 325,
327, 336; strikes in, 440; trade union
leaders in, 275. *See also under* United
States

Jackson, Janet, 456
Jagger, Mick, 370–371
Jakeå, Miloå, 387
James, Harold, 509
Jameson, Storm, 80
Japan, 182, 189, 197, 438, 441, 442, 445
Jaruzelski, Wojciech, 255, 398, 411, 413,
475
Jaurès, Jean, 37, 38
Jazz music, 170, 264, 363, 422
Jeune République, 85, 147
Jeunesse Ouvière Chrétienne, 85
Jews, 2, 3, 4, 16, 18, 63, 64, 75, 141, 173,
174, 175, 185, 339, 340, 361, 405,
471, 505; assimilation of, 208; deporta-
tions of, 201, 202, 207, 208, 210;
euphemisms for killing, 203; exclusions
from education, 65, 66, 209; extermi-

nation of, 199–211, 363, 478, 480,
533, 541; French, 73–74, 186; leaders,
208–209; non-German complicity/
resistance in extermination of Jews,
206–208, 210–211; penalties for help-
ing, 203; in Poland, 200 (*see also*
Poland, Warsaw ghetto in); psycholo-
gists, 92–93; reactions to Nazism, 84,
208–210
John, Augustus, 127
John Paul II (Pope), 409
John XXIII (Pope), 365–366
Joke, The (Kundera), 338, 344, 421–422,
545
Jospin, Lionel, 504, 516
Joyce, James, 91, 101, 488
Judiciary, 512
Junek, Václav, 429–430
Junkers, 185

Kádár, János, 343, 345, 346, 348,
349–350, 353, 365, 401, 509, 510,
529
Kadaré, Ismail, 380, 418, 485, 545
Kadyrov, A., 429
Kalashnikov rifles, 356–357
Kamenev, Lev Borisovich, 163
Károlyi, Michael, 139
Kasztner, Rudolf, 209
Katyn massacre, 241, 477
Kautsky, Karl, 37
Kazakhstan, 466
Kéhayan, Jean, 269
Kelly, Petra, 492
Kennan, George, 267
Kennedy, Paul, 386
Kerensky, Alexander, 56
Keynes, John Maynard, 11, 12–13, 66, 90,
154, 160, 164, 166, 167, 275, 285,
314, 447, 524, 525, 526, 538
KGB, 215, 269, 399, 418–419, 429, 430,
523
Khaldei, Yevgeni, *219, 228–229*
Khanin, Gregory, 268, 269
Khrushchev, Nikita, 242, 252, 266, 270,
354; deposed, 345, 347; secret speech
of, 345–346, 348, 351; and survey of
Soviet rulers, 476; and Tito, 265
Kiesinger, Kurt, 321–322
King, Lord, 456
Kinnock, Neil, 501
Kipling, Rudyard, 80

Kir, Felix, 303
Kirkpatrick, Ivone, 174
Kissinger, Henry, 270
Kitchener (British General), 50
Klaus, Václav, 391
Klemperer, Victor, 204
Klíma, Ivan, 404, 405
Koenig, Franz (Cardinal), 366
Koestler, Arthur, 65
Kohl, Helmut, 70, 479–480, 502, 521
Koïta, Yaguine, 523
Kołakowski. Leszek, 405, 506
Kollontai, Alexandra, 127, 370
Kondratiev cycles, 463
Königsberg, 107
Konrád, György, 480, 506
Korean War, 255
Kornilov (General), 56
Kosovo, 388, 465, 467, 486, 513, 526
Kostov, Traïtcho, 343
Kosygin, Alexei, 428
Kotkin, Stephen, 546
Koudelka, Josef, 232
Kovács, Béla, 251
Kriegel, Annie, 5, 113, 208, 393, 532
Kristallnacht (1938), 202
Kristol, Irving, 506
Kronstadt uprising, 130
KuOan, Milan, 466
Kuehnul, Karel, 351
Kun, Béla, 65, 139
Kundera, Milan, 88, 338, 344, 363, 404, 407, 421, 468, 480, 485, 530, 545
Kye (Tomin), 403

Labor, 26, 121, 153, 163, 169–170, 199, 282, 284–290, 297; conscripted, 273; costs, 433; defeats for, 440, 441; disputes, 277 (see also Strikes); forced/slave labor, 164, 241, 476; Jewish, 201, 210; labor brigades, 340, 361; labor camps, 340, 361, 378; Labor Charter of 1941 (France), 165; labor movements, 32, 38, 103–104, 118–119, 145, 308, 392; labor relations, 292, 436–443, 450, 456, 459 (see also Industry, industrial relations); migrant workers, 4, 16, 17, 18, 285, 286, 296; in Second World War, 190–191; shortages, 376; skilled workers, 131. See also Employment; Trade unions; Working class

Labor Parties of Netherlands, Norway, Sweden, 324
Labor-saving devices, 377
Labour Party (Britain), 32, 37, 40, 131, 132, 166, 280, 300, 301, 307, 313, 314–315, 324, 326, 327, 391, 494; New Labour Party, 501, 517–518
La Cicciolina, 418
Ladurie, Emmanuel Le Roy, 243, 312
Lady Chatterley's Lover (Lawrence), 96, 244, 369, 370
La Garçonne (Margueritte), 96
La Gazette du Bon Ton, 216
Lambert, Kit, 243
La Nausée (Sartre), 370
Lancaster, Osbert, 372–373
Lancet, The, 76
Land ownership, 21, 27, 28–29, 55, 138, 139, 140, 283, 304, 363, 471
Language, 22, 24, 36, 51, 107, 188, 205, 245, 247, 263, 267, 286, 288, 363, 438, 469; English, 484–485; foreign languages, 364; French, 484, 485; multilingual dissidents, 405; political language and fall of communism, 505–506; and sexual morality, 101–102; study of classical, 289; swearing, 149
La Nouvel Observateur, 371–372
La Règle du Jeu (film), 99, 103
Larkin, Philip, 369–370
Lark Rise to Candleford (L. Thompson), 97
Last Tango in Paris (film), 371
Lateran Treaty of 1929, 92
Latin America, 243, 525
Latvia, 176, 206, 249
Laval, Pierre, 70
La Vie Ouvrière (magazine), 231(caption)
Lawrence, D. H., 92, 93, 96, 103, 370, 494
Lawson, Nigel, 449
Leadership, 194–196, 267, 300, 313, 515, 516, 530; age of communist, 421; of business, 391; Church leaders, 310; communist, 253–254, 303, 330, 331, 341, 342, 343–344, 346, 347, 348, 351, 353, 392, 394, 399, 402, 408, 418, 421, 423, 425, 426–427, 427(n), 476, 479 (see also Leadership, Soviet); from dissident movements, 406; of European Union, 468; and fall of communism, 427; Jewish,

208–209; of Moscow coup in 1991, 425; of 1968 protests, 333; Polish leaders in London, 477; purged, 249; socialist, 325, 326; Soviet, 243, 341, 345, 353, 389, 394, 399, 401, 418, 476; survey concerning Soviet, 476; of trade unions, 275, 331, 392, 440; women's loyalty to, 316; of youth culture, 246; youth of, 391–392

League of Nations, 176, 181

League of St. Brigid, 89

Lebanon, 181

Lebed, Alexander, 413

Le Blanc à Lunettes (Simenon), 109

Le Chien Jaune (Simenon), 102

Le Corbusier, 154–155

Légion Française des Combattants, 74

Le Grand Hiver (Kadaré), 545

Lehmann, Rosamond, 127

Leipzig, 397

Leisure, 161, 168–170, 171, 379

Le Midi Libre, 452

Le Monde, 311

Lend-Lease, 196

Lenin, V. I., 41, 56–57, 130, 143, 144, 156, 161, 362, 385(n), 533; Leninism, 387–388, 392, 397, 502, 504; and survey of Soviet rulers, 476, 477

Leningrad, 126, 186, 194, 355

Le Noeud de Vipères (Mauriac), 119

Lepercq, Aimé, 158

Lessing, Doris, 530–531

Levi, Carlo, 20, 30–31, 101

Levi, Primo, 64, 210

Lewin, Moshe, 2, 163, 533

Lewis, Michael, 454

Lewis, Norman, 293

Lewis, Wyndham, 155

Liberal International, 300, 457, 507

Liberal Party (Britain), 166–167

Liberal Party (Netherlands), 457

Libération, 457

Libertarianism, 493

Libya, 46, 387

L'identité (Kundera), 485

Life expectancy, 54

Life magazine, 216

Lira revaluation (1926), 154

Literacy, 18, 20, 22, 24, 25, 31, 159, 288, 438

Lithuania, 2, 16, 64, 146, 173, 176, 177,

206, 206, 249, 387, 466, 481, 503

Little Entente, 176

Liverpool, 187, 439

Living standards, 194, 246, 272, 280, 309, 358, 414, 417, 418, 509–510, 524, 531; urban vs. rural, 283. *See also under* Working class

Lloyd George, David, 50–51, 167

Lloyds Bank (Britain), 34, 44

Loans, 386–387, 414, 446

Lobbying, 282, 290

Locarno Agreement of 1925, 176

Łódź, 201, 208

London, 230(caption), 243, 244, 374, 438, 439, 446, 447, 485, 489, 495; Gay Pride demonstration in (1997), 493; Greater London Council, 493

London, Artur, 328, 342

London School of Economics, 484

Lost generation, 72, 79

Lost Traveller, The (White), 81

Lotta Continua (Italy), 335

Low Countries, 63, 172. *See also individual countries*

Luchaire, Jean, 79

Ludendorff, Erich von, 57, 71

Luftwaffe, 180, 192, 193

Luniku, Kristaq, 473

L'Unita, 311

Luther, Hans, 202

Lutyens, Sir Edwin, 72

Luxembourg, 265

Luxemburg, Rosa, 36

Lvov (Prince), 53, 56

Maastricht treaty, 444, 468

Mabey, Nick, 516

Macarthur, Mary, 118

Macaulay, Thomas Babington, 1

MacDonald, Ramsay, 32, 149, 326

McDonald's, 482–483

Macedonia, 466

McGowan, Cathy, 244

Machines, 151, 154–155, 156, 164, 171, 292, 355, 443, 471. *See also* Mechanization

McKibbin, Ross, 536

McKinsey management consultancy, 448, 484

Macmillan, Harold, 71, 72–73, 312, 314, 489

Madagascar, 63, 200
Mafia, 140, 260, 292–293, 302
Magazines, 216, 218, 283, 317
Maginot line, 172, 176
Magneti Marelli, 102, 153, 154, 158, 159, 160
Magnitogorsk (Soviet Union), 152, 163, 379, 390, 476, 546
Magnum photo agency, 217, 218, *223*, 232(caption)
Major, John, 392
Makine, Andrei, 485
Malaria, 12, 16
Malaya, 108
Malenkov, Georgi, 345, 348
Malraux, André, 81
Managers/management, 158, 160–161, 277, 293, 295, 355, 376, 388, 401, 402, 414, 417, 421, 428, 441, 450, 451, 459, 473, 515, 535; American management techniques, 484; consultancies, 448; and fall of Polish communism, 430; Japanese management techniques, 442; management buyout, 429–431; management vs. unions, 441–442; and ownership, 448, 452; women managers, 492, 496
Manchester Guardian, 311
Mancini, Giacomo, 327
Mandates, 181
Mandelson, Peter, 501
Mangin (Marshal), 182
Mann, Thomas, 406
Mannerheim, Carl Gustav, 51, 189
Mannheim, Karl, 79
Manufacturing, 434, 435(table), 445, 517. *See also* Industry
Mao Tsetung, 333, 345
Marchais, Georges, 264, 479
Marcou, Lilly, 3, 266, 338–339, 344, 375, 533, 545
Margolius, Heda, 342, 352, 353
Margolius, Rudolf, 341, 346
Margueritte, Victor, 96
Marinetti, Filippo, 135
Márquez, Gabriel García, 528
Marriage, 92, 96, 146, 160, 189, 317, 368, 370–371, 378, 379, 380, 487, 493; marriage loans, 111, 112
Marseilles, 287
Marshall Plan, 259, 260, 262, 264–265, 275, 292, 294

Martial law, 398, 413
Marx, Jean, 174
Marxism, 32, 36, 37, 39, 270, 313; reformist, 405, 431
Marxist Social Democrat Federation (Britain), 36
Masaryk, Jan, 352
Masaryk, Tomàå, 51
Masculinity, 76, 79, 89, 94–96, 103, 513, 517
Mason, Tim, 3
Massis, Henri, 79
Matteotti, Giacomo 133
Maugham, W. Somerset, 103
Mauriac, François, 119
Maurras, Charles, 134–135, 142, 311, 507, 516
Maxwell, Robert, 326
Mayo brothers, 217
Mazower, Mark, 536
Mead, Margaret, 93
Mechanization, 273, 274, 282–283. *See also* Machines
Medical issues, 16, 18, 33, 46, 76, 93, 98, 102, 126, 372, 377, 378, 494–495; costs, 452, 453; women's health, 498. *See also* AIDS; Disease
Medvedev, Roy, 425
Meinhof, Ulrike, 334
Meir, Golda, 16
Melchett, Peter, 516
Mendès France, Pierre, 83, 292
Mensheviks, 41
Mental illness, 94, 126
Mentré, François, 79
Merchant ships, 188
Metalwork, 161
Metternich, K. W. von, 270
Michaelis, Georg, 51
Michnik, Adam, 505–506, 519, 520
Microsoft, 451, 454
Middle class, 66, 75, 86, 103–104, 119, 121, 123, 154, 291, 295, 306, 314, 516, 517, 522; expansion of, 122; lower, 34–35, 48, 167, 242, 243, 289, 536; upper, 11; women, 317. *See also* Bourgeoisie
Middle East, 269, 387
Migrant workers. *See under* Labor
Milan, 12, 35, 38, 83, 159, 324. *See also* Magneti Marelli
Military alliances, 266, 466–467

Military/industrial complex, 281
Military service, 22, 25, 30, 46, 124, 340, 361, 389, 410, 412, 491, 514, 515
Military spending, 266, 279–281, 357, 400, 467, 514
Milk, 26, 115, 282
Millennium, 521
Millerand, Alexandre, 37
Miloåeviñ, Slobodan, 379, 465
Miłosz, Czesław, 480
Minc, Hilary, 341
Mindszenty, József, 365, 411
Ministers, 248–249, 327, 328, 339, 341, 427, 453, 478, 516, 524; Ministers of Interior, 251, 258, 323, 339, 348
Minitel, 451
Minorities, 438, 439, 480
Missiles, 270, 400
Mitterrand, François, 70, 197, 302, 444, 479, 492; illness/death of, 507, 521
Mlynář, Zdeněk, 344, 346, 351, 352, 418, 421, 424–425, 426, 546
Moch, Jules, 261
Modernity/modernization, 30, 101, 114–115, 134, 141, 260, 296, 387, 415, 469; of agriculture/industry, 275, 281, 282, 292; military modernization, 180, 388
Moldavia, 240
Moller, Katti Anker, 121
Mollet, Guy, 325
Molotov, Vyacheslav, 253, 345, 347, 378
Monarchies, 137
Monetary systems, 433, 453, 468
Monnet, Jean, 254, 262, 275–276, 281
Mons, battle at, 77
Montenegro, 466, 474
Montini (Monsignor), 107
Montpellier, 439
Morality, 413, 523; and abortion, 371, 519; informal, 99; and Second World War, 197; sexual, 90, 92–93, 100, 101–102, 109, 125, 370, 372, 487, 500
Morning Post, 311
Moro, Aldo, 336
Morrison, Herbert, 501
Mortality rates, 26
Moscow, 267, 360, 525
Moscow Institute for International Relations, 361, 428
Moscow University, 346, 361, 424
Mosley, Nicholas, 99

Mosley, Oswald, 71, 73, 84, 136–137, 167
Motor industry, 291, 294, 369, 441, 442, 454. See also Cars
Mountbatten, Edwina, 109
Mouvement Républicain Populaire (MRP), 119, 320, 321–322, 323
MRP. See Mouvement Répulicain Populaire
Muggeridge, Kitty, 100
Muggeridge, Malcolm, 99–100, 108
Mukosev, Vladimir, 219
Munich conference (1938), 172, 177
Münnich, Ferenc, 349
Munnings, Alfred, 72
Münster, Bishop of, 75
Murders, 138, 139, 163, 512, 527. See also Assassinations
Murdoch, Iris, 277
Murmansk, 187, 188
Murphy, Robert, 107, 261
Music, 31, 86, 156, 170, 243, 244, 264, 363, 413, 421, 423, 476; rock music, 260, 370, 392, 422, 454–456. See also Jazz music
Muslims, 143, 199, 364, 365, 387, 412, 522; Bosnian, 466, 500, 522
Mussolini, Benito, 71, 90, 125, 128, 133, 134, 136, 142, 144, 148, 154, 189, 207, 260; and radio broadcasts, 169
My Life and Work (Ford), 152

Nabokov, Vladimir, 97
Nagy, Imre, 248, 269, 348–349
Naimark, Norman, 185
National Farmers' Union (Britain), 282
National Federation of Women Workers, 118
Nationalism, 20, 24, 36, 40, 44, 49, 51, 55, 60, 66, 84, 117, 132, 133, 135, 144, 166, 265, 299–300, 335, 351, 352, 365, 398, 475, 479, 480–482, 509, 519; Arab, 387; and armies, 412, 413; economic, 482; inclusive/civic, 481; vs. progress, 480
Nationalization, 138, 277, 278, 317, 321, 324, 341, 441, 442, 454, 459
National Union of Mineworkers (Britain), 489, 491, 494
NATO. See North Atlantic Treaty Organization
Natural gas, 284, 472
Nazi Germany, 4, 13, 60, 75, 121, 124,

479, 540–541; agriculture in, 191;
birth rates in, 125–126; Büro
Ribbentrop in, 174; civilians and extermination of Jews, 202–204, 210; economy, 166, 167, 176, 178–179, 189,
190, 191, 273; European allies of, 189;
female employment in, 111–112;
Foreign Office, 173, 202; foreign workers in, 190–191, 199; and homosexuality, 93, 97–98, 372; industry in, 191,
192, 273; invaded by Red Army,
106–107; military spending in, 193;
navy of, 182, 187, 188; Nazi
Agricultural Association, 115; nonaggression pact with Soviet Union, 177;
Nuremberg laws of 1935, 174; and religion, 146, 148; servants in, 123; and
sexual relations between Jews and
Gentiles, 106; Strength Through Joy
program, 169; war economy of, 67,
191; youth organizations in, 86, 88 (*see
also* Hitler Youth). *See also* Hitler,
Adolph
Nazism, 529–530; Nazism/communism
compared, 405–406, 540
Negri, Toni, 514
Nehru, Jawaharlal, 109
Nenni, Pietro, 325
NEP. *See* Soviet Union, New Economic
Policy in
Nepotism, 323, 361, 362, 378, 428
Netherlands, 40, 43, 207, 265, 284, 302,
324, 457; Christian democrats in, 320;
Communist Party in, 492; liberals in,
457; military spending in, 279; work-
ing women in, 488
Networks/contacts, 497. *See also* Politics,
political contacts
Neuilly, Treaty of, 66
Newspapers, 33, 38, 133, 310–311, 327,
378, 419, 420, 450, 472, 524
Newsreels, 180, 240
Newton, Francis, 264
New York (city), 18, 19, 30, 31; St.
Patrick's Cathedral in, 19
Nicaragua, 248, 387
Nicholas II (Tsar), 67, 137, 476, 477
Nicolson, Harold, 101, 122, 137,
173–174
Nineteen Eighty-four (Orwell), 242
Nixdorf computer firm, 452
Nixon, Richard, 270, 385

Nomenklatura, 357, 358, 414, 416,
423–428, 429, 470; and capitalism, 430;
children of, 428; two categories of, 424
Noriel, Gérard, 375
North Atlantic Trading Company, 17
North Atlantic Treaty Organization
(NATO), 260, 266, 267, 269, 299, 301,
306, 324, 327, 356, 388, 464,
466–467; transformation of, 467
North Korea, 431
Norway, 43, 116, 124, 195, 284, 324
Nostalgia, 476, 479, 527
*Notre Temps: La Revue des Nouvelles
Générations,* 79
Nouvelles Équipes Internationales, 300
Nove, Alec, 269
Novels, 91, 96, 241–242, 374, 403, 485,
545
Novotnü, Antonin, 352
Nuclear weapons, 266, 269, 270, 279,
280, 389, 467, 491, 513, 523. *See also*
Atom bomb
Nuremberg trials, 153, 529

OAS. *See* Organisation de L'Armée Secrète
October (film), 216
Odd Man Out (film), 242
Odessa, 359; massacre at (1941), 206
OEEC. *See* Organization for European
Economic Cooperation
Oil, 271, 454, 459, 472, 512, 516. *See also
under* Prices
Old people, 296, 307, 316, 367, 421, 453,
458, 470, 488
Olson, Mancur, 440
Olympic Games of 1936, 200
One Day in the Life of Ivan Denisovich
(Solzhenitsyn), 545
Ophul, Marcel, 114
Opinion polls, 304, 312, 313–314, 315,
317, 419, 481. *See also* Public opinion
Optimism, 245, 409, 414, 523, 524
Organisation de L'Armée Secrète (OAS),
335, 336
Organization for Economic Cooperation
and Development, 299
Organization for European Economic
Cooperation (OEEC), 164–165
Orphans, 70, 75, 82, 120, 344, 379
Ortega y Gasset, José, 79
Orthodox Church, 143, 144, 145, 364,
365, 405

Orwell, George, 33, 78, 79, 81, 103–104, 109, 142(n), 156, 168–169, 242, 512, 536
Osborne, John, 375
Ostpolitik, 366, 367
Ottawa Conference (1932), 176
Ottoman Empire, 58, 363. *See also* Turkey
Owen, Wilfred, 72, 80
Oxford University, 80

Pacem in Terris (encyclical), 310, 366
Pagnol, Marcel, 23, 25, 125
Paix et Liberté, 306
Pakistan, 285
Pale, 16
Palestine, 181
Papon, Maurice, 479
Parents, 75, 82, 88, 90, 120, 121, 125, 210, 245, 346, 373, 374, 379, 423; in lower middle-class, 289, 375; social position of, 361
Paris, 30, 34, 35, 57, 110, 118–119, 153, 154, 216, 217, 332, 336, 374; Disneyland in, 482, 484; gay quarter in, 495; radio in, 507
Paris Soir, 217
Paris, Treaty of (1951), 265
Parti Agraire (France), 141
Parti Catholique (Belgium), 147
Parti Communist Français, 479, 504
Parti Ouvrier Belge, 32
Parti Ouvrier Français, 28, 36, 37, 38
Parti Populaire Français, 135, 136
Parti Socialiste (France), 319, 491–492
Parvulescu, Constantin, 504
Passerini, Luisa, 333, 533, 534
Passports, 174, 175, 483, 484; internal, 361
Paternalism, 169
Patriarchy, 103
Patronage, 251, 308, 322, 362
Pauker, Ana, 340
Paul VI (Pope), 366
Paulus (German commander), 194
Pawlak, Waldemar, 469
Paxton, Robert, 2
Peacekeepers, 514
Pearl Harbor, 189
Pearson Group, 457–458
Peasant Party (Bulgaria), 140
Peasant Party (France), 30, 280
Peasant Party (Poland), 251, 469

Peasants, 7, 19, 21–26, 39, 42, 126, 129, 152, 282, 292, 333, 343, 360, 363, 364, 426, 499, 539; as conservative, 30, 120, 407; executions/deportations of, 139; and First World War, 46, 48, 49, 55–56, 58, 66–67, 75; peasant parties, 30, 140–141, 469; property-owning, 138; prosperity of, 29; rebellions, 141; and religion, 143–144, 145, 147; and sexuality, 100, 101; violence against, 140; and working class, 26, 27, 519. *See also* Countryside; *under* Armies; *individual countries*
Peasants into Frenchmen (Weber), 21–22
Pellizzi, Camillo, 83
Pensions, 70, 92
People's Party (Bavaria), 145
Perestroika, 353, 387, 399–402, 421, 428
Permissive society, 369–373
Pessimism, 241–242, 291
Pétain, Philippe, 43, 48, 71, 74, 90, 136, 137, 141–142, 146–147, 150; Pétainists, 257, 258, 263, 279, 318, 321–322
Peter, Janós, 365
Peter (King of Serbia), 45
Peter Pan (Barrie), 79
Petkov family (Bulgaria), 149, 250
Peyrefitte, Roger, 174
Philosophy, 403
Photography, 215–235, 240, 243, 267; airbrushing, 215, *221,* *228*
Picasso, Pablo, 22
Picture Post magazine, 216, 217
Pieds noirs, 287–288, 293, 297, 335
Pilip, Ivan, 427
Piłsudski, Jósef, 51–52, 71, 139, 398
Pink Floyd, 422
Pinochet, Augusto, 512, 530(n)
Pirenne, Henri, 55
Pius XI (Pope), 142, 144, 145
Pizza Hut, 483
Planning. *See under* Economic issues
Planning (journal), 165
Pleasures, 426
Pleven, René, 304
Pogroms, 206, 209
Poison gas, 57
Poland, 2, 4, 7, 16, 27, 28, 31, 63, 64, 85, 137, 139, 146, 173, 176, 206, 240, 256, 287, 355, 401; abortion in, 410, 497; agriculture in, 469; Church in,

364, 366, 405, 409, 410, 411, 413,
420, 431, 502; Communist Party in,
253, 347, 348, 366, 430, 476, 503;
communist past in, 475–476; computers in, 417; deaths from typhus, 54;
defeat of Red Army (1920), 178, 255;
dissent in, 404–405, 406; economy,
359, 414, 509; emigrants, 15, 18; execution of civilians in, 200; fall of communism in, 398, 407, 430, 510; and
First World War, 47, 51–52, 58;
German invasion (1939), 172, 179,
198, 200; industry in, 409; Jews in,
478 (*see also* Poland, Warsaw ghetto in);
and Lithuania, 177; military in (*see*
Armies, Polish); moonlighting in, 420;
Movement for Democratic Action in,
507; nationalism in, 475; and NATO,
466; purges in, 340, 342; Radio Maryja
in, 507; and Second World War, 477;
Solidarity in, 394, 398, 404, 408, 411,
413, 417, 420, 426(n), 469, 476, 519;
and Soviet Union, 198, 249, 251, 252,
254, 255, 256, 348, 398, 413, 419,
466; Warsaw ghetto in, 198, 201, 208,
209, 255; women in, 377, 496, 498;
workers in, 392–393, 404, 408, 409,
420, 518
Police, 19, 25, 33, 38, 251, 332, 336, 374;
Police Battalion 101 (Nazi Germany),
205; secret police, 343, 351, 475;
Soviet infiltration of, 341
Polish Universal Encyclopaedia, 385
Political science, 1, 242–243, 317
Politics, 26–30, 531; and accusations of
homosexuality, 98; ages of political leaders in 1933, 85(table); and agriculture
(*see* Agriculture, political power of);
apoliticism of some dissidents, 407, 464;
Christian political parties, 147 (*see also*
Christian democrats); coalition politics,
302; consensus politics, 299–337, 459;
convergence of political systems,
300–303; and economics, 314, 393,
401; and engineers, 158, 161–162;
expulsions from political parties, 340;
and First World War, 50–52, 71, 72;
and generational divisions, 83–84,
391–392; hinge parties, 34, 282; ideology in world politics, 270; of information, 507–508; militancy-based parties,
303, 305, 311, 326; multi-dimensional

politics, 460; multiparty systems, 407,
431, 466; new politics, 504–505, 517,
519; notable parties, 303–304, 305; per-
sonal/political as connected, 328; political contacts, 470, 472; political left, 35,
72, 104, 130–132, 138, 139, 143, 149,
150, 156, 166, 170, 216, 243, 245,
254, 262, 318, 319, 321, 325, 333–334,
390, 393, 459, 460, 467, 490, 491, 492,
493–494, 519; political parties, 30, 34,
140–141, 147, 169, 249, 263, 282, 300,
303–306, 308, 317, 326, 335, 340, 407,
469, 490, 502–504, 520, 524, 543;
political prisoners, 199, 247, 475; political right, 4, 20, 21, 27, 30, 35, 72, 73,
74, 84, 124, 128, 133–137, 141, 143,
150, 153, 166, 170, 301, 315, 316, 318,
333–334, 394, 395, 407, 456, 490, 492,
493, 504, 519 (*see also* Conservatism;
Fascism); redistribution of rural property, 140; and servant problem, 123;
and sexual morality, 90; and social
change, 305–306; two-party politics,
302, 304–305; voter-oriented parties,
303, 304, 320, 326; and war pensions,
70; and women, 116–119, 489–493,
506 (*see also* Women, voters)
Pollution, 414–415, 517. *See also*
Environment
Polycentrism, 331, 419
Pompidou, Georges, 23, 333
Pont-à-Mousson, 167–168
Popular Party (Italy), 322, 323
Populations, 16, 93, 107, 123, 124, 154,
174, 181, 200, 208, 239, 246, 268,
287, 354–355, 360, 368–369, 400,
414, 435(table), 436, 478
Porritt, Jonathon, 517
Portillo, Michael, 483
Port of London Authority, 164
Portugal, 4, 7, 43, 84, 86, 117, 129, 137,
145, 146, 285, 299, 386; agriculture in,
150, 152; Christian democrats in, 502;
communism in, 330; democracy in,
337, 390; and European Economic
Community, 443; and First World War,
58; National Syndicalist movement in,
129, 135
Potsdam conference, *219*
Potter, Dennis, 375
Poujade, Pierre, 83, 329–330
Poultry, 114

Poverty, 16, 18, 45, 283, 297, 304, 496, 525

Powell, Anthony, 374

Power issues, 135–136

PPI. *See* Italian Popular Party

Prague, 12, 342, 360, 386, 394, 397, 398, 403, 405, 428, 471, 480, 485, 499; Jewish sites of, 478; Prague Spring, 232(caption), 243, 245, 254, 256, 331, 332, 352–353, 364, 378, 381, 408, 421, 424, 431, 474, 476, 504; statue of Stalin in, 351; unemployment in, 468, 496

Presley, Elvis, 260

Prices, 66, 118, 141, 154, 408, 441, 473–474; and living standards, 159; of oil, 245, 284, 385, 386, 388, 414, 433. *See also* Inflation; *under* Food

Priests, 19, 37, 89, 100, 101, 143, 144, 145, 147, 148, 170, 330, 364, 410, 411; worker-priest movement, 321

Primo de Rivera, Miguel, 140

Prince of Wales, 72

Princip, Gavrilo, 24, 44, 45, 343

Prisoners of war, 40, 103, 105, 112, 186, 190, 198, 199, 273, 274; sexual relations of, 106

Privacy, 126, 376

Private property, 27, 167, 280, 390, 421, 426, 431, 459, 470–471, 472. *See also* Land ownership

Private/public spheres, 276–277, 368, 376

Privatization, 429, 446, 450, 453–454, 471, 473; coupon, 472; false, 471

Privilege(s), 362, 374, 393, 426–427, 428, 470, 486, 495, 515, 525

Productivism, 291–297

Productivity, 162, 281, 288, 440, 454, 458, 496; productivity missions, 274–275

Professions, 295, 373, 377, 410, 450, 495

Profits, 111, 164, 193, 262, 292, 293, 334, 436, 447, 458, 474; and wages, 442

Progress, 12, 30

Proletariat, 26, 33, 65, 99, 112, 116, 139, 170, 321, 331

Propaganda, 50, 51, 55, 98, 106, 149, 197, 258, 266, 275, 294, 349, 375, 386, 388, 429; anticommunist, 328; and television, 418

Prosperity, 4, 16, 20, 29, 33, 34, 66, 167, 169, 175, 242, 243, 248, 275, 307, 378, 434, 443, 476, 524, 525–526, 529, 547; and distribution vs. production, 291–292; and town/country dispute, 292, 468; of Western Europe, 271, 280, 284, 291; and working class, 309; and youth, 373, 374, 455

Prostitution, 90, 94, 100, 102, 103, 105, 109, 260, 499; male, 104

Protestants, 30, 37, 76, 85, 141, 142, 144, 148, 205, 297, 310, 320, 364, 365, 410, 481, 502

Proust, Marcel, 22, 37, 91

Prussia, 25, 28, 38, 82, 141, 146, 173, 185; Franco-Prussian War, 59; Ministry of Social Welfare, 92; public-sector workers in, 39

Psychiatric hospitals, 393, 404

Psychologists, 92–93

Public opinion, 90, 203, 388, 419, 439, 470(table), 487, 516, 522. *See also* Opinion polls

Public/private domains, 126, 325

Public/private sectors, 447–448

Pubs, 33

Purges. *See under* Eastern Europe; Soviet Union; Stalin, Joseph

Putin, Vladimir, 523

Quadragesimo Anno (encyclical), 145

Queuille, Henri, 139, 258

Quintavalle, Bruno Antonio, 160

Quotas, 361

Racial issues, 65, 75, 98, 125–126, 148, 173, 186, 392, 393, 394, 480, 486, 513, 517, 518, 541; and African troops, 182; and sexuality, 105, 106, 108–109, 500. *See also* Anti-Semitism; Jews

Radić, Stefan, 24, 139, 147

Radicalism, 393, 457, 467

Radical Party (France), 139, 259, 304, 305, 308, 316, 318, 319, 322, 323

Radio, 101, 135, 144, 151, 169, 209, 260, 290, 311, 358, 507; Radio Free Europe, 269, 350, 411, 418; Radio Tirana, 418

Railways, 25, 30, 54, 192

Rajk, László, 339, 346, 348, 349

Rákosi, Mátyás, 343, 349

Rand Institution, 268

Rapallo, treaty at, 177

Rape, 90, 105, 106–107, 108, 368, 379, 499–500; of Bosnian women, 500; in

Russia, 499–500; written account of, 107
Raphael, Enid, 89
Rassemblement des Gauches Républicaines (RGR), 318
Rassemblement du Peuple Français, 258, 299
Rathenau, Walther, 53, 161
Rationality, 318–319
Rationalization of production, 155–164, 168
Rationing, 273, 276
Reagan, Ronald, 388
Rear Window (film), 218
Rebellions, 27, 29, 43, 136, 141, 170, 208, 209. *See also* Armies, mutinies in
Recessions, 4, 275
Red Brigade. *See under* Italy
Red Cross, 50, 186
Red Falcons (France), 85
Reed, Carol, 242
Referenda, 481
Reflation, 444–445, 446
Reforms, 5, 29, 37, 38, 40, 166, 277, 307, 324–325, 326, 347, 348, 352, 353, 367, 398, 420, 421, 425, 463, 469, 493; Communist reforms, 431, 503; of Gorbachev, 390, 395, 398, 423, 425, 426, 480 (*see also* Perestroika); sexual, 371
Refugees, 16, 54, 175, 216, 284, 297, 348; economic benefits of, 286–288; numbers of, 174
Regards, 217
Regencies, 137
Regulations, 291, 345, 355; deregulation, 446
Reich Coal Council, 165
Reichstag, *228*
Religion, 30, 37, 76, 117, 142–149, 169, 309–310, 315–316, 328, 352, 363, 364–365, 380, 392, 394, 409–411; Church/state relations, 143, 144, 409–410 (*see also* Catholicism, and secular authorities); visions, 76–77. *See also* Catholicism; Jews; Muslims; Orthodox Church; Protestants
Remarque, Erich Maria, 70
Remittances, 20, 21
Renault cars, 53, 440
Renault, Louis, 153, 160, 216
Renner, Karl, 36

Renoir, Jean, 99
Rentiers, 12, 13, 113, 175
Reparations, 65, 175, 176, 197, 249, 252
Repatriations, 174, 199, 200
Repression, 38, 39, 41, 43, 67, 133, 136, 143, 242, 299, 338, 343, 365, 378, 379, 381, 400, 414
Republicanism, 312
Resettlement projects, 200
Revolution(s), 38, 39, 40, 42, 55, 85, 136, 300, 302, 330, 452; demographic, 373; economic, 434–436; Iranian, 387; of 1989, 407. *See also* Sexual revolution(s)
Rexists (Belgium), 147, 149
Reynaud, Paul, 181
RGR. *See* Rassemblement des Gauches Républicaines
Rhineland, 36, 182, 211
Rhineland Provincial Institute for Neuro-Psychological Eugenic Research, 211
Richthofen, Baron Manfred von, 96
Riots, 41, 56, 73, 118, 300, 302, 332, 390, 408, 526
Rist, Charles, 166
Roads, 25
Robert Capa Gold Medal, 232(caption)
Roberts, Alderman, 170
Robots, 416, 417
Rodger, George, 216, 217, 218, *227*
Röhm, Ernst, 98
Rokossovsky, Konstantin, 255
Rolfe, Samuel, 70
Rolling Stones, 454, 455
Romania, 4, 16, 64, 146, 176, 177, 407, 412, 414, 428, 499, 530; abortion in, 378, 498; agriculture in, 469; communist past in, 475; dissent in, 397–398, 406, 407; fall of communism in, 401–402, 407; and First World War, 43, 58, 66; Iron Guard in, 133, 135, 136, 149; King Michael of Romania, 249; nationalism in, 480, 513; National Salvation Front in, 519; peasants in, 27; privatization in, 471; Protestants in, 410; purges in, 340; and Second World War, 189, 206, 478; and Soviet Union, 363
Romanian Socialist Party of Labor, 504
Rome, Treaty of, 265
Romilly, Giles and Esmond, 85
Rommel (General), 184, 196
Roosevelt, Franklin D., 189, 195

Rossi, Tino, 170
Rostov-on-Don, 360
Roth, Philip, 403
Rothermere (Lord), 137
Roux, Olivier, 448
Rowland, Tiny, 326
Roxburgh, J. F., 81
Royal Dutch Shell, 459
Royal, Ségolène, 489
Rubber, 190
Rugby, 170
Ruhr region, 64, 153, 175, 182, 192, 414
Rule of law, 511, 512
Ruling class. *See* Upper classes
Rupnik, Jacques, 480, 505
Rural areas. *See* Countryside
Rushdie, Salman, 295
Russell, Bertrand, 11
Russia, 16, 18, 38, 172, 401, 413, 431,
    467, 496, 499, 518, 523; army in,
    22–23, 43–44 (*see also* Armies, Red
    Army; Armies, Russian White army);
    attitudes to recent past in, 476–477;
    casualties in, 59, 129; Civil War in, 20,
    50, 64, 82, 110, 129, 130, 137, 138;
    communist parties refounded in,
    503–504; communist youth organiza-
    tions in, 83–84; economy in, 354, 356,
    429, 469, 470(table); education in,
    24–25; Financial Industrial Groups
    (FIGs) in, 472; and First World War,
    40, 41, 43–44, 45, 47, 51, 56, 57, 59;
    food shortages in, 54, 59, 240; homo-
    sexuality in, 97; imbalance between
    sexes in, 113; military spending in,
    193, 514; Muslim Russia, 116; Pamyat
    in, 481; peasants in, 22–23, 24–25,
    28–29, 49, 56, 100, 114; Petrograd
    Soviet in, 56; railways in, 54, 56; rape
    in, 499–500; rebellions in, 27; Russian
    Federation, 399 (*see also* Soviet Union,
    republics of former); Russian
    Revolution, 13, 56, 58, 78, 92, 118,
    128, 138, 143, 145, 149, 150; town-
    country conflict in, 138; War Industry
    Committees, 534. *See also* Soviet Union
Russian Workers Communist Party, 504
Rybkin, Ivan, 472
Rykov (Russian leader), 163

Sabbatarianism, 170
Sachs, Jeffrey, 391

Safety issues, 285, 291, 443, 459
St.-Cyr military school (France), 80
St. Germain, Treaty of, 66
Sakharov, Andrei, 402, 404, 416, 425;
    widow of, 524
Salazar, António, 84, 86, 117, 129, 135,
    146, 147
Salzburg, Archbishop of, 146
Samizdat publications, 404, 417
Sanity/insanity, 76
Sapir, Jacques, 474
Sarajevo, 24
Sartre, Jean-Paul, 81, 88, 91, 99, 370, 403,
    494
Sassoon, Donald, 536
Sassoon, Siegfried, 72, 76, 95
Saudi Arabia, 387, 474
Saukel (Nazi leader), 191
Sauvy, Alfred, 535
Savage, Jon, 455
Scandinavia, 21, 63, 503
Schacht, Hjalmar, 134
Schama, Simon, 2
Schelsky, Helmut, 368
Schumacher, Kurt, 261
Schuman, Robert, 322
Science, 93, 98, 102, 157, 171, 415–416,
    449
Scotland, 501
Scott, Paul, 108
Second International, 32, 40, 131, 261,
    502, 503
Second Sex, The (de Beauvoir), 91
Second World War, 26, 87, 93, 126, 136,
    150, 184–198, 312, 325, 514, 529,
    542; air war in, 192–193, 196 (*see also*
    Aircraft, in Second World War); casual-
    ties in, 64, 172, 184, 185, 186, 188,
    196, 240; civilians in, 185, 186; eastern
    front, 184–187, 189–190, 191, 195,
    203, 205, 211, 215 (*see also* Soviet
    Union, and Second World War);
    economies in, 189–194; foreign work-
    ers in Germany during, 190–191; and
    generational division, 87–88; German
    morale in, 192–193; globalization of,
    187–188, 196; legacies of, 376, 480;
    and living standards, 298; and morale,
    194; munitions in, 190, 191, 193–194,
    196; 1939—1941 period of, 172, 179,
    180, 183, 184, 187, 189; peace initia-
    tives in, 195–196; photography in,

217; postwar period, 3–4, 6, 149, 171, 198, 240, 273, 284, 368, 369, 373; recalled/reassessed, 465, 477–478, 479; sea war, 188 (*see also* Submarines); war damage, 273, 274(table)

Section Française de L'Internationale Ouvrière (SFIO), 32, 131, 167, 305, 324, 325, 326

Secularization, 309–310, 316, 319, 490

Séeberger brothers, 216

Segalen, Martine, 114, 115

Segregation, 108, 198

Séguin, Philippe, 440

Self-control, 76

Self-determination, 66, 176

Self-interest, 419, 421, 426, 427, 431

Sembat, Marcel, 40

Separation of church and state, 92, 144

Serbia, 4, 8, 40, 365, 412, 465, 467, 474, 486; and First World War, 44, 54, 58; Jews in, 202

Servants, 3, 12, 102, 103, 121, 122–123, 280

Service sector, 377, 434, 442, 443, 458, 488, 517

Seton-Watson, Hugh, 23–24, 79, 363

Sexuality, 7, 20, 67, 79, 86, 89, 98, 99, 105–109, 120, 126, 264, 334, 368, 369–373, 530; and class, 102–104, 123; regulating, 92, 371; scientific approaches to, 93; sexual morality (*see* Morality, sexual); study of sexual relations, 90–92. *See also* Celibacy; Homosexuality; Sexual revolution(s); *under* Race

Sexual revolution(s), 243–244, 369–370, 371, 373, 464, 487–500

Seymour, David ("Chim"), 216–217, 218, *222–223*

Seyss-Inquart, Artur, 148

SFIO. *See* Section Française de L'Internationale Ouvrière

Shadow, The (Kadaré, 380

Shareholders, 447, 452, 460, 472–473, 517

Shell shock, 76, 92, 94, 95

Shevardnadze, Eduard, 386

Shipbuilding, 284, 392, 435

Shipping lines, 17, 18

Shonfeld, Andrew, 447

Shopkeepers, 35, 147, 296

Shortages, 360, 376. *See also under* Food

Siberia, 18, 190, 341

Sicily, 260, 292–293, 323, 511, 512

Siemans, 452

Sifton, Clifford, 19

Simenon, Georges, 82, 102, 109, 147

Singer, Isaac Bashevis, 31

Sirinelli, Jean-François, 23

Siroky (Czech leader), 342

SKF manufacturer, 484

Skills, 159, 290, 362, 438, 452, 515

Skvorecky, Josef, 405

Slánskü, Rudolf, 328, 339, 342, 344

Slavs, 44, 49, 141, 185, 389, 390; in Red Army, 412

Slovakia, 149, 206, 351, 477–478, 480, 481–482, 513, 530; unemployment in, 497

Slovenia, 465–466, 468, 474, 482

Slovic, Eddie, 187

Small businesses, 290–291, 292, 293

Smallholders' Party (Hungary), 30, 251

Smith, John, 501

Smith, Paul, 435

Smyrna, 173

Social change, 294, 304, 305–306, 350, 360–361, 370, 393–394, 395, 464. *See also* Change

Social democracy, 390, 419, 502–503, 504. *See also individual parties*

Social Democratic Party (Russia), 41

Social Democratic Party (SPD, Germany), 29, 32, 33, 34, 37, 38, 39, 40, 51, 261, 315, 324, 492, 502, 516

Socialism, 28, 29, 32–42, 84, 104, 131, 142, 145, 147, 166, 205, 259, 261, 263, 303, 324–327, 402, 458–459, 492, 506; national roads to socialism, 254; in 1980s, 394–395, 459; and Social democratic parties, 502–503;

Socialist Internationals (1900, 1951), 39, 300, 458; in western Europe, 390, 391

Social mobility, 23–24, 34, 70–71, 325, 360, 361–362, 373, 375

Social sciences, 289, 313–314, 332

Social security, 440, 488

Société Générale bank, 52

Sociology, 1, 5, 242–243, 283, 419, 469

Soixante-huitards, 332, 333, 334, 457

Solzhenitsyn, Alexander, 402, 404, 545

Somme, Battle of, 43, 49, 76

Soros, George, 546

Sorrow and the Pity, The (film), 114
Soviet Union, 3, 5, 93, 121, 172, 174,
177–178, 412; abortion in, 378, 498;
agriculture in, 115–116, 194, 355;
alcohol consumption in, 390 (*see also*
Alcoholism/drinking; Vodka); Asian
republics of, 399; atomic bomb in, 354
(*see also* Nuclear weapons); birth rates
in, 123, 126, 389–390; black market
in, 359; car production in, 358;
Catholicism in, 366; causalities in
Second World War, 185, 186, 196;
children's social position in, 361; coup
of 1991, 413, 430; debt of, 415(table);
and declining East/West tensions, 389;
deportations from, 341; dissidents in,
394, 402, 404, 405; and eastern
Europe, 249–256; economy, 176,
268–269, 353–354, 355, 356, 357,
359, 386, 388, 400–401, 416,
420–421, 535; education as privilege
in, 393; extra-European commitments
of, 182; fall of communist rule in, 386,
394, 397, 398–399, 466; families in,
119–120, 380; female employment in,
112–113; and Finland, 255–256; five-
year plans in, 163; foreign trade of,
429; grain requisitions in, 138; gray
economy in, 420–421; homosexuality
in, 97–98; industry in, 153, 161–163,
163–164, 166, 187, 189–190, 355;
informal empire of, 265; and Japan,
182; Jews in, 206–207, 209; military
power of, 389–390, 400 (*see also*
Armies, Red Army); Muslims in, 387,
389; nationalities in, 389–390; New
Economic Policy (NEP) in, 138, 163;
NKVD in, 164, 241, 361; orphans in,
82–83; Orthodox Church in, 405;
peasants in, 83, 138, 139, 161; perceptions of Western rivals, 268–269; and
Poland (*see* Poland, and Soviet Union);
Politburo in, 266, 421; *praktiki* in, 161;
purges in, 65, 130, 131, 177, 215, 267,
268, 339, 362, 476 (*see also* Stalin,
Joseph, purges of); rationalization of
production in, 161–163, 168; rehabilitation of Stalin's victims in, 347;
republics of former, 399, 468, 499,
503; science in, 415–416; and Second
World War, 180, 185, 186, 189–190,
196, 201, 209, 240, 241, 376 (*see also*

Second World War, eastern front);
show trials in, 338, 339, 340, 363, 529;
Special Bureau for Women's Affairs,
112; starvation in, 240; state enterprises in, 416; statisticians in, 535; visitors to, 267; weakening of, 386;
Western perceptions of, 267–268;
workers in, 407, 518. *See also* Russia
Spain, 4, 8, 21, 22, 28, 30, 32, 37, 101,
118, 135, 140, 143, 145, 207, 241,
257, 299, 458; abortion in, 487; agriculture in, 150, 152; Basque areas in,
334, 335 (*see also* Basques); birth rates
in, 487; Christian democrats in, 320,
333, 502; Civil War in, 64, 81, 128,
129, 145–146, 174, 175, 178, 180,
182, 217, *222–223,* 340 (*see also*
Franco, Francisco); Communist Party
in, 492; contraception in, 371, 490;
democracy in, 337, 390; divorce in,
487; economy, 274, 354, 437, 525;
education in, 24; and European
Economic Community, 443; Falange
in, 135; and First World War, 43; mar-
riage in, 370; Popular Front in, 132,
158, 333; and protests of 1968,
332–333; and Second World War, 136;
Socialist Party in, 492; working women
in, 488
Spark, Muriel, 113
SPD. *See* Social Democratic Party
Specialization, 161, 162, 435
Speer, Albert, 191
Spending. *See* Government spending;
Military spending
Spiritualism, 76
Sports, 33, 169, 170, 439, 508
Sputnik, 354
Srebrenica, 522
Stability, 12, 58, 60, 80, 87, 136, 175,
367, 433, 476, 525
Stahlhelm, 83
Stakhanovism, 112–113, 155, 162–163
Stalin, Joseph, 65, 112, 130, 131, 138,
144, 163, 177, 184, 195, 248, 252,
256–257, 262, 330, 343–344, 400,
535; and Churchill and Roosevelt, 189,
248; death of, 6, 242, 254, 338, 339,
345, 376, 378, 380; de-Stalinization,
345–353; and economic growth, 353;
and Hitler, 177, 209; purges of, 249,
251, 254, 339–345, 379, 412, 534, 544

(*see also* Soviet Union, purges in);
Stalinism, 67, 88, 132, 162, 164,
250–251, 268, 325, 328, 338, 339,
341, 342, 361, 375, 424, 431, 522,
530, 538–539; and survey of Soviet
rulers, 476, 477; and Tito, 339; and
Trotsky, 207
Stalingrad, 186, 190, 191, 194
Stamboliski, Alexander, 55, 66, 469
State's role, 6, 37–38, 162, 163–164, 165,
167, 169, 272, 275–279, 304, 446,
452–454, 459, 498, 508–511, 520; and
restoration of property, 471; and weak-
ness of European states, 510–511. *See
also* Government spending; Welfare
state
Statistics, 271–272, 280, 313, 434, 477,
524, 535; about marriage, 370; Soviet,
354, 362
Status, 289, 294–295, 296, 361, 488; of
women, 496
Stavropol, 426
Steel, 52, 153, 165, 189, 279, 284, 316,
324, 357, 392, 435, 438, 441, 449,
472, 476, 491
Stepinac (Archbishop), 149
Sterilization, compulsory, 124, 126
Sterling, 446
Stern, 372
Stewart, James, 264
Stock exchanges, 447, 489
Stock options, 448, 452
Stolitchny Bank (Russia), 429
Stolypin, Petr, 28–30
Strachey, John, 137
Strachey, Lytton, 11
Strategic Defense Initiative, 400
Strauss, Franz-Josef, 298
Stresemann, Gustav, 173, 183
Strikes, 36, 37, 38, 39, 41, 48, 54, 56,
104, 118, 129, 132, 158–159, 207,
245, 262, 277, 302, 317, 366, 408,
440–441; and capitalism, 326, 460;
general strike in France (1968), 332; in
industry and transport, 441(table); no-
strike deals, 441; opportunistic, 441;
pacifist, 119; of Polish workers, *234;*
against scientific management, 158
Strummer, Joe, 455
Students, 332–334, 340, 350, 360,
408–409, 410, 451, 457, 484,
513–514, 519

Sturzo, Luigi, 140, 147
Submarines, 188, 192, 255, 535
Subsidies, 121, 123, 124, 169, 197, 262,
278, 292, 437, 451; agricultural, 292;
of West Germany to East Germany,
410
Suburbanization, 121
Suez, 87
Suffering, 527, 528
Suicides, 18, 105, 185, 196, 210, 336,
350, 351, 379
Sunday Times Colour Supplement, 242
Superpower status, 389, 401
Supervisors, 357
Svevo, Italo, 160
Sweden, 43, 67, 93, 124, 166, 207, 324,
458; economy, 300, 445, 449; and
European Economic Community, 443;
King of Sweden, 127; military spend-
ing of, 467; social democrats in, 337;
working women in, 488
Swiss Bank Corporation, 449
Switzerland, 32, 40, 43, 129, 175, 302,
324, 369, 445–446, 491, 525; foreign
workers in, 286
Syndicat National des Entreprises Gaies,
495
Syria, 181, 386

Tajikistan, 116, 468
Tanks, 57, 179, 180, 182, 184, 188, 191,
332, 348, 389, 390, 515; US potential
to produce, 268
Tardieu, André, 167
Tariffs, 444
Taro, Gerda, 217
Tasca, Henry, 261
Taxes, 34, 35, 55, 70, 125, 138, 175, 280,
282, 291, 295, 329, 440, 452, 472
Taylor, A. J. P., 7, 101, 154, 243, 533, 534
Taylor, Frederick Winslow, 155–156, 160;
Taylorism, 155, 156, 157, 160, 161,
162, 168
Teachers, 23, 24, 55, 82, 113, 325, 378,
488, 515
Tebbit, Norman, 437
Technocrats, 161, 360
Technology, 16, 134, 135, 151, 154, 155,
156, 157, 159, 171, 218, 354, 357,
388, 391, 415, 434, 442, 443, 444,
525; and economic success, 449–452;
information technologies, 450, 451;

military, 179–180, 182, 281, 389, 400; and privatization, 450; technical training, 160
Telecommunications, 449, 450, 454, 512
Telegraphy, 25
Telephones, 12, 151, 209, 275, 416, 435, 443, 450, 534
Television, 218, 242, 244, 284, 304, 308, 310–313, 440, 450, 472, 500, 507, 508, 521, 525; and propaganda, 418
Temple, Nina, 492
Terrorism, 334–336, 374, 514, 527
Teschen, 173
Textiles, 110, 280, 316, 377, 435
Thatcher, Margaret, 4, 245, 336–337, 395, 435, 451, 453, 455, 457–458, 459, 493, 500; Thatcherism, 450, 543–544
Third International, 502. *See also* Comintern
Third Man, The (Greene), 242
Third World, 333, 335, 392, 490, 514
Thomas, Albert, 53
Thomas (Nazi leader), 191
Thompson, Edward, 5, 329
Thompson, Flora, 97
Thorez, Maurice, 257
Thorpe, Jeremy, 244
Times, The, 327
Timiçoara (Romania), 397, 498, 522
Tindemans, Leo, 300
Tiso, Josef, 149, 478
Tito (Marshal), 248, 250, 254, 255, 257, 265, 339, 340, 341, 349, 363, 479
Tixier-Vignancour (French presidential candidate), 335
Todd, Emmanuel, 354, 358, 361, 422, 545
Todt (Nazi leader), 191
Togliatti, Palmiro, 330, 331
Tomin, Julius and Lukáå, 403
Toranska, Teresa, 534
Torture, 336, 343, 512, 528
Totalitarianism, 136, 268
Tottenham Conservative Association, 493
Tounkara, Fodé, 523
Tractors, 115, 152, 155, 282
Trade, 254, 272, 429, 443, 444, 445
Trade unions, 32, 33, 34, 36, 37, 40, 41, 52–53, 103–104, 118, 131, 132, 140, 157, 158, 260, 261, 262, 292, 317, 328, 334, 435, 450, 510, 517–518,

520; Catholic, 321, 322, 324; communist controlled, 366, 375; management vs. unions, 441–442; and socialist parties, 326; Solidarity (*see* Poland, Solidarity in). *See also* Labor, labor movements; Leadership, of trade unions
Translations, 269
Transportation, 22, 25, 293, 444; and Second World War, 191, 192
Travel, 417–418, 469
Treason, 99, 186, 456
Treaties, 66, 176, 249, 265
Trianon, Treaty of, 66, 84, 175, 509
Trotsky, Leon, 37, 43, 131, 132, 163, 173, 206, *220–221,* 332, 422
Truman, Harry, 250
Tuberculosis, 239
Tudjman, Franjo, 20, 466
Tukhachevskii, Mikhail, 178, 179
Turkey, 43, 44, 54, 64, 173, 174, 266. *See also* Ottoman Empire
Tymivski, Stanisław, 20
Tynan, Kenneth, 373
Typhus, 54, 239, 240

Udet, Ernst, 192
Ukraine, 174, 206, 240, 363, 387, 468, 481, 514
Ukrainian Uniate Catholic Church, 366
Ulysses (Joyce), 101
Underclass, 518
Unemployment, 28, 73, 82, 84, 103, 110, 111, 131, 150, 154, 243, 284, 285, 286, 297, 298, 305, 325, 388, 393, 436–440, 437(table), 452, 535; benefits, 440; in Czechoslovakia, 468–469; long-term, 438, 439(table), 439; and women, 496; of youth, 437, 438, 439, 455
Union Démocratique et Socialiste de la Résistance, 304
Union of Democratic Miners, 494
Union of the Democratic Center (Spain), 492
Union of the Militant Godless (Russia), 143
Union pour la Nouvelle République, 305
Unità, 504
United Nations, 188–189, 196
United States, 93, 273–274, 363, 445, 523; allies of, 259, 262–263; Black

American GIs, 108, 197–198; and Britain, 188–189, 263; business culture in, 157; consumption in, 294, 296; and eastern Europe, 250; economy, 193, 275, 438, 482; executions in, 514; and First World War, 52, 57–58; and France, 261–262, 263; and German industry, 263–264; and Hungarian uprising, 267; immigrants in, 15, 16, 17(table), 18–19, 31; and Italy, 261, 263; military spending in, 193–194; and NATO, 467; and postwar Europe, 248, 258–264; and Second World War, 187, 193–194, 197; as world power, 197

Universal male suffrage, 16, 26, 29, 36, 44, 303

Universities, 2, 80, 84, 164, 242, 289, 333, 340, 350, 374, 393, 451, 483, 484; entry to, 361, 364; graduates, 362; and social sciences, 332

Un Jeune Homme Seul (Vailland), 99

Upper/ruling classes, 72, 79, 98, 112, 188–189, 195, 267, 374, 538. *See also* Elites

Urbanization, 26, 30, 121, 130, 139, 245, 283, 304, 359, 368, 471. *See also* Cities

Uzbekistan, 390, 430

Vaernet (Doctor), 98

Vailland, Roger, 99, 241

Values, 366, 370, 374, 395, 421, 459; European, 522, 529; family values, 380, 381, 487, 493, 498, 500; and opposition to Hitler and Stalin, 530; sexual, 464

van der Stegen, Tristan, 484

Vandervelde, Emile, 37

Vandivert, Bill, 217, 218

Varga, Eugen, 268

Vatican City, 146, 147, 148

Vatican II council, 310, 411

Vaucluse, 288

Velvet Revolution, 430

Venice, 463; Venice festival of 1977, 403

Verdun, Battle of, 43, 48, 49, 70, 172

Versailles Treaty, 65, 66, 74, 123, 172, 175, 177, 182, 197

Vesely, Jindrich, 340

Veterans, 70, 71, 72, 73, 74–75, 80, 83, 346, 379

Vienna, 12, 107, 239

Vietnam, 431; Vietnam War, 87, 218, 269, 270, 333, 385–386, 387

Villiers, Georges, 279

Violence, 123, 136, 139, 140, 143, 149, 200, *229,* 299, 300, 302, 322, 332, 336, 343, 348, 352, 411, 480, 481, 513–514, 526–527, 527—528; avoiding, 353, 406, 423, 431; domestic, 379–380; legitimate, 514

Virginity, 93, 100, 379

Virgin Records, 456

Vizzini, Don Calò, 293

Vodka, 390, 426. *See also* Alcoholism/drinking

Vogel, Lucien, 216

Vojvodina, 465

von Stauffenberg, Claus, 196

Voynet, Dominique, 492, 516

Vu (magazine), 216

Vyshinsky, Andrei, 197, 251, 529

Vyvyan, Michal, 100(n)

Wages, 4, 21, 33, 67, 190, 242, 262, 282, 286, 292, 334, 362, 393, 408, 420, 435, 436, 439, 445, 459, 531; and profits, 442; wage cuts, 345; of women, 110, 111, 112, 118, 291, 369, 373, 377, 488

Wajda, Andrzej, 242

Waldheim, Kurt, 479

Wales, 135, 153, 414, 501

Wałesa, Lech, 408, 411, 475, 477, 519

Wall Street Crash (1929), 66, 150, 154, 157, 176. *See also* Depression period

Wall Street Journal, 261

Wannsee Conference on Jewish policy, 201, 202

War, attitudes toward, 39

Warburg, Sigismund, 446–447

War Industry Committee (Russia), 41

Warsaw, 239, 394, 417, 480. *See also* Poland, Warsaw ghetto in

Warsaw Pact, 5, 232(caption), 250, 256, 266, 267, 269, 332, 348, 363, 388, 413; dissolved, 466, 467; invasion of Czechoslovakia, 331 (*see also* Prague, Prague Spring)

Washing machines, 294, 377

Water, 292–293

Watergate scandal, 385

Watkins, Alan, 314
Waugh, Evelyn, 78, 79, 80–81, 187
Weather in the Streets, The (Lehmann), 127
Webb, Sidney and Beatrice, 132, 164
Weber, Eugen, 21–22, 533, 536
Weber, Henri, 457
Weber, Max, 514
Weil, Simone and André, 67
Weiss, Louise, 315
Welfare state, 307–308, 317–318, 369, 452, 508, 529
Wessel, Horst, 90
West Germany, 261, 274, 281, 298, 299, 302, 315, 322, 332, 373, 410, 467, 491, 509; abortion in, 371, 497; Basic Law in, 369; and East Germany/eastern Europe, 417, 445; economy, 242, 260, 287, 434, 437, 445, 454, 529; educa- tion in, 288; and France, 197, 444; immigrants in, 286(table); Ministry for the Family in, 369; Parliament, 492, 493; Red Army Faction in, 334, 335, 336, 514; strikes in, 440; and United States, 445; workers in, 442–443
Westphalia, 36
Weygand, Maxime, 129
Wharton business school, 157
White, Antonia, 81
Whitehouse, Mary, 370
Who, The, 373–374
Widmerpool, Kenneth, 87
Widows, 70, 75, 92, 116, 117, 119, 341, 346
Wiener-Neustadt, 239
Wilde, Oscar, 97, 104, 372, 488
Wilno/Vilnius, 173, 206
Wilson, Harold, 312, 313, 326, 327
Wilson, Woodrow, 66
Wine growers, 27–28, 29
Winock, Michel, 243
Wiskemann, Elizabeth, 533
Wisliceny, Dieter, 201
Wolf, Naomi, 496
Women, 20, 33, 40, 76, 82, 92, 93, 94, 95, 103, 154, *229,* 290, 347, 360, 458, 488–493, 539, 547; in agriculture, 113–116; autonomy of, 371, 373; and Christian democrats, 315, 316, 317, 318, 319, 321, 373, 490; in cities, 283; control of, 105, 190, 377; and fall of communism, 496–500; female suffrage, 116, 117, 315, 319, 322, 369, 373; and French liberation, 105–106; new woman, 89, 116, 127; and politics, 116–119, 489–493, 506; power of, 114, 115; returning to the home, 498–499; seduction of wealthy, 102–103; sexuality of, 125, 126, 127; Stakhanovites, 112–113; unmarried, 376; voters, 315–320, 373, 491, 492; and welfare states, 317–318, 541–542; women's movements in East, 498; and work, 109–113, 118, 122, 124, 159, 190, 291, 309, 316–317, 368, 373, 376–378, 436, 439, 442, 488–489, 496, 499, 517. *See also* Abortion; Marriage; Prostitution; Rape; *under* Wages
Woolf, Leonard, 11, 12, 13, 122
Woolf, Virginia, 11, 13, 215, 217, 217(n)
Working class, 26, 27, 32, 34, 36, 37, 38, 39, 73, 86, 102–103, 104, 110, 121, 138, 173, 242, 243, 285, 290, 306, 332, 366, 407–409, 414, 490, 491, 517, 518, 519, 520; apathy of, 409; autonomy of, 156, 443; children of, 428; and Church, 366, 409; and com- munism, 328, 331; cultures of, 33, 36, 308–309; divisions among, 36, 37, 40; East/West comparison, 392–393; French, 374–375; and leisure, 169; liv- ing standards of, 33, 37, 159, 262, 292, 298, 307, 327; protests of, 345 (*see also* France, protests of 1968 in); and rationalization of production, 158–159; and students' interests, 334; worker- priest movement, 321. *See also* Employment; Labor; Proletariat
World Cup (1934), 170
Wright, Gordon, 330
Wyszyvski, Stepan, 365

Xoxe, Koçi, 339

Yeltsin, Boris, 399, 401, 419, 425, 499, 503, 521; and survey of Soviet rulers, 476
Yom Kippur war, 433
Young Plan, 176
Youth, 40, 65, 67, 78–88, 169, 242, 243, 282, 288, 290, 296, 319, 321, 348,

367, 379, 410, 414, 415, 421–423, 448–449, 457, 463, 483, 485; coalition with the wealthy, 495; as commodity, 455; depoliticized, 423; and masculinity, 79; after Second World War, 373–375; unemployed, 437, 438, 439, 455; and war generation, 81; youth culture, 244, 246, 283, 295–296, 370, 374, 392, 421, 422, 423, 455; youth organizations, 429 (*see also* Hitler Youth). *See also* Children; Generational divisions; Students
Yugoslavia, 3, 58, 78, 98, 128, 134, 143, 146, 176, 207, 248, 250, 349, 467, 478, 481, 512; civil war of 1991–95, 500, 513, 526; fall of communism in, 398, 431, 465, 466; as federal state, 466; new class in, 362–363; religious divisions in, 365; and Soviet Union, 363; students in, 360; tuberculosis in, 239. *See also* Tito

Zappa, Frank, 422
Zavodsky, Osvald, 351
Zender, Joseph, 147
Zhukov (Marshal), 195
Zinoviev, Grigory, 163
Ziuganov, Genadii, 503
Zivković, Petar, 98
Zorn, John, 422

DATE DUE

Demco, Inc. 38-293